MCDOUGAL LITTELL

Passport
to **Mathematics**

BOOK 2

RON LARSON

LAURIE BOSWELL

TIMOTHY D. KANOLD

LEE STIFF

McDougal Littell

A HOUGHTON MIFFLIN COMPANY

Evanston, Illinois • Boston • Dallas

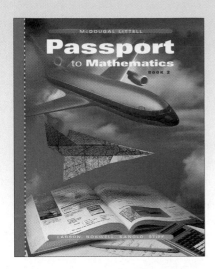

About the Cover

The Passport series brings mathematics to life with many real-life applications. The cover shows a use of mathematics in transportation and engineering. Other examples of mathematics in transportation and engineering are shown on pages 100, 314, 329, 422, 423, 424, 425, 451, 452, and 470. The mathematical statements and diagrams on the cover show some of the material covered in this book—algebra, geometry, and problem solving. Look for exciting applications of these and other topics as you study mathematics this year!

ISBN: 0-395-87985-X   123456789—VJM—01 00 99 98 97

Internet Web Site: http://www.mlmath.com

Ron Larson is a professor of mathematics at the Behrend College of Pennsylvania State University at Erie. He is the author of many well-known high school and college mathematics textbooks, including *Heath: Algebra 1*, *Geometry*, *Algebra 2*, *Precalculus*, *Precalculus with Limits,* and *Calculus*. He is a pioneer in the development of interactive textbooks, and his calculus textbook is published on CD-ROM. Dr. Larson is a member of NCTM and frequently speaks at NCTM and other professional conferences.

Laurie Boswell is a mathematics teacher at Profile Junior-Senior High School in Bethlehem, New Hampshire. She is active in NCTM and local mathematics organizations. A recipient of the 1986 Presidential Award for Excellence in Mathematics Teaching, she is also the 1992 Tandy Technology Scholar and the 1991 recipient of the Richard Balomenos Mathematics Education Service Award presented by the New Hampshire Association of Teachers of Mathematics. She is an author of *Heath Geometry* and Houghton Mifflin *Math Central*.

Timothy D. Kanold is Director of Mathematics and Science and a teacher at Adlai Stevenson High School in Lincolnshire, Illinois. A 1986 recipient of the Presidential Award for Excellence in Mathematics Teaching, he is also the 1993 recipient of the Illinois Council of Teacher of Mathematics Outstanding Leadership Award. A member of NCTM, he served on NCTM's Professional Standards for Teaching Mathematics Commission. He is an author of *Heath: Algebra 1* and *Algebra 2*.

Lee Stiff is an associate professor of mathematics education in the College of Education and Psychology of North Carolina State University at Raleigh and has taught mathematics at the high school and middle school levels. A member of NCTM, he served on the Board of Directors. He is also the 1992 recipient of the W.W. Rankin Award for Excellence in Mathematics Education presented by the North Carolina Council of Teachers of Mathematics. He is an author of *Heath: Algebra 1*, *Geometry*, *Algebra 2*, and Houghton Mifflin *Math Central*.

Reviewers and Contributors

Renee Arrington
Mathematics Specialist
Alief Middle School
Houston, TX

Lyn Baier
Mathematics Teacher
Hopkins West Junior High School
Hopkins, MN

Deborah J. Barrett
Curriculum Coordinator, K-12
Wapato School District
Wapato, WA

Jeff Beatty
Mathematics Teacher
Thomas Harrison Middle School
Harrisonburg, VA

Nancy Belsky
Mathematics Teacher
Westmoreland School
Westmoreland, NH

Marianne Cavanaugh
Head Mathematics Teacher
Gideon Welles Middle School
Glastonbury, CT

Linda Cooke
Mathematics Teacher
Lincoln Middle School
Pullman, WA

Charleen M. DeRidder
Supervisor of Mathematics, K-12
Knox County School District
Knoxville, TN

Betty Erickson
Mathematics Coordinator and Teacher
Kearsarge Regional School District
Bradford, NH

Madelaine Gallin
Mathematics Teacher
Community School District #5
Manhattan, NY

Linda Gojak
Mathematics Teacher/Department Chairperson
Hawken School
Lyndhurst, OH

Margarita Gutiérrez
Curriculum Specialist
Urban Systemic Initiative
El Paso, TX

Thomas Keating
Mathematics Teacher
Chase Middle School
Spokane, WA

Nancy W. Lewis
Mathematics Teacher
Thurmont Middle School
Thurmont, MD

Richard D. Lodholz
Mathematics Coordinator
Parkway School District
St. Louis, MO

Donna J. Long
Title I/Mathematics Coordinator
M.S.D. of Wayne Township
Indianapolis, IN

Carol Mellett
Mathematics Teacher
Lincoln School
Brookline, MA

Dee Ann Meziere
Mathematics Teacher
Putnam City Central Middle School
Oklahoma City, OK

Janice Mosley
Mathematics Teacher
Bellevue Middle School
Nashville, TN

Donna M. Ogle
Professor of Reading and Language
National-Louis University
Evanston, IL

John Peter Penick
District Mathematics Coordinator
Marcus Whitman Junior High School
Port Orchard, WA

Susan Powell
Mathematics Teacher
Burghard Elementary School
Macon, Georgia

Rochelle President-Brown
Mathematics Teacher
Burnside Scholastic Academy
Chicago, IL

Eduardo Reyna
Mathematics Teacher/Department Chairperson
Brown Middle School
McAllen, TX

Krista Rogers
Mathematics Teacher
Hutchinson Junior High School
Lubbock, TX

Marsha Rosenwasser
Mathematics Teacher/Department Head
J. Q. Adams Middle School
Metairie, LA

Frank C. Santoro
Mathematics Teacher
Lincoln School
Brookline, MA

Donna Schneller
Mathematics Teacher
Lake Riviera Middle School
Brick, NJ

Cindy H. Sellars
Mathematics Chairperson
Peet Junior High School
Conroe, TX

Cynthia G. Siebert
Mathematics Teacher
Ballenger Creek Middle School
Frederick, MD

Robyn Silbey
Mathematics Specialist
Montgomery County Public Schools
Rockville, MD

Diana G. Sullivan
Mathematics Teacher
Murray Avenue School
Huntingdon Valley, PA

William F. Tate
Associate Professor of Mathematics Education
University of Wisconsin
Madison, WI

Vicki Vaughan
Mathematics Teacher
Putnam City Central Middle School
Oklahoma City, OK

Beverly Weldon
Senior Mathematics Consultant
Region 10 Educational Service Center
Richardson, TX

Brenda Wright
Mathematics Specialist
Dozier Middle School
Newport News, VA

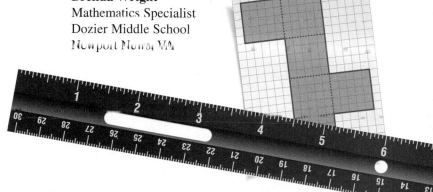

Student Review Panel

Laina Carlos
Greeneville Middle School
Greeneville, TN

Amelia Groeschel
Peet Junior High School
Conroe, TX

Kendra Hudgins
Brewer Middle School
Fort Worth, TX

Jennifer Karr
West Middle School
Holland, MI

Megan Keller
Marinette Middle School
Marinette, WI

Danny Kelly
Norton Middle School
Norton, OH

Frank Kincel, Jr.
West Scranton Intermediate School
Scranton, PA

Jessica Kull
Haven Middle School
Evanston, IL

Jonathan Larason
Woodbury School
Salem, NH

Rebecca Marriott
Southeastern Randolph
   Middle School
Asheboro, NC

Megan McDiffett
Wendler Middle School
Anchorage, AK

Meredith McKenna
Plymouth Community
   Intermediate School
Plymouth, MA

Gaston Prevette
Smithfield Middle School
Smithfield, NC

Gabrielle Ramos
Frederick H. Tuttle Middle School
South Burlington, VT

Reathie Rogers
Durham Magnet School
Durham, NC

Eric Roskens
Thayer Jay Hill Middle School
Naperville, IL

Arlie Sommer
Middleton Middle School
Middleton, ID

Kelly Swift
Anderson High School
Cincinnati, OH

Kelli VanDeusen
Irons Junior High School
Lubbock, TX

Sarah Zanoff
Forestwood Middle School
Lewisville, TX

Problem Solving Together

Applications

Assessment

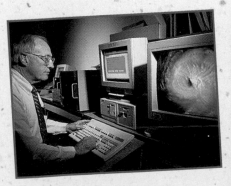

Number Relationships and Fractions

Applications

Assessment

Fractions and Their Operations

Applications

Assessment

CHAPTER 4

Algebra and Integers

Applications

Assessment

Data Analysis and Statistics

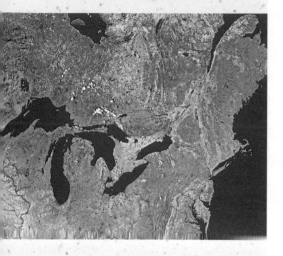

CHAPTER 6

Ratios and Proportions

Applications

Percents and Decimals

Applications

Assessment

Problem Solving Strategies

Interdisciplinary Features

CHAPTER 8

Geometry in the Plane

Applications

Assessment
Ongoing Assessment *375, 381, 387, 391, 397, 401, 407, 413*
Standardized Test Practice *377, 383, 389, 393, 399, 403, 409, 415, 421*
Spiral Review *384, 394, 404*
Mid-Chapter Assessment *395* **Chapter Assessment** *420*

Problem Solving Strategies
Applying Strategies *384, 388, 392, 407, 409, 415*

Interdisciplinary Features
Career Interview: Carpenter and Sculptor *384*
Communicating About Mathematics: Geometry in the Field *405*

CHAPTER 9

Geometry in Space

Applications

Assessment

Algebra: Using Integers

Applications

Assessment

CHAPTER 11

Probability and Discrete Mathematics

Applications

Genetics 531
Basketball 532
Vacation Choices 536
Manufacturing 537
License Plates 538
Psychology 545
Baseball 546
CD Players 547
River Rafting 549
Restaurant Menus 550
Fair Games 557
Recycling 563
Music Preferences 569

Assessment

Ongoing Assessment *531, 537, 545, 549, 557, 561, 567*
Standardized Test Practice *533, 539, 547, 551, 559, 563, 569, 575*
Spiral Review *540, 552, 564*
Mid-Chapter Assessment *553* **Chapter Assessment** *574*

Problem Solving Strategies
Applying Strategies *532, 536, 538, 545, 551, 563, 566*

Interdisciplinary Features
Life Science Connection: Genetics *540*
Communicating About Mathematics: Parrot Talk *565*

CHAPTER 12

Algebra: Equations and Functions

Applications

Assessment

Student Handbook

You can use the reference tools in the Student Handbook to help you find answers to your math questions.

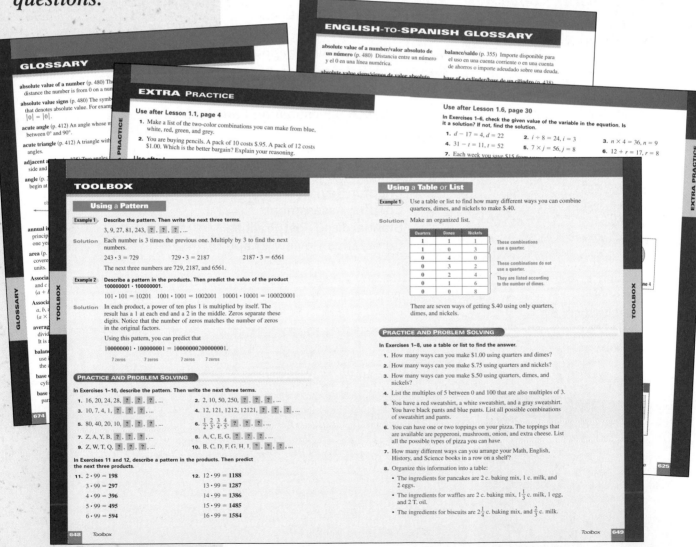

Real-Life Applications

Look through this list for things that interest you. Then find out how they are linked to mathematics.

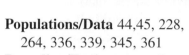

Real Life... Real Math

You may be surprised at all the ways mathematics is connected to daily life and careers.

Real Life... Real People

Real Life... Real Facts

Welcome to the Passport series

Preparing you for success in mathematics in the middle grades and beyond.

As you progress through this course you will see that:

Mathematics makes connections

In this course you will study important middle grade mathematics concepts and see how they are related. You will also find a gradual approach to understanding the underlying principles of algebra and geometry.

Mathematics is accessible

Each lesson in the *Passport* series will help you learn more about math. The interesting activities and the useful pictures, charts, graphs, and models will make it easier for you to learn.

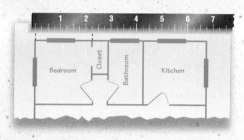

Mathematics is meaningful

Throughout each book in the series, you will explore and discover the importance of mathematics in daily life. In fact, you will find that many of the things you do, see, and hear are linked to mathematics.

Making mathematics relevant.

The emphasis in the Passport series is on real data and real-life applications. Every lesson will show you the real-world importance of mathematics.

The value of math is highlighted through the **LESSON OBJECTIVES** which will explain what you will learn, and why it is important.

3.3 Adding and Subtracting Fractions

What you should learn:

Goal 1 How to add and subtract fractions

Goal 2 How to use addition and subtraction of fractions to solve real-life problems

Why you should learn it:

Knowing how to add and subtract fractions can help you with statistics. An example is interpreting the results of a survey about peanut butter preferences.

Goal 1 ADDING AND SUBTRACTING FRACTIONS

The rules for adding and subtracting fractions depend on whether they have the same denominator or different denominators.

ADDING AND SUBTRACTING FRACTIONS

1. To add or subtract two fractions with a *common denominator*, add or subtract their numerators. Write the sum or difference of the numerators over the denominator.
2. To add or subtract two fractions with *different denominators*, first rewrite the fractions using the least common denominator. Then add or subtract.

Example 1 Adding and Subtracting Fractions

a. $\dfrac{4}{5} - \dfrac{1}{5} = \dfrac{4-1}{5}$ Subtract numerators.

$= \dfrac{3}{5}$ Simplify.

b. To rewrite the fractions $\dfrac{1}{3}$ and $\dfrac{3}{8}$ with the least common denominator of 24, multiply $\dfrac{1}{3}$ by $\dfrac{8}{8}$ and $\dfrac{3}{8}$ by $\dfrac{3}{3}$.

$\dfrac{1}{3} + \dfrac{3}{8} = \dfrac{1 \cdot 8}{3 \cdot 8} + \dfrac{3 \cdot 3}{8 \cdot 3}$ Least common denominator is 24.

$= \dfrac{8}{24} + \dfrac{9}{24}$ Simplify.

$= \dfrac{8+9}{24}$ Add numerators.

$= \dfrac{17}{24}$ Simplify.

c. $\dfrac{5}{6} - \dfrac{1}{2} = \dfrac{5}{6} - \dfrac{1 \cdot 3}{2 \cdot 3}$ Least common denominator is 6.

$= \dfrac{5}{6} - \dfrac{3}{6}$ Simplify.

$= \dfrac{5-3}{6}$ Subtract numerators.

$= \dfrac{2}{6}$ Simplify.

$= \dfrac{1}{3}$ Reduce to lowest terms.

STUDY TIP

The least common denominator of two fractions is the least common multiple of their denominators. For example, the least common denominator of $\dfrac{5}{6}$ and $\dfrac{3}{4}$ is 12 because the least common multiple of 6 and 4 is 12.

Use of **COMPUTERS** and **CALCULATORS** is often demonstrated by showing you how these everyday tools are used to solve problems.

What Percent is Good Enough?

Many people think that getting something 99.9% correct is good enough. Many times in life that's true. But there are some times when it isn't!

Example

a. About 270,000,000 first-class letters are sent each day in the United States. If only 99.9% were delivered to the correct address, how many would be delivered incorrectly?

b. About 44,000,000 hot dogs are eaten each day in the United States. If only 99.9% were fit to eat, how many would not be fit to eat?

Solution

a. 99.9% of 270,000,000 is

0.999 ⊠ 270,000,000 ⊟ 269,730,000.

This means that 270,000,000 − 269,730,000, or 270,000 letters would be delivered incorrectly each day.

b. 99.9% of 44,000,000 is

0.999 ⊠ 44,000,000 ⊟ 43,956,000.

This means that 44,000,000 − 43,956,000, or 44,000 hot dogs would not be fit to eat each day.

CALCULATOR TIP

If your calculator doesn't display enough digits to work with very large numbers, you can do part of the multiplication. For example, to ...999 by ...000, you ...000,000 ...ter ...of ...0). ...e result ...0,000.

...es

...About 31,000,000 households have one car. If only 99.9% of these cars start up one morning, how many do not start?

2. Over 1.6 billion telephone calls are made each day in the United States. If only 99.9% were made to correct numbers, how many would be made to wrong numbers?

3. About 700 million audio compact disks are sold each year in the United States. If only 99.9% are not retu... sellers, how many would...

333

Interesting and informative **TABLES**, **CHARTS**, and **GRAPHS** not only show the real-life value of math, but also develop your critical thinking skills.

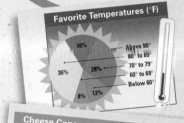
Favorite Temperatures (°F)
16% Above 90°
80° to 89°
36% 28% 70° to 79°
60° to 69°
8% 12% Below 60°

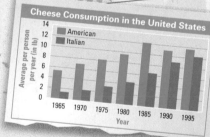
Cheese Consumption in the United States
American
Italian

① SOLVING REAL-LIFE PROBLEMS

To add three or more fractions, you can use the same rules as when you add two fractions. Here are two examples.

$\frac{1}{5} + \frac{2}{5} + \frac{4}{5} = \frac{1+2+4}{5} = \frac{7}{5}$ **Common denominator**

$\frac{1}{2} + \frac{1}{3} + \frac{1}{6} = \frac{3}{6} + \frac{2}{6} + \frac{1}{6} = \frac{6}{6}$ **Different denominators**

Example 2 Using a Survey

REAL LIFE Business

Your company is producing a new type of peanut butter. To help design the product, you conduct a survey to find people's peanut butter preferences. The results of the survey are shown in the circle graph below. Find the sum of the fractions.

PEANUT BUTTER PREFERENCES
Do not like either $\frac{1}{6}$ Like both $\frac{1}{8}$
Prefer smooth $\frac{3}{8}$ Prefer crunchy $\frac{1}{3}$

Solution

The least common denominator is 24.

$\frac{1}{6} + \frac{3}{8} + \frac{1}{8} + \frac{1}{3} = \frac{4}{24} + \frac{9}{24} + \frac{3}{24} + \frac{8}{24}$

$= \frac{4+9+3+8}{24}$

$= \frac{24}{24}$

$= 1$

The sum is 1.

Real Life... Real Facts

Peanut crops are grown in Asia, Africa, Australia, South America, and the southern United States. The flowers grow above ground, but the peanut itsel... beneath the...

ONGOING ASSESSMENT

Write About It

1. Can you use a common ...minator of 48 ...ample 2? ...y and ...

Mathematical **MODELING** shows you math at work in real-life situations and demonstrates the problem-solving power of mathematics.

REAL LIFE, REAL FACTS shows the everyday value and importance of mathematics.

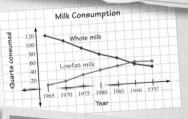
Milk Consumption
Whole milk
Lowfat milk
Quarts consumed

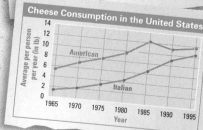
Cheese Consumption in the United States
American
Italian

Making mathematics easy to learn.

Throughout the Passport series, lessons and labs make even the most difficult concepts easier to understand.

Each **LESSON** has two goals: the first goal helps you to understand the math skill, the second goal shows you how the skill is applied to daily life.

6.2 Rates

What you should learn:

Goal ① How to find a rate

Goal ② How to use rates to solve real-life problems

Why you should learn it:

Knowing how to find rates can help you compare speeds. An example is comparing the speeds of two people on mountain bikes.

Important **TERMS** are highlighted and defined clearly, making it easy to understand key math vocabulary.

TOOLBOX

iding Decimals, age 655

STUDY TIP

In real life, rate has many different names. Here are some examples.

speed in miles per hour: 55 mi/h

hourly wage in dollars per hour: $5/h

unit price in dollars per ounce: $1/oz

Goal ① FINDING RATES

A **rate** is a fraction in which the numerator and denominator have different units of measure. For example, if you ride your bicycle for 1 h and travel 4 mi, then your rate is

$$\frac{\text{Distance}}{\text{Time}} = \frac{4 \text{ mi}}{1 \text{ h}}.$$

In words, this rate is read as "4 miles per hour." In real life, rates are usually simplified so that they have a denominator of 1 unit. A rate with a denominator of 1 unit is a **unit rate**.

> **RATE**
>
> If two quantities a and b have different units of measure, then the **rate of a per b** is $\frac{a}{b}$.

Example 1 Finding a Unit Rate

On Saturday, you baby-sit for 2.5 hours and are paid $10. On Sunday, you baby-sit for 3 hours and are paid $10.50. Find the hourly wage that you were paid on each day. Which was greater?

Solution

To find the hourly wage, divide the amount paid by the time.

Saturday: $\frac{\text{Amount paid}}{\text{Time}} = \frac{\$10}{2.5 \text{ h}}$ Set up the rate.

$= \frac{\$10 \div 2.5}{2.5 \text{ h} \div 2.5}$ Divide numerator and denominator by 2.5.

$= \frac{\$4}{1 \text{ h}}$ Simplify.

Sunday: $\frac{\text{Amount paid}}{\text{Time}} = \frac{\$10.50}{3 \text{ h}}$ Set up the rate.

$= \frac{\$10.50 \div 3}{3 \text{ h} \div 3}$ Divide numerator and denominator by 3.

$= \frac{\$3.50}{1 \text{ h}}$ Simplify.

On Saturday, you earned $4 per hour and on Sunday, $3.50 per hour. So, your hourly wage was greater on Saturday.

LAB 4.4

Investigating Integer Addition

Materials Needed
• paper
• number counters
• pencils or pens

Part A ADDING TWO INTEGERS

You can use number counters to model adding integers.

Sum: 3 + 4

Choose 3 tan counters to show positive 3 and 4 tan counters to show positive 4.

Place and count the total number of tan counters.

$$3 + 4 = 7$$
Number sentence

Sum: −3 + (−4)

Choose 3 red counters to show negative 3 and 4 red counters to show negative 4.

Place and count the total number of red counters.

$$-3 + (-4) = -7$$

1. Use number counters to add.

a. 6 + 4   b. 5 + 3   c. −2 + (−4)   d. −3 + (−3)

2. Use the two examples above and Exercise 1 to tell how to add two positive integers and how to add two negative integers.

Part B ZERO PAIRS

When you pair one tan and one red counter, the result is zero. This pair of counters is a *zero pair*.

4
−4

$$4 + (-4) = 0$$

Part C ADDING POSITIVE AND NEGATIVE INTEGERS

When you use number counters to add a positive integer and a negative integer, remember that each pair that has one red counter and one tan counter adds to zero.

Sum: −4 + 2

−4
2

Choose 4 red counters to show negative 4 and 2 tan counters to show positive 2.

Add to zero.

Place the counters and group pairs of tan and red counters. The remaining counters show the sum.

$$-4 + 2 = -2$$

4. Use number counters to add.

a. −3 + 4   b. 5 + (−2)   c. 4 + (−6)   d. −6 + 3

5. Give an example of each addition problem.

a. Positive integer + Negative integer = Negative integer
b. Positive integer + Negative integer = Positive integer
c. Positive integer + Negative integer = Zero

NOW TRY THESE

In Exercises 6–11, use number counters to model the addition problem. Then write a number sentence for the problem.

6. 4 + (−3)   7. 1 + 6   8. −6 + (−4)
9. −4 + (−5)   10. −5 + 2   11. 2 + (−2)

In Exercises 12–14, complete the _____ment. Then use number counters to check _____.

___ is a negative num___
___ is a positive num___
___ is zero.

___cises 12–14, is th___
___plete each ___

LESSON INVESTIGATION

Investigating Finding a Percent of a Number

GROUP ACTIVITY Copy and complete the table below. For each problem, draw a 10-by-10 unit square.

Unit Square Represents	Percent	Number of Small Squares Shaded	Value of a Small Square	Value of Shaded Squares
300 miles	20%	?	?	?
$150	20%	?	?	?
$5.00	80%	20	?	?
200 boats	25%	?	3 miles	60 miles
600 hours	30%	?	?	?
			?	?
				?

Goal 2 SOLVING REAL-LIFE PROBLEMS

Example 2 Comparing Rates

Arnold and Jena went mountain biking on some trails in their town. Based on the information below, which one of them rode at a faster pace?

REAL LIFE
Mountain Biking

• Arnold rode 23 miles in 4 hours.
• Jena rode 16 miles in 3.5 hours.

Solution

Begin by finding each rider's speed. To determine speed, divide the distance that each person traveled by the time that it took. Then simplify to find the unit rates.

Arnold: $\frac{\text{Distance}}{\text{Time}} = \frac{23 \text{ mi}}{4 \text{ h}}$ Set up the rate.

$= \frac{23 \text{ mi} \div 4}{4 \text{ h} \div 4}$ Divide numerator and denominator by 4.

$= \frac{5.75 \text{ mi}}{1 \text{ h}}$ Simplify.

Jena: $\frac{\text{Distance}}{\text{Time}} = \frac{16 \text{ mi}}{3.5 \text{ h}}$ Set up the rate.

$= \frac{16 \text{ mi} \div 3.5}{3.5 \text{ h} \div 3.5}$ Divide numerator and denominator by 3.5.

$\approx \frac{4.6 \text{ mi}}{1 \text{ h}}$ Simplify.

Arnold rode 5.75 mi/h and Jena rode about 4.6 mi/h. So, Arnold rode his bike faster than Jena.

6.2 Rates **277**

ONGOING ASSESSMENT

Talk About

You are shop___
oranges. Wh___
has the sm___
price? Whi___
you buy? D___
reasons.

1. 2 pounds ___
2. 5 pounds fo___
3. 8 pounds for $6.___

LABS and **LESSON INVESTIGATIONS** provide engaging, memorable ways to explore and understand math concepts.

Numerous **EXAMPLES** model how each skill is used. **COLOR-CODING** and **STEP-BY-STEP EXPLANATIONS** make it easy for you to follow each example.

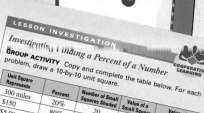

XXV

Providing opportunities to practice and to solve problems.

The Passport series helps you achieve success in each lesson and chapter, in standardized tests, and more.

GUIDED PRACTICE aids you and your teacher in assessing your understanding of each skill.

6.2 Exercises

Extra Practice, page

GUIDED PRACTICE

1. How do rate and ratio differ? Give an example of each.

2. Write each rate below as a unit rate. If you need to complete a 75-question test in 60 minutes, which unit rate would you prefer to use to help you complete the test on time? Explain.

   A. $\dfrac{60 \text{ min}}{75 \text{ questions}}$

   B. $\dfrac{75 \text{ questions}}{60 \text{ min}}$

3. **TRAVEL** You drove 1350 mi in 3 days. Each day you drove for 9 h. What was your average speed?

PRACTICE AND PROBLEM SOLVING

In Exercises 4–7, simplify the quotient. Is the quotient a rate or a ratio? Explain your reasoning.

4. $\dfrac{18 \text{ people}}{54 \text{ people}}$

5. $\dfrac{140 \text{ mi}}{5 \text{ gal}}$

6. $\dfrac{576 \text{ beats}}{8 \text{ min}}$

7. $\dfrac{165 \text{ apples}}{125 \text{ apples}}$

In Exercises 8–11, find the unit rate.

8. It rains 28 inches in 8 hours.

9. You pay $2.73 for 100 sheets of paper.

10. In 3.5 h a plane flies 2275 mi.

11. You are paid $90 for delivering newspapers for 6 days.

Tech Link

Investigation 6,
Interactive
Real-Life
Investigations

In Exercises 12–14, which is the better buy? Explain.

12. **A.** A 16 oz box of cereal for $3.49

    B. A 20 oz box of cereal for $4.19

13. **A.** A 2 lb bag of potatoes for $1.08

    B. A 5 lb bag of potatoes for $2.10

    C. A 10 lb bag of potatoes for $3.95

14. **A.** A 0.5 gal container of frozen yogurt for $2.25

    B. A 2 gal container of frozen yogurt for $8.00

15. **CALORIE CONSUMPTION** For a typical adult, the calorie consumption for 7 days is 17,500. The cal[...] 7 days of an Olympic athlete in train[...] Use this information to find the [...] of a typical adult and an Olym[...]

PRACTICE AND PROBLEM SOLVING gives you the opportunity to master key skills and apply them to real-world situations and problems.

CHAPTER **PROJECTS**

offer you a unique way to develop math skills and demonstrate your problem-solving abilities.

STANDARDIZED **TEST PRACTICE**

not only prepares you for these important tests, but also strengthens your ability to solve problems and to think critically.

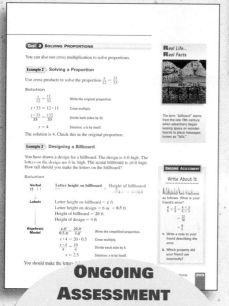

ONGOING **ASSESSMENT**

helps you check your progress by talking and writing about mathematics problems.

COMMUNICATING **About Mathematics**

encourages you to build your communication skills while learning about real-world applications.

Problem Solving Together

TORNADOES A tornado is a funnel-shaped column of spiral winds that can move up to 500 miles an hour. Texas has more tornadoes than any other state.

TECHNOLOGY

Technology resources accompanying this chapter:

• Interactive Real-Life Investigations

• Middle School Tutorial Software

CHAPTER THEME
Weather

THUNDERSTORMS El Niño increases the frequency of thunderstorms in the southwestern states, such as Arizona.

El Niño

REAL LIFE
Weather

Every few years, trade winds off the west coast of South America weaken and the temperature of the Pacific rises. This disturbance is called **El Niño**. When ocean waters warm, the fish die. Fish catches decline as much as 80 percent. In the United States, strong El Niños result in flooding, and increased thunderstorm, tornado, and hurricane activity. Mild El Niños cause drought in the West and severe cold in the East.

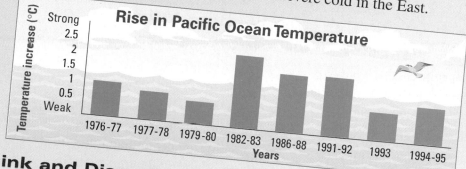

Rise in Pacific Ocean Temperature

Temperature increase (°C)

Strong
2.5
2
1.5
1
0.5
Weak

1976-77 1977-78 1979-80 1982-83 1986-88 1991-92 1993 1994-95

Years

Think and Discuss

1. In which years was El Niño the strongest? In which years was it the weakest?

2. Why is predicting future El Niños important?

PORTFOLIO

CHAPTER PROJECT

Making a Weather Safety Booklet

The National Weather Service tracks severe weather, such as hurricanes, and issues weather warnings and forecasts.

PROJECT DESCRIPTION

Tornadoes, hurricanes, blizzards, and other severe weather can result in the loss of property and lives. Weather forecasters try to minimize the damage by warning people so they can prepare for a storm. Local governments help by building storm shelters. You can become better prepared for weather emergencies by making a weather safety booklet using the **TOPICS** listed on the next page.

GETTING STARTED

Talking It Over

- Discuss in your group what sort of weather emergencies are likely to happen where you live. What kind of problems can severe weather cause? What can you do to prepare for severe weather?

- Discuss what it might be like to be caught in a severe weather emergency. How can being prepared help?

Planning Your Project

- **Materials Needed:** paper, pencils

- You can use the eight topics in the **BUILDING YOUR PROJECT** list on page 3. You may want to include newspaper articles on local weather emergencies and your journal entries in your weather safety booklet. Keep your work in your portfolio and add to it as assigned by your teacher.

Barometers show changes in air pressure.

Evacuation and preparation before a hurricane can save lives and property.

Hurricanes, like the one shown in the photo, often travel up the Atlantic coast of the United States.

BUILDING YOUR PROJECT

These are places throughout the chapter where you will work on your project.

TOPICS

1.1 Estimate the number of tornadoes that occurred in a year. *p. 7*

1.2 Plan for emergency snow removal. *p. 11*

1.3 Determine the extent of a tornado's destruction. *p. 19*

1.4 Interpret a weather forecast. *p. 24*

1.5 Examine the capacity of storm shelters. *p. 29*

1.7 Analyze where tornadoes and hurricanes are most likely to occur. *p. 39*

1.8 Compare the costs of tornadoes and hurricanes. *p. 43*

1.9 Compare the climates of two cities. *p. 47*

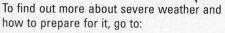

INTERNET

To find out more about severe weather and how to prepare for it, go to:
http://www.mlmath.com

A Problem Solving Plan

Goal 1 USING A PROBLEM SOLVING PLAN

In this chapter, you will study several problem solving strategies, such as Solving a Simpler Problem and Making an Estimate. With each of these strategies, you can use a problem solving plan.

PROBLEM SOLVING PLAN

1. Understand the problem, then make a plan.
2. Collect and organize the necessary information.
3. Solve the problem.
4. Look back at your solution. Is it reasonable?

Example 1 Using a Problem Solving Plan

STRATEGY MAKE AN ESTIMATE You go to a convenience store with $10 to buy items that cost $1.89, $0.40, $1.10, and $2.55. Do you have enough money to buy another item that costs $3.35?

Solution

Understand the Problem
1. You have enough money to buy the four items. Do you have enough to buy the fifth item?

Collect Data
2. You have $10.00. The first four items cost $1.89, $0.40, $1.10, and $2.55. The fifth item costs $3.35.

Solve the Problem
3. You can make an estimate.

$1.89 is about $2.00

$0.40 is about $0.50

$1.10 is about $1.00

$2.55 is about $2.50   Total is about $6.00.

$6.00

After buying the four items, you have about $10 − $6, or $4 left. So, you have enough to buy the item that costs $3.35.

Look Back
4. You could use a calculator to check your answer.

Using a problem solving plan can help you make estimations on the job.

Example 2 **Using a Problem Solving Plan**

You work in a hardware store and are asked to estimate the number of nails in a 20 lb box of nails.

REAL LIFE
Hardware Sales

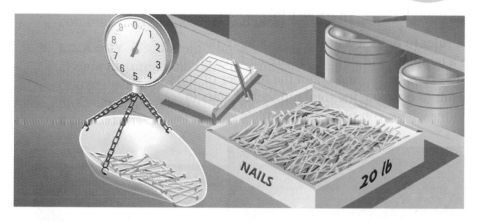

Solution

Understand the Problem

1. You are not asked to count the exact number of nails in the box. You only need to estimate the number.

Collect Data

2. One way to estimate the number of nails in the box is to count and weigh a handful of nails.

   • There are **27** nails in the handful.

   • The handful weighs about $\frac{1}{2}$ lb.

Solve the Problem

3. To solve the problem, you can reason that the 20 lb box must contain **40** half-pounds. So, you can estimate the total number of nails in the box to be

$$\begin{array}{c} \textbf{Total number} \\ \textbf{of nails} \end{array} = \begin{array}{c} \textbf{Nails in} \\ \textbf{1 handful} \end{array} \times \begin{array}{c} \textbf{Number of} \\ \textbf{handfuls} \end{array}$$

$$= 27 \times 40$$

$$= \textbf{1080 nails.}$$

Look Back

4. To check your estimate, you could try counting and weighing another handful of nails.

ONGOING ASSESSMENT

Talk About It
....

You go to a store with $12 to buy items that cost $0.85, $2.15, $0.59, $1.98, and $1.08. Use estimation to find if you have enough money to buy another item that costs the amount shown below.

1. $4.95

2. $7.25

3. $5.82

Discuss your strategy.

GUIDED PRACTICE

1. **LOOKING FOR A PATTERN** Find the sums. Describe any patterns that you see.

   $1 + 2 + 1 =$?

   $1 + 2 + 3 + 2 + 1 =$?

   $1 + 2 + 3 + 4 + 3 + 2 + 1 =$?

2. **FLORAL DISPLAY** You work during weekends at a flower shop. In a floral display you place 20 flowers in the bottom row, 19 flowers in the next higher row, 18 in the next higher, and so on. How many flowers do you need to complete the display? Describe a simpler problem that can help you answer the question.

3. **WRITING** Describe a different problem solving strategy that you could use to solve Exercise 2. Tell how you would apply the strategy.

PRACTICE AND PROBLEM SOLVING

LOOKING FOR A PATTERN In Exercises 4–7, find the missing number in the pattern. Explain your reasoning.

4. 2, 7, 12, 17, ? , 27

5. 3, 7, 12, 18, ? , 33

6. 1, 4, 9, 16, ? , 36

7. 2, 6, 14, 30, ? , 126

8. **GEOMETRY** Count the number of triangles in each polygon below. Describe the pattern. Then find the number of triangles that are formed by drawing lines from *one* point of a polygon with 15 sides.

   | 4 sides | 5 sides | 6 sides | 7 sides |

9. The dots below illustrate the *triangular numbers*. Describe a pattern for triangular numbers. Then find the 20th triangular number. Name two problem solving strategies you could use to solve this problem. Then explain how you would apply these strategies.

10. How many different sizes of non-tilted rectangles can you find in the grid at the right? Before solving this problem, describe and solve a simpler problem. (Recall that a square is a rectangle.)

SKYDIVING In Exercises 11 and 12, solve, then describe your problem solving strategy.

11. After jumping, a skydiver falls 16 ft in the first second, 48 ft in the next second, 80 ft in the third second, and so on. How many feet will the skydiver fall in the tenth second?

12. A skydiving club has 30 members. The club members jump in pairs. How many different pairs of skydivers are possible?

13. In a chess tournament, the loser drops out after each game. If there are 43 players at the start, how many games will be played? Describe the problem solving strategy you used to arrive at your answer.

Real Life... Real Facts

Skydivers jump from airplanes and fall freely before opening their parachutes.

STANDARDIZED TEST PRACTICE

14. How many cans could you use to make a triangular stack in which each row has one can less than the next lower row?

  (**A**) 18   (**B**) 21   (**C**) 25   (**D**) 32

15. At an amusement park, you and 3 friends get into a car that has 4 seats, 2 in front and 2 in back. How many different seating arrangements can you make?

  (**A**) 4   (**B**) 6   (**C**) 12   (**D**) 24

EXPLORATION AND EXTENSION

PORTFOLIO

16. **BUILDING YOUR PROJECT** During a blizzard, the highway department must clear the snow from a 12 ft wide road. Trucks push the snow into two 2 ft wide piles on either side of the road. How many inches of snow will have to fall before the 2 piles reach a height of 3 ft? Explain how you got your answer. Record your results in your journal.

In Exercises 1–3, round to the given place value. (Toolbox, page 652)

1. 3.05 (tenths)

2. 15.89 (ones)

3. 0.2746 (hundredths)

In Exercises 4–6, write two fractions that represent the shaded portion of the figure. (Toolbox, page 653)

4.

5.

6.

In Exercises 7–9, complete the statement. (U. S. Customary Units, page 668)

7. $4 \text{ ft} = \boxed{?} \text{ in.}$

8. $\boxed{?} \text{ yd} = 9 \text{ ft}$

9. $\frac{1}{2} \text{ yd} = \boxed{?} \text{ in.}$

10. **MAKING A LIST** You are buying a sweater. You can choose from a V-neck, turtleneck, or cardigan sweater in red, blue, green, black, or white. How many different sweaters can you choose from? **(1.1)**

CAREER Interview

METEOROLOGIST

Barbara McNaught Watson is a meteorologist for the National Weather Service. She tracks the course of severe storms, makes weather forecasts, and assesses damage caused by severe weather events.

Q What led you to this career?
Growing up, I was always fascinated by lightning and thunderstorms. When I first studied meteorology in ninth grade science, I immediately knew that was what I wanted to do.

Q What is your favorite part of the job?
To me, weather is both interesting and exciting. No two days are the same.

Q How does math help you on your job?
I routinely use a variety of math skills. For example, calculating the reliability of our predictions involves simple arithmetic. Our long-range forecasts, on the other hand, rely on complex equations of motion that are based on calculus.

Q What would you like to tell students about studying math?
I think it's important to learn math no matter what career you end up pursuing. As a student, the importance of math and good writing skills may not always be apparent. But as an adult, it's amazing how much you depend on those skills on a day-to-day basis.

Rounding Numbers

When you round a number, you round down if the next digit is 4 or less and round up if the next digit is 5 or more. For example, 2.364 rounds to 2.36 and 2.365 rounds to 2.37. You can practice rounding in the following example.

CALCULATOR TIP

While most calculators automatically round the last digit of a repeating pattern, some do not. Thus, 23 divided by 3 might look like this.

$$7.6666666$$

Use the digit in the thousandths' place to round to the hundredths' place.

Example

Change the fractions to decimals. Round to the hundredths' place.

$$\frac{23}{1}, \frac{23}{2}, \frac{23}{3}, \frac{23}{4}, \frac{23}{5}, \frac{23}{6}, \frac{23}{7}$$

Solution

Division Problem	Calculator Keystrokes	Display	Decimal
$\frac{23}{1} = 23 \div 1$	23 ÷ 1 =	23.	23.00
$\frac{23}{2} = 23 \div 2$	23 ÷ 2 =	11.5	11.50
$\frac{23}{3} = 23 \div 3$	23 ÷ 3 =	7.666667	7.67
$\frac{23}{4} = 23 \div 4$	23 ÷ 4 =	5.75	5.75
$\frac{23}{5} = 23 \div 5$	23 ÷ 5 =	4.6	4.60
$\frac{23}{6} = 23 \div 6$	23 ÷ 6 =	3.833333	3.83
$\frac{23}{7} = 23 \div 7$	23 ÷ 7 =	3.285714	3.29

Exercises

1. Change the fractions to decimals. Round to the hundredths' place.

$$\frac{22}{1}, \frac{22}{2}, \frac{22}{3}, \frac{22}{4}, \frac{22}{5}, \frac{22}{6}, \frac{22}{7}$$

2. When you change a fraction to a decimal, the decimal can *terminate*, as in $\frac{1}{8} = 0.125$, or it can *repeat*, as in $\frac{1}{7} = 0.142857142857\ldots$(the three dots mean the pattern keeps repeating). Which decimals in Exercise 1 terminate? Which repeat?

LAB
1.3
COOPERATIVE LEARNING

Investigating Geometric Shapes

Materials Needed
- dot paper
- plain paper
- scissors
- ruler
- pencils or pens

Part A CUTTING TANGRAMS

Draw the seven figures below on dot paper and cut them out.

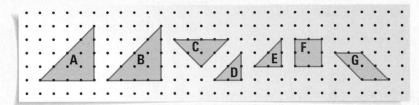

1. The set of 7 pieces above is a tangram. This tangram originated in China. With a partner arrange the 7 pieces to form a square. Sketch your solution.

2. Imagine that you are describing your solution to a friend on the phone. Describe the position of each of the 7 pieces.

Part B COMPARING AREAS

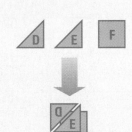

Tangrams can be used to investigate areas. For example, by placing Triangle D and Triangle E on top of Square F, you can see that the square has twice the area of each small triangle.

3. Suppose Triangle D or E has an area of 1 square unit. Copy the table and enter the area of each tangram piece.

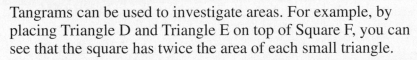

Tangram Piece	A	B	C	D	E	F	G
Area	?	?	?	?	?	?	?

4. Suppose that Square F has an area of 3 square units. Copy the table and enter the area of each tangram piece.

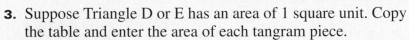

Tangram Piece	A	B	C	D	E	F	G
Area	?	?	?	?	?	?	?

5. Suppose that the square you formed in Exercise 1 has an area of 1 square unit. Copy the table and enter the area of each tangram piece.

Tangram Piece	A	B	C	D	E	F	G
Area	?	?	?	?	?	?	?

There are many ways that tangrams can be used to form geometric shapes. Here are two examples.

Rectangle made with
3 tangram pieces

Parallelogram made with
2 tangram pieces

6. Copy the table. With your group, use the indicated number of tangram pieces to form the geometric shape. The pieces can be flipped to form the shapes. If it is not possible, write "Not Possible" in the table. If it is possible, sketch a solution. Don't use the same sketch twice.

Number of Tangrams	Square	Rectangle	Parallelogram
1	?	?	?
2	?	?	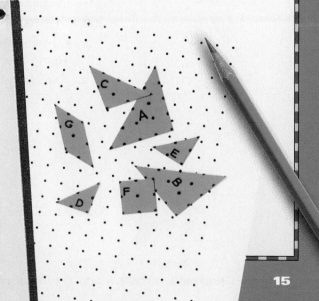
3	?	D G E	?
4	?	?	?
5	?	?	?
6	?	?	?

NOW TRY THESE

CLASSIFYING POLYGONS In Exercises 7–10, use all 7 tangram pieces to form the polygon. Sketch your solution on dot paper.

7. Form a triangle, a polygon with 3 sides.

8. Form a quadrilateral, a polygon with 4 sides.

9. Form a pentagon, a polygon with 5 sides.

10. Form a hexagon, a polygon with 6 sides.

11. Compare the polygons in Exercises 7–10.

What you should learn:

Goal 1 How to identify similar geometric figures

Goal 2 How to compare the perimeters and areas of similar figures

Why you should learn it:

Knowing how to identify similar geometric figures can help you compare the areas and perimeters of floor tiles.

Drawing a Diagram

Goal 1 DIAGRAMMING SIMILAR FIGURES

Two geometric figures are **similar** if they have the same shape. Any two squares are similar. Two triangles may or may not be similar, depending on their shapes.

Example 1 Using a Problem Solving Plan

STRATEGY **DRAW A DIAGRAM** You have several 1 in. square tiles. Draw a diagram showing how to use the tiles to form larger similar figures.

Solution

Four of the tiles can be used to form a similar square that is 2 tiles by 2 tiles. Nine of the tiles can be used to form a similar square that is 3 tiles by 3 tiles. This solution is diagrammed below. How would you form a square that is 4 tiles by 4 tiles?

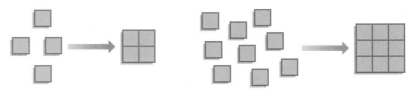

LESSON INVESTIGATION

COOPERATIVE LEARNING

Investigating Similar Shapes

GROUP ACTIVITY Each person in the group should choose one of the shapes below. On dot paper, draw 9 copies of the shape you selected. Cut them out.

1. Can you form a larger similar figure using 4 of the copies? Using 9 of the copies?

2. Sketch the figures you formed. Discuss your findings.

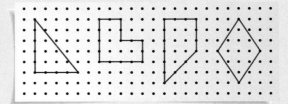

Perimeter is the distance around a figure. **Area** is a measure of how much surface is covered by a figure.

Example 2 **Comparing Perimeters and Areas**

You are tiling a floor using diamond-shaped tiles, as shown below. Find the perimeter and area of each tile. Then form a similar diamond with 4 tiles and find its perimeter and area.

REAL LIFE
Floor Tiling

STUDY TIP

To find the area of a rectangle, multiply the length by the width. To find the area of a triangle, multiply one half by the base by the height.

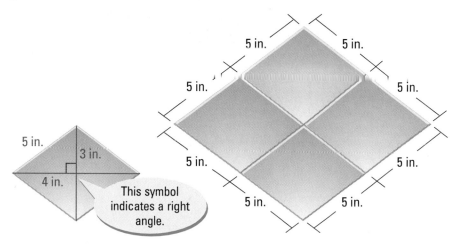

5 in.   5 in.

5 in.   5 in.

5 in.   5 in.

5 in.   5 in.

5 in.

3 in.

4 in.

This symbol indicates a right angle.

Solution

Sum the lengths of the sides of a tile to find the perimeter of 20 in. To find the area of a tile, imagine that it is made of 4 right triangles. (A right triangle is a triangle that has one right angle, which is an angle of 90°.) Then use the following formula to find the area of each triangle.

$$\text{Area of triangle} = \frac{1}{2} \times \textbf{Base} \times \textbf{Height}$$

$$= \frac{1}{2} \times 4 \times 3$$

$$= 6 \text{ in.}^2$$

Four triangles make up a tile, so the area of each tile is 4×6, or 24 square inches (in.²). The large diamond has an area of 4×24, or 96 in.², and a perimeter of 40 in.

ONGOING ASSESSMENT

Write About It

Compare the perimeter and area of the tile with the perimeter and area of the larger diamond in Example 2.

1. How do the two perimeters compare?

2. How do the areas of the two figures compare?

3. Are the comparisons the same?

GUIDED PRACTICE

1. **WRITING** Explain how to identify similar geometric figures. Describe what similar figures are.

2. Which triangles are similar? Explain your reasoning.

A   B   C   D

In Exercises 3 and 4, use the rectangle at the right.

3. Find the perimeter and area of the rectangle at the right.

4. On graph paper, draw a larger similar rectangle. Explain why the two rectangles are similar.

7 cm

15 cm

In Exercises 5 and 6, use the triangle at the right.

5. Find the perimeter and area of the triangle.

6. On graph paper, draw a larger similar triangle. Explain why the two triangles are similar.

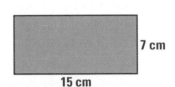

17 cm

8 cm

15 cm

PRACTICE AND PROBLEM SOLVING

In Exercises 7–10, use dot paper to sketch two similar figures of the given shape. Explain how you did it.

7. Triangle   8. Rectangle   9. Square   10. Diamond

In Exercises 11–14, find the perimeter and area of the figure.

11.

8 m
8 m

12.
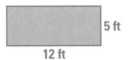
5 ft
12 ft

13.
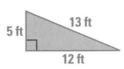
13 ft
5 ft
12 ft

14.
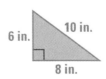
10 in.
6 in.
8 in.

In Exercises 15–17, find the perimeter and area of the figure.

15.
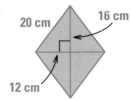
20 cm
16 cm
12 cm

16.
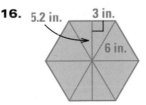
5.2 in.
3 in.
6 in.

17.
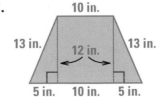
10 in.
13 in.
12 in.
13 in.
5 in.   10 in.   5 in.

18. Show how 4 copies of the figure at the right can be used to form a larger similar figure. Find the area. (The dots are 1 unit apart.)

19. **THINKING SKILLS** Are all right triangles similar? Explain.

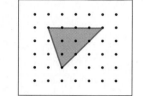

In Exercises 20–25, are the objects similar? Explain.

20. An airplane and its model

21. A pair of socks

22. A baseball and a softball

23. A flute and a clarinet

24. A cassette and a compact disk

25. A photo and its enlargement

TILING A FLOOR **In Exercises 26–29, use the triangle-shaped tile shown at the right.**

26. Find the perimeter and area of the tile.

27. On graph paper, draw a similar triangle with four tiles.

28. Find the perimeter and area of the similar triangle.

29. Compare the perimeters and areas of the two figures. Are the comparisons the same?

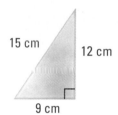

STANDARDIZED TEST PRACTICE

30. Which of the following is *not* always true of similar triangles?

(A) Equal sides   **(B)** Equal angles   **(C)** Same shape   **(D)** Straight sides

31. Which of the following is the measure of a right angle?

(A) 60°   **(B)** 80°   **(C)** 90°   **(D)** 100°

EXPLORATION AND EXTENSION

PORTFOLIO

32. BUILDING YOUR PROJECT The path followed by a tornado is shown on graph paper, where each square equals 100 m². Estimate how far the tornado traveled. How many square meters were touched by the tornado? Record your results in your journal.

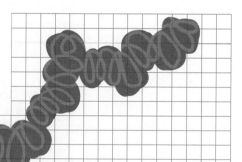

1.4 Experiments and Simulations

What you should learn:

Goal 1 How to make predictions using a mathematical experiment

Goal 2 How to simulate an experiment

Why you should learn it:

Knowing how to perform and analyze experiments and simulations can help you understand advertising contests.

Goal 1 PERFORMING AN EXPERIMENT

Example 1 A Number Cube Experiment

How many times would you have to toss a 6-sided number cube before a number repeats? What is the least number of tosses that could result in a repeat? What is the greatest?

Solution

One way to answer this question is to do the experiment several times. The outcomes of 15 experiments are shown below.

Experiment	Outcome	Number of Tosses
1	2, 4, 2	3
2	4, 3, 1, 5, 1	5
3	1, 1	2
4	4, 6, 1, 4	4
5	5, 6, 2, 5	4
6	6, 3, 1, 5, 3	5
7	2, 3, 5, 6, 5	5
8	3, 4, 4	3
9	4, 5, 2, 6, 3, 1, 6	7
10	6, 3, 2, 6	4
11	4, 3, 3	3
12	5, 5	2
13	3, 2, 4, 5, 2	5
14	3, 3	2
15	3, 6, 1, 4, 1	5

To estimate the number of tosses needed to get a repeat, find the average by dividing the total number of tosses by the number of experiments.

$$\text{Average} = \frac{59}{15}$$ Add the tosses. Divide by 15.

The symbol ≈ means "approximately equal to."

$$\approx 3.9$$ Round the result.

You could expect to get a repeat after about 4 tosses. The least number of tosses that could produce a repeat is 2. The greatest is 7.

Example 2 **Simulating an Experiment**

A yogurt company has announced a contest. Parts of a fractal pattern are printed under the lids of its yogurt containers. There are 6 parts that fit together to make the complete pattern. Your chance of getting each part is the same. To win a fractal poster, you must collect all 6 parts. What is the least number of containers you would expect to buy to win?

REAL LIFE
Advertising

Solution

You can simulate this experiment with a number cube. For each simulation, toss the cube until you get all 6 numbers. In the following simulation, 10 tosses were needed to get all 6 numbers.

The simulation was done 15 times. The number of the tosses needed before all 6 numbers appeared are as follows.

$$10, 15, 9, 13, 12, 10, 9, 13, 10, 11, 12, 22, 11, 18, 15$$

You can find the average of these numbers by finding their sum and dividing the result by 15, the number of simulations.

$$\text{Average} = \frac{\text{Sum}}{15}$$

$$= \frac{10 + 15 + 9 + 13 + 12 + 10 + 9 + \cdots + 11 + 18 + 15}{15}$$

$$= \frac{190}{15}$$

$$\approx 12.7$$

You would expect to buy about 12 or 13 yogurt containers to win.

Fractals are complex geometric figures that represent mathematical equations.

ONGOING ASSESSMENT

Talk About It
· · · · · · · · · · · · · · ·

With a partner, keep tossing number cubes until you get all six numbers. Do this several times and find the average number of tosses required.

1. Is your result similar to the one in Example 2?

2. What is the least number of tosses you would need?

In Exercises 1 and 2, copy and complete the table at the right to find all the possible sums when a red and a blue number cube are tossed.

+	1	2	3	4	5	6
1	2	3				
2	3					
3						
4						
5						
6						

1. If you tossed the number cubes 50 times, what total do you think would come up most often? Explain.

2. Toss two number cubes 50 times and record the results. Was your prediction in Exercise 1 correct?

3. **SIMULATION** You work for a frozen yogurt shop. The shop sells 12 flavors of frozen yogurt. As a special promotion, the shop installs a spinner with the 12 flavors. After a customer orders a cone, you spin the spinner. If it lands on the customer's flavor, the cone is free. Of 100 cones ordered, how many do you think will be free?

4. In the *Number Cube Age Game* you add and subtract numbers to get your age. Toss a number cube twice and add the numbers. If the total is less than your age, add the number on the next toss. If the total is greater than your age, subtract the number on the next toss. Estimate the number of tosses needed to get your age. Then play the game several times and record your results. The sample below was played by a 13-year-old.

Toss:	**5**	**3**	**1**	**6**	**2**
Total:	5	$5 + 3 = 8$	$8 + 1 = 9$	$9 + 6 = 15$	$15 - 2 = 13$

5. **MOUSE MAZE** At any fork in the maze, the mouse is equally likely to go left or right. Notice that there are four possible paths the mouse can travel.

   a. How many times do you think the mouse will travel the maze before it finds the food?

   b. Use a simulation to check your answer.

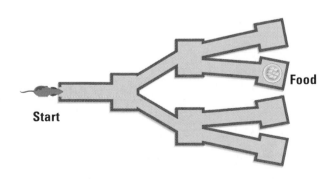

6. **WEATHER REPORTS** A local television station encourages viewers of its weather segment to report daily temperatures. The station estimates that for every 20,000 viewers, 15 will actually report temperatures. About 60,000 people watch the station's weather segment. Estimate the number of viewers that will report daily temperatures.

In Exercises 7 and 8, use the following information. Your coin bank has 5 pennies, 5 nickels, 5 dimes, and 5 quarters. You shake the coins out of the bank one at a time until you have a total of at least $0.50.

7. Estimate the number of coins you will have to shake out of the bank.

8. Describe and do a simulation that could be used to check your answer to Exercise 7.

9. **FIELD STUDY** The interactive investigation for this chapter has a simulation that estimates the population of white-footed mice, meadow voles, short-tailed shrews, and jumping mice in a region. Suppose you are a conservationist and want to estimate these populations. Describe how you might do this.

Tech Link

*Investigation 1,
Interactive
Real-Life
Investigations*

STANDARDIZED TEST PRACTICE

10. In a game, you randomly select one of 4 marbles. The marbles are black, green, red, and blue. You plan to play the game 3 times. Which item can you use to simulate the chance of selecting red, red, green?

   A 6-sided number cube   **B** 2-sided coin

   C Spinner with 4 sections   **D** Spinner with 3 sections

11. You plan to have a game at your party where any guest who picks the 1 cup out of 6 that has a marble under it wins a prize. Which item can you use to estimate how many prizes you will need?

   A 6-sided number cube   **B** 2-sided coin

   C Spinner with 4 sections   **D** Spinner with 3 sections

12. You scatter your button collection onto an 8 in.-by-12 in. tray. In a 2 in.-by-2 in. square of the tray, you count 13 buttons. Estimate how many buttons you have in your collection.

   A 26   **B** 96   **C** 312   **D** 1248

13. BUILDING YOUR PROJECT Thunderstorms are formed by the strong upward movement of warm, unstable, moist air. They always are accompanied by lightning and thunder, and usually produce rain.

The weather forecast for Saturday says that there is a 25% chance of thunderstorms. Design a simulation that can be used to illustrate the chance of a thunderstorm. Explain in your journal what a 25% chance of storms means. Record your answers in your journal.

SPIRAL REVIEW

In Exercises 1–4, write the number in words. (Toolbox, p. 652)

1. 5015   **2.** 16,450   **3.** 412,003   **4.** 180,927

In Exercises 5–8, multiply or divide. (Toolbox, p. 655)

5. 1.45×10 **6.** $612 \div 10$ **7.** $300 \div 1000$ **8.** 7.98×100

In Exercises 9–11, find the area of the figure. (1.3)

9.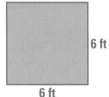
6 ft
6 ft

10.
0.5 m
2.3 m

11.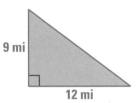
9 mi
12 mi

In Exercises 12–15, match the measurement with the object. (Toolbox, p. 658)

  A. 19 cm   **B.** 80 cm   **C.** 1.2 m   **D.** 11 mm

12. Diameter of a shirt button   **13.** Length of a pencil

14. Depth of a swimming pool   **15.** Length of a skateboard

READING A TABLE In Exercises 16–18, use the table showing the maximum running speed (in miles per hour) of a human compared with various animals. **(1.1)**

16. How much faster can a lion run than a human?

17. Which animal can run twice as fast as a rabbit?

18. How much slower is a human than a cheetah?

	Speed (mi/h)
Cheetah	70
Lion	50
Zebra	40
Rabbit	35
Human	28

Take this test as you would take a test in class. The answers to the exercises are given in the back of the book.

1. **MAKING A LIST** You have the letters that spell the word *MATH* in a bag. How many different ways can you pick 3 letters out of the bag? How many are words? **(1.1)**

2. **FINDING A PATTERN** Find the area of a square that has a side length of 2 units. What happens to the area of the square when its side length doubles? Triples? Quadruples? Describe the pattern of the areas. Then use the pattern to find the area when the side length is multiplied by 5. **(1.1,1.2)**

3. Which of the triangles are similar? Explain your answer. **(1.3)**

A 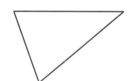 B C D

4. **TILING A FLOOR** You are tiling a floor using six-sided tiles, as shown at the right. Find the area of each tile. **(1.3)**

4 in.
3.5 in.

5. Draw two similar diamond-shaped figures, where each diamond shape is made up of four right triangles. **(1.3)**

In Exercises 6–8, use the perimeter of each figure to find the length of the missing side. (1.3)

6. Perimeter = 22 in.

5 in. 5 in.
?

7. Perimeter = 17 cm

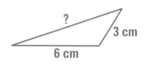
?
3 cm
6 cm

8. Perimeter = 20 m

?

9. **VIDEO RENTALS** A video store is having a special promotion. A customer selects a video and then spins the spinner at the right. The result determines whether the cost will be free or discounted. Out of 50 videos sold, how many do you think will be free or sold at a discount? Explain. **(1.4)**

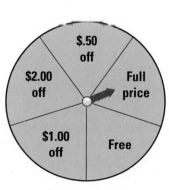
$.50 off
Full price
$2.00 off
$1.00 off
Free

10. Suppose you toss a red and a blue number cube 180 times. How many times do you think doubles will appear? Explain your reasoning. **(1.4)**

11. How could you estimate the grains of rice in 1 cup? **(1.4)**

Guess, Check, and Revise

What you should learn:

Goal 1 How to use a Guess, Check, and Revise strategy

Goal 2 How to use a Guess, Check, and Revise strategy to solve real-life problems

Why you should learn it:

Knowing how to use a Guess, Check, and Revise strategy can help you reconstruct past events.

The United States Postal Service handles more than 100 billion pieces of first-class mail each year.

Goal 1 GUESS, CHECK, AND REVISE

Guess, Check, and Revise involves the following three steps.

GUESS, CHECK, AND REVISE

1. Make an educated *guess* at the solution.
2. Use the given information to *check* the solution.
3. If not correct, *revise* the solution.

You should continue checking and revising your answer until you arrive at a correct solution.

Example 1 Using Guess, Check, and Revise

You took $5 to the post office and bought stamps to mail postcards and letters to 10 friends. You received change of $2.16. On your way home, you forgot how many of your friends were sent postcards and how many were sent letters. A postcard costs $0.20 to mail and a letter costs $0.32 to mail. How many postcards were sent and how many letters were sent?

Solution

STRATEGY **GUESS, CHECK, AND REVISE** You must have spent $5.00 minus $2.16, or $2.84. You can begin by guessing that you sent **5** postcards and **5** letters. You can check this as follows.

$$(5 \times 0.20) + (5 \times 0.32) = 1.00 + 1.60$$
$$= \$2.60$$

This amount is too small, so increase the number of letters. Suppose you sent **4** postcards and **6** letters.

$$(4 \times 0.20) + (6 \times 0.32) = 0.80 + 1.92$$
$$= \$2.72$$

This amount is still too small, so you again increase the number of letters. Suppose you sent **3** postcards and **7** letters.

$$(3 \times 0.20) + (7 \times 0.32) = 0.60 + 2.24$$
$$= \$2.84$$

The solution, $2.84, checks, which means you must have sent 3 postcards and 7 letters to your friends.

Example 2 Using Guess, Check, and Revise

REAL LIFE
Games

Shonda and you are playing a dart game. She tells you that she threw 12 balls at the board below. She hit the board each time and scored a total of 66 points. Can you tell how many balls landed in each region?

Solution

Begin by guessing that **4** balls landed in each region.

$$(4 \times 3) + (4 \times 7) + (4 \times 10) = 12 + 28 + 40$$
$$= 80$$

This guess is too large. Suppose you change it to **5** balls in the red, **4** in the blue, and **3** in the yellow.

$$(5 \times 3) + (4 \times 7) + (3 \times 10) = 15 + 28 + 30$$
$$= 73$$

This guess is still too large. Suppose you change it to **7** balls in the red, **3** in the blue, and **2** in the yellow.

$$(7 \times 3) + (3 \times 7) + (2 \times 10) = 21 + 21 + 20$$
$$= 62$$

This guess is too small. Suppose you change it to **6** balls in the red, **4** in the blue, and **2** in the yellow.

$$(6 \times 3) + (4 \times 7) + (2 \times 10) = 18 + 28 + 20$$
$$= 66$$

The last solution checks. Shonda threw 6 balls in the red region, 4 in the blue region, and 2 in the yellow region.

ONGOING ASSESSMENT

Write About It
· · · · · · · · · · · · · · · ·

Troy, Barb, and Greg were also playing the dart game shown in Example 2. Each person threw 12 balls and hit the board every time. Work with a partner to find the number of balls that landed in each region for each person. Write a description of your work.

1. Troy: 74 points

2. Barb: 70 points

3. Greg: 83 points

GUIDED PRACTICE

GUESS, CHECK, AND REVISE In Exercises 1 and 2, explain why the given guess would not be a good guess when using the Guess, Check, and Revise strategy.

1. The area of a square is 144 m^2. What is the length of each side?

Guess: $\frac{1}{4}$ of 144, or 36 m

2. The perimeter of a square is 36 in. What is the length of each side?

Guess: 2 in.

GUESS, CHECK, AND REVISE In Exercises 3 and 4, find the digits that represent letters in the sum.

3.
$$\begin{array}{r} \text{TWO} \\ + \text{TWO} \\ \hline \text{FIVE} \end{array}$$
Use the digits 1, 2, 4, 5, 6, 7, and 8.

4.
$$\begin{array}{r} \text{ONE} \\ \text{ONE} \\ + \text{ONE} \\ \hline \text{FOUR} \end{array}$$
Use the digits 1, 2, 4, 6, 7, and 8.

GEOMETRY In Exercises 5–10, find the length and width of the rectangle.

5. Perimeter: 38 m; Area: 18 m^2

6. Perimeter: 30 in.; Area: 26 in.^{2}

7. Perimeter: 14 km; Area: 10 km^2

8. Perimeter: 20 ft; Area: 21 ft^2

9. Perimeter: 28 yd; Area: 33 yd^2

10. Perimeter: 12 mi; Area: 5 mi^2

PRACTICE AND PROBLEM SOLVING

PUZZLES In Exercises 11–13, complete the magic polygon so that each number is used once and the sum of the numbers along each side is the same as the number in the center.

11. Use numbers 1–8.

12. Use numbers 1–10.

13. Use numbers 1–12.

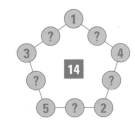

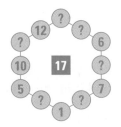

TECHNOLOGY In Exercises 14–16, use a calculator and the Guess, Check, and Revise strategy to find the value of *n*.

14. $n \times n = 289$

15. $n \times n = 676$

16. $n \times n = 2025$

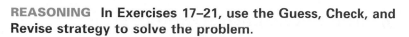

REASONING In Exercises 17–21, use the Guess, Check, and Revise strategy to solve the problem.

17. The length of a swimming pool is 3 times its width. The perimeter is 88 ft. What are the dimensions of the pool?

18. The sum of the scores on 3 science quizzes is 68. One score is 22. The other two scores are the same. What are they?

19. There are 10 nickels, dimes, and quarters in your backpack. You know that you have exactly one nickel and that the total amount is $1.70. How many quarters do you have?

20. You and a friend are playing *Scrabble*®. You spell *ZIG* and receive 13 points. Your friend spells *PIG* and receives 6 points. Then you spell *ZIP* and receive 14 points. An *I* is worth 1 point. How many points are *Z, P,* and *G* worth?

21. **NUMBER RIDDLE** When you add me to 100, you get 5 times my value. What number am I?

STANDARDIZED TEST PRACTICE

22. If the area of a square is 81 in.², what is the length of a side?

   A 3 in.   **B** 5 in.   **C** 7 in.   **D** 9 in.

23. Jeremy's bug collection has 4 more beetles than Lanette's and twice as many as Manuel's. Together the three own 46 beetles. How many beetles does Lanette own?

   A 10   **B** 16   **C** 20   **D** 32

EXPLORATION AND EXTENSION

PORTFOLIO

24. **BUILDING YOUR PROJECT** A hurricane is an intense tropical low pressure area with winds greater than 74 mi/h. Hurricanes start near the equator and travel north along the Gulf and Atlantic coasts. A coastal town has shelters for people to go to in case of a hurricane. Some of the shelters hold 35 people and others hold 64 people. After receiving a hurricane alert, 367 people go to the shelters. All the shelters are full. How many of each size shelter are there? Record your results in your journal.

1.6

Writing an Equation

What you should learn:

Goal ❶ How to use Guess, Check, and Revise to solve an equation

Goal ❷ How to write an equation to represent a real-life problem

Why you should learn it:

Knowing how to write and solve equations can help with your finances. An example is finding the total income at a yard sale.

Goal ❶ USING GUESS, CHECK, AND REVISE

The Guess, Check, and Revise problem solving strategy can be used to *solve an equation*.

EQUATIONS AND VARIABLES

An **equation** is a mathematical statement with an equal sign "=" in it. A letter, such as n or x, in an equation is called the **variable**. A variable can be replaced by any number. When you **solve an equation**, you find the value of the variable that makes the equation true.

Here is an example of an equation.

$3 \times n = 12$ — Equation

In the equation above, the variable is n. The **solution of the equation** is 4, because $3 \times 4 = 12$ is a true statement.

Example 1 **Solving Equations**

Use Guess, Check, and Revise to solve each equation. Check your result by substituting it into the original equation.

CONNECTION
Algebra

a. $12 + p = 23$ **b.** $36 \div m = 4$ **c.** $x - 13 = 27$

Solution

a. You need to find a number that can be added to 12 to get 23. The solution is $p = \mathbf{11}$.

✔**Check:** $12 + p = 23$ Write original equation.
          $12 + \mathbf{11} \overset{?}{=} 23$ Substitute 11 for p.
              $23 = 23$ Solution checks.

b. You need to find a number that 36 can be divided by to get 4. The solution is $m = \mathbf{9}$.

✔**Check:** $36 \div m = 4$ Write original equation.
       $36 \div \mathbf{9} \overset{?}{=} 4$ Substitute 9 for m.
           $4 = 4$ Solution checks.

c. You need to find a number that you can subtract 13 from to get 27. The solution is $x = \mathbf{40}$. You can check this solution.

STUDY TIP

Later in this book and in future math classes, you will study other strategies for solving equations. Whatever strategy you use, be sure that you always check your solution by substituting it into the original equation.

Much of *algebra* is about writing and solving equations. People developed algebra to model and solve real-life problems. When you write an equation that represents a real-life problem, you are **modeling a real-life problem** .

| Example 2 | **Writing an Equation** |

You and three friends had a yard sale. One friend divided the income from the sale by 4 and each person received $21. Write an algebraic equation to find the total income. Then find the solution to the equation.

REAL LIFE
Money

Solution

| **Verbal Model** | **Total** ÷ **Number** = **Share for** |
| | **income** **of people** **each person** |

Labels   Total income = T
Number of people = 4
Share for each person = 21

Algebraic Model $T \div 4 = 21$

You need to find a number that can be divided by 4 to get 21. You guess that the solution is 84. Then you check your solution.

✔**Check:** $T \div 4 = 21$ Write original equation.
$84 \div 4 = 21$ Substitute 84 for *T*.
$21 = 21$ Solution checks.

The solution checks, so the total income must have been $84.

GUIDED PRACTICE

1. COMMUNICATING In your own words, describe what it means to solve an equation. Give an example.

In Exercises 2–4, use the equation $x + 15 = 24$. Complete the statement with the word *solution*, *variable*, or *check*.

2. x is the __?__ .

3. 9 is the __?__ .

4. $9 + 15 = 24$ is the __?__ .

In Exercises 5–8, match the equation with its solution.

A. $n = 14$ B. $n = 12$ C. $n = 24$ D. $n = 20$

5. $21 - n = 1$ **6.** $n + 8 = 22$ **7.** $n \div 4 = 6$ **8.** $n \times 3 = 36$

9. COMPACT DISKS You buy 7 CDs for a total of $83.93. Each CD is the same price. Use the verbal model below. Assign labels and write an equation to represent this problem. Then solve the equation to find the cost of each CD.

$$\begin{array}{ccc} \text{Number of} \\ \text{CDs} \end{array} \times \begin{array}{c} \text{Cost of a} \\ \text{CD} \end{array} = \begin{array}{c} \text{Total} \\ \text{cost} \end{array}$$

PRACTICE AND PROBLEM SOLVING

In Exercises 10–15, check the given value of the variable in the equation. Is it a solution? If not, find the solution.

10. $p + 11 = 14, p = 25$ **11.** $16 - x = 8, x = 12$ **12.** $7 + t = 40, t = 33$

13. $21 \div y = 7, y = 3$ **14.** $m \div 2 = 13, m = 36$ **15.** $z \times 9 = 54, z = 5$

GUESS, CHECK, AND REVISE In Exercises 16–23, solve the equation. Then check your result.

16. $n + 12 = 21$ **17.** $14 + z = 39$ **18.** $50 - t = 14$ **19.** $p - 17 = 18$

20. $y \times 6 = 42$ **21.** $2 \times m = 28$ **22.** $44 \div x = 4$ **23.** $b \div 9 = 7$

WRITING AN EQUATION In Exercises 24–27, write an equation for each question. Then solve the equation to answer the question.

24. What number can be added to 15 to get 30?

25. What number can 16 be subtracted from to get 7?

26. What number can be multiplied by 4 to get 60?

27. What number can be divided by 18 to get 2?

TECHNOLOGY In Exercises 28–33, solve the equation using the Guess, Check, and Revise strategy and a calculator.

28. $8.56 + x = 16.31$ **29.** $28 - p = 8.97$ **30.** $t - 4.7 = 5.39$

31. $m \times 2.05 = 27.06$ **32.** $14.44 \div y = 3.8$ **33.** $d \div 5.25 = 2.6$

34. WRITING Formulate a possible problem situation to go with each equation in Exercises 28–33.

35. PUZZLE Think of a 2-digit number. Add 3, double the number, subtract 6, and divide by 2. What is the result?

36. GOLF You and 2 friends go to a driving range to hit golf balls. You divide a bucket of golf balls among you, each getting 16. Use the verbal model below. Assign labels and write an equation for this problem. Then solve the equation to find the total number of golf balls in the bucket.

$$\begin{array}{ccc} \text{Golf balls} \\ \text{in bucket} \end{array} \div \begin{array}{c} \text{Number} \\ \text{of people} \end{array} = \begin{array}{c} \text{Golf balls} \\ \text{per person} \end{array}$$

37. BASEBALL CARDS You and 3 friends share the cost of a pack of baseball cards evenly. The pack costs $1.80. Use the verbal model below. Assign labels and write an equation. Then solve the equation and find each person's share.

$$\text{Number of people} \times \text{Cost per person} = \text{Cost of a pack}$$

Real Life...
Real People

Card Designers
Krista Lowe and Jessica Mendelowitz produced baseball cards of their school baseball team in LaPorte, Indiana.

STANDARDIZED TEST PRACTICE

38. Choose the equation that represents the sentence, "If you add 7 to some number, you get 30."

   A $m + 7 = 30$ **B** $7 - d = 30$

   C $30 + p = 7$ **D** $r - 7 = 30$

39. Which value is the solution of the equation $j - 17 = 51$?

   A $j = 3$ **B** $j = 17$

   C $j = 68$ **D** $j = 122$

40. Which equation does not represent the perimeter of the figure shown at the right?

   A $P = 21 + 10 + n$ **B** $P = 7 + 10 + 14 + n$

   C $P = n(7 + 10 + 14)$ **D** $P = n + 31$

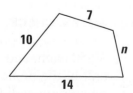

41. **COMMUNICATING ABOUT MATHEMATICS** Giant pandas are one of the most endangered species on Earth. To survive in the wild, pandas need large areas of bamboo forest in which to live.

    To help ensure the future of the panda, China is planning to set aside 14 more areas of bamboo forest as panda reserves. The addition of these reserves will bring the total number up to 26. Write a verbal model to find out how many reserves there were originally. Assign labels and write an algebraic model. Then solve the equation.

| Verbal Model | → | Labels | → | Algebraic Model |

SPIRAL REVIEW

MAKING AN ESTIMATE In Exercises 1–4, match the object with its measurement. (1.1)

A. 6 cm   B. 15 m   C. $3\frac{3}{4}$ in.   D. 1 cm

1. Width of a baseball card   2. Height of a mug

3. Width of a paper clip   4. Height of a tree

5. **MAKING A LIST** You are buying a sherbet cone. You can choose from raspberry, orange, lime, or rainbow sherbet in a cake, sugar, or waffle cone. How many different choices do you have? (1.2)

6. **LOOKING FOR A PATTERN** You deposit money in your savings account each month. You deposit $1 in January, $2 in February, $4 in March, $8 in April. If you continue this pattern, how much will you deposit in September? (1.2)

GEOMETRY In Exercises 7–9, find the area of each figure. (1.3)

7.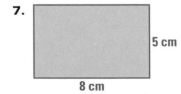

8.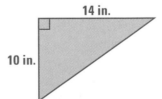

9.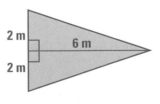

10. **GUESS, CHECK, AND REVISE** You leave home with money to shop for school supplies. You buy 2 notebooks for $2.50 each, 2 folders for $0.50 each, and a pack of pencils for $3. You stop for lunch and spend half of the money you have left. You get back home with $3. How much money did you have when you left home? (1.5)

PANDA Populations

READ About It

Ten years ago, there were only about 1400 giant pandas in the bamboo forests of China. Half lived in the Min Mountains. Another 18 percent were in the Qionglai Mountains. The rest were either in the Liang or the Qinling Mountains.

Panda populations in the wild have been decreasing at a rate of 4 percent per year. In 1996, only about 1000 pandas remained in the mountains of China.

Pandas live to be about 25 years old. They are active for $\frac{5}{8}$ of each day and spend $\frac{14}{15}$ of this time eating. Pandas need to eat at least 30 pounds of bamboo each day.

China is putting aside protected areas, or reserves, of bamboo forest in an effort to save panda populations in the wild. The Chinese plan is to add 14 new panda reserves, bringing the total number of reserves up to 26.

WRITE About It

1. How many pandas were living in the Liang or Qinling Mountains 10 years ago? Explain your answer.

2. How many hours of each day does a panda spend eating bamboo? How many hours does a panda spend resting? Explain.

3. Estimate how much bamboo a panda might eat in a lifetime. How did you arrive at your estimate?

4. Estimate the panda population for 1990. How did you get your answer?

5. Write a verbal model to find the number of hours a panda rests in a year. Assign labels and write the equation. Solve.

Qinling • Xi'an
• Shanghai
Min
Qionglai
CHINA
Liang
TAIWAN
• Kunming
• Hong Kong
VIETNAM

What you should learn:

Goal 1 How to use logical reasoning to solve a problem

Goal 2 How to use a Venn diagram to solve a problem

Why you should learn it:

Knowing how to use logic tables and Venn diagrams can help you solve a logic problem such as who is dancing with whom.

Goal 1 USING LOGICAL REASONING

In this lesson, you will learn how to apply logical reasoning with logic tables and Venn diagrams.

Example 1 Using a Logic Table

Three couples are at a costume dance. One couple is wearing red, one couple is in blue, and one is in green. The couples decide to change dancing partners. The man in green, who is not dancing with the woman in red, says "Not one of us is dancing with the partner we came with." Who is dancing with whom?

Solution

One way to solve this puzzle is to use a logic table. Eliminate the possibilities that are false. Keep going until there is only one possibility left, as shown below.

No one is dancing with a person wearing the same color.

The man in green is not dancing with the woman in red.

The woman in red is dancing with the man in blue. So, the man in blue is not dancing with the woman in green.

The woman in green is dancing with the man in red. So, the man in red is not dancing with the woman in blue.

As you can see, the woman in red is dancing with the man in blue. The woman in blue is dancing with the man in green. The woman in green is dancing with the man in red.

A **Venn diagram** is a drawing that uses geometric shapes to show relationships among sets of objects. The Venn diagram below shows relationships among natural numbers from 1 to 10. Recall that a *prime number* is a number divisible only by itself and 1.

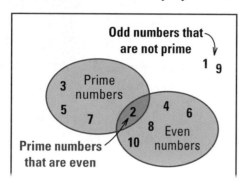

Example 2 Interpreting a Survey

In a survey of 32 students, 21 students say they like blue jeans, 17 say they like black jeans, and 3 say they don't like either color. How many students said they like both colors of jeans?

Solution

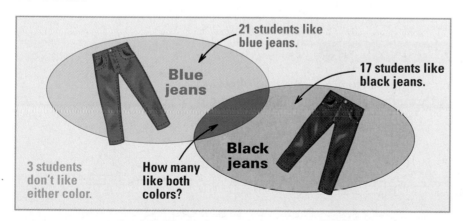

21 students like blue jeans.

17 students like black jeans.

Blue jeans

Black jeans

3 students don't like either color.

How many like both colors?

To find how many students like both colors, you can add the numbers in the three categories.

$$21 + 17 + 3 = 41$$

Because 41 is 9 more than are in the class, you can reason that 9 students like both blue and black jeans.

GUIDED PRACTICE

1. **BASKETBALL** Of the 5 players on a basketball team, 2 are guards, 2 are forwards, and 1 is a center. Cindy, Shawna, and Sheila play on a basketball team. One plays center, one plays forward, and one plays guard. Copy and complete the table below to find who plays which position.

   - Shawna and the center each scored more than Sheila.

   - Shawna is not the forward.

	Center	Forward	Guard
Cindy	?	?	?
Shawna	?	?	?
Sheila	?	?	?

2. **VENN DIAGRAM** You surveyed 50 students. Of those surveyed, 35 have been to a fair, 20 have been to a rodeo, and 3 have been to neither. How many students have been to both a fair and a rodeo? Illustrate your answer using a Venn diagram.

3. Juan, Linda, and Ed are each in a different club: ski, drama, or pep.

   - Linda is not in the drama club.

   - Linda and the student in the ski club are Juan's neighbors.

   Who is in which club?

PRACTICE AND PROBLEM SOLVING

In Exercises 4–6, copy the Venn diagram. Then classify the following figures by writing the letters A through H in the Venn diagram regions.

 A B C D E F G H

4.
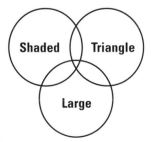

5.
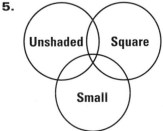

6.
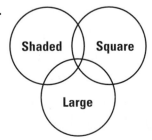

7. USING LOGICAL REASONING Ben, Jen, Ken, and Len are all different heights.

- Ken is taller than Jen and Len.

- Ben is taller than Ken.

- Jen is shorter than Len.

Who is the tallest? Who is the shortest?

9. HOUSEHOLD PETS You take a survey of the 28 students in your class. In the survey, 16 say they have a dog, 13 say they have a cat, and 5 say they have neither a cat nor a dog. How many students have both a cat and a dog?

8. The last names of Ben, Jen, Ken, and Len are Su, Kipp, Lee, and Roi.

- Ken and Ben are not Su or Lee.

- Jen is not Su.

- Ben's last name is longer than Ken's.

Find the names of the four people.

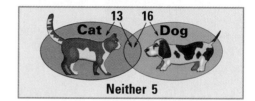

10. Carmine is older than Jasmine. Regina is older than Carmine. Charille is younger than Jasmine. What is the correct order of the four, from oldest to youngest?

- **A** Carmine, Jasmine, Regina, Charille

- **B** Jasmine, Regina, Charille, Carmine

- **C** Regina, Carmine, Jasmine, Charille

- **D** Charille, Carmine, Jasmine, Regina

11. In the set of numbers from 1 to 20, 8 are factors of 36, 5 are multiples of 4, and 9 are neither. How many numbers are both factors of 36 and multiples of 4?

- **A** 2   **B** 3   **C** 4   **D** 6

EXPLORATION AND EXTENSION

PORTFOLIO

12. BUILDING YOUR PROJECT The map shows states where hurricanes occur and states where 10 or more tornadoes occur each year. Make a Venn diagram to determine the number of states where both hurricanes and 10 or more tornadoes occur. Record your Venn diagram in your journal.

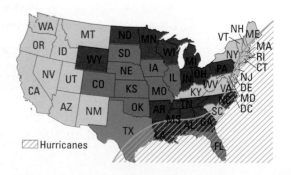

Separating into Cases

What you should learn:

Goal 1 How to use cases to solve a problem

Goal 2 How to use cases to solve a real-life problem

Why you should learn it:

Knowing how to use cases can help you decide what to buy. An example is getting the best buy on a product.

Goal 1 SEPARATING INTO CASES

Some problems are easier to solve when you separate them into different cases. When you do this, you must be sure that you consider *all* possible cases.

Example 1 Separating into Cases

How many squares are in a 4 unit-by-4 unit square?

Solution

One way to solve this problem is to separate it into four different cases, as shown below.

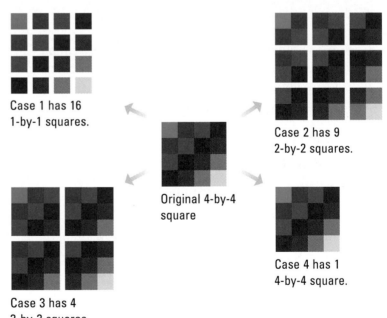

Case 1 has 16 1-by-1 squares.

Case 2 has 9 2-by-2 squares.

Original 4-by-4 square

Case 3 has 4 3-by-3 squares.

Case 4 has 1 4-by-4 square.

STRATEGY **MAKE A TABLE** A table, like the one below, can help you organize your results.

Dimensions	1×1	2×2	3×3	4×4
Number of Squares	16	9	4	1

By adding the number of squares in each case, you can see that the total number of squares is 30.

$$16 + 9 + 4 + 1 = 30$$

| Example 2 | **Separating into Cases** |

REAL LIFE
Shopping

You are buying tomatoes to make a batch of salsa. At the store, you find tomatoes packaged in two different sizes of boxes, as shown below. How many of each size should you buy to get at least 17 lb at the least cost?

3 lb/$2.79   Tomatoes   5 lb/$3.98   Tomatoes

Solution

Consider all the ways you could get at least 17 lb.

3 lb boxes	5 lb boxes	Weight			Cost
6	0	18 lb	$(6 \times 2.79) + (0 \times 3.98)$	=	$16.74
5	1	20 lb	$(5 \times 2.79) + (1 \times 3.98)$	=	$17.93
4	1	17 lb	$(4 \times 2.79) + (1 \times 3.98)$	=	$15.14
3	2	19 lb	$(3 \times 2.79) + (2 \times 3.98)$	=	$16.33
2	3	21 lb	$(2 \times 2.79) + (3 \times 3.98)$	=	$17.52
1	3	18 lb	$(1 \times 2.79) + (3 \times 3.98)$	=	$14.73
0	4	20 lb	$(0 \times 2.79) + (4 \times 3.98)$	=	$15.92

The best buy is one 3 lb box and three 5 lb boxes.

Salsa Mexicana
Combine the following ingredients:
  5–6 ripe tomatoes, chopped
  1/2 cup chopped onion
  4–6 fresh chiles, chopped
  1/3 cup chopped cilantro
  1 tsp. salt
  juice from 1/2 a lime
Let the salsa sit for an hour before serving.
Use on eggs, sandwiches, or chips.

ONGOING ASSESSMENT

Talk About It
· ·

Suppose a 1-by-1 square has 1 square.

A 2-by-2 square has 5, or 4 + 1, squares.

A 3-by-3 square has 14, or 9 + 4 + 1, squares.

1. Predict the number of squares in a 6-by-6 square.

2. Discuss how you arrived at your prediction.

GUIDED PRACTICE

1. How many non-square rectangles can be drawn in the original 4-by-4 square shown in Example 1 on page 40?

2. **BALLPARK** You are driving from your home to the ballpark on the streets shown at the right. The traffic can only flow west and south. How many different routes can you take?

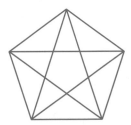

3. **PIZZA** The 2 largest pizzas that the pizza shop offers are shown below. How many of each size should be bought to get at least 70 pieces at the least cost?

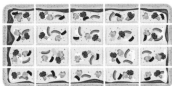

Super: 20 pieces for $15.99   **Large: 8 pieces for $6.99**

PRACTICE AND PROBLEM SOLVING

4. How many different combinations of 3 odd numbers have a sum of 15? (Consider $7 + 7 + 1$ to be the same as $7 + 1 + 7$.)

5. Copy the triangular grid at the right. How many total triangles of different sizes are in the grid?

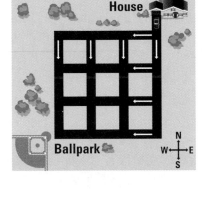

TRACING A PATH In Exercises 6–8, show how the figure can be traced by going over each line exactly once and returning to the starting point without lifting your pencil. (*Hint:* Choosing a different starting point may help you trace the figure.)

6.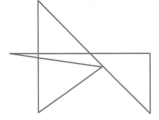

7.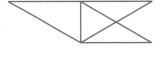

8.

9. **TRACK AND FIELD** Annette, Rita, Sharmain, and Jana compete in the 100-yd dash track-and-field event. How many different ways can the four of them finish first, second, third, and fourth? (Ignore ties.)

10. **MAKING CHANGE** Admission into an amusement park costs $21.75. You give the cashier $22. How many ways can you be given change?

11. Trace the maze below on a sheet of paper. Is there more than one way to travel through the maze? Describe all the routes you can find.

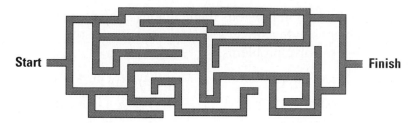

Start   Finish

12. **SEPARATING INTO CASES** You work at a zoological park. You are buying minnows and crayfish for the whooping cranes. You want a total of 7 lb, including at least 2 lb of each food. How many of each weight should you buy to spend as little as possible?

Minnows: 1 lb for $1.75, or 3 lb for $5.00

Crayfish: 1 lb for $2.25, or 3 lb for $6.00

STANDARDIZED TEST PRACTICE

13. How many different combinations of three numbers have a sum of ten? (Numbers may be repeated.)

(A) 6   **(B)** 8   **(C)** 10   **(D)** 12

14. You go to a restaurant with $5. Burgers cost $1.05 and fries cost $0.78. You want to buy the combination that gives you the *least* amount of change. Which combination should you buy?

(A) 1 burger, 4 fries   **(B)** 2 burgers, 3 fries

(C) 3 burgers, 2 fries   **(D)** 4 burgers, 1 fries

EXPLORATION AND EXTENSION

PORTFOLIO

15. **BUILDING YOUR PROJECT** During one year in the United States, there were 1303 tornadoes, causing $800 million in property damage. During the same year, 5 tropical storms and 1 hurricane caused $25 billion of property damage in coastal regions. Explain which kind of storm you think is the most costly and why. Record your answer in your journal.

More Problem Solving Strategies

Goal 1 USING A GRAPH

In this chapter and in previous mathematics courses, you studied many problem solving strategies. Here are some of the strategies you can use to solve problems.

Look for a Pattern	Act It Out
Use a Graph	Draw a Diagram
Classify and Group Data	Work Backward
Solve a Simpler Problem	Use a Simulation
Guess, Check, and Revise	Write an Equation
Use Logical Reasoning	Separate into Cases
Make a List or Table	Make an Estimate

In this lesson, you will practice the strategies of Using a Graph and Working Backward.

Example 1 Using a Graph

The double bar graph below shows the populations of El Paso, Texas, and Knoxville, Tennessee, from 1986 to 1996. Describe their growth.

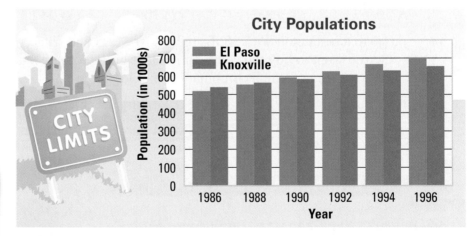

City Populations

Solution

Use the graph to estimate the populations of El Paso and Knoxville from 1986 to 1996. The graph shows that the populations of both cities increased during the period from 1986 to 1996. El Paso's population increased at a faster rate than Knoxville's. In 1986, El Paso had a smaller population than Knoxville. By 1996, the population of El Paso was greater than that of Knoxville.

Example 2 Working Backward

REAL LIFE
Population

In 1996, Omaha, Nebraska, had a population of about 670,000. From 1986 through 1996, the population increased by about 4000 people a year. Use the Working Backward strategy to estimate the population in 1986.

Solution

One way to solve the problem is to start with the 1996 population. Then work backward by repeatedly subtracting 4000 until you reach 1986.

Year	Population
1996	670,000
1995	670,000 − 4000 = 666,000
1994	666,000 − 4000 = 662,000
1993	662,000 − 4000 = 658,000
1992	658,000 − 4000 = 654,000
1991	654,000 − 4000 = 650,000
1990	650,000 − 4000 = 646,000
1989	646,000 − 4000 = 642,000
1988	642,000 − 4000 = 638,000
1987	638,000 − 4000 = 634,000
1986	634,000 − 4000 = 630,000

The 1986 population was about 630,000.

1986

1996

From the calculations above, you can see that the population of Omaha was about 630,000 in 1986. Can you see any difference between the photograph of Omaha taken in 1986 and the one taken in 1996? What differences do you see?

ONGOING ASSESSMENT

Write About It

Estimate the 1990 population for each city listed below.

1. Modesto, California

1980: 266,000
1996: 426,000

2. Erie, Pennsylvania

1980: 280,000
1996: 280,000

3. Cleveland, Ohio

1980: 2,278,000
1996: 2,214,000

WHAT *did you learn?*

WHY *did you learn it?*

Skills

1.1	Use a problem solving plan.	Estimate the number of items in a box.
1.2	Employ the strategy of Solving a Simpler Problem.	Find the number of items needed for a store display.
1.3	Use diagrams to compare similar figures.	Compare the perimeters and areas of similar figures.
1.4	Perform mathematical experiments and simulations.	Estimate the number of items needed to win a contest.
1.5	Use the strategy of Guess, Check, and Revise.	Reconstruct past events.
1.6	Write and solve an algebraic equation.	Compute the amount of money made at a sale.
1.7	Use Logical Reasoning and Venn diagrams.	Solve a logic problem and interpret a survey.
1.8	Employ the strategy of Separating into Cases.	Find the best buy on a food item.
1.9	Interpret a graph and use the strategy of Working Backward.	Estimate the population of a city.

Strategies | **1.1–1.9** Use problem solving strategies. | Solve real-life problems.

Using Data | **1.1–1.9** Use tables and graphs. | Organize data and solve problems.

HOW *does it fit into the bigger picture of mathematics?*

The first steps in solving any problem are to understand the problem and to make a plan. For example, suppose you are told that the population of Charlestown, West Virginia was 270,000 in 1980 and 249,000 in 1997. Then you are asked to estimate the population of Charlestown in 1990. To solve this problem, you could use any or all of the following strategies.

Method **1**   Work Backward

Method **2**   Look for a Pattern

Method **3**   Guess, Check, and Revise

VOCABULARY

- similar (p. 16)
- perimeter (p. 17)
- area (p. 17)
- equation (p. 30)

- variable (p. 30)
- solve an equation (p. 30)
- solution of an equation (p. 30)

- modeling a real-life problem (p. 31)
- Venn diagram (p. 37)

1.1 A PROBLEM SOLVING PLAN

Example   Use the problem solving plan to find the height of a $10 stack of dimes.

Understand the Problem

1. How tall is a stack of 100 dimes?

Collect Data

2. The height of 1 dime is 1 mm.

Solve the Problem

3. 1 mm × 100 = 100 mm

Look Back

4. Check your solution.

1. You are buying a 3 lb bag of Delicious apples for $2.25. Macintosh apples sell for $0.79/lb. Which is the better bargain? Explain the problem solving plan you used.

2. You are planning dinners for the next month. You can choose from 4 different main courses, 3 kinds of vegetables, and 3 desserts. Could you have a different dinner each day? Explain.

1.2 PATTERNS AND PROBLEM SOLVING

Example   You are helping a younger student learn multiplication by 9. You tell the student to look for a pattern.

You list all the products, starting with 2×9 and ending with 10×9.

$2 \times 9 = 18, 3 \times 9 = 27, 4 \times 9 = 36, 5 \times 9 = 45, \ldots, 10 \times 9 = 90$

You find the sum of the digits of each product is 9 and the first digit of the product is one less than the multiplier.

3. Describe the pattern of the figures at the right. Then find how many squares make up the 50th figure.

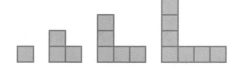

Number Relationships
and Fractions

SERPENT MOUND This mound in Ohio was constructed around 1070 A.D. The Northeast cultural area included about $\frac{31}{168}$ of the major Native American groups in North America.

CHACO CANYON This site in New Mexico was an important cultural center from about 900 A.D. through 1130 A.D. The Southwest cultural area included about $\frac{11}{84}$ of the major Native American groups.

TECHNOLOGY

Technology resources accompanying this chapter:
• Interactive Real-Life Investigations
• Middle School Tutorial Software

CHAPTER **THEME**
Unearthing the Past

MAYA TEMPLE Chichén Itzá in Mexico, built around 514 B.C., includes this temple, El Castillo, and carved stone head of an imaginary beast. The Middle America cultural area included about $\frac{5}{84}$ of the major Native American groups in North America.

Native Americans

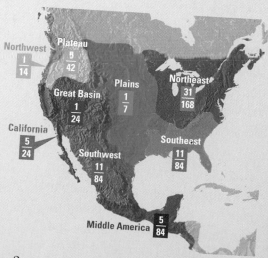

REAL LIFE
Ancient Peoples

The first Americans are thought to have come to North America by crossing the frozen Bering Strait several thousand years ago. These people gradually moved down throughout North America. They had specialized **cultures**, but often traded freely with each other.

By 1492, Native Americans had settled into many different groups throughout North America, most with their own language. The map shows the portion of major groups located in various geographic areas.

Northwest $\frac{1}{14}$
Plateau $\frac{9}{42}$
Plains $\frac{1}{7}$
Northeast $\frac{31}{168}$
Great Basin $\frac{1}{24}$
California $\frac{5}{24}$
Southwest $\frac{11}{84}$
Southeast $\frac{11}{84}$
Middle America $\frac{5}{84}$

Think and Discuss

1. What fraction of groups lived on the Northwest Coast?

2. Which area contained $\frac{1}{7}$ of the major groups of Native Americans?

PORTFOLIO

CHAPTER PROJECT

Keeping a Field Journal

PROJECT DESCRIPTION

Archeology is the scientific study of the remains of past human life and activities. To answer questions about what life was like for people who lived in the past, archeologists keep detailed journals about what they discover, because often a site they are unearthing is destroyed by their digging. Suppose you are helping at several digs. To organize your information, you will keep a field journal containing information about the **TOPICS** listed on the next page.

GETTING STARTED

Talking It Over

- Discuss what you think it was like to live in North America 5000 years ago. What types of houses did Native Americans live in? What clothes did they wear? How did they get their food?

- What do you think an archeologist's job is like? What tasks do you think an archeologist does in a typical day? Ask your librarian to help you find out about archeologists. Then share the information with your group.

Planning Your Project

- **Materials Needed:** paper, pencils or pens

- You can use the seven topics in the **BUILDING YOUR PROJECT** list on page 57. You may want to include photographs of archeological digs or objects (called *artifacts*) along with your journal entries. Keep your work in your portfolio and add to it as assigned.

BUILDING YOUR PROJECT

These are places throughout the chapter where you will work on your project.

TOPICS

INTERNET

To find out more about archeology, go to:
http://www.mlmath.com

2.1

Order of Operations

What you should learn:

Goal 1 How to evaluate a variable expression

Goal 2 How to use order of operations

Why you should learn it:

When more than one operation is used in an expression, it is important to know the order in which the operations must be performed.

In cooking you need to follow the directions in a recipe in the correct order. For example, you must mix bread dough and let it rise before baking.

Goal 1 EVALUATING VARIABLE EXPRESSIONS

An **expression** is a collection of numbers, variables, and symbols such as $+$, $-$, $\times$, and $\div$. An expression can contain grouping symbols, such as parentheses. If the expression has only numbers and symbols, it is a **numerical expression**. If it has a variable, it is a **variable expression**.

Numerical Expression	Variable Expression
$(2 \times 3) + 5$	$13 - (4 \times n)$

In the variable expression $13 - (4 \times n)$, the symbol used for multiplication is $\times$. Three other ways to write a product such as 4 times n are $4 \cdot n$, $4(n)$, and $4n$. The last expression uses no symbol for the operation of multiplication.

Finding the value of an expression is called **evaluating the expression**. Grouping symbols tell you the order in which to do the operations. When evaluating an expression, operations that are within grouping symbols should be done first.

Example 1 Evaluating a Variable Expression

Evaluate $15 + (3 \times m)$ for the given values of m.

a. $m = 1$ **b.** $m = 2$ **c.** $m = 5$

Solution

Value of m	Substitute	Evaluate Numerical Expression
a. $m = 1$	$15 + (3 \times 1)$	$15 + 3 = 18$
b. $m = 2$	$15 + (3 \times 2)$	$15 + 6 = 21$
c. $m = 5$	$15 + (3 \times 5)$	$15 + 15 = 30$

Example 2 Sum of Whole Numbers

The expression $n \times (n + 1) \div 2$ gives the sum of the first n whole numbers. Find the sum of the first 5 whole numbers.

Solution

Evaluate the expression $n \times (n + 1) \div 2$ for $n = 5$.

$5(5 + 1) \div 2 = 5(6) \div 2 = 30 \div 2 = 15$

✔**Check:** $1 + 2 + 3 + 4 + 5 = 15$

Goal 2 ORDER OF OPERATIONS

In the following investigation, you will use a calculator to evaluate expressions that have more than one operation.

LESSON INVESTIGATION

COOPERATIVE LEARNING

Investigating Order of Operations

GROUP ACTIVITY Use a calculator to evaluate each expression. Did you get the same results as others in your group? Discuss the order in which each calculator performed the operations.

1. $18 - 3 \times 4$
2. $8 \times 5 \div 4$
3. $28 \div 4 + 3$
4. $23 - 8 \div 2$
5. $3 \times 6 \div 3 + 2$
6. $12 + 9 - 6$
7. $6 \times 2 + 6 \times 4$
8. $40 - 4 \times 3 + 2$

In the investigation you may have discovered that the value of an expression with two or more operations depends on the order in which you do the operations. Therefore, we need rules for evaluating expressions.

ORDER OF OPERATIONS

1. First do operations within grouping symbols.

2. Then multiply and divide from left to right.

3. Finally add and subtract from left to right.

Example 3 Using Order of Operations

Evaluate the expression.

a. $25 - 3 \cdot 5$

b. $(2 + 4) \div 3 \times 2$

Solution

a. $25 - 3 \cdot 5 = 25 - 15$ Multiply 3 by 5.

$= 10$ Subtract 25 and 15.

b. $(2 + 4) \div 3 \times 2 = 6 \div 3 \times 2$ Operate inside parentheses: 2 + 4.

$= 2 \times 2$ Divide 6 by 3.

$= 4$ Multiply 2 by 2.

ONGOING ASSESSMENT

Write About It

Use the expression $(6 \times 4 + 3) \div 3 - 4 \times 2$.

1. Describe the steps you would use to evaluate the expression.

2. Check to see that your steps match the order of operations listed at the left.

ALGEBRA CONNECTION

Number Properties

Part A COMMUTATIVE PROPERTIES

Materials Needed
- graph paper
- pencil or pen
- colored pencils or markers

1. Explain how the models below represent the sums $5 + 3$ and $3 + 5$. What is the value of each expression?

2. Explain how the models below represent the products 3×5 and 5×3. What is the value of each expression?

3. Draw a model for each expression. Then evaluate the expression.

   a. $7 + 2$ **b.** $2 + 7$ **c.** 4×6 **d.** 6×4

4. What can you say about the values of $a + b$ and $b + a$? What about the values of $a \times b$ and $b \times a$? Explain.

Part B ASSOCIATIVE PROPERTIES

5. Explain how the models below represent the sums $(2 + 4) + 3$ and $2 + (4 + 3)$. What is the value of each expression?

6. Explain how the models below represent the products $(2 \times 3) \times 4$ and $2 \times (3 \times 4)$. What is the value of each expression?

7. Draw a model for each expression. Then evaluate the expression.

   a. $(7 + 3) + 5$; $7 + (3 + 5)$ **b.** $(4 \times 2) \times 5$; $4 \times (2 \times 5)$

8. Consider the values of $(a + b) + c$ and $a + (b + c)$ and the values of $(a \times b) \times c$ and $a \times (b \times c)$. What do you notice?

9. The word *commute* means to move from one
location to another. The *Commutative Property
of Addition* says that you can add two numbers
in either order and get the same sum—the
numbers can switch locations. That is, if *a* and
b are any two numbers, then

$$a + b = b + a.$$ **Commutative Property
of Addition**

Use variables to write the Commutative
Property of Multiplication.

10. Do the commutative properties apply to
decimals? Give examples.

11. The word *associate* means to group together.
The *Associative Property of Addition* says that
when you add three numbers, you can group the numbers in
different ways and still get the same sum. That is, if *a*, *b*, and *c*
are any three numbers, then

$$(a + b) + c = a + (b + c).$$ **Associative Property of Addition**

Use variables to write the Associative Property of Multiplication.

12. Do the associative properties apply to decimals? Give examples.

NOW TRY THESE

13. Draw a model for both expressions. Use the
models to show that the expressions are equal.
Then write the number property demonstrated.

   a. $4 + 7$ and $7 + 4$

   b. $3 \times (5 \times 2)$ and $(3 \times 5) \times 2$

   c. 5×6 and 6×5

   d. $(5 + 2) + 4$ and $5 + (2 + 4)$

14. Decide whether there is only one value of *n* that
makes the equation true or many values of *n*.
Draw models to explain.

   a. $5 + n = n + 5$

   b. $(3 \times n) \times 10 = 3 \times (n \times 10)$

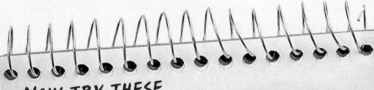

2.2

What you should learn:

Goal 1 How to use exponents to write powers

Goal 2 How to recognize patterns in expressions that have exponents

Why you should learn it:

Exponents allow you to write mathematical expressions in simpler ways. For example, $4 \cdot 4 \cdot 4$ can be written as 4^3.

Some mineral crystals are shaped like cubes. The large crystals shown here are a mineral called *pyrite* (iron sulfide).

Powers and Exponents

Goal 1 USING EXPONENTS TO WRITE POWERS

When two or more numbers are multiplied in an expression, each number is a **factor**. Some expressions, such as $5 \cdot 5 \cdot 5 \cdot 5$, have a repeated factor and can be written in a simpler way using an **exponent**.

$$\underbrace{5 \cdot 5 \cdot 5 \cdot 5}_{\text{Factors}} = 5^{\overset{\text{Exponent}}{4}} \Big\} \text{ Power}$$

In the expression 5^4, the number 5 is the **base** and the number 4 is the exponent. The entire expression is called a **power**.

Written	**Read as**
$5 \cdot 5 = 5^2$	5 to the 2nd power or 5 squared
$7 \times 7 \times 7 = 7^3$	7 to the 3rd power or 7 cubed
$(n)(n)(n)(n) = n^4$	n to the 4th power

Powers need to be added to the list of order of operations given on page 59.

ORDER OF OPERATIONS

1. First do operations within grouping symbols.
2. Then evaluate powers.
3. Then multiply and divide from left to right.
4. Finally add and subtract from left to right.

You can use the order of operations to simplify expressions such as $\left(3 + 5^2\right) \div 7$ and $(6 - 2)^2 \times 3 + 4$ that involve grouping symbols, powers, and operations.

Example 1 Order of Operations

a. $\left(3 + 5^2\right) \div 7 = (3 + 25) \div 7$ Evaluate 5^2.
$= 28 \div 7$ Operate inside parentheses: $3 + 25$.
$= 4$ Divide 28 by 7.

b. $(6 - 2)^2 \times 3 + 4 = 4^2 \times 3 + 4$ Operate inside parentheses: $6 - 2$.
$= 16 \times 3 + 4$ Evaluate 4^2.
$= 48 + 4$ Multiply 16 by 3.
$= 52$ Add 48 and 4.

The word *square* for the second power comes from geometry. The area of a square with sides *s* units long is *s* squared $\left(s^2\right)$. See if you can discover why the word for the third power is *cube*.

LESSON INVESTIGATION

COOPERATIVE
LEARNING

Investigating Volume

STRATEGY **ACT IT OUT** Use 1-by-1-by-1 cubes to build each of these larger cubes. Then count the number of small cubes in each larger cube. Find a pattern that relates the dimensions of the larger cubes to the number of small cubes used.

    2-by-2-by-2   **3-by-3-by-3**   **4-by-4-by-4**

Example 2 **Exploring the Volume of a Cube**

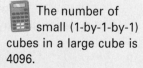
CONNECTION
Geometry

Find the volume of each cube by finding the number of 1-by-1-by-1 cubes.

a. 1-by-1-by-1   **b.** 2-by-2-by-2   **c.** 3-by-3-by-3

d. 4-by-4-by-4   **e.** 5-by-5-by-5   **f.** 6-by-6-by-6

Solution

Dimensions of Large Cube	Volume (Number of Small Cubes)
a. 1-by-1-by-1	1
b. 2-by-2-by-2	$2 \cdot 2 \cdot 2 = 2^3 = 8$
c. 3-by-3-by-3	$3 \cdot 3 \cdot 3 = 3^3 = 27$
d. 4-by-4-by-4	$4 \cdot 4 \cdot 4 = 4^3 = 64$
e. 5-by-5-by-5	$5 \cdot 5 \cdot 5 = 5^3 = 125$
f. 6-by-6-by-6	$6 \cdot 6 \cdot 6 = 6^3 = 216$

From this pattern, you can see that there are s^3 small cubes in an *s*-by-*s*-by-*s* cube.

ONGOING ASSESSMENT

Talk About It

The number of small (1-by-1-by-1) cubes in a large cube is 4096.

1. Use a calculator to find the dimensions of the large cube.

2. Describe the problem solving strategy that you used.

2.2 Exercises   Extra Practice, page 626

GUIDED PRACTICE

1. Write 64 as a power with 8 as the base.   **2.** Write 64 as a power with 3 as the exponent.

In Exercises 3–6, match the expression with the power.

A. 3^5 **B.** 5^3 **C.** 5^5 **D.** 3^3

3. $5 \times 5 \times 5$ **4.** $3 \times 3 \times 3 \times 3 \times 3$ **5.** $3 \times 3 \times 3$ **6.** $5 \times 5 \times 5 \times 5 \times 5$

7. NUMBER SENSE Explain how 2×3 and 2^3 are different.

8. Explain how $3 + 5^2$ and $(3 + 5)^2$ are different.

9. Write a power that represents the volume of a cube with edge c units.

PRACTICE AND PROBLEM SOLVING

In Exercises 10–12, write the product as a power.

10. $6 \times 6 \times 6$ **11.** $m \cdot m \cdot m \cdot m \cdot m$ **12.** $(2)(2)(2)(2)(2)(2)$

In Exercises 13–21, evaluate the expression.

13. 3^4 **14.** 10^2 **15.** 5^3

16. 1^5 **17.** 4 cubed   **18.** 7 squared

19. 1 to the tenth power   **20.** 9 to the second power   **21.** 2 to the fifth power

22. GEOMETRY Which figure does *not* have a volume of $4 \times n^3$?

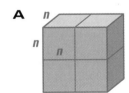

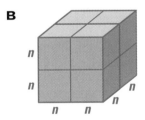

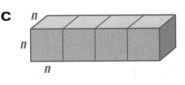

TECHNOLOGY In Exercises 23 and 24, find the missing numbers. Then describe any patterns that you see.

23. $2^2 = \boxed{?}, 2^4 = \boxed{?}, 2^6 = \boxed{?}, 2^8 = \boxed{?}, 2^{10} = \boxed{?}, 2^{12} = \boxed{?}, \ldots$

24. $8^2 = \boxed{?}, 8^3 = \boxed{?}, 8^4 - \boxed{?}, 8^5 = \boxed{?}, 8^6 = \boxed{?}, 8^7 = \boxed{?}, \ldots$

25. THINKING SKILLS Are both of the following correct? Explain.

$$\textbf{a. } 4^2 + 4 \div 2 = 8 + 4 \div 2$$
$$= 8 + 2$$
$$= 10$$

$$\textbf{b. } 4^2 + 4 \div 2 = 16 + 4 \div 2$$
$$= 20 \div 2$$
$$= 10$$

ALGEBRA In Exercises 26–31, evaluate the expression when $m = 1$ and when $m = 3$.

26. $16 - m^2 + 3$

27. $m^3 - 6 \div 6$

28. $\left(3 + m^2\right) \div 2$

29. $(1 + m)^2$

30. $1 + m^2$

31. $(m + 1)^3 - (m - 1)^3$

32. PACKAGING If a cube has an edge of s units, then its volume is s^3 cubic units. How many more cubic units would a cubic package with edge 5 units hold than a cubic package with edge 4 units?

In Exercises 33–38, complete the statement using >, <, or =.

33. 4^3 **?** 3^4

34. 3^4 **?** 9^2

35. 2^4 **?** 2^5

36. 1^{10} **?** 1^6

37. 5^2 **?** 2^5

38. 8^2 **?** 2^6

LOOKING FOR A PATTERN In Exercises 39 and 40, use the diagram at the right.

39. What are the patterns for the rows of the table?

40. **TECHNOLOGY** Add the numbers in each ⌐-shaped region. Write each sum as a power. Describe the pattern.

Row 1	1	3	5	7	9	11	13
Row 2	1	4	7	10	13	16	19
Row 3	1	5	9	13	17	21	25
Row 4	1	6	11	16	21	26	31
Row 5	1	7	13	19	25	31	37
Row 6	1	8	15	22	29	36	43
Row 7	1	9	17	25	33	41	49

41. Evaluate the expression $4 \times 3 + 6^2 \div 2$.

   A 12   **B** 18   **C** 24   **D** 30

42. What is another way to write $d \times d \times d \times d \times d \times d$?

   A $d \times 6$ **B** $6d$ **C** d^6 **D** d cubed

EXPLORATION AND EXTENSION

43. COMMUNICATING ABOUT MATHEMATICS (page 91)
As of September 1996, Dan Marino had thrown 352 touchdown passes. Complete the expression so that it is equal to the number of Dan Marino's touchdown passes.

$$3^{?} \times 4 + 3^3 + 1$$

Explain your solution.

LOOKING FOR A PATTERN In Exercises 1–4, find the missing number in the pattern. Explain your reasoning. (1.2)

1. 6, 12, 24, 48, ?

2. 1, 2, 5, 10, ? , 26

3. 243, 81, ? , 9, 3

4. 8, 16, 24, ? , 40

5. **GUESS, CHECK, AND REVISE** You pay for an $0.85 yogurt cone with nickels, dimes, and quarters, using at least one of each type of coin. You pay with 7 coins. How many of each coin did you use? (1.5)

In Exercises 6–8, check the given value of the variable in the equation. Is it a solution? If not, find the solution. (1.6)

6. $m + 5 = 12, m = 7$

7. $25 = t - 12, t = 13$

8. $9 + d = 15, d = 8$

ALGEBRA AND MENTAL MATH In Exercises 9–12, use mental math to solve the equation. (1.6)

9. $m + 25 = 41$

10. $z \times 3 = 39$

11. $p - 35 = 16$

12. $x \div 5 = 9$

CAREER Interview

ETHNOMUSICOLOGIST

Ethnomusicologist **Charlotte Wilson Heth,** assistant director of public programs at the National Museum of the American Indian in Washington, D.C., explores connections between music and culture, focusing on the music of the American Indian. She has composed and recorded music for albums, film scores, and videos.

Q What led you to this career?
As soon as I could talk, I started singing. From the time I could read, I began studying music. When I got older, I decided to concentrate on music—first the music of my own Cherokee tribe, then American Indian music in general, and eventually other music of the world.

Q Do you use math in your job?
All the time. I review budgets every single day, which involves arithmetic; future planning is based on extrapolations. I use geometry in designing exhibits, as well as for planning a new building for the museum. Moreover, everything in music is mathematically related. For instance, fractions are used to divide time into segments. In my job, math is not only useful, it's essential.

Q What can you say about the importance of studying math?
It's a lifelong tool, and you almost cannot live without it. I suppose you can live without it, but I wouldn't choose to do so.

Doubling Numbers

Some growth patterns follow a pattern that can be described using an exponent. A doubling of population every few years is an example of *exponential growth*.

Example

You are studying population growth patterns. You find that the population of a town is doubling every 5 years. The population is 15,000 now. In how many years will the population reach 500,000?

Solution

STRATEGY **MAKE A LIST** You can organize your work with a list.

Number of Years from Now	Population
0	15,000
5	$15{,}000 \cdot 2 = 30{,}000$
10	$15{,}000 \cdot 2^2 = 60{,}000$
15	$15{,}000 \cdot 2^3 = 120{,}000$
20	$15{,}000 \cdot 2^4 = 240{,}000$
25	$15{,}000 \cdot 2^5 = 480{,}000$

From this list, you can see that the population will reach 500,000 in a little over 25 years.

CALCULATOR TIP

Some calculators have an exponent key that allows you to find powers. The key may be labeled as y^x or as $\boxed{\land}$. For example, to evaluate 2^4 you enter

2 $\boxed{y^x}$ 4 $\boxed{=}$ or

2 $\boxed{\land}$ 4 $\boxed{=}$

to get a display of

$\boxed{\qquad 16.}$.

Exercises

In Exercises 1–8, use a calculator to evaluate the power.

1. 3^7 **2.** 10^6 **3.** 2^{10} **4.** 5^9

5. 4^6 **6.** 11^5 **7.** 8^3 **8.** 15^6

9. GUESS, CHECK, AND REVISE What is the smallest value of n for which 3^n is greater than 100,000?

10. GUESS, CHECK, AND REVISE What is the smallest value of n for which 2^n is greater than 1,000,000?

11. GUESS, CHECK, AND REVISE In the Example, it takes the town about 26 years to reach a population of 500,000. About how many more years would it take to reach a population of 1,000,000?

2.3

Number Patterns: Divisibility Tests

What you should learn:

Goal 1 How to decide whether one number is evenly divisible by another number

Goal 2 How to use divisibility tests to solve real-life problems

Why you should learn it:

Knowing how to use divisibility tests can help you make rectangular arrangements. An example is planning formations for a marching band.

Goal 1 USING DIVISIBILITY TESTS

A number may be *evenly divisible* by another number. If the quotient $n \div m$ is a whole number, then n is evenly divisible by m.

LESSON INVESTIGATION

COOPERATIVE LEARNING

Investigating Whole Number Division

GROUP ACTIVITY Copy the table. Then use a calculator to complete it. Can you predict which answers are whole numbers? If n is evenly divisible by the number, write the quotient. If not, write "Not Divisible."

	$n \div 2$	$n \div 3$	$n \div 4$	$n \div 5$	$n \div 6$	$n \div 9$	$n \div 10$
3120	1560	?	?	?	?	?	?
3121	?	?	?	?	?	?	?
3122	?	?	?	?	?	?	?
3123	?	?	?	?	?	?	?
3124	?	?	?	?	?	?	?
3125	?	?	?	?	?	?	?
3126	?	?	?	?	?	?	?

From this investigation, you may have discovered the following divisibility tests.

STUDY TIP

The divisibility tests for 3 and 9 are similar. For example, to decide whether 5256 is divisible by 3 or 9, add its digits.

$$5 + 2 + 5 + 6 = 18$$

Because the sum is divisible by 3 and by 9, it follows that 5256 is divisible by 3 and by 9.

DIVISIBILITY TESTS

A whole number is divisible by

2 if the number is even.

3 if the sum of its digits is divisible by 3.

4 if the number formed by its last two digits is divisible by 4.

5 if its last digit is 5 or 0.

6 if it is even and divisible by 3.

9 if the sum of its digits is divisible by 9.

10 if its last digit is 0.

For example, the number 78 is divisible by 6 because it is even and it is divisible by 3 ($7 + 8 = 15$; $15 \div 3 = 5$).

Example 1 Using Divisibility Tests

You are planning a half-time show for a marching band. There are 120 players in the band. How many rectangular formations such as the following can you make?

REAL LIFE
Band Formations

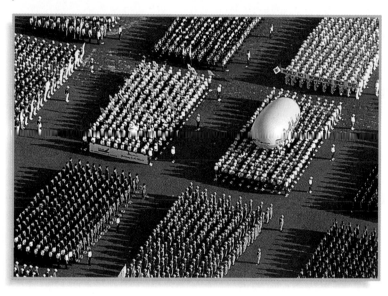

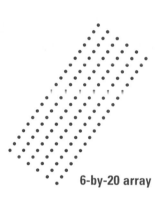

6-by-20 array

Solution

Using divisibility tests, you can conclude that 120 is evenly divisible by 1, 2, 3, 4, 5, 6, and 10. Notice that 120 is also divisible by 8. The possible rectangular formations are listed below.

Number of Players on One Side	Number of Players on Other Side	Number of Players
1	120	$1 \times 120 = 120$
2	60	$2 \times 60 = 120$
3	40	$3 \times 40 = 120$
4	30	$4 \times 30 = 120$
5	24	$5 \times 24 = 120$
6	20	$6 \times 20 = 120$
8	15	$8 \times 15 = 120$
10	12	$10 \times 12 = 120$

There are 8 rectangular formations.

ONGOING ASSESSMENT

Write About It

In Example 1, suppose six other people join the 120-person band.

1. Write a description of how to find the number of rectangular formations that are now possible.

2. Make a sketch of one of the possible formations.

GUIDED PRACTICE

1. What number between 300 and 400 is divisible by 2, 3, 4, 5, 6, 9, and 10? Explain how you found it.

2. Find the missing digit of 81?6 so that the number is divisible by 4 and 9.

3. **THINKING SKILLS** Your friend says that if a number is divisible by 10, then it must also be divisible by 5. Is this friend correct? Explain.

4. **GROUP ACTIVITY** Play the matching game. Make two copies of each card at the right. Place all 24 cards facedown in a 6-by-4 rectangular pattern. Each player takes turns flipping two cards. If they don't match, flip the cards facedown and let your partner take a turn. If they do match, use divisibility tests to decide whether the number is divisible by 2, 3, 4, 5, 6, 9, or 10. If your partner agrees that you are correct, keep the cards and take another turn. The player with the most cards wins.

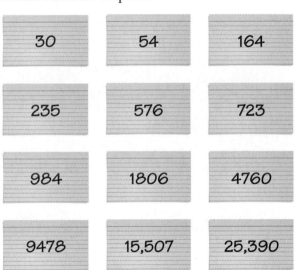

30	54	164
235	576	723
984	1806	4760
9478	15,507	25,390

PRACTICE AND PROBLEM SOLVING

USING LOGICAL REASONING In Exercises 5–7, complete the statement using *sometimes*, *always*, or *never*. Give examples to support your answer.

5. A number that is divisible by 6 is _?_ divisible by 2.

6. A number that is divisible by 5 is _?_ divisible by 4.

7. A number that is divisible by 3 is _?_ divisible by 6.

In Exercises 8–15, use the divisibility tests to decide whether the number is divisible by 2, 3, 4, 5, 6, 9, and 10.

8. 273	**9.** 391	**10.** 5940	**11.** 4164
12. 23,805	**13.** 10,526	**14.** 127,854	**15.** 306,920

In Exercises 16–19, find all the digits that will make the number divisible by 6.

| **16.** ?70 | **17.** 351? | **18.** 96,79? | **19.** 462,1?8 |

TECHNOLOGY In Exercises 20–22, use a calculator to find a number that matches the given description.

20. A 3 digit number that is divisible by 2 and 5.

21. A 4 digit number that is divisible by 3, but not by 6.

22. A 4 digit number that is divisible by 9.

23. Is 2^4 divisible by 2^3? Explain your reasoning.

24. **USING LOGICAL REASONING** What is the smallest number that is divisible by 2, 3, 5, 6, and 9? Explain your reasoning.

25. **THINKING SKILLS** Write a divisibility test for 8.

26. **BANKING** You go to a bank to cash a check for $100. You ask the teller for bills of all the same denomination. Describe the different groups of bills you might receive.

27. **GARDENING** You planted 450 flower bulbs of four different types: crocus, daffodil, tulip, and hyacinth. Is it possible that you planted the same number of each type of bulb?

 STANDARDIZED TEST PRACTICE

28. Without dividing, decide which number is divisible by 9.

    A 425,781   **B** 462,196   **C** 487,232   **D** 495,762

29. Which number is divisible by 2, 3, and 5?

    A 2,107,332   **B** 2,109,138   **C** 2,114,985   **D** 2,115,330

 EXPLORATION AND EXTENSION

PORTFOLIO

30. **BUILDING YOUR PROJECT** You are making a map of an archeological site in West Virginia. Native peoples lived at the site from about 400 A.D. to 1000 A.D. Your map will show some of the items uncovered at the site.

The region you want to map is 24 feet by 48 feet. To make the map, you divide the region into squares of the same size. Describe your different options. Which option would you choose? Explain why.

ceramic shards

wood charcoal

fire-cracked rock

nutshell

seeds

GEOMETRY CONNECTION

Investigating Factors

Materials Needed
- graph paper
- square tiles
- pencils or pens

Part A ARRANGING TILES

With three square tiles, you can make two different arrangements as shown below.

2 Different Arrangements

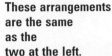

These arrangements are the same as the two at the left.

This one doesn't count. Each tile must have at least one common edge with another tile.

1. Work with your group to make all the possible arrangements of four square tiles. Sketch each arrangement on graph paper.

2. How many of the arrangements of the four tiles in Exercise 1 are rectangles? (Remember that a square is also a rectangle.) What are their dimensions?

3. Work with your group to make all the possible arrangements of five square tiles. Sketch each arrangement on graph paper. Are any of the arrangements rectangles?

Part B FOCUS ON FACTORS

In Exercise 2, you should have found two sizes of rectangles: 4-by-1 and 2-by-2. For each of these, the area is the product of the length and the width. That is, $4 = 4 \times 1$ and $4 = 2 \times 2$. The numbers 1, 2, and 4 are called *factors* of 4.

4. Find the number of different sizes of rectangles that can be formed with n tiles when n is 1, 2, 3, . . . , 20. Sketch them on graph paper. Record your results in a table like this.

Number of Tiles n	Number of Rectangles	Dimensions of Rectangles	Factors of n
1	?	?	?
2	?	?	?
3	?	?	?
4	2	4-by-1, 2-by-2	1, 2, 4
5	?	?	?

Tables like the one in Part B have fascinated people for thousands of years. Answer these questions that some people have asked about factors and patterns.

5. Do any numbers have exactly one factor? If so, what are they?

6. Some numbers have exactly two factors. Of the whole numbers from 1 through 20, which have exactly two factors?

7. Without using tiles, tell which whole numbers from 21 through 30 produce exactly one rectangle. Explain how you can tell.

8. There is something special about the number of factors of these numbers: 2^2, 3^2, 5^2, 7^2, and 11^2. What is it?

NOW TRY THESE

9. Sort the whole numbers from 1 through 20 into two groups: those that have an even number of factors and those that have an odd number of factors. Describe the numbers that have an odd number of factors.

Numbers with an even number of factors 2, 3, . . .	Numbers with an odd number of factors 1, 4, . . .

10. The ancient Greeks were fascinated by numbers that equal the sum of all their factors except the largest factor. For example, $6 = 1 + 2 + 3$. Such numbers are called *perfect numbers*. One of the whole numbers from 21 through 30 is perfect. Which number is it?

11. How many even numbers have exactly two factors? Explain your reasoning.

2.4 Number Patterns: Prime Factorization

What you should learn:

Goal 1 How to write a whole number as the product of prime numbers

Goal 2 How to investigate unsolved problems in mathematics

Why you should learn it:

Knowing how to write a whole number as the product of prime numbers can help you find a least common denominator when adding and subtracting fractions.

Goal 1 FACTORING WHOLE NUMBERS

Whole numbers can be classified by the number of factors they have. Numbers that have exactly two factors are *prime*. Numbers other than 1 that are not prime are *composite*.

PRIME AND COMPOSITE NUMBERS

A **prime number** has exactly two factors: itself and 1. A **composite number** has more than two factors. (The number 1 is neither prime nor composite.)

Writing the **prime factorization** of a number means to write the number as the product of prime numbers.

Example 1 Writing a Prime Factorization

Write the prime factorization of 378.

Solution

To write the prime factorization of a number, it is helpful to use **tree diagrams**, as shown below.

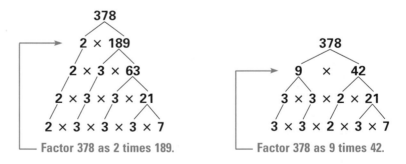

Both factor trees give the same prime factors. The prime factorization of 378 is $2 \cdot 3^3 \cdot 7$.

Example 2 Writing a Prime Factorization

Write the prime factorization of 81.

Solution

$81 = 9 \cdot 9 = 3 \cdot 3 \cdot 3 \cdot 3 = 3^4$

Some people think that everything there is to know about mathematics has already been discovered. But that is not true. People are still discovering things in mathematics that are new.

Example 3 An Unsolved Problem

Conjecture: Every even number greater than 2 can be written as the sum of two primes. Do you think this is true?

Solution

To begin, you can try several examples.

Number	Written as Sum of Two Primes
4	$2 + 2 = 4$
6	$3 + 3 = 6$
8	$3 + 5 = 8$
10	$3 + 7 = 10$
12	$5 + 7 = 12$
14	$3 + 11 = 14$
16	$3 + 13 = 16$
18	$5 + 13 = 18$
20	$3 + 17 = 20$

From the list, you can see that the conjecture is true for the even numbers from 4 to 20. They can all be written as the sum of two primes. No matter how long you continued, however, you could not use a list to show that *every* even number greater than 2 can be written as the sum of two primes.

Example 4 Another Unsolved Problem

Conjecture: Every number that is a square of a prime number has only itself, the prime number, and 1 as its factors. Is this true?

Solution

The prime factorization of a square of a prime would have only the prime number as its branches. The conjecture is correct for all numbers that have been tested.

Example:
49

7   7

**Real Life...
Real People**

Andrew Wiles

After more than 360 years, a conjecture made by Pierre de Fermat was finally proven true. Andrew Wiles, a professor at Princeton University, was able to prove that there are no nonzero integers x, y, and z for which $x^n + y^n = z^n$, when $n > 2$.

ONGOING ASSESSMENT

Talk About It

Use the list in Example 3.

1. Continue the list in Example 3 to show that the even numbers from 22 to 60 can be written as the sum of two primes.

2. Discuss whether or not you think your list proves that this is true for every even number.

GUIDED PRACTICE

1. Copy and complete the tree diagram at the right. Then write the prime factorization represented by the diagram.

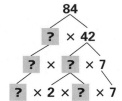

2. Name a whole number that is neither prime nor composite.

3. Name the only even prime number.

4. Explain how to check the prime factorization of a number.

In Exercises 5 and 6, complete the statement.

5. A number with more than two factors is a ? number.

6. Writing a number as the product of primes is called writing its ? .

PRACTICE AND PROBLEM SOLVING

7. Write the numbers from 1 to 25. For each number, decide whether it is *prime*, *composite*, or *neither*.

In Exercises 8–11, use a tree diagram to write the prime factorization of the number.

8. 48   9. 56   10. 150   11. 144

 TECHNOLOGY In Exercises 12–15, use a calculator and the divisibility tests to find the prime factorization.

12. 672   13. 720   14. 1815   15. 2310

In Exercises 16–21, find the number with the given prime factorization.

16. $2 \cdot 3 \cdot 11$ 17. $3 \cdot 5 \cdot 7$ 18. $2^3 \cdot 7$

19. $2 \cdot 3^3$ 20. $2^2 \cdot 3 \cdot 7$ 21. $2 \cdot 3^2 \cdot 5$

ALGEBRA In Exercises 22–24, evaluate $3x + 5$ for the given value of x. Then decide whether the number is *prime* or *composite*.

22. $x = 2$ 23. $x = 7$ 24. $x = 12$

25. Explain how you know that the number 1287 is not prime.

26. **THINKING SKILLS** Make a list of the odd numbers between 6 and 30. Can you write each number as the sum of three prime numbers? Explain why your list does not prove that this is always the case.

27. **DESIGN** You work for a company that sells jewelry-making kits. Your job is to design a package to hold the 195 beads included in the kit. One way to package the beads is to put them in 5 rows with 39 beads in each row as shown. List 3 other rectangular arrangements that would be possible for the beads. Which package design would you choose? Explain your choice.

28. **RIDDLE** I am a composite number between 30 and 40. The sum of my prime factors is 12. What number am I?

29. **RIDDLE** I am a number between 31 and 50. The sum of my two prime factors is 5. I have an odd number of factors. What number am I?

30. **RIDDLE** I am a number between 16 and 30. The product of my two prime factors is 6. I have an even number of factors. What number am I?

31. **THINKING SKILLS** The interactive investigation for this chapter asks you to arrange displays on a wall at the Baseball Hall of Fame in Cooperstown, New York. The displays will show information about Hall of Fame inductees. The display space is 8 feet high and 12 feet wide. Suppose you filled the entire space with rectangular displays of the same size. Each display has a whole-number height and width of at least 2 feet. What size displays are possible? Illustrate each with a sketch.

Tech Link

*Investigation 2,
Interactive
Real-Life
Investigations*

STANDARDIZED TEST PRACTICE

32. Which of the following is a prime number?

    (A) 75   (B) 79   (C) 81   (D) 87

33. Find the number that has the prime factorization $2^3 \cdot 3^3 \cdot 5$.

    (A) 30   (B) 270   (C) 900   (D) 1080

34. A grocery store owner wants to make a display of 72 boxes of crackers. Which of the following is *not* a way that the grocery store owner could make the display?

    (A) 8 rows with 9 boxes in each row

    (B) 18 rows with 4 boxes in each row

    (C) 7 rows with 12 boxes in each row

    (D) 3 rows with 24 boxes in each row

35. BUILDING YOUR PROJECT You and two other archeologists discover some stones with ancient numbers carved into them. You have figured out the meaning of the symbols for the numbers from 1 to 12, and you realize that many of the numerals are composed by multiplying others.

Real Life...
Real People

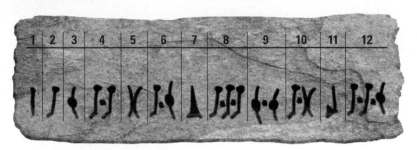

Describe the number system in your journal. What number does the symbol **J·J·⅃** represent? Decide if you have enough information to write the numbers 15, 26, and 33 using symbols. If you do, write that number. If you do not, explain why you cannot write the number. Record your answers in your journal.

Sequoyah

In 1821, a Cherokee named Sequoyah invented a system of writing for the Cherokee people. Each written character stood for a spoken syllable in the Cherokee language.

SPIRAL REVIEW

GEOMETRY In Exercises 1–4, sketch all the different sizes of rectangles with whole-number dimensions that have the given area. **(1.3)**

1. 45 square units
2. 48 square units
3. 72 square units
4. 80 square units

In Exercises 5–7, find the average. **(1.4)**

5. 14, 45, 22
6. 111, 120, 99
7. 65, 80, 26

8. You give a cashier $60 to pay for a pair of shoes. The cashier gives you $8 in change. Write an equation to represent this problem. Then solve the equation to find the cost of the shoes. **(1.6)**

USING LOGICAL REASONING In Exercises 9–14, use the Venn diagram to write the letter of the region where the number belongs. **(1.7)**

9. 6
10. 24
11. 17
12. 7
13. 9
14. 21

ALGEBRA In Exercises 15–18, evaluate the expression when $t = 3$ and when $t = 6$. **(2.1)**

15. $t \times 13$
16. $28 - t$
17. $t + 98$
18. $144 \div t$

Take this test as you would take a test in class. The answers to the exercises are given in the back of the book.

In Exercises 1–4, insert parentheses to make a true statement. (2.1)

1. $5 \times 9 + 2 = 55$ **2.** $45 - 6 \times 2 + 3 = 15$

3. $36 \div 3 + 6 \div 2 = 2$ **4.** $27 - 18 \div 6 - 3 = 3$

In Exercises 5–8, evaluate the expression. (2.2)

5. 5 cubed   **6.** 8 squared   **7.** 3^5 **8.** 2 to the sixth power

In Exercises 9–12, match the divisibility test with its result. (2.3)

A. **The number is divisible by 5.**   **B.** **The number is divisible by 9.**

C. **The number is divisible by 3.**   **D.** **The number is divisible by 6.**

9. The sum of the digits is divisible by 3.   **10.** The last digit is 0 or 5.

11. The number is even and divisible by 3.   **12.** The sum of the digits is divisible by 9.

13. For the science fair, you are making a display of Native American arrowheads. You have 84 arrowheads in your collection. What are the different rectangular arrangements that you could make? **(2.3)**

In Exercises 14–17, find the number with the given prime factorization. (2.4)

14. $2 \cdot 5 \cdot 13$ **15.** $2^2 \cdot 3 \cdot 11$

16. $3^2 \cdot 5^2$ **17.** $2^2 \cdot 3^2 \cdot 7$

In Exercises 18–21, decide whether the statement is *true* or *false*. If it is false, correct it. (2.1, 2.2, 2.4)

18. The power 2^3 is the same as $2 + 2 + 2$, or 6.

19. In the power 5^4, the base is 5.

20. The expression $6 \times 8 - 6 \div 2$ is equal to 21.

21. The prime factorization of 155 is $5 \cdot 31$.

22. **MOSAICS** You are making a mosaic like this Four Seasons mosaic you saw when you were in Chicago. The area of your mosaic will be 36 inches by 78 inches. Can you use 3 in.-by-3 in. tiles for the mosaic? Explain why or why not. **(2.4)**

2.5 Greatest Common Factor

What you should learn:

Goal 1 How to find the greatest common factor of two whole numbers

Goal 2 How to use greatest common factors to solve real-life problems

Why you should learn it:

Knowing how to find the greatest common factor of two whole numbers can help you solve real-life problems. An example is studying ways to create a calendar.

Goal 1 FINDING GREATEST COMMON FACTORS

Finding factors can help you tile the floor of a room.

LESSON INVESTIGATION

Investigating Greatest Common Factors

GROUP ACTIVITY You can buy square tiles that are 1 by 1, 2 by 2, 3 by 3, 4 by 4, and so on up to 24 by 24. Using only one size tile at a time, which kinds of tiles can be used to tile an 18-by-24 rectangular room? Sketch tiles on grid paper to help you answer this question. The 3-by-3 tiling is started below.

1-by-1   **2-by-2**   **3-by-3**   **4-by-4**   **5-by-5**

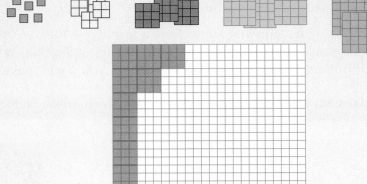

In this investigation, you may have discovered that the only tiles that can be used are 1 by 1, 2 by 2, 3 by 3, and 6 by 6. The numbers 1, 2, 3, and 6 are **common factors** of 18 and 24, and 6 is the **greatest common factor**.

Example 1 Finding a Greatest Common Factor

Find the greatest common factor of 28 and 36.

Solution

Begin by listing all factors of 28 and 36.

Factors of 28: 1, 2, **4**, 7, 14, 28

Greatest common factor

Factors of 36: 1, 2, 3, **4**, 6, 9, 12, 18, 36

The greatest common factor of 28 and 36 is 4.

STUDY TIP

To find all the factors of a number, make an organized list.

Factors of 28:

1 × 28
2 × 14
4 × 7
7 × 4

Stop when the factors repeat.

The factors of 28 are 1, 2, 4, 7, 14, and 28.

Example 2 Using Greatest Common Factors

REAL LIFE
Calendars

Ancient calendars used 28 days as a lunar month and 365 days as a solar year. What is the greatest common factor of these two numbers? Why is it difficult to create a calendar that uses these two numbers?

Lunar Month: Time it takes the moon to orbit Earth.

Earth

Solar Year: Time it takes Earth to orbit the sun.

Moon

Solution

Begin by listing the factors of 28 and 365.

Factors of 28: **1**, 2, 4, 7, 14, 28

Greatest common factor

Factors of 365: **1**, 5, 73, 365

The greatest common factor of 28 and 365 is 1. This causes problems with calendars because there is no way to divide the year evenly into lunar months.

Example 3 Creating a Calendar

Suppose that a lunar month had exactly 28 days and a solar year had exactly 364 days. Describe a calendar that could be used in this system.

Solution

In your calendar, you want the number of days in a "week" to be a common factor of 28 and 364. The common factors are 1, 2, 4, 7, 14, and 28. If you choose 4 days as the length of a week, then your calendar has 13 months, and each month has 7 weeks.

Month 13			
1	2	3	4
5	6	7	8
9	10	11	12
13	14	15	16
17	18	19	20
21	22	23	24
25	26	27	28

ONGOING ASSESSMENT

Write About It

Find the greatest common factor of the three numbers. Write a description of the steps you used.

1. 24, 30, 54

2. 16, 52, 80

3. 32, 40, 72

GUIDED PRACTICE

1. What is the smallest factor of a whole number? the largest factor?

2. **THINKING SKILLS** The prime factorizations of 54 and 60 are shown below. Your friend says that the greatest common factor of 54 and 60 is 30. Is your friend correct? Explain.

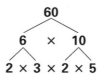

3. **a.** Find the greatest common factor of 32 and 48 by listing all the factors of each number.

   b. Find the greatest common factor of 32 and 48 by writing the prime factorization of each number.

   c. Which way do you prefer? Explain.

4. **PARTY FOOD** Your class purchased an 18 in., a 24 in., and a 36 in. submarine sandwich. You want to cut the sandwiches into equal-sized pieces. How can you make the pieces as long as possible? If you have 24 people in your class, will there be an equal-sized long piece for everyone? If not, what size pieces should be cut?

PRACTICE AND PROBLEM SOLVING

In Exercises 5–8, match the numbers with their greatest common factor.

A. 7   B. 2   C. 6   D. 14

5. 12, 22   **6.** 42, 56   **7.** 24, 30   **8.** 63, 70

In Exercises 9–12, find the greatest common factor by listing all the factors of each number.

9. 14, 21   **10.** 12, 35   **11.** 72, 84   **12.** 66, 96

In Exercises 13–16, find the greatest common factor by writing the prime factorization of each number.

13. 44, 88   **14.** 15, 75   **15.** 27, 45   **16.** 40, 64

NUMBER SENSE In Exercises 17–20, find a pair of numbers that have the given greatest common factor. Tell how you found them.

17. 3   **18.** 11   **19.** 12   **20.** 16

USING LOGICAL REASONING In Exercises 21 and 22, complete the statement using *sometimes*, *always*, or *never*. Explain your reasoning.

21. The greatest common factor of two numbers is __?__ one of the numbers.

22. The greatest common factor of two composite numbers is __?__ 1.

23. **LOOKING FOR A PATTERN** Use the graph at the right.

   a. Find the greatest common factors of 6 and each of the numbers along the bottom of the grid.

   b. Copy the grid and graph each of the greatest common factors.

   c. What patterns do you notice?

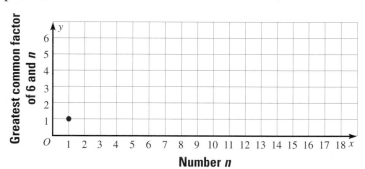

STANDARDIZED TEST PRACTICE

24. The greatest common factor of 88 and 64 is

   (A) 2.   **(B)** 4.   **(C)** 6.   **(D)** 8.

25. Which of the following is *not* a common factor of 24 and 60?

   (A) 3   **(B)** 4   **(C)** 5   **(D)** 6

EXPLORATION AND EXTENSION

PORTFOLIO

26. **BUILDING YOUR PROJECT** You find trading records in the sites of 3 ancient villages. Each village used a year of 360 days. The southern village used months of 15 days each. The village to the north had 20 days in each month, and the village to the east used months of 30 days. Each village trades with another when they have a month that begins on the same day. All three villages meet when they all have a month that begins on the same day. Decide how often in one year

   a. the north trades with the south.
   b. the east trades with the south.
   c. all three meet.

   Record your results in your journal.

The ancient Maya used a calendar, called Haab, with 18 months of 20 days each, and one month of 5 days.

2.6

Fractions in Simplest Form

What you should learn:

Goal 1 How to write fractions in simplest form

Goal 2 How to use fractions to solve real-life problems

Why you should learn it:

Knowing how to simplify fractions can help you solve real-life problems. An example is finding the size of a socket for a bolt.

Fractions are often used in tool measurements, such as socket sizes.

Goal 1 WRITING FRACTIONS IN SIMPLEST FORM

Two fractions are **equivalent fractions** if they represent the same quantity. For example, in the area models below, $\frac{3}{4}$ and $\frac{18}{24}$ are equivalent. Of these two, $\frac{3}{4}$ is in *simplest form*.

$$\frac{3}{4}$$ $$\frac{18}{24}$$

SIMPLEST FORM

A fraction is in **simplest form** if its numerator and denominator have a greatest common factor of 1.

One way to write a fraction in simplest form is to divide its numerator and denominator by their greatest common factor.

Example 1 **Writing a Fraction in Simplest Form**

Write the fractions in simplest form.

a. $\frac{12}{18}$ **b.** $\frac{28}{63}$ **c.** $\frac{48}{80}$

Solution

a. The greatest common factor of the numerator and denominator is 6. Use the greatest common factor to rewrite the numerator and denominator as products.

$$\frac{12}{18} = \frac{\cancel{6} \cdot 2}{\cancel{6} \cdot 3}$$ The greatest common factor is 6.

$$= \frac{2}{3}$$ Divide the numerator and denominator by 6.

b. $$\frac{28}{63} = \frac{\cancel{7} \cdot 4}{\cancel{7} \cdot 9}$$ The greatest common factor is 7.

$$= \frac{4}{9}$$ Divide the numerator and denominator by 7.

c. $$\frac{48}{80} = \frac{\cancel{16} \cdot 3}{\cancel{16} \cdot 5}$$ The greatest common factor is 16.

$$= \frac{3}{5}$$ Divide the numerator and denominator by 16.

Example 2 **Using Fractions in Simplest Form**

REAL LIFE
Bicycle Repair

You are using a socket set to remove bolts from a bicycle. The sockets in your socket set have the following measures.

$$\frac{5}{16}'', \quad \frac{3}{8}'', \quad \frac{7}{16}'', \quad \frac{1}{2}'', \quad \frac{9}{16}'', \quad \frac{5}{8}'', \quad \frac{11}{16}'', \quad \frac{3}{4}'',$$

$$\frac{13}{16}'', \quad \frac{7}{8}'', \quad \frac{15}{16}'', \quad 1'', \quad \frac{17}{16}'', \quad \frac{9}{8}'', \quad \frac{19}{16}'', \quad \frac{5}{4}''$$

Which sockets should you use to remove each of the following bolts?

a. The head of a bolt that you measure to be $\frac{14}{16}$ inch.

b. The head of a bolt that you measure to be $\frac{8}{16}$ inch.

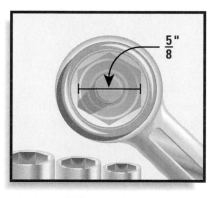

$\frac{5''}{8}$

Solution

a. To find which socket to choose, rewrite $\frac{14}{16}$ in simplest form.

$$\frac{14}{16} = \frac{2 \cdot 7}{2 \cdot 8} = \frac{7}{8}$$

You should choose the socket that is labeled $\frac{7''}{8}$.

b. To find which socket to choose, rewrite $\frac{8}{16}$ in simplest form.

$$\frac{8}{16} = \frac{8 \cdot 1}{8 \cdot 2} = \frac{1}{2}$$

You should choose the socket that is labeled $\frac{1''}{2}$.

ONGOING ASSESSMENT

Talk About It
. . . .
Describe which sockets in Example 2 you would choose for the following measures.

1. $\frac{12''}{16}$

2. $\frac{18''}{16}$

3. $\frac{4''}{16}$

GUIDED PRACTICE

In Exercises 1–3, match the model with its fraction.

A. $\frac{2}{5}$ **B.** $\frac{3}{4}$ **C.** $\frac{1}{2}$

1.    **2.** 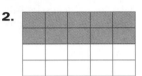   **3.**

4. Which of the fractions are in simplest form? How do you know?

A. $\frac{8}{9}$ **B.** $\frac{12}{27}$ **C.** $\frac{9}{23}$ **D.** $\frac{10}{55}$ **E.** $\frac{13}{52}$

5. SPORTS In racquetball the first player to reach 15 points wins the game. Which fractions below *could not* be the fraction of points out of 15 that a player has?

A. $\frac{1}{5}$ **B.** $\frac{5}{6}$ **C.** $\frac{2}{3}$ **D.** $\frac{3}{10}$ **E.** $\frac{3}{4}$

6. SPINNER GAME Make 2 spinners as shown at the right. With a partner, take turns being Player 1. Player 1 spins the **numerator spinner** and then spins the **denominator spinner** to create a fraction. If the fraction is in simplest form, Player 1 gets 2 points. If the fraction is not in simplest form, Player 2 can get 1 point by writing the fraction in simplest form. The first player to reach 10 points wins.

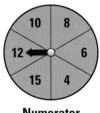 

Numerator spinner   **Denominator spinner**

PRACTICE AND PROBLEM SOLVING

NUMBER SENSE **In Exercises 7–10, find a denominator for the fraction so the greatest common factor of the numerator and denominator is 3.**

7. $\frac{12}{?}$ **8.** $\frac{30}{?}$ **9.** $\frac{42}{?}$ **10.** $\frac{93}{?}$

In Exercises 11–19, write the fraction in simplest form.

11. $\frac{30}{45}$ **12.** $\frac{12}{120}$ **13.** $\frac{27}{63}$

14. $\frac{48}{64}$ **15.** $\frac{35}{55}$ **16.** $\frac{66}{180}$

17. $\frac{15}{90}$ **18.** $\frac{25}{85}$ **19.** $\frac{42}{70}$

In Exercises 20–23, which three fractions are equivalent?

20. $\frac{4}{7}, \frac{14}{28}, \frac{28}{56}, \frac{7}{14}$

21. $\frac{72}{81}, \frac{8}{9}, \frac{24}{27}, \frac{36}{42}$

22. $\frac{24}{28}, \frac{42}{56}, \frac{12}{14}, \frac{6}{7}$

23. $\frac{2}{3}, \frac{15}{25}, \frac{75}{125}, \frac{3}{5}$

In Exercises 24–26, write three other fractions that are equivalent to the given fraction. Include the simplest form of the fraction.

24. $\frac{25}{100}$

25. $\frac{18}{21}$

26. $\frac{32}{36}$

FRUIT The chart shows the number of pounds of different fruits consumed in the United States per person in 1995. The total use of these fruits was 72 pounds. Write the amount of each fruit type used as a fraction of the total in simplest form. (Source: U.S. Department of Agriculture)

27. Bananas

28. Pineapples

29. Oranges

30. Grapes

31. Apples

32. Strawberries

27 lb   19 lb   8 lb

4 lb   2 lb   12 lb

STANDARDIZED TEST PRACTICE

33. Which fraction is in simplest form?

Ⓐ $\frac{3}{12}$ Ⓑ $\frac{5}{19}$ Ⓒ $\frac{7}{49}$ Ⓓ $\frac{8}{30}$

34. Which fraction is equivalent to $\frac{3}{24}$?

Ⓐ $\frac{1}{2}$ Ⓑ $\frac{1}{4}$ Ⓒ $\frac{1}{6}$ Ⓓ $\frac{1}{8}$

35. The table shows the average number of school days for different countries. The fraction of a year (365 days) that is spent in school in South Korea is

Ⓐ $\frac{44}{73}$.   Ⓑ $\frac{180}{220}$.

Ⓒ $\frac{9}{11}$.   Ⓓ $\frac{365}{220}$.

Country	Days in School per Year
United States	180
Canada	188
Israel	215
South Korea	220

EXPLORATION AND EXTENSION

PORTFOLIO

36. BUILDING YOUR PROJECT You find some arrowheads at a dig in Nevada and want to include descriptions in your records. To do this you need to know the lengths of the arrowheads. Use a ruler to measure the length of each arrowhead to the nearest sixteenth of an inch. Write the lengths in simplest form. Then record the descriptions in your journal.

length

SPIRAL REVIEW

1. **MAKING A LIST** You are buying a pair of sneakers. You can choose from low or high top sneakers in white or black, with white, black, blue, or red laces. How many different types of sneakers can you choose from? **(1.1)**

2. **LOOKING FOR A PATTERN** Find the missing number in the pattern 4, 7, ? , 14, 17. **(1.2)**

3. **PERFORMING AN EXPERIMENT** Suppose you toss 2 different coins together 30 times. The tosses that could come up are 2 heads, 1 head and 1 tail, or 2 tails. Which toss do you think would occur most often? Explain your reasoning. Toss two coins 30 times and record your results. Was your prediction correct? **(1.4)**

4. **EATING OUT** You and two of your friends go out for lunch. You share the cost of the meal evenly. The lunch (including tax and tip) costs $19.50. Use the verbal model to find each person's share. **(1.6)**

   Number of people × Cost per person = Total cost of lunch

5. Insert parentheses to make the statement true:
   $22 - 10 \times 16 \div 8 = 24$. **(2.1)**

In Exercises 6–8, evaluate the expression. (2.2)

6. 13^2 7. 5 cubed   8. 2 to the fourth power

9. **RIDDLE** I am a composite number between 40 and 50. I have an odd number of factors. What number am I? **(2.4)**

In Exercises 10–13, use a tree diagram to write the prime factorization of the number. (2.4)

10. 360   11. 675   12. 1470   13. 1183

14. What is the greatest common factor of 72 and 108? **(2.5)**

On *the*

Record

READ About It

In football, a touchdown pass occurs when one player passes the ball and the receiver makes a touchdown—for 6 points. In September 1996, Dan Marino set an NFL record for touchdown passes. Over 13 years, he had thrown 352 of these passes.

In an article about Dan Marino, *Sports Illustrated for Kids* magazine made the following observations.

• Dan Marino's 48,841 career passing yards equal 28 trips on Space Mountain at Disneyland.

• His 3913 completions equal enough dollars to buy 300 CDs.

• And, if you had one scoop of ice cream for each of his touchdown passes, you'd have two 30-foot-tall ice cream cones.

WRITE About It

1. A field goal equals $\frac{1}{2}$ of a touchdown score. A safety and a running conversion each is $\frac{1}{3}$ of a touchdown score. How many points are awarded to each of the three plays?

2. Could Dan Marino have passed the same number of yards in each of the 13 years? Explain why or why not.

3. *Sports Illustrated for Kids* estimates the height of a scoop of ice cream as what value? Write your answer as a sentence.

4. Decide whether one trip on the Space Mountain ride equals a whole number of yards passed. Explain how you could decide this without dividing.

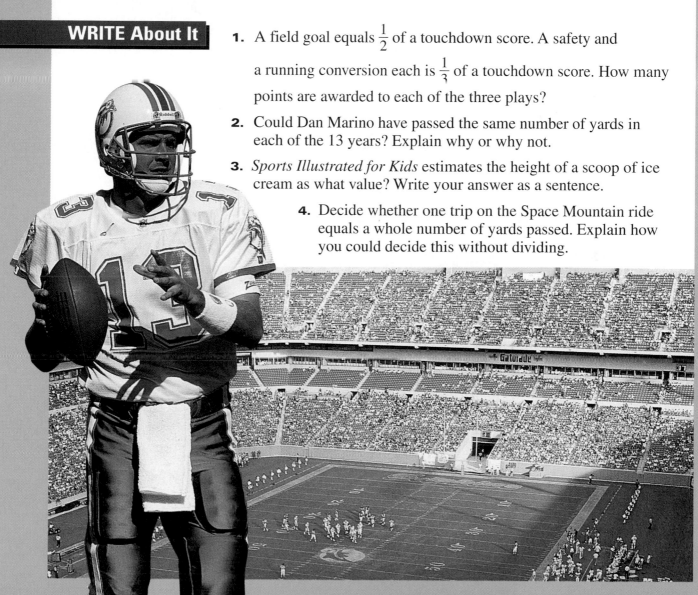

Investigating Models for Fractions

Part A PART-TO-WHOLE MODELS FOR FRACTIONS

Materials Needed
- plain paper
- pencils or pens
- scissors

You can use models to represent fractions. For example, each model below represents $\frac{4}{3}$.

Model 1

Each whole has 3 parts.

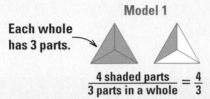

$$\frac{4 \text{ shaded parts}}{3 \text{ parts in a whole}} = \frac{4}{3}$$

Model 2

Each whole has 6 parts.

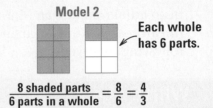

$$\frac{8 \text{ shaded parts}}{6 \text{ parts in a whole}} = \frac{8}{6} = \frac{4}{3}$$

1. Which of the following models also represents $\frac{4}{3}$?

A   B   C

2. Draw a part-to-whole model for each fraction.

   a. $\frac{1}{2}$ **b.** $\frac{3}{8}$ **c.** $\frac{5}{6}$ **d.** $\frac{3}{2}$

Part B SET MODELS FOR FRACTIONS

The fraction $\frac{3}{4}$ describes the number of red cars in relation to the total number of cars.

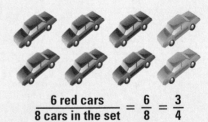

3. Which of the following models also represents the fraction $\frac{3}{4}$?

$$\frac{6 \text{ red cars}}{8 \text{ cars in the set}} = \frac{6}{8} = \frac{3}{4}$$

A   B   C

4. Draw a set model for the fraction $\frac{5}{6}$.

Suppose that a strip of paper is 3 units long.

There are many ways to fold the strip to show $\frac{3}{4}$.

Reggie's way

Fold the strip into thirds.

Fold a unit into fourths and shade three of them.

Rhonda's way

Fold the strip into fourths and shade one of them.

5. Fold a strip of paper Reggie's way. Fold another strip with the same length Rhonda's way. Do the two ways show $\frac{3}{4}$ as the same length?

6. Fold strips of paper in two ways to show each fraction. Then sketch the strips.

  a. $\frac{2}{3}$ (Let the strips be 2 units long.)

  b. $\frac{4}{3}$ (Let the strips be 4 units long.)

NOW TRY THESE

7. You have three small pizzas to be shared by four people. How can you cut the pizzas so that each person gets the same amount? Illustrate your solution with a sketch.

8. You have 5 feet of ribbon. You want to cut the ribbon to wrap four identical presents.

  a. How long should each piece of ribbon be?

  b. Without using a ruler, how could you decide where to cut the ribbon?

9. The distance from your apartment to the subway station is 5 blocks. How far is one third of the distance? Sketch your solution.

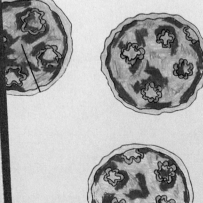

2.7

A Division Model
for Fractions

What you should learn:

Goal 1 How to write a fraction as a division problem

Goal 2 How to write fractions as decimals

Why you should learn it:

Knowing how to write a fraction as a division problem can help you solve real-life problems. An example is dividing an amount into equal shares.

Goal 1 FRACTIONS AND DIVISION

Example 1 Fractions and Division

You and two friends want to share 7 pounds of clay in your art class. How much should each person get?

Solution

STRATEGY **DRAW A DIAGRAM** One way to solve this problem is to draw a diagram, as shown below.

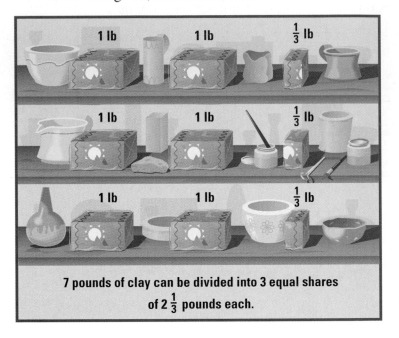

7 pounds of clay can be divided into 3 equal shares
of $2\frac{1}{3}$ pounds each.

From the diagram, you can see that each person will get 2 pounds and $\frac{1}{3}$ of the seventh pound. That is, each person will get $2\frac{1}{3}$ pounds.

$$7 \div 3 = 2\frac{1}{3} = \frac{7}{3} \qquad \text{Summary equation}$$

Dividing 7 by 3 produces the fraction $\frac{7}{3}$.

THE DIVISION MODEL FOR FRACTIONS

The fraction $\frac{a}{b}$ is equivalent to the expression $a \div b$.

$$\frac{a}{b} = a \div b$$

You can use a calculator to find decimal forms of fractions.

LESSON INVESTIGATION

COOPERATIVE LEARNING

Investigating Decimal Forms of Fractions

GROUP ACTIVITY The decimal forms of the fractions $\frac{6}{2}$ and $\frac{5}{2}$ have 0 decimal places and 1 decimal place, respectively.

$\frac{6}{2} = 3$ **0 decimal places** $\frac{5}{2} = 2.5$ **1 decimal place**

Use a calculator to find fractions whose decimal forms have 2, 3, and 4 decimal places. Can you find a fraction whose decimal form has an unending number of decimal places?

Example 2 **Writing Fractions as Decimals**

Write each fraction as a decimal. Round the result to the nearest hundredth.

a. $\frac{2}{9}$ **b.** $\frac{7}{8}$

Solution

In each case, use a calculator to divide the numerator by the denominator.

a. $\frac{2}{9} = 2 \div 9$

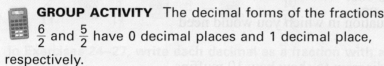

2/9
.2222222222

The calculator shows 0.2222222 .... You can write $0.\overline{2}$ to show that the 2 keeps repeating.

$\frac{2}{9} = 0.\overline{2}$ **Use a calculator.**

≈ 0.22 **Round. Use the symbol $\approx$ ("is approximately equal to") whenever you round a number.**

b. $\frac{7}{8} = 7 \div 8$ **Divide numerator by denominator.**

$= 0.875$ **Use a calculator.**

≈ 0.88 **Round.**

ONGOING ASSESSMENT

Write About It

Each decimal is approximately equal to a fraction with a single-digit numerator and denominator. Find the fractions. Explain the problem solving strategy you used.

1. 0.11

2. 0.29

3. 0.17

GUIDED PRACTICE

1. Give two real-life examples of ordering fractions or decimals.

2. Estimate the values of the fractions *a* and *b* on the number line. Then use > or < to write a statement that relates the values.

3. **TRUE OR FALSE?** Is the following statement *true* or *false*? *Two fifths is greater than one half.* Draw a number line and plot the numbers to support your answer.

In Exercises 4 and 5, plot the numbers on a number line. Then order the numbers from least to greatest.

4. $2.05, \frac{4}{5}, \frac{1}{3}, \frac{6}{5}, 1.4, \frac{3}{4}$

5. $2.9, 3.3, \frac{5}{4}, \frac{8}{3}, \frac{7}{2}, 2.85$

6. **RUNNING** You, Sheila, and Marin run together to practice for a cross-country meet. You run 3.6 miles, Sheila runs $\frac{17}{5}$ miles, and Marin runs $\frac{15}{4}$ miles. Who ran the farthest? Explain.

PRACTICE AND PROBLEM SOLVING

In Exercises 7 and 8, estimate the values of the fractions *a* and *b* on the number line. Then use > or < to write a statement that relates the values.

7.

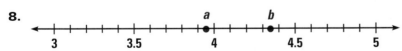

8.

9. **TRANSPORTATION** You visited museums in Washington, D.C., and recorded the following inventions and their dates in the history of transportation. Use a time line to organize the dates.

- 1807 Steamboat
- 1907 Helicopter
- 1825 Steam railroad
- 1939 Jet engine aircraft
- 1885 Gas automobile
- 1976 Supersonic passenger airliner
- 1903 Airplane

Real Life...
Real Facts

Steam railroad trains have fascinated people for over 170 years. The photo shows the world's oldest operable steam engine on its 150th anniversary, being driven by Smithsonian Institution employees dressed in costume.

In Exercises 10–12, plot the numbers on a number line. Then order the numbers from least to greatest.

10. 5.4, 7.05, 6.8, 6.75, 7.5, 5.45   **11.** $\dfrac{8}{7}, \dfrac{18}{6}, \dfrac{7}{3}, \dfrac{7}{9}, \dfrac{7}{2}, \dfrac{13}{4}$ **12.** $\dfrac{28}{9}, \dfrac{14}{3}, \dfrac{17}{4}, 4.35, \dfrac{18}{5}, 3.75$

TRUE OR FALSE? In Exercises 13 and 14, is the statement *true* or *false*? Draw a number line and plot the numbers to support your answer.

13. Eleven thirds is greater than eleven eighths.

14. Three and four fifths is less than three and seventy-five hundredths.

LOOKING FOR A PATTERN In Exercises 15 and 16, plot the numbers on a number line. Describe the pattern and write the next two numbers.

15. $\dfrac{1}{5}, 0.5, 0.8, \dfrac{11}{10}, \dfrac{7}{5}$ **16.** $\dfrac{21}{10}, \dfrac{13}{5}, 3.1, \dfrac{36}{10}, 4.1$

STANDARDIZED TEST PRACTICE

17. If the numbers are ordered from least to greatest, which number could you use to replace n in the list of numbers 0.38, $\dfrac{2}{5}$, $\dfrac{1}{2}$, n, and $\dfrac{3}{4}$?

Ⓐ 0.47   **Ⓑ** 0.64   **Ⓒ** $\dfrac{5}{6}$ **Ⓓ** $\dfrac{375}{100}$

18. Which list of numbers is in the correct order from least to greatest?

Ⓐ 0.1, $\dfrac{2}{15}$, 0.4, $\dfrac{7}{10}$, $\dfrac{7}{8}$ **Ⓑ** 0.1, 0.13, $\dfrac{1}{15}$, $\dfrac{3}{8}$, $\dfrac{4}{11}$

Ⓒ $\dfrac{1}{2}$, $\dfrac{1}{3}$, $\dfrac{1}{4}$, $\dfrac{1}{5}$, $\dfrac{1}{6}$ **Ⓓ** 0.32, $\dfrac{3}{8}$, $\dfrac{4}{5}$, $\dfrac{5}{6}$, 0.81

EXPLORATION AND EXTENSION

PORTFOLIO

19. BUILDING YOUR PROJECT Use a time line to organize these dates. Record them in your journal.

- In 1100 A.D., the Native American settlement at Cahokia (near present-day St. Louis) had a population of about 40,000.
- The Maya civilization at Teotihuacán, Mexico, collapsed around 600 A.D.
- In 1000 A.D., the cultivation of maize, beans, and squash reached the southeastern Atlantic region of North America.

Pyramid of the Moon, Teotihuacán, Mexico

WHAT *did you learn?*

WHY *did you learn it?*

Skills	2.1	Evaluate a variable expression and use the order of operations to evaluate an expression.	Simplify expressions by doing operations in a given order.
	2.2	Use commutative and associative properties and evaluate powers.	Follow order of operations and find volumes.
	2.3	Use divisibility tests.	Find all possible rectangles of a given area.
	2.4	Identify prime and composite numbers and write the prime factorization of a number.	Make conjectures about number properties and patterns.
	2.5	Find the greatest common factor of two numbers.	Investigate the difficulties in creating calendars.
	2.6	Write a fraction in simplest form.	Choose the correct tool for a repair job.
	2.7	Write a fraction as a division problem and as a decimal.	Divide materials among a number of people.
	2.8	Use a number line to order numbers.	Make a time line to organize dates in history.
Strategies	2.1–2.8	Use problem solving strategies.	Solve a wide variety of real-world problems.
Using Data	2.1–2.8	Use tables, graphs, and time lines.	Organize data and solve problems.

HOW *does it fit in the bigger picture of mathematics?*

After having developed mathematics for practical reasons, many people became fascinated with its properties. For example, they began to recognize differences between numbers such as prime and composite.

Example Look for a pattern in the numbers 4, 9, 25, 49, 121, 169, 289, and so on. Can you name the last number in the list?

Solution All the numbers in the list are composite. In fact, they arc all perfect squares. But the group does not include *every* perfect square (for example, 16 is missing). The group does include the squares of the prime numbers: $4 = 2^2$, $9 = 3^2$, $25 = 5^2$, $49 = 7^2$, and so on. The last number in this list would be the square of the last prime (which is not known).

VOCABULARY

- expression (p. 58)
- numerical expression (p. 58)
- variable expression (p. 58)
- evaluating an expression (p. 58)
- factor (p. 64)
- exponent (p. 64)

- base (p. 64)
- power (p. 64)
- prime number (p. 76)
- composite number (p. 76)
- prime factorization (p. 76)
- tree diagram (p. 76)

- common factor (p. 82)
- greatest common factor (p. 82)
- equivalent fractions (p. 86)
- simplest form (p. 86)
- number line (p. 98)

2.1 ORDER OF OPERATIONS

You may need to use the order of operations to evaluate some numerical and variable expressions.

Examples   **a.** Evaluate the expression $22 - (10 \times n)$ when $n = 2$.

b. Evaluate the expression $9 + 4(12 - 7)$.

Solution   **a.** $22 - (10 \times n) = 22 - (10 \times 2)$ Substitute 2 for n.

$$= 22 - 20$$ Then do operations within grouping symbols.

$$= 2$$

b. $9 + 4(12 - 7) = 9 + 4(5)$ First do operations within grouping symbols.

$$= 9 + 20$$ Then multiply and divide from left to right.

$$= 29$$ Finally add and subtract from left to right.

1. Evaluate the expression $9 - (2 + 7) \div 3$.

2. Evaluate the expression $2 \times (x + 5)$ when $x = 6$.

3. Insert parentheses to make the statement true: $24 \div 8 - 2 + 6 \cdot 3 = 22$.

2.2 POWERS AND EXPONENTS

You can write an expression that has repeated factors as a power.

$$4 \cdot 4 \cdot 4 \cdot 4 \cdot 4 = 4^5 \overset{\text{Exponent}}{\Big\}} \text{Power}$$

Factors   Base

Example   Evaluate the expression $(13 - 6) + 2 \times 3^2$.

Solution $(13 - 6) + 2 \times 3^2 = 7 + 2 \times 3^2$ First do operations within grouping symbols.

$$= 7 + 2 \times 9$$ Then evaluate powers.

$$= 7 + 18$$ Then multiply and divide from left to right.

$$= 25$$ Finally add and subtract from left to right.

4. Complete the statement using $>$, $<$, or $=$: 6^2 **?** 2^5

5. Evaluate $m(11 - 2^3)$ when $m = 4$.

2.3 NUMBER PATTERNS: DIVISIBILITY TESTS

You can determine whether a number is evenly divisible by another number using the divisibility tests given on page 70.

Example The number 414 is divisible by 6 because it is even, and the sum of its digits is divisible by 3: $4 + 1 + 4 = 9$; $9 \div 3 = 3$.

6. Use the divisibility tests to decide whether 1788 is divisible by 2, 3, 4, 5, 6, 9, and 10.

7. Sketch the different sizes of rectangles with whole-number dimensions that have an area of 64 square units.

2.4 NUMBER PATTERNS: PRIME FACTORIZATION

Example Write the prime factorization of 405.

Solution To write the prime factorization of a number, you can use a tree diagram.

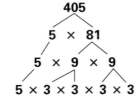

405
5 × 81
5 × 9 × 9
5 × 3 × 3 × 3 × 3

The prime factorization of 405 is $3^4 \cdot 5$.

8. Explain how you know that the number 117 is not prime.

9. Use a tree diagram to write the prime factorization of 750.

2.5 GREATEST COMMON FACTOR

Example Find the greatest common factor of 18 and 30.

Solution List the factors for each number. Find the largest number common to both lists.

Factors of 18: 1, 2, 3, **6**, 9, 18
Factors of 30: 1, 2, 3, 5, **6**, 10, 15, 30

The greatest common factor of 18 and 30 is 6.

10. Find the greatest common factor of 64 and 96.

11. **FLOOR TILING** You want to tile your bedroom floor and bathroom floor with the same-sized square tiles. The bedroom is 8×10 and the bathroom is 6×6. Find the common factors of 80 and 36 to determine the largest size of square tiles you can use.

2.6 FRACTIONS IN SIMPLEST FORM

Example Write $\dfrac{28}{42}$ in simplest form.

Solution $\dfrac{28}{42} = \dfrac{14 \times 2}{14 \times 3} = \dfrac{2}{3}$ Divide by the greatest common factor.

12. Which three fractions are equivalent? $\dfrac{5}{8}, \dfrac{30}{48}, \dfrac{15}{16}, \dfrac{70}{112}$

13. Write the fraction $\dfrac{36}{42}$ in simplest form.

2.7 A DIVISION MODEL FOR FRACTIONS

Example $\dfrac{5}{8} = 5 \div 8$ Write the fraction as a division problem.

$= 0.625$ Divide the numerator by the denominator.

FOOD CHOICES In Exercises 14–16, use the diagram.
It shows the fraction of people in a survey that chose
each vegetable as his or her favorite. Write each
fraction as a decimal.

14. Broccoli   **15.** Beans   **16.** Potatoes

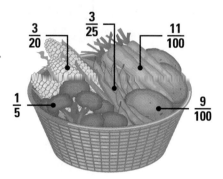

2.8 ORDERING NUMBERS ON A NUMBER LINE

You can order numbers by graphing them on a number line.

Example Plot the numbers $\dfrac{4}{5}$, 0.75, $\dfrac{7}{8}$, 0.23, and $\dfrac{2}{3}$ on a number line.
Then order the numbers from least to greatest.

Solution $\dfrac{4}{5} = 4 \div 5 = 0.8$ $\dfrac{7}{8} = 7 \div 8 = 0.875$ $\dfrac{2}{3} = 2 \div 3 \approx 0.67$

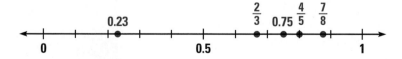

$0.23, \dfrac{2}{3}, 0.75, \dfrac{4}{5}, \dfrac{7}{8}$ Read the number line from left to right.

17. Use a number line to order the numbers $0.95, \dfrac{8}{9}, 0.85, \dfrac{9}{11}$, and $\dfrac{9}{10}$.

18. Name a fraction that could complete this list of ordered numbers:

$0.24, \boxed{?}, \dfrac{8}{25}, 0.36$

In Exercises 1–6, evaluate the expression when *t* = 5.

1. $13 - t + 8$　　　　**2.** $2^2 \cdot 10 \div t$　　　　**3.** $t + 12 \div 6$

4. $(2 + t) \times (t - 2)$　　**5.** $2^6 - (3^3 + t)$　　**6.** $t^2 - 15 \div t + 9$

In Exercises 7–9, use the divisibility tests to decide whether the number is divisible by 2, 3, 4, 5, 6, 9, and 10.

7. 738　　　　　　**8.** $35{,}640$　　　　　**9.** $129{,}003$

In Exercises 10–12, use a tree diagram to write the prime factorization of the number.

10. 78　　　　　　**11.** 112　　　　　　**12.** 135

In Exercises 13–15, find the greatest common factor of the numbers.

13. $16, 24$　　　　**14.** $20, 35$　　　　**15.** $44, 66$

In Exercises 16–18, write the fraction in simplest form.

16. $\dfrac{7}{63}$　　　　　　**17.** $\dfrac{26}{39}$　　　　　　**18.** $\dfrac{60}{75}$

In Exercises 19–21, write the fraction as a decimal. Round your answer to the nearest hundredth.

19. $\dfrac{2}{5}$　　　　　　**20.** $\dfrac{3}{8}$　　　　　　**21.** $\dfrac{7}{9}$

In Exercises 22 and 23, plot the numbers on a number line. Then order the numbers from least to greatest.

22. $\dfrac{7}{5}, \dfrac{21}{20}, 2.35, \dfrac{1}{5}, \dfrac{11}{6}, \dfrac{3}{2}$

23. $5.2, \dfrac{13}{4}, \dfrac{29}{7}, 3.85, \dfrac{9}{2}, \dfrac{10}{3}$

24. INVENTIONS While visiting a museum, you record the following dates of different inventions through history. Use a time line to organize the dates.

- 1816　Stethoscope
- 1837　Telegraph
- 1826　Photography
- 1846　Sewing machine
- 1867　Typewriter
- 1877　Phonograph
- 1876　Telephone
- 1895　Radio

1. Evaluate the expression $12 + 20 \cdot x$ when $x = 6$.

   Ⓐ 38   Ⓑ 132

   Ⓒ 192   Ⓓ 360

2. What is the next number in the pattern?

   1, 8, 27, 64, ?

   Ⓐ 125   Ⓑ 137

   Ⓒ 525   Ⓓ 729

3. What is the prime factorization of 756?

   Ⓐ $3 \cdot 4 \cdot 7 \cdot 9$ Ⓑ $2^2 \cdot 3 \cdot 7 \cdot 9$

   Ⓒ $2^2 \cdot 3^2 \cdot 7$ Ⓓ $2^2 \cdot 3^3 \cdot 7$

4. What is the greatest common factor of 120, 315, and 225?

   Ⓐ 5   Ⓑ 9

   Ⓒ 15   Ⓓ 25

5. Which number is *not* equivalent to the other three?

   Ⓐ $\frac{27}{8}$ Ⓑ $\frac{61}{24}$

   Ⓒ 3.375   Ⓓ $3\frac{3}{8}$

6. Which of the following sets of numbers is ordered from least to greatest?

   Ⓐ $\frac{3}{4}, \frac{5}{6}, \frac{4}{3}, \frac{10}{9}, 1.37$

   Ⓑ $\frac{3}{4}, \frac{5}{6}, \frac{10}{9}, 1.37, \frac{4}{3}$

   Ⓒ $\frac{3}{4}, \frac{4}{3}, \frac{5}{6}, \frac{10}{9}, 1.37$

   Ⓓ $\frac{3}{4}, \frac{5}{6}, \frac{10}{9}, \frac{4}{3}, 1.37$

7. You bake brownies in a pan that is 9 inches by 12 inches. What size square brownies can you cut from the pan after it has cooled?

   Ⓐ 2 inch squares

   Ⓑ 3 inch squares

   Ⓒ 4 inch squares

   Ⓓ 5 inch squares

8. In the library, there were 5 shelves that each held an equal number of books. The librarian rearranged the books and moved them to 9 shelves. Each shelf still has an equal number of books. You know there are more than 140 books but fewer than 200 on each shelf. How many books are on each of the 9 shelves now?

   Ⓐ 172   Ⓑ 145

   Ⓒ 160   Ⓓ 180

9. You are setting up chairs in the gym for a class assembly. You need to arrange 126 chairs into a rectangular array and you want each row to have the same number of seats. Pick the number of rows that you *cannot* use.

   Ⓐ 9   Ⓑ 15

   Ⓒ 18   Ⓓ 14

10. You are designing a rectangular plate to set hot pans on. You are making the plate out of square tiles. If the finished size of the plate is to be 21 cm by 45 cm, what size tiles should you buy?

    Ⓐ 3 cm   Ⓑ 5 cm

    Ⓒ 9 cm   Ⓓ 2 cm

Fractions and Their Operations

SINGLE PROPRIETORSHIPS A fashion designer just starting out may own her business as well as handle every aspect of the business, including sewing, accounting, and marketing.

TECHNOLOGY

Technology resources accompanying this chapter:

• Interactive Real-Life Investigations

• Middle School Tutorial Software

CHAPTER THEME
Business

CORPORATIONS The largest corporations employ thousands of workers, and may own several factories, warehouses, and office buildings.

PARTNERSHIPS Street vendors may form partnerships to grow and sell fresh fruits and vegetables.

Ownership and Management

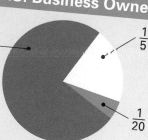

REAL LIFE Business

The way a business is run is often determined by the number of owners. For example, if thousands of people own a business, they need to select a small group of managers to run it. On the other hand, a business owned by one person is usually operated by that person. The circle graph below classifies the businesses in the United States by **ownership**.

U.S. Business Ownership

$\frac{3}{4}$ **Single proprietorships** owned and operated by one person

$\frac{1}{5}$ **Corporations** owned by many shareholders, but operated by managers

$\frac{1}{20}$ **Partnerships** owned and operated by two or more people

Think and Discuss

1. There are about 16 million businesses in the United States. Use the graph to estimate the number of each type.

2. Estimate the fraction of businesses that are either single proprietorships or partnerships. How did you get your answer?

PORTFOLIO

CHAPTER **PROJECT**

Managing a T-Shirt Company

PROJECT DESCRIPTION

Suppose you manage a T-shirt company. There are many things you have to take into consideration. You must plan how to manufacture and sell your products. Because public opinion determines which products will sell, you must adjust your production when peoples' tastes change. It's also your job to report the company's performance and plans to the stockholders. Write a letter to the stockholders addressing each of the **TOPICS** listed on the next page.

GETTING STARTED

Talking It Over

- Discuss in your group what you think a manager of a T-shirt company does. What math skills do you think are needed?

- In a newspaper, look up the values of stocks of several companies. Find a magazine about a current business. Describe some of the ways that the businesses use mathematics.

Planning Your Project

- **Materials Needed:** paper, pencils or pens

- You can use the six topics in the **BUILDING YOUR PROJECT** list on the next page. Begin your letter to the stockholders. Give a brief description of the company and the product. Keep the letter in your portfolio.

BUILDING YOUR PROJECT

These are places throughout the chapter where you will work on your project.

TOPICS

INTERNET

To find out about starting your own business, go to:

http://www.mlmath.com

LAB 3.1

COOPERATIVE LEARNING

Investigating Common Multiples

Materials Needed

- pencils or pens
- colored pencils or markers
- colored paper
- scissors

Part A LOOKING FOR A PATTERN

1. Describe the pattern for each list. Then write the next three numbers in the list.

a. 3, 6, 9, ? , ? , ?   **b.** 2, 4, 6, ? , ? , ?

Part B PATTERNS AND MULTIPLES

The pattern in Exercise 1(a) is graphed on the number line below using •'s. The pattern in Exercise 1(b) is graphed using ×'s.

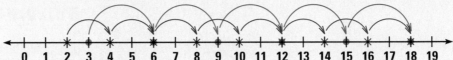

The numbers listed in Exercise 1(a) are called *multiples* of 3. They can be written as 3×1, 3×2, 3×3, and so on.

2. a. List the multiples of 3 that are graphed above.

b. List the multiples of 2 that are graphed above.

c. List the numbers that are marked with both a • and an ×. These numbers are *common multiples* of 3 and 2. What is the *least* common multiple of 3 and 2?

3. The number line below illustrates the multiples of two numbers. What are the numbers? What is their least common multiple?

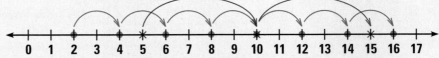

4. a. List the multiples of 3 that are less than or equal to 40.

b. List the multiples of 5 that are less than or equal to 40.

c. Graph the numbers you listed in parts (a) and (b).

d. What is the least common multiple of 3 and 5?

5. Find the least common multiple of each pair of numbers.

a. 3 and 4   **b.** 4 and 12   **c.** 8 and 12   **d.** 5 and 12

Cut out several 2-inch strips of red paper and several 3-inch strips of blue paper. Place a red strip next to a blue strip as shown below. Add more red strips end-to-end until they reach past the blue strip. Then add more blue strips until they reach past the red strips. Continue adding strips until the total lengths of the two rows match. The total length of the two rows in inches will be the least common multiple of 2 and 3.

2	
3	

→

2	2
3	

→

2	2
3	3

→

2	2	2
3	3	

6. Use the method above to find the least common multiple of each pair of numbers.

    a. 2 and 4   **b.** 4 and 5

    c. 6 and 10   **d.** 5 and 6

NOW TRY THESE

7. Use a number line to find the least common multiple of 4 and 6.

8. The prime factorizations of 12 and 20 are shown below.

$$12 = 2 \times 2 \times 3 \qquad 20 = 2 \times 2 \times 5$$

   a. Find the least common multiple of 12 and 20. Compare its prime factorization to the prime factorizations of 12 and 20.

   b. Repeat part (a) for the numbers 18 and 45.

   c. Repeat part (a) for the numbers 25 and 30.

   d. Look back at your answers to parts (a)–(c). What patterns do you see?

9. Write a complete sentence that describes the least common multiple illustrated below.

   a.

2	2	2	2	2
5		5		

   b.

4	4	4
6		6

3.1

Least Common Multiples

What you should learn:

Goal 1 How to use a list to find the least common multiple of two numbers

Goal 2 How to use prime factorization to find the least common multiple of two numbers

Why you should learn it:

Knowing how to find the least common multiple of two numbers can help you predict events. An example is knowing when two runners will meet on a track.

Goal 1 LISTING COMMON MULTIPLES

The *multiples* of 5 are 1×5, 2×5, 3×5, and so on. A **multiple** of a number is the product of the number and any whole number greater than zero.

Example 1 Finding Common Multiples

STRATEGY **MAKE A LIST** List the multiples of 2 and the multiples of 3 less than 25. Which multiples are common to both lists?

Solution

Multiples of 2:   2, 4, **6**, 8, 10, **12**, 14, 16, **18**, 20, 22, **24**

Multiples of 3:   3, **6**, 9, **12**, 15, **18**, 21, **24**

The common multiples of 2 and 3 less than 25 are 6, 12, 18, and 24.

> ### LEAST COMMON MULTIPLE
>
> Of all common multiples of two numbers, the smallest is called the **least common multiple** . For example, the least common multiple of 2 and 3 is 6.

Example 2 Using a Least Common Multiple

Meg and Nara are running laps on a track. Meg circles the track in 3 minutes and Nara circles the track in 4 minutes. They started running together at the same time. When will they be together again at the starting point?

REAL LIFE
Running

Solution

Meg crosses the starting point every 3 min. Nara crosses the starting point every 4 min. At 12 min, they will be together again at the starting point, because 12 is the least common multiple of 3 and 4.

Meg: 3 min
Nara: 4 min
Meg: 6 min
Nara: 8 min
Meg: 9 min
Nara: 12 min
Meg: 12 min

Another way to find the least common multiple of two numbers is to compare their prime factorizations.

  1. List the prime factorization of the first number.

  2. List the prime factorization of the second number.

  3. Circle any factors the numbers have in common.

  4. List the factors of both, writing any circled factors only once.

  5. Multiply the factors in the last list to get the least common multiple.

Example 3 **Using Prime Factorization**

Find the least common multiple of 24 and 30.

Solution

  1. Write the prime factorization of 24. $24 = 2 \times 2 \times 2 \times 3$

  2. Write the prime factorization of 30. $30 = 2 \times 3 \times 5$

  3. Circle the factors that are the same.

$$24 = ⟨2⟩ \times 2 \times 2 \times ⟨3⟩$$
$$30 = ⟨2⟩ \times \qquad ⟨3⟩ \times 5$$

  4. List the factors of both, writing any circled factors only once. **2, 2, 2, 3, 5**

  5. Multiply the factors in the list to get the least common multiple. $2 \times 2 \times 2 \times 3 \times 5 = 120$

The least common multiple of 24 and 30 is 120.

Example 4 **Using Prime Factorization**

Find the least common multiple of 9, 10, and 12.

Solution

$$9 = \qquad\quad ⟨3⟩ \times 3$$
$$10 = ⟨2⟩ \times \qquad\quad 5$$
$$12 = ⟨2⟩ \times 2 \times ⟨3⟩$$
$$2 \times 2 \times 3 \times 3 \times 5 = 180$$

ONGOING ASSESSMENT

Talk About It
....

Work with a partner to find the least common multiple of each pair of numbers. Each of you should use a different method. Discuss your work. Which method do you prefer? Explain.

  1. 12 and 15

  2. 8 and 10

  3. 6 and 15

GUIDED PRACTICE

USING LOGICAL REASONING **In Exercises 1–4, decide whether the statement is** *true* **or** *false***. If it is false, rewrite the sentence so that it is true.**

1. The least common multiple of 12 and 15 is 3.

2. The greatest common factor of 12 and 15 is 3.

3. The least common multiple of 12 and 19 is 228.

4. The least common multiple of 12 and 20 is 240.

5. Find two numbers whose least common multiple is 504 and whose greatest common factor is 6.

6. **AUTO MAINTENANCE** The owner's manual for a new car suggests that the oil be changed every 2000 mi, the tires be rotated every 5000 mi, and the brakes be checked every 7500 mi. After how many miles will all three things need to be done at the same time?

PRACTICE AND PROBLEM SOLVING

 In Exercises 7–11, list the first eight multiples of each number. Use your lists to find the least common multiple.

7. 2, 7   **8.** 6, 9   **9.** 4, 20   **10.** 12, 14   **11.** 4, 6, 8

In Exercises 12–16, find the least common multiple of the numbers.

12. 28, 32   **13.** 46, 115   **14.** 35, 40   **15.** 64, 72   **16.** 2, 3, 5

17. **BUSINESS** You own a business and are hiring a new employee. You want the employee's salary to be between $23,000 and $24,000. Your employee can choose to be paid every two weeks (26 times a year) or once a month (12 times a year). You want each paycheck to be an exact dollar amount. What are the possible salaries of the new employee?

ALGEBRA **In Exercises 18–20, find the values of** $2 \cdot n$ **and** $3 \cdot n$**. Then find the least common multiple of the two values.**

18. $n = 2$ **19.** $n = 3$ **20.** $n = 5$

21. **LOOKING FOR A PATTERN** Use the results of Exercises 18–20 to write an expression that represents the least common multiple of $2 \cdot n$ and $3 \cdot n$ for any value of n.

22. **INTERIOR DECORATING** You want to put a wallpaper border at the top of your bathroom walls. The room is 5 ft by 10 ft. Which pattern is a better choice for your room? Why? (*Hint:* 1 ft = 12 in.)

one full pattern

one full pattern

23. **LANDSCAPING** You are planting three different kinds of plants in parallel rows that are 50 ft long. Every 2 ft you plant a rose bush, every 3 ft you plant a juniper bush, and every 9 ft you plant a dogwood tree. The three plants line up at the beginning of the rows. Will they ever line up again? If so, where?

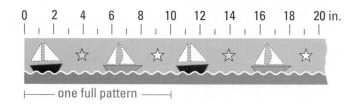

STANDARDIZED TEST PRACTICE

24. Which regions of the Venn diagram represent the common multiples of 4 and 5?

(A) A and B   (B) B and D

(C) B and E   (D) D and E

25. In which region does the number 30 belong?

(A) C   (B) D   (C) E   (D) G

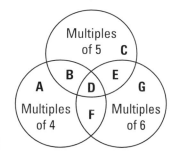

Multiples of 5 C
B E
A D G
Multiples of 4 F Multiples of 6

EXPLORATION AND EXTENSION

PORTFOLIO

26. **BUILDING YOUR PROJECT** To promote a new style of T-shirt, you put a gold sticker in every 15th package and a silver sticker in every 25th package. Customers who get a package with both stickers get a free T-shirt. When you sell 1000 packages, how many T-shirts will you give away? Explain this promotion to your stockholders and suggest variations that could be used.

3.2 Mixed Numbers and Improper Fractions

What you should learn:

Goal 1 How to write mixed numbers and improper fractions

Goal 2 How to write mixed numbers as decimals

Why you should learn it:

Knowing how to rewrite mixed numbers and improper fractions can help you in business situations. An example is weighing items at a deli.

Goal 1 MIXED NUMBERS AND FRACTIONS

A fraction is a **proper fraction** if it is less than 1. It is an **improper fraction** if it is greater than or equal to 1. An improper fraction greater than 1 can be rewritten as a **mixed number**.

LESSON INVESTIGATION

Rewriting Improper Fractions

GROUP ACTIVITY The model below shows that the improper fraction $\frac{8}{3}$ is equal to the mixed number $2\frac{2}{3}$.

Cut five circles into fourths and three circles into eighths. Use the above method to write each fraction as a mixed number.

$$\frac{7}{4} \qquad \frac{9}{4} \qquad \frac{18}{4} \qquad \frac{19}{8} \qquad \frac{13}{8} \qquad \frac{24}{8}$$

Example 1 Writing Mixed Numbers

Rewrite the improper fraction $\frac{14}{3}$ as a mixed number.

Solution

Begin by dividing 14 by 3. The remainder will be the numerator of the mixed number's fraction.

$$\frac{14}{3} \qquad \Longrightarrow \qquad 3\overline{)14} \; {}^{4} \text{ R } 2 \qquad \Longrightarrow \qquad 4\frac{2}{3}$$

STUDY TIP

Remember that a mixed number can be written as the sum of a whole number and a fraction.

$$3\frac{2}{5} \quad = \quad 3 \quad + \quad \frac{2}{5}$$

mixed number = whole number + fraction

Example 2 Writing Improper Fractions

$$4\frac{1}{5} = 4 + \frac{1}{5} \qquad \text{Rewrite as a sum.}$$

$$= \frac{20}{5} + \frac{1}{5} \qquad \text{Rewrite 4 as } \frac{20}{5}.$$

$$= \frac{21}{5} \qquad \text{Add fractions.}$$

When working with computers and other machines, it is useful to know how to express a mixed number as a decimal.

Example 3 **Writing Mixed Numbers as Decimals**

You work at a deli. A customer asks for the following items. Your scale shows decimal amounts using only two decimal places. Find the decimal weight of each item.

REAL LIFE
Food Service

a. $1\frac{1}{4}$ lb roast turkey

b. $2\frac{3}{8}$ lb potato salad

c. $1\frac{1}{3}$ lb sliced Swiss cheese

Solution

a. $1\frac{1}{4} = 1 + \frac{1}{4}$ Rewrite the mixed number as a sum.

$= 1 + (1 \div 4)$ Rewrite $\frac{1}{4}$ as $1 \div 4$.

$= 1 + 0.25$ Divide.

$= 1.25$ Add.

b. $2\frac{3}{8} = 2 + \frac{3}{8}$ Rewrite the mixed number as a sum.

$= 2 + (3 \div 8)$ Rewrite $\frac{3}{8}$ as $3 \div 8$.

$= 2 + 0.375$ Divide.

$= 2.375$ Add.

≈ 2.38 Round to two decimal places.

c. $1\frac{1}{3} = 1 + \frac{1}{3}$ Rewrite the mixed number as a sum.

$= 1 + (1 \div 3)$ Rewrite $\frac{1}{3}$ as $1 \div 3$.

$= 1 + 0.333\ldots$ Divide.

$= 1.333\ldots$ Add.

≈ 1.33 Round to two decimal places.

ONGOING ASSESSMENT

Write About It

Write a sentence that uses each number in a real-life setting.

1. $2\frac{3}{5}$

2. $\frac{8}{3}$

GUIDED PRACTICE

1. Explain how to decide whether a fraction is proper or improper. Give examples of each type.

ERROR ANALYSIS In Exercises 2 and 3, find and correct the error.

2. $\dfrac{16}{5} = 1\dfrac{3}{5}$ $5\overline{)16}$ ✗
$\qquad\qquad\quad \dfrac{3}{\underline{}}$
$\qquad\qquad\quad \underline{15}$
$\qquad\qquad\quad \ 1$

3. $8\dfrac{2}{3} = 8 + \dfrac{2}{3}$ ✗
$\qquad\quad = \dfrac{10}{3}$

4. Write the the mixed number and the equivalent improper fraction represented by the model at the right.

5. **FOOD SERVICE** At the deli, a customer asks for $2\dfrac{3}{4}$ lb of fruit salad. Find the decimal weight of the fruit salad.

PRACTICE AND PROBLEM SOLVING

In Exercises 6–9, is the fraction *proper* or *improper*? Explain.

6. $\dfrac{1}{6}$ **7.** $\dfrac{5}{5}$ **8.** $\dfrac{17}{4}$ **9.** $\dfrac{8}{9}$

10. **USING LOGICAL REASONING** Are there any improper fractions that can be written as a whole number? If so, give an example to support your answer.

NUMBER SENSE In Exercises 11–14, match the mixed number with its equivalent improper fraction or decimal.

A. 3.2   **B.** $\dfrac{24}{5}$ **C.** $\dfrac{18}{5}$ **D.** 4.4

11. $4\dfrac{2}{5}$ **12.** $3\dfrac{1}{5}$ **13.** $3\dfrac{3}{5}$ **14.** $4\dfrac{4}{5}$

In Exercises 15–18, rewrite the improper fraction as a mixed number.

15. $\dfrac{11}{6}$ **16.** $\dfrac{27}{4}$ **17.** $\dfrac{28}{9}$ **18.** $\dfrac{35}{8}$

In Exercises 19–22, rewrite the mixed number as an improper fraction.

19. $1\dfrac{5}{11}$ **20.** $2\dfrac{6}{7}$ **21.** $8\dfrac{1}{3}$ **22.** $10\dfrac{1}{2}$

In Exercises 23–26, rewrite the number as a decimal.

23. $\dfrac{17}{4}$ **24.** $\dfrac{8}{5}$ **25.** $9\dfrac{1}{2}$ **26.** $1\dfrac{3}{20}$

27. LAUNDROMATS At a laundromat, it costs $1.75 to wash a load of laundry and $1.25 to dry a load of laundry.

    a. Write each price as an improper fraction in simplest form.

    b. How many quarters do you need to wash a load of laundry? to dry a load of laundry? How do your answers relate to the fractions you wrote in part (a)?

STANDARDIZED TEST PRACTICE

28. Which mixed number is equal to the improper fraction $\dfrac{17}{5}$?

    (A) $1\dfrac{2}{5}$ **(B)** $2\dfrac{1}{5}$ **(C)** $3\dfrac{1}{5}$ **(D)** $3\dfrac{2}{5}$

29. Which fraction is equal to the mixed number $4\dfrac{6}{11}$?

    (A) $\dfrac{10}{11}$ **(B)** $\dfrac{24}{11}$ **(C)** $\dfrac{38}{11}$ **(D)** $\dfrac{50}{11}$

EXPLORATION AND EXTENSION

PORTFOLIO

30. BUILDING YOUR PROJECT In the past, stock prices have been quoted as mixed numbers. For example, if the price of a stock is listed at $9\dfrac{1}{2}$, one share of the stock will cost you $9.50. The prices of your company's stock in one week are as follows.

MONDAY	TUESDAY	WEDNESDAY	THURSDAY	FRIDAY
$13\dfrac{3}{4}$	$13\dfrac{7}{8}$	$13\dfrac{1}{2}$	$13\dfrac{3}{8}$	$13\dfrac{1}{4}$

    a. Write each price as a decimal.

    b. On what day was the price the highest?

    c. On what day was the price lowest?

Include this information in your letter to the stockholders.

1. LOOKING FOR A PATTERN You are practicing for the cross-country team. You run 2 mi on Monday, 4 mi on Tuesday, and 6 mi on Wednesday. If this pattern continues through the rest of the week, how many miles will you run on Friday? **(1.2)**

In Exercises 2–4, tell whether the statement is *true* or *false*. If it is false, insert parentheses to make it true. (2.1)

2. $15 + 9 \cdot 3 = 42$ **3.** $20 \div 2 \times 5 + 7 = 9$ **4.** $28 - 16 \div 2 + 4 = 2$

In Exercises 5–8, find the greatest common factor. (2.5)

5. $25, 36$ **6.** $34, 68$ **7.** $51, 57$ **8.** $81, 108$

In Exercises 9–12, write the fraction in simplest form. (2.6)

9. $\dfrac{6}{27}$ **10.** $\dfrac{13}{52}$ **11.** $\dfrac{30}{42}$ **12.** $\dfrac{84}{96}$

Social Studies Connection

THE STOCK MARKET

Until recently, stocks in the United States were priced in eighths of dollars, or units of 12.5 cents. This system was based on the Spanish dollar of the 1700s, which was denominated in "pieces of eight," or eighths. Then in 1997, stock markets began pricing stocks in sixteenths, as a step towards converting to a decimal-based system.

1. What would the following stock prices total?

$$22\frac{7}{8}; \ 50\frac{1}{4}; \ 19\frac{3}{16}$$

Express this total in dollars and cents.

2. If a stockbroker charges an extra $\dfrac{1}{16}$ of a dollar over the actual stock price of $41\frac{7}{8}$, how much money will one share of the stock cost you?

Accuracy and Rounding

You can make your answers accurate when doing a series of computations. Solve this simple problem two ways to see which way is more accurate.

Example

Find the sum $\frac{1}{3} + \frac{4}{3}$ to the nearest hundredth.

Solution

Method **1**   Change each fraction to a decimal rounded to the nearest hundredth. Then add.

Rounded, the fractions are $\frac{1}{3} \approx 0.33$ and $\frac{4}{3} \approx 1.33$.

$$0.33 \;\boxed{+}\; 1.33 \;\boxed{=}\; \boxed{1.66}$$

Method **2**   Use a calculator to add the fractions. Then round the final result.

You can use the Memory feature of a calculator to add the fractions. First be sure the Memory is cleared (set to 0). Then use the following keystrokes.

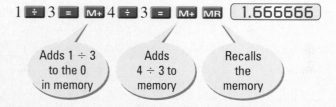

$$1 \;\boxed{÷}\; 3 \;\boxed{=}\; \boxed{M+}\; 4 \;\boxed{÷}\; 3 \;\boxed{=}\; \boxed{M+}\; \boxed{MR}\; \boxed{1.666666}$$

| Adds 1 ÷ 3 to the 0 in memory | Adds 4 ÷ 3 to memory | Recalls the memory |

Rounded to the nearest hundredth, the answer is 1.67.

The actual result is $\frac{1}{3} + \frac{4}{3} = \frac{5}{3}$, which rounds to 1.67.

To get accurate results with a calculator, do all the calculations and round only the final answer.

CALCULATOR TIP

Some calculators have parentheses keys. To use one of these calculators for Method 2, you would use the keystrokes below.

$$\boxed{(}\; 1 \;\boxed{÷}\; 3 \;\boxed{)}\; \boxed{+}$$
$$\boxed{(}\; 4 \;\boxed{÷}\; 3 \;\boxed{)}\; \boxed{=}$$

Exercises

Find the sum to the nearest hundredth.

1. $\frac{5}{7} + \frac{4}{11}$ **2.** $\frac{1}{3} + \frac{1}{7}$ **3.** $\frac{4}{9} + \frac{2}{13}$ **4.** $\frac{5}{17} + \frac{5}{13}$

5. $\frac{2}{9} + \frac{4}{9}$ **6.** $\frac{7}{12} + \frac{7}{300}$ **7.** $\frac{1}{6} + \frac{1}{15}$ **8.** $\frac{4}{30} + \frac{7}{30}$

LAB 3.3

COOPERATIVE LEARNING

Addition and Subtraction of Fractions

Materials Needed
- plain paper
- pencils or pens
- colored pencils or markers

Part A FRACTIONS WITH A COMMON DENOMINATOR

1. Write the addition or subtraction fact represented by the diagram. (1 square = 1 unit)

   a.  **b.**

2. Draw a diagram to model each problem. Then use the diagram to solve the problem.

   a. $\dfrac{1}{3} + \dfrac{2}{3}$ **b.** $\dfrac{4}{6} - \dfrac{2}{6}$ **c.** $\dfrac{2}{4} + \dfrac{1}{4}$

3. Use a diagram to explain how to add or subtract two fractions with a common denominator.

Part B ADDING WITH DIFFERENT DENOMINATORS

The model below shows how to add $\dfrac{1}{3}$ and $\dfrac{2}{5}$.

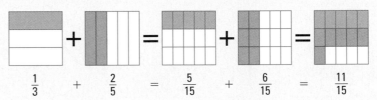

$$\frac{1}{3} \quad + \quad \frac{2}{5} \quad = \quad \frac{5}{15} \quad + \quad \frac{6}{15} \quad = \quad \frac{11}{15}$$

4. Write the equations represented by the diagram below.

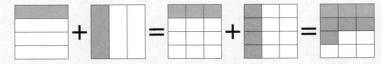

5. Draw a diagram to model each problem. Use the diagram to solve the problem.

   a. $\dfrac{1}{3} + \dfrac{1}{2}$ **b.** $\dfrac{2}{5} + \dfrac{1}{3}$ **c.** $\dfrac{1}{8} + \dfrac{2}{3}$

6. Use the results of Exercises 4 and 5 to explain how to add two fractions that have different denominators. Give examples.

The model below shows how to subtract $\frac{1}{3}$ from $\frac{3}{4}$.

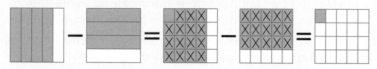

$$\frac{3}{4} \quad - \quad \frac{1}{3} \quad = \quad \frac{9}{12} \quad - \quad \frac{4}{12} \quad = \quad \frac{5}{12}$$

7. Write the equations represented by the diagram below.

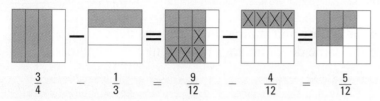

8. Draw a diagram to solve each problem.

a. $\frac{1}{3} - \frac{1}{4}$ **b.** $\frac{5}{6} - \frac{1}{3}$ **c.** $\frac{3}{8} - \frac{1}{4}$

9. Use the results of Exercises 7 and 8 to explain how to subtract two fractions with different denominators. Give examples.

NOW TRY THESE

10. Use a diagram to find each sum or difference. Then write equations that correspond to the diagrams. What denominator do you use to add and subtract the fractions?

a. $\frac{2}{5} + \frac{1}{6}$ **b.** $\frac{1}{4} + \frac{5}{7}$ **c.** $\frac{3}{8} + \frac{1}{3}$

d. $\frac{3}{5} - \frac{1}{9}$ **e.** $\frac{3}{8} - \frac{1}{5}$ **f.** $\frac{1}{2} - \frac{1}{3}$

11. Find the least common multiple. Explain how the result is related to the answers in Exercise 10.

a. 5 and 6 **b.** 4 and 7 **c.** 8 and 3

d. 5 and 9 **e.** 8 and 5 **f.** 2 and 3

12. Explain how to add and subtract fractions without using a diagram. Use your method to find each sum or difference below.

a. $\frac{4}{9} + \frac{1}{4}$ **b.** $\frac{5}{6} - \frac{3}{10}$ **c.** $\frac{7}{8} - \frac{2}{3}$

3.3 Adding and Subtracting Fractions

What you should learn:

Goal 1 How to add and subtract fractions

Goal 2 How to use addition and subtraction of fractions to solve real-life problems

Why you should learn it:

Knowing how to add and subtract fractions can help you with statistics. An example is interpreting the results of a survey about peanut butter preferences.

Goal 1 ADDING AND SUBTRACTING FRACTIONS

The rules for adding and subtracting fractions depend on whether they have the same denominator or different denominators.

ADDING AND SUBTRACTING FRACTIONS

1. To add or subtract two fractions with a *common denominator*, add or subtract their numerators. Write the sum or difference of the numerators over the denominator.

2. To add or subtract two fractions with *different denominators*, first rewrite the fractions using the least common denominator. Then add or subtract.

Example 1 Adding and Subtracting Fractions

a. $\dfrac{4}{5} - \dfrac{1}{5} = \dfrac{4-1}{5}$ Subtract numerators.

$= \dfrac{3}{5}$ Simplify.

b. To rewrite the fractions $\dfrac{1}{3}$ and $\dfrac{3}{8}$ with the least common denominator of 24, multiply $\dfrac{1}{3}$ by $\dfrac{8}{8}$ and $\dfrac{3}{8}$ by $\dfrac{3}{3}$.

$\dfrac{1}{3} + \dfrac{3}{8} = \dfrac{1 \cdot 8}{3 \cdot 8} + \dfrac{3 \cdot 3}{8 \cdot 3}$ Least common denominator is 24.

$= \dfrac{8}{24} + \dfrac{9}{24}$ Simplify.

$= \dfrac{8 + 9}{24}$ Add numerators.

$= \dfrac{17}{24}$ Simplify.

c. $\dfrac{5}{6} - \dfrac{1}{2} = \dfrac{5}{6} - \dfrac{1 \cdot 3}{2 \cdot 3}$ Least common denominator is 6.

$= \dfrac{5}{6} - \dfrac{3}{6}$ Simplify.

$= \dfrac{5 - 3}{6}$ Subtract numerators.

$= \dfrac{2}{6}$ Simplify.

$= \dfrac{1}{3}$ Reduce to lowest terms.

STUDY TIP

The least common denominator of two fractions is the least common multiple of their denominators. For example, the least common denominator of $\dfrac{5}{6}$ and $\dfrac{3}{4}$ is 12 because the least common multiple of 6 and 4 is 12.

Goal 2 SOLVING REAL-LIFE PROBLEMS

To add three or more fractions, you can use the same rules as when you add two fractions. Here are two examples.

$$\frac{1}{5} + \frac{2}{5} + \frac{4}{5} = \frac{1+2+4}{5} = \frac{7}{5}$$ Common denominator

$$\frac{1}{2} + \frac{1}{3} + \frac{1}{6} = \frac{3}{6} + \frac{2}{6} + \frac{1}{6} = \frac{6}{6}$$ Different denominators

Example 2 Using a Survey

Your company is producing a new type of peanut butter. To help design the product, you conduct a survey to find people's peanut butter preferences. The results of the survey are shown in the circle graph below. Find the sum of the fractions.

**Real Life...
Real Facts**

Peanut crops are grown in Asia, Africa, Australia, South America, and the southern United States. The flowers grow above ground, but the peanut itself grows beneath the soil.

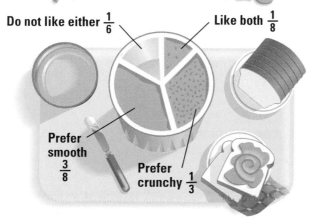

PEANUT BUTTER PREFERENCES

Do not like either $\frac{1}{6}$

Like both $\frac{1}{8}$

Prefer smooth $\frac{3}{8}$

Prefer crunchy $\frac{1}{3}$

Solution

The least common denominator is 24.

$$\frac{1}{6} + \frac{3}{8} + \frac{1}{8} + \frac{1}{3} = \frac{4}{24} + \frac{9}{24} + \frac{3}{24} + \frac{8}{24}$$

$$= \frac{4+9+3+8}{24}$$

$$= \frac{24}{24}$$

$$= 1$$

The sum is 1.

ONGOING ASSESSMENT

Write About It

1. Can you use a common denominator of 48 to solve Example 2? If so, show how and explain your steps. If not, explain why not.

3.3 Exercises

Extra Practice, page 628

GUIDED PRACTICE

1. Two fractions have denominators of 12 and 8. What is their least common denominator? How did you get your answer?

2. **WRITING** Explain how to add or subtract two fractions with a common denominator and with different denominators.

3. **BIKE RIDING** You bike $\frac{1}{2}$ mi and your friend bikes $\frac{3}{5}$ mi. Who had the longer bike ride? How much longer?

4. **YOU BE THE TEACHER** One of your students adds two fractions as follows. Is your student correct? Explain.

$$\frac{5}{8} + \frac{1}{4} = \frac{20}{32} + \frac{8}{32} = \frac{28}{32} = \frac{7}{8}$$

PRACTICE AND PROBLEM SOLVING

In Exercises 5–12, add or subtract. Simplify if possible.

5. $\frac{4}{7} + \frac{5}{7}$
6. $\frac{8}{9} - \frac{2}{9}$
7. $\frac{4}{5} - \frac{1}{7}$
8. $\frac{2}{3} + \frac{1}{5}$

9. $\frac{2}{5} - \frac{3}{10}$
10. $\frac{5}{6} - \frac{3}{8}$
11. $\frac{3}{8} + \frac{1}{8} + \frac{5}{8}$
12. $\frac{3}{5} + \frac{1}{10} + \frac{1}{4}$

13. **USING LOGICAL REASONING** Can the sum of two fractions that are each less than 1 be greater than 1? Give examples to support your answer.

LOOKING FOR A PATTERN In Exercises 14–16, find the sums or differences. Then continue the pattern to find the next two sums or differences.

14. $\frac{1}{3} - \frac{1}{18}$

   $\frac{1}{3} - \frac{1}{15}$

   $\frac{1}{3} - \frac{1}{12}$

15. $\frac{1}{5} + \frac{1}{2}$

   $\frac{2}{5} + \frac{1}{2}$

   $\frac{3}{5} + \frac{1}{2}$

16. $\frac{1}{2} + \frac{1}{2} + \frac{1}{4}$

   $\frac{2}{3} + \frac{1}{3} + \frac{1}{6}$

   $\frac{3}{4} + \frac{1}{4} + \frac{1}{8}$

GUESS, CHECK, AND REVISE In Exercises 17–22, use the Guess, Check, and Revise strategy to find the missing fraction in simplest form.

17. $\boxed{?} + \frac{3}{4} = 1$
18. $\frac{9}{11} - \boxed{?} = \frac{7}{11}$
19. $\frac{1}{2} - \boxed{?} = \frac{1}{6}$

20. $\boxed{?} + \frac{1}{2} = \frac{15}{14}$
21. $\frac{1}{8} + \boxed{?} = \frac{7}{24}$
22. $\boxed{?} - \frac{7}{10} = \frac{1}{20}$

COMPANY SIZES In Exercises 23–25, use the circle graph at the right. It shows a summary of the $94\frac{1}{2}$ million employees who worked in U.S. companies of various sizes in 1996. Find the fraction of employees who worked in companies having

23. fewer than 100 employees.

24. fewer than 500 employees.

25. 100–999 employees.

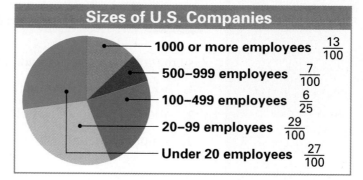

Sizes of U.S. Companies

1000 or more employees $\frac{13}{100}$

500–999 employees $\frac{7}{100}$

100–499 employees $\frac{6}{25}$

20–99 employees $\frac{29}{100}$

Under 20 employees $\frac{27}{100}$

STANDARDIZED TEST PRACTICE

26. You rode a go-cart for $\frac{2}{3}$ mi. Your friend rode for $\frac{8}{9}$ mi. How much farther did your friend ride than you did?

A $\frac{1}{9}$ mi   **B** $\frac{2}{9}$ mi   **C** $\frac{1}{3}$ mi   **D** $\frac{2}{3}$ mi

27. $\frac{1}{3} + \frac{3}{5} =$

A $\frac{4}{5}$ **B** $\frac{4}{8}$ **C** $\frac{4}{15}$ **D** $\frac{14}{15}$

EXPLORATION AND EXTENSION

PORTFOLIO

28. BUILDING YOUR PROJECT You conduct a survey to find out how people choose the T-shirts they buy. The results are shown at the right. What fraction of people would you say are mostly concerned with the outward appearance of the T-shirt? What fraction are concerned with fabric quality or brand name? Include this information in the letter to your stockholders.

Fabric quality $\frac{1}{4}$

Color $\frac{1}{10}$

Name brand $\frac{2}{15}$

Price $\frac{3}{20}$

Style $\frac{1}{6}$

Logo/sayings $\frac{1}{5}$

Adding and Subtracting Mixed Numbers

What you should learn:

Goal ① How to add and subtract mixed numbers

Goal ② How to use regrouping to subtract mixed numbers

Why you should learn it:

Knowing how to add and subtract mixed numbers can help you with carpentry projects. An example is finding the heights of stacks of boards.

Goal ① Operations with Mixed Numbers

Use the following steps to add or subtract two mixed numbers.

1. Add or subtract the fractions.
2. Add or subtract the whole numbers.
3. Simplify when possible.

Example 1 ▷ **Common Denominators**

$$2\frac{2}{5} + 1\frac{4}{5} = 3\frac{6}{5}$$ Add fractions and whole numbers.

$$= 3 + \frac{5}{5} + \frac{1}{5}$$ Rewrite the improper fraction.

$$= 3 + 1 + \frac{1}{5}$$ Simplify.

$$= 4 + \frac{1}{5}$$ Add whole numbers.

$$= 4\frac{1}{5}$$ Write as a mixed number.

Example 2 ▷ **Different Denominators**

a. $5\frac{3}{4} + 3\frac{1}{2} = 5\frac{3}{4} + 3\frac{2}{4}$ Rewrite fractions with a common denominator.

$$= 8\frac{5}{4}$$ Add fractions and whole numbers.

$$= 8 + \frac{4}{4} + \frac{1}{4}$$ Rewrite the improper fraction.

$$= 8 + 1 + \frac{1}{4}$$ Simplify.

$$= 9 + \frac{1}{4}$$ Add whole numbers.

$$= 9\frac{1}{4}$$ Write as a mixed number.

b. $9\frac{5}{6} - 3\frac{1}{2} = 9\frac{5}{6} - 3\frac{3}{6}$ Rewrite fractions with a common denominator.

$$= 6\frac{2}{6}$$ Subtract fractions and whole numbers.

$$= 6\frac{1}{3}$$ Simplify.

When you subtract mixed numbers, the fractional part of the second number may be larger than the fractional part of the first number. In such cases you should *regroup*.

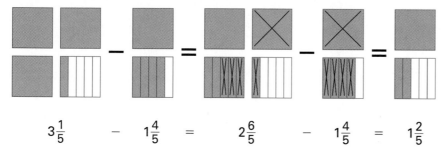

$$3\frac{1}{5} \qquad - \qquad 1\frac{4}{5} \qquad = \qquad 2\frac{6}{5} \qquad - \qquad 1\frac{4}{5} \qquad = \qquad 1\frac{2}{5}$$

Writing $3\frac{1}{5}$ as $2\frac{6}{5}$ is called **regrouping** because the 3 is regrouped as $2 + 1$, as follows.

$$3\frac{1}{5} = 2 + 1 + \frac{1}{5} \qquad \text{Rewrite 3 as } 2 + 1.$$

$$= 2 + \frac{5}{5} + \frac{1}{5} \qquad \text{Rewrite 1 as } \frac{5}{5}.$$

$$= 2 + \frac{6}{5} \qquad \text{Add fractions.}$$

$$= 2\frac{6}{5} \qquad \text{Write as a mixed number.}$$

Example 3 ▷ **Regrouping to Subtract**

a. $5\frac{1}{4} - 2\frac{3}{4} = 4\frac{5}{4} - 2\frac{3}{4} \qquad$ Regroup $5\frac{1}{4}$ as $4\frac{5}{4}$.

$$= 2\frac{2}{4} \qquad \text{Subtract mixed numbers.}$$

$$= 2\frac{1}{2} \qquad \text{Simplify.}$$

b. $6\frac{1}{6} - 3\frac{1}{2} = 6\frac{1}{6} - 3\frac{3}{6} \qquad$ Rewrite with a common denominator.

$$= 5\frac{7}{6} - 3\frac{3}{6} \qquad \text{Regroup } 6\frac{1}{6} \text{ as } 5\frac{7}{6}.$$

$$= 2\frac{4}{6} \qquad \text{Subtract mixed numbers.}$$

$$= 2\frac{2}{3} \qquad \text{Simplify.}$$

ONGOING ASSESSMENT

Talk About It

With another student, solve the following problems. In each problem, discuss whether you had to find a common denominator, regroup, or simplify the answer.

1. $7\frac{5}{6} - 2\frac{1}{3}$

2. $7\frac{2}{3} - 2\frac{1}{3}$

3. $7\frac{1}{6} - 2\frac{1}{3}$

Extra Practice, page 628

GUIDED PRACTICE

In Exercises 1 and 2, the steps for solving the problem are out of order.
Rewrite the steps in order.

1. $1\frac{5}{6} + 2\frac{9}{10}$

   A. $= 3\frac{52}{30}$ **B.** $= 4\frac{11}{15}$ **C.** $= 1\frac{25}{30} + 2\frac{27}{30}$ **D.** $= 4\frac{22}{30}$

2. $5\frac{1}{10} - 2\frac{1}{2}$

   A. $= 2\frac{3}{5}$ **B.** $= 2\frac{6}{10}$ **C.** $= 4\frac{11}{10} - 2\frac{5}{10}$ **D.** $= 5\frac{1}{10} - 2\frac{5}{10}$

In Exercises 3–5, complete the equation.

3. $3\frac{5}{6} = 2\frac{?}{6}$ **4.** $5\frac{9}{5} = 6\frac{?}{5}$ **5.** $1\frac{1}{12} = \frac{?}{12}$

6. OPEN-ENDED PROBLEM Write a subtraction problem that requires regrouping a mixed number. Then solve the problem.

PRACTICE AND PROBLEM SOLVING

In Exercises 7–10, simplify the mixed number.

7. $4\frac{9}{5}$ **8.** $6\frac{6}{8}$ **9.** $1\frac{26}{22}$ **10.** $2\frac{15}{10}$

In Exercises 11–14, complete the statement.

11. $7\frac{1}{2} = 6\frac{?}{2}$ **12.** $4\frac{3}{10} = 3\frac{?}{10}$ **13.** $9\frac{2}{7} = 8\frac{?}{7}$ **14.** $2\frac{2}{3} = 1\frac{?}{3}$

In Exercises 15–22, add or subtract. Simplify if possible.

15. $5\frac{2}{9} + 2\frac{8}{9}$ **16.** $2\frac{5}{12} + 6\frac{1}{6}$ **17.** $3\frac{4}{15} - 1\frac{7}{15}$ **18.** $7\frac{2}{3} - 2\frac{11}{12}$

19. $4\frac{5}{6} + 2\frac{1}{6}$ **20.** $5\frac{2}{3} + 2\frac{1}{8}$ **21.** $3 - 1\frac{5}{8}$ **22.** $6\frac{1}{4} - 1\frac{7}{16}$

In Exercises 23–30, solve. Simplify if possible.

23. $2\frac{5}{12} + 1\frac{3}{12}$ **24.** $6\frac{8}{9} + 2\frac{2}{9}$ **25.** $5\frac{3}{4} - 1\frac{1}{3}$ **26.** $3\frac{1}{8} + 5\frac{5}{6}$

27. $2\frac{3}{10} + 6\frac{9}{10}$ **28.** $4\frac{1}{6} - 2\frac{5}{6}$ **29.** $6 - 3\frac{3}{4}$ **30.** $9\frac{3}{8} - 4\frac{1}{12}$

GEOMETRY In Exercises 31–33, how much of the given fencing will be left over after the yard is fenced? Explain.

31. Fencing: 60 ft

$9\frac{1}{2}$ ft

$17\frac{1}{3}$ ft

32. Fencing: 75 ft

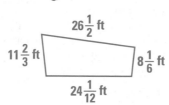

$26\frac{1}{2}$ ft

$11\frac{2}{3}$ ft

$8\frac{1}{6}$ ft

$24\frac{1}{12}$ ft

33. Fencing: 40 ft

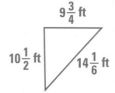

$9\frac{3}{4}$ ft

$10\frac{1}{2}$ ft $14\frac{1}{6}$ ft

BUSINESS CAREERS In Exercises 34 and 35, use the bar graph at the right. It shows the average number of hours worked per day by a person in each career. (Source: The Jobs Rated)

34. On average, how many more hours per day does a dairy farmer work than an accountant?

35. Find the length of the sum of the average workdays for firefighters and receptionists.

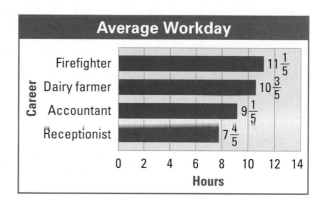

Average Workday

Firefighter — $11\frac{1}{5}$
Dairy farmer — $10\frac{3}{5}$
Accountant — $9\frac{1}{5}$
Receptionist — $7\frac{4}{5}$

0 2 4 6 8 10 12 14
Hours

WOODWORKING Boards are named for their dimensions when they are cut from logs. When they are planed smooth, these dimensions decrease, as shown in the table at the right. In Exercises 36–38, find the height of each stack of boards.

36.

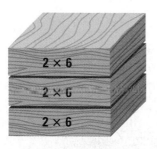

2 × 6

2 × 6

2 × 6

37.

1×2
1×2
1×2
2×2

38.

2 × 4

2 × 4

4 × 4

Name of board	Actual size (inches)
1 × 2	$\frac{3}{4} \times 1\frac{1}{2}$
2 × 2	$1\frac{1}{2} \times 1\frac{1}{2}$
2 × 4	$1\frac{1}{2} \times 3\frac{1}{2}$
2 × 6	$1\frac{1}{2} \times 5\frac{1}{2}$
4 × 4	$3\frac{1}{2} \times 3\frac{1}{2}$

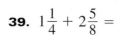

STANDARDIZED TEST PRACTICE

39. $1\frac{1}{4} + 2\frac{5}{8} =$

(A) $3\frac{3}{8}$ (B) $3\frac{5}{8}$ (C) $3\frac{7}{8}$ (D) $4\frac{1}{8}$

40. BUILDING YOUR PROJECT When you first opened your T-shirt company in January, you sold each share for $10\frac{1}{2}$. When the weather got warmer in April, stock prices rose to $13\frac{7}{8}$. The weather got even warmer in July, and the stock price rose by $2\frac{1}{4}$. In October the price fell by $5\frac{1}{16}$. By the next January, holiday sales had driven the stock up by $3\frac{3}{16}$. Include the following information in your letter to the stockholders.

a. How much did your stock rise between January and April?

b. What did your stock sell for in July? What did it sell for in October?

c. One year after the initial sale, was the price of your stock higher or lower than what it was when you first sold it in January? By how much had the stock price changed?

How to Read a Stock Listing

High and low prices for the day — Price at the close of the market

Stock	Sales 100s	High	Low	LastChg.
FrnkRs s	2791	$72^3/_4$	$72^9/_{16}$	$72^5/_8$ +$^1/_6$
FrkUnv	888	$9^1/_2$	$9^3/_8$	$9^1/_2$ +$^1/_6$
FrMeyer	2225	$52^{13}/_{16}$	$51^{15}/_{16}$	$52^1/_2$ +$^{13}/_{16}$
FredMac s	8269	$36^1/_8$	$34^{11}/_{16}$	$35^5/_8$ +$^5/_8$
FMCG A	1225	$28^3/_4$	$27^7/_8$	28 $-1^1/_4$

Stock symbol — Number of shares bought and sold — Change in price from day before

---

SPIRAL REVIEW

DRAWING A DIAGRAM In Exercises 1 and 2, use the figure at the right. **(1.1)**

1. The area of the large square is 64 square units. What is the area of each small triangle?

2. How many triangles and squares are in the figure?

GUESS, CHECK, AND REVISE In Exercises 3 and 4, you are given the perimeter and area of a rectangle. Find its dimensions. **(1.5)**

3. Perimeter: 18 m; Area: 18 m^2

4. Perimeter: 28 in.; Area: 45 in.^{2}

5. You are tiling a floor using parallelogram-shaped tiles, as shown at the right. Find the area of each tile. **(1.3)**

6 in.

12 in.

In Exercises 6–8, evaluate the expression. **(2.2)**

6. 5 cubed

7. 4 to the fourth power

8. 11 squared

In Exercises 9–14, write the prime factorization of the number. **(2.6)**

9. 64

10. 72

11. 105

12. 47

13. 80

14. 216

Take this test as you would take a test in class. The answers to the exercises are given in the back of the book.

In Exercises 1–4, find the least common multiple. (3.1)

1. 6, 42   **2.** 4, 34   **3.** 2, 5, 11   **4.** 4, 5, 15

5. TRAVEL A travel agent offers a tour to Bermuda every three weeks, to Jamaica every four weeks, and to Aruba every six weeks. How often will the agent offer all three tours during the same week? **(3.1)**

Match the improper fraction with its mixed number or decimal. (3.2)

A. 5.2   **B.** 2.125   **C.** $7\frac{1}{2}$ **D.** $3\frac{2}{9}$

6. $\dfrac{17}{8}$ **7.** $\dfrac{29}{9}$ **8.** $\dfrac{45}{6}$ **9.** $\dfrac{26}{5}$

In Exercises 10–12, use the circle graph at the right. It shows the types of flowers that are planted.
(Source: Professional Plant Growers Association) **(3.3)**

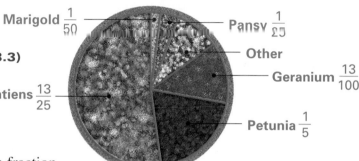

Marigold $\frac{1}{50}$ Pansy $\frac{1}{25}$ Other   Geranium $\frac{13}{100}$ Impatiens $\frac{13}{25}$ Petunia $\frac{1}{5}$

10. Find the difference between the fraction of petunias and the fraction of pansies.

11. Find the difference between the fraction of impatiens and the fraction of geraniums.

12. What fraction of flowers is in the "other" category?

In Exercises 13–20, add or subtract. Simplify if possible. (3.3, 3.4)

13. $\dfrac{7}{6} - \dfrac{1}{6}$ **14.** $\dfrac{4}{9} + \dfrac{4}{3}$ **15.** $2\dfrac{7}{10} + 3\dfrac{9}{10}$ **16.** $5\dfrac{8}{9} - 1\dfrac{4}{9}$

17. $3\dfrac{1}{3} + 6\dfrac{1}{8}$ **18.** $7\dfrac{2}{5} - 4\dfrac{3}{10}$ **19.** $4\dfrac{1}{12} - 1\dfrac{5}{6}$ **20.** $8\dfrac{3}{8} - 2\dfrac{2}{3}$

NAUTICAL SIGNAL FLAGS Each flag represents a letter of the alphabet. They are used as signals between ships. Write, both as a fraction and as a decimal, the portion of the flag that is blue. **(3.2)**

21.

C

22.

J

23.

G

24.
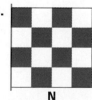
N

LAB 3.5

COOPERATIVE LEARNING

Investigating Multiplication and Area Models

Part A MULTIPLYING FRACTIONS

Materials Needed
- plain paper
- pencils or pens
- colored pencils or markers

The diagram below is an area model for multiplying $\frac{1}{3}$ and $\frac{3}{4}$.

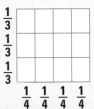

Divide a unit square horizontally into thirds and vertically into fourths.

Color one third of the square one color.

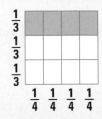

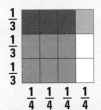

Color three fourths of the square another color. Find the area of the region where the colors overlap.

Because $\frac{3}{12}$ of the square is colored with both colors, the product of $\frac{1}{3}$ and $\frac{3}{4}$ is $\frac{3}{12}$, or $\frac{1}{4}$.

1. Write the multiplication problem that is represented by the area model. Then use the model to find the product.

   a. 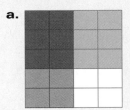   b. 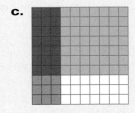   c.

2. Draw an area model to find the product.

   a. $\frac{2}{5} \times \frac{2}{3}$ b. $\frac{1}{2} \times \frac{1}{2}$ c. $\frac{1}{2} \times \frac{3}{2}$ d. $\frac{4}{5} \times \frac{3}{3}$

3. Use any patterns you see in Exercise 2 to explain how to multiply fractions without using an area model. Then use your method to find the following products.

   a. $\frac{2}{7} \times \frac{3}{4}$ b. $\frac{1}{3} \times \frac{2}{3}$ c. $\frac{1}{2} \times \frac{3}{2}$ d. $\frac{4}{5} \times \frac{7}{1}$

4. Find the following products. Explain your method.

   a. $2 \times \frac{2}{5}$ b. $3 \times \frac{5}{3}$ c. $\frac{1}{2} \times 4$ d. $\frac{3}{4} \times 6$

5. The area model below represents the product of $1\frac{1}{3}$ and $2\frac{1}{2}$. Explain how the model is used to find the product.

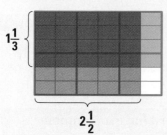

$1\frac{1}{3}$

$2\frac{1}{2}$

You can see that $\frac{20}{6}$ (or $3\frac{1}{3}$) of the region is colored by both colors.

6. Draw an area model to find the product.

a. $1\frac{1}{3} \times 2\frac{2}{3}$ b. $2 \times 3\frac{1}{2}$

c. $\frac{1}{2} \times 2\frac{1}{4}$ d. $3\frac{2}{3} \times \frac{1}{5}$

NOW TRY THESE

7. USING LOGICAL REASONING If two fractions are each less than $\frac{1}{2}$, what can you say about their product? Use an area model to explain your reasoning.

In Exercises 8–10, match the product of fractions with the product of decimals. Then check your answers by finding each product.

A. 0.4×0.2 B. 0.1×0.5 C. 0.75×0.8

8. $\frac{1}{10} \times \frac{1}{2}$ **9.** $\frac{2}{5} \times \frac{1}{5}$ **10.** $\frac{3}{4} \times \frac{4}{5}$

11. Each model represents a product. Find the product in decimal form and in fraction form.

a. 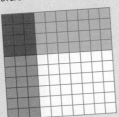   b.

Multiplying Fractions and **Mixed Numbers**

Why you should learn it:

Knowing how to multiply fractions and mixed numbers can help you find areas. An example is finding the area of the region of a park to be planted with trees.

Goal 1 MULTIPLYING FRACTIONS

MULTIPLYING FRACTIONS

To multiply two fractions, multiply their numerators and multiply their denominators.

When you add or subtract fractions, they must have a common denominator. That is not necessary when you multiply fractions.

Example 1 **Multiplying Fractions**

$$\frac{4}{9} \times \frac{3}{4} = \frac{4 \times 3}{9 \times 4}$$ **Multiply the numerators and denominators.**

$$= \frac{12}{36}$$ **Find products.**

$$= \frac{1}{3}$$ **Simplify.**

Example 2 **Finding an Area**

You are planning a park that has an area of three fourths of an acre. You want to plant four fifths of the park with trees. What is the area of the region that will be planted with trees?

REAL LIFE
Parks

Solution

This is the same as asking "*What is $\frac{4}{5}$ of $\frac{3}{4}$?*"

Method **1** Multiply the two fractions.

$$\frac{4}{5} \times \frac{3}{4} = \frac{12}{20}$$ **Find products.**

$$= \frac{3}{5}$$ **Simplify.**

The region planted with trees has an area of $\frac{3}{5}$ acre.

Method **2** **DRAW A DIAGRAM** You could also use an area model to find the area planted with trees.

STRATEGY

The model shows that $\frac{12}{20}$ or $\frac{3}{5}$ acre will be planted with trees.

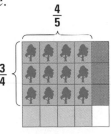

Goal 2 MULTIPLYING MIXED NUMBERS

MULTIPLYING MIXED NUMBERS

To multiply mixed numbers, first rewrite them as improper fractions. Then multiply numerators and multiply denominators.

Example 3 **Multiplying Mixed Numbers**

a. $1\frac{1}{2} \times 3\frac{1}{4} = \frac{3}{2} \times \frac{13}{4}$ Rewrite as improper fractions.

$= \frac{3 \times 13}{2 \times 4}$ Multiply fractions.

$= \frac{39}{8}$ Find products.

$= 4\frac{7}{8}$ Simplify.

b. $4 \times 2\frac{1}{4} = \frac{4}{1} \times \frac{9}{4}$ Rewrite as improper fractions.

$= \frac{4 \times 9}{1 \times 4}$ Multiply fractions.

$= \frac{36}{4}$ Find products.

$= 9$ Simplify.

Example 4 **Changing a Recipe**

A recipe calls for $1\frac{1}{3}$ cups of rice. If you cut the amounts in half, how much rice do you need?

REAL LIFE
Cooking

Solution

$\frac{1}{2} \times 1\frac{1}{3} = \frac{1}{2} \times \frac{4}{3}$ Rewrite as an improper fraction.

$= \frac{1 \times 4}{2 \times 3}$ Multiply fractions.

$= \frac{4}{6}$ Find products.

$= \frac{2}{3}$ Simplify.

You need two-thirds cup of rice.

GUIDED PRACTICE

In Exercises 1 and 2, write the multiplication problem that is represented by the area model. Then use the model to find the product.

1. 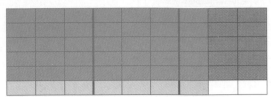   **2.**

3. Explain how to multiply two mixed numbers.

4. **WRITING** Write a rule for multiplying the fractions $\frac{a}{b}$ and $\frac{c}{d}$.

5. Your teacher asks, "What is $\frac{1}{8}$ of $\frac{4}{5}$?" You write the problem as $\frac{4}{5} \times \frac{1}{8}$. Your friend writes the problem as $\frac{1}{8} \times \frac{4}{5}$. Who do you think is correct?

PRACTICE AND PROBLEM SOLVING

6. **GRAVITY** The table compares the weights of an object on different planets. An object that weighs 1 lb on Earth weighs $2\frac{1}{2}$ lb on Jupiter. Find the weight of a 100-lb person on each planet.

Mercury	Venus	Earth	Mars	Jupiter	Saturn	Uranus	Neptune	Pluto
$\frac{2}{5}$	$\frac{22}{25}$	1	$\frac{19}{50}$	$2\frac{1}{2}$	$1\frac{1}{20}$	$\frac{9}{10}$	$1\frac{7}{50}$	$\frac{1}{20}$

USING LOGICAL REASONING In Exercises 7–9, complete the statement with *sometimes*, *always*, or *never*.

7. The product of two mixed numbers is __?__ greater than 1.

8. The product of a whole number and a proper fraction is __?__ less than 1.

9. The product of a mixed number and zero is __?__ greater than 1.

In Exercises 10–21, multiply. Simplify if possible.

10. $\frac{1}{2} \times \frac{6}{7}$ **11.** $\frac{5}{9} \cdot \frac{2}{3}$ **12.** $\frac{3}{5} \cdot 8$ **13.** $10 \times \frac{1}{4}$

14. $1\frac{2}{5} \cdot 3\frac{1}{3}$ **15.** $4\frac{1}{2} \times 2\frac{3}{4}$ **16.** $\frac{1}{9} \times 5\frac{2}{7}$ **17.** $3\frac{1}{6} \cdot \frac{1}{3}$

18. $2\frac{1}{5} \times 10$ **19.** $8 \times 1\frac{5}{8}$ **20.** $\frac{2}{5} \times \frac{1}{2} \times 3\frac{1}{3}$ **21.** $6 \cdot \frac{2}{5} \cdot 3\frac{1}{2}$

GEOMETRY In Exercises 22 and 23, find the area of the region.

22.

$1\frac{1}{8}$ in.

$1\frac{1}{8}$ in.

23.

$1\frac{5}{6}$ ft

4 ft

24. You ran $1\frac{1}{3}$ times around a $\frac{1}{4}$-mi track. How far did you run?

25. GARDENING You are planning a rectangular vegetable garden that is $2\frac{1}{2}$ m by $1\frac{3}{4}$ m. Use an area model to find the area of the garden.

STANDARDIZED TEST PRACTICE

26. You have six pieces of string that are each $2\frac{3}{8}$ in. long. What is the total length of the string if you lay the pieces end to end?

A $8\frac{3}{8}$ in. **B** $12\frac{1}{6}$ in. **C** $12\frac{3}{8}$ in. **D** $14\frac{1}{4}$ in.

27. $2\frac{1}{3} \times 3\frac{5}{12} =$

A $6\frac{5}{6}$ **B** $6\frac{5}{36}$ **C** $7\frac{2}{3}$ **D** $7\frac{35}{36}$

EXPLORATION AND EXTENSION

PORTFOLIO

28. BUILDING YOUR PROJECT The table shows the amount of material needed for each size T-shirt.

Size	Sm	Med	Lg	XL
Yards	$1\frac{3}{4}$	$2\frac{1}{8}$	$2\frac{1}{2}$	$2\frac{7}{8}$

a. How much material is needed to make one shirt of each size?

b. Can you make ten of each size from one 100-yd bolt of material?

Include this information in your letter to the stockholders.

3.6

What you should learn:

Goal ➊ How to use the Distributive Property with numbers

Goal ➋ How to use the Distributive Property with variables

Why you should learn it:

Knowing how to use the Distributive Property can help you change difficult problems into easy ones. An example is finding the amount of money earned at a car wash.

The Distributive Property

Goal ➊ **THE DISTRIBUTIVE PROPERTY**

LESSON INVESTIGATION

Investigating the Distributive Property

GROUP ACTIVITY Which diagram below illustrates the expression 3(2 + 4)? Which diagram illustrates the expression 3 × 2 + 3 × 4? Are the expressions equivalent? How do you know?

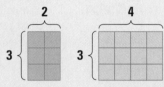

Draw a similar diagram to show that 4(3 + 5) = 4 × 3 + 4 × 5.

In this investigation, you may have discovered the **Distributive Property** defined below.

THE DISTRIBUTIVE PROPERTY

For all numbers *a*, *b*, and *c*, $a(b + c) = a \times b + a \times c$.

Example: $3(2 + 4) = 3 \times 2 + 3 \times 4$

Example 1 **Using the Distributive Property**

Evaluate $3 \times \frac{2}{5} + 3 \times \frac{3}{5}$.

Solution

Method ➊ $3 \times \frac{2}{5} + 3 \times \frac{3}{5} = \frac{6}{5} + \frac{9}{5}$ Use order of operations.

$= \frac{15}{5}$ Add.

$= 3$ Simplify.

Method ➋ $3 \times \frac{2}{5} + 3 \times \frac{3}{5} = 3\left(\frac{2}{5} + \frac{3}{5}\right)$ Use the Distributive Property.

$= 3(1)$ Add inside parentheses.

$= 3$ Multiply.

In algebra, when you write the product of a number and a variable, you can omit the multiplication sign. For example, the product $3 \times n$ can be written as $3n$.

Example 2 Evaluating Expressions

Evaluate each expression when $x = 4$.

a. $5(x + 2)$ **b.** $5x + 5(2)$

Solution

a. $5(x + 2) = 5(4 + 2)$ Substitute 4 for x.

             $= 5(6)$ Add inside parentheses.

             $= 30$ Multiply.

b. $5x + 5(2) = 5(4) + 5(2)$ Substitute 4 for x.

               $= 20 + 10$ Multiply.

               $= 30$ Add.

Both expressions have the same value. This is an example of the Distributive Property.

$$5(x + 2) = 5x + 5(2)$$

Example 3 Using Mental Math

You and some friends washed 12 cars for $5.25 each. Find the total amount you earned.

REAL LIFE
Car Wash

Solution

Instead of multiplying 12 by 5.25, you can find the products 12×5 and 12×0.25 and add the results.

$12 \times 5.25 = 12(5 + 0.25)$ Regroup 5.25 as 5 + 0.25.

             $= 12 \times 5 + 12 \times 0.25$ Distributive Property

             $= 60 + 3$ Mental math multiplication

             $= 63$ Mental math addition

You earned $63 washing cars.

ONGOING ASSESSMENT

Write About It

Look at the two methods for evaluating the expression in Example 1.

1. Which uses the Distributive Property?

2. Do you think one method is easier than the other? Explain.

GUIDED PRACTICE

In Exercises 1 and 2, complete the statement using + or ×.

1. $3 \; ? \; (6 + 8) = 3 \; ? \; 6 + 3 \; ? \; 8$

2. $(5 + 2) \; ? \; 3 = 5 \times 3 \; ? \; 2 \times 3$

ERROR ANALYSIS In Exercises 3 and 4, describe and correct the error.

3.
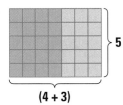

4.
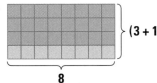

5. Write the product of 5 and t in as many ways as possible.

6. Which of these correctly uses the Distributive Property?

    a. $4(12 + x) = 48 + 12x$ **b.** $4\left(5 + \dfrac{2}{3}\right) = 4 \times 5 + \dfrac{2}{3}$ **c.** $3t + \dfrac{4}{5}t = \left(3 + \dfrac{4}{5}\right)t$

PRACTICE AND PROBLEM SOLVING

In Exercises 7 and 8, use the Distributive Property to write two expressions that are represented by the area model.

7.

5

$(4 + 3)$

8.

$(3 + 1)$

8

In Exercises 9–14, evaluate the expression. Tell whether you used the Distributive Property.

9. $5(3 + 8)$ **10.** $17(85 + 15)$ **11.** $10(5.9 + 1.2)$

12. $4\left(\dfrac{5}{6} + \dfrac{1}{4}\right)$ **13.** $6\left(\dfrac{1}{3} + \dfrac{1}{5}\right)$ **14.** $9\left(\dfrac{7}{9} + \dfrac{1}{3}\right)$

In Exercises 15–20, use the Distributive Property to rewrite the expression.

15. $3(t + 4)$ **16.** $12(5 + b)$ **17.** $c(4 + 6)$

18. $n(15 + 25)$ **19.** $1(x + 24)$ **20.** $5(p + q)$

In Exercises 21 and 22, evaluate the two expressions when $x = 5$. What can you conclude?

21. $4(x + 7)$ and $4x + 4(7)$ **22.** $4\left(\dfrac{1}{2} + x\right)$ and $4\left(\dfrac{1}{2}\right) + 4x$

MENTAL MATH In Exercises 23–28, complete the statement without using pencil and paper or a calculator.

23. $3(11.2) = 3(11 + 0.2) = \boxed{?}$

24. $5(20.1) = 5(20 + 0.1) = \boxed{?}$

25. $50(2.5) = 50(2 + 0.5) = \boxed{?}$

26. $11(2.03) = 11(2 + 0.03) = \boxed{?}$

27. $18(5.4) = 18(5 + 0.4) = \boxed{?}$

28. $3(12.04) = 3(2 + 0.4) = \boxed{?}$

29. TALENT SHOW You are organizing a talent show. You allow each person 2 min to set up, $\frac{1}{2}$ min for an introduction, and 5 min for the act. There are 20 people performing. How long will the talent show be? Explain.

30. COMMUNITY SERVICE You are helping deliver Thanksgiving packages to the elderly. Each package contains a 12-lb turkey, 3 lb of vegetables, and 4 lb of potatoes. Assume that you can only carry 50 lb. Can you carry three of these packages?

31. LANDSCAPING During the summer, you mow lawns. You charge $10.75 to mow a small lawn and $15.50 to mow a large lawn. In one week, you mow ten small lawns and six large lawns. Use the Distributive Property to find the total amount you earned during the week.

STANDARDIZED TEST PRACTICE

32. Which of the following is *not* equal to $x(6 + 8)$?

(A) $14x$ **(B)** $6x + 8x$ **(C)** $6x + 8$ **(D)** $(6 + 8)x$

33. Choose the equation that best demonstrates the Distributive Property.

(A) $5 \times 3 + 1 = 15 + 1$ **(B)** $\left(\frac{3}{4} + \frac{1}{2}\right) \times 8 = 6 + 4$

(C) $17 \times 23 = 23 \times 17$ **(D)** $3 + (9 + 7) = (3 + 9) + 7$

34. You take three friends to the zoo. The admission is $3.25 per person, and you buy four train tickets for $1.35 each. Which expression could you use to find the total amount of money that you spent?

(A) $3.25 + 3 \times 1.35$ **(B)** $4 \times (3.25 + 1.35)$

(C) $3 \times (3.25 + 1.35)$ **(D)** $4 \times (3.25 \times 1.35)$

35. COMMUNICATING ABOUT MATHEMATICS
Amelia Earhart's plane, a Lockhead Electra, burned about 38 gallons of fuel per hour. When she was last heard from, Earhart had traveled $20\frac{1}{4}$ hours after leaving Lae, Guinea.

At that point, she had about 4 hours of fuel left. How many gallons did the plane contain when it took off from Lae? Explain.

GUESS, CHECK, AND REVISE In Exercises 1–4, solve the equation. **(1.6)**

1. $12 + x = 27$ **2.** $n - 11 = 9$ **3.** $y \times 5 = 45$ **4.** $36 \div b = 18$

5. USING LOGICAL REASONING A survey asked 50 people to name what type of bread they like for sandwiches. Thirty-eight people said white bread and 21 said wheat. How many said either white bread or wheat bread? **(1.7)**

In Exercises 6–8, use the divisibility tests to decide whether the number is divisible by 2, 3, 4, 5, 6, 9, or 10. **(2.3)**

6. 519   **7.** 1842   **8.** 3960

In Exercises 9–14, find the greatest common factor by listing all the factors of each number. **(2.5)**

9. 51, 68   **10.** 72, 98   **11.** 27, 64

12. 36, 57   **13.** 35, 210   **14.** 48, 100

In Exercises 15–23, write the fraction in simplest form. **(2.6)**

15. $\frac{39}{78}$ **16.** $\frac{28}{48}$ **17.** $\frac{99}{132}$

18. $\frac{7}{196}$ **19.** $\frac{6}{15}$ **20.** $\frac{39}{52}$

21. $\frac{16}{40}$ **22.** $\frac{34}{51}$ **23.** $\frac{64}{80}$

In Exercises 24 and 25, plot the numbers on a number line. Then list the numbers from least to greatest. **(2.8)**

24. $1\frac{1}{4}, \frac{10}{3}, \frac{33}{10}, \frac{7}{2}, \frac{13}{5}$ **25.** $\frac{7}{4}, 1\frac{1}{2}, 1.7, 1.45, \frac{4}{5}, 1.04, \frac{7}{5}$

26. Samuel, Jessica, and Latasha ride the same bus home from school. Samuel rides the bus every other day. Jessica rides the bus every day. Latasha rides the bus home every fourth day. They all ride the bus home on Monday. When will they ride the bus together again? **(3.1)**

AMELIA EARHART

READ About It

Amelia Earhart was a pioneer of early aviation. In 1928, she was the first woman to fly across the Atlantic as a passenger. Today, a DC-9 flying from New York to London takes only $6\frac{5}{6}$ hours, but Earhart's flight took $20\frac{1}{6}$ hours. In 1932 she crossed the Atlantic alone and cut $7\frac{1}{6}$ hours off of her earlier flight as a passenger. Earhart set many records for speed and distance traveled.

In 1937, Amelia Earhart tried to break another record. She attempted to fly over 24,000 miles around the world.

During part of the trip, in the Pacific Ocean, Earhart began a flight of about 2500 miles from Lae, New Guinea, to Howland Island. Twenty and a quarter hours after leaving Lae, Earhart made her last radio transmission. Experts guess she had about 4 hours worth of fuel left, but she was never seen again.

WRITE About It

1. How much longer did the transatlantic flight take in 1928 than it did in 1932? Write your answer as a sentence.

2. How many times longer did it take Earhart to cross the Atlantic than it would take for you to fly from New York to London today in a DC-9? What does this tell you about airplane travel?

3. What fraction of the total flight was the last hop to Howland Island? How many separate flights do you think the whole trip would have taken? Why?

4. Before her last flight, Earhart's record distance was $2026\frac{1}{2}$ miles.

   How many more miles than her previous distance record was the flight to Howland Island supposed to be? Explain whether you think this would have mattered.

LAB
3.7
COOPERATIVE LEARNING

Investigating Division of Fractions

Part A **USING MODELS FOR DIVISION**

Materials Needed
- plain paper
- colored pencils or markers
- pencils

You need to measure $3\frac{1}{3}$ cups of water. You have a $\frac{1}{3}$ cup measure. How many times do you need to fill the measure? To find the answer, divide $3\frac{1}{3}$ by $\frac{1}{3}$, as shown in the following model.

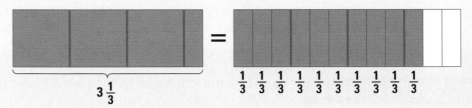

$3\frac{1}{3}$

$\frac{1}{3}$ $\frac{1}{3}$ $\frac{1}{3}$ $\frac{1}{3}$ $\frac{1}{3}$ $\frac{1}{3}$ $\frac{1}{3}$ $\frac{1}{3}$ $\frac{1}{3}$ $\frac{1}{3}$

1. Use the above model to rewrite the problem $3\frac{1}{3} \div \frac{1}{3}$ with no mixed numbers. Then solve.

2. The following model represents $4\frac{1}{6}$. Copy the model. Explain how you can use the model to rewrite the problem $4\frac{1}{6} \div \frac{5}{6}$ with no mixed numbers. Then solve.

3. Use a model to find the quotient.

   a. $4\frac{4}{5} \div \frac{3}{5}$ **b.** $4\frac{2}{3} \div \frac{2}{3}$ **c.** $7\frac{1}{2} \div 1\frac{1}{2}$

4. Describe any patterns you see in Exercises 1–3. With others in your group, discuss how you could solve these division problems without drawing a model. Then solve the following problems without using a model.

   a. $2\frac{4}{7} \div \frac{3}{7}$ **b.** $2\frac{2}{5} \div 1\frac{1}{5}$ **c.** $10\frac{2}{3} \div 1\frac{1}{3}$

5. Explain how to divide two fractions that have the same denominator.

Below is a model for $1\frac{1}{2} \div \frac{3}{4}$. You can think of this division problem as asking the question "How many times do you need to fill a $\frac{3}{4}$ cup container to get $1\frac{1}{2}$ cups?"

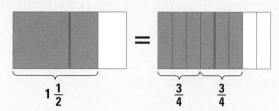

$$1\frac{1}{2} \qquad \frac{3}{4} \qquad \frac{3}{4}$$

6. Use the above model to help you solve the problem $1\frac{1}{2} \div \frac{2}{4}$.

7. Copy and complete the following.

	Mixed Numbers	Improper Fractions	Rewritten with Common Denominators	Solution
a.	$3\frac{1}{3} \div \frac{5}{6}$	? ÷ ?	? ÷ ?	?
b.	$2\frac{2}{5} \div 1\frac{1}{2}$	? ÷ ?	? ÷ ?	?

NOW TRY THESE

8. Solve each division problem.

   a. $\frac{3}{4} \div \frac{1}{8}$ b. $\frac{7}{8} \div \frac{1}{4}$ c. $2\frac{2}{3} \div \frac{1}{6}$ d. $4\frac{1}{2} \div \frac{3}{4}$

9. Explain how to divide two fractions that have different denominators.

In Exercises 10–13, match the division problem with the equivalent multiplication problem.

   A. $\frac{1}{3} \times \frac{3}{4}$ B. $\frac{3}{5} \times \frac{2}{3}$ C. $\frac{9}{8} \times \frac{1}{4}$ D. $\frac{7}{3} \times \frac{5}{6}$

   10. $\frac{9}{8} \div 4$ 11. $\frac{3}{5} \div \frac{3}{2}$ 12. $\frac{7}{3} \div \frac{6}{5}$ 13. $\frac{1}{3} \div \frac{4}{3}$

14. Use the results of Exercises 11–13 to describe a shortcut for dividing fractions that have different denominators.

3.7 Dividing Fractions and Mixed Numbers

What you should learn:

Goal 1 How to divide fractions

Goal 2 How to divide mixed numbers

Why you should learn it:

Knowing how to divide fractions and mixed numbers can help you make equal divisions. An example is dividing a page into columns of equal widths.

Goal 1 DIVIDING FRACTIONS

In Lab 3.7, you may have found that you can divide by a fraction by multiplying by its *reciprocal*. Two fractions are **reciprocals** if their product is 1. So, $\frac{2}{3}$ and $\frac{3}{2}$ are reciprocals because $\frac{2}{3} \times \frac{3}{2} = 1$.

Example 1 Finding Reciprocals

Write the reciprocal of the number.

a. $\frac{5}{12}$ **b.** 6

Solution

Write the number as a fraction. Then invert the fraction.

	Original number	Write as fraction	Invert to get reciprocal	Check by multiplying
a.	$\frac{5}{12}$	$\frac{5}{12}$	$\frac{12}{5}$	$\frac{5}{12} \times \frac{12}{5} = \frac{60}{60} = 1$
b.	6	$\frac{6}{1}$	$\frac{1}{6}$	$6 \times \frac{1}{6} = \frac{6}{6} = 1$

USING RECIPROCALS TO DIVIDE FRACTIONS

To divide one fraction by another fraction, multiply the first fraction by the reciprocal of the second fraction.

Example 2 Dividing Fractions

a. $\frac{7}{4} \div \frac{1}{3} = \frac{7}{4} \times \frac{3}{1}$ Multiply by the reciprocal.

$= \frac{21}{4}$ Multiply fractions.

$= 5\frac{1}{4}$ Simplify.

b. $\frac{3}{5} \div 3 = \frac{3}{5} \times \frac{1}{3}$ Multiply by the reciprocal.

$= \frac{3}{15}$ Multiply fractions.

$= \frac{1}{5}$ Simplify.

Goal 2 DIVIDING MIXED NUMBERS

To solve a division problem that involves mixed numbers, first rewrite the mixed numbers as improper fractions.

> ### DIVIDING MIXED NUMBERS
>
> To divide two mixed numbers, first rewrite them as improper fractions. Then multiply the first fraction by the reciprocal of the second fraction.

Example 3 — Dividing Mixed Numbers

$$3\frac{1}{5} \div 1\frac{1}{3} = \frac{16}{5} \div \frac{4}{3}$$ Rewrite as improper fractions.

$$= \frac{16}{5} \times \frac{3}{4}$$ Multiply by the reciprocal.

$$= \frac{48}{20}$$ Multiply fractions.

$$= \frac{12}{5}$$ Simplify fraction.

$$= 2\frac{2}{5}$$ Rewrite as a mixed number.

Example 4 — Using Division in Real Life

REAL LIFE
Newspapers

You work on a school newspaper. You need to know how many $1\frac{3}{4}$ in. columns of text you can fit into a region that is 7 in. wide.

Solution

Divide the width of the region by the width of each column.

$$7 \div 1\frac{3}{4} = \frac{7}{1} \div \frac{7}{4}$$ Rewrite as improper fractions.

$$= \frac{7}{1} \times \frac{4}{7}$$ Multiply by the reciprocal.

$$= \frac{28}{7}$$ Multiply fractions.

$$= 4$$ Simplify.

You can fit four columns in the space.

1. **WRITING** Choose three problem solving strategies from Chapter 1. Write a sentence describing how to use each strategy.

Decide whether the figures are *congruent,* *similar,* **or** *neither.* **(1.3)**

2.

3.

4.

GUESS, CHECK, AND REVISE In Exercises 5 and 6, you are given the perimeter and area of a rectangle. Find its dimensions. **(1.5)**

5. Perimeter: 36 m; Area: 80 m^2

6. Perimeter: 50 in.; Area: 144 in.^{2}

In Exercises 7–9, write an equation. Then solve the equation to answer the question. (1.6)

7. What number can be subtracted from 102 to get 54?

8. What number can be multiplied by 15 to get 75?

9. What number can you divide by 8 to get 9?

10. **USING LOGICAL REASONING** In a survey of 36 people taken at a mall, 22 said they were going to a clothing store, 17 said they were going to a restaurant, and 2 said they were going to neither. How many people were going to both a clothing store and a restaurant? Illustrate your answer using a Venn diagram. **(1.7)**

In Exercises 11–16, evaluate the expression. (2.1, 2.2)

11. $15 - 6 \div 3 + 4$

12. $3 \times 9 + 12 \div 6$

13. $(25 - 3) \div (5 + 6)$

14. 4 squared

15. 1^7

16. 6^3

USING LOGICAL REASONING In Exercises 17–22, decide whether the statement is *true* or *false*. If it is false, make it true. **(2.3, 2.4, 2.5)**

17. A number that is divisible by 3 is also divisible by 6.

18. A number that is divisible by 3 is also divisible by 9.

19. The prime factorization of 72 is $2^3 \cdot 3^2$.

20. The only whole number that is even and prime is 2.

21. The greatest common factor of 25 and 125 is 5.

22. The greatest common factor of two prime numbers is 1.

In Exercises 23–28, write the fraction in simplest form. (2.6)

23. $\dfrac{14}{140}$ **24.** $\dfrac{36}{72}$ **25.** $\dfrac{35}{49}$ **26.** $\dfrac{44}{48}$ **27.** $\dfrac{25}{150}$ **28.** $\dfrac{300}{450}$

In Exercises 29–34, use division to write the fraction as a decimal. Round your answer to the nearest hundredth. (2.7)

29. $\dfrac{3}{8}$ **30.** $\dfrac{5}{12}$ **31.** $\dfrac{1}{6}$ **32.** $\dfrac{2}{9}$ **33.** $\dfrac{3}{15}$ **34.** $\dfrac{7}{20}$

In Exercises 35–37, plot the numbers on a number line. Then order the numbers from least to greatest. (2.8)

35. $\dfrac{1}{4}, \dfrac{3}{11}, \dfrac{2}{5}, \dfrac{2}{9}$ **36.** 4.04, 5.40, 4.45, 5.05   **37.** $\dfrac{7}{5}$, 1.04, $\dfrac{4}{9}$, 0.49

In Exercises 38–43, find the least common multiple of the numbers. (3.1)

38. 12, 20   **39.** 7, 11   **40.** 24, 34

41. 5, 6, 8   **42.** 3, 4, 15   **43.** 5, 16, 20

44. Use the Distributive Property to rewrite the expression $16(t + 6)$. (3.6)

INTERPRETING A SURVEY In Exercises 45 and 46, use the circle graph at the right. It shows the results of a survey that asked people how long they talked on the phone after 5 P.M. (Source: NFO Research, Inc.) **(3.3)**

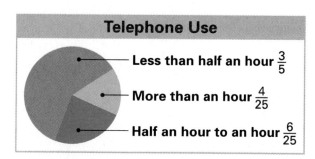

Telephone Use

Less than half an hour $\dfrac{3}{5}$

More than an hour $\dfrac{4}{25}$

Half an hour to an hour $\dfrac{6}{25}$

45. Find the difference between the fraction of people who talked less than half an hour and the fraction who talked more than an hour.

46. Did more people talk less than half an hour, or half an hour or more? Explain.

COMPUTER USE The table shows the number of times per week that people use their home computers. (Source: Consumer Electronics Manufacturers Association) **(3.3)**

47. What fraction of people use their computers two days per week or more?

48. What fraction of people use their computers less than four days per week?

Use each week	Fraction of users
1 day or less	$\dfrac{7}{20}$
2-3 days	$\dfrac{1}{3}$
4-5 days	$\dfrac{17}{100}$
6-7 days	$\dfrac{11}{75}$

Algebra and Integers

BASKETBALL In 1891, a physical education instructor named Dr. James Naismith invented basketball to combine indoor recreation with competitive fun.

TECHNOLOGY

Technology resources accompanying this chapter:
• Interactive Real-Life Investigations
• Middle School Tutorial Software

CHAPTER THEME
Sports

SOCCER Soccer is the world's most popular sport. Known as "football" in over 80 countries, it is the direct ancestor of American football.

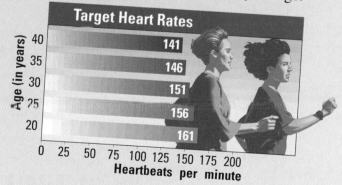

SOFTBALL Softball was first developed as an indoor version of baseball using a larger and softer ball.

Target Heart Rates

REAL LIFE
Sports

Participants in **athletics** keep their heart and circulation system fit by exercising strenuously enough to maintain their target heart rate. When you first start exercising, you should maintain a lower heart rate, and gradually increase it until you have reached the target heart rate for your age.

Target Heart Rates

Age (in years)

40	141
35	146
30	151
25	156
20	161

0   25   50   75   100 125 150 175 200
Heartbeats per minute

Think and Discuss

1. What pattern can you notice in the target heart rates? Explain why you think this pattern exists.

2. The formula to find target heart rates is *Target heart rate = 181 − Age of the athlete*. Use this formula to estimate the target heart rate for a 45 year old. Estimate your own target heart rate.

PORTFOLIO

CHAPTER **PROJECT**

Making a Poster for Sports Night

PROJECT DESCRIPTION

To celebrate National Physical Fitness and Sports month, your school is planning a Sports Night for students and their families. As part of a display, you are making a poster that depicts various aspects of your school's sports teams. To create your poster, you will use the list of **TOPICS** on the next page.

GETTING STARTED

Talking It Over

- Discuss in your group what other sorts of activities and displays your school might have at Sports Night. What sorts of demonstrations might the various teams give?

- What types of sports do you like to play? What sports do you like to watch? What do you enjoy most about sports? Do you prefer sports where you compete as a team or as an individual? Explain why.

Planning Your Project

- **Materials Needed:** posterboard, colored pencils or markers, pencils or pens, tape

- Look through magazines and newspapers to find pictures to depict the kinds of teams in each of the **TOPICS**. Decide if you will make one large poster or six smaller ones. As you answer the **BUILDING YOUR PROJECT** questions, include your results on your poster.

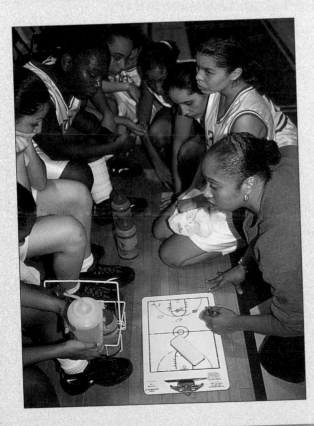

I N T E R N E T

To find out more about sports, go to:

http://www.mlmath.com

LAB 4.1

COOPERATIVE LEARNING

Investigating Patterns and Expressions

Part A LOOKING FOR A PATTERN

Materials Needed
- grid paper
- plain paper
- pencils or pens
- colored pencils or markers

The first four figures in a sequence are shown below.

1. a. Copy the four figures shown below on grid paper. Discuss the pattern with others in your group. Then draw the next four figures on grid paper.

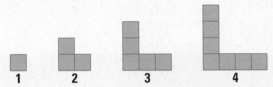

b. Copy the table shown below. Then use the eight figures that you have drawn to complete the table.

Figure Number (n)	Number of Squares	Expression for Number of Squares
1	1	$2 \times 1 - 1$
2	3	$2 \times 2 - 1$
3	5	$2 \times 3 - 1$
4	7	$2 \times 4 - 1$
5	?	?
6	?	?
7	?	?
8	?	?

c. Write an expression for the number of squares in the nth figure in the sequence. Evaluate your expression when $n = 11$. Explain how you could check your result.

2. The numbers in the sequence

4, 6, 8, 10, 12, ...

can be represented by the expression $2n + 2$. Use grid paper to draw a sequence of figures that have the same pattern. Make a table like the one you completed above. Then use the sequence of numbers, the expression, and the figures that you have drawn to complete the table.

The first four figures in a sequence are shown below.

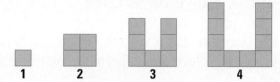

1   2   3   4

3. **a.** Copy the four figures on grid paper. Discuss the pattern with others in your group. Then draw the next six figures on grid paper.

   b. Count the number of squares in each figure. Then use a table to organize your results.

   c. Write an expression for the number of squares in the *n*th figure in the pattern. Evaluate the expression when *n* is 1, 2, 3, 4, 5, 6, 7, 8, 9, and 10. Do the values agree with those given in your table?

NOW TRY THESE

4. **a.** Copy the three figures on grid paper. Then draw the next six figures in the sequence.

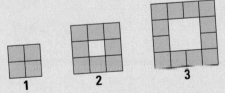

1   2   3

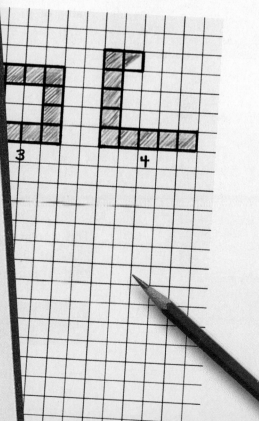

   b. Count the number of squares in each figure. Then use a table to organize your results.

   c. Write an expression for the number of squares in the *n*th figure in the sequence.

5. The numbers in the sequence

   1, 4, 9, 16, 25, 36, . . .

   can be represented by the expression n^2. Use grid paper to draw a sequence of figures that has the same pattern.

Patterns, Tables, and Expressions

What you should learn:

Goal 1 How to use an expression to make a table of values

Goal 2 How to write an expression that represents the values in a table

Why you should learn it:

Knowing how to make tables, recognize patterns, and write expressions can save you money. An example is choosing the least expensive place to swim.

Goal 1 MAKING A TABLE OF VALUES

A **table of values** is a table that is used to organize several values of an expression. A table of values can help you recognize patterns.

Example 1 Making a Table of Values

A health club charges a monthly fee of $10. The club also charges $2 each time you use the swimming pool. The total cost for swimming n times in a month is

$$10 + 2n = \text{Total Cost.}$$

Write a table of values that shows the total cost if you swim 0, 1, 2, 3, 4, 5, 6, 7, and 8 times in a month.

Solution

Begin by evaluating the expression for different values of n.

Value of n	Substitute in $10 + 2n$	Value of Expression
0	$10 + 2(0) = 10 + 0$	$10
1	$10 + 2(1) = 10 + 2$	$12
2	$10 + 2(2) = 10 + 4$	$14
3	$10 + 2(3) = 10 + 6$	$16
4	$10 + 2(4) = 10 + 8$	$18
5	$10 + 2(5) = 10 + 10$	$20
6	$10 + 2(6) = 10 + 12$	$22
7	$10 + 2(7) = 10 + 14$	$24
8	$10 + 2(8) = 10 + 16$	$26

The value of n describes the number of times that you swam. The value of the expression shows your total cost for swimming at the club. You can use a table of values to organize your results.

Times Swam	0	1	2	3	4	5	6	7	8
Total Cost ($)	10	12	14	16	18	20	22	24	26

From the table, you can see the following pattern. *The value of the expression begins at 10. Then each time n increases by 1, the value of the expression increases by 2.*

Example 2 **Writing an Expression**

REAL LIFE
Health Club

A community center charges a monthly fee of **$5**, plus **$3** each time you use the swimming pool. Write an expression for the total cost of swimming *n* times a month.

Solution

STRATEGY **MAKE A LIST** Begin by making a list that shows the total cost for swimming *n* times in a month.

Times Swam	Computation	Total Cost
0	$5 + 3(0) = 5 + 0$	$5
1	$5 + 3(1) = 5 + 3$	$8
2	$5 + 3(2) = 5 + 6$	$11
3	$5 + 3(3) = 5 + 9$	$14
4	$5 + 3(4) = 5 + 12$	$17
5	$5 + 3(5) = 5 + 15$	$20
6	$5 + 3(6) = 5 + 18$	$23
7	$5 + 3(7) = 5 + 21$	$26
8	$5 + 3(8) = 5 + 24$	$29

From this list, you can see that the total cost to swim *n* times in a month is given by the expression $5 + 3n =$ Total Cost.

Example 3 **Comparing Two Expressions**

Compare the swimming plans from Examples 1 and 2.

Solution

One way to compare the two plans is to make a table.

Times Swam	0	1	2	3	4	5	6	7	8
Example 1 ($)	10	12	14	16	18	20	22	24	26
Example 2 ($)	5	8	11	14	17	20	23	26	29

You can see that if you swim 5 times, both clubs cost the same. If you swim less than 5 times, the health club in Example 2 is less expensive. If you swim more than 5 times, it is more expensive.

ONGOING ASSESSMENT

Talk About It
·····················

A youth club charges no monthly fee. Instead, it charges $4 each time you swim.

1. Make a list to describe this plan.

2. Write an expression for this plan.

3. Make a table to compare all three swimming plans.

4. Discuss when each swimming plan is least expensive.

Extra Practice, page 630

GUIDED PRACTICE

In Exercises 1 and 2, complete the table of values.

1.

n	0	1	2	3	4
$5n + 1$	?	?	?	?	?

2.

n	0	1	2	3	4
$20 - 0.3n$	?	?	?	?	?

In Exercises 3–5, match the expression with its table of values.

A.

n	1	2	3	4
	1	6	11	16

B.

n	1	2	3	4
	$\frac{1}{2}$	1	$\frac{3}{2}$	2

C.

n	1	2	3	4
	14	25	36	47

3. $5n - 4$

4. $3 + 11n$

5. $n \div 2$

6. FIELD HOCKEY Your coach schedules field hockey practice every day for 45 minutes. Make a table to show the total number of minutes you practice in n days when n is 1, 2, 3, 4, and 5. Write an expression that gives the total practice time in minutes for n days.

In Exercises 7–12, make a table of values. Use $x = 1, 2, 3, 4, 5,$ and 6.

7. $3x - 1$

8. $x \div 3$

9. $4 + 5x$

10. $33 - 2x$

11. $7 - 4x$

12. $3x \div 4$

PRACTICE AND PROBLEM SOLVING

In Exercises 13–15, write an expression for the pattern. Then use the expression to make a table of values for $m = 1, 2, 3, 4, 5,$ and 6 that fits the expression of the pattern.

13. The value of the expression begins at 5. Each time m increases by 1, the value of the expression increases by 3.

14. The value of the expression begins at 14. Each time m increases by 1, the value of the expression decreases by 2.

15. The value of the expression begins at 0. Each time m increases by 1, the value of the expression increases by 10.

In Exercises 16 and 17, write a description of the pattern in the table.

16.

n	0	1	2	3	4	5
Time (sec)	30	27	24	21	18	15

17.

n	0	1	2	3	4	5
Time (sec)	50	56	62	68	74	80

18. **BUSINESS** The table shows the prices a company charges for a soccer trophy. Each price depends on the number of letters, *n*, to be engraved. Write an expression that gives the price of a trophy engraved with *n* letters.

n	0	1	2	3	4	5	6
Price ($)	3.90	4.00	4.10	4.20	4.30	4.40	4.50

19. The table below shows the prices a second company charges for a soccer trophy. Which company offers the better deal? Explain?

n	0	1	2	3	4	5	6
Price ($)	4.25	4.30	4.35	4.40	4.45	4.50	4.55

STANDARDIZED TEST PRACTICE

20. Which value best completes the pattern in the table?

x	1	2	3	4	5
y	45	43	41	?	37

(**A**) 35   (**B**) 39   (**C**) 41   (**D**) 43

21. Which expression best describes the pattern in the table?

x	1	2	3	4	5
y	7	10	13	16	19

(**A**) $y = 7x$ (**B**) $y = x + 3$ (**C**) $y = 4x - 1$ (**D**) $y = 3x + 4$

EXPLORATION AND EXTENSION

PORTFOLIO

22. **BUILDING YOUR PROJECT** Going into the season, swim team members are expected to swim 4 laps in the pool. After each week of practice they are expected to be able to swim two more laps than the week before. So, for example, after week 1 they swim 6 laps. Make a table to track their progress. Then write an expression describing how many laps they will be swimming after *w* weeks of practice.

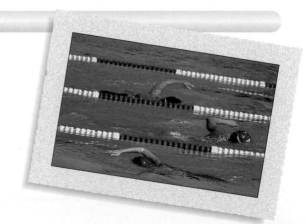

4.2

Scatter Plots and the Coordinate Plane

What you should learn:

Goal 1 How to plot points in a coordinate plane

Goal 2 How to draw a scatter plot

Why you should learn it:

Knowing how to plot points in a coordinate plane can help you find patterns in data. An example is finding the energy saved by recycling glass bottles.

Goal 1 POINTS IN A COORDINATE PLANE

A **coordinate plane** uses **ordered pairs** such as (**3, 5**) to name points. The numbers are the **coordinates** of the point.

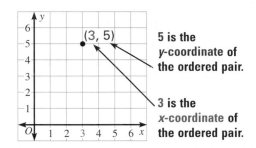

5 is the **y-coordinate** of the ordered pair.

3 is the **x-coordinate** of the ordered pair.

A coordinate plane has two axes, the **x-axis** and the **y-axis**. The first coordinate of a point is the **x-coordinate** and the second coordinate is the **y-coordinate**. The **origin** is located where the two axes cross. The origin has the ordered pair (0, 0).

Example 1 Plotting Points

Plot the points represented by the ordered pairs.

a. (6, 2)   **b.** (0, 5) and (5, 0)

Solution

a.

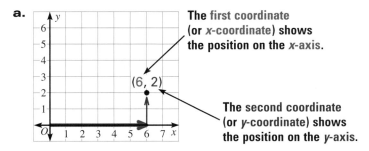

The **first coordinate** (or **x-coordinate**) shows the position on the **x-axis**.

The **second coordinate** (or **y-coordinate**) shows the position on the **y-axis**.

b. If either one of the coordinates is 0, the point will lie on an axis.

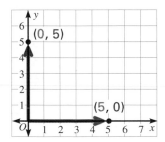

A **scatter plot** is a collection of points in a coordinate plane that represents a relationship between two quantities.

Example 2 **Drawing a Scatter Plot**

Draw a scatter plot that represents the equation $y = 7 - \frac{1}{2}x$. Use x-values of 1, 2, 3, 4, 5, and 6.

Solution

Begin by substituting the x-values into the equation to determine the corresponding y-values.

Value of x	Substitute.	Value of y
1	$y = 7 - \left(\frac{1}{2}\right)(1)$	$6\frac{1}{2}$
2	$y = 7 - \left(\frac{1}{2}\right)(2)$	6
3	$y = 7 - \left(\frac{1}{2}\right)(3)$	$5\frac{1}{2}$
4	$y = 7 - \left(\frac{1}{2}\right)(4)$	5
5	$y = 7 - \left(\frac{1}{2}\right)(5)$	$4\frac{1}{2}$
6	$y = 7 - \left(\frac{1}{2}\right)(6)$	4

Next, you can organize the results of your list in a table of values.

x	1	2	3	4	5	6
y	$6\frac{1}{2}$	6	$5\frac{1}{2}$	5	$4\frac{1}{2}$	4

These results can be written as ordered pairs. For example, the first pair of values are represented by the ordered pair $\left(1, 6\frac{1}{2}\right)$. The ordered pairs can then be used to plot points in a coordinate plane. The points on the coordinate plane allow you to see the general pattern of the equation.

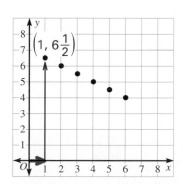

Trend Lines are plotted lines which most accurately describe a group of data points. They are used in the business world to predict such things as future stock prices, sales volumes, or company growth.

ONGOING ASSESSMENT

Write About It
• • • • • • • • • • • • • • • • • • •

Investigate the equation $y = 2x - 1$. Use x-values of 1, 2, 3, 4, 5, 6, and 7.

1. Make a table of values for the equation.

2. Draw a scatter plot for the equation.

GUIDED PRACTICE

In Exercises 1–6, match the letters on the coordinate plane with the terms below.

1. x-coordinate   **2.** x-axis

3. y-coordinate   **4.** y-axis

5. origin   **6.** ordered pair

7. Name the coordinates of the point where the x-axis meets the y-axis.

8. **BOWLING** When you go bowling it costs $1 to rent bowling shoes and $2 to bowl each game. The cost of bowling x games can be expressed as $y = 2x + 1$. Copy and complete the table below. Then draw a scatter plot of the data in the table.

Games Bowled, x	1	2	3	4	5	6
Total Cost, y	?	?	?	?	?	?

PRACTICE AND PROBLEM SOLVING

In Exercises 9–14, write the ordered pair that is represented by the letter.

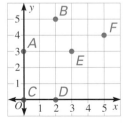

9. A **10.** B **11.** C

12. D **13.** E **14.** F

In Exercises 15 and 16, write the ordered pairs represented by the table. Then draw a scatter plot of the data.

15.

x	1	2	3	4	5	6
y	2	4	6	8	10	12

16.

x	1	2	3	4	5	6
y	8	7	6	5	4	3

In Exercises 17–19, copy and complete the table. Then draw a scatter plot using the data in the table. Describe any patterns that you see in the scatter plot.

17. $y = 4x$ **18.** $y = x + \dfrac{1}{2}$ **19.** $y = 30 - 1.5x$

x	1	2	3	4	5
y	?	?	?	?	?

x	1	2	3	4	5
y	?	?	?	?	?

x	1	2	3	4	5
y	?	?	?	?	?

20. CONSUMER SPENDING For a telephone call, Company A has an initial charge of 25 cents and charges 10 cents for each minute. So, the cost for x minutes is $y = 25 + 10x$. Company B charges 30 cents initially and 8 cents for each minute of the call. The cost for x minutes is $y = 30 + 8x$ for Company B. Copy and complete the tables at the right. Then draw a scatter plot for each table. When is it less expensive to make a phone call using Company A? When is it cheaper to use Company B?

A	Minutes	1	2	3	4	5	6
	Cost	35	?	?	?	?	?

B	Minutes	1	2	3	4	5	6
	Cost	38	?	?	?	?	?

21. RECYCLING Recycling 1 glass bottle saves enough energy to light a 100-watt light bulb for 4.1 hours. This means that the number of hours of energy saved by recycling x glass bottles is given by $y = 4.1x$. Draw a scatter plot that represents this equation. Use x values of 1 through 10. Describe any patterns in the scatter plot.

STANDARDIZED TEST PRACTICE

In Exercises 22 and 23, use the scatter plot at the right.

22. Which point is not plotted in the scatter plot?

A $(2, 3)$ **B** $(3, 2)$ **C** $(6, 2)$ **D** $(5, 5)$

23. For which point is the value of the x-coordinate greater than the value of the y-coordinate?

A A **B** B **C** C **D** D

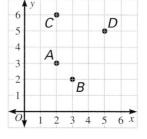

EXPLORATION AND EXTENSION

PORTFOLIO

24. BUILDING YOUR PROJECT The table below gives the runs scored and results for the games played by the baseball team. Draw a scatter plot of the data. Mark each point with a w for a win or an l for a loss. What conclusions about the team's season can you make from the scatter plot?

Game	1	2	3	4	5	6	7	8	9	10
Runs Scored	10	3	8	11	6	7	8	9	1	12
Result	w	l	w	w	l	l	w	w	l	w

1. **LOOKING FOR A PATTERN** Fold a piece of paper in half to form two regions. Repeat the process three more times, each time counting the number of regions. Describe the pattern. **(1.1)**

ALGEBRA AND MENTAL MATH **In Exercises 2–4, solve the equation. Then check your solution. (1.6)**

2. $19 - x = 14$

3. $n \div 7 = 4$

4. $m + 16 = 30$

In Exercises 5–7, use order of operations to evaluate the expression. (2.1)

5. $3 \cdot 6 - 4$

6. $6 \div 2 + 4 \cdot 2$

7. $7 - 4 + 6 \div 6$

In Exercises 8–11, compare using >, <, or =. (2.8)

8. 0.45 ? $\dfrac{4}{9}$

9. $\dfrac{3}{5}$? $\dfrac{4}{9}$

10. $\dfrac{11}{8}$? $\dfrac{4}{9}$

11. $\dfrac{9}{5}$? $\dfrac{4}{9}$

GEOMETRY **In Exercises 12–14, find the perimeter and area. (3.3–3.5)**

12.

$\dfrac{3}{4}$ mi
$\dfrac{3}{4}$ mi

13.
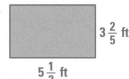
$3\dfrac{2}{5}$ ft
$5\dfrac{1}{2}$ ft

14.
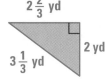
$2\dfrac{2}{3}$ yd
2 yd
$3\dfrac{1}{3}$ yd

CAREER Interview

TEACHER, COACH

Fred Leon teaches Spanish in Worcester, Massachusetts. He also coaches the Girl's Junior Varsity Basketball and Boy's Varsity Baseball teams.

Q What led you to this career?
Spanish is my native language and I wanted to teach, so teaching Spanish was a great choice. In high school, I played sports; we had a winning tradition. The great teachers and coaches I had also influenced me.

Q What kind of math do you use as a coach?
We use statistics and basic math to find averages and describe performances of all kinds. In basketball, the clock is the key. Numbers are involved in all aspects of sports.

Q What would you like to tell kids in school?
I took algebra and geometry in high school, and statistics in college. Be sure to take math and work at it. Don't avoid mathematics, and don't let anyone hold you back from studying math.

Area of a **Frame**

Example

Find the area of each square "picture frame." Can you see a pattern between the area of the frames and the widths?

a.   b.   c.

←3 in.→   ←2.5 in.→   ←2.7 in.→
←4 in.→   ←3.5 in.→   ← 3.7 in.→

Solution

In each case, you can find the area of the frame by subtracting the area of the square "hole" from the area of the larger square.

a. The area of the frame is $4^2 - 3^2$.

   Keystrokes   **Display**

   (4 x 4) − (3 x 3) =   7.

b. The area of the frame is $3.5^2 - 2.5^2$.

   Keystrokes   **Display**

   (3.5 x 3.5) − (2.5 x 2.5) =   6.

c. The area of the frame is $3.7^2 - 2.7^2$.

   Keystrokes   **Display**

   (3.7 x 3.7) − (2.7 x 2.7) =   6.4

In each case, the area is the sum of the two widths.
That is, $4 + 3 = 7$, $3.5 + 2.5 = 6$, and $3.7 + 2.7 = 6.4$.

CALCULATOR TIP

If your calculator has a squaring key or an exponent key, you can use it to evaluate the expressions in the example.

Squaring Key

4 x^2 − 3 x^2 =

Exponent Key

4 y^x 2 − 3 y^x 2 =

Exercises

In Exercises 1–4, you are given the inside and outside dimensions of a square picture frame. Find the area of the frame. Does the result follow the same pattern described in the example? Explain.

1. Outside: 5.1; Inside: 4.1
2. Outside: 7.2; Inside: 6.2
3. Outside: 12.6; Inside: 11.6
4. Outside: 18.4; Inside: 17.4

5. Does the pattern shown in the example depend on the outer width being exactly 1 more than the inner width? Explain.

4.3

What you should learn:

Goal 1 How to graph and order integers

Goal 2 How to use integers to solve real-life problems

Why you should learn it:

Knowing how to use integers can help you solve problems that involve increases and decreases. An example is comparing business profits.

Goal 1 GRAPHING AND ORDERING INTEGERS

The numbers ..., $-4, -3, -2, -1, 0, 1, 2, 3, 4, ...$ are **integers**. Integers are divided into three categories: **negative integers**, zero, and **positive integers**. On a number line, negative integers are to the left of zero and positive integers are to the right of zero.

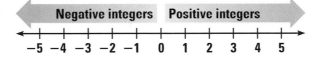

A number line can be used to order integers.

The symbol "$-$" used to represent negative numbers is a **negative sign**. You read "-4" as "negative 4."

LESSON INVESTIGATION

Ordering Integers

GROUP ACTIVITY Name the two integers shown on each number line. Which integer is greater? Write your answer in the form $n < m$. How can you tell which integer is greater? Discuss your reasoning with your group. Then write your answer in words.

1. [number line: -4 -3 -2 -1 0 1]

2. [number line: -3 -2 -1 0 1 2]

3. [number line: -7 -6 -5 -4 -3 -2]

4. [number line: -12 -11 -10 -9 -8 -7]

In the investigation above, you may have discovered that smaller numbers are to the left and greater numbers are to the right.

Example 1 Ordering Integers

Use a number line to complete the statement -4 ? -1 with $<$ or $>$.

Solution

Begin by graphing -4 and -1 on a number line.

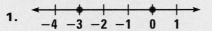

From the number line, -4 is to the left of -1, so $-4 < -1$.

Goal 2 SOLVING REAL-LIFE PROBLEMS

Example 2 **Ordering Numbers**

REAL LIFE
Business

You are starting a part-time lawn mowing business. Your profits for six months are shown below. Use a number line to order these profits. Which profit is least? What is another word for a negative profit?

Month	Apr.	May	June	July	Aug.	Sept.
Profit ($)	−50	−120	70	50	100	−10

Solution

Draw a number line and locate the six integers on the line.

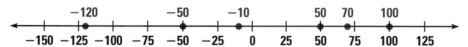

From the number line, you can order the profits as follows.

$$-120, -50, -10, 50, 70, 100$$

We can now see that −$120 is least because it is furthest to the left in our list. In business, another word for *negative profit* is *loss*. For example, a profit of **−$120** is the same as a **loss of $120**.

Example 3 **Plotting Nonintegers**

Plot the numbers 1.3, $-2\frac{1}{2}$, −2.6, and $\frac{3}{8}$ on a number line. Use the result to order the numbers from least to greatest.

Solution

Begin by writing the mixed numbers and fractions as decimals: $-2\frac{1}{2} = -2.5$ and $\frac{3}{8} = 0.375$. Then draw a number line and use estimation to plot the points.

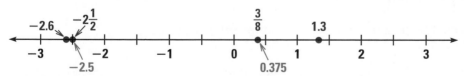

You can order the numbers as follows: $-2.6, -2\frac{1}{2}, \frac{3}{8}, 1.3$.

ONGOING ASSESSMENT

Write About It
....

Draw a number line with tick marks from −5 to 5. Graph each number below on the number line. Explain how you decided to plot each number.

1. 3.5   **2.** −2.5

3. $-3\frac{1}{2}$ **4.** $-\frac{9}{2}$

GUIDED PRACTICE

1. Which of the following numbers are *not* integers? Plot the numbers on a number line.

   $-9, \, 3.5, \, -6\frac{1}{2}, \, 0, \, -2.75$

2. **USING LOGICAL REASONING** Use the following clues to decide which integers are represented by the letters a, b, c, d, and e.

   - c lies halfway between b and d.
   - e lies 6 units to the right of d.
   - d is the least possible positive integer.
   - b lies halfway between a and c.
   - c is the greatest possible negative integer.

3. What integer is neither positive nor negative?

WRITING In Exercises 4 and 5, write a statement that compares the two integers shown on the number line.

4.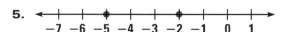

5.

PRACTICE AND PROBLEM SOLVING

LOOKING FOR A PATTERN In Exercises 6–9, graph the numbers on a number line. Describe the pattern and find the missing integers.

6. $-9, -5, -1, 3, 7, \boxed{?}, \boxed{?}$

7. $6, 4, 2, 0, -2, \boxed{?}, \boxed{?}$

8. $-5, 5, -4, 4, -3, \boxed{?}, \boxed{?}$

9. $-8, -7, -5, -2, 2, \boxed{?}, \boxed{?}$

In Exercises 10–13, complete the statement using < or >.

10. $-6 \; \boxed{?} \; 0$

11. $7 \; \boxed{?} \; -7$

12. $-4 \; \boxed{?} \; -5$

13. $-2 \; \boxed{?} \; 3$

In Exercises 14–16, is the statement *true* or *false*? Support your answer with a number-line drawing.

14. Four and negative four are the same distance from one.

15. Negative one is less than negative two.

16. Eight is greater than negative nine.

NUMBER SENSE In Exercises 17–20, write the integer represented by the real-life situation.

17. 12 degrees below zero

18. 5 bonus points

19. Withdraw $45 from an account.

20. 9 feet underground

In Exercises 21–24, order the numbers from least to greatest.

21. $-3, -8, 3, -9, 0$

22. $5.5, -\frac{9}{4}, 2, -\frac{1}{2}, -2.5$

23. $-4.25, -7, -\frac{7}{2}, -1\frac{3}{4}, -5$

24. $-6.8, \frac{3}{8}, -2\frac{1}{5}, -2.3$

MARINE SCIENCE In Exercises 25 and 26, use the information provided at the right. The graph shows the depth at which each fish has been found. (Source: Big Book of Animal Records)

Viperfish:	6000 ft
Lantern fish:	3300 ft
Sole:	36,000 ft
Hatchet fish:	1800 ft
Rat-tail fish:	15,500 ft

25. Which fish has been found at the greatest depth?

26. Order the depths from least to greatest.

STANDARDIZED TEST PRACTICE

27. The following integers should be ordered from least to greatest. Which integers need to be interchanged so that this is true?

$$-12, -6, -1, -3, 0, 5, 8$$

(A) -6 and -1 **(B)** -1 and -3 **(C)** -3 and 0 **(D)** 0 and 5

28. Which integer lies halfway between -8 and 6?

(A) -1 **(B)** 0 **(C)** 1 **(D)** 7

29. If the following integers were ordered least to greatest, which integer would come first in the list?

$$20, 13, -3, 10, -11, 5, -6$$

(A) -6 **(B)** 5 **(C)** 10 **(D)** -11

EXPLORATION AND EXTENSION

PORTFOLIO

30. BUILDING YOUR PROJECT The marching band operated a souvenir stand at the first football game. On some items they made money. For other items, they lost money. The profit or loss for each item sold is shown in the graph. Write each profit and loss as a positive or negative number. Order the numbers from least to greatest. Did the band have an overall profit or loss for the first game?

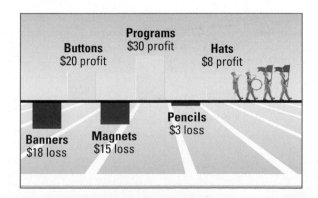

Buttons $20 profit
Programs $30 profit
Hats $8 profit
Banners $18 loss
Magnets $15 loss
Pencils $3 loss

Investigating Integer Addition

Materials Needed
- paper
- number counters
- pencils or pens

Part A ADDING TWO INTEGERS

You can use number counters to model adding integers.

Sum: 3 + 4

3 ⊕ ⊕ ⊕
4 ⊕ ⊕ ⊕ ⊕

3 + 4 = 7
Number sentence

Choose 3 tan counters to show positive 3 and 4 tan counters to show positive 4.

Place and count the total number of tan counters.

Sum: −3 + (−4)

−3 ⊖ ⊖ ⊖
−4 ⊖ ⊖ ⊖ ⊖

−3 + (−4) = −7

Choose 3 red counters to show negative 3 and 4 red counters to show negative 4.

Place and count the total number of red counters.

1. Use number counters to add.

  a. 6 + 4   **b.** 5 + 3   **c.** −2 + (−4) **d.** −3 + (−3)

2. Use the two examples above and Exercise 1 to tell how to add two positive integers and how to add two negative integers.

Part B ZERO PAIRS

When you pair one tan and one red counter, the result is zero. This pair of counters is a *zero pair*.

4 ⊕ ⊕ ⊕ ⊕
−4 ⊖ ⊖ ⊖ ⊖

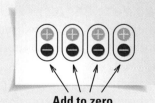

4 + (−4) = 0

Add to zero.

3. Use number counters to add.

  a. −2 + 2   **b.** 5 + (−5)   **c.** −6 + 6   **d.** 1 + (−1)

When you use number counters to add a positive integer and a negative integer, remember that each pair that has one red counter and one tan counter adds to zero.

Sum: $-4 + 2$

-4 ⊖⊖⊖⊖

2 ⊕⊕

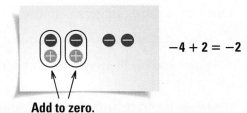

$-4 + 2 = -2$

Add to zero.

Choose 4 red counters to show negative 4 and 2 tan counters to show positive 2.

Place the counters and group pairs of tan and red counters. The remaining counters show the sum.

4. Use number counters to add.

   a. $-3 + 4$ **b.** $5 + (-2)$ **c.** $4 + (-6)$ **d.** $-6 + 3$

5. Give an example of each addition problem.

   a. Positive integer + Negative integer = Negative integer

   b. Positive integer + Negative integer = Positive integer

   c. Positive integer + Negative integer = Zero

NOW TRY THESE

In Exercises 6–11, use number counters to model the addition problem. Then write a number sentence for the problem.

6. $4 + (-3)$ 7. $1 + 6$ 8. $-6 + (-4)$

9. $-4 + (-5)$ 10. $-5 + 2$ 11. $2 + (-2)$

In Exercises 12–14, complete the statement. Then use number counters to check your answer.

12. $8 + \boxed{?}$ is a negative number.

13. $8 + \boxed{?}$ is a positive number.

14. $8 + \boxed{?}$ is zero.

15. In Exercises 12–14, is there more than one way to complete each statement correctly? Explain.

4.4

Adding Integers

What you should learn:

Goal 1 How to use a number line to add integers

Goal 2 How to use integer addition to solve real-life problems

Why you should learn it:

Knowing how to add integers can help you solve problems that involve increases and decreases. An example is accuracy of a tire-making machine.

Goal 1 ADDING INTEGERS

One way to add integers is to use a number line.

• When you add a **positive** number, move to the *right*.

• When you add a **negative** number, move to the *left*.

Example 1 Adding Two Integers

Use a number line to solve the addition problems.

a. $-2 + (-3)$ **b.** $-6 + 8$ **c.** $-3 + 3$

Solution

a. Begin at -2.
Move **3** units to the *left*.

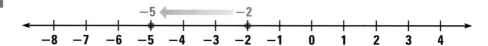

Your final position is -5. So, $-2 + (-3) = -5$.

b. Begin at -6.
Move **8** units to the *right*.

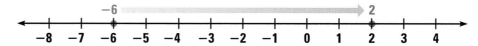

Your final position is **2**. So, $-6 + 8 = 2$.

c. The numbers -3 and 3 are **opposites** because they are the same distance from 0 on the number line. The sum of any two opposites is 0, as shown below.

Begin at -3.
Move **3** units to the *right*.

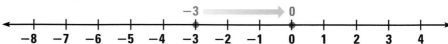

Your final position is **0**. So, $-3 + 3 = 0$.

STUDY TIP

You can check the results of Example 1 with a calculator. If your calculator has a change-sign key, $\boxed{+/-}$, then you can check part (b) using the following keystrokes.

$6 \boxed{+/-} \boxed{+} 8 \boxed{=}$

Example 2 Using an Average

Your company manufactures tires. To check the accuracy of one of the molding machines, you measure the width of five tires that it produced.

REAL LIFE
Manufacturing

Measure (in millimeters)	Number
Tire 1: 2 mm too wide.	2
Tire 2: 1 mm too narrow.	−1
Tire 3: correct width.	0
Tire 4: 2 mm too narrow.	−2
Tire 5: 3 mm too wide.	3

From this sample, would you say the machine is tending to make the tires too wide or too narrow?

Solution

One way to answer the question is to find the average of the numbers. To find the average, add the five integers and divide the result by 5.

$$2 \boxed{+} 1 \boxed{+/-} \boxed{+} 0 \boxed{+} 2 \boxed{+/-} \boxed{+} 3 \boxed{=} \quad \boxed{2.}$$

The sum is 2, which means that the average is $2 \div 5$ or 0.4. Because the average is positive, the machine is tending to make the tires a little too wide.

ONGOING ASSESSMENT

Talk About It
....

Use a number line to add the integers. You should use one order and your partner should use the other order. What can you conclude? What is the name of the property that is being illustrated?

1. $-3 + 4$ and $4 + (-3)$

2. $-5 + (-2)$ and $-2 + (-5)$

GUIDED PRACTICE

In Exercises 1–3, match the addition problem with the description of the answer.

1. $-14 + 8$
2. $-14 + (-8)$
3. $14 + (-8)$

A. A positive number less than 14

B. A negative number greater than negative 14

C. A negative number less than negative 14

COMPLETE THE SENTENCE In Exercises 4–6, complete the statement using the words *sometimes, always,* or *never.*

4. The sum of two negative numbers is __?__ positive.

5. The sum of a positive number and a negative number is __?__ negative.

6. The sum of a number and its opposite is __?__ zero.

ERROR ANALYSIS In Exercises 7 and 8, find and correct the error in the calculator keystrokes.

7. Expression: $-5 + 5$

   Keystrokes: 5 [−] [+] 5 [=]

8. Expression: $-4 + (-6)$

   Keystrokes: 4 [+/−] 6 [+/−] [=]

PRACTICE AND PROBLEM SOLVING

In Exercises 9 and 10, write the addition problem that is illustrated by the number line. Then solve the problem.

9.
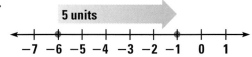

10.
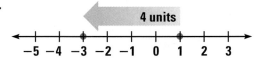

In Exercises 11–18, use a number line to find the sum.

11. $4 + 9$
12. $-8 + 8$
13. $-3 + 10$
14. $13 + (-2)$

15. $-4 + (-11)$
16. $16 + (-16)$
17. $5 + 18$
18. $11 + (-24)$

TECHNOLOGY In Exercises 19–21, match the addition problem with the keystrokes. Then solve the problem.

A. 3 [+] 2 [+/−] [=]

B. 3 [+/−] [+] 2 [+/−] [=]

C. 3 [+/−] [+] 2 [=]

19. $-3 + 2$

20. $-3 + (-2)$

21. $3 + (-2)$

LOOKING FOR A PATTERN In Exercises 22 and 23, integers are being added to form new integers. Use a number line to find the pattern. Then determine what the next two integers in the list should be.

22. $2, 3, 1, 2, 0, 1, -1, 0,$ [?] , [?]

23. $3, -3, 1, -5, -1, -7, -3,$ [?] , [?]

TECHNOLOGY In Exercises 24–27, use a calculator to find the average.

24. $-13, 25, -9$

25. $-42, -32, 89$

26. $-64, 125, -31, -22$

27. $-13, 38, -25$

NUMBER SENSE In Exercises 28–30, decide whether the expression $-5 + x$ is *positive*, *negative*, or *zero*.

28. x is greater than 6

29. x is 5

30. x is less than 4

ALGEBRA In Exercises 31–33, evaluate the expression when $n = -1$.

31. $-3 + n$

32. $5 + n$

33. $n + 1$

DEEP-SEA DIVING In Exercises 34 and 35, you are a marine biologist. The table below shows the deep-sea dives you have taken in the last 2 months.

Location	Gulf of Mexico	Caribbean	Hawaii
Depth	-575 ft	-340 ft	-1000 ft

34. Find the sum of the depths of the Caribbean and Gulf of Mexico dives.

35. After you reached your depth in Hawaii, you swam up 633 ft to investigate an interesting coral formation. At what depth was the coral formation?

36. TEST SCORES The interactive investigation for this chapter asks you to determine how far test scores lie above or below the average. If you were to take the average of 10 test scores, and then add the amount each score differed from the average, what do you think the sum would be? Explain your reasoning.

Tech Link

Investigation 4, Larson Interactive Real-Life Investigations

 **STANDARDIZED TEST PRACTICE**

37. Which problem is illustrated by the number line below?

−6 −5 −4 −3 −2 −1 0 1 2 3 4 5

    A $-5 + 8$ **B** $-5 + (-8)$ **C** $-5 + 2$ **D** $2 - (-5)$

38. Evaluate the expression $-3 + (-7)$.

    A -10 **B** -4 **C** 4   **D** 10

39. BUILDING YOUR PROJECT The golf team gives you one of their scorecards. Instead of recording the number of strokes that a player had, they recorded the number of strokes above or below par that the player had on each hole. Complete the scorecard based on how many strokes each player is above or below the par score of 36. Which player had the lowest score? List the players in order of lowest to highest score.

HOLE	1	2	3	4	5	6	7	8	9	Total
PAR	4	3	5	5	4	3	5	3	4	36
Chris P.	+3	0	−1	−1	−1	+4	+3	+2	−1	?
Pat S.	+2	−1	+4	+3	0	0	−1	+3	−1	?
Fran B.	−1	+2	+2	0	+4	+5	−1	+1	−1	?
Sam F.	+3	−1	−1	+4	+3	+3	+2	0	−1	?

SPIRAL REVIEW

1. **SEPARATING INTO CASES** You are buying apples to make applesauce. At the store, you find apples packaged in 3-pound and 5-pound bags. A 3-pound bag costs $2.58 and a 5-pound bag costs $4.09. How many of each size bag should you buy to get at least 14 pounds at the least cost? **(1.8)**

In Exercises 2–4, evaluate the expression. **(2.1, 2.2)**

2. $9 + 14 \div 7 - 6$

3. $(12 - 3^2) \cdot (9 + 3)$

4. $20 - 2(5 + 11) \div 8$

In Exercises 5–8, find all the digits that will make the number divisible by 3. **(2.3)**

5. $9\boxed{?}7$

6. $812\boxed{?}$

7. $\boxed{?}7396$

8. $150,\boxed{?}99$

NUMBER SENSE In Exercises 9–11, use the Guess, Check, and Revise strategy to find the missing number. **(3.3, 3.5, 3.7)**

9. $\dfrac{3}{4} + \boxed{?} = 1\dfrac{1}{12}$

10. $10 \div \boxed{?} = \dfrac{1}{7}$

11. $\boxed{?} \times 1\dfrac{3}{10} = 6\dfrac{1}{2}$

In Exercises 12–15, use the Distributive Property to rewrite the expression. Then evaluate. **(3.6)**

12. $5(8 + 4)$

13. $\dfrac{1}{4}(8 + 6)$

14. $3 \times \dfrac{2}{9} + 3 \times \dfrac{1}{9}$

15. $2 \cdot 3.2 + 2 \cdot 4.8$

Take this test as you would take a test in class. The answers to the exercises are given in the back of the book.

In Exercises 1–3, make a table of values. Use $x = 1, 2, 3, 4, 5$, and 6. **(4.1)**

1. $3x + 8$

2. $100 - 5x$

3. $120 \div x$

In Exercises 4 and 5, describe the pattern in the table. **(4.1)**

4.

x	0	1	2	3	4	5
Cost ($)	4	9	14	19	24	29

5.

x	0	1	2	3	4	5
Cost ($)	75	68	61	54	47	40

In Exercises 6 and 7, write the ordered pairs shown in the scatter plot. **(4.2)**

6.
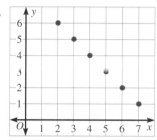

7.
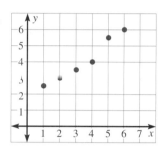

In Exercises 8–10, make a table of values for the equation. Use *x*-values of 1, 2, 3, 4, 5, and 6. Write the ordered pairs represented by the table. Then draw a scatter plot of the data. Describe any patterns in the scatter plot. **(4.2)**

8. $y = x + 0.5$

9. $y = 7\frac{1}{2} - x$

10. $y = -1 + x$

In Exercises 11 and 12, order the numbers from least to greatest. **(4.3)**

11. $-10, -1, 4, -5$

12. $-13, -12, -11, -15$

In Exercises 13 and 14, use a number line to find the sum. **(4.4)**

13. $6 + (-17)$

14. $-7 + 11$

15. TRACK AND FIELD In a 4-mile race, a runner's time for each mile was compared to his best previous time. The results are shown in the table. Write each comparison using an integer. How did his time for the whole race compare with his best previous time? **(4.4)**

	1st mile	2nd mile	3rd mile	4th mile
Previous Time	6 min 45 s	7 min 5 s	7 min 28 s	7 min
Current Time	6 min 49 s	7 min 2 s	7 min 28 s	6 min 58 s
Comparison	4 more	3 less	same time	2 less

LAB
4.5

COOPERATIVE LEARNING

Investigating Integer Subtraction

Part A SUBTRACTING TWO POSITIVE INTEGERS

Materials Needed
- **number counters**
- **pencils or pens**
- **paper**

1. This example shows how number counters can model $6 - 8$.

2 zero pairs

$$6 - 8 = -2$$

Number sentence

Start with 6 tan counters.

Add enough zero pairs to get 8 tan counters.

Subtract positive 8 by removing 8 tan counters.

Use number counters to subtract.

a. $3 - 8$ **b.** $4 - 7$ **c.** $1 - 5$ **d.** $7 - 8$

Part B SUBTRACTING TWO NEGATIVE INTEGERS

2. Here is a number counter model of $-8 - (-3)$.

$$-8 - (-3) = -5$$

Start with 8 red counters.

Subtract negative 3 by removing 3 red counters.

Use number counters to subtract.

a. $-5 - (-2)$ **b.** $-9 - (-5)$ **c.** $-7 - (-1)$

3. Here is a number counter model of $-3 - (-5)$.

2 zero pairs

$$-3 - (-5) = 2$$

Start with 3 red counters.

Add enough zero pairs to get 5 red counters.

Subtract negative 5 by removing 5 red counters.

Use number counters to subtract.

a. $-2 - (-5)$ **b.** $-1 - (-3)$ **c.** $-4 - (-7)$ **d.** $-3 - (-8)$

4. *Subtracting a Negative Integer from a Positive Integer*
Here is an example showing a model of 4 − (−3).

3 zero pairs

4 − (−3) = 7

Start with 4 tan counters.

Add enough zero pairs to get 3 red counters.

Subtract negative 3 by removing 3 red counters.

5. *Subtracting a Positive Integer from a Negative Integer*
Here is an example showing a model of −2 − 3.

3 zero pairs

−2 − 3 = −5

Start with 2 red counters.

Add enough zero pairs to get 3 tan counters.

Subtract positive 3 by removing 3 tan counters.

Use number counters to subtract.

a. 6 − (−5)   **b.** 5 − (−2)   **c.** −2 − 4

NOW TRY THESE

In Exercises 6–11, use counters to subtract.

6. 6 − 4   7. 7 − 9   8. −4 − (−1)

9. −5 − (−5)   10. 5 − (−3)   11. −4 − 3

12. If possible, give an example of each type of subtraction problem. If not possible, explain.

a. Positive number − Negative number = Positive number

b. Positive number − Negative number = Negative number

c. Negative number − Positive number = Positive number

d. Negative number − Positive number = Negative number

Subtracting Integers

What you should learn:

Goal 1 How to use a number line to subtract integers

Goal 2 How to use integer subtraction to solve real-life problems

Why you should learn it:

Knowing how to subtract integers can help you solve problems that involve increases and decreases. An example is finding the change in elevation as you descend into Death Valley.

Scotty's Castle, Death Valley

Goal 1 SUBTRACTING INTEGERS

In Lesson 4.4, you used a number line to add integers. You can also use a number line to subtract integers.

• When you subtract a **positive** number, move to the *left*.

• When you subtract a **negative** number, move to the *right*.

Compare these rules with the rules for adding a number on page 184. Notice that with subtraction, you move the opposite direction than you move with addition.

Example 1 **Subtracting Two Integers**

Use a number line to solve the subtraction problems.

a. $-6 - 4$ **b.** $3 - (-5)$ **c.** $3 - 7$

Solution

a. Begin at -6.

Move **4** units to the *left*.

Your final position is -10. So, $-6 - 4 = -10$.

b. Begin at 3.

Move **5** units to the *right*.

Your final position is 8. So, $3 - (-5) = 8$.

c. Begin at 3.

Move **7** units to the *left*.

Your final position is -4. So, $3 - 7 = -4$.

COOPERATIVE
LEARNING

LESSON INVESTIGATION

Investigating Subtraction with a Calculator

GROUP ACTIVITY Use a calculator to evaluate each expression. Then compare the result to the distance between the two points on a number line. What can you conclude?

Expression	Number Line
1. $2 - (-4)$	
2. $-1 - (-3)$	

Example 2 **Finding Changes in Elevation**

REAL LIFE
Geography

You visit Death Valley National Monument located in California and Nevada. As you begin your descent into the valley, you see a sign which states that your current elevation is 2600 feet *above* sea level. As you proceed towards the valley floor, you see a sign that says that your elevation is now 200 feet *below* sea level. How much did your elevation decrease as you descended into the valley?

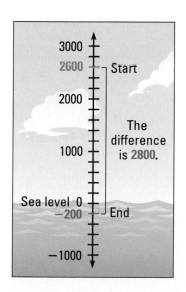

Solution

You can use integer subtraction to solve this problem. If you think of sea level as the point 0 on your number line then the number of feet that your elevation decreased is the difference between 2600 and -200. To find this difference, subtract -200 from 2600.

$$2600 - (-200) = 2800$$

From this you can see that your elevation dropped a total of 2800 ft between the two signs that you saw as you traveled down into the valley.

ONGOING ASSESSMENT

Write About It

At the beginning of the month, your Spanish Club's treasury had a balance of $65. By the end of the month, the balance was $-$25.

1. What do you think the negative balance means?

2. What is the difference between these two balances? Explain your answer in a sentence.

GUIDED PRACTICE

In Exercises 1–4, without solving the problem, decide whether the difference is *positive* or *negative*.

1. $12 - 13$

2. $-8 - 6$

3. $13 - (-14)$

4. $-9 - (-5)$

ENVIRONMENT In Exercises 5 and 6, use the following information. The table shows the percent changes in air pollutants from 1987 to 1996. (Source: American Petroleum Institute)

5. What is the difference between the percent changes in carbon monoxide and sulfur dioxide?

6. What is the difference between the percent changes in airborne lead and carbon monoxide?

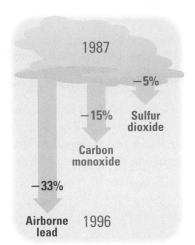

PRACTICE AND PROBLEM SOLVING

ERROR ANALYSIS In Exercises 7 and 8, describe and correct the error in the number-line model. Then solve the problem.

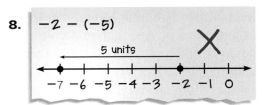

7. $-4 - 3$

8. $-2 - (-5)$

In Exercises 9–11, match the expression with its description.

A. Positive

B. Negative

C. Zero

9. $-6 - 6$

10. $-6 - (-6)$

11. $0 - (-6)$

In Exercises 12–20, use a number line to find the difference.

12. $-6 - 3$

13. $-11 - 8$

14. $6 - (-13)$

15. $14 - (-3)$

16. $-14 - (-16)$

17. $-21 - (-10)$

18. $-20 - (-5)$

19. $-16 - 32$

20. $17 - (-45)$

In Exercises 21–29, use a calculator to solve each of the following expressions.

21. $-45 - 56$

22. $-120 - 63$

23. $36 - (-75)$

24. $148 - (-99)$

25. $-121 - (-156)$

26. $-218 - (-188)$

27. $152 - 186$

28. $-89 - (-89)$

29. $323 - (-59)$

30. NUMBER RIDDLE I am an integer. I am less than zero but greater than −13. When you subtract me from −11, the result is positive. What number am I?

GARDENING In Exercises 31–33, use the list below. It shows the depths to plant various vegetable seeds.
(Source: Taylor's Guide to Vegetables & Herbs)

Beets $\frac{1}{4}$ inch   Carrots $\frac{1}{8}$ inch

Corn   1 inch   Garlic   3 inches

Peas $\frac{1}{2}$ inch

31. How much deeper do you plant garlic than beets?

32. How much deeper do you plant corn than carrots?

33. How much deeper do you plant garlic than peas?

STANDARDIZED TEST PRACTICE

34. Solve $4 - (-17) = $? .

    A −21   **B** −13   **C** 13   **D** 21

35. Which statement is always true?

    A A negative number minus a negative number is negative.

    B A negative number plus a negative number is negative.

    C A positive number plus a negative number is positive.

    D A positive number minus a negative number is negative.

EXPLORATION AND EXTENSION

36. COMMUNICATING ABOUT MATHEMATICS (page 203)
Snorkel divers observe underwater objects while swimming along the surface and then dive down when they want to get a closer look. Most amateur divers can hold their breath long enough to dive about 30 feet. Very skilled divers can often dive down 100 feet. Using 0 to represent surface level, write a subtraction expression to find how much deeper than an amateur diver a skilled diver can go. Then solve the problem.

Investigating Algebra Tiles

Materials Needed
- algebra tiles
- pencils or pens
- paper

Algebra tiles, like those shown below, can be used to solve equations.

 1
 1

The smaller tile is a 1-by-1
square whose area is 1 square unit.
It represents the number 1.

The larger tile is a 1-by-x rectangle
whose area is x square units.
It represents the variable x.

Part A MODELING EXPRESSIONS

Algebra tiles can be used to model expressions. Here are some
examples of this.

       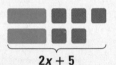

$2x + 3$ $x + 6$ $2x + 5$

1. Write the expression that is modeled by the tiles.

a.    b.    c.

2. Use algebra tiles to model each expression. Sketch each model.

a. $2x + 1$ b. $x + 8$ c. $3x + 4$

Part B SOLVING EQUATIONS

Algebra tiles can also be used to solve equations. The example below
shows how to solve the equation $x + 2 = 8$.

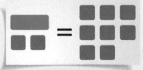   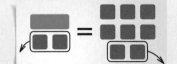   

Model the equation with
algebra tiles.

You need to get the x-tile by itself
on one side. Remove two 1-tiles
from each side.

The solution is $x = 6$.

3. Write the equation that is being modeled. Then remove enough tiles from both sides of the equation so that one x-tile is left on one side. What is the solution?

a.

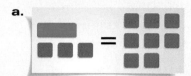

b.

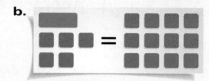

c. With others in your group, discuss how you know how many 1-tiles to remove from each side of the equation.

4. Use algebra tiles to solve each equation. Sketch the steps that you took to solve the equation.

a. $x + 6 = 10$ **b.** $x + 7 = 9$ **c.** $x + 3 = 12$

5. In the following model, three tiles are removed from each side of the equation. What operation does this represent?

   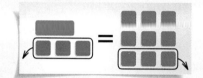

NOW TRY THESE

In Exercises 6–9, use algebra tiles to solve the equation. Sketch the tiles that you used.

6. $x + 6 = 9$

7. $x + 7 = 13$

8. $x + 4 = 10$

9. $x + 2 = 14$

10. To solve the equation $x + 6 = 4$, which of the following operations could you use? Explain your reasoning.

A. Subtract 4 from each side of the equation.

B. Subtract 6 from the left side of the equation.

C. Subtract 4 from the right side of the equation.

D. Subtract 6 from each side of the equation.

4.6

Solving Addition Equations

What you should learn:

Goal 1 How to solve addition equations by subtracting the same number from both sides

Goal 2 How to use addition equations to solve real-life problems

Why you should learn it:

Knowing how to solve addition equations can help you solve problems involving increases and decreases. An example is finding the yards gained or lost on a 4th down.

Goal 1 SOLVING ADDITION EQUATIONS

An *addition equation* is an equation with a sum, such as

$$n + 3 = 2 \text{ or } 8 = 2 + x.$$

SOLVING AN ADDITION EQUATION

To solve an addition equation, you subtract the same number from both sides of the equation so that the variable will be by itself on one side of the equation.

Example 1 Solving an Addition Equation

Solve each equation.

a. $n + 8 = -2$ **b.** $4 = x + 9$

Solution

a. Subtract 8 from both sides of the equation.

$$
\begin{array}{lll}
n + 8 = & -2 & \text{Write original equation.} \\
\underline{-8} & \underline{-8} & \text{Subtract 8 from both sides.} \\
n & = -10 & \text{Solution: } n \text{ is by itself.}
\end{array}
$$

The solution is $n = -10$. Check this as follows.

✔**Check:** Substitute for the variable in the original equation.

$$
\begin{array}{ll}
n + 8 = -2 & \text{Write original equation.} \\
-10 + 8 \stackrel{?}{=} -2 & \text{Substitute } -10 \text{ for } n. \\
-2 = -2 & \text{Both sides are the same. ✔}
\end{array}
$$

b. Subtract 9 from both sides of the equation.

$$
\begin{array}{lll}
4 = x + 9 & & \text{Write original equation.} \\
\underline{-9} & \underline{-9} & \text{Subtract 9 from both sides.} \\
-5 = x & & \text{Solution: } x \text{ is by itself.}
\end{array}
$$

The solution is $x = -5$. Check this as follows.

✔**Check:** Substitute for the variable in the original equation.

$$
\begin{array}{ll}
4 = x + 9 & \text{Write original equation.} \\
4 \stackrel{?}{=} -5 + 9 & \text{Substitute } -5 \text{ for } x. \\
4 = 4 & \text{Both sides are the same. ✔}
\end{array}
$$

STUDY TIP

You can probably solve many of the equations in Lessons 4.6 and 4.7 using mental math. This is good as a check that your answer is reasonable.

Be sure that you also can solve the equations by writing out your steps. This will help you solve harder equations.

Example 2 Writing an Addition Equation

A friend keeps a record of your football team's gains and losses on each play of a game. The record for a sequence of downs is shown below, but part of it is missing. Find the missing information by writing and solving an addition equation.

REAL LIFE
Football

Play	Play Gain or Loss	Overall Gain or Loss
1st Down	Gain of 2 yards	Gain of 2 yards
2nd Down	Loss of 5 yards	Loss of 3 yards
3rd Down	Gain of 7 yards	Gain of 4 yards
4th Down	?	Loss of 7 yards

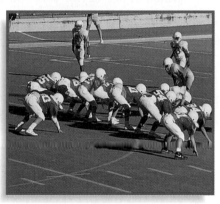

Solution

One way to solve this problem is to use a **verbal model**. Let x represent the unknown amount.

Verbal Model $\quad$ **Yards on 4th down** $+$ **Yards after 3 downs** $=$ **Total yards**

Labels $\quad$ Yards on 4th down $= x$

$\qquad\qquad$ Yards after 3 downs $= 4$

$\qquad\qquad$ Total yards $= -7$

Equation $\quad x + 4 = -7$

To solve this equation, you can subtract 4 from both sides of the equation.

$$x + 4 = -7 \qquad \text{Write original equation.}$$
$$\underline{-4 \quad -4} \qquad \text{Subtract 4 from both sides.}$$
$$x = -11 \qquad \text{Solution: } x \text{ is by itself.}$$

The solution is -11. This means that your team lost 11 yards on its 4th down. Check this using a number line.

ONGOING ASSESSMENT

Write About It

1. Write two different addition equations that have a solution of -2.

2. For each equation, write about a real-life problem that can be represented by the equation.

GUIDED PRACTICE

In Exercises 1 and 2, describe how the equation was solved.

1.
$$-12 + x = \quad 8$$
$$\underline{-12 \qquad -12}$$
$$x = \quad -4$$

2.
$$-6 = y + 7$$
$$\underline{-7 \qquad -7}$$
$$-13 = y$$

In Exercises 3–5, which value is the solution of the equation?

3. $m + 1 = 1$ **A.** $m = -2$ **B.** $m = 0$ **C.** $m = 2$

4. $11 + t = 5$ **A.** $t = -6$ **B.** $t = 16$ **C.** $t = 6$

5. $-3 = p + 10$ **A.** $7 = p$ **B.** $-7 = p$ **C.** $-13 = p$

In Exercises 6 and 7, do the equations have the same solution? Explain your reasoning.

6. $n + 4 = -5,\ 5 = n + 4$

7. $z + 9 = 15,\ 15 = 9 + z$

8. PERSONAL FINANCE After you deposit a check for $65, your new total balance is $315. Write a verbal model, labels, and equation to find the amount that was in your account before you made the deposit.

PRACTICE AND PROBLEM SOLVING

In Exercises 9–17, solve the equation. Then check your solution.

9. $n + 7 = -7$ **10.** $2 = t + 15$ **11.** $-12 = 11 + p$

12. $37 + k = 28$ **13.** $-4 = 46 + b$ **14.** $z + 16 = -23$

15. $c + 1.7 = 2.6$ **16.** $\dfrac{5}{12} = m + \dfrac{1}{12}$ **17.** $\dfrac{3}{10} + x = \dfrac{4}{5}$

TREADMILL SALES In Exercises 18 and 19, use the bar graph at the right and a calculator. The graph shows treadmill sales in America from 1990 to 1995.
(Source: National Sporting Goods Association)

18. Write and solve an addition equation to determine how many more treadmills were sold in 1993 than in 1992.

19. In what year did sales increase the least from the previous year? In what year did they increase the most? Use addition equations to prove your answers.

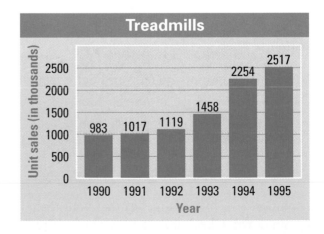

Treadmills

Unit sales (in thousands)

2500 — 2000 — 1500 — 1000 — 500 — 0

983   1017   1119   1458   2254   2517

1990   1991   1992   1993   1994   1995

Year

20. Write 3 different addition equations that have a solution of -6.

In Exercises 21–24, write the equation that represents the statement. Then solve it.

21. The sum of a number and ten is ten.

22. The sum of fifteen and a number is negative fifteen.

23. Negative twenty is the sum of fourteen and a number.

24. Twenty-six is the sum of a number and seventeen.

25. SCIENCE Ice melts to become water at its melting point of 32°F. Water then boils and becomes steam at its boiling point of 212°F. Write an addition equation to find the increase in temperature that it takes to turn ice into steam.

26. WRITING Describe a real-life situation that can be modeled by the equation $x + 12 = 70$.

27. MUSIC STORE You go to a music store to buy either a CD single for $8.50, an album CD for $15.85, or a double CD set for $24.50. You have a total of $28 when you go to the store, but you have to buy some blank cassette tapes which cost $8.75. Write a verbal model, labels, and an equation to find out how much you can spend on CDs. Which CDs could you buy? Can you buy more than one? Explain.

 STANDARDIZED TEST PRACTICE

28. Which value of c makes $-6 + c = 9$ a true statement?

    A $c = -15$ **B** $c = -3$ **C** $c = 3$ **D** $c = 15$

29. The figure shown to the right is a right angle. Which equation can you use to find the angle labeled m?

    A $63 + m = 180$ **B** $m + 180 = 63$

    C $63 + m = 90$ **D** $m + 90 = 63$

30. Which equation can you use to find the angle labeled x in the triangle shown at the right?

    A $x + 72 + 45 = 180$ **B** $x + 72 + 45 = -90$

    C $x + 72 + 45 = -180$ **D** $x + 72 + 45 = 90$

31. COLLEGE FOOTBALL The table at the right contains information about the ten Division 1-A college football teams with the most wins through their 1995 season. Using the table and the verbal model below, assign labels and write an equation to find how many wins each team has. (Source: Sports Illustrated 1997 Sports Almanac)

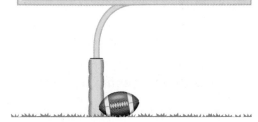

Teams	Games played	Losses or ties	Winning percentage
Notre Dame	999	261	76.0%
Michigan	1042	286	74.3%
Alabama	996	285	73.6%
Oklahoma	974	304	71.5%
Texas	1017	312	70.9%
Ohio State	1003	324	70.3%
Southern Cal.	959	312	70.3%
Nebraska	1028	330	69.8%
Penn State	1030	335	69.5%
Tennessee	989	334	68.9%

$$\text{Number of games won} + \text{Games lost or tied} = \text{Total games played}$$

a. Which team has the most wins?

b. Rank the teams in the order from team with the greatest number of wins to the team with the least number of wins. Is the order the same as the order in the table? If not, how can you explain the difference between the two lists?

SPIRAL REVIEW

1. Find the perimeter and area of the figure shown at the right. **(1.3)**

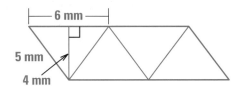

6 mm

5 mm

4 mm

2. USING LOGICAL REASONING Ashley, Carmen, Felicia, and Ricardo are ages 8, 11, 14, and 16. Ricardo is 3 years older than Carmen. Felicia is the youngest. How old is each person? **(1.7)**

In Exercises 3–6, use a tree diagram to write the prime factorization of the number. (2.4)

3. 81   **4.** 90   **5.** 112   **6.** 165

In Exercises 7–10, write the fraction in simplest form. (2.6)

7. $\dfrac{72}{120}$ **8.** $\dfrac{112}{14}$ **9.** $\dfrac{256}{288}$ **10.** $\dfrac{17}{300}$

In Exercises 11–14, match the multiplication or division problem with the letter that provides its correct answer. (3.5, 3.7)

A. $\dfrac{30}{77}$ **B.** 1   **C.** $\dfrac{8}{13}$ **D.** $\dfrac{4}{21}$

11. $\dfrac{4}{9} \cdot \dfrac{3}{7} =$ **12.** $\dfrac{6}{11} \div \dfrac{7}{5} =$ **13.** $5 \cdot \dfrac{1}{5} =$ **14.** $\dfrac{12}{13} \div \dfrac{3}{2} =$

In Exercises 15–18, write the integer represented by the real-life situation. (4.3)

15. A loss of 3 yards   **16.** A deposit of $55 into an account

17. 10 points extra credit   **18.** 5 degrees below zero

Diving to EXPLORE

READ About It

People began to explore sunken ships after Jacques Cousteau invented underwater breathing gear in 1943. Now diving to explore wrecks is a popular hobby. New Jersey attracts tourists with a site called "Dual Wrecks" which consists of two ships which lie 25 feet under the sea. A ship named the *Lowrance* can be found off the coast of Florida. This ship was built in 1953. It rests partly upright in the water, 210 feet below the surface at the bow (front) and only 150 feet below the surface at the stern (back). A tanker named the *British Splendour* lies 110 feet beneath the surface off Ocracoke Island, North Carolina.

In 1982, a Canaanite ship was found 150 feet under water off the southern coast of Turkey. The ship had been built around 1300 B.C. and required careful excavation. This depth would really test an amateur diver, as most amateurs don't go deeper than about 130 feet. Even the most skilled professional divers are limited to diving about 800 feet. New devices let professionals explore the deepest wrecks. To probe the *Titanic*, lying 13,000 feet under the surface, explorers used a deep submergence vehicle named *Alvin*.

WRITE About It

1. Using the water level as 0, make a number line showing the shipwreck depths described above. Include both depths for the *Lowrance*.

2. On your number line, mark the furthest depths that amateur and professional divers usually go. How much deeper is the *Titanic* than the professional divers' furthest depth? Explain.

3. If a diver dove to the bow of the *Lowrance* and then halfway back up to the stern, what would be his depth? Explain.

4. About how many years had the Cananite ship been in existence when it was discovered in 1982? What operation did you use to get your answer?

5. If a diver dove off a boat rail that was 7 ft above the surface to the "Dual Wrecks" site, how far would she have descended?

Solving Subtraction Equations

What you should learn:

Goal 1 How to solve subtraction equations by adding the same number to both sides

Goal 2 How to use subtraction equations to solve real-life problems

Why you should learn it:

Knowing how to solve subtraction equations can help you determine increases or decreases. An example is finding how much more money is needed for a hockey club field trip.

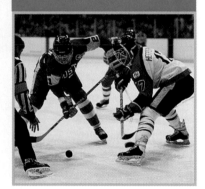

Goal 1 SOLVING SUBTRACTION EQUATIONS

A *subtraction equation* is an equation with a difference, such as

$$x - 4 = -2 \text{ or } 7 = x - 5.$$

SOLVING A SUBTRACTION EQUATION

To solve a subtraction equation, you add the same number to both sides of the equation so that the variable will be by itself on one side of the equation.

Example 1 Solving a Subtraction Equation

Solve each equation.

a. $n - 3 = 9$ **b.** $-5 = x - 8$

Solution

a. Add 3 to both sides of the equation.

$n - 3 = -9$	**Write original equation.**
$\underline{+3 \quad +3}$	**Add 3 to both sides.**
$n \quad = -6$	**Solution: *n* is by itself.**

The solution is $n = -6$. Check this as follows.

✔ **Check:** Substitute for the variable in the original equation.

$n - 3 = -9$	**Write original equation.**
$-6 - 3 \stackrel{?}{=} -9$	**Substitute −6 for *n*.**
$-9 = -9$	**Both sides are the same.** ✔

b. Add 8 to both sides of the equation.

$-5 = x - 8$	**Write original equation.**
$\underline{+8 \qquad +8}$	**Add 8 to both sides.**
$3 = x$	**Solution: *x* is by itself.**

The solution is $x = 3$. Check this as follows.

✔ **Check:** Substitute for the variable in the original equation.

$-5 = x - 8$	**Write original equation.**
$-5 \stackrel{?}{=} 3 - 8$	**Substitute 3 for *x*.**
$-5 = -5$	**Both sides are the same.** ✔

Example 2 Writing a Subtraction Equation

REAL LIFE
Field Trip

Your hockey club is taking a field trip. You have raised $234 for the trip. Your adviser says that you still need $164. What is the total amount of money needed?

Solution

Use a verbal model. Let x represent the unknown amount.

Verbal Model	$\dfrac{\text{Total}}{\text{amount}}$	$-$	$\dfrac{\text{Amount}}{\text{raised}}$	$=$	$\dfrac{\text{Amount left}}{\text{to raise}}$

Labels   Total amount $= \$x$
Amount raised $= \$234$
Amount left to raise $= \$164$

Equation

$$x - 234 = 164 \qquad \text{Write the equation.}$$
$$\underline{+\,234 \quad +\,234} \qquad \text{Add 234 to both sides.}$$
$$x \qquad = 398 \qquad \text{Solution: } x \text{ is by itself.}$$

So, the total amount needed is $398.

Example 3 Modeling a Real-Life Problem

The temperature fell 14° to -32°F. Which equation models this situation? What information does the solution provide?

a. $x - 14 = -32$ **b.** $-14 - n = -32$ **c.** $-32 - m = -14$

Solution

The equation in (a) models the situation.

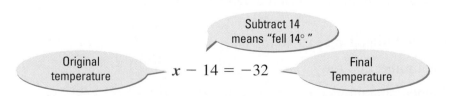

Subtract 14 means "fell 14°."

Original temperature $x - 14 = -32$ Final Temperature

Using methods from Examples 1 and 2, the solution is found to be -18. This means that the **original temperature was -18°F**.

ONGOING ASSESSMENT

Talk About It
....

Solve each equation by adding or subtracting the same number from both sides. Explain how you decided to add or subtract. Also explain how you decided what to add or subtract.

1. $x + 21 = 13$

2. $n - \dfrac{1}{2} = -1$

3. $-4 + m = 14$

4. $-7.3 = 2.5 + p$

4.7 Exercises

Extra Practice, page 631

GUIDED PRACTICE

In Exercises 1–4, describe how to solve the equation.

1. $11 + t = 9$
2. $-4 = p - 7$
3. $-15 + m = 21$
4. $-8 = 13 + x$

In Exercises 5–8, match the equation with its solution.

A. $n = 8$
B. $n = 2$
C. $n = -8$
D. $n = 10$

5. $6 = n - 2$
6. $n - 9 = 1$
7. $-5 + n = -3$
8. $-10 = -2 + n$

9. **TEST SCORING** You get a score of 56 points on a math test. You missed 9 points on the test. Use the verbal model below to find the number of points the test was worth.

$$\text{Total points} - \text{Points missed} = \text{Score}$$

10. **WRITING** Write a real-life problem that uses a subtraction equation to find a temperature.

PRACTICE AND PROBLEM SOLVING

In Exercises 11–13, without solving the equation, decide whether the solution is *positive* or *negative*. Then check your result by solving the equation.

11. $14 + x = 6$
12. $-18 = p - 12$
13. $-19 + y = 4$

WRITING EQUATIONS In Exercises 14–16, write an addition equation and a subtraction equation that has the given solution.

14. $z = -9$
15. $-16 = b$
16. $12 = k$

In Exercises 17–25, solve the equation. Then check the solution.

17. $x - 8 = -8$
18. $-1 = t - 17$
19. $-20 + p = 14$

20. $m - 25 = -33$
21. $-11 = y + 12$
22. $36 + k = 47$

23. $-18.03 + z = -14.7$
24. $n - 9.32 = 16.2$
25. $2\frac{1}{6} = a - 1\frac{1}{3}$

In Exercises 26–28, write the equation that is represented by the statement. Then solve the equation.

26. The difference of a number and fifteen is negative fifteen.

27. Twenty-six is the sum of a number and forty.

28. Seven eighths is the difference of a number and one fourth.

29. **THINKING SKILLS** Do the equations $-3 + x = 5$ and $x - 3 = 5$ have the same solution? Explain your reasoning.

30. TIDES The tide fell $14\frac{3}{4}$ feet to low tide at $12\frac{1}{2}$ feet. Use a subtraction equation to find the elevation of the water at high tide.

31. RIDDLE When I am added to myself and two is subtracted, the result is the same as when I am added to one. Who am I?

32. TEMPERATURE On the radio you hear that the temperature fell 13°F in the last two hours. When you look at the thermometer, it reads 25°F. Write an equation to find out what the temperature was two hours ago.

Real Life... Real Facts

The Bay of Fundy in eastern Canada has the highest tides in the world. The difference between low and high tides can be as much as 60 feet in a day.

33. VIDEO GAMES You go shopping to purchase a video game that has a sale price of $27. The sale was $9 off the original price. Write a verbal model, labels, and equation to find the original price.

34. RETAIL SALES You pay tax on the video game in Exercise 33. The total cost including tax is $28.35. Write a verbal model, labels, and equation to find the tax.

STANDARDIZED TEST PRACTICE

35. Which value of p makes $p - (-3) = 7$ a true statement?

   A $p = -10$ **B** $p = -4$ **C** $p = 4$ **D** $p = 10$

36. $s = 6$ is a solution to which equation?

   A $12 - s = 18$ **B** $s - (-5) = 1$ **C** $s - 9 = -3$ **D** $-4 - s = 2$

EXPLORATION AND EXTENSION

PORTFOLIO

37. BUILDING YOUR PROJECT Your track team finished the 1600-meter relay race in 3.35 minutes. Your team's time is 0.15 minute more than the first-place team's time, and 0.05 minute less than the third place team's time. Write verbal models, labels, and subtraction equations to find the times of the other teams.

WHAT *did you learn?*

WHY *did you learn it?*

		WHAT did you learn?	WHY did you learn it?
Skills	4.1	Make a table of values for an expression and write an expression that represents a table.	Compare fees for using a swimming pool at different health clubs.
	4.2	Plot points on a coordinate plane and draw a scatter plot.	To find and represent patterns in data.
	4.3	Graph and order integers.	Order profits from a part-time business.
	4.4	Use a number line to add integers.	Check the accuracy of a manufacturing machine.
	4.5	Use a number line to subtract integers.	Find the change in elevation while driving in Death Valley.
	4.6	Solve addition equations.	Find the yards gained or lost in a football play.
	4.7	Solve subtraction equations.	Find the amount of money needed for a field trip.
Strategies	4.1–4.7	Use problem solving strategies.	Solve a wide variety of real-world problems.
Using Data	4.1–4.7	Use tables, graphs, and time lines.	Organize data and solve problems.

HOW *does it fit into the bigger picture of mathematics?*

Mathematics can be used to model and explain many real-life problems. In this chapter, you saw how algebra equations can be used to model real-life problems that involve increases and decreases.

You used the steps shown to outline which part of the problem went with which part of the equation. Even though some of the problems of the chapter could be solved using mental math, it is important to understand the algebraic models of the problems. Later, you will encounter more complex problems that cannot be solved by mental math.

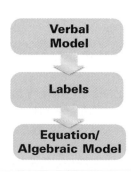

That's when you will see the true value of algebra as a problem solving language.

VOCABULARY

- **table of values** (p. 168)
- **coordinate plane** (p. 172)
- **ordered pairs** (p. 172)
- **coordinates** (p. 172)
- **x-axis** (p. 172)
- **y-axis** (p. 172)

- **x-coordinate** (p. 172)
- **y-coordinate** (p. 172)
- **origin** (p. 172)
- **scatter plot** (p. 173)
- **integers** (p. 178)
- **negative integers** (p. 178)

- **positive integers** (p. 178)
- **negative sign** (p. 178)
- **opposites** (p. 184)
- **verbal model** (p. 199)

4.1 PATTERNS, TABLES, AND EXPRESSIONS

Example Make a table of values for the expression $2m + 7$ for $m = 0, 1, 2,$ and 3.

Solution

Value of m	Substitute.	Value of Expression
0	$2(0) + 7 = 0 + 7$	7
1	$2(1) + 7 = 2 + 7$	9
2	$2(2) + 7 = 4 + 7$	11
3	$2(3) + 7 = 6 + 7$	13

Value of m	0	1	2	3
Value of Expression	7	9	11	13

In Exercises 1–4, make a table for the expression for $n = 1, 2, 3, 4, 5, 6$.

1. $n + 4$ **2.** $6 - 2n$ **3.** $3n - 13$ **4.** $-n + 3$

5. Write a description of the pattern in the table. Then write the expression based on the description.

Value of t	1	2	3	4	5	6	7
Value of Expression	23	22	21	20	19	18	17

4.2 SCATTER PLOTS AND THE COORDINATE PLANE

In an ordered pair, the x-coordinate shows the position on the x-axis and the y-coordinate shows the position on the y-axis.

In Exercises 6–8, write the ordered pair given by the letter.

6. A **7.** B **8.** C

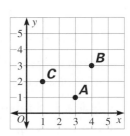

9. Write the ordered pairs represented by the data in the table. Then draw a scatter plot of the data.

x	1	2	3	4	5
y	5	4	2	3	1

4.3 INTEGERS AND THE NUMBER LINE

You can order integers by graphing them on a number line. Smaller numbers are to the left. Larger numbers are to the right.

Example To order the integers -9, 3, 0, 4, and -8 from least to greatest, begin by graphing them on a number line.

From the number line you can see that the numbers in order from least to greatest are -9, -8, 0, 3, and 4.

10. Use a number line to order 1, -6, -7, 6, and -2 from least to greatest.

RECORD LOWS In Exercises 11 and 12, use the table of record low temperatures for 1995.
(Source: National Climatic Data Center)

11. Use a number line to order the temperatures from least to greatest.

12. Which state had the lowest temperature? Which had the highest low temperature?

State	°F
Connecticut	-32
Maine	-48
New Hampshire	-46
New Jersey	-34
Massachusetts	-35
Oregon	-54
Montana	-70
California	-45

4.4 ADDING INTEGERS

You can use a number line to add integers.

Example Find the sum: $5 + (-3)$.

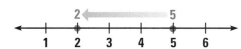

Your final position is 2. So, $5 + (-3) = 2$

In Exercises 13–16, use a number line to find the sum.

13. $-12 + (-5)$ **14.** $8 + (-12)$ **15.** $-9 + 9$ **16.** $0 + (-5)$

17. ADVERTISING A bakery advertises that they average 50 raisins in each cookie they sell. You count the raisins in four cookies.

Cookie 1: 5 raisins under average   Cookie 3: 2 raisins under average
Cookie 2: 6 raisins over average   Cookie 4: 1 raisins over average
Is the bakery's advertising correct?

4.5   SUBTRACTING INTEGERS

You can use a number line to subtract integers.

Example   Find the difference: $7 - (-4)$.

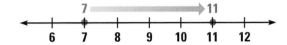

Your final position is 11. So, $7 - (-4) = 11$

In Exercises 18–21, use a number line to find the difference.

18. $-1 - (-7)$ **19.** $8 - (-8)$ **20.** $9 - 13$ **21.** $0 - 5$

4.6   SOLVING ADDITION EQUATIONS

To solve an addition equation, subtract to isolate the variable.

Example   Solve the equation $m + 6 = -10$.

Solution

$m + 6 = -10$	Rewrite original equation.
$\underline{ -6 \quad -6}$	Subtract 6 from both sides.
$m = -16$	Solution: m is by itself.

Check your solution by substituting $m = -16$ into the original equation.

In Exercises 22–24, solve the equation and check your solution.

22. $13 + x = 6$ **23.** $n + (-13) = 13$ **24.** $7 + d = 15$

25. PERSONAL FINANCE You receive an allowance of $8.00, and spend
$3.25 on a movie. Write an addition equation that you can use to
find the amount of money you have left. Then solve the equation.

4.7   SOLVING SUBTRACTION EQUATIONS

To solve a subtraction equation, add to isolate the variable .

Example   Solve the equation $b - 5 = -8$.

Solution

$b - 5 = -8$	Write the original equation.
$\underline{ +5 \quad +5}$	Add 5 to both sides.
$b -3$	Solution: b is by itself.

Check your solution by substituting $b = -3$ into the original equation.

In Exercises 26–28, solve the equation and check your solution.

26. $x - 13 = 6$ **27.** $m - 7 = -7$ **28.** $y - (-6) = -11$

In Questions 1–3, make a table of values. Use $t = 0, 1, 2, 3, 4, 5,$ and 6.

1. $2t + 6$ **2.** $t \div 4$ **3.** $15 - 3t$

In Questions 4–6, copy and complete the table. Then draw a scatter plot of the data. Describe any patterns in the scatter plot.

4. $y = 3x$

x	1	2	3	4	5
y	?	?	?	?	?

5. $n = m - \frac{1}{2}$

m	1	2	3	4	5
n	?	?	?	?	?

6. $b = 18 - 3a$

a	1	2	3	4	5
b	?	?	?	?	?

In Questions 7–9, complete the statement using < or >.

7. $5 \; ? \; -2$ **8.** $-9 \; ? \; -8$ **9.** $0 \; ? \; -1$

In Questions 10–15, find the sum or difference.

10. $13 + (-6)$ **11.** $5 - (-9)$ **12.** $-7 - 12$

13. $-11 + (-17)$ **14.** $-2 + 21$ **15.** $-15 - (-8)$

In Questions 16–21, solve the equation. Then check your solution.

16. $m + 16 = 7$ **17.** $-14 = y + 22$ **18.** $-11 = t - 11$

19. $27 = -30 + p$ **20.** $\frac{1}{6} + x = \frac{3}{4}$ **21.** $11.8 = 7.25 + z$

22. The table below shows the cost for a school jacket. The cost depends on the number of letters, n, that will be on the jacket. Write an expression for the cost using the variable n. How much would the jacket cost if you bought one with your first and last names on it?

n	0	1	2	3	4
Cost ($)	40.00	40.75	41.50	42.25	43.00

23. SPORTS RETAIL You buy a badminton set on sale for $63.75. The original price for the set was $85. Use the verbal model below to assign labels and to write an equation. Then solve the equation and find the discount on the badminton set.

$$\text{Sale Price} + \text{Discount} = \text{Original Price}$$

1. Which expression is represented by the table of values?

x	1	2	3	4	5
y	7	9	11	13	15

   (A) $x + 6$ (B) $8x - 1$
   (C) $2x + 5$ (D) $3x + 4$

2. A long-distance telephone call costs $1 for the first minute and $0.15 for each additional minute. Which expression can be used to represent the problem?

   (A) $m + 0.15$ (B) $1 + 0.15m$
   (C) $1 - 0.15m$ (D) $0.15m - 1$

3. Which set of ordered pairs represents the scatter plot?

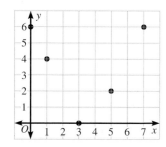

   (A) $(3, 0), (4, 1), (5, 2), (0, 6), (7, 6)$
   (B) $(7, 6), (5, 2), (0, 3), (6, 0), (1, 4)$
   (C) $(2, 5), (6, 0), (4, 1), (6, 7), (0, 3)$
   (D) $(0, 6), (3, 0), (7, 6), (1, 4), (5, 2)$

4. Order the integers $-3, 0, -6, 7, -4$, and 3 from least to greatest.

   (A) $7, -6, -4, 3, -3, 0$
   (B) $-6, -4, -3, 0, 3, 7$
   (C) $-3, -4, -6, 0, 3, 7$
   (D) $0, -6, -4, -3, 3, 7$

5. Find the sum: $-8 + (-3)$.

   (A) -11 (B) -5
   (C) 5 (D) 11

6. Which statement could be used to represent $-1 + 6$?

   (A) The elevator ascended 6 floors to the 5th floor.
   (B) The elevator descended 1 floor to the 6th floor.
   (C) The elevator ascended 1 floor from the 6th floor.
   (D) The elevator ascended 6 floors from the 1st floor.

7. Which statement could be used to represent $-2 - 5$?

   (A) The temperature fell 5 degrees from 2 degrees.
   (B) The temperature rose 5 degrees from -2 degrees.
   (C) The temperature fell 5 degrees from -2 degrees.
   (D) The temperature rose 2 degrees from -5 degrees.

8. You buy a pair of tennis shoes that have a sale price of $41.25. The sale was $13.75 off the original price. Which equation could be used to find the original price of the shoes?

   (A) $p - 13.75 = 41.25$
   (B) $41.25 - 13.75 = p$
   (C) $p + 13.75 = 41.25$
   (D) $p + 55 = 13.75$

Data Analysis
and Statistics

TECHNOLOGY

Technology resources accompanying this chapter:

- Interactive Real-Life Investigations
- Middle School Tutorial Software

NEWS National and international reports make up $\frac{13}{30}$ of a typical half-hour newscast.

ADVERTISING Nearly $\frac{4}{15}$ of a half-hour newscast is taken up by advertisements.

CHAPTER THEME
Reporting the News

WEATHER The weather report makes up $\frac{1}{10}$ of a half-hour news show.

SPORTS About $\frac{2}{15}$ of a half-hour news program is devoted to sports.

REAL LIFE Reporting

Television News

Television newscasters want to report stories that are important, interesting, and accurate. They also must be concerned with how long the stories take to tell! An average newscast, including advertisements, is 30 minutes long. It cannot run any longer or shorter, so producers must plan exactly how much time will be given to each segment.

News programmers start with an **ideal mix** of times that will be allotted to news, sports, and weather. Then they adjust those times depending on what is going on that day. The way one station assigns the time in a 30-minute news broadcast is shown by the circle graph at the right.

$\frac{13}{30}$ News

$\frac{4}{15}$ Advertising

$\frac{2}{15}$ Sports

$\frac{1}{15}$ Other

$\frac{1}{10}$ Weather

Think and Discuss

1. What takes up the most time in the news broadcast? How many more minutes are spent on this item than on the item that takes up the second longest time?

2. Suppose there is a large hurricane approaching the southeastern United States. How might this affect the ideal mix? Referring to the circle graph, revise the schedule to allow for more storm coverage.

PORTFOLIO

Reporting on TV Viewing

PROJECT DESCRIPTION

As a reporter, you have to be able to analyze information and present it clearly to your readers or viewers. Sometimes you may write short pieces for TV or newspapers. Other times you may do in-depth studies for magazines or documentary programs. In this project, you are a reporter writing an article about TV-viewing habits. To organize your information you can use the list of **TOPICS** on the next page.

GETTING STARTED

Talking It Over

- Discuss in your group what sorts of stories reporters investigate. Would you rather cover politics or sports? Would you prefer reporting on local, national, or international news? Is it important to know what your audience would like to see or read?

- Think of some possible topics that would be interesting to an audience and that you might like to research. Discuss in your group where you would go to find information about each topic. Try searching the **Internet**.

Planning Your Project

- **Materials Needed:** paper, pencils or pens, colored pencils or markers, camera, tape recorder, computer (optional)

- Design a layout for your story. Decide if you will include photographs. Interview some of your friends about their TV-viewing habits. Use your school library or other resource to gather additional information. Include the five topics in the **BUILDING YOUR PROJECT** list on page 217. Keep your work in your portfolio and add to it as assigned.

LAB 5.1

COOPERATIVE LEARNING

Gathering and Interpreting Data

Materials Needed
• ruler
• map of the United States
• colored pencils
• markers
• roll of paper
• masking tape
• measuring tape

Part A ORGANIZING DATA IN A TABLE

Estimated 1996 populations (in millions) of the 26 eastern United States are as follows. (Source: U.S. Bureau of the Census)

AL	4.3	GA	7.4	ME	1.2	MS	2.7	NC	7.3	SC	3.7	WI	5.2
CT	3.3	IL	11.8	MD	5.1	NH	1.2	OH	11.2	TN	5.3	WV	1.8
DE	**0.7**	IN	5.8	MA	6.1	NJ	8.0	PA	12.1	VT	0.6		
FL	14.4	KY	3.9	MI	9.6	NY	18.2	RI	1.0	VA	6.7		

1. Copy and complete the table at the right. Draw a tally mark for each state whose population falls within each interval. A sample tally mark is shown for Delaware (**DE**). *Frequency* refers to the sum of the tally marks for each interval.

Population interval (in millions)	Tally	Freq.
0.0 – 2.9	I	
3.0 – 5.9		
6.0 – 8.9		
9.0 – 11.9		
12.0 – 14.9		
15.0 – 17.9		
18.0 – 20.9		

2. Describe which population intervals have the greatest frequencies. What does this suggest about the populations of the eastern states?

Part B MAKING A FREQUENCY TABLE

Estimated 1996 populations (in millions) of the 24 western United States are as follows. (Source: U.S. Bureau of the Census)

AK	0.6	CO	3.8	KS	2.6	MT	0.9	ND	0.6	TX	19.1
AZ	4.4	HI	1.2	LA	4.4	NE	1.7	OK	3.3	UT	2.0
AR	2.5	ID	1.2	MN	4.7	NV	1.6	OR	3.2	WA	5.5
CA	31.9	IA	2.9	MO	5.4	NM	1.7	SD	0.7	WY	0.5

3. Make a frequency table similar to the one shown in Part A. Complete the table using the data above. How do the most frequent population intervals for western states compare with those for eastern states?

4. Assign a color to each population interval. Then color the map of the United States. Use the map to describe state populations.

The number of homerooms in 15 middle schools in a city are

17, 21, 14, 15, 12, 16, 15, 15, 16, 14, 18, 15, 16, 17, 15.

5. Complete this sentence.

Each school has about ? homerooms.

Which number did you select? Explain why.

6. Here are three ways that students answered Exercise 5.

a. Marlene found the average of the 15 numbers by adding the numbers and dividing the total by 15.

b. Ki Tae wrote the numbers in order from smallest to largest and chose the middle number.

c. Esther found the number that occurs most often.

What number did each student use? Which number do you think best represents the typical number of homerooms? Why?

NOW TRY THESE

7. Record the heights of all the students in your math class. Then do the following.

a. Use Marlene's method to find the average height.

b. Use Ki Tae's method of ordering the heights from least to greatest and choosing the middle height.

c. Use Esther's method of selecting the height that occurs most often.

8. ACT IT OUT Tape a long piece of paper along a hallway wall. Line up your math class from shortest to tallest. Mark each person's height on the paper. Look at the pattern of heights. Which of the methods used above best represents the typical height of a student?

5.1

Measures of Central Tendency

What you should learn:

Goal 1 How to find the mean, median, and mode of data

Goal 2 How to use measures of central tendency to represent data

Why you should learn it:

Knowing how to find measures of central tendency can help you describe data. An example is describing the typical length of a jury trial.

Goal 1 MEASURES OF CENTRAL TENDENCY

A **measure of central tendency** is a single number that is used to represent a set of data. Measures of central tendency help you describe a data set and interpret it.

MEAN, MEDIAN, AND MODE

The **mean**, or average, is the sum of a set of numbers divided by how many numbers are in the set.

The **median** is the middle number (or the mean of the two middle numbers) of a set of numbers that have been written in numerical order.

$$3, 5, 5, 7, 10, 11, 12 \qquad 4, 6, 6, 7, 9, 10, 10, 11$$

Median $\qquad\qquad$ Median: $\dfrac{7 + 9}{2} = 8$

The **mode** is the number that occurs most often in a set.

The set 4, 6, 8, 10, and 13 has no mode, because no number occurs more often than the rest. The set 3, 4, 4, 7, 7 has two modes: 4 and 7.

Example 1 Measures of Central Tendency

You interview 15 students in your class and ask how many times each has flown in an airplane. The results are shown below. Find the mean, the median, and the mode of the data.

$$0, 0, 1, 2, 2, 2, 2, 4, 4, 4, 5, 6, 10, 18, 32$$

Solution

To find the mean, add the numbers to get 92. Then divide by 15.

$$\text{Mean} = \frac{92}{15} \approx 6$$

The median is the middle number, which is 4.

Median

$$0, 0, 1, 2, 2, 2, 2, 4, 4, 4, 5, 6, 10, 18, 32$$

The mode is 2, the number that occurs most often in the data set.

Example 2 **Measures of Central Tendency**

STRATEGY **MAKE A TABLE** You are writing a story about the length of jury trials. From courthouse records, you find the lengths of 25 recent trials and record them in a table.

REAL LIFE
Reporting

Length of Trial (days)	1	2	3	4	5	6	8	13	183
Number of Trials	10	6	3	1	1	1	1	1	1

Which measure of central tendency best represents the typical length of a jury trial?

NEED TO KNOW

If a set has an odd number of numbers, then the median is the middle number. If it has an even number of numbers, then the median is the average of the two middle numbers of the set.

Solution

Ten of the trials each lasted 1 day, so 1 day is the mode. List the lengths in numerical order to find the median of **2** days. Here the trial lengths are listed in order.

1, 1, 1, 1, 1, 1, 1, 1, 1, 1, 2, 2, **2**, 2, 2, 2, 3, 3, 3, 4, 5, 6, 8, 13, 183

The sum of these numbers is 250, so the mean is 250 ÷ 25, or 10.

The mean is not a good representation, because it gives the impression that a typical jury trial lasts 10 days, which is not so. The median and mode are better representations.

Example 3 **Using a Mean**

In your math class, your semester grade will be determined by your mean score on 8 tests. To get an A, you need a mean of 92 or more. So far, your scores are 85, 97, 92, 94, 84, 98, and 88. What is the minimum score you need on your last test to get an A?

Solution

The sum of the 8 scores must be 8 × 92, or 736, because

$$\frac{736}{8} = 92.$$

The sum of your first seven scores is 638. You need to get at least 736 − 638, or 98, on your last test.

ONGOING ASSESSMENT

Write About It
....

Consider the following.

3, 6, 2, 7, 2, 8, 5, 5, 4, **?**

1. If the mean is 8, what is the missing number?

2. If the median is 5, what is the missing number?

3. If the mode is 2, what is the missing number?

GUIDED PRACTICE

In Exercises 1–3, explain why the statement is false.

1. The mean and median of 10, 14, 17, and 19 is 15.

2. The mode of 14, 33, 45, 67, and 77 is 45.

3. The median of 15, 13, 16, 14, and 11 is 16.

GUESS, CHECK, AND REVISE **In Exercises 4–6, complete the statement.**

4. The mean of 44, 54, 43, and ? is 49.

5. The median of 112, 115, 117, 121, 122, and ? is 118.5.

6. The median and mean of 75, 73, 72, 78, and ? is 75.

PRACTICE AND PROBLEM SOLVING

In Exercises 7–10, order the data from least to greatest. Then find the mean, median, and mode of the data.

7. Price per pound of 10 types of fruit:

$3.25, $5.00, $2.45, $3.25, $4.00, $3.00, $3.25, $4.00, $2.45, $3.15

8. Number of board games owned by 15 people:

5, 3, 4, 4, 5, 2, 4, 5, 3, 4, 3, 2, 2, 4, 2

9. Number of birthday cards received by 21 people:

4, 4, 3, 5, 1, 1, 4, 4, 3, 3, 4, 3, 8, 3, 4, 6, 5, 7, 6, 3, 3

10. Number of times 20 people have each flown in an airplane in the past year:

0, 0, 2, 8, 1, 2, 0, 1, 0, 1, 4, 3, 0, 1, 5, 0, 0, 0, 2, 0

11. STATE NAMES The data below represent the numbers of letters in the names of the 50 states. Find the mean, median, and mode. What number do you think best represents the typical length of a state name? Explain your reasoning.

7, 6, 7, 8, 10, 8, 11, 8, 7, 7,

6, 5, 8, 7, 4, 6, 8, 9, 5,

8, 13, 8, 9, 11, 8, 7, 8, 6, 12, 9,

9, 7, 13, 11, 4, 8, 6, 12, 11, 13,

11, 9, 5, 4, 7, 8, 10, 12, 9, 7

THINKING SKILLS In Exercises 12 and 13, create a data set of 5 numbers with the given measures of central tendency.

12. Mean: 10, Median: 10, Mode: 8

13. Mean: 26, Median: 25, Mode: 25

SALARIES In Exercises 14 and 15, use the table showing the salaries of employees of a TV station.

14. Find the mean, median, and mode of the salaries. Which do you think best represents the salary of a typical TV station employee? Explain.

15. If the station hires a vice president at a salary of $125,000, how would it change the mean, median, and mode?

Job	Number employed	Salary
Owner	1	$200,000
Newscaster	5	60,000
Meteorologist	1	52,000
Reporter	5	38,000
Set designer	2	32,000
Camera operator	10	27,000
Technician	10	25,000

STANDARDIZED TEST PRACTICE

16. Which measures of central tendency are the same for the data?

2, 3, 3, 3, 5, 6, 6

(**A**) Mean and median

(**B**) Mean and mode

(**C**) Median and mode

(**D**) All are the same

17. Which measures of central tendency are the same for the data?

1, 1, 4, 4, 5, 6, 6, 6, 7

(**A**) Mean and median

(**B**) Mean and mode

(**C**) Median and mode

(**D**) None are the same

EXPLORATION AND EXTENSION

PORTFOLIO

18. BUILDING YOUR PROJECT You want to report the number of people who watch nature programs on TV. The results below are from 10 surveys. The data show the number (in millions) of 14 to 19-year-olds who watch at least one nature program each week. Which measure of central tendency will you use? Why?

1.5, 2.4, 2.1, 1.4, 2.5, 2.2, 1.6, 1.7, 1.9, 1.7

LAB 5.2

COOPERATIVE LEARNING

Investigating Range and Scale

Materials Needed
- grid paper
- pencils or pens
- ruler
- colored pencils or markers

Part A SELECTING INTERVALS

You are studying your city bus system. For 18 days, you count the number of people who are on the 8:15 A.M. bus at the corner of First and Walnut Streets. Your results are as follows.

12, 15, 24, 18, 11, 15, 18, 23, 10,

27, 17, 17, 22, 24, 17, 13, 11, 27

Because the numbers vary from 10 to 27, the *range* is 27–10, or 17. One way to simplify the information in the list is to make a frequency table as shown at the right.

Interval	Tally	Freq.
10 – 12	IIII	4
13 – 15	III	3
16 – 18	HH	5
19 – 21		0
22 – 24	IIII	4
25 – 27	II	2

1. Each interval in the frequency table contains 3 numbers. Make a frequency table in which the intervals contain 4 numbers. Begin with the interval 10–13.

2. Make another frequency table in which the intervals contain 2 numbers. Begin with the interval 10–11.

3. Of the three frequency tables, which do you think best represents the data? Explain your reasoning.

Part B SCALING A NUMBER LINE

When you use a graph to represent data, you need to decide which numbers to put on the number line. Sometimes the numbers increase by ones, but they can also increase by twos, threes, and so on.

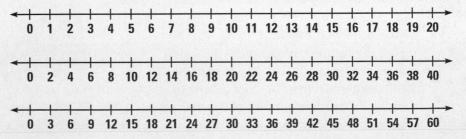

4. Draw a number line that has a scale from 0 to 40 by fours.

5. Draw a number line that has a scale from 15 to 45 by threes.

6. Copy the coordinate plane twice on grid paper. Without changing the number of grid lines, add scales to the *x*-axis and *y*-axis. Then plot the ordered pairs for parts (a) and (b).

a. (1, 5), (3, 2), (4, 8),
(4, 12), (5, 5), (5, 14),
(6, 1), (7, 13), (7, 3),
(8, 10)

b. (1, 90), (1, 85), (2, 80),
(2, 75), (3, 70), (3, 65),
(4, 60), (4, 55), (5, 50),
(5, 45)

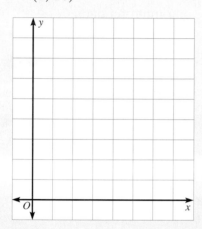

NOW TRY THESE

7. Listed below are the average low and high temperatures for several western states. What is the range of each data set? Make a frequency table for each data set. Choose appropriate intervals for your frequency tables.

Average Low Temperatures (°F)

AZ 59	**CO** 36	**KS** 45	**MT** 33	**NM** 42	**OR** 45	**UT** 40
AR 51	**ID** 39	**MN** 35	**NE** 40	**ND** 29	**SD** 34	**WA** 45
CA 48	**IA** 40	**MO** 44	**NV** 35	**OK** 49	**TX** 55	**WY** 33

Average High Temperatures (°F)

AZ 86	**CO** 64	**KS** 67	**MT** 56	**NM** 70	**OR** 63	**UT** 64
AR 73	**ID** 63	**MN** 54	**NE** 62	**ND** 54	**SD** 57	**WA** 59
CA 74	**IA** 60	**MO** 64	**NV** 67	**OK** 71	**TX** 76	**WY** 58

8. Use the data above to write an ordered pair for each state. Use the low temperatures as the first coordinates. Then graph the data. Describe any patterns that you see in the graph.

5.2

Histograms

What you should learn:

Goal 1 How to make a frequency table

Goal 2 How to draw a histogram

Why you should learn it:

Knowing how to draw histograms can help you organize data. An example is organizing data about state taxes on gasoline.

Goal 1 MAKING A FREQUENCY TABLE

STRATEGY **MAKE A TABLE** A **frequency table** groups large amounts of data into intervals. The **frequency** is the number of times an item occurs within an interval. The intervals must cover the **range**, or difference between the extremes, of a data set. A frequency table helps you organize and interpret data.

Example 1 **Making a Frequency Table**

Make a frequency table showing the gasoline tax (in cents per gallon) for each state. The tax for each of the 50 states is given below. (Source: Statistical Abstract of the United States, 1996)

REAL LIFE
Gasoline Taxes

AL 18	HI 16	MA 21	NM 21	SD 20
AK 8	ID 22	MI 16	NY 23	TN 21
AZ 18	IL 19	MN 20	NC 22	TX 20
AR 19	IN 16	MS 18	ND 18	UT 20
CA 19	IA 20	MO 15	OH 22	VT 16
CO 27	KS 18	MT 27	OK 17	VA 18
CT 31	KY 15	NE 25	OR 24	WA 23
DE 22	LA 20	NV 24	PA 22	WV 21
FL 12	ME 19	NH 19	RI 28	WI 26
GA 8	MD 24	NJ 15	SC 17	WY 9

Solution

The frequency table is shown at the left. The columns are completed as follows.

Interval	Tally	Freq.
0–2		0
3–5		0
6–8	||	2
9–11			1
12–14			1
15–17	⊪⊪ IIII	9
18–20	⊪⊪ ⊪⊪ ⊪⊪ II	17
21–23	⊪⊪ ⊪⊪ I	11
24–26	⊪⊪	5
27–29	III	3
30–32			1

Interval: The data are grouped into intervals of 3 cents. The first interval is 0–2 cents. The last interval is 30–32 cents. The 11 intervals cover the range of the data, which is 31 minus 8, or 23.

Tally: The tax for each state is recorded with a tally mark. The tax and tally mark for Alabama (AL) are shown in red.

Frequency: The frequency of each interval is the number of tally marks in the interval.

From the frequency table, you can see that the gasoline tax in most states is between 15 and 23 cents per gallon.

Goal 2 DRAWING A HISTOGRAM

A **histogram** is a bar graph that represents data in a frequency table. In a histogram, there is a bar (or space for a bar) for each interval of the frequency table.

Example 2 > Drawing a Histogram

STRATEGY **USE A GRAPH** Use the data in the frequency table on page 226 to draw a histogram for state gasoline taxes.

Solution

To draw a histogram, use the following steps.

1. Draw a rectangle and divide the base into the intervals shown in the frequency table. Label each interval.

2. Scale the left side of the rectangle to allow for the greatest frequency in the table. Label the scale with numbers.

3. Use the scale to draw horizontal lines. Then use the horizontal lines to draw bars whose heights represent the frequencies.

4. Label the vertical scale, the intervals, and the entire histogram.

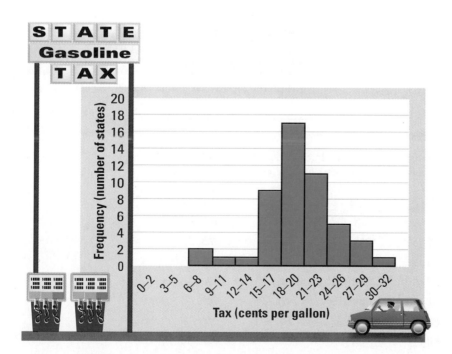

STATE Gasoline TAX

Frequency (number of states)

Tax (cents per gallon)

ONGOING ASSESSMENT

Talk About It

Make a frequency table of the data in Example 1. Use intervals of 0–1, 2–3, 4–5, and so on. Then draw a histogram of the data in the table.

1. How does your histogram compare with the histogram in Example 2?

2. Discuss the advantages and disadvantages of each histogram.

GUIDED PRACTICE

In Exercises 1 and 2, copy and complete the frequency tables using the data below. Which table best represents the data? Why?

4.5, 1.1, 2.5, 3.9, 4.2, 5.6, 3.3, 1.3, 1.8, 5.7, 2.1, 9, 18.4, 3.3, 2.4, 3, 5.1,
1.2, 10.9, 5, 2.9, 5.8, 3.4, 2.8, 4.6, 2, 5.5, 2.2, 2.6, 5.5

1.

Interval	Tally	Frequency
1–1.9		
2–2.9		
3–3.9		
4–4.9		
5–5.9		
6 plus		

2.

Interval	Tally	Frequency
1–3.9		
4–6.9		
7–9.9		
10–12.9		
13–15.9		
16–18.9		

PRACTICE AND PROBLEM SOLVING

USING A GRAPH In Exercises 4 and 5, use the histogram at the right. (Source: U.S. Bureau of the Census)

3. What age interval has the greatest population? What age interval has the least?

4. Write a statement about the age distribution of the population in the United States in 1997.

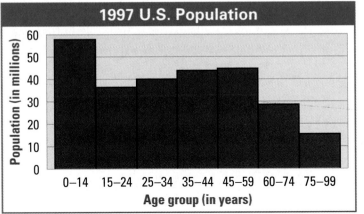

5. The data below show the number of English-language daily newspapers published in 1996. Make a frequency table and a histogram of the data. (Source: Information Please Almanac, 1997)

AL 26	**HI** 6	**MA** 36	**NM** 18	**SD** 11	**AK** 7
ID 12	**MI** 50	**NY** 69	**TN** 27	**AZ** 22	**IL** 68
MN 25	**NC** 50	**TX** 89	**AR** 31	**IN** 71	**MS** 22
ND 10	**UT** 6	**CA** 98	**IA** 38	**MO** 44	**OH** 84
VT 8	**CO** 30	**KS** 47	**MT** 11	**OK** 46	**VA** 28
CT 18	**KY** 23	**NE** 17	**OR** 19	**WA** 24	**DE** 3
LA 26	**NV** 9	**PA** 87	**WV** 22	**FL** 40	**ME** 9
NH 12	**RI** 6	**WI** 35	**GA** 35	**MD** 14	**NJ** 20
SC 15	**WY** 9				

6. U.S. CONGRESS Use the data below to make two frequency tables and histograms, one for **Democrats** and one for **Republicans** in the United States House of Representatives.

(Source: Statistical Abstract of the United States, 1996)

AL	4	3	HI	2	0	MA	8	2	NM	1	2	SD	1	0
AK	0	1	ID	0	2	MI	9	7	NY	17	14	TN	4	5
AZ	1	5	IL	10	10	MN	6	2	NC	4	8	TX	18	12
AR	2	2	IN	4	6	MS	3	2	ND	1	0	UT	1	2
CA	25	26	IA	0	5	MO	6	3	OH	6	13	VT	0	0
CO	2	4	KS	0	4	MT	1	0	OK	1	5	VA	6	5
CT	3	3	KY	2	4	NE	0	3	OR	3	2	WA	2	7
DE	0	1	LA	2	5	NV	0	2	PA	11	10	WV	3	6
FL	8	15	ME	1	1	NH	0	2	RI	2	0	WI	3	0
GA	3	8	MD	4	4	NJ	5	8	SC	2	4	WY	0	1

Senator Campbell is the only Native American in the United States Congress.

STANDARDIZED TEST PRACTICE

7. Which of the following is shown by the graph?

(A) Consumption rose steadily from 1975.

(B) Consumption was the same in 1975 and 1990.

(C) Consumption in 1985 was twice that in 1980.

(D) Consumption was lowest in 1975.

8. What was the peanut consumption in 1995?

(A) 6.9 lb   (B) 5.7 lb   (C) 6.0 lb   (D) 4.8 lb

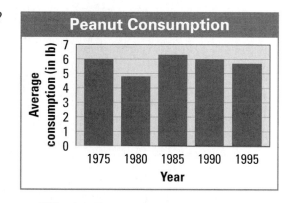

Peanut Consumption

EXPLORATION AND EXTENSION

PORTFOLIO

9. BUILDING YOUR PROJECT Two groups of parents were interviewed. The table shows how many hours of TV their children watched each week. Draw a histogram for each age group. (To do a simulated survey, see the interactive investigation for this chapter.)

Tech Link

Investigation 5, Interactive Real-Life Investigations

Ages 5–9	22, 25, 29, 30, 24, 28, 27, 26, 25, 21, 30, 26, 25, 29, 22, 20, 27, 24, 25, 26
Ages 10–14	22, 19, 20, 26, 21, 18, 23, 20, 18, 16, 24, 25, 17, 23, 24, 19, 23, 26, 23, 20

1. **USING LOGICAL REASONING** Each letter represents a digit from 0 through 9. Find the value of each letter. **(1.7)**

$$\begin{array}{r} A \\ + F \\ \hline F \end{array} \qquad \begin{array}{r} H \\ \times C \\ \hline H \end{array} \qquad \begin{array}{r} F \\ - I \\ \hline G \end{array} \qquad \begin{array}{r} G \\ \times G \\ \hline B \end{array} \qquad \begin{array}{r} J \\ J \\ + J \\ \hline C\,J \end{array} \qquad \begin{array}{r} G \\ + G \\ \hline H \end{array} \qquad \begin{array}{r} F \\ \times G \\ \hline E\,C \end{array} \qquad \begin{array}{r} J \\ E\,\overline{)\,C\,A} \end{array}$$

$$\begin{array}{r} I \\ E\,\overline{)\,D} \end{array}$$

In Exercises 2–5, find a denominator so that the fraction is proper and the greatest common factor of the numerator and denominator is 4. **(2.6)**

2. $\dfrac{12}{?}$ **3.** $\dfrac{20}{?}$ **4.** $\dfrac{32}{?}$ **5.** $\dfrac{68}{?}$

In Exercises 6–9, make a table of values. Use $x = 1, 2, 3, 4, 5,$ and 6. Then graph the data. Describe any patterns you see. **(4.1, 4.2)**

6. $y = 4 + x$ **7.** $y = x \div 5$ **8.** $y = 3x + 1$ **9.** $12 - 2x = y$

HEALTH Connection

FLORENCE NIGHTINGALE

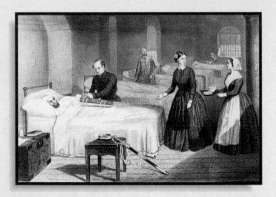

Florence Nightingale (1820–1910) was the founder of modern nursing. Nightingale used statistics to convince the British army that sanitary conditions could save lives. She compiled data about the survival rates of those wounded in the Crimean War. A year after she instituted sanitary conditions in hospitals, the death rate had declined from 43 percent to 2 percent. Nightingale invented the circle graph to display her data.

1. Food and medicine were carried by ox cart in the Crimean War. Suppose 20 ox carts were used. If each cart can carry supplies for 100 soldiers and 50 horses, how many trips would be needed to supply 25,000 troops and 13,000 horses?

2. Three British hospitals were to be supplied with fuel, mattresses, pork, and rice. Each hospital was to receive one cartload of each supply. Instead, one hospital received 3 carts of rice, another received 3 loads of mattresses and 3 loads of pork, and a third received 3 loads of rice. What is the minimum number of trips it will take for one cart to redistribute the supplies properly?

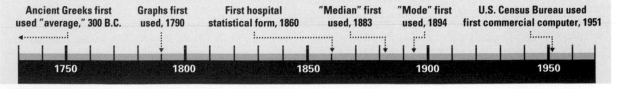

| Ancient Greeks first used "average," 300 B.C. | Graphs first used, 1790 | First hospital statistical form, 1860 | "Median" first used, 1883 | "Mode" first used, 1894 | U.S. Census Bureau used first commercial computer, 1951 |

| 1750 | 1800 | 1850 | 1900 | 1950 |

Creating Graphs on **Computers**

Most computer spreadsheet programs can be used to draw bar graphs and line graphs.

....

Example

Use a spreadsheet to draw a bar graph for the data in the table at the left. The data show the number of VCRs per 100 TV households. (Source: Veronis, Suhler & Associates)

Year	VCRs per 100 homes
1991	73
1992	76
1993	77
1994	77
1995	80
1996	82

Solution

STRATEGY **USING A GRAPH** Begin by entering the data in a spreadsheet. Then use the program's commands to draw a bar graph. You should obtain a graph that is similar to the one shown below.

	A	B	C	D
1	1991	73		
2	1992	76		
3	1993	77		
4	1994	77		
5	1995	80		
6	1996	82		

VCRs per 100 TV Households

Exercises

1. Use a spreadsheet to draw a line graph for the data given in the example above. Use the line graph to predict the number of VCRs per 100 TV households in 1998.

2. The table below shows the average yearly admission price for a movie. Enter the data in a spreadsheet. Then use the spreadsheet to draw a bar graph and a line graph for the data. (Source: Motion Picture Association of America)

1991	1992	1993	1994	1995	1996
$4.21	$4.15	$4.14	$4.18	$4.35	$4.42

Investigating Quartiles

Part A DESCRIBING DATA

Materials Needed
• paper
• pencils or pens
• ruler

The average number of days of precipitation (0.01 inch or more) per year for a city in each state is listed below.

(Source: Statistical Abstract of the United States, 1996)

CONNECTION
Earth Science

AL 122	**HI** 98	**MA** 127	**NM** 61	**SD** 98
AK 222	**ID** 90	**MI** 136	**NY** 135	**TN** 107
AZ 36	**IL** 126	**MN** 134	**NC** 111	**TX** 79
AR 105	**IN** 126	**MS** 109	**ND** 96	**UT** 91
CA 57	**IA** 108	**MO** 106	**OH** 130	**VT** 154
CO 89	**KS** 86	**MT** 101	**OK** 83	**VA** 115
CT 127	**KY** 124	**NE** 99	**OR** 151	**WA** 154
DE 116	**LA** 114	**NV** 50	**PA** 153	**WV** 151
FL 116	**ME** 129	**NH** 126	**RI** 124	**WI** 125
GA 115	**MD** 113	**NJ** 112	**SC** 110	**WY** 100

1. List this data in increasing order. Use the ordered list to find the median of the data. Explain your reasoning.

2. Divide the data into two groups: the smallest 25 numbers and the largest 25 numbers. The median of the first group is called the *first quartile,* and the median of the second group is called the *third quartile*. Find the first and third quartiles.

3. Copy the number line below.

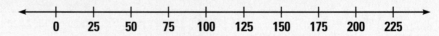

On the number line, plot the following numbers.
- The least number in the list
- The first quartile of the list
- The median or second quartile of the list
- The third quartile of the list
- The greatest number in the list

These five numbers divide the data into four groups. About what fraction of the numbers lie in each group? Why do you think the name "quartile" is used?

4. What can you conclude by looking at your graph?

The average yearly precipitation (to the nearest inch) for a city in each state is listed below. (Source: Statistical Abstract of the United States, 1996)

AL 64	**HI** 22	**MA** 42	**NM** 9	**SD** 24
AK 54	**ID** 12	**MI** 33	**NY** 36	**TN** 52
AZ 8	**IL** 36	**MN** 30	**NC** 43	**TX** 34
AR 51	**IN** 40	**MS** 55	**ND** 15	**UT** 16
CA 18	**IA** 33	**MO** 38	**OH** 41	**VT** 34
CO 15	**KS** 29	**MT** 15	**OK** 33	**VA** 45
CT 44	**KY** 44	**NE** 30	**OR** 36	**WA** 37
DE 41	**LA** 62	**NV** 8	**PA** 37	**WV** 43
FL 51	**ME** 44	**NH** 36	**RI** 46	**WI** 33
GA 51	**MD** 41	**NJ** 40	**SC** 50	**WY** 14

5. Write the data above in increasing order.

6. Use your ordered data to find the (a) smallest number, (b) first quartile, (c) median, (d) third quartile, and (e) greatest number. Graph these numbers on a number line.

7. Compare the data in Part A and Part B. Are the places with a lot of rain the same places where precipitation occurs often? Explain.

NOW TRY THESE

In Exercises 8–11, match the data set with the corresponding number line.

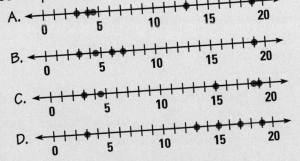

A.

B.

C.

D.

8. 4, 14, 4, 4, 3, 12, 19, 4, 14, 3, 5, 8

9. 4, 7, 3, 5, 5, 19, 4, 8, 6, 6, 6, 7

10. 15, 17, 19, 12, 17, 17, 15, 3, 18, 14, 15, 12

11. 5, 13, 19, 4, 19, 18, 5, 19, 18, 3, 4, 17

5.3

Box-and-Whisker Plots

What you should learn:

Goal 1 How to organize data with box-and-whisker plots

Goal 2 How to use box-and-whisker plots to interpret data

Why you should learn it:

You can use box-and-whisker plots to help interpret real-life data. An example is interpreting the price ranges of cars.

Goal 1 DRAWING A BOX-AND-WHISKER PLOT

The median or **second quartile** of an ordered set of numbers separates the set into two halves: those below the median and those above the median. The **first quartile** is the median of the lower half. The **third quartile** is the median of the upper half.

$$\frac{14 + 16}{2} = 15$$
Second quartile

3, 6, 8, | 10, 13, 14, | 16, 18, 20, | 20, 25, 27

First quartile
$$\frac{8 + 10}{2} = 9$$

Third quartile
$$\frac{20 + 20}{2} = 20$$

A **box-and-whisker plot** of this data is shown below.

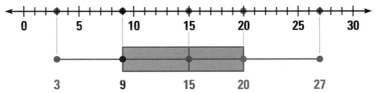

3 — Least number 9 — First quartile 15 — Second quartile 20 — Third quartile 27 — Greatest number

Example 1 Making a Box-and-Whisker Plot

Draw a box-and-whisker plot for the following data.

16, 20, 23, 12, 18, 26, 2, 9, 16, 32, 35, 3, 25, 28

Solution

Begin by writing the numbers in increasing order.

2, 3, 9, **12**, 16, 16, 18, | 20, 23, 25, **26**, 28, 32, 35

From this ordering, you can see that the first quartile is **12**, the second quartile is **19**, and the third quartile is **26**. A box-and-whisker plot for this data is shown below.

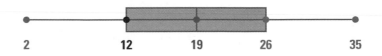

STUDY TIP

When you draw a box-and-whisker plot, you should graph five numbers: the least number, the three quartiles, and the greatest number. These five numbers should be spaced as they would be on a number line.

Example 2 Interpreting Box-and-Whisker Plots

REAL LIFE
Car Prices

In 1997, a survey was taken of the prices of 50 compact cars and 50 luxury cars. The box-and-whisker plots show the results. What do the plots tell you about the prices of these two types of cars?

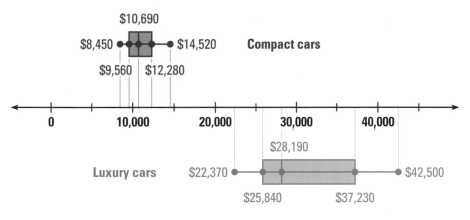

Driver's Education courses result in lower insurance costs in many states.

Solution

From these box-and-whisker plots, you can make many observations.

- The compact cars ranged between $8,450 and $14,520.

- Half of the compact cars were between $9,560 and $12,280.

- The median compact car price was $10,690.

- The luxury cars ranged between $22,370 and $42,500.

- Half of the luxury cars were between $25,840 and $37,230.

- The median luxury car price was $28,190.

There are many other observations you can make. For example, you can observe that the least expensive luxury car was about $8,000 more than the most expensive compact car.

Ford Aspire

Lincoln Continental

ONGOING ASSESSMENT

Write About It

Suppose you wanted to survey the prices of 50 1997 midsize cars.

1. Use the information in Example 2 to estimate the prices of 1997 midsize cars.

2. Draw a box-and-whisker plot of your estimated data.

GUIDED PRACTICE

In Exercises 1–4, complete the statement with the correct word.

1. The median of the lower half of the ordered data is the __?__ quartile.

2. The second quartile is the __?__ of the data.

3. The third quartile is the median of the __?__ half of the ordered data.

4. The first step in making a box-and-whisker plot is to write the data in __?__ order.

In Exercises 5 and 6, use the tables at the right. They show the weekly grocery bills for two households of 4 people for 6 weeks.

Week	1	2	3	4	5	6
Bill	108	110	91	102	95	101

5. For each household, draw a box-and-whisker plot that shows the grocery bill in dollars.

Week	1	2	3	4	5	6
Bill	99	101	102	102	103	100

6. Use the box-and-whisker plots to compare the amounts spent by each household.

PRACTICE AND PROBLEM SOLVING

In Exercises 7–10, match the data with the box-and-whisker plot.

A.
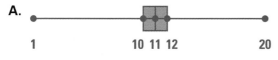

B.

C.

D.

7. 2, 1, 8, 13, 6, 8, 9, 15, 20, 18

8. 6, 7, 3, 1, 6, 11, 20, 3, 2, 1

9. 14, 15, 1, 8, 18, 20, 17, 19, 13, 15

10. 11, 10, 11, 12, 1, 13, 11, 10, 11, 20

In Exercises 11 and 12, draw a box-and-whisker plot of the data.

11. 3, 6, 8, 11, 14, 17, 19, 20, 25, 25, 26, 26, 29, 30

12. 15, 20, 33, 34, 41, 44, 48, 48, 52, 63, 64, 67, 68, 75

13. BOSTON MARATHON The box-and-whisker plots below show the winning times (to the nearest minute) of the Boston Marathon from 1978 to 1997 for men and women. Describe the winning times. (Source: Boston Athletic Association)

Men

127   129 129.5 131.5   140

Women

142 145   146.5   154.5   169

Real Life...
Real People

Lameck Aguta of Kenya won the 1997 Boston Marathon with a time of 2:10:33.

STANDARDIZED TEST PRACTICE

14. What conclusion can you draw from the box-and-whisker plot at the right?

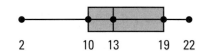

2   10 13   19 22

(A) The least number is 10.   **(B)** The mean is 13.

(C) Most of the data are greater than 19.   **(D)** The greatest number is 22.

15. What is *not* true of the data shown in the box-and-whisker plot?

(A) About half of the data falls between 10 and 19.   **(B)** Most of the data are greater than 10.

(C) The mode is 13.   **(D)** About one fourth of the data are greater than 19.

EXPLORATION AND EXTENSION

PORTFOLIO

16. BUILDING YOUR PROJECT Out of 100 people surveyed, the number (by age group) who watched network television and the number who watched cable television are shown in the table at the right.

Age Group	18–24	25–34	35–44	45–54	55–64	65 and over
TV	89	89	90	91	92	95
Cable	62	64	66	68	68	57

In your article, include a graph that you think best represents this data. Explain your choice. What patterns do you see?

(Source: Statistical Abstract of the United States, 1996)

Scatter Plots

What you should learn:

Goal 1 How to plot points in a coordinate plane

Goal 2 How to draw a scatter plot that represents real-life data

Why you should learn it:

You can use a scatter plot to represent real-life data, such as the relationship between Fahrenheit and Celsius temperature scales.

Goal 1 POINTS IN A COORDINATE PLANE

In Lesson 4.2, you learned how to plot points that have positive coordinates. In this lesson, you will extend the coordinate plane to include points with negative coordinates. A complete coordinate plane has four **quadrants** identified by Roman numerals.

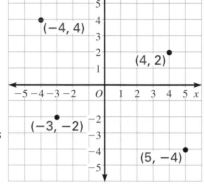

Quadrant II
x-coordinate is negative.

Quadrant I
Both coordinates are positive.

Quadrant III
Both coordinates are negative.

Quadrant IV
y-coordinate is negative.

Example 1 **Plotting Points in a Coordinate Plane**

Plot the following points. Identify each point's quadrant.

$(-3, 4), (-2, 0), (-5, -4), (0, -4), (2, -2), (2, 4)$

Solution

The *x*-coordinate tells you how far left or right you are from the origin. The *y*-coordinate tells you how far to move up or down. To plot $(-3, 4)$, move 3 units left and 4 units up in Quadrant II.

Each point's quadrant is shown below. Notice that $(-2, 0)$ and $(0, -4)$ lie on an axis and are in no particular quadrant.

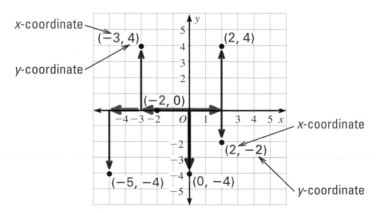

Goal 2 REPRESENTING REAL-LIFE DATA

Recall that a *scatter plot* is a collection of points in a coordinate plane that represents a relationship between two quantities.

Example 2 › Drawing a Scatter Plot

CONNECTION
Science

STRATEGY **MAKE A TABLE** You have a Fahrenheit thermometer and a Celsius thermometer. To figure out how the two temperature scales relate, you read both thermometers at several different temperatures. You record your results in a table, as shown below. Find a pattern for this data.

°F	−4	−2	8	14	24	32	45
°C	−20	−19	−13	−10	−4	0	7

Solution

One way to find a pattern is to write the data as ordered pairs. Then draw a scatter plot of the ordered pairs.

$$(-4, -20), (-2, -19), (8, -13), (14, -10), (24, -4), (32, 0), (45, 7)$$

With real-life data, it often is not convenient to use scales whose tick marks increase by one. With the data above, it is more convenient to use tick marks that increase by three or five, as shown in the scatter plot below.

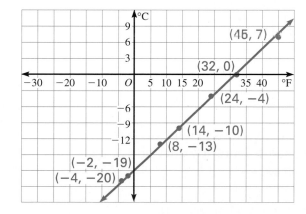

The scatter plot shows that the points lie nearly on a line. You can use the scatter plot to convert temperatures from one scale to the other.

In Exercises 1–6, refer to the coordinate plane at the right and write the ordered pair that is represented by the letter.

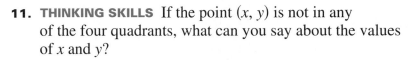

1. *A*
2. *B*
3. *C*
4. *D*
5. *E*
6. *F*

In Exercises 7–10, name the quadrant in which the point lies.

7. $(-6, 4)$
8. $(-2, -7)$
9. $(5, 3)$
10. $(1, -8)$

11. **THINKING SKILLS** If the point (x, y) is not in any of the four quadrants, what can you say about the values of x and y?

12. **LATITUDE** The distance north or south of the equator is called a location's latitude. It is measured in degrees north (°N) or degrees south (°S). The latitudes and the average high temperatures in January are listed in the table for selected cities. Draw a scatter plot of the data and describe any patterns that you see.

Latitude (°N)	4	12	20	26	33	40	45	49	59	61
Temperature (°C)	19	33	19	23	13	6	−6	5	−24	−7

In Exercises 13–16, plot the points in a coordinate plane.

13. $(0, -3), (6, 4), (1, -1), (-5, -5), (-1, 2)$
14. $(4, 5), (-7, 1), (-2, 0), (5, -6), (-3, -1)$
15. $(-6, -2), (2, 0), (-4, 3), (8, 1), (0, 0)$
16. $(-9, 7), (0, 5), (-5, -2), (3, 2), (1, -6)$

17. **AIR TEMPERATURES** The temperatures at various heights (in km) above Earth's surface are listed in the table. Draw a scatter plot of the data and describe any patterns that you see.

Height (km)	2	4	6	8	10	12	14	16
Temperature (°C)	11	−2	−15	−28	−41	−54	−67	−80

18. **ASTRONOMY** The table below lists the distances of the nine planets from the sun. The distances are given in astronomical units (AU) with Earth's distance as 1. Revolution times are given in Earth years. Draw a scatter plot of the data. If there were a planet 25 AU from the sun, how many Earth years would you expect it to take to revolve around the sun?

	Mercury	Venus	Earth	Mars	Jupiter	Saturn	Uranus	Neptune	Pluto
Distance from sun (AU)	0.4	0.7	1	1.5	5.2	9.6	19.2	30.1	39.5
Years for 1 revolution	0.2	0.6	1	1.9	11.9	29.5	84	165	248

The Great Red Spot on Jupiter is a huge hurricane-like feature that was first observed by Gailileo in 1610.

SPORTING GOODS In Exercises 19–22, use the table below. It shows the profits or losses your business had each month for a year. (Positive numbers represent profits and negative numbers represent losses.)

	Jan.	Feb.	Mar.	Apr.	May	June	July	Aug.	Sept.	Oct.	Nov.	Dec.
Equipment	$832	$325	$275	−$120	$450	$875	$761	$0	−$104	−$515	$290	$650
Clothing	$515	$98	$104	−$52	$317	$608	$384	$25	−$30	−$324	$363	$521

19. Draw a scatter plot of the data.

20. Describe any patterns you see in the scatter plot.

21. If the profit on equipment was $200 in a month, what would you expect the profit on clothing to be?

22. If there was a $200 loss (−$200) on clothing, what would you expect to have on equipment?

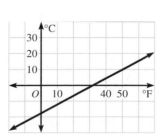

STANDARDIZED TEST PRACTICE

23. In which quadrant of a coordinate plane would you find the coordinates (−3, −4)?

    A Quadrant I   **B** Quadrant II

    C Quadrant III   **D** Quadrant IV

24. Use the graph to convert 50°F to degrees Celsius.

    A 0°C   **B** 8°C   **C** 10°C   **D** 13°C

25. BUILDING YOUR PROJECT A survey of 100 women and 100 men tells how they find the programs they want to watch on TV. Among the women, 45 use program listings, 31 flip channels, and 18 use both methods. Among the men, 34 use program listings, 43 flip channels, and 20 use both methods.

a. Include a graph representing this data in your article. You may use a bar graph or a scatter plot.

b. Explain why you chose the graph you did, and write a paragraph that interprets the graph for your readers.

SPIRAL REVIEW

In Exercises 1–6, evaluate the expression. (2.1)

1. $3 - 6 \div 2 + 7$ **2.** $5 \times 20 - 8 \div 4$ **3.** $6 + 15 \div 3 - 1$

4. $25 + 5 \div 5 - 2$ **5.** $20 + 10 \times 15 \div 5$ **6.** $8 + 12 \div 2 \times 3$

7. GEOMETRY Square tiles are available whose sides are a whole number of feet. Find the different sizes that can be used to tile a 24 ft-by-32 ft rectangular room. Use only one size tile at a time. How many tiles are used for each tiling? **(2.5)**

In Exercises 8–10, use the number line to find the letter that represents the solution of the problem. (3.3–3.5)

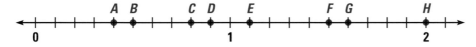

8. $A + B$ **9.** $F - A$ **10.** $H \times C$

In Exercises 11–16, solve the equation. Then check the solution. (4.6, 4.7)

11. $m + 16 = 7$ **12.** $-18 = 3 + x$ **13.** $-8 + p = -8$

14. $t - 26 = -12$ **15.** $8.2 = n - 6.2$ **16.** $1\frac{4}{5} + y = 2\frac{9}{10}$

PRESIDENTS In Exercises 17 and 18, use the following data showing the ages of the presidents of the United States when they were inaugurated. (5.2)

57, 61, 57, 57, 58, 57, 61, 54, 68, 51, 49, 64, 50, 48, 65, 52,
56, 46, 54, 49, 51, 47, 55, 55, 54, 42, 51, 56, 55, 51, 54, 51,
60, 62, 43, 55, 56, 61, 52, 69, 64, 46

17. Create a frequency table for the data.

18. Draw a histogram for the data and describe the patterns you see.

Take this test as you would take a test in class. The answers to the exercises are given in the back of the book.

In Exercises 1–3, find the mean, median, and mode of the data. (5.1)

1. Number of CDs purchased in one year by 20 teenagers:

4, 2, 3, 0, 5, 6, 4, 4, 0, 6, 2, 2, 5, 1, 6, 4, 3, 4, 6, 5

2. Price of 10 types of sneakers:

$60, $45, $65, $65, $45, $35, $55, $40, $45, $35

3. Number of points scored in 13 football games:

14, 23, 30, 21, 3, 10, 9, 19, 21, 13, 27, 24, 7

4. FARMLAND The data below show the amount of land (in millions of acres) used for farming in 1996. (States with less than half a million acres of farmland are not included.) Make a frequency table for the data and draw a histogram. (Source: U.S. Department of Agriculture) **(5.2)**

AL 10	**CO** 33	**ID** 14	**KY** 14	**MI** 11	**NE** 47	**NC** 9	**PA** 8	**UT** 11
AK 1	**DE** 1	**IL** 28	**LA** 9	**MN** 30	**NV** 9	**ND** 40	**SC** 5	**VT** 1
AZ 35	**FL** 10	**IN** 16	**ME** 1	**MS** 13	**NJ** 1	**OH** 15	**SD** 44	**VA** 9
AR 15	**GA** 12	**IA** 33	**MD** 2	**MO** 30	**NM** 44	**OK** 34	**TN** 12	**WA** 16
CA 30	**HI** 2	**KS** 48	**MA** 1	**MT** 60	**NY** 8	**OR** 18	**TX** 129	**WV** 4
WI 17	**WY** 35							

SOAP **In Exercises 5 and 6, use the data for number of hand washes possible from 14 kinds of soap bars.** (Source: Consumer Reports) **(5.3)**

90, 80, 80, 81, 100, 67, 90, 62, 52, 70, 71, 70, 41, 62

5. Make a box-and-whisker plot for the data.

6. Use the box-and-whisker plot in Exercise 5 to write a statement about the data.

In Exercises 7 and 8, plot the points in a coordinate plane. (5.4)

7. $(0, -4), (5, 6), (-3, -3), (-5, 1), (2, -7)$

8. $(-1, 0), (7, -7), (-6, 2), (3, 8), (-2, -4)$

MINIATURE GOLF **In Exercises 9 and 10, use the table at the right showing scores for the first nine holes of a miniature golf game. A minus score represents the amount under par. A plus score represents the amount over par. (5.4)**

9. Draw a scatter plot of the data.

10. Describe any patterns you see in your scatter plot.

Hole	Score
1	+3
2	+1
3	+2
4	+1
5	−1
6	−2
7	−2
8	−2
9	−1

5.5

Using Appropriate Graphs

What you should learn:

Goal 1 How to use bar graphs and pictographs

Goal 2 How to use line graphs

Why you should learn it:

You can use different types of graphs to represent real-life data. An example is drawing a graph to show the amount of cheese that Americans eat.

Goal 1 DOUBLE BAR GRAPHS AND PICTOGRAPHS

In a double bar graph, different colored bars are used to compare two data sets. A **pictograph** uses pictures or symbols to represent data.

Example 1 Reading a Double Bar Graph

Use the double bar graph to compare the amount of American cheese and Italian cheese eaten per person in the United States.

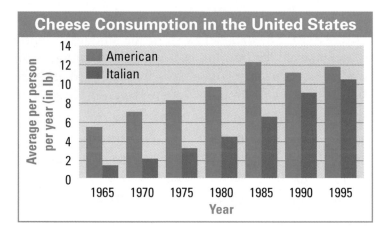

From 1965 to 1985, people ate much more American cheese than Italian cheese. By 1995, consumption of the two types of cheese was nearly equal.

Example 2 Using a Pictograph

Another way to graph data is with a pictograph. Each symbol in the pictograph below represents 2 pounds of cheese.

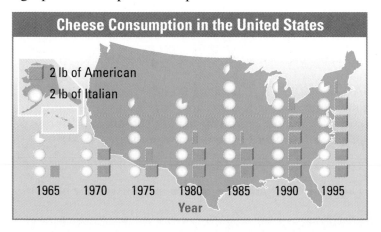

Example 3 **Reading a Line Graph**

REAL LIFE
Eating Trends

What patterns can you see in the line graph?

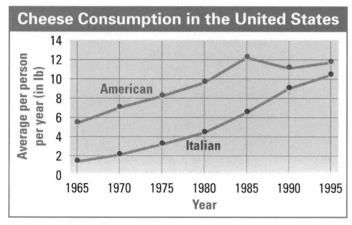

Cheese Consumption in the United States

Average per person per year (in lb)

American

Italian

Year

After 1985, consumption of American cheese decreased, while consumption of Italian cheese kept increasing.

Example 4 **Drawing a Line Graph**

Draw a line graph for the average amount (in quarts) of milk consumed per person as shown in the table below.

Year	1965	1970	1975	1980	1985	1990	1995
Whole	120	106	87	71	60	44	36
Lowfat	9	15	27	35	42	49	48

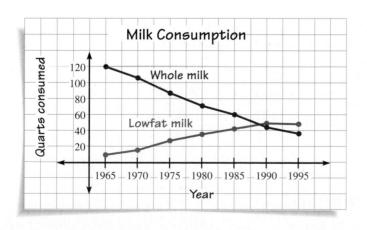

Milk Consumption

Quarts consumed

Whole milk

Lowfat milk

Year

ONGOING ASSESSMENT

Write About It

Use the line graphs in Examples 3 and 4 to predict the consumption of the following foods in the year 2000. Explain your reasoning.

1. American cheese

2. Italian cheese

3. Whole milk

4. Lowfat milk

GUIDED PRACTICE

In Exercises 1 and 2, use the table at the right. It shows the average number of visits to a doctor per person per year for each age group in 1994. (Source: Statistical Abstact of the United States, 1996)

Age	Number
2–4	6.8
5–17	3.5
18–24	3.9
25–44	5.5
45–64	7.3

1. Make a bar graph of the data in the table.

2. Explain why making a line graph of the data in the table would not make sense.

USING A GRAPH In Exercises 3–5, use the pictograph at the right. It shows the number of feet per second that insects can fly.

3. Estimate the number of feet per second that each insect flies.

4. How many insects can fly four or more feet in one second?

5. How many more feet can a bumblebee fly in one second than a damselfly?

How Far Insects Fly in 1 second

Damselfly	
Bumblebee	
Honeybee	
Housefly	
Mosquito	= 2 ft

PRACTICE AND PROBLEM SOLVING

In Exercises 6–9, use a line graph or a bar graph to represent the data in the table. Use your graph to write a statement about the data.

6.

Age	9	10	11	12	13
Height (in.)	48	49	51	54	58

7.

Year	1993	1994	1995	1996	1997
Number	15	18	20	21	24

8.

Age	0	1	2	3	4
Value	$98	$86	$74	$58	$42

9.

Year	1993	1994	1995	1996	1997
Value	$7	$6	$4	$2	$1

FRUIT JUICE SALES In Exercises 10–12, use the data below showing the amount (in millions of gallons) of fruit juice sold for the five top-selling juices in 1996. (Source: Florida Department of Citrus)

Juice	Orange	Grape	Apple	Grapefruit	Blends
Amount	722	63	170	42	92

10. Make a bar graph of the data.

11. Make a pictograph of the data.

12. Which kind of graph do you prefer? Why?

13. SPECIAL OLYMPICS The table below shows the number of athletes (in thousands) who participated in the New Jersey Special Olympics. Draw a line graph of the data.

Year	1987	1988	1989	1990	1991	1992	1993	1994	1995	1996
Number	5	4	5	5	7	7	9	10	10	12

14. USING A GRAPH The data below show the average number of hours worked in a week by each of 30 people. Select a type of graph to represent the data. Explain your selection. Then make the graph.

40, 42, 40, 38, 51, 39, 40, 40, 62, 45, 35, 43, 44, 74, 45, 40, 40, 36, 40, 60, 50, 40, 37, 40, 46, 40, 64, 42, 40, 40

15. PICKLES One hundred people were asked to name their favorite pickle. The results are shown in the table below. Make a pictograph of the data.

Type	Dill	Sweet	Garlic	Bread & Butter	All Others
Number	83	45	24	48	10

STANDARDIZED TEST PRACTICE

16. In a pictograph, one symbol represents three units. How many units do three symbols represent?

(**A**) 2 (**B**) 6 (**C**) 9 (**D**) 12

17. In a pictograph, one symbol represents 2 units. How many symbols should you draw to represent 12 units?

(**A**) 2 (**B**) 6 (**C**) 9 (**D**) 12

PORTFOLIO

EXPLORATION AND EXTENSION

18. BUILDING YOUR PROJECT The data below show the average number of television sets per household in the United States. Represent this data with a graph. Explain the meaning of the graph in your article and explain why you chose the graph you did.

Year	1986	1987	1988	1989	1990	1991	1992	1993	1994	1995	1996
Number	1.8	1.9	1.9	1.9	2.1	2.1	2.1	2.2	2.2	2.2	2.3

Misleading Graphs

Goal 1 **MISLEADING BAR GRAPHS**

Sometimes graphs can be misleading. You need to be able to recognize distortions in graphs so that you can interpret them correctly.

LESSON INVESTIGATION

COOPERATIVE LEARNING

Investigating Bar Graphs

GROUP ACTIVITY Both bar graphs represent the same data. Which graph is misleading? Why?

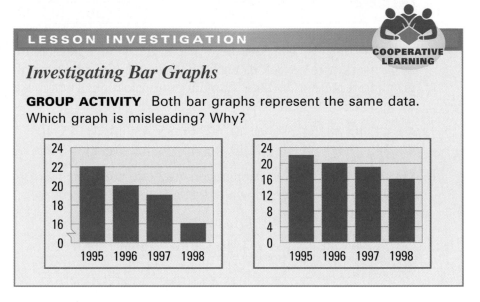

Example 1 **Interpreting a Bar Graph**

Use the graph below to compare the amount of chocolate eaten in Switzerland with the amount eaten in the United States.

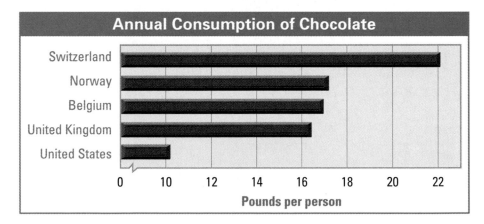

Annual Consumption of Chocolate

Solution

The lengths of the bars make it appear that about five times as much chocolate is eaten in Switzerland as in the United States. From the scale, however, you can see that only a little more than twice as much chocolate is consumed by the Swiss.

Goal ② MISLEADING LINE GRAPHS

When the vertical axis of a graph is broken, the scale distorts the data.

Example 2 **Interpreting Line Graphs**

REAL LIFE
Florists

Each of the line graphs below shows the wholesale cost (in millions of dollars) of cut flowers used by florist shops from 1990 through 1995. Compare the top two graphs with the bottom two graphs. Describe the differences.

(Source: Statistical Abstract of the United States, 1996)

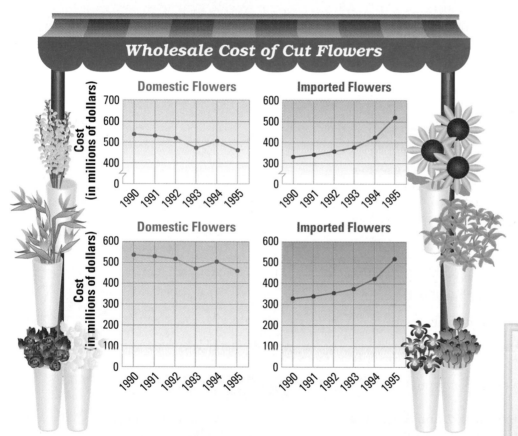

Wholesale Cost of Cut Flowers

Solution

The top two graphs are misleading. The bottom two are not. The top two graphs make it appear that the amount of imported cut flowers has greatly exceeded the amount of cut flowers grown in the United States. The broken vertical scales in the top two graphs exaggerate the changes from one year to the next.

ONGOING ASSESSMENT

Talk About It

Search newspapers and magazines to find graphs that are misleading.

1. Discuss the graphs with your partner.

2. Do you think the graphs were intended to be misleading? Explain why.

GUIDED PRACTICE

1. **WRITING** State how a graph can be misleading. Give an example.

MUSIC In Exercises 2 and 3, use the graph showing the average number of hours Americans spend listening to recorded music in a year. (Source: Veronis, Suhler & Associates)

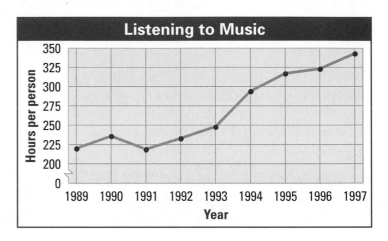

2. Without looking at the scale of the graph, compare the number of hours of recorded music listened to by a person in 1991 with the number of hours in 1996.

3. Use the scale to determine the answer to Exercise 2. Explain why the graph is misleading.

PRACTICE AND PROBLEM SOLVING

SPORTS ACTIVITIES In Exercises 4–6, use the bar graph at the right. It shows the number of Americans (in millions), ages 12 to 17, who participated in various sports activities in 1994. (Source: National Sporting Goods Association)

4. By looking at the length of the bars, compare the number of people who bicycled to the number of people who played volleyball.

5. Use the scale to determine the answer to Exercise 4. Then explain why the graph is misleading.

6. Create a bar graph that is *not* misleading.

USING A GRAPH In Exercises 7 and 8, use the bar graph at the right. It shows the number of people out of 100 from different regions of the United States who prefer the Summer or Winter Olympics. (Source: ESPN/Chilton Sport Poll)

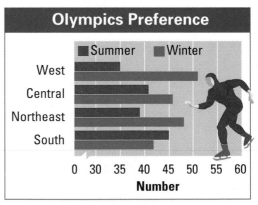

7. Without looking at the scale, compare the data. Then explain why the graph is misleading.

8. Create a bar graph that is *not* misleading.

MOTION PICTURES In Exercises 9–13, use the two line graphs at the right. They show the amount of money in (billions of dollars) Americans spent to see motion pictures from 1990 through 1996. (Source: U.S. Bureau of Census)

9. Describe the general trend in spending shown by the two graphs.

10. Compare the dollar amount spent in 1996 with the dollar amount spent in 1990. What was the amount of increase?

11. Compute the average amount of increase each year.

12. Which graph is misleading? Explain your reasoning.

13. Draw another set of graphs, one that accurately shows the data and one that is misleading.

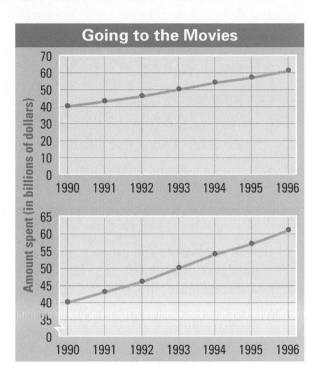

14. Which of the following is *not* a misleading part of the graph at the right?

   (A) Vertical scale uses only even numbers.

   (B) Vertical scale is broken.

   (C) Horizontal scale is uneven.

   (D) Meaning of vertical scale is unknown.

15. Which of the following conclusions can you make from the graph at the right?

   (A) Data values increased steadily each year.

   (B) Data values more than doubled between 1980 and 1991.

   (C) Data value reached a minimum in 1992.

   (D) Data values were equal in 1991 and 1995.

16. The number of units a company produces in a day ranges from 12 to 18. Estimate a reasonable total number of units produced in 5 days.

   (A) 30 units   (B) 55 units   (C) 75 units   (D) 100 units

17. COMMUNICATING ABOUT MATHEMATICS The table shows the number of hours people spent each year watching network stations and the number of hours they spent watching basic cable stations.

Year	1990	1991	1992	1993	1994	1995	1996
Network	780	838	914	920	919	913	909
Cable	260	340	359	375	388	398	408

a. Draw two line graphs of this data. One graph should mislead your readers; the other should not.

b. Explain how the misleading graph distorts the data.

SPIRAL REVIEW

1. USING A GRAPH The graph at the right shows the number of students out of 100 that prefer to study in a certain room. Order the rooms from least used for study to most used for study. (Source: Federal National Mortgage Association) **(1.9)**

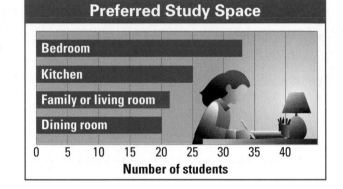

Preferred Study Space

2. PROBLEM SOLVING Imagine that you are a chef planning food for a wedding. You are preparing a total of 80 lb of potatoes. If you divide up the potatoes evenly among the 15 tables, how many pounds will each table receive? How many pounds will each person receive if there are 8 people to a table? **(2.7, 3.7)**

In Exercises 3–6, match the number with its equivalent fraction or decimal. (3.2)

A. 2.2

B. $\dfrac{5}{2}$

C. $\dfrac{12}{5}$

D. 2.25

3. $\dfrac{9}{4}$

4. $2\dfrac{1}{2}$

5. $2\dfrac{1}{5}$

6. $2\dfrac{2}{5}$

7. Use the following description to make a table of values for $c = 1, 2, 3, 4,$ and 5. Write an expression that represents the table. **(4.1, 4.4)**

The value of the expression begins at −3. Each time c increases by 1, the value of the expression increases by 2.

In Exercises 8 and 9, order the data from least to greatest. Use a calculator to find the mean. Then find the median and mode. (5.1)

8. 11, 10, 10, 13, 11, 12, 14, 11, 8, 12, 13, 14, 11

9. 4, 2, 5, 3, 3, 4, 4, 4, 4, 7, 2, 1, 0, 5, 5, 4

WHO'S WATCHING WHAT?

READ About It

A dvertisers want to know who watches TV. They also are interested in the hours during which people watch and the programs that people favor, as shown in the chart below. With this data, advertisers can run ads aimed at viewers who are the most likely to buy their products. The next time you watch TV, pay attention to the products that are advertised. Were they products that interest you?

One hundred homes were polled about their TV-viewing habits. During prime time from 8:00 P.M. to 11:00 P.M., the viewers included 60 men and 76 women over the age of 18. During the same time period, 12 teens (ages 12 to 17) and 14 children (ages 2 to 11) were watching TV. The pattern was different on Saturday mornings, where viewers included 40 adult men, 45 adult women, 13 teens, and 36 children.

WRITE About It

1. How did the number of men watching TV during prime time compare with the number of men watching on Saturday morning? Draw a bar graph to illustrate these statistics.

2. How many more men than children watch TV during prime time? How might the answer to this question be different if only men between the ages of 18 and 25 had been studied instead of all men over 18? Explain your reasoning.

3. Use the chart to find how many hours per week the average viewer watched sitcoms in 1985 compared with 1995.

4. Referring to the chart, describe the popularity of drama series from 1985 to 1995.

5. From the chart, create a line graph comparing sports viewing time with newscast viewing time.

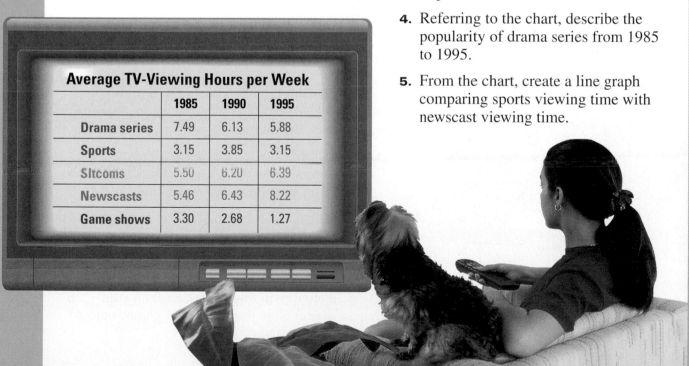

Average TV-Viewing Hours per Week

	1985	1990	1995
Drama series	7.49	6.13	5.88
Sports	3.15	3.85	3.15
Sitcoms	5.50	6.20	6.39
Newscasts	5.46	6.43	8.22
Game shows	3.30	2.68	1.27

LAB 5.7
COOPERATIVE LEARNING

Investigating Probability

Materials Needed
• number cube

Everyone in your class is going to analyze a game of chance. To begin, copy the table shown below. Then for each of the ten games, circle two numbers.

Game	My Numbers	Winning Numbers	Win or Lose?	Number of Winners in Class
1	1 2 3 4 5 6			
2	1 2 3 4 5 6			
3	1 2 3 4 5 6			
4	1 2 3 4 5 6			
5	1 2 3 4 5 6			
6	1 2 3 4 5 6			
7	1 2 3 4 5 6			
8	1 2 3 4 5 6			
9	1 2 3 4 5 6			
10	1 2 3 4 5 6			

Now you are ready to play ten games. Your teacher will toss a number cube once and read the number. Then your teacher will toss the number cube again until a different number comes up. If *both* your numbers are called, you win that game. After each game, count the number of winners in your class.

1. You played only ten games. If you had played 100 games, how many do you think you would have won? Explain your reasoning.

2. Multiply the number of students in your class by 10. This is the total number of games played by your class. How many winners were there?

3. After answering Exercise 2, does it seem as though a person is very likely to win this game? Explain your reasoning. Does your answer change the number of games out of 100 you think a person is likely to win? Explain.

In Part A, you played a game and used the results to find the experimental probability of winning the game. Now you will use mathematics to find the *theoretical probability* of winning.

4. Count the number of different pairs of numbers that could be tossed. Organize your results with a list. Here are some of the possibilities. Note that "1 and 2" is the same as "2 and 1."

5. Use the results of Exercise 4 to find the probability of winning the game. Write your answer as a fraction.

$$\text{Probability of winning} = \frac{\text{Number of pairs that win}}{\text{Total number of pairs}}$$

$$= \frac{1}{\text{Total number of pairs}}$$

6. Multiply the fraction in Exercise 5 by 100. This is the theoretical number of games you could expect to win out of 100 games.

NOW TRY THESE

ACT IT OUT In Exercises 7 and 8, choose 3 numbers for each game instead of 2 numbers. Here are some of the possible tosses.

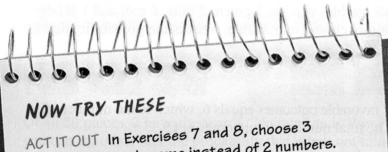

7. Describe and perform an experiment that allows you to estimate the number of times out of 100 that you would win this game.

8. List all the different triples of numbers that could be tossed. How many times out of 100 would you expect to win this game?

WHAT did you learn?

WHY did you learn it?

Skills

5.1	Find the mean, median, and mode of data.	Describe the average length of a jury trial.
5.2	Organize data with a frequency table. Draw a histogram.	Compare state gasoline taxes.
5.3	Draw a box-and-whisker plot for data.	Analyze the price ranges of cars.
5.4	Plot points in a coordinate plane. Draw a scatter plot.	Represent and compare two temperature scales.
5.5	Select and use an appropriate graph.	Compare food consumption data.
5.6	Recognize misleading graphs.	Analyze how a graph is misleading.
5.7	Find the probability of an event.	Use probability analysis to plan an event.

Strategies

5.1–5.7	Use problem solving strategies.	Solve a wide variety of real-life problems.

Using Data

5.1–5.7	Use tables and graphs.	Organize and graph real-life data.

HOW does it fit into the bigger picture of mathematics?

Some people have a poor opinion of data analysis and statistics. They say, "You can prove anything you want with statistics."

Tables and graphs appear in company annual reports, books, magazines, and newspapers. You need to be able to interpret different kinds of graphs and recognize when a graph is intentionally misleading.

You may need to analyze and present data in a school or work situation. Suppose your manager asked you to present sales figures to the Board of Directors. You should select the graph that best represents the data.

Method **1** Use a bar graph to compare sales for different years.

Method **2** Draw a pictograph to compare sales of different products.

Method **3** Prepare a line graph to show the monthly change in sales.

VOCABULARY

- measure of central tendency (p. 220)
- mean (p. 220)
- median (p. 220)
- mode (p. 220)
- frequency table (p. 226)

- frequency (p. 226)
- range (p. 226)
- histogram (p. 227)
- second quartile (p. 234)
- first quartile (p. 234)
- third quartile (p. 234)

- box-and-whisker plot (p. 234)
- quadrant (p. 238)
- pictograph (p. 244)
- probability of an event (p. 256)

5.1 MEASURES OF CENTRAL TENDENCY

A measure of central tendency is a single number that is used to represent a set of data. The mean, median, and mode are measures of central tendency.

Example The ordered list of data below shows the number of books 10 students read in a summer. Find the mean, median, and mode of the data.

3, 6, 6, 6, 8, 8, 11, 12, 15, 15

Solution The mean of the data is 90 divided by 10, or 9 books. The median is 8. The mode is 6, the number that occurs most often.

In Exercises 1–3, use the following costs of 18 models of CD players.

$315, $400, $250, $470, $195, $370, $290, $400, $425
$350, $500, $350, $220, $420, $250, $310, $400, $385

1. Find the mean. **2.** Find the median. **3.** Find the mode.

5.2 HISTOGRAMS

A frequency table is used to organize and summarize large amounts of data. You can represent the data in a frequency table by using a bar graph known as a histogram.

Example The frequency table at the right shows the quiz scores of 20 students in a math class.

14, 7, 18, 15, 13, 5, 11, 20, 17, 16, 19, 12, 10, 14, 17, 18, 17, 16, 20, 17

Interval	Tally	Frequency
0–2		0
3–5	I	1
6–8	I	1
9–11	II	2
12–14	IIII	4
15–17	JHT II	7
18–20	JHT	5

In Exercises 4 and 5, use the data above and the table at the right.

4. Make another frequency table for the data using intervals of 4. Compare the two.

5. Draw histograms for the frequency table you drew for Exercise 4 and the frequency table at the right. How do the two histograms compare?

1. **TALLEST BUILDINGS** The data below show the heights (in meters) of the world's 10 tallest buildings. Find the mean, median and mode of the data.

    374, 415, 452, 348, 442, 381, 421, 417, 452, 369

2. **POPULATIONS** The data below show the projected urban populations (in millions) for the year 2000. Make a frequency table and histogram for the data.

Tokyo	27.9	**Calcutta**	12.7
New York City	16.6	**Buenos Aires**	11.4
Mexico City	16.4	**Seoul**	12.3
São Paulo	17.8	**Osaka**	10.6
Shanghai	17.2	**Rio de Janeiro**	10.2
Bombay	18.1	**Paris**	9.6
Los Angeles	13.1	**Tianjin**	12.4
Beijing	14.2		

3. Draw a box-and-whisker plot for the following data.

    24, 12, 26, 9, 13, 30, 19, 22, 16, 4, 24, 28, 26, 20

4. The table lists the average heights and weights of five breeds of dogs. Draw a scatter plot of the data and describe any patterns that you see.

	Cocker spaniel	St. Bernard	Chihuahua	Irish wolfhound	Collie
Height (in.)	15	25	5	33	24
Weight (lb)	25	183	3	136	65

5. **FITNESS** In 1995, Americans were asked to name the fitness activities that they participated in most often. The data (millions of people) were as follows: fitness walking, 17.2; free weights, 11.3; stationary biking, 9.4; running or jogging, 9.4; treadmill, 7; and resistance machines, 6.2. Choose a type of graph to represent the data. Explain your choice. Draw the graph and use it to write a statement about fitness. (Source: The Fitness Products Council)

BASEBALL In Questions 6 and 7, use the following record showing how you did your last 100 times at bat. You got 8 home runs, 4 triples, 10 doubles, 20 singles, 6 walks, 2 sacrifices, and 50 outs.

6. From this record, estimate the probability that you will get a home run your next time at bat.

7. From this record, estimate the probability that you will not get a walk your next time at bat.

1. Songs on a CD are 4.8, 3.9, 4.2, 5.0, 4.4, 4.4, 5.5, 4.2, 3.1, 4.8, 4.2, 5.5 min long. Which statement is *false*?

   (A) The mode of the data is 4.4.

   (B) Twelve songs are on the CD.

   (C) The mean of the data is 4.5.

   (D) The median of the data is 4.4.

Questions 2 and 3 refer to the histogram.

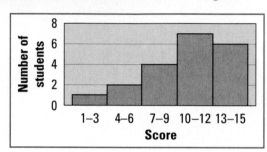

2. The most frequent point range is

   (A) 4–6.   (B) 7–9.

   (C) 10–12.   (D) 13–15.

3. How many scored in the 7–9 range?

   (A) 2   (B) 3

   (C) 4   (D) 5

4. Which set of data is represented by the box-and-whisker plot?

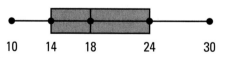

   (A) 23, 14, 25, 28, 15, 11, 30, 21, 14, 27, 12, 20, 14, 16, 11, 20

   (B) 14, 25, 20, 10, 28, 15, 23, 12, 14, 27, 11, 14, 21, 16, 20, 28

   (C) 21, 15, 10, 14, 27, 20, 28, 23, 14, 30, 12, 25, 20, 14, 16, 11

   (D) 18, 27, 14, 23, 25, 30, 10, 12, 20, 15, 28, 11, 14, 21, 14, 20

5. The scatter plot shows temperatures from 7:00 A.M. to 11:00 A.M. If the rate of increase stays the same, what will the temperature be at noon?

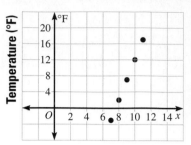

   Time

   (A) 22°F   (B) 31°F

   (C) 33°F   (D) 38°F

6. The bar graph shows your highest bowling score for each year. Which statement is false?

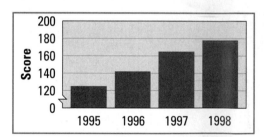

   (A) The data also can be shown as a line graph.

   (B) Your high score in 1997 was twice your high score in 1995.

   (C) Your score got higher each year.

   (D) The bar graph is misleading.

7. A box has 3 orange, 5 apple, and 4 grape juice bars. If you randomly choose one, what is the probability that it is grape?

   (A) $\frac{5}{12}$ (B) $\frac{1}{8}$

   (C) $\frac{1}{4}$ (D) $\frac{1}{3}$

Ratios and Proportions

TECHNOLOGY

Technology resources accompanying this chapter:
• Interactive Real-Life Investigations
• Middle School Tutorial Software

UNDERWATER PHOTOGRAPHY This photograph shows a scuba diving photographer maneuvering to take a deep sea picture.

MICROSCOPIC PHOTOGRAPHY This photo of a young storage cell of a leaf was taken using a transmission electron microscope.

CHAPTER THEME
Photography

SATELLITE PHOTOGRAPHY This photographic image gathered by satellites shows the five Great Lakes and their surrounding region.

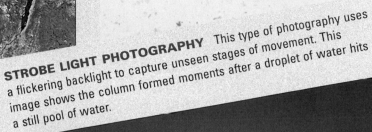

STROBE LIGHT PHOTOGRAPHY This type of photography uses a flickering backlight to capture unseen stages of movement. This image shows the column formed moments after a droplet of water hits a still pool of water.

Make a Camera

REAL LIFE
Photography

Various types of **photography** can be done using different cameras. The simplest cameras are pinhole cameras. You can make one with a box, some tape, scissors, a sheet of waxed paper, and a pin.

Cut an opening (about 3 in. by 3 in.) in one side of the box and tape waxed paper over it. Use the pin to make a small hole in the side opposite the waxed paper. Tape the box shut so light enters only through the pinhole.

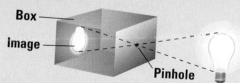

Box
Image
Pinhole

Think and Discuss

1. In a darkened room, point the pinhole at a bright object such as a lightbulb. Measure the image of the light on the waxed paper and measure the distance between the pinhole and the lightbulb.

2. Make the distance between the pinhole and the lightbulb twice the original distance and measure the height of the image.

3. Make measurements at other distances and describe how the height of the image is related to the distance between the pinhole and the lightbulb.

CHAPTER 6

PORTFOLIO

CHAPTER PROJECT

Writing a Photography Manual

PROJECT DESCRIPTION

Imagine that you are a professional photographer. You keep a log of certain aspects of your work to teach your assistant some photography basics. To create your manual, you will use the list of **TOPICS** on the next page.

GETTING STARTED

Talking It Over

- Discuss in your group what you know about cameras. Do you like to take pictures? Do you know how film is developed? Do you know how the shutter works?

- Imagine that you are a professional photographer. Would you like to specialize in taking portraits, nature pictures, or something else? Discuss how your specialty would affect your work and the way you sold your pictures. Discuss the different ways photographs are used in the real world.

Planning Your Project

- **Materials Needed:** paper, pencils or pens, tape, glue, scissors

- Fold several pieces of paper in half to make a booklet. On the front cover, write your name and "Photography Manual." If you like, decorate the cover of your booklet with drawings or photographs. Place the booklet in your portfolio. As you complete the **BUILDING YOUR PROJECT** exercises throughout the chapter, keep track of your results in the booklet.

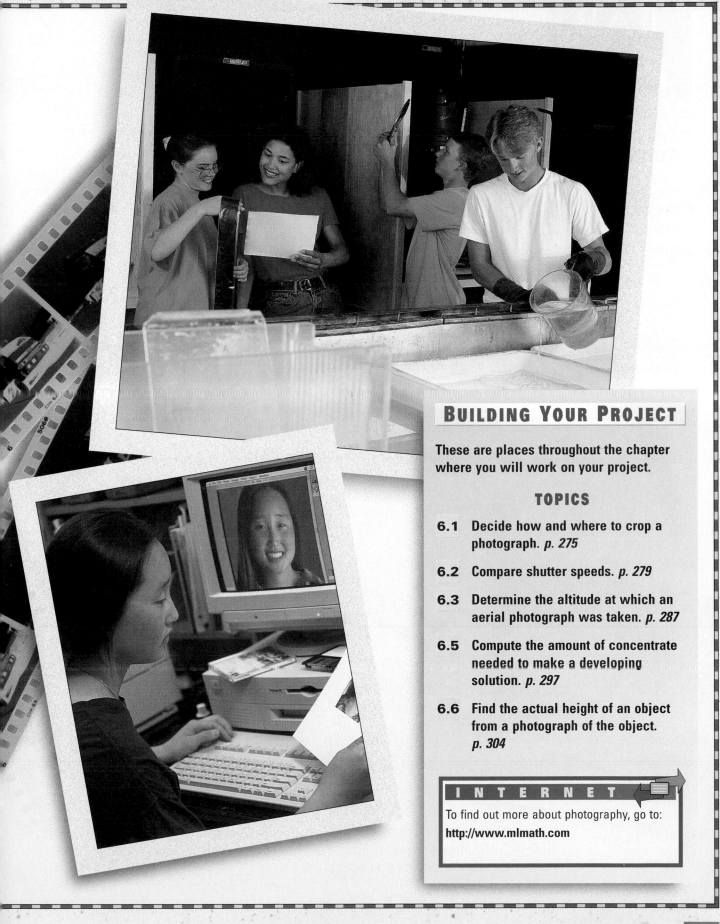

BUILDING YOUR PROJECT

These are places throughout the chapter where you will work on your project.

TOPICS

6.1 Decide how and where to crop a photograph. *p. 275*

6.2 Compare shutter speeds. *p. 279*

6.3 Determine the altitude at which an aerial photograph was taken. *p. 287*

6.5 Compute the amount of concentrate needed to make a developing solution. *p. 297*

6.6 Find the actual height of an object from a photograph of the object. *p. 304*

I N T E R N E T

To find out more about photography, go to:
http://www.mlmath.com

LAB 6.1

COOPERATIVE LEARNING

Investigating Ratios

Materials Needed
- paper
- pencils or pens

Part A COMPARING SETS

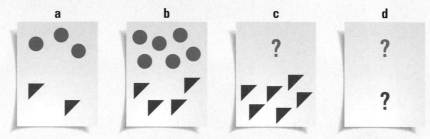

a   b   c   d

1. With your partner, discuss the relationship between the numbers of circles and triangles in **a** and **b**.

2. Copy boxes **a** through **d**. If the relationship between the numbers of circles and triangles continues, how many circles should be in **c**? Sketch your solution and explain your reasoning.

3. Sketch the appropriate numbers of circles and triangles in **d**. Explain your reasoning.

Part B DESCRIBING A RELATIONSHIP

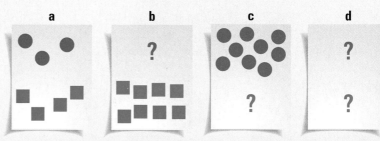

a   b   c   d

4. Write the fraction that is represented by the numbers of circles and squares in **a**.

$$\frac{\text{Number of circles}}{\text{Number of squares}} = \frac{?}{?}$$

5. Copy the boxes. Complete **b** and **c** so that their fractions will simplify to the same fraction as the fraction for **a**.

6. Sketch the appropriate numbers of circles and squares in **d**. Explain your reasoning. Find and simplify the fraction for this box. What can you conclude?

Commission	$3600	$5400	?	$9000
Cost of house	$60,000	$90,000	$120,000	?

7. Suppose you are a real-estate agent. Your commission for selling a house is based on the cost of the house. You are given two examples of commissions. With your partner, decide how much commission you would charge for selling the third house and find the cost of the fourth house.

8. For each of the houses, write the following fraction.

$$\frac{\text{Commission}}{\text{Cost of house}} = \frac{?}{?}$$

Simplify each fraction. What can you conclude?

NOW TRY THESE

In Exercises 9–12, use a fraction to compare the number of blue regions to the number of red regions in the shaded figure. Simplify the fraction. Then copy the second figure and shade it completely so that its "blue to red" fraction simplifies to the same fraction.

9.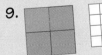

10.

11.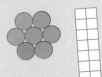

12.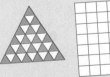

6.1

Ratios

What you should learn:

Goal 1 How to find a ratio

Goal 2 How to decide whether two ratios are equivalent

Why you should learn it:

Knowing how to find ratios can help you compare two quantities. An example is comparing the number of fish in two aquariums.

Goal 1 FINDING RATIOS

One of the ways that you can compare the measures of two quantities is with a quotient called a *ratio*.

> **RATIO**
>
> If two quantities a and b have the same unit of measure, then the **ratio** of a to b is $\dfrac{a}{b}$.

Example 1 Finding Ratios

For the two tanks below, find the ratio of fish in Tank A to Tank B. Then find the ratio of the volume of water in Tank A to Tank B. What can you conclude about the two ratios?

A.

10 gallons

B.

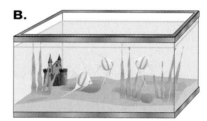

15 gallons

Solution

The ratio of fish in Tank A to Tank B is

$$\frac{\text{Fish in Tank A}}{\text{Fish in Tank B}} = \frac{2 \text{ fish}}{3 \text{ fish}}$$

> You can simplify ratios by dividing out units.

$$= \frac{2}{3}. \qquad \textbf{Find the ratio.}$$

The ratio of the volume of Tank A to Tank B is

$$\frac{\text{Volume of Tank A}}{\text{Volume of Tank B}} = \frac{10 \text{ gallons}}{15 \text{ gallons}} \qquad \textbf{Set up the ratio.}$$

$$= \frac{5 \cdot 2}{5 \cdot 3} \qquad \textbf{Factor.}$$

$$= \frac{2}{3}. \qquad \textbf{Simplify.}$$

The two ratios are equal.

Example 2 **Comparing Records**

REAL LIFE
Baseball

Use ratios to compare the records for the baseball teams at three different schools.

SCHOOL	WINS	LOSSES
Chestnut Hills School	10	8
Mae Jemison School	12	8
Buena Vista School	15	12

Which team had the best record?

Solution

One way to compare the team records is to find the ratio of wins to losses for each team.

a. For Chestnut Hills School, the ratio of wins to losses is

$$\frac{\text{Games won}}{\text{Games lost}} = \frac{10 \text{ games}}{8 \text{ games}}$$
$$= \frac{2 \cdot 5 \text{ games}}{2 \cdot 4 \text{ games}} = \frac{5}{4}.$$

b. For Mae Jemison School, the ratio of wins to losses is

$$\frac{\text{Games won}}{\text{Games lost}} = \frac{12 \text{ games}}{8 \text{ games}}$$
$$= \frac{4 \cdot 3 \text{ games}}{4 \cdot 2 \text{ games}} = \frac{3}{2}.$$

c. For Buena Vista School, the ratio of wins to losses is

$$\frac{\text{Games won}}{\text{Games lost}} = \frac{15 \text{ games}}{12 \text{ games}}$$
$$= \frac{3 \cdot 5 \text{ games}}{3 \cdot 4 \text{ games}} = \frac{5}{4}.$$

Because $\frac{3}{2}$ is greater than $\frac{5}{4}$, you can conclude that the Mae Jemison School had the best record of the three baseball teams.

ONGOING ASSESSMENT

Write About It

1. Using the information given in Example 2, find the ratio of the games won to the games played for each team.

2. Judging from these ratios, which team had the best record?

6.1 Exercises

Extra Practice, page 634

GUIDED PRACTICE

In Exercises 1 and 2, use a ratio to describe the situation.

1. One out of 3 households in the United States owns a dog.

2. A U.S. Presidential election occurs once every 4 years.

In Exercises 3 and 4, which ratio is not equal to the others?

3. $\dfrac{3 \text{ balloons}}{5 \text{ balloons}}, \dfrac{5 \text{ balloons}}{3 \text{ balloons}}, \dfrac{6 \text{ people}}{10 \text{ people}}$

4. $\dfrac{3 \text{ in.}}{12 \text{ in.}}, \dfrac{15 \text{ ft}}{60 \text{ ft}}, \dfrac{1 \text{ in.}}{12 \text{ in.}}$

5. The quotient $\dfrac{9 \text{ ft}}{5 \text{ yd}}$ is not a ratio because the units are not the same. Change the quotient to a ratio of feet to feet and to a ratio of yards to yards. Are the two ratios equal?

6. **GROUP ACTIVITY** Measure the distance from your elbow to the tip of your little finger. Then measure the distance between the tip of your thumb and the tip of your little finger when they are spread apart. What is the ratio of the first of these distances to the second? Compare your ratio with others in your group.

PRACTICE AND PROBLEM SOLVING

In Exercises 7–10, decide whether the quotient is a ratio. Explain your reasoning for each.

7. $\dfrac{5 \text{ in.}}{11}$

8. $\dfrac{4 \text{ in.}}{3 \text{ ft}}$

9. $\dfrac{6 \text{ in.}}{9 \text{ in.}}$

10. $\dfrac{10 \text{ ft}}{1 \text{ s}}$

In Exercises 11–14, rewrite the quotient as a ratio using the units in the denominator. Then rewrite as a ratio using the units in the numerator. Are the two ratios equal for each side?

11. $\dfrac{108 \text{ in.}}{2 \text{ yd}}$

12. $\dfrac{64 \text{ oz}}{1 \text{ lb}}$

13. $\dfrac{1 \text{ mi}}{10{,}560 \text{ ft}}$

14. $\dfrac{8 \text{ quarts}}{3 \text{ gal}}$

GEOMETRY In Exercises 15–17, write the ratio of the perimeter of the green region to the perimeter of the entire region.

15.
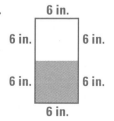

16.
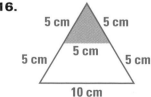

17.
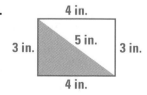

CARS In Exercises 18 and 19, use the following information about the wiring systems of cars in 1948 and in 1994. (Source: Electrical Wiring Component Application Partnership)

1948: 55 wires, 150 feet of wiring

1994: 1500 wires, 1 mile of wiring

18. Find the ratio of the number of wires in a 1948 car to the number of wires in a 1994 car.

19. Find the ratio of the length of wiring in a 1948 car to the length of wiring in a 1994 car.

HOCKEY In Exercises 20 and 21, use the bar graph at the right. It shows the nationalities of 1996 National Hockey League players. (Source: NHL)

20. Find the ratio of the number from the United States to the number from Canada.

21. Find the ratio of the number from Russia to the number from the Czech Republic.

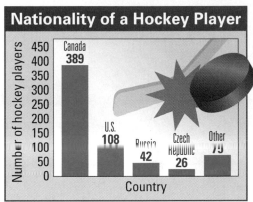

Nationality of a Hockey Player

Number of hockey players

450 400 350 300 250 200 150 100 50 0

Canada 389
U.S. 108
Russia 42
Czech Republic 26
Other 79

Country

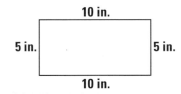 **STANDARDIZED TEST PRACTICE**

22. What is the ratio of the width of the rectangle to the perimeter of the rectangle?

   A 1 to 3   **B** 3 to 1

   C 1 to 6   **D** 6 to 1

10 in.

5 in.   5 in.

10 in.

23. During baseball season, a stadium can seat 1000 people. During football season, the stadium can seat 1500 people. What is the ratio of baseball seating to football seating?

   A 2 to 3   **B** 3 to 2   **C** 2 to 5   **D** 5 to 2

 EXPLORATION AND EXTENSION

PORTFOLIO

24. **BUILDING YOUR PROJECT** You want to enlarge a negative to be an 8 in.-by-10 in. photograph. The negative is 1 in. by $\frac{11}{8}$ in. Draw a diagram of this problem. Will you have to crop (cut off) some of the photograph? Explain your answer.

6.2

Rates

What you should learn:

Goal 1 How to find a rate

Goal 2 How to use rates to solve real-life problems

Why you should learn it:

Knowing how to find rates can help you compare speeds. An example is comparing the speeds of two people on mountain bikes.

Goal 1 FINDING RATES

A **rate** is a fraction in which the numerator and denominator have different units of measure. For example, if you ride your bicycle for 1 h and travel 4 mi, then your rate is

$$\frac{\text{Distance}}{\text{Time}} = \frac{4 \text{ mi}}{1 \text{ h}}.$$

In words, this rate is read as "4 miles per hour." In real life, rates are usually simplified so that they have a denominator of 1 unit. A rate with a denominator of 1 unit is a **unit rate**.

RATE

If two quantities a and b have different units of measure, then the **rate of a per b is $\frac{a}{b}$**.

Example 1 **Finding a Unit Rate**

TOOLBOX

Dividing Decimals, page 655

On Saturday, you baby-sit for 2.5 hours and are paid $10. On Sunday, you baby-sit for 3 hours and are paid $10.50. Find the hourly wage that you were paid on each day. Which was greater?

Solution

To find the hourly wage, divide the amount paid by the time.

$$\text{Saturday:} \quad \frac{\textbf{Amount paid}}{\textbf{Time}} = \frac{\$10}{2.5 \text{ h}} \qquad \text{Set up the rate.}$$

$$= \frac{\$10 \div 2.5}{2.5 \text{ h} \div 2.5} \qquad \text{Divide numerator and denominator by 2.5.}$$

$$= \frac{\$4}{1 \text{ h}} \qquad \text{Simplify.}$$

$$\text{Sunday:} \quad \frac{\textbf{Amount paid}}{\textbf{Time}} = \frac{\$10.50}{3 \text{ h}} \qquad \text{Set up the rate.}$$

$$= \frac{\$10.50 \div 3}{3 \text{ h} \div 3} \qquad \text{Divide numerator and denominator by 3.}$$

$$= \frac{\$3.50}{1 \text{ h}} \qquad \text{Simplify.}$$

On Saturday, you earned $4 per hour and on Sunday, $3.50 per hour. So, your hourly wage was greater on Saturday.

STUDY TIP

In real life, rate has many different names. Here are some examples.

speed in miles per hour: 55 mi/h

hourly wage in dollars per hour: $5/h

unit price in dollars per ounce: $1/oz

Example 2 **Comparing Rates**

REAL LIFE
Mountain Biking

Arnold and Jena went mountain biking on some trails in their town. Based on the information below, which one of them rode at a faster pace?

- Arnold rode 23 miles in 4 hours.
- Jena rode 16 miles in 3.5 hours.

Solution

Begin by finding each rider's speed. To determine speed, divide the distance that each person traveled by the time that it took. Then simplify to find the unit rates.

Arnold: $\dfrac{\text{Distance}}{\text{Time}} = \dfrac{23 \text{ mi}}{4 \text{ h}}$ Set up the rate.

$= \dfrac{23 \text{ mi} \div 4}{4 \text{ h} \div 4}$ Divide numerator and denominator by 4.

$= \dfrac{5.75 \text{ mi}}{1 \text{ h}}$ Simplify.

Jena: $\dfrac{\text{Distance}}{\text{Time}} = \dfrac{16 \text{ mi}}{3.5 \text{ h}}$ Set up the rate.

$= \dfrac{16 \text{ mi} \div 3.5}{3.5 \text{ h} \div 3.5}$ Divide numerator and denominator by 3.5.

$\approx \dfrac{4.6 \text{ mi}}{1 \text{ h}}$ Simplify.

Arnold rode 5.75 mi/h and Jena rode about 4.6 mi/h. So, Arnold rode his bike faster than Jena.

ONGOING ASSESSMENT

Talk About It
....

You are shopping for oranges. Which package has the smallest unit price? Which one would you buy? Discuss your reasons.

1. 2 pounds for $2.58

2. 5 pounds for $4.75

3. 8 pounds for $6.58

6.2 Exercises

GUIDED PRACTICE

1. How do rate and ratio differ? Give an example of each.

2. Write each rate below as a unit rate. If you need to complete a 75-question test in 60 minutes, which unit rate would you prefer to use to help you complete the test on time? Explain.

   A. $\dfrac{60 \text{ min}}{75 \text{ questions}}$

   B. $\dfrac{75 \text{ questions}}{60 \text{ min}}$

3. **TRAVEL** You drove 1350 mi in 3 days. Each day you drove for 9 h. What was your average speed?

PRACTICE AND PROBLEM SOLVING

In Exercises 4–7, simplify the quotient. Is the quotient a rate or a ratio? Explain your reasoning.

4. $\dfrac{18 \text{ people}}{54 \text{ people}}$

5. $\dfrac{140 \text{ mi}}{5 \text{ gal}}$

6. $\dfrac{576 \text{ beats}}{8 \text{ min}}$

7. $\dfrac{165 \text{ apples}}{125 \text{ apples}}$

In Exercises 8–11, find the unit rate.

8. It rains 28 inches in 8 hours.

9. You pay $2.73 for 100 sheets of paper.

10. In 3.5 h a plane flies 2275 mi.

11. You are paid $90 for delivering newspapers for 6 days.

Investigation 6, Interactive Real-Life Investigations

In Exercises 12–14, which is the better buy? Explain.

12. **A.** A 16 oz box of cereal for $3.49

    B. A 20 oz box of cereal for $4.19

13. **A.** A 2 lb bag of potatoes for $1.08

    B. A 5 lb bag of potatoes for $2.10

    C. A 10 lb bag of potatoes for $3.95

14. **A.** A 0.5 gal container of frozen yogurt for $2.25

    B. A 2 gal container of frozen yogurt for $8.00

15. **CALORIE CONSUMPTION** For a typical adult, the calorie consumption for 7 days is 17,500. The caloric intake for 7 days of an Olympic athlete in training can reach 70,000. Use this information to find the daily calorie consumption of a typical adult and an Olympic athlete. (Source: USA Today)

16. **MARATHON RACING** Refer to the caption below the photograph at the right. Find Jean Driscoll's average speed in miles per hour (mi/h) using the information given about the 1993 marathon.

17. **MOVIE RENTALS** For the 5-year period from 1991 through 1995, Americans averaged 243 h watching video movies. Find the average number of hours watched *per year*. The average length of a movie is about 1.5 h. Estimate the number of movies watched per year. (Source: Veronis, Suhler, & Associates)

18. **STUDENT–TEACHER RATIO** A high school has 1508 students in grades 9–12. The school has 52 teachers. Find the unit rate of students per teacher for the school.

19. **TYPING** Three students learned to type in computer class. Who typed the fastest? Explain.
    - Chung typed 126 words in 3 min.
    - Shana typed 240 words in 5 min.
    - Randy typed 180 words in 4 min.

Real Life...
Real People

Jean Driscoll has won the women's wheelchair division of the Boston Marathon six times. Her fastest time came in 1993 when she covered the 26.2 mi in about 96 minutes.

STANDARDIZED TEST PRACTICE

20. You are a sales representative. You make 30 sales calls and sell $2400 of merchandise. Estimate the amount of sales, in dollars per sales call.

    (A) $8 per sales call   **(B)** $80 per sales call

    (C) $125 per sales call   **(D)** $800 per sales call

21. Which is **not** a rate?

    (A) 5 meters per second   **(B)** 10 dollars per hour

    (C) 3 seconds per second   **(D)** 7 dollars per pound

PORTFOLIO

EXPLORATION AND EXTENSION

22. **BUILDING YOUR PROJECT** Your camera has shutter speed settings that vary from

    $$\frac{1 \text{ picture}}{1 \text{ second}} \quad \text{to} \quad \frac{1 \text{ picture}}{0.001 \text{ second}} .$$

    Which of these shutter speeds is faster? If you were taking a picture of a moving bicycle, which shutter speed would be better? Explain your reasoning.

In Exercises 1–4, evaluate the expression. (2.2)

1. 9 squared   **2.** 1^8 **3.** 4^4 **4.** 2 cubed

In Exercises 5–8, write the fraction as a decimal. Round your answer to the nearest hundredth. (2.7)

5. $\dfrac{5}{9}$ **6.** $\dfrac{7}{12}$ **7.** $\dfrac{4}{15}$ **8.** $\dfrac{7}{11}$

9. A survey asked 30 students whether they ride the bus, get a ride from a friend or family member, or walk to school. Three fifths said they ride the bus, one tenth said they get a ride from a friend or family member, and three tenths said they walk to school. What fraction of students said that they either ride the bus or walk to school? **(3.3)**

In Exercises 10–13, write the integer represented by the real-life situation. (4.3)

10. 20 feet below sea level   **11.** 25 degrees above zero

12. A deposit of $15 in an account   **13.** A loss of 10 points

In Exercises 14–16, plot the points in a coordinate plane. (5.4)

14. $(1, -5), (-1, 3)$ **15.** $(-4, -2), (3, 6)$ **16.** $(0, -6), (-4, 2)$

CAREER Interview   PHOTOGRAPHER AND ARTIST

Shan Goshorn is a Native American photographer who specializes in exhibition work for museums and galleries. As an artist-in-residence, she has taught students at many levels.

Q What kind of math do you use on the job?
I mostly use math in managing my business. I use math to keep track of income and expenses, balance accounts, and pay taxes. I also use math and spatial relationships to design exhibit spaces.

Q What math did you take in high school and college?
In high school, I took Algebras I and II and Geometry. Unfortunately, no math courses were offered at the art institute. Everyone should take courses in business and computers. Artists and other professionals need them to successfully run their own businesses.

Q What would you like to tell kids who are in school?
Take math, even if you think it won't apply to your career choice. Math provides discipline. It encourages creative and abstract thinking. Achieving success in math builds self-confidence.

Rates of **Speed**

It is often interesting to compare the rates of objects whose units of speed differ.

Example

Two common units for speed are miles per hour (mi/h) and feet per second (ft/s). Which of the following is faster?

a. A car driven at a speed of 66 mi/h

b. A baseball thrown at a speed of 100 feet per second

Solution

To decide which is faster, you can write the car's speed in feet per second. To do this, you need to change miles to feet and hours to seconds.

$$\frac{66 \text{ mi}}{1 \text{ h}} \cdot \frac{1 \text{ h}}{60 \text{ min}} \cdot \frac{1 \text{ min}}{60 \text{ s}} \cdot \frac{5280 \text{ ft}}{1 \text{ mi}} = \frac{66 \cdot 5280 \text{ ft}}{60 \cdot 60 \text{ s}}$$

To evaluate this rate, you can use the following keystrokes.

(66 × 5280) ÷ (60 × 60) =

or

66 × 5280 ÷ 60 ÷ 60 =

The display is 96.8, so the car is moving at a speed of 96.8 ft/s. This means that the baseball is moving slightly faster than the car.

> ### STUDY TIP
>
> When you rewrite a rate in different units, you can multiply by convenient forms of the number 1. For example, because there are 5280 ft in 1 mi, the following are forms of the number 1:
>
> $$1 = \frac{1 \text{ mi}}{1 \text{ mi}} = \frac{5280 \text{ ft}}{1 \text{ mi}}$$
>
> $$1 = \frac{1 \text{ mi}}{1 \text{ mi}} = \frac{1 \text{ mi}}{5280 \text{ ft}}$$

Exercises

1. Another way to compare the two speeds in the example is to write the baseball's speed in miles per hour. Simplify the following expression to find the baseball's speed in miles per hour.

$$\frac{100 \text{ ft}}{1 \text{ s}} \cdot \frac{60 \text{ s}}{1 \text{ min}} \cdot \frac{60 \text{ min}}{1 \text{ h}} \cdot \frac{1 \text{ mi}}{5280 \text{ ft}}$$

2. Which of the following rates are equal to 1? Explain.

a. $\frac{60 \text{ s}}{1 \text{ min}}$ **b.** $\frac{3 \text{ ft}}{1 \text{ yd}}$ **c.** $\frac{1000 \text{ cm}}{1 \text{ m}}$ **d.** $\frac{1 \text{ lb}}{16 \text{ oz}}$

3. A cheetah can run at a maximum speed of about 80 mi/h. At this speed, how many feet does a cheetah run in one second? Explain.

4. A parachutist falls at a speed of about 20 ft/s. What is this speed in miles per hour?

LAB 6.3

COOPERATIVE LEARNING

Proportions

Part A COMPARING PHOTOS

Materials Needed
- graph paper
- plain paper
- pencils or pens
- centimeter ruler

1. You are a photographer and have taken the photo shown at the right. You are trying to decide which photo dimensions to use in a story about polar bears. To begin, you find the width-to-height ratio of the photo.

$$\frac{\textbf{Width of photo}}{\textbf{Height of photo}} = \frac{?}{?}$$

What is this ratio?

2. Use a centimeter ruler to measure each of the following photos. Find the width-to-height ratio of each photo. Which ones have the same ratio as the original photo? Explain.

8 cm

6 cm

a.

b.

c.

d.

3. Write each of the width-to-height ratios you found in Exercise 2 as an ordered pair. For example, the ratio for the original photo can be written as (**6**, **8**).

4. Copy the coordinate plane and the point at the right onto graph paper. Plot the ordered pairs you found in Exercise 3.

5. Of the 5 points that you plotted, which 3 lie on a line? What can you conclude about the width-to-height ratios of these ordered pairs?

6. Two of the photos found on page 282 are distortions of the image of the polar bear. How do their points differ with respect to the line? What can you conclude? Find two other possible photo sizes that are not distortions of the original image.

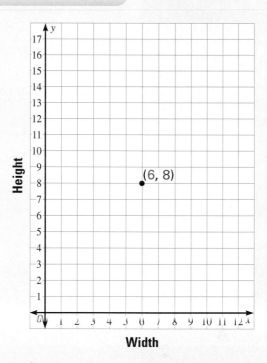

Height

Width

NOW TRY THESE

7. Measure all five of the photos on page 282 in millimeters. Then copy and complete the table. What can you conclude?

Photo	Original	a.	b.	c.	d.
Width (mm)	?	?	?	?	?
Height (mm)	?	?	?	?	?
Width-to-Height Ratio	?	?	?	?	?

8. You want to enlarge the original photo so that it has a width of 9 inches. Use the original width-to-height ratio to find the new height.

9. You want to enlarge the original photo so that it has a height of 20 inches. Use the original width-to-height ratio find the new width.

10. Two photos are *proportional* if they have the same width-to-height ratio. Is a 5 inch-by-7 inch photograph proportional to an 8 inch-by-10 inch photograph? Explain.

6.3

Solving Proportions

What you should learn:

Goal 1 How to solve a proportion

Goal 2 How to solve an equation that equates two rates

Why you should learn it:

Knowing how to solve proportions can help you make plans. An example is planning the amount of juice you need at a party.

Goal 1 SOLVING A PROPORTION

An equation that equates two ratios is a **proportion**.

$$\frac{6}{5} = \frac{n}{30}$$ — Proportion

This is read as "6 is to 5 as n is to 30." When you solve this equation for n, you are solving the proportion. One way to solve a proportion is to write both fractions with the same denominator.

$$\frac{6 \cdot 6}{6 \cdot 5} = \frac{n}{30}$$ **Multiply numerator and denominator by 6.**

$$\frac{36}{30} = \frac{n}{30}$$ **The denominators are equal.**

Because the denominators are equal, it follows that $n = 36$.

So, $\frac{6}{5} = \frac{36}{30}$.

Example 1 **Using Proportional Measurements**

You are making a scale drawing of a room. The actual room has a width of 18 ft and a length of 24 ft. Your scale drawing of the room has a length of 4 in. Use the following proportion to find the width of the room on the scale drawing.

$$\frac{\text{Width of drawing}}{\text{Length of drawing}} = \frac{\text{Width of room}}{\text{Length of room}}$$

$$\frac{x \text{ in.}}{4 \text{ in.}} = \frac{18 \text{ ft}}{24 \text{ ft}}$$

Solution

$$\frac{x}{4} = \frac{18}{24}$$ **Write the proportion.**

$$\frac{x}{4} = \frac{6 \cdot 3}{6 \cdot 4}$$ **Factor.**

$$\frac{x}{4} = \frac{3}{4}$$ **Simplify: the denominators are equal.**

Because the denominators are equal, the solution is $x = 3$. The scale drawing of the room is 3 inches wide.

The methods you use to solve a proportion (an equation equating two ratios) can also be used to solve an equation that equates two rates.

Example 2 **Using Rates in Real Life**

A punch recipe calls for 4 cups of orange juice. The recipe will serve 8 people. You are making punch for a party with 32 people. How many cups of orange juice will you need?

REAL LIFE
Party Planning

Solution

Method ① One way to answer the question is to write a proportion. Let x be the number of cups of orange juice you will need to serve 32 people. You can solve the proportion by writing both rates so they have the same denominator.

$$\frac{4 \text{ cups}}{8 \text{ people}} = \frac{x \text{ cups}}{32 \text{ people}}$$ **Set up the proportion.**

$$\frac{4 \cdot 4 \text{ cups}}{4 \cdot 8 \text{ people}} = \frac{x \text{ cups}}{32 \text{ people}}$$ **Multiply numerator and denominator by 4.**

$$\frac{16 \text{ cups}}{32 \text{ people}} = \frac{x \text{ cups}}{32 \text{ people}}$$ **Simplify.**

Because the denominators are equal, the numerators must also be equal. So, $x = 16$. You will need 16 cups of orange juice to serve 32 people.

Method ② You can also use unit rates.

$$\text{Unit rate} = \frac{4 \text{ cups}}{8 \text{ people}}$$ **Set up the rate.**

$$= \frac{4 \text{ cups} \div 8}{8 \text{ people} \div 8}$$ **Divide.**

$$= \frac{0.5 \text{ cup}}{1 \text{ person}}$$ **Simplify.**

The unit rate is half a cup of juice per person. So, for 32 people, you need 32×0.5, or 16 cups of juice.

As you can see, both methods give the same solution.

ONGOING ASSESSMENT

Talk About It

You and your partner should each solve one of the proportions. Then, take turns describing your solution steps to the other.

1. $\dfrac{\$24}{2.5 \text{ h}} = \dfrac{\$m}{15 \text{ h}}$

2. $\dfrac{18 \text{ ft}}{2 \text{ s}} = \dfrac{y \text{ ft}}{9 \text{ s}}$

GUIDED PRACTICE

In Exercises 1–3, match the statement with the value of x that makes the proportion true.

A. $x = 2$ B. $x = 3$ C. $x = 4$

1. $\dfrac{x}{2} = \dfrac{6}{4}$ **2.** $\dfrac{x}{2} = \dfrac{8}{4}$ **3.** $\dfrac{x}{4} = \dfrac{3}{6}$

In Exercises 4–6, match the proportion with its description. Then solve the proportion.

A. 3 is to 4 as x is to 12.   B. x is to 3 as 16 is to 12.   C. x is to 4 as 3 is to 12.

4. $\dfrac{x}{3} = \dfrac{16}{12}$ **5.** $\dfrac{x}{4} = \dfrac{3}{12}$ **6.** $\dfrac{3}{4} = \dfrac{x}{12}$

PRACTICE AND PROBLEM SOLVING

In Exercises 7–9, decide whether the statement is true.

7. $\dfrac{4}{5} \overset{?}{=} \dfrac{15}{20}$ **8.** $\dfrac{15}{12} \overset{?}{=} \dfrac{5}{3}$ **9.** $\dfrac{8}{18} \overset{?}{=} \dfrac{16}{36}$

In Exercises 10–15, write the description as a proportion. Then solve for the variable to complete the proportion.

10. n is to 9 as 10 is to 18.   **11.** p is to 21 as 11 is to 33.

12. 35 is to 25 as z is to 5.   **13.** 9 is to 6 as m is to 18.

14. 4 is to x as 6 is to 24.   **15.** 28 is to w as 36 is to 9.

In Exercises 16–18, use each one of the given digits in a single space to make the proportion true.

16. 2, 4, 5, and 7   **17.** 1, 2, 3, and 5   **18.** 1, 5, 7, and 9

$\dfrac{3}{6} = \dfrac{\boxed{?}\,\boxed{?}}{\boxed{?}\,\boxed{?}}$ $\dfrac{4}{16} = \dfrac{\boxed{?}\,\boxed{?}}{\boxed{?}\,\boxed{?}}$ $\dfrac{3}{9} = \dfrac{\boxed{?}\,\boxed{?}}{\boxed{?}\,\boxed{?}}$

In Exercises 19–24, solve the proportion.

19. $\dfrac{m}{6} = \dfrac{9}{54}$ **20.** $\dfrac{3}{8} = \dfrac{n}{32}$ **21.** $\dfrac{15}{75} = \dfrac{b}{5}$

22. $\dfrac{d}{5} = \dfrac{40}{100}$ **23.** $\dfrac{36}{9} = \dfrac{z}{3}$ **24.** $\dfrac{x}{8} = \dfrac{18}{2}$

25. WRITING Describe a real-life situation that can be modeled by one of the proportions in Exercises 19–24. Write a verbal model to show how the proportion describes the situation. Include the units of measure in your description.

GIANT PIZZA In Exercises 26–28, use the recipe at the right. This recipe was used at the Singapore Food Festival in 1996 to make a pizza for 10,000 people. (Source: Singapore Tourist Information Board)

PIZZA

Flour 2205 lb Mozzarella cheese 1102 lb
Yeast 26.5 lb Tomato sauce 1058 lb
Olive oil 7.9 gal Cooking oil 21 gal
Salt 88 lb

26. Find the unit rate for mozzarella cheese in pounds per person. Round your answer to the nearest hundredth.

27. How many pounds of mozzarella cheese are needed to make pizza for 500 people?

28. Find the unit rate for flour in pounds per person. Round your answer to the nearest hundredth.

29. PHOTOCOPYING You are using a photocopier to reduce an image on an 11 in.-by-17 in. piece of paper. The reduced image will be 8.5 in. long. Find how wide the reduced image will be by solving the proportion $\frac{11}{17} = \frac{x}{8.5}$.

STANDARDIZED TEST PRACTICE

30. You are hiring counselors for summer camp. You need 2 counselors for every 15 campers. There are 180 campers. Which of the following proportions can be used to find the number of counselors you need?

Ⓐ $\frac{x}{15} = \frac{2}{180}$ Ⓑ $\frac{15}{2} = \frac{x}{180}$ Ⓒ $\frac{2}{15} = \frac{x}{180}$ Ⓓ $\frac{x}{2} = \frac{15}{180}$

31. Solve the proportion: $\frac{x}{15} = \frac{36}{30}$.

Ⓐ 4   Ⓑ 8   Ⓒ 9   Ⓓ 18

EXPLORATION AND EXTENSION

PORTFOLIO

32. BUILDING YOUR PROJECT You photographed a river from an airplane. The 300 foot wide river is 0.25 inch wide on the negative. Your camera has a focal length (distance from lens to film) of 6 inches. Solve the following proportion to find the altitude at which you took the picture.

$$\frac{\text{Focal length (inches)}}{\text{Width on negative (inches)}} = \frac{\text{Altitude of plane (feet)}}{\text{Width of region (feet)}}$$

6.4

More about Solving Proportions

What you should learn:

Goal 1 How to form cross products of a proportion

Goal 2 How to use the Cross Products Property to solve proportions

Why you should learn it:

Knowing how to solve proportions can help you solve real-life problems, such as determining sizes of letters on a billboard.

Goal 1 FORMING CROSS PRODUCTS

Each proportion has two **cross products** as shown in the diagram below. The process of forming the cross products of a proportion is called *cross multiplying*.

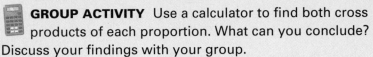

$$\frac{a}{b} \times \frac{c}{d} \longrightarrow \begin{array}{c} b \cdot c \\ a \cdot d \end{array}$$ Cross products

LESSON INVESTIGATION

COOPERATIVE LEARNING

Investigating Cross Products

GROUP ACTIVITY Use a calculator to find both cross products of each proportion. What can you conclude? Discuss your findings with your group.

1. $\frac{2}{3} = \frac{18}{27}$ **2.** $\frac{5}{4} = \frac{30}{24}$ **3.** $\frac{7}{6} = \frac{49}{42}$ **4.** $\frac{3}{4} = \frac{60}{80}$

In this investigation, you may have discovered that the cross products of a proportion are equal.

CROSS PRODUCTS PROPERTY

In the proportion $\frac{a}{b} = \frac{c}{d}$, the products of $a \cdot d$ and $b \cdot c$ are called the cross products of the proportion. By the cross-products property, **if $\frac{a}{b} = \frac{c}{d}$, then $a \cdot d = b \cdot c$.**

Example 1 **Comparing Cross Products**

Use cross multiplication to show that the proportion below has equal cross products.

$$\frac{5}{6} = \frac{35}{42}$$

Solution

$\dfrac{5}{6} = \dfrac{35}{42}$ Write the original proportion.

$5 \cdot 42 \stackrel{?}{=} 6 \cdot 35$ Cross multiply.

$210 = 210$ The cross products are equal.

Goal 2 SOLVING PROPORTIONS

You can also use cross multiplication to solve proportions.

Example 2 Solving a Proportion

Use cross products to solve the proportion $\frac{x}{12} = \frac{11}{33}$.

Solution

$\frac{x}{12} = \frac{11}{33}$ **Write the original proportion.**

$x \cdot 33 = 12 \cdot 11$ **Cross multiply.**

$\frac{x \cdot 33}{33} = \frac{132}{33}$ **Divide both sides by 33.**

$x = 4$ **Solution: x is by itself.**

The solution is 4. Check this in the original proportion.

Example 3 Designing a Billboard

You have drawn a design for a billboard. The design is 4 ft high. The letters on the design are 6 in. high. The actual billboard is 20 ft high. How tall should you make the letters on the billboard?

Solution

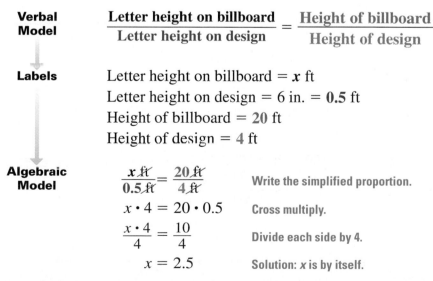

Verbal Model

$$\frac{\text{Letter height on billboard}}{\text{Letter height on design}} = \frac{\text{Height of billboard}}{\text{Height of design}}$$

Labels

Letter height on billboard $= x$ ft
Letter height on design $= 6$ in. $= \mathbf{0.5}$ ft
Height of billboard $= \mathbf{20}$ ft
Height of design $= \mathbf{4}$ ft

Algebraic Model

$\frac{x \text{ ft}}{0.5 \text{ ft}} = \frac{20 \text{ ft}}{4 \text{ ft}}$ **Write the simplified proportion.**

$x \cdot 4 = 20 \cdot 0.5$ **Cross multiply.**

$\frac{x \cdot 4}{4} = \frac{10}{4}$ **Divide each side by 4.**

$x = 2.5$ **Solution: x is by itself.**

You should make the letters 2.5 ft, or 30 in., tall.

ONGOING ASSESSMENT

Write About It

A friend of yours multiplied two fractions as follows. What is your friend's error?

$$\frac{4}{5} \times \frac{2}{3} = \frac{4 \times 3}{5 \times 2}$$

$$= \frac{12}{10}$$

$$= \frac{6}{5}$$

1. Write a note to your friend describing the error.

2. Which property did your friend use incorrectly?

GUIDED PRACTICE

1. Solve $\dfrac{4}{13} = \dfrac{n}{52}$ using two different methods.

   a. Rewrite with the same denominators.

   b. Use cross products.

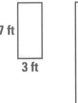 

7 ft

3 ft

14 ft

6 ft

2. **GEOMETRY** Show that the two rectangles at the right have the same width-to-length ratio.

In Exercises 3–6, use cross products to match the proportion with its solution.

A. $x = 3$ **B.** $x = 10$ **C.** $x = 5$ **D.** $x = 2$

3. $\dfrac{x}{9} = \dfrac{10}{45}$ 4. $\dfrac{6}{15} = \dfrac{4}{x}$ 5. $\dfrac{20}{x} = \dfrac{36}{9}$ 6. $\dfrac{75}{50} = \dfrac{x}{2}$

PRACTICE AND PROBLEM SOLVING

In Exercises 7–14, use cross products to decide whether the proportion is true.

7. $\dfrac{6}{7} \overset{?}{=} \dfrac{72}{84}$ 8. $\dfrac{13}{36} \overset{?}{=} \dfrac{1}{3}$ 9. $\dfrac{56}{8} \overset{?}{=} \dfrac{15}{2}$ 10. $\dfrac{48}{4} \overset{?}{=} \dfrac{60}{5}$

11. $\dfrac{3}{4} \overset{?}{=} \dfrac{4.5}{6}$ 12. $\dfrac{10.8}{12} \overset{?}{=} \dfrac{4}{5}$ 13. $\dfrac{36}{7.2} \overset{?}{=} \dfrac{25}{4}$ 14. $\dfrac{8.8}{11} \overset{?}{=} \dfrac{2}{2.5}$

In Exercises 15–22, use cross products to solve the proportion. Then check the solution.

15. $\dfrac{2}{5} = \dfrac{m}{30}$ 16. $\dfrac{42}{54} = \dfrac{7}{x}$ 17. $\dfrac{a}{29} = \dfrac{21}{7}$ 18. $\dfrac{t}{8} = \dfrac{56}{14}$

19. $\dfrac{9}{10} = \dfrac{3.6}{n}$ 20. $\dfrac{5}{r} = \dfrac{6}{8.4}$ 21. $\dfrac{18}{b} = \dfrac{5}{1.25}$ 22. $\dfrac{24.8}{8} = \dfrac{k}{3}$

GEOMETRY In Exercises 23 and 24, show that the polygons have the same width-to-length or base-to-height ratio.

23.

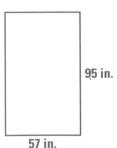

90 in.

95 in.

54 in.

57 in.

24.

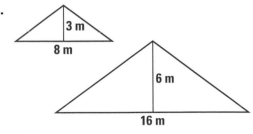

3 m

8 m

6 m

16 m

TECHNOLOGY In Exercises 25–28, use a calculator to help solve the proportion. Round your result to the nearest hundredth.

25. $\dfrac{13}{14} = \dfrac{x}{26}$ **26.** $\dfrac{18}{32} = \dfrac{a}{7}$ **27.** $\dfrac{35}{11} = \dfrac{t}{20}$ **28.** $\dfrac{m}{12} = \dfrac{94}{51}$

THINKING SKILLS In Exercises 29 and 30, is the statement *true* or *false*? Give an example to support your answer.

29. If $\dfrac{a}{b} = \dfrac{c}{d}$, then $\dfrac{d}{b} = \dfrac{c}{a}$.

30. If $\dfrac{a}{b} = \dfrac{c}{d}$, then $\dfrac{a}{b} = \dfrac{d}{c}$.

31. **TRAVEL** On vacation, you drive 125 mi in 3 h. Estimate the time it will take you to complete the 400-mi trip by solving the proportion.

$$\dfrac{3 \text{ h}}{x \text{ h}} = \dfrac{125 \text{ mi}}{400 \text{ mi}}$$

32. **USING A GRAPH** A survey asked 25 students in a class to name their favorite weather temperature range. The results of the survey are shown in the circle graph at the right. Solve the following proportions. What do the solutions represent?

a. $\dfrac{n}{25} = \dfrac{36}{100}$ **b.** $\dfrac{n}{25} = \dfrac{16}{100}$

c. $\dfrac{n}{25} = \dfrac{12}{100}$ **d.** $\dfrac{n}{25} = \dfrac{28}{100}$

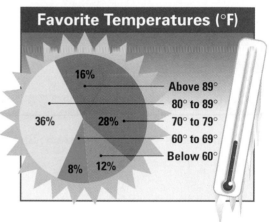

Favorite Temperatures (°F)

16% — Above 89°
80° to 89°
36%   28% — 70° to 79°
60° to 69°
Below 60°
8% 12%

STANDARDIZED TEST PRACTICE

33. What is a cross product of the proportion $\dfrac{6}{18} = \dfrac{3}{9}$?

(**A**) 6   (**B**) 18
(**C**) 54   (**D**) 162

34. A company pays a set hourly amount for overtime. In January, the company paid employees $2100 for overtime hours. Using the graph at the right, estimate how much the company paid for overtime in June.

(**A**) $17.50   (**B**) $1575
(**C**) $1750   (**D**) $2450

Overtime Hours

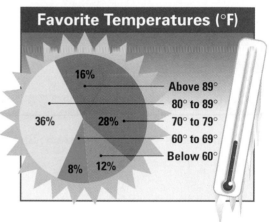

Number of hours — 160 140 120 100 80 60 40 20 0

Jan. Feb. Mar. Apr. May June

35. Solve the proportion $\dfrac{12}{x} = \dfrac{3}{4}$.

(**A**) 8   (**B**) 12   (**C**) 16   (**D**) 20

36. GOLDEN RATIO The *golden ratio* is used by artists, architects, and photographers to plan rectangles that are "pleasing to the eye." The photo at the right shows the Greek Parthenon located in Athens. This building, originally built as a temple to the god Athena Parthenos, shows the *golden ratio* used in architecture. Use a ruler to measure the width and height of the rectangle in the photo at the right. Estimate the golden ratio by calculating the *width-to-height ratio* of the rectangle. If you wanted to crop a photograph using the golden ratio, how wide would the photo be if it was 5 in. high?

37. USING LOGICAL REASONING Use the following clues to match the values of a, b, c, d, e, f, g, and h with 3, 4, 5, 6, 15, 20, 25, and 30.

$a = 5$ $\qquad \dfrac{a}{b} > 1 \qquad\qquad \dfrac{a}{e} = \dfrac{c}{f}$

$h = 15$ $\qquad \dfrac{a}{b} = \dfrac{c}{d} \qquad\qquad \dfrac{e}{f} = \dfrac{g}{h}$

In Exercises 1–4, add or subtract. Simplify if possible. (3.3)

1. $\dfrac{3}{8} + \dfrac{1}{3}$ $\qquad$ **2.** $\dfrac{4}{5} - \dfrac{1}{9}$ $\qquad$ **3.** $\dfrac{1}{6} + \dfrac{6}{15}$ $\qquad$ **4.** $\dfrac{11}{12} - \dfrac{1}{5}$

5. NUMBER SENSE I am a mixed number between 5 and 6. When I am divided by 4, the result is the same as when 4 is subtracted from me. What mixed number am I? **(3.4, 3.7)**

In Exercises 6–9, add or subtract. (4.4, 4.5)

6. $-9 + 4$ $\qquad$ **7.** $-3 + (-12)$ $\qquad$ **8.** $-1 - 8$ $\qquad$ **9.** $-5 - (-10)$

10. PERSONAL SAVINGS You are saving money to buy a bicycle that costs $189. You have already saved $95. Write a verbal model, labels, and an algebraic equation to find how much more you need to save to buy the bicycle. **(4.6)**

In Exercises 11–13, find the probability of the spinner landing on red. (5.7)

11.

12.

13.

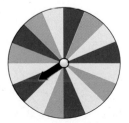

Take this test as you would take a test in class. The answers to the exercises are given in the back of the book.

In Exercises 1–3, rewrite the quotient as a ratio. (6.1)

1. $\dfrac{49 \text{ cm}}{3 \text{ m}}$

2. $\dfrac{4 \text{ lb}}{50 \text{ oz}}$

3. $\dfrac{220 \text{ min}}{5 \text{ h}}$

In Exercises 4 and 5, change the rate to a unit rate. (6.2)

4. Beef has 222 calories in 3 oz.

5. There are 125 pieces of paper in a stack that is 0.25 in. high.

In Exercises 6–9, write a proportion and solve it. (6.3)

6. k is to 12 as 5 is to 60.

7. x is to 6 as 6 is to 2.

8. 4 is to 7 as m is to 35.

9. 72 is to 9 as s is to 4.

In Exercises 10–12, decide whether the proportion is true. (6.4)

10. $\dfrac{18}{6} \overset{?}{=} \dfrac{33}{11}$

11. $\dfrac{8}{30} \overset{?}{=} \dfrac{12}{40}$

12. $\dfrac{27}{135} \overset{?}{=} \dfrac{13}{65}$

13. Find the unit rate for each toll road in the table. Which toll road is most expensive? Explain. (Source: American Automobile Association) **(6.2)**

Name	Toll	Miles
Sam Houston Tollway	$5.40	28
Delaware Turnpike	$1.25	11
Daniel Boone Parkway	$2.10	63
Chicago Skyway	$2.00	7.8

14. **STAIR CLIMBING** It took Geoff Case 618 seconds to climb the 1575 steps of the Empire State Building. Which equation below could you use to find the average number of stairs he climbed in 1 minute? Use a calculator to solve the correct equation. (Source: Guinness Book of World Records) **(6.4)**

a. $\dfrac{1575 \text{ steps}}{618 \text{ s}} = \dfrac{x \text{ steps}}{1 \text{ min}}$

b. $\dfrac{x \text{ steps}}{1575 \text{ steps}} = \dfrac{60 \text{ s}}{618 \text{ s}}$

15. **MINING DIAMONDS** About 6000 pounds of rock must be mined to produce 0.007 ounce (1 carat) of diamonds. Use the proportion below and a calculator to find how much rock must be mined to produce 1 ounce of diamonds. **(6.3)**

$$\dfrac{6000 \text{ lb}}{0.007 \text{ oz}} = \dfrac{x \text{ lb}}{1 \text{ oz}}$$

6.5

Writing Proportions

What you should learn:

Goal 1 How to use ratios to solve real-life problems

Goal 2 How to use rates to solve real-life problems

Why you should learn it:

Knowing how to write proportions can help you make models. An example is planning a replica of Lincoln's statue.

Goal 1 WRITING PROPORTION MODELS

Example 1 Writing a Proportion

You want to make a model of the statue of Abraham Lincoln that is located in the Lincoln Memorial in Washington, D.C. You want your model to have a height of 38 cm. Use the dimensions of the real statue shown below to find the height that Lincoln's chair should be in the model that you make.

Solution

STRATEGY **WRITE AN EQUATION** You reason that your model should have the same part-to-whole ratio as the real statue. You can use the following verbal model to set up the proportion. Then you can use cross products to solve the proportion and find the height of the model of the chair.

Verbal Model	$\dfrac{\text{Model chair height}}{\text{Total model height}} = \dfrac{\text{Statue chair height}}{\text{Total statue height}}$

Labels

Model chair height $= x$ cm

Total model height $= \textbf{38}$ cm

Statue chair height $= \textbf{8}$ ft

Total statue height $= \textbf{19}$ ft

Algebraic Model

$\dfrac{x \,\cancel{cm}}{38\,\cancel{cm}} = \dfrac{8\,\cancel{ft}}{19\,\cancel{ft}}$ Write the proportion.

$x \cdot 19 = 38 \cdot 8$ Cross multiply.

$\dfrac{x \cdot 19}{19} = \dfrac{304}{19}$ Divide each side by 19.

$x = 16$ Solution: x is by itself.

The model of the chair should be 16 cm high.

Notice that the following problem-solving plan was used to solve the proportion problem above. You will find that using a plan such as this one is very helpful in setting up and solving real-life problems.

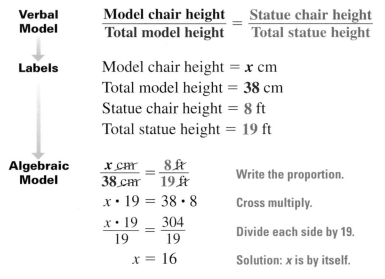

Write verbal models. > Assign labels. > Write proportion. > Solve proportion.

Goal 2 SOLVING REAL-LIFE RATE PROBLEMS

Example 2 Solving a Rate Problem

You are a geologist studying the growth rate of the underwater volcano Loihi Seamount. Loihi's peak is now about 3100 ft below the surface of the ocean. You estimate that the volcano has grown 200 ft during the last 1000 years. If Loihi continues to grow at this rate, when will it reach the surface and begin forming a new Hawaiian island?

CONNECTION
Earth Science

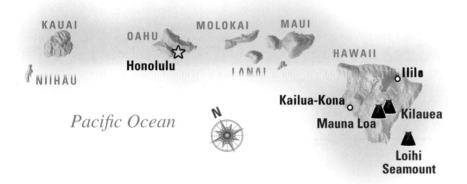

KAUAI OAHU MOLOKAI MAUI
Honolulu LANAI HAWAII
NIIHAU Ilila
Kailua-Kona Kilauea
Pacific Ocean Mauna Loa
N Loihi
Seamount

Solution

Verbal Model	$\dfrac{\text{Height to grow}}{\text{Time to grow}} = \dfrac{\text{Past growth}}{\text{Past time}}$

Labels
Height to grow = **3100** ft
Time to grow = x years
Past growth = **200** ft
Past time = **1000** years

Algebraic Model

$$\frac{3100 \text{ ft}}{x \text{ years}} = \frac{200 \text{ ft}}{1000 \text{ years}}$$ Write the proportion.

$$3100 \cdot 1000 = 200 \cdot x$$ Cross multiply.

$$\frac{3100 \cdot 1000}{200} = \frac{200 \cdot x}{200}$$ Divide each side by 200.

$$15,500 \approx x$$ Solution: x is by itself.

From this, you can estimate that Loihi will reach the ocean's surface in about 15,500 years. (Geologists who study Loihi have generally estimated this time as between 10,000 and 30,000 years.)

GUIDED PRACTICE

1. You have to read a 220-page book. It takes you 15 min to read 10 pages. Use the following equation to estimate the time it will take you to read the entire book.

$$\frac{10 \text{ pages}}{15 \text{ min}} = \frac{220 \text{ pages}}{x \text{ min}}$$

2. You have started a job as a photographer. During your first 5 months, you saved $1220. At this rate, how much will you have saved after 1 year of work?

In Exercises 3 and 4, use the photograph of the rug to the right. The rug was made in the 1700s and is located in the Cha'ien Lung Palace. The actual rug is 154 inches long.

3. Use an inch ruler to measure the photograph. Write a proportion to estimate the width of the actual rug. Solve the proportion using cross products. Round your answer to the nearest inch.

4. You have a different photograph of the rug. The rug is 16 cm wide. How long is it?

PRACTICE AND PROBLEM SOLVING

In Exercises 5 and 6, decide which of the equations you could not use to solve the problem. Then solve the problem.

5. You are an artist designing a new postage stamp. The stamp must be 2 cm tall by 3 cm wide. You make a sketch of the stamp that is 6 in. tall. How wide should the sketch of the stamp be? Explain how you got your answer.

   A. $\dfrac{3 \text{ cm}}{2 \text{ cm}} = \dfrac{x \text{ in.}}{6 \text{ in.}}$ B. $\dfrac{3 \text{ cm}}{x \text{ in.}} = \dfrac{2 \text{ cm}}{6 \text{ in.}}$ C. $\dfrac{3 \text{ cm}}{6 \text{ in.}} = \dfrac{2 \text{ cm}}{x \text{ in.}}$

6. One gallon of paint covers 900 ft². How much does a quart of the same paint cover?

   A. $\dfrac{4 \text{ qt}}{900 \text{ ft}^2} = \dfrac{1 \text{ qt}}{x \text{ ft}^2}$ B. $\dfrac{1 \text{ gal}}{1 \text{ qt}} = \dfrac{900 \text{ ft}^2}{x \text{ ft}^2}$ C. $\dfrac{4 \text{ qt}}{1 \text{ qt}} = \dfrac{900 \text{ ft}^2}{x \text{ ft}^2}$

7. **WRITING** Think of a real-life situation that can be modeled by a proportion. Write a verbal model for the proportion and explain how it models the situation.

In Exercises 8–11, write a proportion to solve the problem.

8. **ELECTRICITY** The electricity used by a 100-watt light bulb if it was left on for 1 full month is 72 kilowatt hours. The cost of this electricity is $5.76. Find the cost of 1 kilowatt hour of electricity.

9. **REAL ESTATE** You are considering renting an office that has 325 ft^2 of space. The rent is $1300 per month. In the same building a larger office is available for $2500 per month. Estimate the number of square feet in the larger office.

10. **EXCHANGE RATE** The exchange rate for money in Kenya is 52 shillings to $1.00. How many shillings can you get for $5.50?

11. **POPULATION DENSITY** The ratio of the number of people per square mile in Kentucky to the number of people per square mile in the United States is approximately 4 to 3. There are 97 people per square mile in Kentucky. Estimate how many people per square mile there are in the United States.

 STANDARDIZED TEST PRACTICE

12. A person who weighs 120 lb on Earth would weigh only 20 lb on the moon. How much would a person who weighs 150 lb on Earth weigh on the moon?

    (A) 22 lb   (B) 25 lb   (C) 26 lb   (D) 30 lb

13. The scale of the map at the right is 1 in. = 75 mi. What is the distance between Kenton and Loweville?

    (A) 30 mi   (B) 150 mi

    (C) 187.5 mi   (D) 225 mi

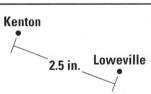

Kenton

2.5 in.   Loweville

 EXPLORATION AND EXTENSION

PORTFOLIO

14. **BUILDING YOUR PROJECT** You are developing film. You need to make a developing solution containing 1 part concentrate to 4 parts water. How many ounces of concentrate should you use if you use 3 cups of water? (1 cup = 8 oz) Include this information in a film developing section of your photography manual.

GEOMETRY CONNECTION

Similar Polygons

Part A COMPARING RECTANGLES

Materials Needed
- graph paper
- plain paper
- pencils or pens
- ruler

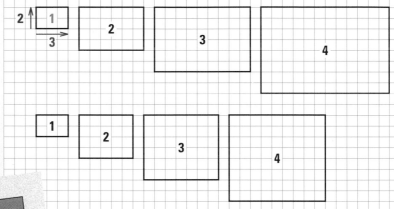

1. Two sequences of rectangles are shown above. For each sequence, copy and complete the table.

Rectangle	1	2	3	4
Width	**2 units**	?	?	?
Length	**3 units**	?	?	?
Width-to-Length Ratio	$\frac{2}{3}$	?	?	?

2. Two rectangles are *similar* if they have the same width-to-length ratio. Which of the above sequences consists of similar rectangles? Explain your reasoning.

3. To draw a rectangle that is similar to a given rectangle, should you change the given rectangle's width and length by multiplying by the same *factor* or by adding the same *amount*? Explain your answer.

4. On graph paper, draw a rectangle that is 5 units by 10 units. Explain how to draw two rectangles that are similar to it: one that is smaller and one that is larger.

a. 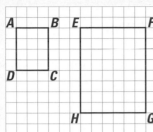 **b.** 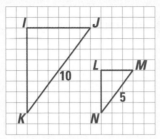 **c.**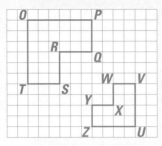

5. The above polygons are similar. Find the following ratios. What can you conclude?

a. $\dfrac{AB}{EF}, \dfrac{BC}{FG}, \dfrac{CD}{GH}, \dfrac{AD}{EH}$

b. $\dfrac{IJ}{LM}, \dfrac{IK}{LN}, \dfrac{JK}{MN}$

c. $\dfrac{UV}{OP}, \dfrac{VW}{PQ}, \dfrac{WX}{QR}, \dfrac{XY}{RS}, \dfrac{YZ}{ST}, \dfrac{UZ}{OT}$

6. The sides of rectangle *ABCD* that are matched with sides of rectangle *EFGH* in the ratios in Exercise 5(a) are *corresponding sides*. For example, $\overline{AB}$ corresponds with $\overline{EF}$. List the corresponding sides of the triangles in 5(b). List the corresponding sides of the hexagons in 5(c).

NOW TRY THESE

7. Draw each polygon on graph paper. Then draw a larger or smaller similar polygon and label its corners.

a. 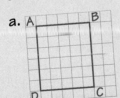   **b.** 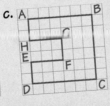   **c.**

8. Write the pairs of corresponding sides for the two similar polygons in Exercise 7(a). Write the ratios of their lengths. The ratios should be equal. Are they?

9. Write the pairs of corresponding sides for the two similar polygons in Exercise 7(c). Write the ratios of their lengths. The ratios should be equal. Are they?

6.6 Similar Polygons

Goal 1 RECOGNIZING SIMILAR POLYGONS

The two triangles shown below are similar. If you match their sides, the ratios of the lengths of matched sides are equal:

$$\frac{AB}{DE} = \frac{BC}{EF} = \frac{CA}{FD}$$

Matched sides (such as $\overline{AB}$ and $\overline{DE}$) are called **corresponding sides** . When the ratios of their lengths are equal, you can say that the sides are **proportional** . Matching angles (such as angle B and angle E) are called **corresponding angles** .

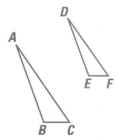

SIMILAR POLYGONS

Two polygons are **similar** if their corresponding angles have the same measure and their corresponding sides are proportional to one another.

Example 1 **Similar Triangles**

Show that the two triangles are similar.

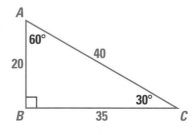 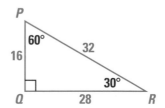

Solution

Corresponding angles have the same measures. For example, angles A and P both have measures of $60°$. The ratios of corresponding sides are as follows.

$$\frac{AB}{PQ} = \frac{20}{16} \qquad \frac{BC}{QR} = \frac{35}{28} \qquad \frac{AC}{PR} = \frac{40}{32}$$

$$= \frac{5}{4} \qquad\qquad = \frac{5}{4} \qquad\qquad = \frac{5}{4}$$

Because all three ratios are equal, the corresponding sides are proportional and, therefore, the triangles are similar.

Goal 2 MAKING INDIRECT MEASUREMENTS

Similar triangles can be used in real life to indirectly measure objects. For example, in the drawing at the right, the ratio of the two heights is equal to the ratio of the two shadow lengths.

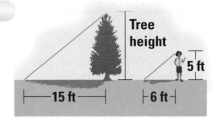

Tree height

5 ft

15 ft   6 ft

LESSON INVESTIGATION

COOPERATIVE LEARNING

Investigating Indirect Measurements

GROUP ACTIVITY Copy the drawing above. Label the height of the tree as *x*. Use the verbal model to write a proportion. Solve the proportion. How tall is the tree?

Verbal Model	Height of tree	Length of tree's shadow
	Height of person	Length of person's shadow

Example 2 **Finding the Height of a Pole**

You measure the shadow of a telephone pole to be 24 ft. The shadow of a 5-ft stick is 4 ft long. How tall is the telephone pole?

Solution

Model the situation. Label the height of the pole as *x*.

Verbal Model

$$\frac{\text{Height of pole}}{\text{Height of stick}} = \frac{\text{Length of pole's shadow}}{\text{Length of stick's shadow}}$$

Labels

Height of pole = x ft

Height of stick = **5** ft

Length of pole's shadow = **24** ft

Length of stick's shadow = **4** ft

Algebraic Model

$$\frac{x \text{ ft}}{5 \text{ ft}} = \frac{24 \text{ ft}}{4 \text{ ft}}$$ Write the simplified proportion.

$$x \cdot 4 = 5 \cdot 24$$ Cross multiply.

$$\frac{x \cdot 4}{4} = \frac{5 \cdot 24}{4}$$ Divide each side by 4.

$$x = 30$$ Solution: *x* is by itself.

The telephone pole is 30 ft high.

6.6 Exercises

GUIDED PRACTICE

1. Draw two similar polygons of different sizes.

REASONING In Exercises 2 and 3, use the figures shown below and the following information.

You ask your friend to sketch two similar figures on grid paper. Your friend's sketches are shown below. Are your friend's sketches correct?

2.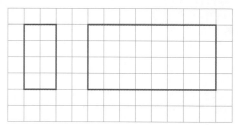

3.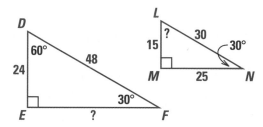

In Exercises 4–7, use the similar triangles shown at the right.

4. Match the sides of triangle *LMN* with the corresponding sides of triangle *DEF*.

5. What is the measure of angle *L*?

6. What is $\overline{EF}$?

7. Show that $\overline{DE}$ is to $\overline{EF}$ as $\overline{LM}$ is to $\overline{MN}$.

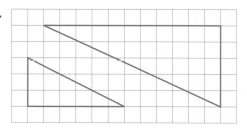

PRACTICE AND PROBLEM SOLVING

In Exercises 8 and 9, show that the two polygons are similar.

8.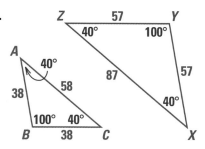

9.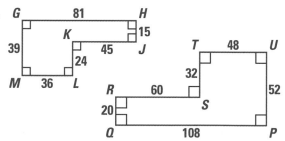

THINKING SKILLS In Exercises 10–12, answer the questions and explain your reasoning.

10. Are all triangles similar?

11. Are all squares similar?

12. Are all rectangles similar?

In Exercises 13–16, find the missing measures in these similar figures.

13.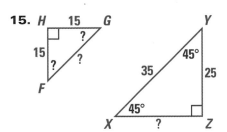

14.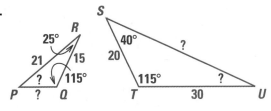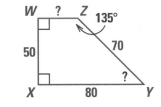

15.

16.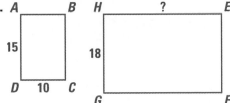

17.  **AMUSEMENT PARK** You are at Yokohama City, Japan, where the world's largest Ferris wheel, the Cosmoclock 21, is located. You want to find the height of the Ferris wheel. The Ferris wheel casts a 40 ft shadow. An $86\frac{1}{8}$ ft building nearby casts a 10 ft shadow.

Draw a diagram of the situation. Then make a verbal model of the diagram you drew. Use the model and a calculator to determine how tall the Cosmoclock 21 is.

STANDARDIZED TEST PRACTICE

In Exercises 18 and 19, use the rectangles shown at the right.

18. Rectangle A is similar to Rectangle B. What is the perimeter of Rectangle B?

    A 15 units   **B** 30 units

    C 35 units   **D** 50 units

19. What is the area of Rectangle B?

    A 54 sq units **B** 60 sq units

    C 80 sq units **D** 150 sq units

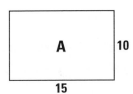

EXPLORATION AND EXTENSION

20. **BUILDING YOUR PROJECT** From the shore, you take a picture of your friend who is windsurfing in the harbor. In the photo, your friend is 3 inches tall and the mast of the sailboard is 9.6 inches tall. Your friend is 5 ft tall. How tall is the actual mast? Include this information in a section of your manual.

SPIRAL REVIEW

1. **SEPARATING INTO CASES** You are buying frozen yogurt for a party. At the store, frozen yogurt comes in 0.5 gal containers for $2.49 and 2 gal containers for $8.99. How many of each size should you buy to get at least 7 gal at the least cost? **(1.8)**

In Exercises 2–4, complete the statement using >, < or =. **(2.2)**

2. 5^3 ? 3^5 3. 9^2 ? 3^4 4. 6^2 ? 2^5

NUMBER SENSE In Exercises 5–8, match the number with its equivalent fraction or decimal. **(3.2)**

A. $\frac{26}{8}$ B. 2.25   C. $\frac{33}{8}$ D. 4.75

5. $2\frac{2}{8}$ 6. $4\frac{1}{8}$ 7. $3\frac{2}{8}$ 8. $4\frac{6}{8}$

ALGEBRA AND MENTAL MATH In Exercises 9–11, use mental math to solve the equation. **(3.7)**

9. $? \div 5 = \frac{1}{9}$ 10. $\frac{7}{11} \cdot ? = 1$ 11. $\frac{1}{12} \div ? = \frac{7}{12}$

In Exercises 12 and 13, write the equation that represents the statement. Then solve it. **(4.6, 4.7)**

12. The sum of eight and a number is negative five.

13. Negative nine is the difference of a number and sixteen.

14. **GAMES** The table below shows the number (in millions) of the best-selling games sold in the United States. Make a bar graph of the data. (Source: NPD Group) **(5.5)**

Game	Uno®	Monopoly®	Jenga®	Candyland®
Number	1.9	1.8	1.3	1.1

In Exercises 15–17, rewrite the quotient as a ratio. **(6.1)**

15. $\frac{7 \text{ ft}}{1 \text{ yd}}$ 16. $\frac{2 \text{ lb}}{8 \text{ oz}}$ 17. $\frac{15 \text{ min}}{3 \text{ h}}$

Powered by *Electricity*

READ About It

When Dan Sturges was only fourteen years old, he earned a commission for helping a salesperson sell a 4000 lb Cadillac.

Dan's taste in the weight of his cars has gotten smaller since then. He realized that air pollution and crowded streets were major problems in big cities. So he designed the Trans 2. It weighs only 875 lb. Dan wants the price of the car to be about $2000.

With a top speed of 22 mi/h, the Trans 2 is designed for very short trips. Its electric power can take it 25 mi without recharging.

New environmental laws may help vehicles like the Trans 2 become popular. For example, California has passed a law which says that by the year 2003, one tenth of all cars sold must be electrically powered. Would you drive a Trans 2 someday?

WRITE About It

1. Compare the weight of the Cadillac with the weight of the Trans 2 by writing a ratio. Explain why this is a ratio and not a rate.

2. Estimate the price of a new full-size car. Then find the ratio of this price to the planned price of the Trans 2. Write your answer as a sentence.

3. You live 5 mi from a grocery store. How many trips could you make to the grocery store and back in a Trans 2 without recharging the battery? Express your answer in the following form.

$$\frac{\text{trips}}{\text{battery charge}}$$

Is this a rate or a ratio? Explain.

4. Is the top speed of the Trans 2 expressed in the form of a rate, a ratio, or neither? Explain your answer.

5. Many cities have a 25 mi/h speed limit. How much longer would a 10 mi trip take if you drove a Trans 2 than if you drove a big car and did not exceed the speed limit? Do you think this is a big difference? Why?

6. In the year 2003, there will be about 6 million passenger cars produced in the United States. If the California law mandating electric cars applied in all states, how many of the cars produced in 2003 would be electric cars? Explain your reasoning.

6.7

Scale Drawings

What you should learn:

Goal 1 How to read a scale drawing

Goal 2 How to use similarity to find distances on a map

Why you should learn it:

Knowing how to make and read scale drawings can help you read blueprints. An example is finding the width of an actual room.

Goal 1 USING SCALE DRAWINGS

A **scale drawing** is a drawing in which the measurements are proportional to the actual dimensions of an object.

Scale drawings are used by many people, including architects, engineers, designers, builders, and landscapers. The ratio of measurements in a scale drawing to the actual measurements is called the **scale factor**.

Example 1 Reading a Scale Drawing

The partial blueprint below has a scale factor of $\frac{1}{8}$ in. to 1 ft. On the blueprint, the bedroom is $2\frac{1}{4}$ in. wide. How wide is the actual bedroom?

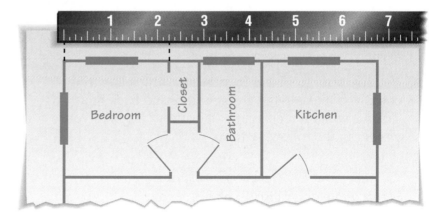

Solution

There are 12 inches in a foot and 8 "eighth inches" in an inch. This implies that there are 12×8, or 96, "eighth inches" in a foot. So, the scale factor is 1 to 96, usually written as 1:96. Let x represent the actual width of the room.

$$\frac{\textbf{Blueprint width}}{\textbf{Actual width}} = \frac{1}{96} \qquad \text{Scale factor is 1:96.}$$

$$\frac{2.25}{x} = \frac{1}{96} \qquad \text{Substitute the measurement.}$$

$$2.25 \cdot 96 = x \cdot 1 \qquad \text{Cross multiply.}$$

$$216 = x \qquad \text{Solution: } x \text{ is by itself.}$$

The room is 216 in. or 18 ft wide.

Example 2 **Using a Map**

STRATEGY **MAKE AN ESTIMATE** A placemat shows a map of Virginia, but no scale is given. You know that the distance from Charlottesville to Richmond is about 70 mi. To find the distance from Charlottesville to Roanoke, you use a ruler to measure the distances on the map, as shown below. Estimate the distance from Charlottesville to Roanoke.

CONNECTION
Geography

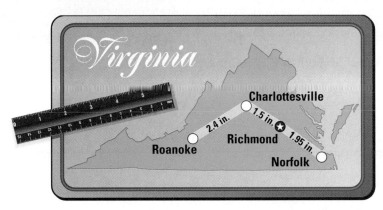

Solution

Verbal Model	$\dfrac{\text{Actual distance to Richmond}}{\text{Actual distance to Roanoke}} = \dfrac{\text{Map distance to Richmond}}{\text{Map distance to Roanoke}}$

Labels   Actual distance to Richmond = **70** mi
Actual distance to Roanoke = x mi
Map distance to Richmond = **1.5** in.
Map distance to Roanoke = **2.4** in.

Algebraic Model

$\dfrac{70 \text{ mi}}{x \text{ mi}} = \dfrac{1.5 \text{ in.}}{2.4 \text{ in.}}$ Write the proportion.

$70 \cdot 2.4 = 1.5 \cdot x$ Cross multiply.

$\dfrac{70 \cdot 2.4}{1.5} = \dfrac{1.5 \cdot x}{1.5}$ Divide each side by 1.5.

$112 = x$ Solution: x is by itself.

The distance to Roanoke is 112 miles.

ONGOING ASSESSMENT

Write About It
....

Use the map to estimate the distance from Richmond to Norfolk.

1. What is the distance in inches on the map?

2. What is the distance in miles? Explain your answer.

GUIDED PRACTICE

In Exercises 1–3, match the scale factor with the description.

A. 1 cm to 4 mi **B. 1 mm to 4 km** **C. 1 in. to 4 ft**

1. Scale drawing: 4 in.
Actual: 16 ft

2. Scale drawing: 3 cm
Actual: 12 mi

3. Scale drawing: 55 mm
Actual: 220 km

4. BIOLOGY You are drawing a diatom that is 0.0025 cm wide. Your drawing has a scale factor of 0.01 cm to 10 cm. How wide should you draw the cell?

5. MODELS A student built a model of Earth using a scale factor of 0.5 in., to 500 km. The distance around Earth is about 40,000 km. What is the distance around the model?

6. The blueprint for a house has a scale factor of $\frac{1}{8}$ in. to 1 ft.

On the blueprint, a room has a perimeter of 7 in. What is the actual perimeter?

7. GROUP ACTIVITY Make a scale drawing of a room in your school. Explain how you chose the scale factor.

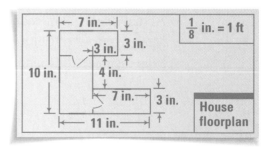

Diatoms are single-celled algae.

PRACTICE AND PROBLEM SOLVING

In Exercises 8–11, the scale of a map is 3 cm to 2 mi. You are given the distance on the map. Find the actual distance.

8. 18 cm **9.** 4 cm **10.** 2.4 cm **11.** 32.4 cm

In Exercises 12 and 13, find the perimeter of the actual object using the scale factor shown on the blueprint.

12.

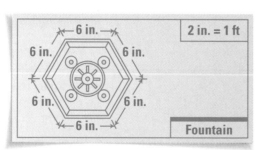

13.

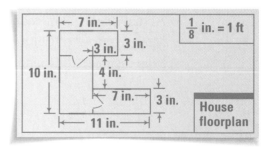

14. DINOSAUR MODEL On a museum tour you see a model depiction of a Brachiosaurus. Your tour guide says that the model was built using a scale factor of 1:5. If the model is 16 ft long, how long was the actual Brachiosaurus?

MAPPING TEXAS In Exercises 15–18, use the map of Texas at the right. The scale factor is 1 cm to 130 mi. Use a centimeter ruler to estimate the distance between the cities.

15. Lubbock and Dallas   **16.** Dallas and San Antonio

17. Houston and Austin   **18.** Austin and Lubbock

19. INTERIOR DESIGN You are designing a new kitchen for a home. The scale factor for the design of the kitchen is 0.25 in. to 1.5 ft. How long should you make a counter in your drawing if it has an actual length of 9 ft?

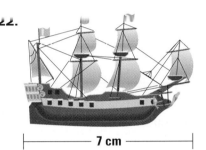

MODEL SHIPS In Exercises 20–22, a scale drawing of a model ship is shown. The scale factor for the drawings is 5 cm to 100 feet. Find the length of the actual ship.

20.

├─── 4 cm ───┤

21.

├─── 5 cm ───┤

22.

├─── 7 cm ───┤

STANDARDIZED TEST PRACTICE

23. The rooms in a dollhouse are 12 in. high, while the rooms in an actual house are 8 ft high. A desk in the actual house is 6 ft long. What is the length of a proportionate dollhouse desk?

(A) 1 ft   **(B)** 4 in.   **(C)** 6 in.   **(D)** 9 in.

EXPLORATION AND EXTENSION

24. COMMUNICATING ABOUT MATHEMATICS (page 305)
Suppose that you were making a design for a new electric car. What would you want it to look like? Make rough sketches of some designs. Choose a single design for your scale drawing. Then decide what dimensions (length, width, height) you would like the car to have. Choose an appropriate scale factor and make an accurate scale drawing of your car.

WHAT *did you learn?*

WHY *did you learn it?*

Skills

| 6.1 | Find a ratio. | Compare win-loss records. |

| 6.2 | Find a rate. | Evaluate the speeds of two bicyclists. |

| 6.3 | Solve proportions by making the denominators equal and by using unit rates. | Expand a recipe. |

| 6.4 | Solve proportions using cross multiplication. | Determine actual dimensions of an object from a drawing. |

| 6.5 | Write a proportion. | Estimate when a new volcanic island will appear. |

| 6.6 | Decide whether two polygons are similar. Use similar triangles to measure indirectly. | Indirectly measure heights. |

| 6.7 | Read and make scale drawings and maps. | Read and use blueprints. |

Strategies

| 6.1–6.7 | Use problem-solving strategies. | Solve a wide variety of real-world problems. |

Using Data

| 6.1–6.7 | Use tables, graphs, and time lines. | Organize data and solve problems. |

HOW *does it fit in the bigger picture of mathematics?*

Proportions can be closely connected to what some people consider "fair" in life.

For instance, a 5-year-old pours more orange juice into her glass than into her 3-year-old sister's glass. When asked why, the 5-year-old explains that she gets more because she is older. Her reasoning can actually be modeled by the following proportion.

$$\frac{\text{Age of 5-year-old}}{\text{Age of 3-year-old}} = \frac{\text{Amount in 5-year-old's glass}}{\text{Amount in 3-year-old's glass}}$$

Many everyday occurrences can be explained using proportions and mathematics.

VOCABULARY

- ratio (p. 272)
- rate (p. 276)
- unit rate (p. 276)
- proportion (p. 284)

- cross products (p. 288)
- corresponding sides (p. 300)
- proportional (p. 300)
- corresponding angles (p. 300)

- similar polygons (p. 300)
- scale drawing (p. 306)
- scale factor (p. 306)

6.1 RATIOS

If a and b have the same unit of measure, then the ratio of a to b is $\dfrac{a}{b}$.

Example Rewrite the quotient as a ratio. $\dfrac{25 \text{ s}}{4 \text{ min}}$

Solution You need to write both quantities in the same unit of measure.

$$\frac{25 \text{ s}}{4 \text{ min}} = \frac{25 \cancel{s}}{240 \cancel{s}} = \frac{5 \cdot 5}{5 \cdot 48} = \frac{5}{48}$$

For Exercises 1–4, rewrite the quotient as a ratio.

1. $\dfrac{10 \text{ ft}}{1 \text{ yd}}$

2. $\dfrac{6 \text{ h}}{17 \text{ min}}$

3. $\dfrac{4 \text{ lb}}{3 \text{ oz}}$

4. $\dfrac{2.5 \text{ gal}}{8 \text{ qt}}$

5. **GEOMETRY** Write the ratio of the area of the small rectangle to the area of the large rectangle.

3 in. | 5 in.

6 in. | 10 in.

6.2 RATES

If a and b have different units of measure, then the rate of a per b is $\dfrac{a}{b}$.

A rate with a denominator of 1 unit is a unit rate.

Example In 8 hours it snows 10 inches. Find the unit rate.

Solution $\dfrac{10 \text{ in.}}{8 \text{ h}} = \dfrac{10 \text{ in.} \div 8}{8 \text{ h} \div 8} = \dfrac{1.25 \text{ in.}}{1 \text{ h}}$

In Exercises 6 and 7, find the unit rate.

6. A heart beats 252 times in 3 min.

7. A car uses 3 gal of gas to travel 78 mi.

8. Find the unit rate for each. Which is the better buy? Explain.

   a. A 32-oz can of tomatoes for $1.60

   b. A 16-oz can of tomatoes for $0.96

6.3 SOLVING PROPORTIONS

An equation that equates two ratios is a proportion. To solve a proportion, you can rewrite both fractions to have the same denominator.

Example Solve the proportion $\frac{n}{42} = \frac{9}{14}$.

Solution $\frac{n}{42} = \frac{9 \cdot 3}{14 \cdot 3} \longrightarrow \frac{n}{42} = \frac{27}{42}$

Since both denominators are equal, $n = 27$.

In Exercises 9–12, solve the proportions.

9. $\frac{s}{5} = \frac{18}{30}$ **10.** $\frac{h}{7} = \frac{4}{70}$ **11.** $\frac{m}{3} = \frac{7}{27}$ **12.** $\frac{32}{11} = \frac{96}{x}$

6.4 MORE ABOUT SOLVING PROPORTIONS

You can also solve a proportion by using the Cross Products Property.

If $\frac{a}{b} = \frac{c}{d}$, then $a \cdot d = b \cdot c$.

Example Solve the proportion $\frac{7}{21} = \frac{y}{9}$ using cross products.

Solution $\frac{7}{21} = \frac{y}{9} \longrightarrow 9 \cdot 7 = 21 \cdot y \longrightarrow \frac{63}{21} = \frac{21 \cdot y}{21} \longrightarrow 3 = y$

Since $y = 3$, $\frac{7}{21} = \frac{3}{9}$.

In Exercises 13–16, use cross products to solve the proportion.

13. $\frac{20}{z} = \frac{4}{13}$ **14.** $\frac{t}{13} = \frac{7}{52}$ **15.** $\frac{6}{17} = \frac{18}{w}$ **16.** $\frac{y}{7.5} = \frac{4}{3}$

6.5 WRITING PROPORTIONS

Writing proportions can help you solve real-life problems. You can use a problem solving plan to write proportions.

Example You are taking a trip. Your destination is 330 mi from home. You travel 55 mi in the first hour. At this rate, how long will the car ride be?

Solution $\frac{\textbf{Distance driven}}{\textbf{Time traveled}} = \frac{\textbf{Total miles}}{\textbf{Total time}} \longrightarrow \frac{55 \text{ mi}}{1 \text{ h}} = \frac{330 \text{ mi}}{x \text{ h}} \longrightarrow$ $55 \cdot x = 1 \cdot 330$
$55x = 330$
$x = 6$

Your trip will take 6 hours at your current rate.

17. NIAGARA FALLS Approximately 750,000 gal/s of water flows over Niagara Falls. Write a verbal model, labels, and a proportion to find how many seconds it takes for 3 million gallons to go over the falls.

6.6 SIMILAR POLYGONS

Two polygons are similar if their corresponding angles have the same measure and their corresponding sides are proportional.

Example Show that the two rectangles are similar.

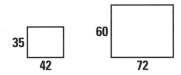

Solution Show that the ratios of the corresponding sides are equal.

$$\frac{35}{60} = \frac{35 \div 5}{60 \div 5} = \frac{7}{12}$$

$$\frac{42}{72} = \frac{42 \div 6}{72 \div 6} = \frac{7}{12}$$

Because the ratios of corresponding sides are equal, it follows that the two rectangles are similar.

18. Show that the two triangles are similar.

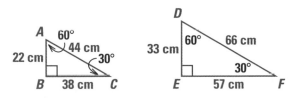

6.7 SCALE DRAWINGS

Scale drawings are used to provide a smaller picture of an actual structure.

Example A pool on a blueprint is 4 inches wide. The scale factor for the drawing is **1 to 48**. How wide is the actual pool?

Solution $\dfrac{\text{Blueprint width}}{\text{Actual width}} = \dfrac{1}{48}$ ⟶ $\dfrac{4 \text{ in.}}{x \text{ in.}} = \dfrac{1}{48}$ ⟶ $4 \cdot 48 = x \cdot 1$ ⟶ $192 = x$

The pool is 192 inches or 16 feet wide.

19. You are making a scale drawing of your classroom using a scale factor of 1 to 96. The actual classroom is 32 ft long and 24 ft wide. What are the dimensions, in inches, of the classroom on the drawing?

In Questions 1–4, is the quotient a rate or a ratio? Explain your reasoning. Then simplify the quotient.

1. $\dfrac{10 \text{ cats}}{15 \text{ dogs}}$

2. $\dfrac{50 \text{ questions}}{45 \text{ min}}$

3. $\dfrac{18 \text{ days}}{30 \text{ days}}$

4. $\dfrac{\$44}{8 \text{ h}}$

5. **HOURLY WAGE** What is the hourly wage of Exercise 4?

In Questions 6–8, which is the better buy? Explain.

6. **A.** A 3 pack of cassette tapes for $6.45   **B.** A 4 pack of cassette tapes for $7.80

7. **A.** A 2 lb bag of apples for $1.82   **B.** A 5 lb bag of apples for $4.45

8. **A.** One-half gallon of gasoline for $0.56   **B.** 7 gal of gasoline for $9.03

In Questions 9–14, solve the proportion. Then check your solution.

9. $\dfrac{2}{5} = \dfrac{x}{35}$

10. $\dfrac{m}{78} = \dfrac{7}{6}$

11. $\dfrac{36}{t} = \dfrac{27}{3}$

12. $\dfrac{17}{8} = \dfrac{8.5}{n}$

13. $\dfrac{7}{15} = \dfrac{k}{12}$

14. $\dfrac{15.9}{z} = \dfrac{3}{4}$

In Questions 15 and 16, find the missing measures of the similar figures.

15.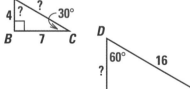

16.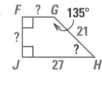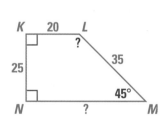

17. **U.S. FLAG** The width-to-length ratio of the flag of the United States is 10 to 19. You are making a flag that is 2 ft long. Write a verbal model, labels, and a proportion to find the width of the flag.

MODEL AIRPLANE You are building a model of a Ford Tri-Motor airplane. The scale factor of model length to actual length is 1 in. to 4 ft. The wingspan of the model airplane is 18 in.

18. Write the given scale factor as a simplified ratio.

19. What is the wingspan of the actual airplane?

20. If the length of the actual airplane is 50 ft, how long is the model airplane?

1. What is the ratio of the perimeter of the shaded region to the perimeter of the entire region?

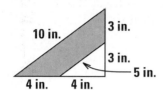

10 in. 3 in. 3 in. 5 in. 4 in. 4 in.

Ⓐ $\frac{1}{4}$ Ⓑ $\frac{1}{2}$

Ⓒ $\frac{11}{12}$ Ⓓ $\frac{11}{6}$

2. Which quotient is not equivalent to the other three?

Ⓐ $\frac{1 \text{ yd}}{6 \text{ yd}}$ Ⓑ $\frac{1 \text{ ft}}{18 \text{ ft}}$

Ⓒ $\frac{3 \text{ ft}}{6 \text{ yd}}$ Ⓓ $\frac{3 \text{ ft}}{18 \text{ ft}}$

3. Which of the following is the better buy?

Ⓐ A 2 lb bag of nails for $1.98

Ⓑ A 3 lb bag of nails for $2.10

Ⓒ A 5 lb bag of nails for $2.79

Ⓓ A 10 lb bag of nails for $5.75

4. Solve the proportion $\frac{9}{12} = \frac{n}{4}$.

Ⓐ 3 Ⓑ 12

Ⓒ 17 Ⓓ 27

5. You are at the top of a roller coaster hill that casts a 54-ft shadow. Your 5-ft tall friend watching below casts a 1.5-ft shadow. How tall is the roller coaster hill?

Ⓐ 16.2 ft Ⓑ 81 ft

Ⓒ 180 ft Ⓓ 270 ft

In Questions 6 and 7, use the following information. Your class of 24 students is having a pizza party. Your teacher estimates that 1 sheet pizza will feed 8 students. The pizza shop is having a special of two sheet pizzas for $25.

6. Which proportion could be used to find the number of sheet pizzas that are needed for the party?

Ⓐ $\frac{8}{1} = \frac{p}{24}$ Ⓑ $\frac{1}{p} = \frac{24}{8}$

Ⓒ $\frac{8}{1} = \frac{24}{p}$ Ⓓ $\frac{8}{24} = \frac{p}{1}$

7. How much will the pizzas cost?

Ⓐ $16.67 Ⓑ $25

Ⓒ $37.50 Ⓓ $75

In Questions 8 and 9, use the following information. The figures are similar.

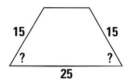

9 9 60° 60° ? 15 15 ? ? 25

8. What is the missing side length?

Ⓐ 12 Ⓑ 15

Ⓒ 18 Ⓓ 25

9. What is the missing angle measure?

Ⓐ 30° Ⓑ 60°

Ⓒ 90° Ⓓ 100°

10. You have a model train car that is 10 in. long and has a scale factor of 1 in. to 6 ft. How long is the actual train?

Ⓐ 16 ft Ⓑ 700 in.

Ⓒ 60 ft Ⓓ 66 ft

In Exercises 1–3, use dot paper to sketch a polygon of the given shape. (1.3)

1. Quadrilateral
2. Pentagon
3. Triangle

4. **GUESS, CHECK, AND REVISE** The diagram at the right represents a long-division problem. Each polygon represents a different digit. What is the long-division problem? **(1.5, 2.7)**

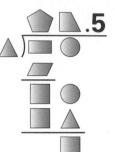

5. **USING LOGICAL REASONING** May, Ray, Kay, and Fay are all different ages. **(1.7)**

   - Kay is older than May.
   - Fay is younger than Ray.
   - May is older than Ray.

   Order the people from oldest to youngest.

In Exercises 6–8, evaluate the expression. (2.1, 2.2)

6. $9 + 3^3 \div 9$
7. $115 - 3(7 + 4) \times (11 - 8)$
8. $8 \times 10 - 2^5 \div 16$

In Exercises 9–12, write the prime factorization of the number. (2.4)

9. 72
10. 75
11. 112
12. 189

In Exercises 13–15, find the greatest common factor and the least common multiple of the numbers. (2.5, 3.1)

13. 6, 14
14. 24, 56
15. 25, 30

In Exercises 16–19, match the fraction with its equivalent fraction or mixed number. (2.6, 3.2)

A. $2\frac{1}{3}$
B. $\frac{3}{5}$
C. $4\frac{2}{3}$
D. $\frac{5}{3}$

16. $\frac{14}{3}$
17. $\frac{15}{25}$
18. $\frac{30}{18}$
19. $\frac{42}{18}$

In Exercises 20 and 21, order the numbers from least to greatest. (2.8)

20. $1.75, \frac{9}{5}, \frac{8}{3}, \frac{7}{2}, \frac{5}{9}, 2.65$
21. $\frac{9}{8}, 1.25, 1.05, \frac{3}{2}, \frac{6}{5}, 1.1$

In Exercises 22–29, add, subtract, multiply, or divide. (3.3–3.5, 3.7)

22. $\frac{2}{3} + \frac{1}{6}$
23. $\frac{3}{4} - \frac{3}{5}$
24. $6\frac{1}{4} - 4\frac{3}{8}$
25. $2\frac{5}{8} + 7\frac{5}{12}$

26. $\frac{1}{4}$ of $\frac{6}{7}$
27. $2\frac{1}{2} \times 3\frac{2}{5}$
28. $\frac{14}{9} \div \frac{7}{8}$
29. $4\frac{1}{6} \div 4$

In Exercises 30 and 31, use the description of the pattern to make a table of values for $x = 1, 2, 3, 4, 5,$ and 6. Then draw a scatter plot of the data. (4.1, 4.2)

30. The value of the expression begins at -4. Each time x increases by 1, the value of the expression increases by 3.

31. The value of the expression begins at 4. Each time x increases by 1, the value of the expression decreases by 2.

SCUBA DIVING In Exercises 32 and 33, you are scuba diving. The table below shows the dives you took at different times of the day. (4.3–4.5)

Time	10:00 A.M.	1:00 P.M.	4:00 P.M.
Depth	-55 ft	-25 ft	-80 ft

32. Find the sum of all three dives.

33. Find the difference between the 4:00 P.M. dive and the 10:00 A.M. dive.

In Exercises 34 and 35, find the mean, median, and mode of the data. (5.1)

34. Number of minutes of piano practice each day for 7 days: 10, 35, 25, 45, 15, 20, 25

35. Scores of 10 bowling games: 131, 167, 155, 111, 132, 149, 131, 102, 148, 134

36. Make a box-and-whisker plot of the data in Exercise 35. (5.3)

HOCKEY The table shows the number of games played and the number of points scored by the Pittsburgh Penguins for several hockey seasons. (5.5, 6.2)

Season	1991–92	1992–93	1993–94	1994–95	1995–96
Games	80	84	84	48	82
Points	87	119	101	61	102

(Source: National Hockey League)

37. Make a line graph of the number of points scored. Describe any patterns that you see.

38. Find the unit rate in points per game for each season.

In Exercises 39–41, use cross products to solve the proportion. Then check the solution. (6.4)

39. $\dfrac{x}{45} = \dfrac{3}{27}$

40. $\dfrac{8}{5} = \dfrac{m}{45}$

41. $\dfrac{33}{36} = \dfrac{11}{n}$

Percents and Decimals

BIRDS Keel-billed toucans can be found in Costa Rica, Central America. The rain forests are the home of many different bird species.

TECHNOLOGY

Technology resources accompanying this chapter:

- Interactive Real-Life Investigations
- Middle School Tutorial Software

CHAPTER THEME
Animals

FISH AND REPTILES A green sea turtle swims in the Pacific Ocean off Borneo, Malaysia.

AMPHIBIANS This three-lined salamander can hide by blending in well with the leaves around it.

MAMMALS Hamsters and guinea pigs are two species of small mammals.

Animal Species

REAL LIFE
Animals

More than a million and a half species of animals have been named, and scientists think that there may be many more species yet to be discovered! The **vertebrate** animals are familiar to us; they are animals with backbones: fish, amphibians, reptiles, birds, and mammals. There are about 45,700 species of vertebrates.

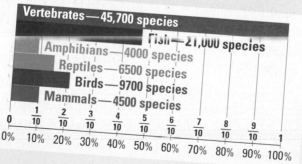

Vertebrates—45,700 species

Fish—21,000 species
Amphibians—4000 species
Reptiles—6500 species
Birds—9700 species
Mammals—4500 species

$0 \quad \frac{1}{10} \quad \frac{2}{10} \quad \frac{3}{10} \quad \frac{4}{10} \quad \frac{5}{10} \quad \frac{6}{10} \quad \frac{7}{10} \quad \frac{8}{10} \quad \frac{9}{10} \quad 1$

0% 10% 20% 30% 40% 50% 60% 70% 80% 90% 100%

Think and Discuss

1. About what fraction of the vertebrate species are fish? About what percent are fish?

2. About what fraction of the vertebrate species are mammals? About what percent are mammals?

PORTFOLIO

CHAPTER PROJECT

Helping a Veterinarian

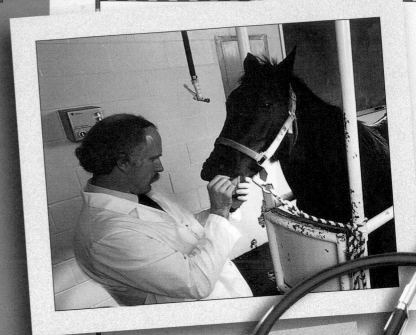

PROJECT DESCRIPTION

Suppose that you are spending your winter school vacation helping a veterinarian. You want to share your experiences with your math class by making one or more posters to accompany an oral or a written report. The posters and report contain information and data about the **TOPICS** listed on the next page. You may want to do your report and poster drawings on a computer if one is available.

GETTING STARTED

Talking It Over

- Discuss in your group what animals you think a veterinarian might treat and what tasks a veterinarian might perform.

- How much education is needed to become a veterinarian? What subjects does one need to study to become a veterinarian? Talk with a veterinarian or a librarian about these questions or explore them on the **Internet**; then report to your group.

Planning Your Project

- **Materials Needed:** poster board, colored pencils or markers, computer drawing software (optional)

- You may choose to make one large poster or several smaller posters. You can use the four topics in the **BUILDING YOUR PROJECT** list on page 321. You may want to include photographs of the animals, along with your data displays. Keep your work in your portfolio and add to it as assigned.

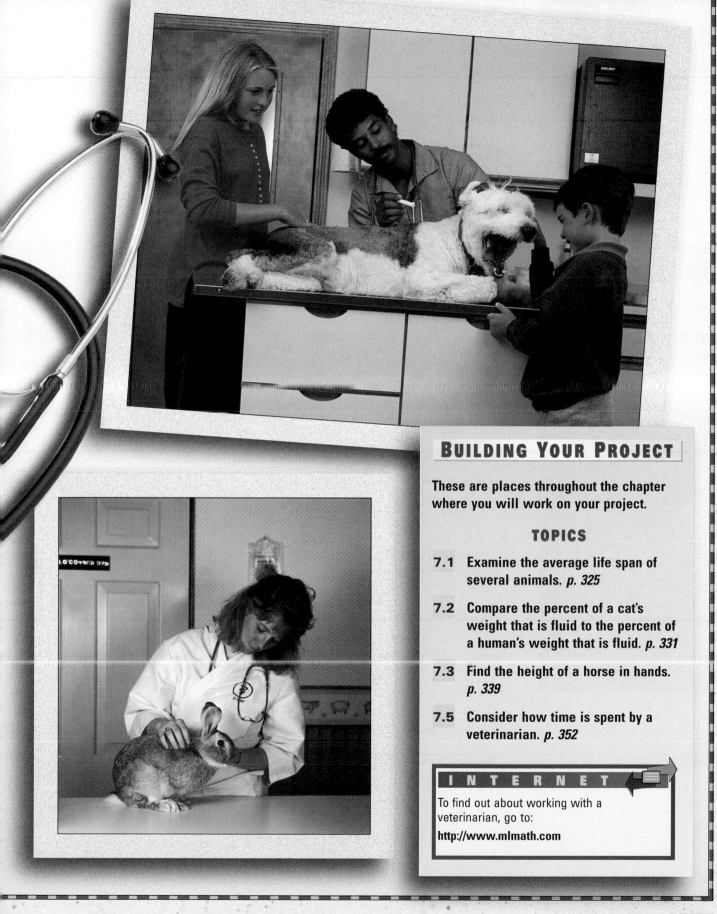

BUILDING YOUR PROJECT

These are places throughout the chapter where you will work on your project.

TOPICS

7.1 Examine the average life span of several animals. *p. 325*

7.2 Compare the percent of a cat's weight that is fluid to the percent of a human's weight that is fluid. *p. 331*

7.3 Find the height of a horse in hands. *p. 339*

7.5 Consider how time is spent by a veterinarian. *p. 352*

INTERNET

To find out about working with a veterinarian, go to:

http://www.mlmath.com

7.1

Percents, Fractions, and Decimals

What you should learn:

Goal 1 How to write numbers as percents, fractions, and decimals

Goal 2 How to use percents in real life

Why you should learn it:

Knowing how to write numbers as percents, fractions, and decimals can help you interpret survey results. An example is interpreting the results of a survey about cars.

Goal 1 PERCENTS, FRACTIONS, AND DECIMALS

The word *percent* means "per hundred." The symbol for percent is %. For example, in the square at the right, 25 of the 100 squares are red, so you can say that 25% of the squares are red.

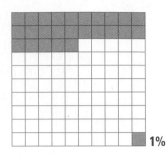

1%

PERCENT

A **percent** is a ratio whose denominator is 100.

Fraction form	Percent symbol form	Decimal form
$\dfrac{25}{100}$	25%	0.25

---

1. To write a fraction or a decimal as a percent, first rewrite it as a fraction with a denominator of 100.

$$\frac{1}{4} = \frac{1 \times 25}{4 \times 25} = \frac{25}{100} = 25\% \qquad 0.75 = \frac{75}{100} = 75\%$$

2. To write a percent as a fraction or a decimal, first rewrite it as a fraction with a denominator of 100.

$$86\% = \frac{86}{100} = 0.86$$

Example 1 Writing Numbers in Different Forms

a. Write 15% as a fraction and as a decimal.

$$15\% = \frac{15}{\mathbf{100}} = 0.15$$

b. Write 0.8 as a fraction and as a percent.

$$0.8 = \frac{8}{10} = \frac{8 \times \mathbf{10}}{10 \times \mathbf{10}} = \frac{80}{100} = 80\%$$

c. Write $\dfrac{2}{5}$ as a decimal and as a percent.

$$\frac{2}{5} = \frac{2 \times 20}{5 \times 20} = \frac{40}{100} = 0.40 = 40\%$$

Example 2 **Rounding Percents**

a. Write $\frac{1}{8}$ as a percent, rounded to one decimal place.

$$\frac{1}{8} = 0.125 = \frac{125}{1000} = \frac{125 \div \mathbf{10}}{1000 \div \mathbf{10}} = \frac{12.5}{100} = 12.5\%$$

b. Write $\frac{1}{3}$ as a percent, rounded to one decimal place.

$$\frac{1}{3} = 0.\overline{3} \approx 0.333 = \frac{333}{1000} = \frac{333 \div \mathbf{10}}{1000 \div \mathbf{10}} = \frac{33.3}{100} = 33.3\%$$

Example 3 **Interpreting a Survey**

In a survey, 120 people who bought new cars were asked which brand they bought. Write the results as percents. What is the total of the four percents?

REAL LIFE
Automobiles

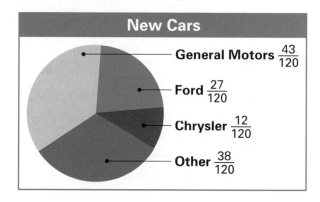

New Cars

General Motors $\frac{43}{120}$

Ford $\frac{27}{120}$

Chrysler $\frac{12}{120}$

Other $\frac{38}{120}$

Solution

General Motors	$\frac{43}{120} \approx 0.358 = \frac{35.8}{100} = 35.8\%$
Ford	$\frac{27}{120} = 0.225 = \frac{22.5}{100} = 22.5\%$
Chrysler	$\frac{12}{120} = 0.10 = \frac{10}{100} = 10\%$
Other	$\frac{38}{120} \approx 0.317 = \frac{31.7}{100} = 31.7\%$

The sum of the four percents is 100%. This means that all 120 people in the survey are accounted for.

ONGOING ASSESSMENT

Talk About It
. . . .

With a partner, use mental math to write each common percent as a fraction in simplest form. Talk about how you did it.

1. 1% **2.** 25%

3. $33\frac{1}{3}\%$ **4.** 40%

5. 50% **6.** 75%

GUIDED PRACTICE

1. THINKING SKILLS How did the word "percent" get its name?

In Exercises 2 and 3, explain the steps in the problem.

2. $36\% = \dfrac{36}{100} = \dfrac{9}{25}$

3. $0.625 = \dfrac{625}{1000} = \dfrac{62.5}{100} = 62.5\%$

4. Write 55% as a decimal and as a simplified fraction.

5. GROUP ACTIVITY Take a survey in your class of how many people can play a musical instrument. Write the result as a fraction, a decimal, and a percent. Use the result to estimate how many people out of 100 can play a musical instrument.

	Fraction	Decimal	Percent
Piano			
Clarinet			
Saxophone			

6. TEST GRADE You got a score of 42 out of 50 correct on a test.

As a fraction, you got $\dfrac{42}{50}$ correct.

As a percent, how much did you get correct?

PRACTICE AND PROBLEM SOLVING

In Exercises 7–10, write the percent as a decimal and a fraction in simplest form.

7. 8%

8. 22%

9. 45%

10. 90%

In Exercises 11–14, write the decimal as a fraction with a denominator of 100, then as a percent.

11. 0.78

12. 0.04

13. 0.095

14. 0.4

In Exercises 15–18, write the fraction as a percent.

15. $\dfrac{14}{25}$

16. $\dfrac{3}{50}$

17. $\dfrac{7}{8}$

18. $\dfrac{3}{4}$

In Exercises 19–22, what percent of the figure is shaded green?

19.

20.

21.

22.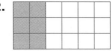

USING LOGICAL REASONING In Exercises 23 and 24, which number doesn't fit in the list? Explain.

23. $0.68, \dfrac{34}{50}, 68\%, \dfrac{14}{25}, \dfrac{68}{100}$

24. $\dfrac{20}{22}, 9.1\%, 0.909, \dfrac{10}{11}, 90.9\%$

MAKING AN ESTIMATE In Exercises 25–28, estimate the time (in hours) you spend in the activity during a typical weekday. Write your answer as a fraction with a denominator of 24. Then write it as a percent.

25. Attend school   **26.** Watch T.V.   **27.** Sleep   **28.** Do homework

GAMES In Exercises 29 and 30, use the results shown in the circle graph at the right. The survey asked 160 Trivial Pursuit® board-game owners which category was their favorite.

29. Write the results as percents. What is the total of the percents? What can you conclude?

30. Which percent is twice as large as another? What does this mean?

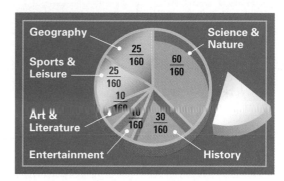

STANDARDIZED TEST PRACTICE

31. The fraction $\dfrac{15}{120}$ is the same as which percent?

Ⓐ 8.13%   Ⓑ 12.5%   Ⓒ 15%   Ⓓ 20%

32. Which fraction is the same as 28%?

Ⓐ $\dfrac{7}{25}$ Ⓑ $\dfrac{7}{50}$ Ⓒ $\dfrac{28}{50}$ Ⓓ $\dfrac{14}{100}$

EXPLORATION AND EXTENSION

PORTFOLIO

33. BUILDING YOUR PROJECT When you visit the veterinarian, you are given a chart that shows the average life span of several common pets. The average human life span (in the United States) is 76 years. What percent of a human life span is each animal's life span?

$$\text{Percent} = \frac{\text{Animal life span}}{\text{Human life span}}$$

Animal	Average life span
Cat	12 years
Dog	12 years
Goat	8 years
Horse	20 years
Rabbit	5 years

LAB 7.2

COOPERATIVE LEARNING

Modeling Percents

Materials Needed
- 10-by-10 unit square paper
- pencils or pens
- colored pencils

Part A PERCENT MODELS

1. Each 10-by-10 grid has 100 small squares. Because *percent* means per hundred, each small square represents 1%. The first figure models 50% because 50 of the 100 squares are shaded. What percents do the other figures model?

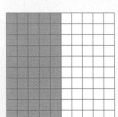 **a.** 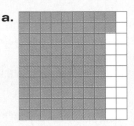 **b.**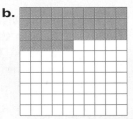

2. A second way to model 50% is shown at the right. Sketch two other ways. Which of the four models for 50% is clearest? Explain.

3. Use a 10-by-10 grid to skctch a model for each percent.

   a. 25%   **b.** 80%   **c.** 40%

   d. 17%   **e.** 1%   **f.** 100%

4. In Exercise 3(b), what percent of the model is *not* shaded?

5. Shade one fifth of all the small squares in a 10-by-10 grid. What percent are shaded?

Part B THE UNIT SQUARE

In the 10-by-10 grids in Part A, the large square represents 100%, or 1 whole unit. That is, the 10-by-10 grid is a *unit square* and each small square is one hundredth of the unit.

6. Draw a unit square that represents the 100 points on a test.

   a. What does each small square represent?

   b. Shade the portion that represents a score of 90 points.

7. Draw a unit square that represents a dollar. Shade the portion that represents $.35.

8. The unit squares below represent 200 frogs in a jumping contest. The 46 frogs that jumped more than 8 feet are represented by the shading in the second model. What percent of the frogs jumped more than 8 feet? Explain.

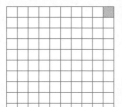 **Each small square represents 1%, or 2 frogs.**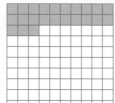

9. Draw a unit square that represents 50 apples.

   a. What does each small square represent?

   b. Shade the number of small squares that represents the 10 apples that are ripe.

   c. What percent of the 50 apples are ripe?

10. Draw a unit square that represents 300 trucks.

   a. What does each small square represent?

   b. Shade the number of small squares that represents the 81 trucks that are blue.

   c. What percent of the 300 trucks are blue?

NOW TRY THESE

11. Sketch a model for each percent.

   a. 24%   **b.** 75%   **c.** 33%

12. Draw a unit square that represents $500.

   a. What does each small square represent?

   b. Explain how to find the number of small squares that represents $200. Shade that number of small squares.

   c. What percent of $500 is $200?

13. If you shaded three fifths of a unit square, what percent of the square would be shaded?

Finding a Percent of a Number

What you should learn:

Goal 1 How to find a percent of a number

Goal 2 How to use percents to solve real-life problems

Why you should learn it:

Knowing how to find a percent of a number can help you understand the results of a survey. An example is finding the number of people who choose a certain method of transportation to get to work.

Many commuters travel by subway in New York City.

Goal 1 FINDING A PERCENT OF A NUMBER

You can use a 10-by-10 unit square to find a percent of a number.

Suppose you are driving 300 miles. The first 20% of the road is under construction. To find this distance, find 20% of 300 miles as follows. The entire unit square represents 300 miles.

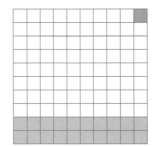

Each small square represents 1%, or 3 miles.

20% of 300 miles is represented by 20 small squares, which represent 60 miles.

You traveled 60 miles on roads that are under construction.

LESSON INVESTIGATION

COOPERATIVE LEARNING

Investigating Finding a Percent of a Number

GROUP ACTIVITY Copy and complete the table below. For each problem, draw a 10-by-10 unit square.

Unit Square Represents	Percent	Number of Small Squares Shaded	Value of a Small Square	Value of Shaded Squares
300 miles	20%	20	3 miles	60 miles
$150	80%	?	?	?
$5.00	25%	?	?	?
200 boats	30%	?	?	?
600 hours	75%	?	?	?

One way to find a percent of a number is to (1) find the value of 1% of the number and then (2) multiply that value by the number of percent given.

$$20\% \text{ of } 300 = 20 \times (1\% \text{ of } 300)$$
$$= 20 \times \left(\frac{1}{100} \times 300\right)$$
$$= 20 \times 3$$
$$= 60$$

A second way to find a percent of a number is to (1) rewrite the percent as a decimal and (2) multiply the decimal by the number.

$$20\% \text{ of } 300 = 0.20 \times 300 = 60$$

Example 1 **Finding a Percent of a Number**

REAL LIFE
Transportation

Two hundred workers in New York and 200 workers in New Jersey were asked how they got to work. The responses to the survey are shown below. How many people are in each category?

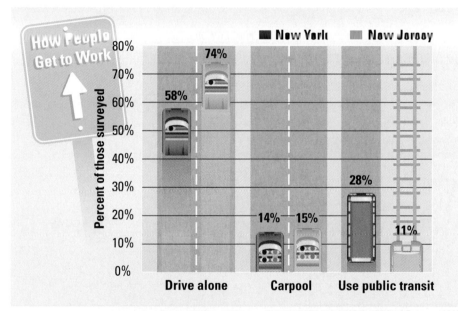

(Source: Statistical Abstract of the United States, 1996)

Solution

Drives Alone (NY)	58% of 200 = 0.58 × 200 = 116
Carpools (NY)	14% of 200 = 0.14 × 200 = 28
Public Transit (NY)	28% of 200 = 0.28 × 200 = 56
Drives Alone (NJ)	74% of 200 = 0.74 × 200 = 148
Carpools (NJ)	15% of 200 = 0.15 × 200 = 30
Public Transit (NJ)	11% of 200 = 0.11 × 200 = 22

You can check this by adding the amounts in each state. For example, in New York, the total is 116 + 28 + 56, or 200 people.

GUIDED PRACTICE

In Exercises 1–3, state what a small square of the unit square represents. Then use your answer to find the given percent.

1. 30% of 250 miles   **2.** 15% of 80 sandwiches   **3.** 60% of 45 oranges

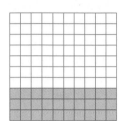 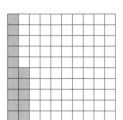 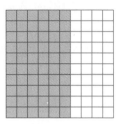

4. Draw a 10-by-10 unit square that represents 200 baseball cards. What does each small square represent?

5. **a.** Use the result of Exercise 4 to find 33% of 200 baseball cards.

   b. Describe a different way to find 33% of 200.

6. **WRITING** Describe a real-life problem that can be solved using the equation $0.30 \times 150 = 45$.

PRACTICE AND PROBLEM SOLVING

In Exercises 7–9, write the percent and the value represented by the shaded area.

7. 100 squares = 50 hours   **8.** 100 squares = 150 kg   **9.** 100 squares = 500 cups

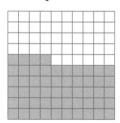 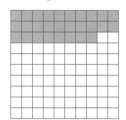 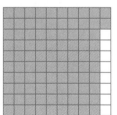

In Exercises 10–12, use a unit-square model to find the value.

10. 25% of 160 cars   **11.** 80% of 50 questions   **12.** 6% of $4.00

In Exercises 13–15, find 1% of the number. Then find 40%.

13. 50   **14.** 250   **15.** 800

In Exercises 16–23, find the percent of the number.

16. 16% of 425   **17.** 52% of 300   **18.** 8% of 150   **19.** 96% of 125

20. 48% of 50   **21.** 18% of 250   **22.** 4% of 600   **23.** 72% of 75

MAKING AN ESTIMATE In Exercises 24 and 25, use the given information to estimate the percent.

24. Estimate 55% of 110. Given: **50% of 110 = 55** and **60% of 110 = 66**

25. Estimate 85% of 40. Given: **80% of 40 = 32** and **90% of 40 = 36**

26. SCIENCE The supply of water on Earth is 326 million cubic miles. About 97% of this amount is salt water. How many million cubic miles of salt water does Earth contain?

27. RECYCLING Your class is collecting used telephone books to recycle. The class goal is to collect 300 phone books. So far, you have reached 73% of your goal. How many phone books have you collected?

28. GOLD PRODUCTION In 1995, there were about 2250 metric tons of gold mined in the world. The bar graph at the right shows the percents that were mined in South Africa, the United States, and Russia. How much gold was mined in each of these three countries?

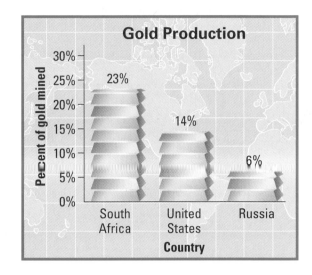

Gold Production

STANDARDIZED TEST PRACTICE

29. 150 people are surveyed. 120 of them say they are satisfied with their jobs. What percent of the people are satisfied?

   (A) 20%   **(B)** 40%   **(C)** 60%   **(D)** 80%

30. Judd's sister weighs 45% as much as Judd does. Judd weighs 80 pounds. How much does his sister weigh?

   (A) 22 pounds   **(B)** 36 pounds   **(C)** 45 pounds   **(D)** 52 pounds

EXPLORATION AND EXTENSION

PORTFOLIO

31. BUILDING YOUR PROJECT The amount of fluid in a cat's body is about 50% of its weight. In a human, fluids are about 72% of the weight. What is the weight of the fluid in a 12-pound cat? In a 12-pound baby? Write a statement comparing these weights.

In Exercises 1–4, write two fractions that represent the shaded portion of the model. (2.6)

1.

2.

3.

4.

5. You have a piece of ribbon that is $4\frac{2}{3}$ feet long. You are going to use it in wrapping four door prizes for a banquet. You divide the ribbon evenly among the door prizes. How long is each piece? **(3.7)**

6. Draw a frequency table and a histogram of the data. **(5.2)**

   19, 32, 56, 21, 48, 11, 13, 24, 67, 45, 14, 60, 25, 22, 39, 20, 16, 18, 31, 27, 40

In Exercises 7–10, solve the proportion. (6.3, 6.4)

7. $\dfrac{7}{12} = \dfrac{x}{60}$

8. $\dfrac{54}{15} = \dfrac{n}{5}$

9. $\dfrac{m}{3} = \dfrac{36}{4}$

10. $\dfrac{y}{6.9} = \dfrac{2}{3}$

Social Studies Connection

THE U.S. CENSUS

The United States Census is a special kind of *tally*, or counting. The Census counts the population and gathers all sorts of data. A new census has been taken every ten years since 1790. The jug at the right shows the figures from the first United States Census.

How old are Americans? How large are their families? What languages do they speak at home? These are just a few questions that the Census answers.

The chart below came from the 1990 census in one Massachusetts town.

Age of children (years)	under 3	3 and 4	5	6 to 11	12 and 13	14	15 to 17
Number of children	993	480	175	1407	252	107	573

1. Which age group is about 25% of the total number of children (3987 children)?

2. About what percent of the total number of children is the "12 and 13 years" group?

What Percent is Good Enough?

Many people think that getting something 99.9% correct is good enough. Many times in life that's true. But there are some times when it isn't!

Example

a. About 270,000,000 first-class letters are sent each day in the United States. If only 99.9% were delivered to the correct address, how many would be delivered incorrectly?

b. About 44,000,000 hot dogs are eaten each day in the United States. If only 99.9% were fit to eat, how many would not be fit to eat?

Solution

a. 99.9% of 270,000,000 is

0.999 ⊠ 270,000,000 ▤ (269,730,000).

This means that 270,000,000 − 269,730,000, or 270,000 letters would be delivered incorrectly each day.

b. 99.9% of 44,000,000 is

0.999 ⊠ 44,000,000 ▤ (43,956,000).

This means that 44,000,000 − 43,956,000, or 44,000 hot dogs would not be fit to eat each day.

CALCULATOR TIP

If your calculator doesn't display enough digits to work with very large numbers, you can do part of the multiplication mentally. For example, to multiply 0.999 by 2,000,000,000, you divide 2,000,000,000 by 1000 and enter

0.999 ⊠ 2,000,000 ▤

to get a display of

(1,998,000).

Then, multiply the result by 1000 to get
   1,998,000,000.

Exercises

1. About 31,000,000 households have one car. If only 99.9% of these cars start up one morning, how many do not start?

2. Over 1.6 billion telephone calls are made each day in the United States. If only 99.9% were made to correct numbers, how many would be made to wrong numbers?

3. About 700 million audio compact disks are sold each year in the United States. If only 99.9% are not returned to the sellers, how many would be returned?

4. Use your library or some other reference source to find a statistic that you think would make an interesting "What Percent is Good Enough?" problem. Then write the problem and its answer.

Investigating Large and Small Percents

Materials Needed
- grid paper
- pencils or pens
- colored pencils or markers

The number represented by the shaded portion of the model below can be written in three ways.

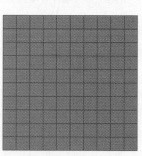

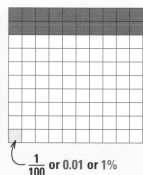

as a Fraction . . .
120 squares = $1\frac{20}{100}$

as a Decimal . . .
120 squares = 1.20

as a Percent . . .
120 squares = 120%

$\frac{1}{100}$ or 0.01 or 1%

1. Write three names (percent, fraction, and decimal) for the model.

 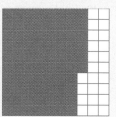

2. Use 10-by-10 grids to sketch a model for each percent.

   a. 125%   **b.** 180%   **c.** 140%

   d. 200%   **e.** 250%   **f.** 400%

3. Consider a 10-by-10 unit square that represents the 100 points on a test.

   a. What does each small square represent?

   b. Suppose the 100-point test has a bonus question, and you score 105 points. Use 10-by-10 grids to sketch a model of this score.

You know that each small square in a unit square represents 1%. To model percents that are less than 1%, use part of a small square.

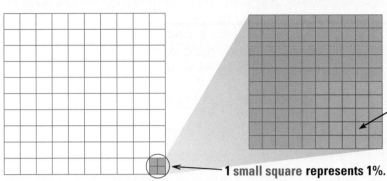

Each 1% small square can be divided into 100 smaller squares. One fourth of a 1% square is 25 smaller squares and represents $\frac{1}{4}$% or 0.25%.

1 small square represents 1%.

4. What portion of one of the small squares in a unit square represents each percent?

   a. $\frac{3}{4}$% or 0.75%   **b.** $\frac{2}{5}$% or 0.4%   **c.** $\frac{1}{10}$% or 0.1%

5. Consider a 10-by-10 unit square that represents 200 people.

   a. What does each small square represent?

   b. How many people does half a small square represent?

   c. What percent does half a small square represent?

   d. What is $\frac{1}{2}$% of 200 people? Explain your reasoning.

NOW TRY THESE

6. Draw a unit square that represents $1000.

   a. What does each small square represent?

   b. How much does one fifth of a small square represent?

   c. What percent does one fifth of a small square represent?

   d. What is $\frac{1}{5}$% of $1000? Explain.

7. What is 100% of 30? What is 50% of 30? Use these two results to find 150% of 30. Explain.

Large and Small Percents

What you should learn:

Goal 1 How to use large and small percents

Goal 2 How to estimate the percent of a number

Why you should learn it:

Knowing how to use large and small percents can help you estimate percents of a population. An example is estimating the percent of births that are identical twins.

In 1992, only about 0.33% of births were identical twins.

Goal 1 USING LARGE AND SMALL PERCENTS

It is possible to have percents that are greater than 100% or less than 1%. Here are some examples. Study the examples to see the relationship between a decimal, a fraction, and a percent.

a. $1.4 = 1\frac{4}{10} = \frac{14}{10} = \frac{14 \times 10}{10 \times 10} = \frac{140}{100} = 140\%$

b. $\frac{1}{2}\% = 0.5\% = \frac{0.5}{100} = \frac{0.5 \times 10}{100 \times 10} = \frac{5}{1000} = 0.005$

c. $\frac{5}{4} = 1\frac{1}{4} = 1.25 = 1\frac{25}{100} = \frac{125}{100} = 125\%$

Example 1 **Finding a Percent of a Number (Percent > 100)**

You can use two methods to find 130% of 250.

Method **1** Rewrite 130% as a decimal.

130% of 250 = **1.3** × 250 = 325

Method **2** Use a unit square model to show that 130 × 2.5 = 325.

 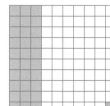

Each unit square (100 small squares) represents 250.

130 small squares represent 130% of 250.

Each small square represents 2.5.

Example 2 **Finding a Percent of a Number (Percent < 1)**

You can use two methods to find 0.5% of 40.

Method **1** Rewrite 0.5% as a decimal.

0.5% of 40 = **0.005** × 40 = 0.2

Method **2** Use a unit square model to show that 0.5 × 0.4 = 0.2.

1 unit square (100 small squares) represents 40.

0.5 small square represents 0.5% of 40.

Each small square represents 0.4.

In many real-life situations, it is helpful to use mental math to estimate the percent of a number.

LESSON INVESTIGATION

COOPERATIVE LEARNING

Investigating Estimation Techniques

GROUP ACTIVITY Copy the table. Use mental math to complete the table. Discuss your strategy.

Unit Square Represents	1%	10%	50%	200%
$48	?	?	?	?
600 people	?	?	?	?
180 grams	?	?	?	?

Example 3 — Estimating Percents

Use mental math to estimate the number.

a. 148% of 84

b. $\frac{1}{2}$% of 140

Solution

a. 148% is about **150%**.

$$
\begin{array}{rcl}
100\% \text{ of } 84 &=& 84 \\
+\ 50\% \text{ of } 84 &=& 42 \\
\hline
150\% \text{ of } 84 &=& 126
\end{array}
$$

Use mental math to break up the problem.

So, 148% of 84 is a little less than 126.

b. $\frac{1}{2}$% is **half** of **1%**.

1% of 140 = **1.4** — Use mental math.

Half of **1.4** is **0.7**.

So, $\frac{1}{2}$% of 140 is 0.7.

UNGOING ASSESSMENT

Talk About It

Use mental math to estimate the number. Describe your steps.

1. 220% of 48

2. $\frac{1}{3}$% of 60

3. 324% of 40

GUIDED PRACTICE

In Exercises 1 and 2, write the percent modeled by the unit square(s).

1.

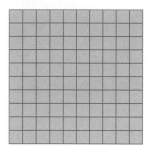

2.

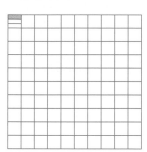

In Exercises 3–6, match the percent with its equivalent decimal.

  A. 0.018   **B. 1.8**   **C. 0.18**   **D. 0.0018**

3. 180% **4.** 0.18% **5.** 1.8% **6.** 18%

In Exercises 7 and 8, use mental math to estimate.

7. 325% of 120 **8.** $\frac{1}{4}\%$ of 400

9. MAKING AN ESTIMATE The average height in your class is 60 inches. John's height is 120% of the average. How tall is John?

10. WRITING Write a real-life problem that uses percents greater than 100%.

PRACTICE AND PROBLEM SOLVING

In Exercises 11–15, write the percent as (a) a decimal and (b) a fraction in simplest form.

11. 170% **12.** $\frac{4}{5}\%$ **13.** $\frac{3}{8}\%$ **14.** 232% **15.** 450%

In Exercises 16–20, write the fraction or decimal as a percent.

16. 1.95 **17.** $\frac{13}{2}$ **18.** $\frac{3}{400}$ **19.** 0.00875 **20.** $\frac{81}{25}$

In Exercises 21–23, use mental math.

21. 110% of 50 points   **22.** 160% of \$450   **23.** $\frac{1}{4}\%$ of 200 days

In Exercises 24–27, complete the statement using >, <, or =.

24. 280% ? 0.28 **25.** 0.0125 ? $\frac{1}{8}\%$ **26.** $\frac{2}{5}\%$? $\frac{2}{50}$ **27.** $\frac{34}{25}$? 136%

LOOKING FOR A PATTERN In Exercises 28 and 29, find the percent of each number. Then describe the pattern and list the next two numbers.

28. $\frac{1}{5}$% of 125, $\frac{2}{5}$% of 125, $\frac{3}{5}$% of 125, $\frac{4}{5}$% of 125

29. 110% of 150, 120% of 200, 130% of 250, 140% of 300

30. IMMIGRATION In 1995, approximately 720,000 people immigrated to the United States. The table at the right shows the number of immigrants who settled in various metropolitan areas. Estimate the percent of immigrants who settled in each area.

Metropolitan Area	Number of Immigrants Settling There in 1995
New York, NY	111,687
Chicago, IL	31,730
Boston, MA	16,750
Houston, TX	14,379
Atlanta, GA	9,494

(Source: Immigration and Naturalization Service)

31. TWINS How many of the approximately 4 million births in 1992 were identical twins? (*Hint.* See page 336.)

32. **TECHNOLOGY** It costs you $12 to publish a book. You sell the book for 175% of your cost. How much do you sell the book for?

STANDARDIZED TEST PRACTICE

33. All of the following are the same as $\frac{4}{25}$% except

A 0.0016.   **B** 0.16%.   **C** $\frac{32}{200}$%.   **D** $\frac{16}{100}$.

34. Out of 80 students taking Algebra I, 95% passed the final exam. About 80% of those who passed the exam got a grade better than a C. How many students got an A or a B?

A 19   **B** 76   **C** 61   **D** 64

EXPLORATION AND EXTENSION

PORTFOLIO

35. BUILDING YOUR PROJECT The veterinarian is checking the height of a horse to make sure it is growing properly. As a foal, the horse was 7 hands tall. After measuring the horse, the veterinarian finds that it is 230% of its height as a foal. How many hands tall is the horse? In inches, how tall is the horse? (1 hand = 4 inches) Write a statement about *your* height in hands.

LAB 7.4

COOPERATIVE LEARNING

Investigating Percent Problems

Part A MODELING PERCENT PROBLEMS

Materials Needed
- 10-by-10 unit square paper
- pencils or pens
- colored pencils or markers

1. In one of their basketball games, the Chicago Bulls scored 120 points. Of those points, Michael Jordan scored 30%.

   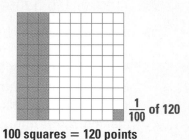

   $\frac{1}{100}$ of 120

   100 squares = 120 points

   a. How many points does one small square represent?

   b. How many small squares represent the number of points scored by Michael Jordan?

   c. How many points did Michael Jordan score? Explain how you found the number.

2. You see a basketball on sale for $13.50. This is 75% of the regular price.

   100 squares represents the regular price.

   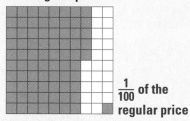

   $\frac{1}{100}$ of the regular price

   75 squares = $13.50

   a. How much money does one small square represent?

   b. The whole unit square represents the regular price. What is the regular price?

   c. What value is represented by the 25 unshaded squares?

Part B WRITING PERCENT PROBLEMS

3. Each person in your group should write a real-life problem that can be modeled by one of these unit squares. Exchange problems and solve them. When everyone is done, discuss the solutions.

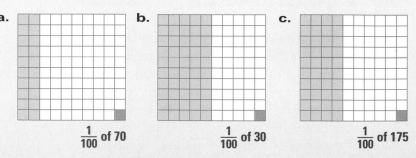

a. $\frac{1}{100}$ of 70   b. $\frac{1}{100}$ of 30   c. $\frac{1}{100}$ of 175

4. Over the past several weeks, you have earned $180 for baby-sitting. Of this amount, you saved $72.

100 squares = $180

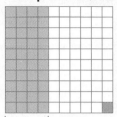

$\frac{1}{100}$ of 180 = 1.8

72 ÷ 1.8 = 40

a. The unit square represents all 180 dollars. How much money is represented by each small square?

b. How many small squares represent the amount of money you saved?

c. What percent of the $180 did you save? Explain how you found the number.

5. There are 700 students in your school. On one day, 28 of the students were absent.

a. Draw a 10-by-10 unit square that represents 700 students. How many students are represented by each small square?

b. How many small squares represent 28 students? Shade that number of squares.

c. The shaded portion represents the percent of absent students. What percent is this?

NOW TRY THESE

6. A concert was attended by 3240 people under 18 years old. This was 60% of the audience.

a. Shade 60% of a 10-by-10 unit square to represent 3240 people.

b. What does each small square represent?

c. How many people are represented by the whole unit square?

d. What does the unshaded portion of the unit square represent? Explain.

7. Use a 10-by-10 unit square to solve each problem. In each case, state what each small square represents.

a. 120 books is 40% of how many books?

b. 1050 people is what percent of 1400 people?

c. $2.88 is what percent of $8.00?

7.4

The Percent Equation

Why you should learn it:

Knowing how to use the percent equation can help you solve percent problems. An example is finding the percent of softball games you won.

Goal 1 FINDING PERCENTS

In Lesson 6.3, you learned how to solve proportions. You can use this skill to solve different kinds of percent problems. To do that, use the **percent equation** described below.

THE PERCENT EQUATION

The statement "*a* is *p* percent of *b*" is equivalent to the equation

$$\frac{a}{b} = \frac{p}{100}.$$ **Percent equation**

In this equation, *b* is the **base of a percent** and *a* is the number that is compared to the base.

Substitute known values into the percent equation. Then solve the proportion for the unknown value as shown in Example 1.

Example 1 ▷ Finding Percents

a. Your team won 19 of its 25 softball games. You can find the percent, *p*, that you won as follows.

$$\frac{19}{25} = \frac{p}{100}$$ **Write a percent equation.**

$$0.76 = \frac{p}{100}$$ **Divide 19 by 25 to obtain the decimal form.**

$$0.76 \times \mathbf{100} = \frac{p}{\cancel{100}} \times \cancel{\mathbf{100}}$$ **Multiply each side by 100.**

$$76 = p$$ **Simplify.**

Your team won 76% of its games.

b. You ordered 40 batteries, but were sent 46 batteries. You can find what percent 46 is of 40 as follows.

$$\frac{46}{40} = \frac{p}{100}$$ **Write a percent equation.**

$$1.15 = \frac{p}{100}$$ **Divide to obtain the decimal form.**

$$1.15 \times \mathbf{100} = \frac{p}{\cancel{100}} \times \cancel{\mathbf{100}}$$ **Multiply each side by 100.**

$$115 = p$$ **Simplify.**

You were sent 115% of the amount you ordered.

NEED TO KNOW

If you start with a true equation and multiply each side of the equation by the same number, the result is a true equation.

$$0.54 = \frac{54}{100}$$

$$0.54 \times 100 = \frac{54}{\cancel{100}} \times \cancel{100}$$

$$54 = 54$$

Example 2 ▷ **Finding the Number**

You bought a pair of jeans on sale. The price you paid was 80% of the full price of $24.50. What was the sale price?

Solution

One way to find the sale price, a, of the pair of jeans is to use the percent equation.

$$\frac{a}{24.50} = \frac{80}{100} \qquad \text{Write a percent equation.}$$

$$\frac{a}{24.50} = 0.80 \qquad \text{Write in decimal form.}$$

$$24.5 \times \frac{a}{24.50} = 24.5 \times 0.8 \qquad \text{Multiply each side by 24.5.}$$

$$a = 19.6 \qquad \text{Simplify.}$$

The sale price for the jeans was $19.60.

Example 3 ▷ **Finding the Base**

A survey of people who suffered injuries at home found that 32% of all the accidents involved falls. If 80 accidents involved falls, how many accidents were there?

REAL LIFE
Safety

Solution

To find the total number of home accidents counted in the survey, use the percent equation.

$$\frac{80}{b} = \frac{32}{100} \qquad \text{Write a percent equation.}$$

$$80 \cdot 100 = 32 \cdot b \qquad \text{Cross multiply.}$$

$$8000 = 32b \qquad \text{Simplify.}$$

$$\frac{8000}{32} = \frac{32b}{32} \qquad \text{Divide each side by 32.}$$

$$250 = b \qquad \text{Simplify.}$$

The respondents in the survey had 250 home accidents.

Real Life...
Real Facts

Levi Strauss & Co. paid $25,000 for an ancient pair of blue jeans. The single back pocket and the leather patch on the waistband show that the pair of jeans was made between 1886 and 1902. The jeans will be placed in the Levi Strauss & Co. Archives.

ONGOING ASSESSMENT

Write About It
....

Write a real-life problem that is similar to Example 3.

1. Trade problems with a partner and solve each other's problem.

2. Discuss your solutions.

GUIDED PRACTICE

In Exercises 1–3, complete the percent equation. Then solve the percent equation and answer the question.

1. What percent of 20 is 17?

$$\frac{?}{?} = \frac{p}{100}$$

2. What is 33% of 300?

$$\frac{a}{?} = \frac{?}{100}$$

3. 25 is 20% of what?

$$\frac{?}{b} = \frac{?}{100}$$

4. PETS Copy and complete the table. It shows the number or percent of the 177,090,000 pets in the United States that are the four most favorite pets. (Source: Pet Industry Joint Advisory Council)

Animal	Cats	Dogs	Small animals*	Parakeets and other birds
Number	?	58,262,610	?	40,022,340
Percent	37.3%	?	7.2%	?

*hamsters, rabbits, gerbils, guinea pigs, ferrets, etc.

ERROR ANALYSIS **In Exercises 5 and 6, an error was made in the percent equation. Correct the error and answer the question.**

5. 36 is what percent of 150?

$$\frac{a}{150} = \frac{36}{100} \quad \times$$

6. 4 is 8% of what number?

$$\frac{a}{8} = \frac{4}{100} \quad \times$$

PRACTICE AND PROBLEM SOLVING

In Exercises 7–10, use a percent equation to solve.

7. A person ate 2500 calories in a day. Of these, 30% came from fat. How many calories came from fat?

8. You spend about 30% of a 24-hour day at school. How many hours are you at school?

9. In a survey, 15% or 30 people said that pretzels were their favorite snack food. How many people were surveyed?

10. DISCOUNT PRICES You bought a jacket that was reduced to 70% of the original price. The original price was $35.00. How much did you pay for the jacket?

In Exercises 11–16, solve the percent problem.

11. What is 24% of 75?

12. What percent of 145 is 29?

13. 99 is what percent of 396?

14. 12% of what number is 42?

15. $33\frac{1}{3}$% of what number is 3?

16. 30 is 250% of what number?

LOOKING FOR A PATTERN **In Exercises 17–19, solve the percent problems. Describe any patterns that you see.**

17. 1% of 800

2% of 400

4% of 200

18. 1% of 100

2% of 200

3% of 300

19. 25% of 60

50% of 60

75% of 60

In Exercises 20 and 21, solve the percent problem.

20. **SUNNY SKIES** In Phoenix, Arizona, the weather is clear about 60% of the time. About how many days of the year is it clear?

21. **HEALTH** Your gym teacher says that your heart rate will be around 90 beats per minute when you are exercising. This is 125% of your heart rate at rest. How many beats per minute is your resting heart rate?

22. **WORLD POPULATION** The population of the world is about 5,850,000,000 people. Use the pictograph to estimate the percent of the world population in each of the listed countries.

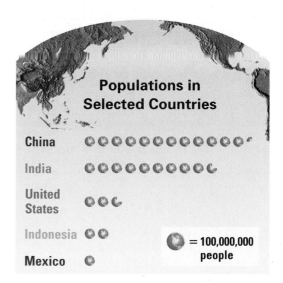

Populations in Selected Countries

China

India

United States

Indonesia

Mexico

= 100,000,000 people

 STANDARDIZED TEST PRACTICE

23. Which angle has a measure that is about 33% of 360°?

Ⓐ Ⓑ Ⓒ Ⓓ

24. **STUDENT GOVERNMENT** You ran for treasurer of the Student Council. Of the 500 students who voted in the election, 325 voted for you. What percent of the votes did you get?

Ⓐ 35%   Ⓑ 154%   Ⓒ 65%   Ⓓ 175%

PERCENT ERROR In Exercises 25 and 26, use the following information. In manufacturing, parts are made according to specifications. To maintain quality, inspectors measure the parts to see that the percent error is within a certain range. The percent error can be calculated as follows:

$$\text{Percent error} = \frac{\text{Specified}\atop\text{dimension} - {\text{Measured}\atop\text{dimension}}}{\text{Specified}\atop\text{dimension}} \times 100$$

The specified dimension of a part is 40 inches. Find the percent error for the given measured dimension.

25. 38 inches   **26.** 39 inches

Real Life... **R**eal Facts

Baseball bats may not exceed 42 inches in length, and the largest diameter may not exceed $2\frac{3}{4}$ inches.

SPIRAL REVIEW

In Exercises 1–4, add or subtract. Simplify if possible. **(3.3, 3.4)**

1. $\dfrac{4}{9} + \dfrac{2}{9}$ **2.** $\dfrac{7}{8} - \dfrac{5}{12}$ **3.** $7\dfrac{1}{6} - 5\dfrac{1}{2}$ **4.** $1\dfrac{2}{5} + 4\dfrac{2}{3}$

GEOMETRY In Exercises 5–7, find the area of the region. **(3.5)**

5.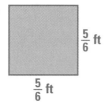

$\frac{5}{6}$ ft

$\frac{5}{6}$ ft

6.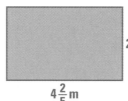

$2\frac{4}{5}$ m

$4\frac{2}{5}$ m

7.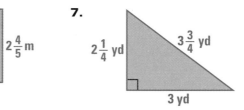

$2\frac{1}{4}$ yd $3\frac{3}{4}$ yd

3 yd

In Exercises 8–13, solve the equation. **(4.6, 4.7)**

8. $x + 18 = -6$ **9.** $17 = t + 24$ **10.** $5 + m = 21$

11. $n - 11 = -13$ **12.** $-32 = b - 19$ **13.** $y - 36 = 25$

14. Draw a box-and-whisker plot of the data. **(5.3)**

24, 17, 22, 30, 18, 28, 25, 28, 15, 26, 19, 28, 22, 17

15. BOWLING In the '95–'96 season, on average, 589 bowlers bowled a perfect game of 300 every 7 days. Find this rate in bowlers per day. **(6.2)**

16. You are making a banner for School Spirit Day. You have drawn a sketch of your planned banner. The letters on the sketch are each 3 inches tall. The sketch is 15 inches tall. The actual banner will be 5 feet tall. How tall should you make the letters on the banner? **(6.4)**

Take this test as you would take a test in class. The answers to the exercises are given in the back of the book.

In Exercises 1–8, write the number as a percent. (7.1)

1. 0.124

2. $\frac{7}{20}$

3. 0.067

4. $\frac{24}{32}$

5. 2.89

6. $\frac{2}{360}$

7. 0.037

8. $\frac{65}{16}$

In Exercises 9–11, write the percent and the value represented by the shaded region. (7.2)

9. 100 squares = 240 feet

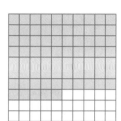

10. 100 squares = 25 muffins

11. 100 squares = 160 pounds

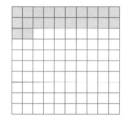

In Exercises 12–14, complete the statement using >, <, or =. (7.3)

12. 0.625% **?** $\frac{1}{16}$

13. $\frac{11}{8}$ **?** 137%

14. $\frac{13}{200}$ **?** 6.5%

In Exercises 15–21, solve the percent problem. (7.4)

15. What is 44% of 300?

16. 9% of what number is 54?

17. Find 150% of 78.

18. 6 is 75% of what number?

19. You bought a tennis racket for 60% of the original price. You paid $60.00. What was the original price of the racket?

20. You are making pottery bowls to sell at a craft show. The materials cost you $8.25 per bowl. You are selling the bowls for 300% of the cost. What is the price of a bowl?

21. UNUSUAL FOODS In a survey, 13.9% or 3475 people said they had eaten snails.

a. How many people were surveyed?

b. 7.6% of the people in the survey had eaten eel. How many people was that?

7.5

What you should learn:

Goal ① How to find angle measures for parts of a circle graph

Goal ② How to make a circle graph

Why you should learn it:

Knowing how to make a circle graph can help you organize data. An example is organizing data about types of trees in an orchard.

Circle Graphs

Goal ① ANGLE MEASURES OF A CIRCLE GRAPH

A **circle graph** represents data as parts of a circle. The parts of the circle are labeled as fractions, decimals, or percents. Because the entire circle graph represents 1 unit, the sum of all parts must be 1 (or 100%).

The measure of an entire circle is 360°. To make a circle graph, you need to find the measure of each part's angle. For example, to find 30% of a circle, find 30% of 360°.

$$30\% \text{ of } 360° = 0.30 \cdot 360°$$
$$= 108°$$

Example 1 **Angle Measures of a Circle Graph**

STRATEGY **DRAWING A DIAGRAM**
You are planting an orchard that has 24 apple trees, 20 peach trees, 16 cherry trees, 12 apricot trees, and 8 plum trees. A circle graph can be used to organize this data. What are the angle measures in the circle graph? (*Hint:* The angle measure for apples is 108°.)

Solution

Your orchard has 80 trees. Find the percent and degrees for each type of tree.

Tree	Number	Percent	Degrees
Apple	24	$\frac{24}{80} = 30\%$	$0.30 \times 360° = 108°$
Peach	20	$\frac{20}{80} = 25\%$	$0.25 \times 360° = 90°$
Cherry	16	$\frac{16}{80} = 20\%$	$0.20 \times 360° = 72°$
Apricot	12	$\frac{12}{80} = 15\%$	$0.15 \times 360° = 54°$
Plum	8	$\frac{8}{80} = 10\%$	$0.10 \times 360° = 36°$

Goal 2 MAKING A CIRCLE GRAPH

To make a circle graph, you can use a protractor to measure and draw each angle in the graph or you can use *circle graph paper*, as shown at the right. Each section on the graph paper represents 5°.

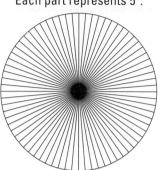

Example 2 Making a Circle Graph

The energy used in American homes falls in the following categories. Represent this data with a circle graph. (Source: 1993 Residential Energy Consumption Survey, Energy Information Administration)

Space heating	54%
Water heating	18%
Refrigerator	5%
Air conditioning	7%
Appliances	16%

Solution

To make a circle graph, you can round each angle measure to the nearest degree.

Energy Use	Percent	Degrees
Space heating	54%	$0.54 \times 360° \approx 194°$
Water heating	18%	$0.18 \times 360° \approx 65°$
Refrigerator	5%	$0.05 \times 360° = 18°$
Air conditioning	7%	$0.07 \times 360° \approx 25°$
Appliances	16%	$0.16 \times 360° \approx 58°$

To make the circle graph, you can use circle graph paper, as shown.

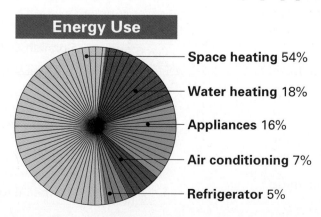

Energy Use

- Space heating 54%
- Water heating 18%
- Appliances 16%
- Air conditioning 7%
- Refrigerator 5%

ONGOING ASSESSMENT

Talk About It

In a survey, 120 people were asked about their vision: 45 had no vision problems, 30 were near-sighted, 20 were far-sighted, 10 were both near-sighted and far-sighted, and 15 had other vision problems.

1. Discuss with a partner how to represent this vision data with a circle graph.

GUIDED PRACTICE

1. Explain how to organize data with a circle graph. How can you check that you have drawn the graph correctly?

In Exercises 2–4, find the missing measures.

2.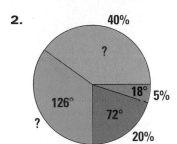

3.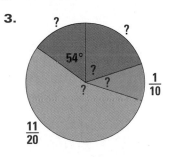

4.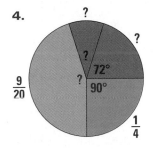

USING LOGICAL REASONING In Exercises 5 and 6, decide whether the data can be organized with a circle graph. Explain your reasoning. If it can, make a circle graph of the data. If it can't, make another type of graph.

5. Two hundred people were asked which professional sporting event they most like to attend. The numbers who chose the six categories were: baseball, 70; basketball, 50; football, 40; hockey, 20; soccer, 12; and other, 8.

6. Two hundred people were asked to name ways they help the environment. The numbers who chose the four categories were: recycle at home, 180; buy biodegradable products, 142; recycle at work, 124; support environmental groups, 74. (Source: Opinion Research Corporation)

PRACTICE AND PROBLEM SOLVING

BUSINESS LANGUAGES In Exercises 7–10, use the circle graph at the right. It shows the results of a survey in which 150 executives from large companies were asked to name the most valuable second language in business in the United States.
(Source: Accountemps)

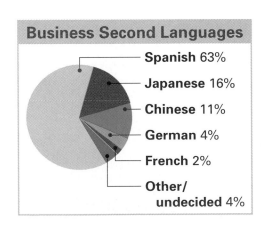

Business Second Languages

Spanish 63%
Japanese 16%
Chinese 11%
German 4%
French 2%
Other/ undecided 4%

7. About how many executives chose Spanish?

8. About how many more executives chose Spanish than Chinese?

9. About how many times as many executives chose Spanish as Japanese?

10. What is the angle measure of the "Japanese" part of the circle?

TELEVISION SHOWS In Exercises 11–13, use the following information. A survey asked 150 teenagers to name their favorite type of show. The choices were: situation comedies, 60; drama, 42; cartoons, 27; news shows, 18; and other, 3.

11. Use a circle graph to organize the data.

12. What percent of the teenagers surveyed chose drama and news shows?

13. Show how to check the results of your circle graph.

MAKING A CIRCLE GRAPH In Exercises 14 and 15, make a circle graph of the data.

14. The percents of electricity used in the United States are: residential buildings, 34.6%; commercial buildings, 28.6%; industrial uses, 33.6%; and other uses, 3.2%. (Source: Energy Information Administration)

15. A survey asked 250 people to name their favorite zoo animal. Data for the top five choices were as follows: elephants, 85; giraffes, 80; tigers, 50; monkeys, 23; and other animals, 12. (For information about zoo animals and their diets, see the interactive investigation for this chapter.)

STANDARDIZED TEST PRACTICE

16. One shaded part of a circle graph represents 60%. This represents how many degrees of the circle?

   (A) 60°   **(B)** 108°   **(C)** 120°   **(D)** 216°

17. 120 out of 300 people surveyed said that they walk for exercise. How many degrees of a circle graph should represent these 120 people?

   (A) 40°   **(B)** 120°   **(C)** 144°   **(D)** 162°

In Exercises 18 and 19, use the circle graph at the right. It shows the results of a recent survey of 600 people.

18. Which part of the circle corresponds to the results of 90 responses?

   (A) Part A   **(B)** Part B   **(C)** Part C   **(D)** Part D

19. Part B represents approximately how many responses?

   (A) 180 responses   **(B)** 90 responses

   (C) 300 responses   **(D)** 150 responses

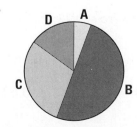

20. **BUILDING YOUR PROJECT** During one week a veterinarian spent 9 hours examining animals, 11 hours talking with owners, 8 hours traveling to make "barn calls," 9 hours keeping records, 6 hours ordering and stocking supplies, and 5 hours reading journals. Find the percent of working hours spent on each task and draw a circle graph of the information.

SPIRAL REVIEW

LOOKING FOR A PATTERN In Exercises 1 and 2, find the missing number or letter in the pattern. Explain your reasoning. **(1.2)**

1. 60, 57, 54, 51, ? , 45

2. a, y, c, w, ? , u

In Exercises 3–6, find the least common multiple of the numbers. **(3.1)**

3. 20, 50

4. 15, 18

5. 64, 80

6. 4, 6, 8

In Exercises 7 and 8, copy and complete the table. Then draw a scatter plot of the data. Describe any patterns in the scatter plot. **(4.2, 4.4, 4.5)**

7. $y = -x + 3$

x	1	2	3	4	5
y	?	?	?	?	?

8. $y = 2x - 1$

x	1	2	3	4	5
y	?	?	?	?	?

9. The data below show the lengths (in minutes) of songs on a compact disk. Find the mean, median, and mode of the data. **(5.1)**

   3.6, 5.75, 4.4, 3.25, 3.5, 5.1, 4.2, 4.85, 4.4, 3.45

10. **WALKATHON** You are walking to raise money for a charity organization. You walk at a rate of 3 miles per hour. The walk covers a total of 8 miles. Use a proportion to find how many hours and minutes it will take you to finish the walk. **(6.5)**

11. You measure the length of the shadow of a flagpole to be 18 feet long. Your friend's shadow is 9 feet long. If your friend is 5 feet tall, how tall is the flagpole? **(6.6)**

In Exercises 12 and 13, which number doesn't fit in the list? Explain. **(7.1)**

12. $45\%, \frac{9}{20}, 0.45, \frac{4}{5}, \frac{45}{100}$

13. $\frac{25}{40}, 625\%, \frac{5}{8}, 0.625, 62.5\%$

Monitoring
Whale
Migration

READ About It

In an aerial survey in 1994, scientists observed migrating bowhead whales, an endangered species, in the Beaufort Sea north of Alaska. Each day from August 31 through October 18, the observers recorded the numbers of whale sightings and numbers of whales in each sighting over a certain period of hours. The majority of whales were seen on two peak days. On September 2, the crew had 29 sightings of a total of 63 whales over 3.97 hours. On September 9, the crew spotted a total of 65 whales out of 20 sightings, calculating that they saw 12.38 whales per hour.

WRITE About It

1. What was the number of sightings per hour on September 2? (Round your answer to two decimal places.) Explain how you found the answer.

2. On October 7, four whales were seen. Calculate a decimal that represents the number of whales seen on October 7 as a fraction of the whales seen on September 9. Explain your reasoning.

3. The total number of whales seen during the survey was 204. Write a percent equation and find the percent of total whales that were seen on the two peak days (September 2 and 9).

4. How long did the survey last on September 9? Explain your reasoning.

5. Two out of the 46 whales observed between September 16–30 were diving. What percentage does this represent? Explain how you found your answer.

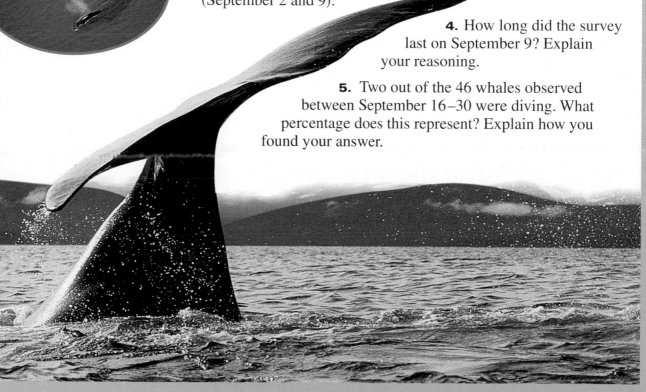

7.6

Simple Interest

What you should learn:

Goal 1 How to find simple interest

Goal 2 How to use the formula for simple interest to solve real-life problems

Why you should learn it:

Knowing how to find simple interest can help you analyze finances. An example is analyzing the record of a savings account.

Goal 1 FINDING SIMPLE INTEREST

When you save money in a bank, the bank pays you interest. When you borrow money from a bank, you must pay interest to the bank (in addition to paying back the amount you borrowed). The amount of interest depends on the amount of money borrowed or saved, the rate of interest, and the length of time.

SIMPLE INTEREST

A **principal** is an amount borrowed, loaned, or in savings. An **annual interest rate** is the percent of the principal you would earn (or pay) as interest based on one year. **Simple interest** is the product of the principal, the annual interest rate, and the time in years.

$$I = P \times r \times t$$

Interest   Principal   Rate   Time

STUDY TIP

When you compute simple interest for a time that is less than 1 year, you should write the time as a fraction of a year. Here are some examples.

1 month	$\frac{1}{12}$ year
2 months	$\frac{2}{12} = \frac{1}{6}$ year
3 months	$\frac{3}{12} = \frac{1}{4}$ year
4 months	$\frac{4}{12} = \frac{1}{3}$ year

Example 1 Finding Simple Interest

a. You borrowed $18,000 for a new car. The annual interest rate is 12%. You can find the simple interest you will pay in 1 year as follows.

$I = P \times r \times t$ **Formula for simple interest**

$= 18,000 \times 0.12 \times 1$ **Substitute. Write 12% as 0.12.**

$= 2160$ **Use a calculator.**

The simple interest for 1 year is $2160.

b. You deposit $300 in a savings account. The annual interest rate is 6%. You can find the simple interest you will earn in 1 month as follows.

$I = P \times r \times t$ **Formula for simple interest**

$= 300 \times 0.06 \times \dfrac{1}{12}$ **Substitute values. Write 6% as 0.06.**

$= 1.5$ **Use a calculator.**

The simple interest for 1 month is $1.50.

Goal 2 SOLVING REAL-LIFE PROBLEMS

The interest you earned in part (b) of Example 1 doesn't seem like much. But, when you leave the money in the bank for several years, the interest can really build up!

Example 2 Finding Interest

REAL LIFE Savings

You deposit $300 in a savings account. This is your beginning **balance**. The annual interest rate is 6%. Each month the simple interest is computed and added to the beginning balance to get the balance at the end of the month. The partial spreadsheet shows the balance after 10 years. Explain how the monthly interest is computed.

First National Bank

Month	Beginning balance	Interest	Ending balance
1	$300.00	$1.50	$301.50
2	$301.50	$1.51	$303.01
3	$303.01	$1.52	$304.53
4	$304.53	$1.52	$306.05
118	$537.72	$2.69	$540.41
119	$540.41	$2.70	$543.11
120	$543.11	$2.72	$545.83

Solution

The monthly interest is computed by using the beginning balance for the month as the principal. For example, the simple interest for the 119th month is as follows.

$$I = P \times r \times t \qquad \text{Formula for simple interest}$$

$$= 540.41 \times 0.06 \times \frac{1}{12} \qquad \text{Substitute values.}$$

$$\approx 2.70 \qquad \text{Use a calculator and round.}$$

The simple interest for the 119th month is $2.70.

Real Life... Real Facts

Automated teller machines were first introduced at bank branches in 1968. ATMs are now available at shopping centers and grocery stores and have become a convenient way to access your bank account to withdraw or deposit funds.

ONGOING ASSESSMENT

Write About It

Complete the 5th, 6th, and 7th rows of the spreadsheet shown in Example 2.

1. Describe the pattern in the interest.

2. Use your pattern to estimate the interest in the 8th row. Then check your estimate.

Extra Practice, page 637

In Exercises 1–4, match the word with its description.

A. A percent of the principal
B. Fee paid to lender or saver
C. Amount of money loaned or saved
D. Principal plus the interest

1. Principal   **2.** Interest rate   **3.** Balance   **4.** Interest

NUMBER SENSE **In Exercises 5 and 6, decide whether your answer is reasonable. Explain why or why not.**

5. A friend borrows $50.00 from you for 6 months. You charge an annual interest rate of 10%. You calculate that your friend has to pay you $30.00 in simple interest after 6 months.

6. A bank advertises that they pay 5% annual interest on a savings account. You put $100 in the bank and calculate that your balance after 6 months will be $250.00.

In Exercises 7–10, write the months as a fraction of a year.

7. 3 months   **8.** 6 months   **9.** 8 months   **10.** 9 months

In Exercises 11–14, find the simple interest earned for the given time on a deposit of $6000 in an account that pays 4% annual interest.

11. 1 month   **12.** 4 months   **13.** 10 months   **14.** 12 months

In Exercises 15–18, find the amount of simple interest paid on $8000 borrowed for 6 months at the given annual interest rate.

15. 8%   **16.** 11%   **17.** 14%   **18.** 18%

19.  **TECHNOLOGY** The photo shows the National Debt Clock in New York City, in June, 1995. By the end of 1996, the federal debt (the money the federal government owes) was about 5300 billion dollars. If the annual interest rate was 8%, how much interest did the government pay in 1 month? (Source: U.S. Office of Management and Budget)

In Exercises 20–22, find the interest earned for depositing the given principal in an account. Then find the account balance.

20. $P = \$600$, $r = 5\%$, $t = 4$ months

21. $P = \$1250$, $r = 3\%$, $t = 6$ months

22. $P = \$7000$, $r = 5.5\%$, $t = 18$ months

In Exercises 23–25, find the interest you will pay for borrowing the given principal. Then find the total you must pay back.

23. $P = \$12{,}000$, $r = 15\%$, $t = 9$ months

24. $P = \$4500$, $r = 9\%$, $t = 5$ months

25. $P = \$900$, $r = 12\%$, $t = 15$ months

26. GUESS, CHECK, AND REVISE You deposit $8000 in a savings account. What interest rate would you have to get to earn $200 interest in 1 year?

CREDIT CARDS In Exercises 27–30, use the table below. It shows the average annual interest rate for credit cards from 1991 to 1995. Find the interest paid for one month using the given year and amount of debt.

Year	1991	1992	1993	1994	1995
Rate	18.2%	17.8%	16.8%	15.7%	16.0%

27. A debt of $850 in 1991

28. A debt of $900 in 1993

29. A debt of $1000 in 1994

30. A debt of $1050 in 1995

STANDARDIZED TEST PRACTICE

31. In which of the following situations do you earn the most interest during one year?

(A) Invest $100 at 8% interest. **(B)** Invest $150 at 4% interest.

(C) Invest $50 at 12% interest. **(D)** Invest $200 at 3% interest.

32. What is the simple interest paid on $300 borrowed for 4 months at an annual interest rate of 5%?

(A) $4 **(B)** $60 **(C)** $5 **(D)** $75

EXPLORATION AND EXTENSION

33. RESEARCH PROJECT Use your school library or talk to an adult to estimate the annual interest rates of the following financial activities. Record the rates. Put the activities in order from least interest rate to greatest interest rate.

a. Borrow money for a car

b. Put money in a savings account

c. Buy a U.S. Savings Bond

d. Borrow money using a credit card

7.7 Percent Increase and Percent Decrease

What you should learn:

 Goal 1
How to find a percent increase

 Goal 2
How to find a percent decrease

Why you should learn it:

Knowing how to find a percent increase or percent decrease can help you compare populations of pairs of bald eagles.

Goal 1 FINDING A PERCENT INCREASE

Percents can be used as a measure of how much a quantity changes. For example, if the price of a bottle of juice increases from $1.00 to $1.25, it has increased by 25%.

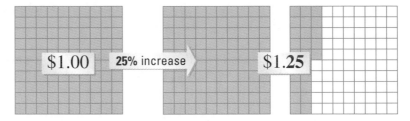

PERCENT INCREASE OR DECREASE

The **percent increase** or **percent decrease** from one amount to another is the ratio of the amount of increase or decrease to the original amount.

Example 1 **Finding a Percent Increase**

The bar graph at the left shows the number of bald eagle pairs in 48 states (excluding Alaska and Hawaii). Find the amount of increase and the percent increase from 1990 to 1995.

CONNECTION
Life Science

Solution

The amount of increase from 1990 to 1995 was

$$4712 - 3020 = \mathbf{1692} \text{ pairs of eagles.}$$

The original amount was 3020. This means that the percent increase was as follows.

$$\text{Percent increase} = \frac{\textbf{Amount of increase}}{\textbf{Original amount}} \quad \text{Percent change ratio}$$

$$= \frac{\mathbf{1692}}{\mathbf{3020}} \qquad \text{Substitute values.}$$

$$\approx 0.56 \qquad \text{Use a calculator.}$$

$$= 56\% \qquad \text{Write as a percent.}$$

The population increased by about 56%.

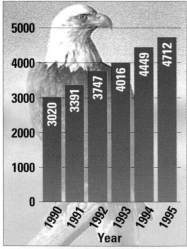

Bald Eagle Pairs

(values: 3020, 3391, 3747, 4016, 4449, 4712 for years 1990, 1991, 1992, 1993, 1994, 1995)

Year

(Source: Fish and Wildlife Service)

Goal 2 FINDING A PERCENT DECREASE

Example 2 ▸ Finding a Percent Decrease

The average amount of milk bought by Americans from 1975 through 1995 is shown in the bar graph. Find the percent decrease in whole milk sales from 1975 to 1995.

REAL LIFE
Trends

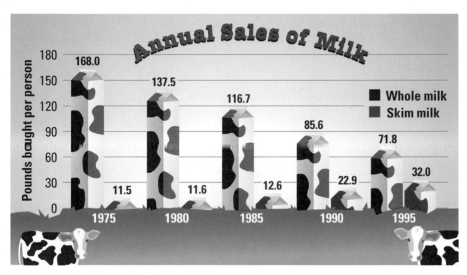

Solution

The amount of decrease from 1975 to 1995 was

$168 - 71.8 = \textbf{96.2}$ pounds.

To find the percent decrease, divide this amount by the 1975 amount.

$$\text{Percent decrease} = \frac{\textbf{Amount of decrease}}{\textbf{Original amount}}$$

Percent change ratio

$$= \frac{\textbf{96.2}}{\textbf{168}} \qquad \text{Substitute values}.$$

$$\approx 0.57 \qquad \text{Use a calculator}.$$

$$= 57\% \qquad \text{Write as a percent}.$$

The sales of whole milk decreased by about 57%.

Example 3 ▸ Finding a Percent Change

Before: 24   **After:** 10

$$\frac{24 - 10}{24} = \frac{14}{24} \approx 0.58 = 58\% \text{ decrease}$$

> **ONGOING ASSESSMENT**
>
> ## Write About It
> ....
>
> Answer these questions after reading Example 2.
>
> 1. During which five-year period did skim milk sales increase by the greatest amount?
>
> 2. During which period did sales increase by the greatest percent?

7.7 Exercises   Extra Practice, page 637

GUIDED PRACTICE

In Exercises 1–4, match the percent increase or decrease with the description.

A. 50% decrease   **B.** 100% increase   **C.** 120% increase   **D.** 0% decrease

1. The number more than doubled.   **2.** The number doubled.

3. The number was halved.   **4.** The number stayed the same.

In Exercises 5 and 6, decide whether the statement is *true* or *false*. Explain.

5. 100% of a number is the number itself.

6. The percent increase is the ratio of the amount of increase to the new amount.

7. **THINKING SKILLS** Your teacher wants to help raise everyone's math grade. There are 200 total points for the grading period. Which of the following would you rather that the teacher did? Explain.

   a. Increase everyone's score by 5%.

   b. Increase everyone's score by 5 points.

PRACTICE AND PROBLEM SOLVING

8. Write the percent increase shown by the unit squares.

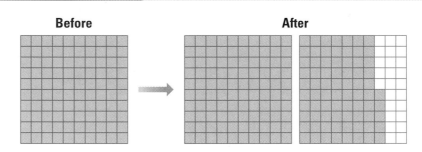

Before   After

In Exercises 9–14, find the percent increase or decrease.

9. **Before:** 30   **After:** 45

10. **Before:** 24   **After:** 42

11. **Before:** 115   **After:** 46

12. **Before:** 128   **After:** 32

13. **Before:** 116   **After:** 145

14. **Before:** 250   **After:** 220

15. **RABIES CASES** The table shows the number of animal rabies cases reported. Find the percent decrease from 1992 to 1995. (Source: U.S. Center for Disease Control and Prevention)

Year	1992	1993	1994	1995
Cases	8589	9377	8147	7811

16. VETERINARIANS In 1996, there were about 55,000 veterinarians. Find the percent increase from an earlier year when there were about 52,000 veterinarians. (Source: Pet Industry Joint Advisory Council)

MAKING AN ESTIMATE In Exercises 17–20, is the percent decrease about 10%, 30%, 50%, or 75%?

17. Original: $15.00   **Sale:** $8.25

18. Original: $95.00   **Sale:** $63.65

19. Original: $57.00   **Sale:** $14.00

20. Original: $22.50   **Sale:** $20.00

POPULATION DATA In Exercises 21–23, the tables show the populations for three metropolitan areas. Find the percent increase from 1990 to 1995. (Source: U.S. Bureau of the Census)

21.

Dallas	
1990	2,689,625
1995	2,937,910

22.

St. Louis	
1990	2,496,146
1995	2,547,688

23.

Orlando	
1990	1,239,119
1995	1,390,374

STANDARDIZED TEST PRACTICE

24. The initial deposit in a savings account is $500. Four years later, the balance of the account is $1250. What is the percent increase?

  (A) 40%   **(B)** 67%   **(C)** 150%   **(D)** 167%

25. Find the percent decrease from 362 to 115.

  (A) about 32%   **(B)** about 215%   **(C)** about 247%   **(D)** about 68%

EXPLORATION AND EXTENSION

26. COMMUNICATING ABOUT MATHEMATICS
(page 353) In September 1986, 65 whales were sighted in the Beaufort Sea. In September 1990, 401 whales were seen, while 183 whales were sighted in September 1994. Find the percent change from 1986 to 1990 and from 1990 to 1994.

WHAT *did you learn?*   **WHY** *did you learn it?*

Skills

7.1	Write numbers as percents, fractions, and decimals. Round percents.	Analyze and interpret surveys.
7.2	Find a percent of a number.	Compare the ways people travel to work.
7.3	Use large and small percents. Estimate the percent of a number.	Work with and estimate percents in real-life situations.
7.4	Use the percent equation.	Solve problems involving percents.
7.5	Make a circle graph.	Analyze the different ways energy is used in homes.
7.6	Find simple interest.	Find the balance in a savings account.
7.7	Find a percent increase or percent decrease.	Find the percent change in animal populations.

Strategies 7.1–7.7 Use problem solving strategies.   Solve a wide variety of real-life problems.

Using Data 7.1–7.7 Use tables and graphs.   Organize data and solve problems.

HOW *does it fit in the bigger picture of mathematics?*

In mathematics, there are always different ways to solve problems. For example, suppose you were asked to find 24% of 150. In this chapter, you studied three ways to answer this question.

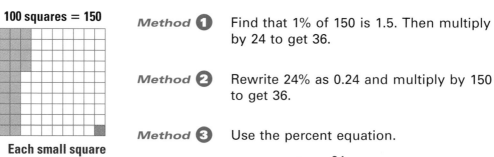

100 squares = 150

Each small square represents 1.5.

Method ❶ Find that 1% of 150 is 1.5. Then multiply by 24 to get 36.

Method ❷ Rewrite 24% as 0.24 and multiply by 150 to get 36.

Method ❸ Use the percent equation.

$$\frac{a}{150} = \frac{24}{100}$$

You should use the method that you understand the best.

VOCABULARY

- percent (p. 322)
- percent equation (p. 342)
- base of a percent (p. 342)
- circle graph (p. 348)
- principal (p. 354)
- annual interest rate (p. 354)
- simple interest (p. 354)
- percent increase (p. 358)
- percent decrease (p. 358)

7.1 PERCENTS, FRACTIONS, AND DECIMALS

A number can be written as a **percent**, a **fraction**, or a **decimal**.

Examples $20\% = \dfrac{20}{100} = \dfrac{1}{5} = 0.2$ $\qquad$ $\dfrac{7}{45} \approx 0.156 = \dfrac{156}{1000} = \dfrac{15.6}{100} = \mathbf{15.6\%}$

1. Write 0.32 as a percent.

2. Write $\dfrac{17}{25}$ as a decimal and a percent.

In Exercises 3–6, write the percent as a decimal and as a fraction in simplest form.

3. 40% $\qquad$ **4.** 15% $\qquad$ **5.** 72% $\qquad$ **6.** 37%

7.2 FINDING A PERCENT OF A NUMBER

You can use a unit square to find a percent of a number.

Example To find 40% of 500 meters, let the entire unit square represent 500 meters. Then each small square represents 1%, or 5 meters. Then 40% of the unit square is represented by 40 small squares, which is 40 × 5, or 200 meters.

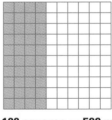

100 squares = 500 m

Another way to find the percent of a number is to change the percent to a decimal and multiply.

Example 25% of 60 = 0.25 × 60 = 15

7. a. Write the percent represented by the shaded area below.
 b. How many feet does the shaded area represent?

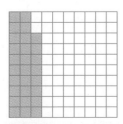

100 squares = 450 ft

8. Find the percent of each number. Then describe the pattern and find the next two numbers.
25% of 32, 50% of 34, 75% of 36, 100% of 38

9. Find 7% of 84.

10. Find 35% of 210.

7.3 LARGE AND SMALL PERCENTS

Example   **a.** Use mental math to estimate 178% of 60.
b. Then find the exact answer.

Solution   **a.** 178% is about **175%** ⟶ $\underbrace{\mathbf{100\%} \text{ of } 60}_{60}$ + $\underbrace{\mathbf{75\%} \text{ of } 60}_{45}$ = 105

So 178% of 60 is a little more than 105.
b. $\mathbf{178\%} \times 60 \longrightarrow \mathbf{1.78} \times 60 = 106.8$

11. Find 0.25% of 10.

12. Use mental math to find $\frac{1}{10}$% of 400.

13. Find 120% of 250.

14. Use mental math to estimate 152% of 80.

7.4 THE PERCENT EQUATION

Examples   What percent of **120** is **48**?

$$\frac{48}{120} = \frac{p}{100}$$

$$0.4 = \frac{p}{100}$$

$$40 = p$$

Find **27%** of **50**.

$$\frac{a}{50} = \frac{27}{100}$$

$$\frac{a}{50} = 0.27$$

$$a = 13.5$$

15. What percent of 160 is 96?

16. Find 18% of 120.

17. In a survey, 45% of respondents, or 81 people, said that their favorite color was blue. How many people were surveyed?

7.5 CIRCLE GRAPHS

Example   In a recent season, the Springfield Stars had 18 wins, 18 losses, and 12 ties. Represent the data with a circle graph.

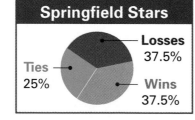

Springfield Stars
Losses 37.5%
Ties 25%
Wins 37.5%

$18 + 18 + 12 = 48$ parts of the circle

$\frac{18}{48} = 0.375;\ 0.375 \times 360° = 135°$

$\frac{12}{48} = 0.25;\ 0.25 \times 360° = 90°$

So, the angles in the circle graph are **135°**, **135°**, and **90°**.

18. LIFE SCIENCE A survey asked 200 people to name their blood type. The results were: O+, 76; A+, 68; B+, 18; O−, 14; A−, 12; AB+, 6; B−, 4; AB−, 2. Make a circle graph of the data.

7.6 SIMPLE INTEREST

You can find simple interest using the formula $I = P \times r \times t$, where I is the interest, P is the number of dollars borrowed, loaned, or invested, r is the annual interest rate written as a decimal, and t is the time in years.

Example If you put **$150** in an account that pays **5%** annual interest, then the simple interest earned at the end of **4 months** is

$$I = P \times r \times t$$
$$= 150 \times 0.05 \times \frac{4}{12}$$
$$= \textbf{2.5, or \$2.50}$$

19. **CREDIT CARDS** You buy a $150 bike with a credit card with annual interest rate 18%. How much simple interest will you pay in 1 month?

20. On the day that your cousin was born, your grandparents deposited $3000 in a trust fund. The annual interest on the fund is 4%. What is the balance in the trust fund on your cousin's first birthday?

7.7 PERCENT INCREASE AND PERCENT DECREASE

$$\text{Percent increase or decrease} = \frac{\text{Amount of \textbf{increase} or \textbf{decrease}}}{\text{Original amount}}$$

Example The value of a car is **$14,000** in 1995 and $11,480 in 1996.

amount of decrease $\longrightarrow$ **$14,000** $-$ $11,480 = **$2520**

percent of decrease $\longrightarrow \dfrac{2520}{14,000} = 0.18 = 18\%$

21. **GOVERNMENT** In 1990, Texas had 27 representatives in the United States House of Representatives. In 1996, Texas had 30 representatives. Find the percent increase from 1990 to 1996.

22. The bar graph shows the number of pounds, in millions, of fish processed in the United States. Find the percent decrease in fresh and frozen fish from 1993 to 1995.

23. Use the bar graph. Find the percent increase in canned fish from 1993 to 1995.

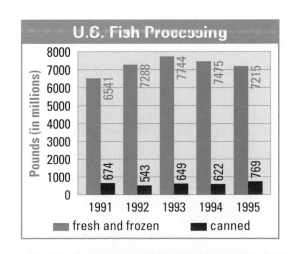

U.S. Fish Processing

Year	fresh and frozen	canned
1991	6541	674
1992	7288	543
1993	7744	649
1994	7475	622
1995	7215	769

Pounds (in millions)

In Questions 1–4, write the percent as (a) a decimal and (b) a fraction in simplest form.

1. 74% **2.** 5% **3.** $\frac{3}{5}$% **4.** 216%

In Questions 5–12, write the fraction or decimal as a percent.

5. 0.88 **6.** $\frac{7}{16}$ **7.** $\frac{22}{5}$ **8.** 0.00625

9. $\frac{11}{4000}$ **10.** $\frac{3}{75}$ **11.** 0.062 **12.** 3.03

In Questions 13–16, use mental math to estimate.

13. 75% of 24 hours **14.** 5% of $145

15. 220% of 5 goals **16.** $\frac{1}{5}$% of 500 people

17. PERSONAL PREFERENCES A survey asked 200 people to name their favorite sea mammal. The results were: dolphin, 76; seal, 68; killer whale, 32; and other, 24. Make a circle graph of this data.

18. CONSUMER SPENDING You borrow $1650 to buy a computer. The annual interest rate is 16%. How much simple interest will you pay in 2 months?

In Questions 19–22, solve the percent problem.

19. 60% of what number is 63? **20.** 22 is 4% of what number?

21. 84 is what percent of 25? **22.** What percent of 400 is 2?

MUSIC SALES In Questions 23–25, use the bar graph at the right. It shows the sales (in millions of dollars) of compact disks and cassettes from 1992 to 1996.

23. Find the percent increase for compact disks from 1992 to 1996.

24. Find the percent decrease for cassettes from 1992 to 1996.

25. In which year did compact-disk sales increase by the greatest percent? What is the percent increase?

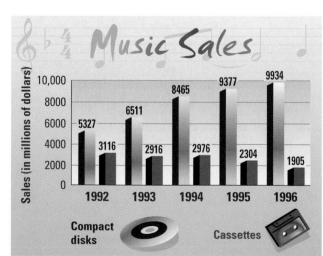

1. Which number does not belong in this list? 3.6%, 0.36, $\frac{9}{25}$, $\frac{27}{75}$

   A 3.6%　　　　**B** 0.36

   C $\frac{9}{25}$　　　　**D** $\frac{27}{75}$

2. A store charges 138% of the cost for a pair of sneakers. The store's cost was $28. How much does the store charge the customer?

   A $14.44　　　　**B** $17.36

   C $38.64　　　　**D** $66.64

3. A store marks jeans at 60% of the original price of $32. For final clearance, the store takes $5 off the sale price. What is the final clearance price of the jeans?

   A $48.33　　　　**B** $19.20

   C $14.20　　　　**D** $9.60

4. In a survey, 28 seventh graders said that their favorite lunch was spaghetti. This was 16% of the class. How many students are in the class?

   A 4　　　　**B** 32

   C 175　　　　**D** 448

5. You deposit $750 in a savings account for six months. The annual interest rate is 5%. How much interest will you earn on the account?

   A $375.00　　　　**B** $187.50

   C $37.50　　　　**D** $18.75

6. What is the percent change from 144 to 72?

   A 72% decrease　　**B** 50% increase

   C 72% increase　　**D** 50% decrease

7. The decimal number 0.00068 is not the same as

   A 0.068%.　　　　**B** $\frac{68}{100,000}$.

   C $\frac{51}{75,000}$.　　　　**D** $\frac{16}{100}$.

8. A survey states that 20% of high school students have gone out of state on vacation. Out of 200 students, how many went out of state on vacation?

   A 5　　　　**B** 10

   C 20　　　　**D** 40

9. This year, 592 students said they recycle. That is 320% of the number who recycled eight years ago. How many recycled eight years ago?

   A 54 students　　**B** 185 students

   C 189 students　　**D** 1894 students

10. Find the missing measure.

    A 135°

    B 164°

    C 144°

    D 154°

    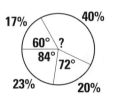

11. Your brother buys a car for $800, fixes it up, and sells it for $1000. What was the percent increase in the car's price?

    A 20%　　　　**B** 25%

    C 120%　　　　**D** 125%

12. Which equation could be used to solve this question? 14 is 25% of what number?

    A $\frac{25}{x} = \frac{14}{100}$　　**B** $\frac{x}{14} = \frac{25}{100}$

    C $\frac{14}{x} = \frac{25}{100}$　　**D** $\frac{x}{25} = \frac{100}{14}$

CHAPTER 8

Geometry in the Plane

TECHNOLOGY

Technology resources accompanying this chapter:
- Interactive Real-Life Investigations
- Middle School Tutorial Software

STAIRCASE CONSTRUCTION When building a staircase, each step should have the same height, or rise, and the same width, or run.

CHAPTER THEME
Carpentry

All the steps of a straight staircase are parallel.

CIRCULAR STAIRCASE Each step of a circular staircase is a trapezoid.

Staircases

REAL LIFE
Carpentry

Geometry is an important part of any carpentry project. For example, the area of a structure tells the builder how much wood and paint are needed and how long it will take to sand the wood. To find the area of an unusual shape like the side of a **staircase**, it helps to divide the shape into rectangles or triangles.

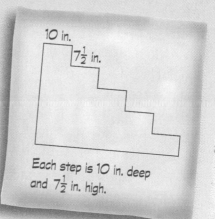

10 in.

$7\frac{1}{2}$ in.

Each step is 10 in. deep and $7\frac{1}{2}$ in. high.

Think and Discuss

1. Divide the shape shown above into rectangles. Use these rectangles to find the area of the side of the staircase.

2. Describe how to use triangles to find the area of the side of the staircase.

PORTFOLIO

CHAPTER PROJECT

Building a Birdhouse

PROJECT DESCRIPTION

Suppose you want to build a birdhouse. For beginning woodworkers, it helps to begin with a cardboard model. As you assemble your model, you should take notes that you can refer to when building the actual birdhouse. The **TOPICS** and plans on the next page will help you construct your model.

GETTING STARTED

Talking It Over

- Have you ever built something out of wood? What sorts of tools does a carpenter use? How do you make sure that corners are square? How do you smooth the rough edges of the wood?

- Think of some wooden things in your home. When you are done with your birdhouse, what would you like your next project to be? Would you rather build functional things or things that are used just for decoration? Search the **Internet** for ideas and instructions.

Planning Your Project

- **Materials Needed:** pencils or pens, cardboard, ruler, scissors, tape, colored pencils or markers

- Draw the front, back, floor, and roof pieces of the birdhouse on cardboard and cut them out. After you draw and cut out the side pieces in Lesson 8.1, tape all six pieces together. Use your model to help you complete the **BUILDING YOUR PROJECT** assignments. Keep the assignments in your portfolio as notes to refer to when you build your real birdhouse.

BIRDHOUSE CONSTRUCTION

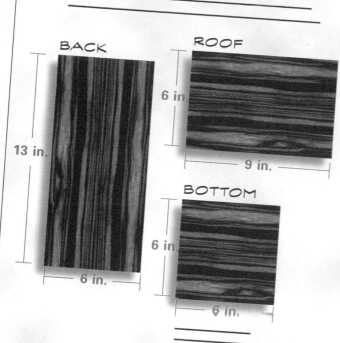

BACK

13 in.

6 in.

ROOF

6 in.

9 in.

BOTTOM

6 in.

6 in.

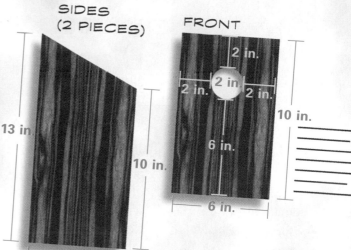

SIDES (2 PIECES)

13 in.

10 in.

6 in.

FRONT

2 in.

2 in. 2 in. 2 in.

10 in.

6 in.

6 in.

INTERNET

To find out about birdhouses, go to:
http://www.mlmath.com

LAB 8.1

COOPERATIVE LEARNING

Investigating Angle Measures

Part A USING A PROTRACTOR

To measure an angle, place the protractor's center on the vertex of the angle. Line up the 0° line with one side of the angle. Read the measure where the other side of the angle crosses the protractor.

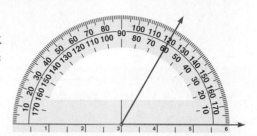

To draw an angle, first draw a line segment. Choose one end of the segment to be the vertex of the angle. Place the center of the protractor at the vertex, and line up the 0° line with the segment. Mark the measure that you want the angle to be. Draw another segment from the vertex through the point you marked.

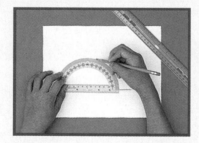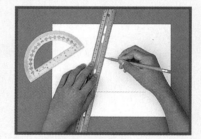

1. Draw angles that measure 50°, 90°, and 125°. Have another student check your work.

Part B ANGLES AND INTERSECTING LINES

2. Copy the intersecting lines on dot paper. Then use a protractor to measure each angle. What patterns do you see?

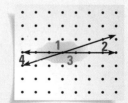

a.

b.

c.

d. Do you think the same patterns exist for all intersecting lines? Draw two more pairs of intersecting lines and check.

Materials Needed
- plain paper
- dot paper
- pencils or pens
- colored pencils
- protractor
- ruler

3. Copy the diagrams on dot paper. Use a protractor to measure each angle. Label each angle with its measure. How are the measures in each pair of angles related?

a. 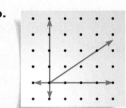 **b.** 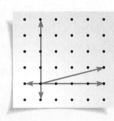 **c.**

4. Draw a right angle and a segment that divides it into two smaller angles. How do you think the measures of the two smaller angles are related? Check your answer by measuring.

5. Copy the diagrams on dot paper. Measure each angle and label it with its measure. How are the measures in each pair related?

a. 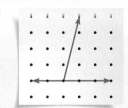 **b.** 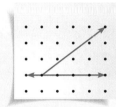 **c.**

6. Draw a straight line. Form two angles by drawing a segment with one endpoint on the line. How are the measures of the two angles related?

NOW TRY THESE

7. Draw an angle with the given measure.

   a. 35°   **b.** 65°   **c.** 105°   **d.** 145°

8. Two of the angles in Exercise 7 can be formed by drawing two intersecting lines. Draw two intersecting lines that form angles with these measures.

9. Two intersecting lines always form four angles. What is the sum of the four angle measures?

10. Make three conjectures about how the position of two angles can tell you how their measures are related.

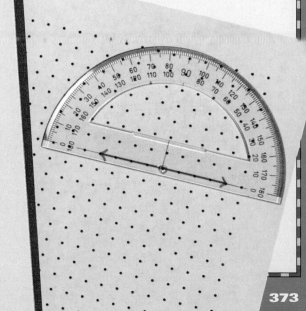

Intersecting Lines and **Angle Measures**

What you should learn:

Goal 1 How to identify parallel lines and vertical angles

Goal 2 How to identify complementary and supplementary angles

Why you should learn it:

Knowing how to calculate measures of angles can help you solve real-life problems. An example is calculating the angles of a gate.

Goal 1 PARALLEL AND INTERSECTING LINES

A **plane** is a flat surface that extends in all directions. In a plane, two lines that never meet are **parallel**. Any two lines in a plane are either parallel or **intersecting**.

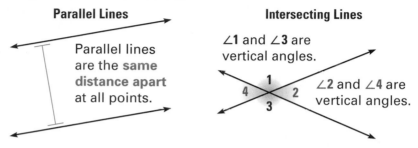

Parallel Lines

Parallel lines are the **same distance apart** at all points.

Intersecting Lines

∠1 and ∠3 are vertical angles.

∠2 and ∠4 are vertical angles.

Intersecting lines form two pairs of **vertical angles**. In each pair, the two angles are **congruent**, which means that they have the same measure. The symbol for congruence is "≅".

VERTICAL ANGLES

Vertical angles are congruent to each other. In the diagram above, ∠1 ≅ ∠3 and ∠2 ≅ ∠4.

Example 1 **Identifying Vertical Angles**

Use the diagram below. Tell which lines appear parallel and identify all sets of vertical angles.

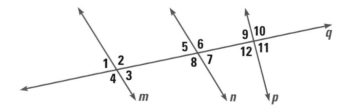

Solution

Lines *m* and *n* appear parallel. All other pairs of lines are intersecting. Line *q* intersects lines *m*, *n*, and *p*, and it appears that line *p* will intersect lines *m* and *n* if the diagram is extended downward.

The diagram has six pairs of vertical angles.

∠1 and ∠3	∠2 and ∠4	∠5 and ∠7
∠6 and ∠8	∠9 and ∠11	∠10 and ∠12

Two angles that share a side and a vertex but do not overlap are called **adjacent angles** . Below are two pairs of adjacent angles.

 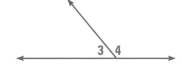

The angles in each pair are also related by their measures.

COMPLEMENTS AND SUPPLEMENTS

Two angles are **complements** if their measures add up to 90°.
Two angles are **supplements** if their measures add up to 180°.

$\angle 1 + \angle 2 = 90°$, so $\angle 1$ and $\angle 2$ are *complementary angles.*

$\angle 3 + \angle 4 = 180°$, so $\angle 3$ and $\angle 4$ are *supplementary angles.*

Complements and supplements do not have to be adjacent. The only requirement is that the sum of their measures be 90° or 180°.

Example 2 **Finding Angle Measures**

REAL LIFE
Carpentry

You are building a gate like the one shown, where $\angle 1$ and $\angle 2$ are complements and $\angle 3$ and $\angle 4$ are supplements. If $\angle 1 = 30°$ and $\angle 4 = 120°$, what are the measures of $\angle 2$ and $\angle 3$?

Solution

$$\angle 2 = 90 - \angle 1$$
$$= 90 - 30$$
$$= 60$$

$$\angle 3 = 180 - \angle 4$$
$$= 180 - 120$$
$$= 60$$

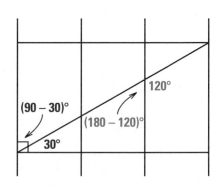

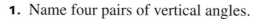

GUIDED PRACTICE

In Exercises 1–4, use the diagram and the fact that ∠3 and ∠6 are supplementary.

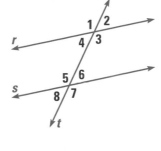

1. Name four pairs of vertical angles.

2. Name four pairs of adjacent angles.

3. Tell whether the statement is *true* or *false*.

   a. ∠1 and ∠4 are complementary angles.

   b. ∠1 and ∠3 are adjacent angles.

   c. ∠5 and ∠6 are supplementary angles.

   d. ∠3 and ∠7 are congruent.

4. Find the measure of each angle if ∠1 measures 125°.

   a. ∠3   **b.** ∠2   **c.** ∠5

PRACTICE AND PROBLEM SOLVING

In Exercises 5–8, use the figure at the right. Find the measure of the angle.

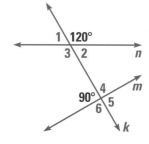

5. ∠1   **6.** ∠4

7. ∠5   **8.** ∠2

SOMETIMES, ALWAYS, NEVER Complete the statement using *sometimes*, *always*, or *never*.

9. Parallel lines ? meet.

10. Vertical angles are ? congruent.

11. Complementary angles are ? congruent.

12. Supplementary angles are ? adjacent.

13. The sum of the measures of supplementary angles is ? 90°.

In Exercises 14–16, find the measures of ∠1 and ∠2.

14.

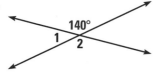

15.

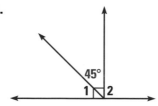

16.

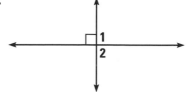

17. An angle measures 40°. What is the measure of its complement?

18. An angle measures 10°. What is the measure of its supplement?

19. **OPEN-ENDED PROBLEMS** Draw two intersecting lines and label the four angles formed. Name a pair of vertical angles, a pair of adjacent angles, and a pair of supplementary angles.

CITY PLANNING In Exercises 20–22, use the diagram at the right. It shows a street map for the downtown portion of a city.

20. Which street appears parallel to West 5th Street?

21. Which streets intersect West 6th Street?

22. Find the measures of the angles labeled *a, b,* and *c.*

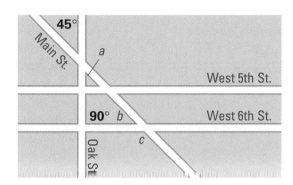

STANDARDIZED TEST PRACTICE

In Exercises 23 and 24, use the diagram at the right.

23. Which angle is congruent to ∠1?

  (A) ∠2   **(B)** ∠3

  (C) ∠4   **(D)** None of these

24. ∠3 and ∠4 arc

  (A) vertical angles   **(B)** complementary angles

  (C) adjacent angles   **(D)** parallel

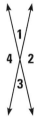

EXPLORATION AND EXTENSION

PORTFOLIO

25. **BUILDING YOUR PROJECT** Use a ruler to draw a 23 in.-by-6 in. rectangle on cardboard. Divide the rectangle in half, as shown at the right. If you cut along the lines, will the two pieces have the same side lengths and angle measures? How do you know?

Check your answer by cutting out the pieces and matching them up. Make a note for yourself about the best way to cut out the sides of the birdhouse.

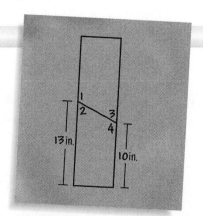

LAB
8.2

COOPERATIVE
LEARNING

Slides in the Coordinate Plane

Materials Needed
- graph paper
- pencils or pens
- ruler
- scissors

Part A HORIZONTAL SLIDES

1. Copy triangle *ABC* in a coordinate plane. Make another copy and cut it out. Lay the cutout triangle exactly on top of the drawn one. Slide the triangle three units to the right. Trace the triangle and label its vertices *D*, *E*, and *F*. Write the coordinates of each vertex.

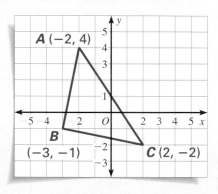

2. Compare the *x*-coordinates of the vertices of the triangles. Then compare the *y*-coordinates. What do you notice?

3. Slide the cutout triangle two units to the left of triangle *ABC* and trace around it to form triangle *GHJ*. Label each vertex with its coordinates.

4. Compare the *x*-coordinates of the vertices of triangles *ABC* and *GHJ*. Then compare the *y*-coordinates. What do you notice?

5. How do the coordinates of a point change as the point moves to the right or left?

Part B VERTICAL SLIDES

6. Slide the cutout triangle four units down from triangle *ABC* and trace around it to form triangle *KLM*. Label each vertex with its coordinates.

7. Compare the *x*-coordinates of the vertices of triangles *ABC* and *KLM*. Then compare the *y*-coordinates. What do you notice?

8. Slide the cutout triangle three units up from triangle *ABC* and trace around it to form triangle *NPQ*. Label each vertex with its coordinates.

9. Compare the *x*-coordinates of the vertices of triangles *ABC* and *NPQ*. Then compare the *y*-coordinates. What do you notice?

10. How do the coordinates of a point change as the point moves up or down?

11. Copy rectangle *ABCD* in a coordinate plane. Make another copy and cut it out. Slide the cutout rectangle four units to the left and two units down from rectangle *ABCD*. Trace around the rectangle to form rectangle *EFGH*. Label each vertex with its coordinates.

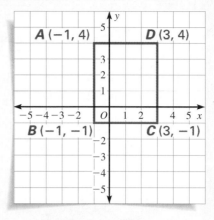

12. Compare the *x*-coordinates of rectangles *ABCD* and *EFGH*. Then compare the *y*-coordinates. What do you notice?

NOW TRY THESE

13. In a coordinate plane, draw a triangle with vertices A(−3, 3), B(−2, −2), and C(3, 1). Then slide the triangle each way.

   a. Up four units   **b.** Left two units

   c. Down three units and right one unit

14. In a coordinate plane, draw a quadrilateral with vertices A(−1, 0), B(−2, −3), C(2, −2), and D(1, 1). Then describe how you could slide the quadrilateral to the position shown below.

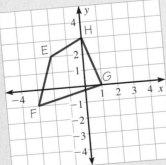

15. The point (5, 4) has been slid to the point (6, 7). Describe the slide.

8.2

Translations

What you should learn:

Goal ① How to find the coordinates of a figure that is translated in the plane

Goal ② How to use translations to solve real-life problems

Why you should learn it:

Knowing how to use translations can help you analyze computer graphics. An example is analyzing motion in a computer animation.

Goal ① TRANSLATIONS AND COORDINATES

In a **translation**, every point on a figure slides the same direction and the same distance.

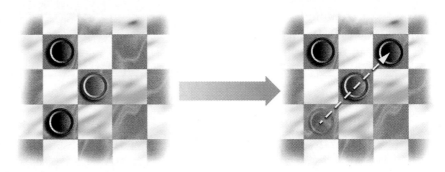

Example 1 **Translating Polygons**

Compare the coordinates of the vertices of the original (blue) and translated (red) triangles.

a.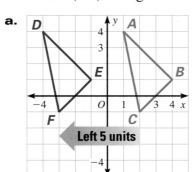

b.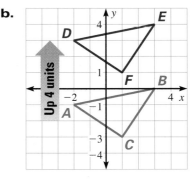

Solution

a. The triangle is translated **5 units to the left**. Notice that each x-coordinate is **decreased by 5**.

$$A(1, 4) \quad \rightarrow \quad D(1 - 5, 4) \text{ or } D(-4, 4)$$
$$B(4, 1) \quad \rightarrow \quad E(4 - 5, 1) \text{ or } E(-1, 1)$$
$$C(2, -1) \quad \rightarrow \quad F(2 - 5, -1) \text{ or } F(-3, -1)$$

b. The triangle is translated **4 units up**. Notice that each y-coordinate is **increased by 4**.

$$A(-2, -1) \rightarrow \quad D(-2, -1 + 4) \text{ or } D(-2, 3)$$
$$B(3, 0) \quad \rightarrow \quad E(3, 0 + 4) \text{ or } E(3, 4)$$
$$C(1, -3) \quad \rightarrow \quad F(1, -3 + 4) \text{ or } F(1, 1)$$

NEED TO KNOW

When a figure is translated in the plane, the translated figure and the original figure are congruent. This means they have exactly the same size and shape.

Goal 2 USING TRANSLATIONS IN REAL LIFE

Real Life...
Real People

Lynn Smith, award-winning animation filmmaker, is working on her film, "Pearl's Diner." She repositions paper cutouts under the camera for each two frames shot. A completed film is projected at 24 frames a second.

Example 2 Recognizing a Translation

To create an animated sequence, different poses are filmed in many locations. Which of the figures below is a translation? Describe the translation.

REAL LIFE
Animation

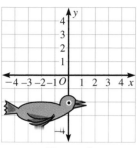

Figure A

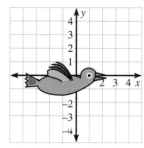

Figure B

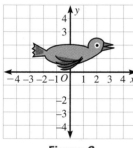

Figure C

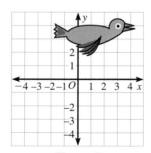

Figure D

Solution

A translated figure is congruent to the original figure. Figures *A* and *C* are congruent with Figure *C* being a translation of Figure *A*. Figure *C* is 2 units to the right and 5 units up from Figure *A*.

Example 3 Describing a Translation

In the animation above, $(-2, -2)$ is a point on Figure *A*. What is the corresponding point on Figure *C*?

REAL LIFE
Animation

Solution

Figure *C* is **2 units to the right** and **4 units up** from Figure *A*. Sliding 2 units to the right means **adding 2 to the *x*-coordinate**. Sliding 4 units up means **adding 4 to the *y*-coordinate**. So the corresponding point in Figure *C* is $(-2 + 2, -2 + 4)$, or $(0, 2)$.

ONGOING ASSESSMENT

Write About It

Suppose that the bird continues to move in the same pattern.

1. Describe the locations of the next four figures.

2. Which figures are they translations of?

GUIDED PRACTICE

Describe the translation of the blue figure to the red figure.

1.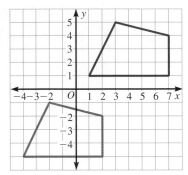

2.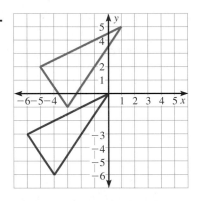

3. Fold a piece of paper in half three times, as shown at the right. Draw and cut out a quadrilateral and unfold the paper. Which of the eight quadrilaterals are translations of each other?

4. Describe a real-life translation.

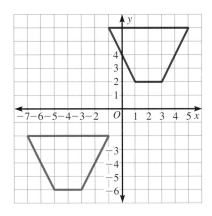

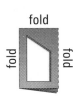

PRACTICE AND PROBLEM SOLVING

Describe the translation of the blue figure to the red figure.

5.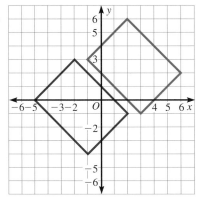

6.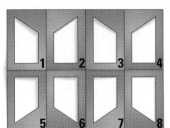

In Exercises 7 and 8, write the coordinates of the translated figure.

7. $G(0, 4)$, $H(6, 4)$, $J(6, -2)$; 2 units down and 2 units to the right

8. $L(-7, 0)$, $M(-6, -4)$, $N(-1, 2)$, $P(-2, -6)$; 3 units down

9. **OPEN-ENDED PROBLEM** Use translations to draw your own animation. Draw the figures by hand or use a computer drawing progam.

10. **THINKING SKILLS** If you translate a figure and then translate it again, is the result a translation of the original figure? Explain.

11. **COMPUTER ANIMATION** The diagram below shows part of a computer animation. When the full animation is shown, it appears that the fish is swimming. Which figures are translations of each other? Describe each translation.

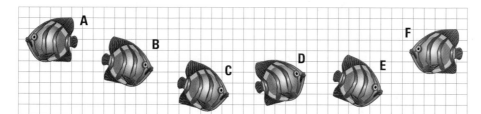

12. What are the triangle's coordinates after it is translated two units to the right and three units up?

  A (2, 2), (3, 4), (1, 7)

  B (−2, 2), (4, 3), (1, 7)

  C (−2, 2), (3, 4), (1, 7)

  D (2, −2), (3, 3), (1, 7)

13. Which set of coordinates represents the vertices of a translation of the triangle?

  A (−8, −2), (2, 2), (−2, 8)   **B** (0, −2), (5, 0), (3, 3)

  C (4, 1), (−1, −1), (1, −4)   **D** (−2, 1), (0, 0), (−1, 4)

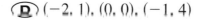
EXPLORATION AND EXTENSION

PORTFOLIO

14. **BUILDING YOUR PROJECT** You drill holes to place the roosting perches inside the birdhouse as shown, drilling hole A first.

  a. Describe how to measure from hole A to hole B, and from hole A to hole C.

  b. Explain how this is like the slides discussed in this chapter.

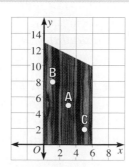

1. **GUESS, CHECK, AND REVISE** You buy a bottle of juice for $0.65 with quarters, dimes, and nickels. You use seven coins for the exact change. How many quarters, dimes, and nickels did you use to buy your juice? **(1.5)**

Find the greatest common factor of the numbers. (2.4)

2. 51, 85

3. 78, 108

4. 180, 126

Find the least common multiple of the numbers. (3.1)

5. 6, 21

6. 8, 20

7. 12, 15

Multiply or divide. Simplify if possible. (3.5, 3.7)

8. $\dfrac{1}{2} \cdot \dfrac{4}{5}$

9. $\dfrac{1}{9} \cdot \dfrac{3}{7}$

10. $\dfrac{3}{5} \cdot 2\dfrac{1}{8}$

11. $\dfrac{6}{7} \div \dfrac{3}{7}$

12. $1\dfrac{1}{2} \div \dfrac{3}{8}$

13. $4\dfrac{1}{3} \div 2\dfrac{1}{4}$

CAREER Interview

CARPENTER AND SCULPTOR

Ellen Gibson owns her own custom woodworking business and is a sculptor who works in wood, steel, and mixed media. She is also a part-time studio manager for a college, where she teaches, fixes equipment, and orders supplies.

Q *What led you into your career?*
I always made things. While I was in college, the school opened a program in artisanry, where I studied ceramics and woodworking.

Q *What kind of math do you use on the job?*
Math is second nature to me now. I am constantly measuring, both with a tape measure or ruler, and also with my eyes. I can estimate short lengths—fractions of inches—visually and add them in my head rapidly. I also figure angles, work with proportions, and calculate "balance" to determine the weight load of a structure.

Q *What would you like to tell kids who are in school?*
Math isn't just pages of problems or rules to be memorized. You'll use math every day and discover that numbers are a tool. Learn to use numbers, make them real, and play with them.

Drawing a Tessellation

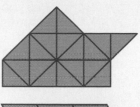

A *tessellation* is a covering of the plane with congruent figures. For example, tessellations can be made using triangles or parallelograms, as shown at the right.

Example

Draw a tessellation based on a parallelogram.

Solution

Draw any parallelogram	Draw a pattern on one side.	Translate pattern to opposite side.
Draw a pattern on third side.	Translate pattern to opposite side.	Add features and color.

Exercise

1. Use a parallelogram to create your own tessellation. Draw the tessellation by hand or use a computer drawing program. A computer drawing program is helpful when creating tessellations, because the program can duplicate patterns and translate them in the plane.

Circumference

What you should learn:

Goal 1 How to find the circumference of a circle

Goal 2 How to use circumference to solve real-life problems

Why you should learn it:

Knowing how to find circumferences can help you solve real-life problems. An example is finding the amount of metal needed for the edge of a drum.

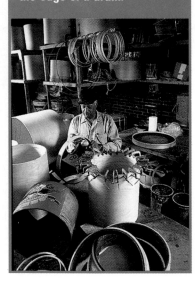

Goal 1 **FINDING CIRCUMFERENCE**

The distance from the edge of a circle to its center is the circle's **radius**, *r*. The distance across the circle through its center is the circle's **diameter**, *d*. The perimeter of a circle is called its **circumference**, *C*.

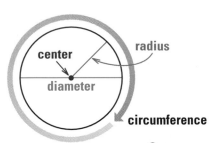

LESSON INVESTIGATION

COOPERATIVE LEARNING

Investigating Circumference

GROUP ACTIVITY Collect five cans with different diameters. Use a string and a ruler to measure the circumference, *C*, and the diameter, *d*. Record the data in a table like the one below.

	Circumference, C (in cm)	diameter, d (in cm)	$\frac{C}{d}$
Can 1	24.6	7.8	3.15

How do you think the circumference of a circle is related to its diameter? Explain your reasoning.

The ratio of a circle's circumference to its diameter is always about 3.14159. This number is represented by the Greek letter *pi*, π.

CIRCUMFERENCE OF A CIRCLE

To find the circumference of a circle, multiply its diameter by π. That is, $C = \pi \cdot d$, where $\pi \approx 3.14$.

Example 1 **Finding a Circumference**

You find that the diameter of a circle is 4 inches. Find the circumference of the circle.

Solution

$$C = \pi \cdot d \qquad \text{Use the circumference formula.}$$
$$\approx 3.14 \cdot 4 \qquad \text{Substitute 3.14 for } \pi \text{ and 4 for } d.$$
$$= 12.56 \qquad \text{Multiply.}$$

Goal 2 CIRCUMFERENCE IN THE REAL WORLD

Example 2 Finding a Circumference

Find the circumference
of the drum.

REAL LIFE
Music

Solution

First find the diameter of the drum.

$$d = 2r \qquad \text{The diameter is twice the radius.}$$
$$= 2 \cdot 7\frac{1}{2} \qquad \text{Substitute } 7\frac{1}{2} \text{ for } r.$$
$$= 15 \qquad \text{Multiply.}$$

Then use the diameter to find the circumference.

$$C = \pi \cdot d \qquad \text{Use the circumference formula.}$$
$$\approx 3.14 \cdot 15 \qquad \text{Substitute 3.14 for } \pi \text{ and 15 for } d.$$
$$= 47.1 \qquad \text{Multiply.}$$

Example 3 Finding a Diameter and Radius

A basketball hoop has a circumference of 56.5 in.
Find the diameter and radius of the hoop.

REAL LIFE
Basketball

Solution

You are given that $C = 56.5$ inches. To find d, use the formula for the
circumference and solve for d.

$$C = \pi \cdot d \qquad \text{Write formula for circumference.}$$
$$56.5 \approx 3.14 \cdot d \qquad \text{Substitute 56.5 for } C \text{ and 3.14 for } \pi.$$
$$\frac{56.5}{3.14} \approx \frac{3.14 \cdot d}{3.14} \qquad \text{Divide each side by 3.14.}$$
$$18.0 \approx d \qquad \text{Use a calculator.}$$

The diameter is about 18 in., so the radius is about 9 in.

ONGOING ASSESSMENT

Talk About It
· · · · · · · · · · · · · · · · · · · ·

The circumference of a
basketball is about 30 in.
Discuss the following
questions with another
person.

1. How does the
   circumference of the
   ball compare to the
   circumference of the
   hoop?

2. How does the radius of
   the ball compare to the
   radius of the hoop?

GUIDED PRACTICE

1. In your own words, describe the circumference, diameter, and radius of a circle.

In Exercises 2–4, find the circumference of the circle. Use $\pi \approx 3.14$.

2.

3 in.

3.

4 ft

4.

8 m

5. Find the circumference of a compact disk having a diameter of $4\frac{3}{4}$ in.

6. Find the diameter of a circle having a circumference of 15.7 cm.

PRACTICE AND PROBLEM SOLVING

In Exercises 7–9, find the circumference of the circle. Use $\pi \approx 3.14$.

7.
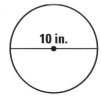
10 in.

8.
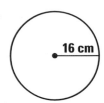
16 cm

9.

10 ft

10. LANDSCAPING You are a landscape architect. As part of your design for a new park, you want to plant flowers around a water fountain. The diameter of the round fountain is 20 ft. You want to plant a flower every 2 ft. How many flowers can you plant around the fountain?

11. REASONING What happens to the circumference of a circle if you double its diameter? What happens if you double its radius? Give examples to support your answer.

MAKING AN ESTIMATE Match the object with its circumference.

A. $3\frac{7}{10}$ ft

B. 75 ft

C. $\frac{6}{25}$ ft

12. A pizza

13. A quarter

14. Base of a lighthouse

In Exercises 15–17, find the dimension labeled *x*.

15. Circumference = 11.3 cm

16. Circumference = 47.1 m

17. Circumference = 1 in.

SPORTS **In Exercises 18 and 19, find the circumference.**

18.

16 ft.

19.

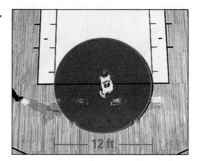

12 ft

STANDARDIZED TEST PRACTICE

20. A circle has a circumference of 226.08 cm. Which value best approximates the circle's radius?

   A 36 cm   **B** 72 cm   **C** 226 cm   **D** 1017 cm

21. The front tire on your bicycle has a diameter of 26 in. How far will you travel when the tire makes one complete revolution?

   A 26 in.   **B** 40.84 in.   **C** 81.64 in.   **D** 163.36 in.

EXPLORATION AND EXTENSION

22. COMMUNICATING ABOUT MATHEMATICS (p. 405)
Crop circles are flattened areas of grain that were first observed in England in the 1970s. Later, it was discovered that the circles were the work of two men. Even though the mystery of the circles has been solved, they continue to appear in fields all over the world.

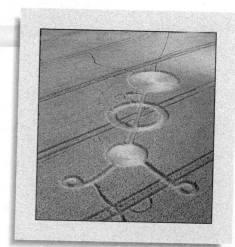

One of the largest known crop circles had a diameter of 60 ft. Find the circumference of the circle.

Area of a Parallelogram

Goal 1 FINDING AN AREA

A **parallelogram** is a quadrilateral whose opposite sides are parallel. The diagram at the right shows the **base** and **height** of a parallelogram.

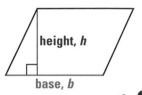

LESSON INVESTIGATION

Finding an Area Formula

GROUP ACTIVITY Draw two horizontal segments of the same length on dot paper. Connect the endpoints of the segments to form a parallelogram. Cut the parallelogram out. Cut a triangle off the end of the parallelogram as shown, and rearrange the pieces to form a rectangle. How does the area of the rectangle relate to the area of the original parallelogram? How does the area of the parallelogram relate to its height and base? Explain.

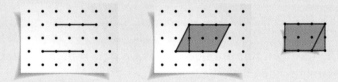

In the Lesson Investigation, you may have discovered the formula for the area of a parallelogram.

AREA OF A PARALLELOGRAM

To find the area A of a parallelogram, multiply its base, b, by its height, h. That is, $A = b \cdot h$.

Example 1 Finding the Area of a Parallelogram

Find the area of the parallelogram at the left.

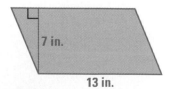

7 in.

13 in.

Solution

$$\text{Area} = b \cdot h \qquad \text{Use the formula given above.}$$
$$= 13 \cdot 7 \qquad \text{Substitute 13 for } b \text{ and 7 for } h.$$
$$= 91 \qquad \text{Multiply.}$$

The area of the parallelogram is 91 square inches.

| Example 2 | **Finding the Area of a Parallelogram** |

Use the map below to estimate the area of Tennessee.

CONNECTION
Geography

Scale 0   Miles   400

Solution

Begin by drawing a parallelogram that approximates the outline of the state. Then measure the base and height of the parallelogram. Use the map's scale to estimate the base and height in miles.

The base is about 350 mi and the height is about 120 mi. Use these values in the formula for the area of a parallelogram.

$$\text{Area} = b \cdot h \qquad \text{Write formula for area of parallelogram.}$$
$$= 350 \cdot 120 \qquad \text{Substitute 350 for } b \text{ and 120 for } h.$$
$$= 42{,}000 \qquad \text{Simplify.}$$

The area is approximately 42,000 mi². (The actual area of Tennessee is 42,146 mi².)

ONGOING ASSESSMENT

Write About It

Look at the map at the top of the page.

1. Use a parallelogram to estimate the area of Georgia. Explain your steps.

2. For which other states could you use a parallelogram to find the area?

GUIDED PRACTICE

In Exercises 1–3, use the parallelogram shown below. Each small square formed by the dots represents one square unit.

1. What are the base and height of the parallelogram?

2. Find the area of the parallelogram using the formula $A = b \cdot h$.

3. Find the area of the parallelogram using the dot paper.

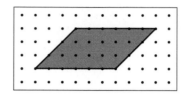

4. **ERROR ANALYSIS** Describe and correct the error.

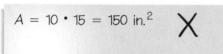

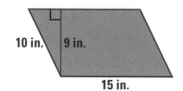

10 in.   9 in.

15 in.

5. Find the missing measure.

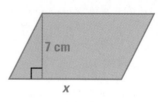

7 cm

x

$A = 84 \text{ cm}^2$

PRACTICE AND PROBLEM SOLVING

In Exercises 6–8, find the area of the parallelogram.

6.
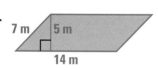
7 m   5 m
14 m

7.
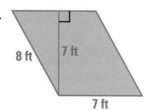
8 ft   7 ft
7 ft

8.
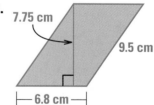
7.75 cm
9.5 cm
6.8 cm

OPEN-ENDED PROBLEMS In Exercises 9–11, draw on dot paper two different parallelograms that have the given area.

9. 12 square units   10. 30 square units   11. 36 square units

12. **LOOKING FOR A PATTERN** Find the area of each parallelogram. Use a table to organize your results. Write a statement to describe the pattern.

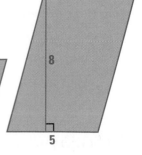

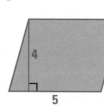

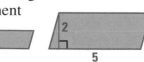

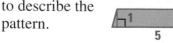

ALGEBRA In Exercises 13–15, find the missing measure.

13. $A = 238$ in.^{2}

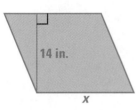

14 in.

x

14. $A = 58.08$ m^2

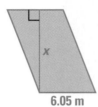

x

6.05 m

15. $A = 9\frac{5}{8}$ ft^2

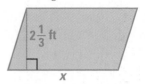

$2\frac{1}{3}$ ft

x

16. Copy the parallelogram at the right and divide it into two triangles and a rectangle.

   a. Find the area of each part. Then add the three areas to obtain the area of the parallelogram.

   b. Compare the result with that obtained using the formula for the area of a parallelogram.

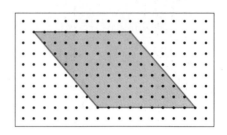

ALL, SOME, OR NO In Exercises 17–20, complete the statement using *all, some,* or *no.* Explain your reasoning.

17. _?_ parallelograms are quadrilaterals.

18. _?_ squares are parallelograms.

19. _?_ parallelograms are rectangles.

20. _?_ triangles are parallelograms.

21. QUILTING The quilt at the right is made up of parallelograms. Each parallelogram has a base of 2 in. and a height of $1\frac{3}{4}$ in. What is the area of each parallelogram in the quilt?

 STANDARDIZED TEST PRACTICE

22. Which expression can you use to find the area of the parallelogram?

   A 5×9 **B** 4×9

   C 4×6 **D** 3×5

5   4

3   6

23. What is the area of the parallelogram?

   A 15   **B** 39

   C 60   **D** 75

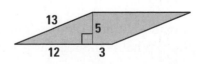

13   5

12   3

24. **BUILDING YOUR PROJECT** Suppose you want to paint the entire outside of your birdhouse. Which pieces of the birdhouse are solid parallelograms? Calculate the area of each.

Bottom: 6 in. by 6 in.
Back: 6 in. by 13 in.
Sides (2): 13 in. by 6 in. by 10 in.

Front: 6 in. by 10 in. minus
            hole that has a diameter
            of 2 in.

Roof: 6 in. by 9 in.

SPIRAL REVIEW

In Exercises 1–6, decide whether the equation is *true* or *false*. If it is false, insert parentheses to make it true. (2.1)

1. $3 + 7 \times 9 - 4 = 38$ **2.** $4 + 3 \times 2 \times 5 = 70$ **3.** $10 - 3 \times 2 - 3 = 1$

4. $4 + 6 \div 2 \times 3 + 4 = 9$ **5.** $13 - 5 \div 4 + 2 = 4$ **6.** $38 \div 2 + 17 \times 4 = 8$

SPORTS In Exercises 7–10, each list shows the number of points scored in several games by a basketball player. Find the mean, median, and mode of the data. **(5.1)**

7. 11, 9, 14, 12, 8, 10, 7, 9, 20, 9   **8.** 13, 19, 21, 23, 13, 15, 24, 10, 13

9. 18, 12, 20, 10, 8, 22, 17, 12, 19   **10.** 23, 10, 5, 7, 23, 9, 23, 4, 11

Solve each proportion. (6.3, 6.4)

11. $\dfrac{k}{5} = \dfrac{12}{4}$ **12.** $\dfrac{6}{15} = \dfrac{8}{m}$ **13.** $\dfrac{5}{60} = \dfrac{x}{72}$

GEOMETRY The figures in each exercise are similar. Find the missing lengths. **(6.6)**

14.

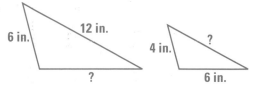

15.

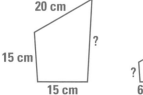

16. **SHOPPING** You paid $36 for a remote control car. The price was 75% of the regular price. What is the regular price? **(7.2)**

Take this test as you would take a test in class. The answers to the exercises are given in the back of the book.

In Exercises 1–4, is the statement *true* or *false*? (8.1–8.4)

1. Complementary angles are always congruent.

2. A translated figure has the same dimensions as the original figure.

3. Dividing a diameter in half divides the circumference in half.

4. A rectangle is a parallelogram.

In the figure at the right, ∠2 and ∠5 are supplementary and ∠4 measures 55°. (8.1)

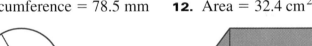

5. Name two angles that are congruent to ∠1. Explain why they are congruent.

6. Name two pairs of adjacent angles.

7. Find the measure of ∠5. Explain.

In Exercises 8 and 9, you are given the coordinates of the vertices of a figure. Find the coordinates of the vertices of the translated figure. (8.2)

8. $L(-2, 2)$, $M(-3, -2)$, $N(3, 1)$; 3 units to the left

9. $G(-1, 1)$, $H(-3, -2)$, $J(2, -3)$, $K(4, 0)$; 5 units up

In Exercises 10–12, find the dimension labeled *x*. (8.3, 8.4)

10. Circumference = 18.84 m 11. Circumference = 78.5 mm 12. Area = 32.4 cm^2

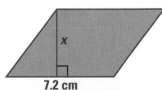

7.2 cm

KITES In Exercises 13 and 14, find the amount of blue material necessary to make the kite. (8.4)

13.

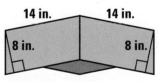

14 in. 14 in.

8 in. 8 in.

14.

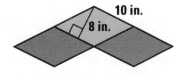

10 in.

8 in.

Area of a Trapezoid

What you should learn:

Goal 1 Find a formula for the area of a trapezoid

Goal 2 How to use the area of a trapezoid to solve real-life problems

Why you should learn it:

Knowing how to find the area of a trapezoid can help you solve real-life problems. An example is finding the area of the side of a house.

Goal 1 FINDING A FORMULA

A **trapezoid** is a quadrilateral that has two opposite sides that are parallel and two opposite sides that are not parallel. The parallel sides are called the **bases** and are labeled b_1 and b_2 (read as "b sub 1" and "b sub 2.") The two bases and the **height**, h, of a trapezoid are shown in the diagram at the right.

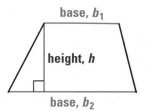

base, b_1

height, h

base, b_2

LESSON INVESTIGATION

Investigating the Area of a Trapezoid

GROUP ACTIVITY Draw two horizontal line segments of different lengths on dot paper. Connect the endpoints of the segments to form a trapezoid. Draw a second trapezoid exactly like the first.

On each trapezoid, label the bases b_1 and b_2 and the height h. Cut the trapezoids out and arrange them to form a parallelogram. Write an expression for the area of the parallelogram in terms of b_1, b_2, and h. Use your expression to find the area of each trapezoid in terms of b_1, b_2, and h.

In the Lesson Investigation, you may have discovered the following formula for the area of a trapezoid.

AREA OF A TRAPEZOID

To find the area A of a trapezoid, multiply half the sum of the two bases by the height.

$$A = \frac{1}{2} \cdot (b_1 + b_2) \cdot h$$

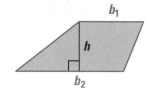

b_1

h

b_2

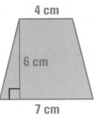

4 cm

6 cm

7 cm

Example 1 > **Finding the Area of a Trapezoid**

Find the area of the trapezoid shown at the right.

Solution

$$\text{Area} = \frac{1}{2} \cdot (b_1 + b_2) \cdot h \qquad \text{Write formula for area of trapezoid.}$$

$$= \frac{1}{2} \cdot (4 + 7) \cdot 6 \qquad \text{Substitute 4 for } b_1, 7 \text{ for } b_2, \text{ and 6 for } h.$$

$$= \frac{1}{2} \cdot 11 \cdot 6 \qquad \text{Add.}$$

$$= 33 \qquad \text{Multiply.}$$

The area of the trapezoid is 33 cm^2.

Example 2 > **Finding the Area of a Trapezoid**

Find the area of the side of the house shown below.

REAL LIFE
Construction

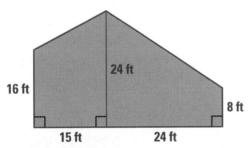

24 ft

16 ft

8 ft

15 ft   24 ft

Solution

One way to find the area is to divide the side into two trapezoids.

$$\text{Area of left trapezoid} = \frac{1}{2} \cdot (16 + 24) \cdot 15$$

$$= 300$$

$$\text{Area of right trapezoid} = \frac{1}{2} \cdot (8 + 24) \cdot 24$$

$$= 384$$

To find the total area, add the areas of the two trapezoids.

$$300 + 384 = 684 \text{ ft}^2$$

ONGOING ASSESSMENT

Write About It

Use the following rule to find the area of the trapezoid with the given dimensions. "Multiply the average of the two bases by the height."

1. $b_1 = 4$, $b_2 = 10$, $h = 5$

2. $b_1 = 3$, $b_2 = 9$, $h = 8$

3. $b_1 = 5$, $b_2 = 15$, $h = 9$

Do you the think the rule always works? Explain.

GUIDED PRACTICE

1. On dot paper, draw a trapezoid that has one base of 2 units and another base of 5 units.

In Exercises 2–4, match the figure with an area formula.

A. Area $= \frac{1}{2} \cdot b \cdot h$ **B.** Area $= b \cdot h$ **C.** Area $= \frac{1}{2} \cdot (b_1 + b_2) \cdot h$

2.    **3.** 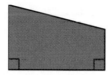   **4.**

5. **ERROR ANALYSIS** Find and correct the error.

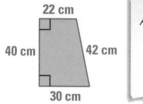

$$A = \frac{1}{2} \cdot (b_1 + b_2) \cdot h$$

$$= \frac{1}{2} \cdot (22 + 30) \cdot 42$$

$$= 1092 \ cm^2 \quad \times$$

6. **WRITING** In your own words, describe the difference between a trapezoid and a parallelogram.

PRACTICE AND PROBLEM SOLVING

In Exercises 7–9, find the area of the trapezoid.

7. 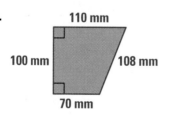   **8.** 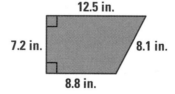   **9.**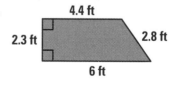

In Exercises 10–13, find the area of the trapezoid.

10. $b_1 = 3$ in., $b_2 = 4$ in., $h = 5$ in.   **11.** $b_1 = 5.3$ m, $b_2 = 3.6$ m, $h = 3.2$ m

12. $b_1 = 2$ cm, $b_2 = 17$ cm, $h = 12$ cm   **13.** $b_1 = 2\frac{1}{2}$ mi, $b_2 = 6$ mi, $h = 4\frac{1}{4}$ mi

14. Show how to divide a rectangle into two trapezoids.

In Exercises 15 and 16, draw a trapezoid to fit the description.

15. Two right angles   **16.** Two sides of equal length

In Exercises 17 and 18, find the dimension labeled *x*.

17. $A = 10 \text{ mi}^2$

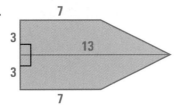

18. $A = 450 \text{ cm}^2$

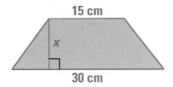

In Exercises 19 and 20, find the area of the region.

19.

20.

STANDARDIZED TEST PRACTICE

21. What is the area of the trapezoid?

   A 15.75   **B** 27

   C 31.5   **D** 37.8

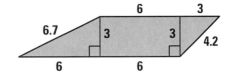

22. Which expression does *not* give the area of the trapezoid?

   A $\frac{1}{2} \cdot (6 + 9) \cdot 4$ **B** $\frac{1}{2} \cdot (3 \cdot 4) + (4 \cdot 6)$

   C $\frac{1}{2} \cdot (6 + 6 + 3) \cdot 4$ **D** $(3 \cdot 4) + (4 \cdot 6)$

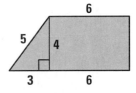

EXPLORATION AND EXTENSION

PORTFOLIO

23. BUILDING YOUR PROJECT Use the formula for the area of a trapezoid to calculate the area of the sides of your birdhouse. (See page 371.)

   a. Refer to the way you laid the sides out on cardboard in Lesson 8.1 (page 377). Use this layout to find the area of each side of your birdhouse.

   b. Explain how the two methods are related.

8.6 **Area** of a **Circle**

What you should learn:

Goal 1 How to find the area of a circle

Goal 2 How to use the area of a circle to solve real-life problems

Why you should learn it:

Knowing how to find the area of a circle can help you solve real-life problems. An example is finding the area of the part of a lawn that is not watered.

Goal 1 THE AREA OF A CIRCLE

In the following investigation, you will discover a relationship between the area of a circle and its radius.

LESSON INVESTIGATION

Investigating the Area of a Circle

GROUP ACTIVITY Cut a circle into 16 congruent parts. Rearrange the parts to approximate a parallelogram, as shown. Explain how the formula for the area of a parallelogram can be used to find a formula for the area of a circle.

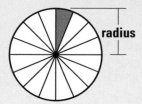 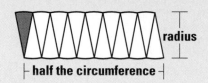

AREA OF A CIRCLE

To find the area, *A*, of a circle, multiply the square of the radius, *r*, by π. That is, $A = \pi \cdot r^2$, where $\pi \approx 3.14$.

Example 1 **Finding the Area of a Circle**

Find the area of the circle below.

1.5 ft

Solution

$$A = \boldsymbol{\pi} \cdot \boldsymbol{r}^2 \qquad \text{Write formula for area of a circle.}$$
$$\approx \mathbf{3.14} \cdot \mathbf{1.5}^2 \qquad \text{Substitute 3.14 for } \pi \text{ and 1.5 for } r.$$
$$\approx 7.1 \qquad \text{Use a calculator.}$$

The area of the circle is about 7.1 ft^2.

Goal 2 SOLVING REAL-LIFE PROBLEMS

Example 2 Finding the Area of a Circle

REAL LIFE
Music

A compact disk has a diameter of 12.1 cm. Find the area of a compact disk.

Solution

The radius of the compact disk is one half the diameter, or 6.05 cm.

$A = \pi \cdot r^2$ Write formula for area of a circle.

$\approx 3.14 \cdot 6.05^2$ Substitute 3.14 for π and 6.05 for r.

$\approx 114.9 \text{ cm}^2$ Multiply.

Example 3 Difference in Areas

REAL LIFE
Gardening

You use a rotating sprinkler to water a circular portion of your rectangular yard. What is the area of the yard that is *not* watered?

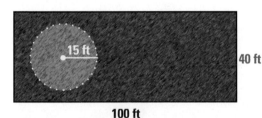

15 ft

40 ft

100 ft

Solution

First find the area of the entire garden.

$A = b \cdot h$ Write formula for area of a rectangle.

$= 100 \cdot 40$ Substitute 100 for b and 40 for h.

$= 4000$ Multiply.

Then find the area of the circular patch being watered.

$A = \pi \cdot r^2$ Write formula for area of a circle.

$\approx 3.14 \cdot 15^2$ Substitute 3.14 for π and 15 for r.

$= 706.5$ Multiply.

Subtract to find the area that is not watered.

$$4000 - 706.5 = 3293.5$$

About 3300 ft^2 of the garden is not being watered.

ONGOING ASSESSMENT

Talk About It
. . . .

Which of the following give you enough information to find the area of the circle? Work together to find the area of each circle, if possible.

1. $r = 8$ in.

2. $d = 10$ m

3. Center is at $(-2, 3)$.

4. $C = 31.4$ ft

GUIDED PRACTICE

In Exercises 1–4, match the expression with the measurement.

A. $\pi \cdot d$ **B.** $\pi \cdot r^2$ **C.** $b \cdot h$ **D.** $2 \cdot \ell + 2 \cdot w$

1. Circumference of a circle

2. Area of a parallelogram

3. Perimeter of a rectangle

4. Area of a circle

5. You are painting a ceiling with a large round light fixture in the middle of it. If the ceiling is 12 ft by 8 ft and the light is 2 ft in diameter, what is the area of the region that you need to paint?

6. **WRITING** Describe a real-life problem that can be solved using the area of a circle. Then solve the problem.

PRACTICE AND PROBLEM SOLVING

In Exercises 7–9, find the area of the circle. Use $\pi \approx 3.14$.

7. $d = 30.5$ cm

8. $d = 29$ in.

9. $r = 8$ in.

In Exercises 10–13, find the area and circumference of the circle.

10. Radius = 5 ft

11. Diameter = 20 cm

12. Diameter = 19 in.

13. Radius = 14 mi

In Exercises 14–16, find the area of the shaded region. Use $\pi \approx 3.14$.

14.

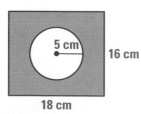

5 cm   16 cm   18 cm

15.

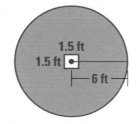

1.5 ft   1.5 ft   6 ft

16.

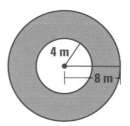

4 m   8 m

17. FORESTRY You work for a lumber company. Suppose you are buying logs that are 10 feet long. Which of the following is the largest?

   a. a 10-foot log with a radius of 8 in.

   b. a 10-foot log with a circumference of 43.96 in.

   c. a 10-foot log with a cross-sectional area of 78.5 in.^{2}

(To find out more about forestry, use Investigation 8 in *Interactive Real-Life Investigations*.)

18. GRANITE WORLD MAP Outside the United States Navy Memorial in Washington, D.C., is a circular granite map of the world, as shown in the photo at the right. Find the area of the circular map using the information in the caption.

19. RADIO WAVES A radio station broadcasts a signal that extends in a 75-mile radius from the station. Find the area of the region that receives the radio station's broadcasts.

Tech Link

Investigation 8, Interactive Real-Life Investigations

Real Life...
Real Facts

The U.S. Navy Memorial in Washington, D.C., has a circular map of the world that is 100 feet in diameter.

ARCHERY In Exercises 20–23, find the area of the target that represents the indicated score. The archery target at the right has a radius of 2 ft.

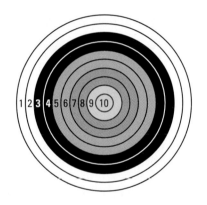

20. 10 points

21. 5 or more points

22. 1 or 2 points

23. More than 2 points

 STANDARDIZED TEST PRACTICE

24. Estimate the area of the shaded region.

   A 6.75 cm^2 **B** 7.74 cm^2

   C 17.15 cm^2 **D** 23.43 cm^2

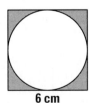

6 cm

25. The circle has a radius of 4 cm. The shaded region in the circle has an area of 10.05 cm^2. What percent of the circle is shaded?

   A 10%   **B** 15%

   C 20%   **D** 25%

EXPLORATION AND EXTENSION

26. BUILDING YOUR PROJECT Find the area of the wood surface on the front of your birdhouse. Explain your method. Combine this figure with your results from Lessons 8.4 and 8.5 to find the total area that you will need to paint.

If it takes you five minutes to paint a region that is one square foot, how long will it take you to paint your birdhouse? Explain your answer.

SPIRAL REVIEW

1. Find all the digits that will make the four-digit number 18**?**6 divisible by 4. **(2.3)**

2. You and four friends want to share 7 lb of trail mix equally. How much should each of you receive? **(2.7)**

In Exercises 3–6, match the improper fraction with its equivalent mixed number. (3.2)

A. $1\frac{1}{8}$ **B.** $2\frac{3}{4}$ **C.** $1\frac{5}{8}$ **D.** $3\frac{1}{4}$

3. $\dfrac{13}{4}$ **4.** $\dfrac{22}{8}$ **5.** $\dfrac{27}{24}$ **6.** $\dfrac{13}{8}$

In Exercises 7–12, decide whether the solution is *positive, negative,* or *zero*. Then solve the equation to check your answer. (4.6, 4.7)

7. $p + 11 = 11$ **8.** $7 = -7 + n$ **9.** $12 + y = 6$

10. $k - 5 = -13$ **11.** $-19 + x = 9$ **12.** $-23 = m - 23$

GEOMETRY **In Exercises 13 and 14, the figures are similar. Find the missing measures. (6.6)**

13.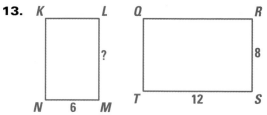

14.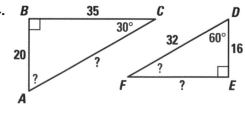

In Exercises 15–18, solve the percent problem. (7.4)

15. 12 is 48% of what number?   **16.** What percent of 105 is 63?

17. 30% of 80 is what number?   **18.** 72 is 9% of what number?

GE⬤METRY in the Field

Crop circles first started appearing in England in the late 1970s. At first nobody had any idea what was causing the patterns of flattened grain. People blamed UFOs, weather patterns, even mysterious energy fields. Finally two men confessed to making the circles.

A mathematician noticed that in the triangular pattern, the ratio of the areas of the outer and the inner circles is 4 to 1.

Some of the crop circle patterns are large. A pattern in Indiana had a central circle that measured 45 feet across. Two of the outside circles were 36 feet across, and one of them was 20 feet across.

The largest ring observed in the "bubble pattern" was a circle with a diameter of $25\frac{1}{2}$ feet enclosed by $4\frac{1}{3}$ feet of flattened grain around the circumference.

WRITE About It

1. What is the diameter of the largest ring in the bubble pattern, measured from the outside edges of the flattened grain? Explain in words how this is related to the circle's radius.

2. Figure out how much grain was flattened to make the largest ring of the bubble pattern. Explain how you found your answer.

3. The radius of a circle inside an equilateral triangle is 18 feet. What is the area of the *outer* circle that touches the apexes of the triangle? Explain your answer.

8.7 Square Roots

What you should learn:

Goal 1 How to find a square root

Goal 2 How to estimate a square root

Why you should learn it:

Knowing how to find square roots can help you solve real-life problems. An example is planning a work space for a business.

Goal 1 THE SQUARE ROOT OF A NUMBER

The **square root** of a number n is the number that when multiplied by itself will equal n. For example, the square root of 16 is 4, because $4 \times 4 = 16$. A table of squares and square roots appears on page 671 in the back of this book.

SQUARE ROOT OF A NUMBER

The square root of n is denoted by $\sqrt{n}$. The symbol $\sqrt{}$ is called a **radical sign**.

Example 1 Finding Square Roots

a. $\sqrt{49} = 7$

   ✔**Check:** $7 \times 7 = 49$

b. $\sqrt{6.25} = 2.5$

   ✔**Check:** $2.5 \times 2.5 = 6.25$

c. $\sqrt{8} \approx 2.83$

   ✔**Check:** $2.83 \times 2.83 \approx 8$

In Example 1, the number 49 is a **perfect square** because its square root is a whole number. The numbers 0, 1, 4, 9, and 16 are some other examples of perfect squares. More examples can be found in the table on page 671.

CALCULATOR TIP

You can use a calculator to approximate the square root of a number. For instance,

8 $\boxed{\sqrt{x}}$ $\approx 2.828427\ldots$

Example 2 Finding a Square Root

CONNECTION
Geometry

A square has an area of 10 yd². What is the length of each side of the square?

Solution

The area of a square is s^2, where s is the length of each side. Because the area is 10, it follows that the length of each side is the square root of 10.

Length of a side $= \sqrt{10}$ **Write square root of the area.**

≈ 3.16 **Use a calculator.**

The length of each side is about 3.16 yd.

Goal 2 ESTIMATING SQUARE ROOTS

Example 3 Using Mental Math

Use mental math and the table of squares and square roots on page 671 to estimate each square root.

a. $\sqrt{200}$ **b.** $\sqrt{60}$

Solution

a. The perfect square closest to 200 is 196. Since $\sqrt{196} = 14$, $\sqrt{200} \approx 14$. So, $\sqrt{200}$ is a little more than 14.

b. 60 is between the perfect squares 49 and 64. Since $\sqrt{49} = 7$ and $\sqrt{64} = 8$, $\sqrt{60}$ is between 7 and 8.

Example 4 Finding a Square Root

You are partitioning an office into rectangular work spaces, each with an area of 120 ft². Suggest two possible rectangles that could be used.

REAL LIFE
Office planning

Solution

Because Area = Length × Width, the length and width of a work space will be two numbers whose product is 120.

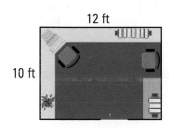
12 ft
10 ft

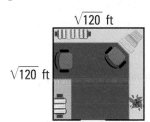
$\sqrt{120}$ ft
$\sqrt{120}$ ft

Area = Length × Width
   = 12 × 10
   = 120

Area = Length × Width
   = $\sqrt{120} \times \sqrt{120}$
   = 120

STRATEGY **MAKE AN ESTIMATE** The perfect square closest to 120 is 121.

Since $\sqrt{121} = 11$, $\sqrt{120} \approx 11$.

So, $\sqrt{120}$ is a little less than 11. You can use a calculator to find that each wall should be about 10.95 ft long.

ONGOING ASSESSMENT

Talk About It

Use mental math to estimate each square root. In each case explain your reasoning to your partner. Then, use a calculator to check your estimates.

1. $\sqrt{94}$

2. $\sqrt{28}$

3. $\sqrt{145}$

8.7 Exercises

Extra Practice, page 639

GUIDED PRACTICE

1. What number times itself is 81? Write two number sentences that answer the question.

2. Is 20 a perfect square? Explain.

3. Use the table of squares and square roots on page 671 to find three perfect squares that are greater than 100.

MENTAL MATH In Exercises 4–6, which is the best estimate? Explain your reasoning.

4. $\sqrt{143}$ **A.** 11.96   **B.** 12.1   **C.** 7.15

5. $\sqrt{108}$ **A.** 10.8   **B.** 11.04   **C.** 10.39

6. $\sqrt{170}$ **A.** 14.24   **B.** 13.04   **C.** 13.98

PRACTICE AND PROBLEM SOLVING

 TECHNOLOGY In Exercises 7–14, use a calculator to find the square root of the number.

7. $\sqrt{25}$ 8. $\sqrt{289}$ 9. $\sqrt{1}$ 10. $\sqrt{7.84}$

11. $\sqrt{82.81}$ 12. $\sqrt{12}$ 13. $\sqrt{60}$ 14. $\sqrt{43.25}$

 TECHNOLOGY In Exercises 15–17, use a calculator to find the value of *s*. Explain your method.

15. $A = 94.09$ yd^2 16. $A = 150$ yd^2 17. $A = 30$ yd^2

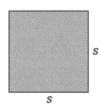   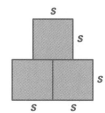   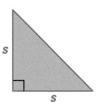

MENTAL MATH In Exercises 18–25, use mental math and the table of squares and square roots on page 671 to estimate the square root. Then use a calculator to check your estimate.

18. $\sqrt{3}$ 19. $\sqrt{10}$ 20. $\sqrt{75}$ 21. $\sqrt{183}$

22. $\sqrt{82}$ 23. $\sqrt{24}$ 24. $\sqrt{288}$ 25. $\sqrt{401}$

26. **LOOKING FOR A PATTERN** Evaluate each expression. What is the pattern?

$$\sqrt{1}, \sqrt{1+3}, \sqrt{1+3+5}, \sqrt{1+3+5+7}, \sqrt{1+3+5+7+9}$$

408   **Chapter 8** *Geometry in the Plane*

27. USING LOGICAL REASONING Use the clues to find the values of a, b, c, and d.

$$\sqrt{a} = b \qquad c^2 = b \qquad \sqrt{c} = d \qquad d \text{ is even and prime.}$$

GEOMETRY In Exercises 28 and 29, use the figure at the right.

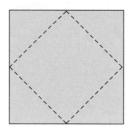

28. The outer square has an area of 64 square units. How long are its sides?

29. Copy the diagram. Cut it out and fold on the dotted lines. What is the area of the inner square? How long are its sides?

30. HORSESHOE PITCHING You are playing a game of horseshoe pitching. The figure below shows a horseshoe-pitching court. The area of each pitching box is 36 ft^2. Find the total area of the horseshoe pitching court.

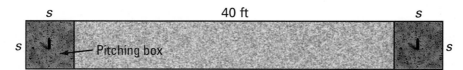

31. Estimate $\sqrt{96}$.

    A 8.7   **B** 9.1   **C** 9.8   **D** 10.1

32. A square has an area of 155 mm^2. Estimate the length of a side.

    A 12.0 mm   **B** 12.45 mm   **C** 12.8 mm   **D** 12.95 mm

EXPLORATION AND EXTENSION

PORTFOLIO

33. BUILDING YOUR PROJECT The floor of a birdhouse must be at least 100 in.^{2} for a bluebird to nest in it.

    a. If the floor is square, how long must each side be? Will your birdhouse be big enough for a bluebird? Explain.

    b. Suppose you want to change your birdhouse so that it is the minimum size required for a bluebird. How does each piece of the birdhouse have to change?

LAB 8.8

COOPERATIVE LEARNING

Discovering the Pythagorean Theorem

Part A GETTING READY

Materials Needed
- dot paper
- colored pencils or pens
- scissors
- ruler

1. Draw a right triangle in the middle of a piece of dot paper. Use different dimensions than the ones below. Label the shorter sides (the *legs*) a and b. Label the hypotenuse, the longest side, c.

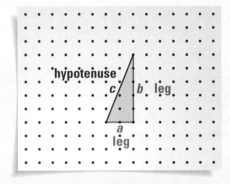

2. Draw a square on each of the triangle's three sides. Label the areas a^2, b^2, and c^2, and color them as shown.

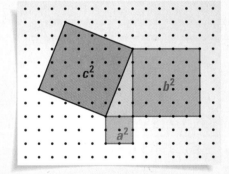

3. Draw and color seven copies of the triangle. Then cut out all eight triangles and all three squares.

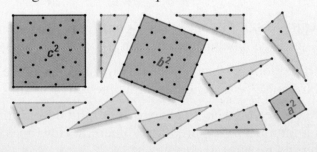

4. Arrange the red square and four triangles as shown. What is the length of each side of the figure? Use your answer to complete the equations below. What is the area of the entire figure?

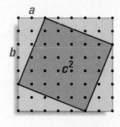

$$\text{Area} = 4 \cdot (\text{Area of triangle}) + \boxed{?}$$
$$= 4 \cdot \boxed{?} + \boxed{?}$$

5. Arrange the blue and green squares and the four triangles as shown. What is the length of each side of the figure? Use your answer to complete the equations below. What is the area of the entire figure?

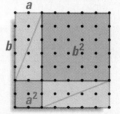

$$\text{Area} = 4 \cdot (\text{Area of triangle}) + \boxed{?} + \boxed{?}$$
$$= 4 \cdot \boxed{?} + \boxed{?} + \boxed{?}$$

6. Explain why the two figures you formed in Exercises 4 and 5 have the same area.

7. How are the areas of the blue and green squares related to the area of the red square? Explain your reasoning. Then write this relationship as an equation.

NOW TRY THESE

8. Do you think that the equation you wrote in Exercise 7 applies to any triangle? Explain your reasoning and draw an example.

9. Do you think that the equation you wrote in Exercise 7 applies to any right triangle? Explain your reasoning and draw an example.

10. Draw a right triangle on dot paper and use the equation you wrote in Exercise 7 to find the length of the side labeled c. To check your answer, measure the side with a strip of dot paper.

11. Explain the relationship between the measures of the legs and the hypotenuse in Exercise 10.

8.8 The **Pythagorean Theorem**

What you should learn:

Goal 1 How to identify types of triangles

Goal 2 How to use the Pythagorean Theorem to find the lengths of the sides of a right triangle

Why you should learn it:

Knowing how to use the Pythagorean Theorem can help you solve real-life problems. An example is finding the measurements of a roof.

Goal 1 TYPES OF TRIANGLES

Each angle of a triangle can be classified by its measure, as shown in the examples below.

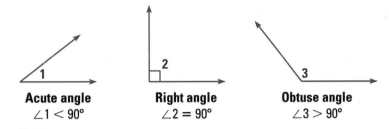

Acute angle
$\angle 1 < 90°$

Right angle
$\angle 2 = 90°$

Obtuse angle
$\angle 3 > 90°$

These classifications also apply to triangles. An **acute triangle** has three acute angles. A **right triangle** has one right angle. An **obtuse triangle** has one obtuse angle.

Example 1 Identifying Triangles

Identify each triangle as acute, right, or obtuse.

a. **b.** **c.**

Solution

a. One of the angles of this triangle is a right angle. So, this triangle is a right triangle.

b. All three angles are acute (each has a measure that is less than 90°). So, this triangle is an acute triangle.

c. One of the angles is obtuse. (Its measure is greater than 90°). So, this triangle is an obtuse triangle.

In a right triangle the side opposite the right angle is the **hypotenuse**. The other two sides are the **legs**.

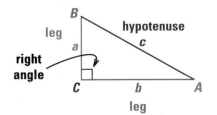

$\angle A$ is opposite leg a.
$\angle B$ is opposite leg b.
$\angle C$ is opposite hypotenuse c.

The side lengths of any right triangle are related by a rule called the **Pythagorean Theorem** .

THE PYTHAGOREAN THEOREM

For any right triangle, the sum of the squares of the lengths of the legs equals the square of the length of the hypotenuse.

$$a^2 + b^2 = c^2$$

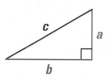

Example 2 **Finding the Hypotenuse**

You are designing a roof, as shown at the right. What is the distance from the ridge to the eave?

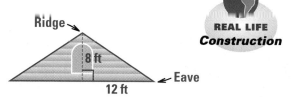

Solution

$c^2 = a^2 + b^2$	Write the Pythagorean Theorem.
$c^2 = 12^2 + 8^2$	Substitute 12 for a and 8 for b.
$c^2 = 208$	Simplify.
$c = \sqrt{208}$	Take the square root.
$c \approx 14.4$	Use a calculator.

The distance from the ridge to the eave is about 14.4 ft.

Example 3 **Finding the Length of a Leg**

Find the value of a.

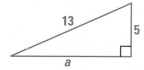

Solution

$c^2 = a^2 + b^2$	Write the Pythagorean Theorem.
$13^2 = a^2 + 5^2$	Substitute 13 for c and 5 for b.
$169 = a^2 + 25$	Simplify.
$144 = a^2$	Subtract 25 from both sides.
$12 = a$	The square root of 144 is 12.

ONGOING ASSESSMENT

Talk About It
....

Work with a partner to find the hypotenuse of a right triangle with the given leg lengths.

1. 5, 5

2. 7, 24

3. 30, 40

GUIDED PRACTICE

1. Complete the statement of the Pythagorean Theorem below.

For any ? triangle, the sum of the squares of the lengths of the ? equals the square of the length of the ? .

In Exercises 2 and 3, find the missing numbers.

2.
$$a^2 + b^2 = c^2$$
$$15^2 + 20^2 = c^2$$
$$\boxed{?} + \boxed{?} = c^2$$
$$\boxed{?} = c^2$$
$$\boxed{?} = c$$

3.
$$a^2 + b^2 = c^2$$
$$30^2 + b^2 = 50^2$$
$$\boxed{?} + b^2 = \boxed{?}$$
$$b^2 = \boxed{?}$$
$$b = \boxed{?}$$

In Exercises 4–6, refer to the triangle at the right.

4. Which sides of the triangle are the legs?

5. Which side is the hypotenuse?

6. Find the missing side length of the triangle.

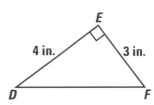

PRACTICE AND PROBLEM SOLVING

In Exercises 7–9, decide whether the triangle is *right, acute,* or *obtuse*. If it is a right triangle, name the hypotenuse.

7.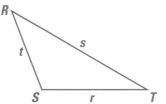

8.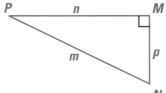

9.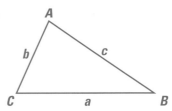

TECHNOLOGY In Exercises 10–12, decide whether the triangle is *right, acute,* or *obtuse*. If it is a right triangle, use a calculator to find the length of the hypotenuse.

10.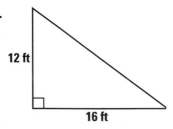

11.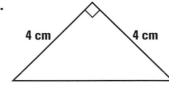

12.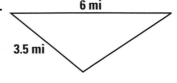

TECHNOLOGY In Exercises 13–15, you are given the lengths of the legs of a right triangle. Use a calculator to find the length of the hypotenuse to the nearest hundredth.

13. $a = 25, b = 30$ **14.** $a = 35, b = 65$ **15.** $a = 55, b = 100$

GUESS, CHECK, AND REVISE In Exercises 16–18, find the missing side lengths.

16.

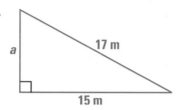

17.

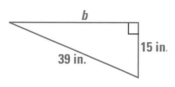

18.

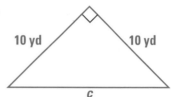

19. BICYCLES You are making a ramp for a BMX bike trail. You want the ramp to be $1\frac{1}{2}$ ft high at the end and 10 ft long. How long should the board for the ramp be?

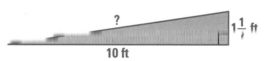

20. Which triangle is obtuse?

Ⓐ 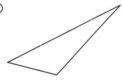 Ⓑ Ⓒ Ⓓ

21. Which set of lengths can be the side lengths of a right triangle?

Ⓐ 9, 16, 25 Ⓑ 9, 13, 22 Ⓒ 6, 8, 10 Ⓓ 7, 7, 7

EXPLORATION AND EXTENSION

 PORTFOLIO

22. BUILDING YOUR PROJECT You want the roof of your birdhouse to extend at least 2 in. past the front to protect the opening from the rain.

a. How far will the roof extend past the front?

b. Explain how you got your answer.

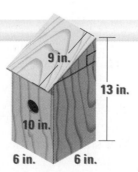

WHAT *did you learn?*

WHY *did you learn it?*

Skills

8.1 Identify parallel and intersecting lines, and special pairs of angles.

Analyze angles found in carpentry.

8.2 Translate a figure in a coordinate plane.

Understand cartoon animation.

8.3 Find the circumference of a circle.

Determine the material needed to manufacture round items.

8.4 Find the area of a parallelogram.

Estimate the area of a geographic region.

8.5 Find the area of a trapezoid.

Calculate areas found on structures such as buildings.

8.6 Find the area of a circle.

Determine areas in gardens.

8.7 Find the square root of a number.

Design square regions, such as work spaces for a business.

8.8 Use the Pythagorean Theorem.

Design a structure with a slant, such as a roof.

Strategies 8.1–8.8 Use problem solving strategies.

Solve a wide variety of real-life problems.

Using Data 8.1–8.8 Use graphs and diagrams.

Solve geometric problems.

HOW *does it fit in the bigger picture of mathematics?*

There are many different ways to view the things around you. For example, the shape below can be divided into several different combinations of **rectangles**, **triangles**, **parallelograms**, and **trapezoids**.

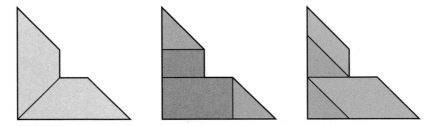

You should use the combinations that you understand best.

VOCABULARY

- plane (p. 374)
- parallel (p. 374)
- intersecting (p. 374)
- vertical angles (p. 374)
- congruent (p. 374)
- adjacent angles (p. 375)
- complements (p. 375)
- supplements (p. 375)
- translation (p. 380)

- radius (p. 386)
- diameter (p. 386)
- circumference (p. 386)
- parallelogram (p. 390)
- base of a parallelogram (p. 390)
- height of a parallelogram (p. 390)
- trapezoid (p. 396)
- bases of a trapezoid (p. 396)
- height of a trapezoid (p. 396)

- square root (p. 406)
- radical sign (p. 406)
- perfect square (p. 406)
- acute triangle (p. 412)
- right triangle (p. 412)
- obtuse triangle (p. 412)
- hypotenuse (p. 412)
- legs (p. 412)
- Pythagorean Theorem (p. 413)

8.1 INTERSECTING AND PARALLEL LINES

Example

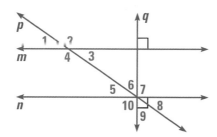

Lines m and n are parallel.

$\angle 6$ and $\angle 7$ are adjacent angles.

$\angle 2$ and $\angle 4$ are vertical angles.

$$\angle 2 \cong \angle 4$$

$\angle 5$ and $\angle 6$ are complements.

$$\angle 5 = 35°$$

$\angle 3$ and $\angle 4$ are supplements.

$$\angle 3 + \angle 4 = 180°$$

1. Find the measures of $\angle 3$, $\angle 7$, $\angle 8$, and $\angle 9$ in the diagram above.

8.2 TRANSLATIONS

When you slide a figure, you are translating the figure.

Example

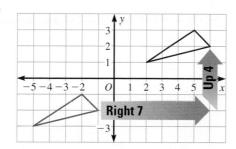

The coordinates of the vertices of a quadrilateral are (0, 0), (3, 3), (5, 4), and (4, −2). Give the coordinates of the vertices after each translation.

2. down 6 units   **3.** right 3 units   **4.** up 4 units and left 2 units

8.3 CIRCUMFERENCE

To find the circumference of a circle, multiply the diameter by π.

Example

$$\text{Circumference} = \pi \cdot d$$
$$\approx 3.14 \cdot 7$$
$$= 21.98$$

Find the value of *x* for each circle with the dimensions given.

5. Circumference = *x* ft
Diameter = 11 ft

6. Circumference = *x* in.
Radius = 14 in.

7. Circumference = 25.12 m
Diameter = *x* m

8.4 AREA OF A PARALLELOGRAM

To find the area of a parallelogram, multiply its base by its height.

Example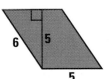

$$\text{Area} = b \cdot h$$
$$= 9 \cdot 4$$
$$= 36$$

Find the area of the parallelogram.

8.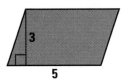

9.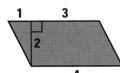

10.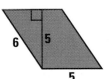

8.5 AREA OF A TRAPEZOID

To find the area of a trapezoid, multiply half the sum of the two bases by
the height.

Example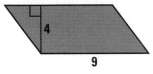

$$\text{Area} = \frac{1}{2} \cdot (b_1 + b_2) \cdot h$$
$$= \frac{1}{2} \cdot (13 + 7) \cdot 5$$
$$= 50$$

Find the area of the trapezoid.

11.

12.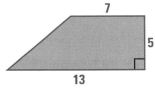

13.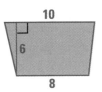

8.6 AREA OF A CIRCLE

To find the area of a circle, multiply the square of the radius by π.

Example
$$\begin{aligned}
\text{Area} &= \pi \cdot r^2 \\
&\approx 3.14 \cdot 10^2 \\
&= 3.14 \cdot 100 \\
&= 314
\end{aligned}$$

14. Find the area of a circle with radius 7 ft.

15. Find the area of a circle with diameter 12 in.

8.7 SQUARE ROOTS

To find the square root of a number n, find a number that when multiplied by itself will equal n. To find a square root you can use a calculator or the table of squares and square roots on page 671.

Examples $\sqrt{64} = 8$ because $8^2 = 64$ $\sqrt{1.69} = 1.3$ because $1.3^2 = 1.69$

16. Find the value of $\sqrt{121}$.

17. Find the value of $\sqrt{33.64}$.

18. Estimate the value of $\sqrt{17}$.

19. Estimate the value of $\sqrt{90}$.

8.8 THE PYTHAGOREAN THEOREM

Traingles can be classified as acute, right, or obtuse.

To find the length of the hypotenuse of a right triangle, use the Pythagorean Theorem.

Example
$$\begin{aligned}
c^2 &= a^2 + b^2 \\
c^2 &= 4^2 + 3^2 \\
c^2 &= 25 \\
c &= \sqrt{25} \\
c &= 5
\end{aligned}$$

Identify the triangle as acute, right, or obtuse. If the triangle is a right triangle, find the missing side length.

20.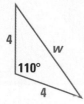

21.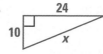

22.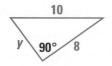

In Questions 1–4, use the figure at the right to complete the statement. The lines *m* and *n* are parallel.

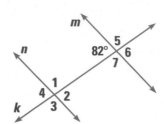

1. ∠1 and ∠3 are __?__ angles.

2. ∠2 and ∠3 are __?__ angles.

3. The measure of ∠6 is **?** .

4. The measure of ∠7 is **?** .

In Questions 5–7, find the area of the figure.

5.

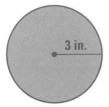

3 in.

6.

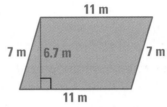

11 m
7 m | 6.7 m | 7 m
11 m

7.

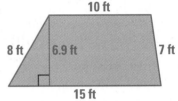

10 ft
8 ft | 6.9 ft | 7 ft
15 ft

8. Find the circumference of the circle in Question 5.

9. A triangle is slid so that one of its vertices moves from (4, 3) to (7, 21). Describe this translation.

10. A triangle with vertices of (1, 21), (4, 3), and (22, 1) is translated two units to the left and three units up. What are the vertices of the translated triangle?

 In Questions 11–14, use a calculator to evaluate the square roots. Use estimation to check that your answers are reasonable.

11. $\sqrt{17}$ 12. $\sqrt{42}$ 13. $\sqrt{168}$ 14. $\sqrt{200}$

STAINED GLASS In Questions 15–18, imagine that you have designed the stained glass window at the right.

15. What is the height of a red trapezoid?

16. What is the area of a red trapezoid?

17. What is the area of the green trapezoid?

18. What is the hypotenuse of a yellow triangle?

19. What is the area of the blue parallelogram?

20. **WRITING** Explain how a square root is related to the dimensions of a square. Illustrate your explanation with a diagram.

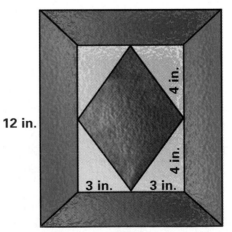

12 in.
4 in.
4 in.
3 in. | 3 in.
10 in.

For Questions 1–3, use the figure:

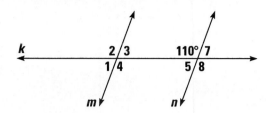

1. Which statement is *false*?

  (A) Lines *m* and *n* are parallel.

  (B) ∠5 and ∠8 are complements.

  (C) ∠1 and ∠3 are vertical angles.

  (D) ∠2 and ∠4 are congruent.

2. What is the measure of ∠7?

  (A) 20°   **(B)** 70°

  (C) 90°   **(D)** 110°

3. What is the measure of ∠8?

  (A) 20°   **(B)** 70°

  (C) 90°   **(D)** 110°

4. The vertices of triangle *A* are at $(-4, -1)$, $(-1, 0)$, and $(1, -3)$. The vertices of triangle *B* are at $(-1, 4)$, $(2, 5)$, and $(4, 2)$. Which statement describes the translation from triangle *A* to triangle *B*?

  (A) 5 down, 3 left

  (B) 4 up, 3 right

  (C) 2 up, 5 right

  (D) 5 up, 3 right

5. A parallelogram has an area of 162 m^2 and a height of 9 m. What is the base of the parallelogram?

  (A) 6 m   **(B)** 18 m

  (C) 22.5 m   **(D)** 36 m

Questions 6–8 refer to a circular swimming pool with a radius of 9 ft.

6. The diameter of the pool is

  (A) 6 ft.   **(B)** 18 ft.

  (C) 27 ft.   **(D)** 36 ft.

7. The circumference of the swimming pool is

  (A) 28.3 ft^2.   **(B)** 56.5 ft.

  (C) 254.3 ft^2. **(D)** 28.3 ft.

8. The area of the bottom of the pool is

  (A) 56.5 ft.   **(B)** 254.3 ft.

  (C) 254.3 ft^2. **(D)** 1017.4 ft^2.

9. What is the area of a trapezoid that has bases of 6 in. and 9 in. and a height of 4 in.?

  (A) 27 in.^2 **(B)** 30 in.^2

  (C) 37.5 in.^2 **(D)** 40.5 in.^2

10. Which equation is true?

  (A) $\sqrt{1.21} = 1.1$ **(B)** $\sqrt{7} = 49$

  (C) $\sqrt{3.6} = 0.6$ **(D)** $\sqrt{100} = 50$

11. Find the height of the triangle.

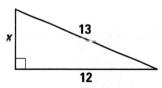

  (A) 1   **(B)** 3.6

  (C) 5   **(D)** 17.7

12. Find the area of a parallelogram with a base of 4 ft and a height of 3.2 ft.

  (A) 6.4 ft^2 **(B)** 6.4 ft.

  (C) 12.8 ft   **(D)** 12.8 ft^2

Geometry in Space

NATIONAL AQUARIUM Baltimore's National Aquarium features a cylindrical tank with a neon wave going around it and buildings with triangular faces.

TECHNOLOGY

Technology resources accompanying this chapter:

• Interactive Real-Life Investigations

• Middle School Tutorial Software

CHAPTER THEME
Engineering

REUNION TOWER This Dallas landmark, shown at the right in the photo above, is made up of four slender concrete cylinders topped by a geodesic dome.

FRED HARTMAN BRIDGE When this bridge over the Houston ship channel was completed in 1995, it became the largest suspension bridge in the world.

Solid Geometry

REAL LIFE
Engineering

The structures in the photos contain many shapes that lie in a plane—triangles, rectangles, and circles, for example. These plane figures are joined together to form the **three-dimensional structures** you see in the photos. In this chapter, you will use many of the ideas and figures from plane geometry to study the geometry of figures in space.

Think and Discuss

1. What plane figures can you find in each of the three-dimensional figures below?

   a.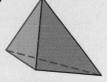

   b.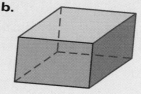

   c.

2. How many plane figures can you identify in the three-dimensional structures shown in the photos?

PORTFOLIO

CHAPTER PROJECT

Building a Playground

PROJECT DESCRIPTION

Engineers design many structures, including equipment for playgrounds. Before their designs are approved, engineers often build models of their proposed structures. Like a real-life engineer, you will design and build models of the playground equipment listed in the **TOPICS** on the next page.

GETTING STARTED

Talking It Over

- Is there a playground in your neighborhood? What kind of equipment does it have? How is the equipment constructed?

- What things do you think an engineer must take into consideration when designing playground equipment?

- If you were asked to design the ideal playground for your community, what would it be like? What equipment would you include? How would you make sure the playground was safe and accessible to all?

Planning Your Project

- **Materials Needed:** cardboard, construction paper, straws, scissors, tape or glue, popsicle sticks, toothpicks, string

- Decide what you would like to include in your playground. Draw a layout of your playground on construction paper.

- Build a model of your playground, where 1 in. represents 1 ft of the real playground. Use the topics in the **BUILDING YOUR PROJECT** list on page 425. Keep your written work in your portfolio and add to it as assigned.

BUILDING YOUR PROJECT

These are places throughout the chapter where you will work on your project.

TOPICS

9.2 Build a model swing set. *p. 435*

9.3 Construct models of two climbing poles. *p. 441*

9.4 Design a wheelchair access ramp for your playground. *p. 446*

9.5 Build a model sandbox. *p. 453*

9.6 Compute the volume of supports for a swing set. *p. 458*

INTERNET

To find out more about engineering and playground design, go to:

http://www.mlmath.com

Building Solids from Nets

Part A FOLDING A NET

Materials Needed
• grid paper
• pencils or pens
• ruler
• scissors
• tape

The figure at the right is called a *net*. When a net is cut out, it can be folded along its dotted lines to form a solid—a three-dimensional figure.

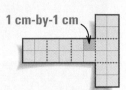

1 cm-by-1 cm

1. With your partner, describe the solid that can be formed with the net at the right.

2. Copy the net on centimeter grid paper. Cut out the net and fold it to form a solid. Did you get the solid you expected? The name of this solid is a *cube*.

3. Each flat surface of the cube is a *face*. Is it possible to hold the cube so that your partner sees (a) exactly one face, (b) exactly two faces, (c) exactly three faces, and (d) more than three faces?

4. Describe four common objects that have the shape of a cube.

Part B NETS AND AREA

5. Find the total area of the faces of the cube that you folded in Exercise 2.

Each face is a 4 cm-by-4 cm square.

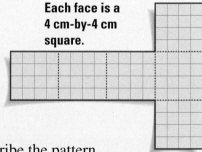

6. Copy this net, cut it out, and fold it on the dotted lines to form a cube. Find the total area of the faces of this cube.

7. Copy and complete the table. Describe the pattern. Use your description to predict the total area of the faces of a cube in which each face is an 8 cm-by-8 cm square.

Dimensions of Each Face	Number of 1 cm-by-1 cm Squares per Face	Area of Each Face	Total Area of All Faces
1 cm-by-1 cm	?	?	?
2 cm-by-2 cm	4	?	?
3 cm-by-3 cm	?	?	?
4 cm-by-4 cm	16	?	?
5 cm-by-5 cm	?	?	?

8. With your partner, describe the solid that can be formed with the net at the right.

9. Copy the net on centimeter grid paper. Cut the net out and fold it to form a solid. Did you get the solid you expected? The name of this solid is a *pyramid*.

10. Find the total area of the faces of the pyramid.

11. Sketch a net that can be cut out and folded to form the solid.

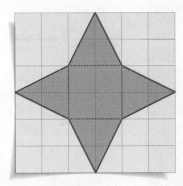

a.

b.

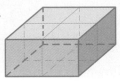

c.

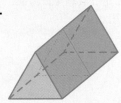

d.

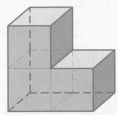

NOW TRY THESE

12. Describe the solid that could be formed by cutting and folding the net.

a.

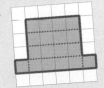

b.

13. Find the total area of the faces of each of the solids in Exercise 12.

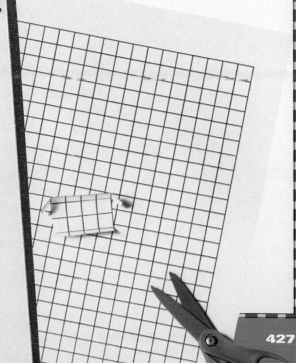

9.1

Exploring Polyhedrons

What you should learn:

Goal 1 How to identify polyhedrons

Goal 2 How to identify parts of polyhedrons

Why you should learn it:

Knowing how to identify polyhedrons and their parts can help you describe the shapes of buildings.

Goal 1 IDENTIFYING POLYHEDRONS

The solid figures below have polygons as sides. Such figures are called **polyhedrons**. Two common types of polyhedrons are prisms and pyramids. Notice that the prisms and pyramids shown below have either rectangular or triangular bases.

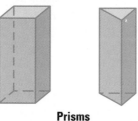

Prisms   **Pyramids**

Polyhedrons are named by their number of sides. A triangular pyramid has 4 sides and is a tetrahedron. A triangular prism and a rectangular pyramid are pentahedrons, because they each have 5 sides. The rectangular prism has 6 sides and is a hexahedron. A polyhedron with 8 sides is called an octahedron.

Example 1 Identifying Polyhedrons

The photograph at the left is of San Francisco. Describe the different shapes of the buildings.

CONNECTION
Architecture

Solution

Most of the skyscrapers shown in the photograph have 6 rectangular sides. This is the most common shape of a skyscraper.

The Transamerica Building is a pyramid. It has 4 triangular sides and a square side on the bottom, so it is a pentahedron.

Some of the buildings are irregular polyhedrons. For example, the lower part of the building to the right of the Transamerica Building has two trapezoidal sides. One of the buildings to the left has a top with trapezoidal sides.

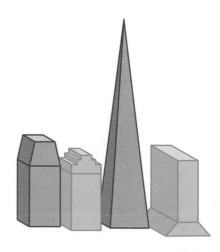

The polygons that are the sides of a polyhedron are its **faces**. The line segments where the faces meet are **edges**. Each point where the edges meet is called a **vertex** (plural: vertices). How many faces, edges, and vertices can you find in the rectangular pyramid below?

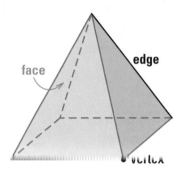

face   edge

vertex

Example 2   Identifying Parts of Polyhedrons

Count the faces, vertices, and edges of the polyhedrons at the top of page 428. What patterns can you find?

Solution

STRATEGY   **MAKE A TABLE** Sometimes it is easier to find a pattern if you make a table of your data.

	Rectangular prism	Triangular prism	Rectangular pyramid	Triangular pyramid
Faces	6	5	5	4
Vertices	8	6	5	4
Edges	12	9	8	6

You should find the following pattern. The sum of the number of faces and the number of vertices is 2 more than the number of edges. In the rectangular prism: $6 + 8 = 12 + 2$. In the triangular prism: $5 + 6 = 9 + 2$. In the rectangular pyramid: $5 + 5 = 8 + 2$. In the triangular pyramid: $4 + 4 = 6 + 2$. Do the pentagonal prism and the hexagonal prism at the right show the same pattern?

ONGOING ASSESSMENT

Write About It

Count the faces, edges, and vertices of these prisms. Describe the pattern.

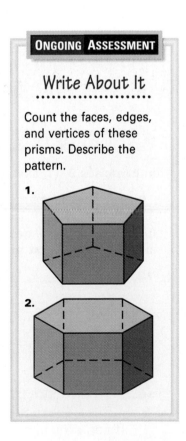

1.

2.

GUIDED PRACTICE

In Exercises 1–4, is the figure a polyhedron? If yes, name the polyhedron. If no, explain your reasoning.

1.

2.

3.

4.

5. Identify and describe the parts labeled *a*, *b*, and *c* of the polyhedron shown at the right.

6. **WRITING AN EQUATION** Write an equation that relates the number of faces, vertices, and edges of polyhedrons. (See Example 2 on page 429.)

7. **DRAWING** To draw a rectangular prism, lightly sketch a rectangle and then a congruent rectangle as in Step 1 at the right. Join corresponding vertices as in Step 2. Then darken the visible edges and make the hidden edges dashed as in Step 3. Draw several rectangular solids.

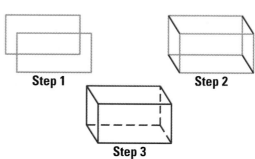

Step 1 Step 2 Step 3

8. **WRITING** Describe a real-life polyhedron.

PRACTICE AND PROBLEM SOLVING

In Exercises 9–11, sketch a polyhedron of the given type.

9. Rectangular pyramid   **10.** Hexagonal prism   **11.** Cube

In Exercises 12–15, decide whether the net can be folded to form a cube. If it can, what number will be on the face opposite 1?

12.

13.

14.

15.

16. **THINKING SKILLS** Is it possible to build a polyhedron that has 4 faces, 4 vertices, and 6 edges? If so, sketch one and describe it. If not, explain why.

17. PACKAGING Which of the following nets could be used as a pattern for a cereal box? Explain your reasoning.

A.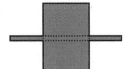

B.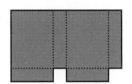

C.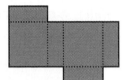

18. ARCHITECTURE The Citicorp Center in New York City has the shape of two stacked prisms. The lower one is a rectangular prism. The upper one has two faces that are trapezoids, as shown at the right. Count the number of faces, edges, and vertices of the upper prism.

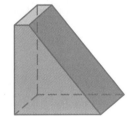

STANDARDIZED TEST PRACTICE

19. What is the name of the figure at the right?

    (**A**) Tetrahedron   (**B**) Pentahedron

    (**C**) Hexahedron   (**D**) Octahedron

20. How many vertices does the figure have?

    (**A**) 3   (**B**) 4

    (**C**) 5   (**D**) 6

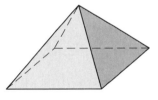

EXPLORATION AND EXTENSION

POLYHEDRON Use the glossary to match the polyhedron with its name. Count the number of faces, edges, and vertices. Do the numbers fit the pattern described in Example 2 on page 429?

A. Octahedron   **B. Hexahedron**   **C. Nonahedron**

21.   **22.**   **23.**

9.2

Surface Area of a Prism

What you should learn:

Goal 1 How to find the surface area of a prism

Goal 2 How to use the surface area of a prism to solve real-life problems

Why you should learn it:

Knowing how to find the surface area of a prism can help you decide how much paint to buy for a set of building blocks.

Goal 1 FINDING SURFACE AREA

The **surface area of a polyhedron** is the sum of the areas of all its faces.

LESSON INVESTIGATION

COOPERATIVE LEARNING

Investigating Surface Area

GROUP ACTIVITY Draw the nets shown below on centimeter grid paper. Cut them out and fold them to form prisms. Find the surface area of each. Which prism has the greater surface area? Discuss your reasoning.

1.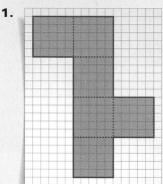

2.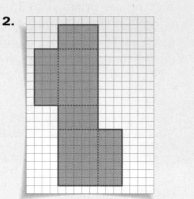

Example 1 Finding Surface Area

Find the surface area of the triangular prism at the left.

Solution

To find the surface area, you need to find the area of each face. Then find the sum of all the faces.

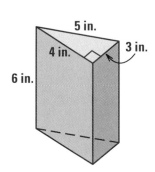

$$\text{Area of two triangular faces} = 2\left(\frac{1}{2} \cdot 3 \cdot 4\right) = 12 \text{ in.}^2$$

$$\text{Area of } \mathbf{3} \text{ in.-by-} \mathbf{6} \text{ in. rectangular face} = \mathbf{3} \cdot \mathbf{6} = 18 \text{ in.}^2$$

$$\text{Area of } \mathbf{4} \text{ in.-by-} \mathbf{6} \text{ in. rectangular face} = \mathbf{4} \cdot \mathbf{6} = 24 \text{ in.}^2$$

$$\text{Area of } \mathbf{5} \text{ in.-by-} \mathbf{6} \text{ in. rectangular face} = \mathbf{5} \cdot \mathbf{6} = 30 \text{ in.}^2$$

$$\text{Surface area} = 12 + 18 + 24 + 30 = 84 \text{ in.}^2$$

The surface area of the triangular prism is 84 in.^{2}

> **Example 2** Finding Surface Area

REAL LIFE
Crafts

You are making a set of wooden building blocks. The set has three types of blocks, and there are 24 of each type. A small can of enamel paint will cover 10 ft^2. If you want to paint each type of block a different color, how many cans of paint will you need?

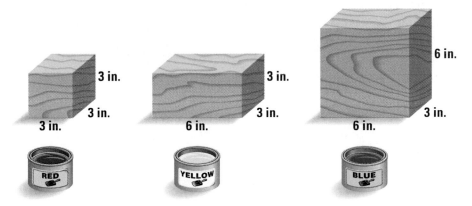

Solution

Red Blocks: Each red block has six faces that are 3 in. by 3 in.

$$6 \times (3 \times 3) = 54 \text{ in.}^2 \qquad \text{Find surface area.}$$
$$24 \times 54 = 1296 \text{ in.}^2 \qquad \text{Multiply by 24.}$$

Yellow Blocks: Each yellow block has two faces that are 3 in. by 3 in. and four faces that are 3 in. by 6 in.

$$2 \times (3 \times 3) + 4 \times (3 \times 6) = 90 \text{ in.}^2 \qquad \text{Find surface area.}$$
$$24 \times 90 = 2160 \text{ in.}^2 \qquad \text{Multiply by 24.}$$

Blue Blocks: Each blue block has four faces that are 3 in. by 6 in. and two faces that are 6 in. by 6 in.

$$4 \times (3 \times 6) + 2 \times (6 \times 6) = 144 \text{ in.}^2 \qquad \text{Find surface area.}$$
$$24 \times 144 = 3456 \text{ in.}^2 \qquad \text{Multiply by 24.}$$

One square foot is equal to 144 in.^{2}, so 10 ft^2 is equal to 1440 in.^{2} You will need one can of red paint, two cans of yellow paint, and three cans of blue paint.

ONGOING ASSESSMENT

Write About It
· · · · · · · · · · · · · · ·

You decide to add two other types of blocks to the set: 24 green blocks that are 3 in. by 3 in. by 9 in. and 24 purple blocks that are 6 in. by 6 in. by 6 in.

1. How many cans of green paint will you need?

2. How many cans of purple paint will you need?

GUIDED PRACTICE

In Exercises 1 and 2, use the prism at the right.

1. Find the area of each face of the prism.

2. Find the surface area of the prism.

3. **WRAPPING** You have a sheet of brown paper to mail a package. The sheet is 36 inches by 48 inches. Which of the packages can you cover without cutting the paper?

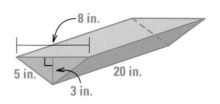

A.

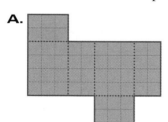

10 in.
10 in.
10 in.

B.

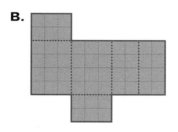

6 in.
24 in.
30 in.

C.

24 in.
10 in.
16 in.

4. Draw a net for a rectangular prism with a surface area of 40 cm^2. What are the dimensions of the prism?

PRACTICE AND PROBLEM SOLVING

5. **NETS** Which of the nets could you fold to make the prism? What is the surface area of the prism?

A.

B.

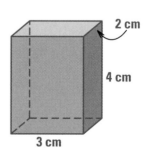

2 cm
4 cm
3 cm

In Exercises 6–8, find the surface area of the prism.

6.

2 ft
2 ft
2 ft

7.

$4\frac{1}{8}$ in.
1 in.
1 in.
4 in.

8.

10 cm
1 cm
6 cm

9. **GUESS, CHECK, AND REVISE** Find the length of each edge of a cube that has a surface area of 864 square inches. Sketch the cube and label the lengths of its edges.

In Exercises 10–12, find the surface area of the prism.

10.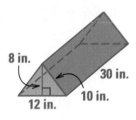
8 in.
30 in.
10 in.
12 in.

11. 6 cm
2.8 cm
8 cm
10 cm
2 cm
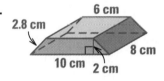

12. 10 in.
30 in.
8 in.
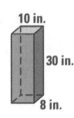

MAKING AN ESTIMATE In Exercises 13 and 14, decide which is the best estimate of the surface area of the object. Explain your reasoning.

13. Sugar cube   **A.** 1.5 in.^2 **B.** 5.5 in.^2 **C.** 10.5 in.^2

14. Standard door   **A.** 8.5 ft^2 **B.** 43.5 ft^2 **C.** 105 ft^2

CRAFTS In Exercises 15 and 16, how much gold foil will you need to cover all the surfaces except the bottom of the jewelry box?

15.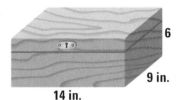
6
9 in.
14 in.

16. 11 in.
4 in.
7 in.
5 in.
5 in.
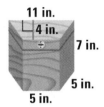

STANDARDIZED TEST PRACTICE

17. The hexagon at the right is the base of a prism. What is the area of the hexagon?

   Ⓐ 216 cm^2 Ⓑ 187.2 cm^2

   Ⓒ 103.2 cm^2 Ⓓ 93.6 cm^2

3 cm
5.2 cm
6 cm

18. The hexagonal prism has 6 rectangular sides, each measuring 6 cm by 6 cm. What is the surface area of the prism?

   Ⓐ 187.2 cm^2 Ⓑ 403.2 cm^2 Ⓒ 525.6 cm^2 Ⓓ 619.2 cm^2

EXPLORATION AND EXTENSION

PORTFOLIO

19. **BUILDING YOUR PROJECT** Your playground will contain a swing set. The seats of the swings are cut from boards, as shown at the right. Find the surface area of one of the boards. Then build a model swing set.

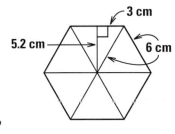
1 in.
8 in.
14 in.

In Exercises 1–8, multiply or divide. Simplify if possible. (3.5, 3.7)

1. $\frac{2}{9} \times \frac{3}{8}$

2. $\frac{2}{5}$ of 12

3. $3 \div \frac{1}{4}$

4. $\frac{7}{8} \div \frac{5}{2}$

5. $3\frac{2}{3} \times 1\frac{1}{8}$

6. $4 \times 3\frac{1}{16}$

7. $1\frac{7}{12} \div \frac{3}{4}$

8. $2\frac{3}{5} \div 3\frac{3}{8}$

9. **VIDEO RENTALS** The data below show the number of videos rented from a video store for 14 days. Make a histogram of the data. What other type of graph could you make? **(5.2, 5.5)**

49, 60, 78, 80, 85, 59, 60, 65, 63, 75, 88, 90, 59, 65

10. The track-and-field team is practicing for a track meet. Kelsey ran 100 m in 13 s, Julian ran 200 m in 27 s, and Byron ran 400 m in 50 s. Who ran the greatest average speed? **(6.2)**

In Exercises 11–16, solve the percent problem. (7.4)

11. What is 30% of 80?

12. 8 is 40% of what number?

13. What percent of 32 is 40?

14. What is 98% of 250?

15. 19 is 20% of what number?

16. 153 is what percent of 204?

Life Science Connection

ANIMAL ARCHITECTURE

Beekeepers provide places for honeybees to live, but the bees build their own honeycombs inside. Each honeycomb houses 40 to 80 thousand bees and provides storage for pollen and honey. The bees construct the cells of the comb with wax from their own bodies. The inside of each cell is a hexagonal prism.

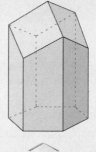

The design of the honeycomb is perfect, because it takes the least amount of material and effort to build. The hexagonal shape provides the most usable space and structural strength in the smallest area. Because of shared sides, bees use the perimeters of five hexagons to obtain an area equal to seven hexagons.

1. Refer to the drawing above to find how many faces, edges, and vertices each bee's cell contains.

2. What percentage of wax is saved building 5 hexagons instead of 7 circles in the same amount of space? (*Hint:* The perimeter of 5 hexagons is equal to $20r\sqrt{3}$ and the circumference of 7 circles is equal to $14\pi r$.)

Comparing Surface Areas

In Lesson 9.2, you found the surface area of a prism by adding the areas of all the faces. When you use a spreadsheet to find the surface area of a rectangular prism, it is convenient to use a formula.

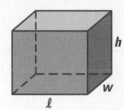

$$\text{Surface Area} = (2 \cdot \ell \cdot w) + (2 \cdot \ell \cdot h) + (2 \cdot w \cdot h)$$

COMPUTER TIP

If you use a spreadsheet to find the surface area of a rectangular prism, you will need to enter the formula for surface area. For example, the formula entered in cell D2 of the spreadsheet is

2*A2*B2 + 2*A2*C2 + 2*B2*C2.

Example

The spreadsheet below shows the surface areas for several rectangular prisms. When you double the dimensions of a prism, how is the surface area affected?

	A	B	C	D
	Surface Areas			
	Length	Width	Height	Surface area
2	2	3	9	102
3	4	6	18	408
4	5	7	4	166
5	10	14	8	664
6	8	6	10	376
7	16	12	20	1504

Solution

Compare the dimensions of the first two prisms, the second two prisms, and the third two prisms. In each case, the dimensions are doubled; the surface area is multiplied by 4.

Exercises

1. Use a spreadsheet to compare other prisms whose dimensions have been doubled. In each case, do you obtain a surface area that is 4 times as large as the smaller prism?

2. Use a spreadsheet to compare 3 pairs of prisms whose dimensions have been tripled. What happens to the surface area when the length, width, and height are tripled?

What you should learn:

Goal 1 How to find the surface area of a cylinder

Goal 2 How to use the surface area of a cylinder to solve real-life problems

Why you should learn it:

Knowing how to find the surface area of a cylinder can help you solve real-life problems. An example is finding the surface area of a paint can.

Goal 1 FINDING SURFACE AREA

A **cylinder** is a solid figure that has two circular **bases** and a curved **lateral surface** . The **surface area of a cylinder** is the sum of the areas of the bases and the area of the lateral surface.

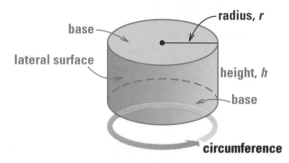

LESSON INVESTIGATION

Investigating Surface Area of a Tube

GROUP ACTIVITY You and your partner should each cut a rectangle out of construction paper. Measure your rectangle and find its area. Roll and tape the rectangle to form a circular tube. Exchange tubes with your partner. Without unrolling the tube, find its surface area. Explain how you did it. Does the surface area equal the area of the original rectangle?

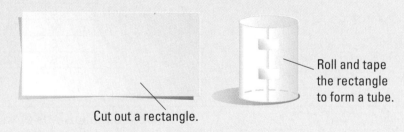

Cut out a rectangle.

Roll and tape the rectangle to form a tube.

You may have discovered that the lateral surface area of a cylinder equals its circumference times its height.

SURFACE AREA OF A CYLINDER

The surface area of a cylinder is the sum of the lateral surface area plus the area of the 2 bases.

$$\text{Surface area} = \underbrace{2\pi r \cdot h}_{\text{lateral surface area}} + \underbrace{2\pi r^2}_{\text{area of 2 bases}}$$

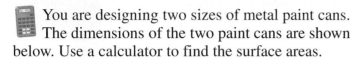

Example 1 Comparing Surface Areas

You are designing two sizes of metal paint cans. The dimensions of the two paint cans are shown below. Use a calculator to find the surface areas.

REAL LIFE
Packaging

a. Find the amount (area) of metal needed for each can.

b. What is the ratio of the surface areas of the two cans?

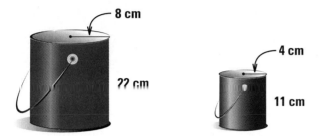

8 cm

22 cm

4 cm

11 cm

Solution

a. Use the formula for the surface area of a cylinder to find the surface areas of the large and small paint cans.

Large Can: The radius of the large can is **8** cm and the height is **22** cm.

$$\text{Surface Area} = 2\pi r \cdot h + 2\pi r^2 \qquad \text{Write the formula.}$$
$$\approx (2 \cdot 3.14 \cdot \mathbf{8} \cdot \mathbf{22}) + \left(2 \cdot 3.14 \cdot \mathbf{8}^2\right) \qquad \text{Substitute values.}$$
$$= 1105.28 + 401.92 \qquad \text{Solve for areas.}$$
$$= 1507.20 \text{ cm}^2 \qquad \text{Simplify.}$$

Small Can: The radius of the small can is **4** cm and the height is **11** cm.

$$\text{Surface Area} = 2\pi r \cdot h + 2\pi r^2 \qquad \text{Write the formula.}$$
$$\approx (2 \cdot 3.14 \cdot \mathbf{4} \cdot \mathbf{11}) + \left(2 \cdot 3.14 \cdot \mathbf{4}^2\right) \qquad \text{Substitute values.}$$
$$= 276.32 + 100.48 \qquad \text{Solve for areas.}$$
$$= 376.8 \text{ cm}^2 \qquad \text{Simplify.}$$

b. To find the ratio of the two surface areas, divide the surface area of the large can by the surface area of the small can.

$$\frac{\text{Larger Surface Area}}{\text{Smaller Surface Area}} = \frac{1507.20}{376.8} = 4$$

The large can has 4 times the surface area as the small can.

ONGOING ASSESSMENT

Write About It
. . . .

A third paint can has dimensions that are twice those of the large can in the example.

1. Draw a diagram of the third can and label its dimensions.

2. Find the amount of metal used to make the can.

3. Compare the amount of metal to that used to make the large can in Example 1.

GUIDED PRACTICE

1. Name the parts of the cylinder labeled *a, b, c, d,* and *e.*

2. **VISUAL THINKING** A rectangle can be rolled to form the lateral surface of a cylinder. Can any parallelogram be rolled to form the lateral surface of a cylinder? Explain.

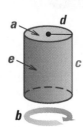

In Exercises 3–6, use the cylinder at the right to match the description with its measurement.

A. ≈ 197.8 in.² 　　　　　 B. ≈ 127.2 in.²

C. ≈ 325.0 in.² 　　　　　 D. ≈ 63.6 in.²

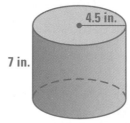

3. Area of one base 　　　 **4.** Surface area

5. Lateral surface area 　　 **6.** Area of two bases

7. **WRITING** Descibe three real-life cylinders and how they are used.

PRACTICE AND PROBLEM SOLVING

In Exercises 8–11, decide whether the net can be folded to form a cylinder. Explain your reasoning.

8. 　　 **9.** 　　 **10.** 　　 **11.**

OIL TANKS In Exercises 12–14, find the surface area of the cylinder.

12. 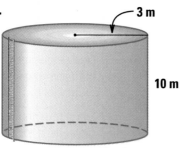　3 m
10 m

13. 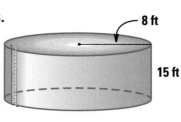　8 ft
15 ft

14. 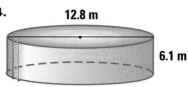　12.8 m
6.1 m

MAKING AN ESTIMATE In Exercises 15–18, match the figure with its dimensions. Then find the surface area of the figure.

A. $h = 190$ mm; $r = 4$ mm 　　　　　 B. $h = 6\frac{3}{4}$ in.; $r = 1\frac{1}{4}$ in.

C. $h = 1$ mm; $d = 19$ mm 　　　　　 D. $h = 4.2$ cm; $d = 1$ cm

15. Pencil 　　　 **16.** AAA Battery 　　　 **17.** Juice bottle 　　　 **18.** Penny

19. **GUESS, CHECK, AND REVISE** Sketch two cylinders that each have a surface area of about 300 square inches.

20. **DECISION MAKING** Each of the containers below holds the same amount of liquid. Which do you think has the least surface area? Check your guess by finding the surface area of each container.

a.

16 cm

4 cm

9.42 cm

b.

12 cm

├8 cm┤

21. **CAMPING** Your sleeping bag fits in a cylindrical stuff sack. When you unroll the bag, it is in the shape of a prism as shown at the right. Do you think that the surface areas of the stuff sack and the unrolled sleeping bag are the same? Find the surface areas to check your guess.

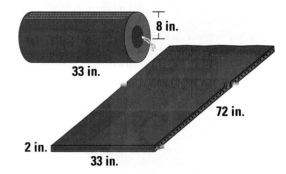

8 in.

33 in.

72 in.

2 in.

33 in.

STANDARDIZED TEST PRACTICE

22. Which formula gives the lateral surface area of a cylinder?

(A) $2\pi r^2$ (B) $2\pi r \cdot h$ (C) πr^2 (D) $2\pi \cdot d$

23. You are frosting the top and sides of a circular cake that has a 9 in. diameter. The cake is 6 in. tall. How much of the cake's surface do you need to cover?

(A) 233.15 in.^{2} (B) 296.73 in.^{2}

(C) 593.46 in.^{2} (D) 847.80 in.^{2}

EXPLORATION AND EXTENSION

PORTFOLIO

24. **BUILDING YOUR PROJECT** Build two model climbing poles for your playground. Make each model pole 10 inches long with a diameter of $\frac{1}{4}$ inch. Find the lateral surface of a model pole and of an actual climbing pole. The scale is 1 inch : 1 foot.

What you should learn:

Goal 1 How to draw different views of a solid

Goal 2 How to analyze different views of a solid

Why you should learn it:

Knowing how to draw and analyze different views of a solid can help you draw blueprints. An example is drawing a three-view blueprint for a metal part.

Computers can be used to create three-dimensional images of blueprint drawings.

Spatial Visualization

Goal 1 DRAWING VIEWS OF A SOLID

There are several different ways that engineers, designers, and architects draw objects. A common way is to draw three different views of the object: a top view, a front view, and a side view.

Example 1 Comparing Three Views

STRATEGY **DRAW A DIAGRAM** A metal part is shown below. Draw a top view, a front view, and a side view of the metal part. Check the drawing of each view to make sure it accurately shows the object in two dimensions.

CONNECTION
Mechanical Drawing

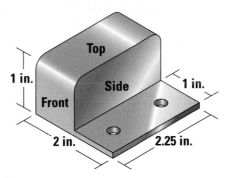

Solution

The three views are shown below.

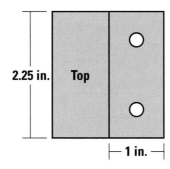

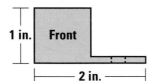
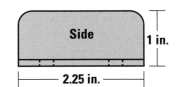

Why do you think that three views are necessary?

To see the relationship between a solid object and a drawing, it helps if you know how to analyze the three views that are drawn.

Example 2 **Analyzing a Drawing**

Draw a top view, front view, and side view for the stack of 9 cubes shown below.

Solution

One way to do this is to build the stack out of blocks and look at the 3 views. When you do this, you should see the views shown at the right. Notice that the top view is usually drawn on the top. The front view is shown at the lower left, and the side view is shown at the lower right.

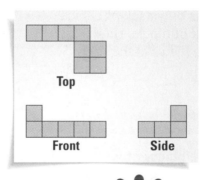

Top

Front   Side

LESSON INVESTIGATION

COOPERATIVE
LEARNING

Investigating Views of Solids

GROUP ACTIVITY You are shown 3 views of a stack of cubes.

Top

Front   Side

Use the views to build a stack of cubes that has the same structure as shown in the drawings. Discuss how you did it.

ONGOING ASSESSMENT

Talk About it

In the Lesson Investigation at the left, you built a stack of cubes that have the three given views.

1. Can you build another stack that has the same three views? If so, do it. If not, explain why it's not possible.

GUIDED PRACTICE

DRAWING In Exercises 1–3, draw a top view, a front view, and a side view of the cone and the two block structures.

1.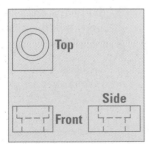

2.

3.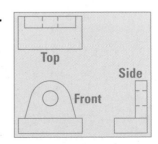

4. **PARTNER ACTIVITY** Choose a simple object in your classroom. Sketch the top view, front view, and side view of the object. Can your partner name the object by looking at your sketch?

Top

5. You are shown 3 views of a stack of cubical blocks. Draw the stack of blocks shown by the top, front, and side views at the right.

Front

Side

PRACTICE AND PROBLEM SOLVING

In Exercises 6–8, match the blueprint with the object.

A.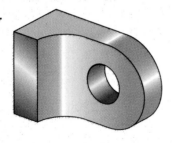

B.

C.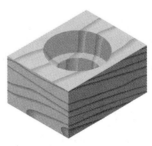

6.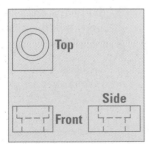

7.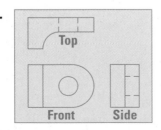

8.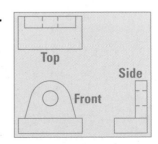

In Exercises 9–11, use the views to name the solid.

9.

Top

Front
Side

10.
Top

Front Side

11.

Top

Front
Side

FAMOUS BUILDINGS In Exercises 12–14, match the top view of the building in Washington, D.C., with its name.

A. The White House

B. Jefferson Memorial

C. Washington Monument

12.
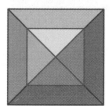

13.
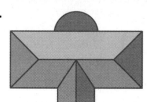

14.
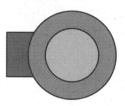

 STANDARDIZED TEST PRACTICE

Consider the solid shown at the right and the views below.

A

B
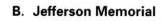 

C

D

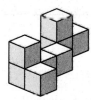

15. Which view is the front view?

  Ⓐ View A   Ⓑ View B   Ⓒ View C   Ⓓ View D

16. Which is the top view?

  Ⓐ View A   Ⓑ View B   Ⓒ View C   Ⓓ View D

17. BUILDING YOUR PROJECT You are putting a wheelchair access ramp at the street curb near your playground. Draw the front, back, side, and top views of the ramp shown below. Build a model of the ramp. Use a scale of 1 inch : 1 foot.

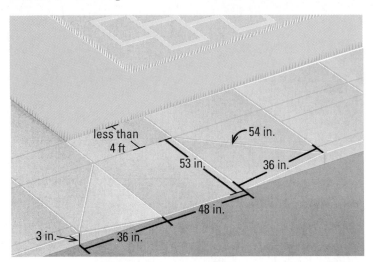

SPIRAL REVIEW

1. USING A DIAGRAM Of 28 students surveyed, 24 had traveled to another state, 7 had traveled to another country, and 3 had done neither. How many had traveled to both another state and another country? Use a Venn diagram to find your answer. **(1.7)**

 TECHNOLOGY In Exercises 2–5, use a calculator to find the mean of each data set. **(4.4)**

2. $-38, 75, -16$ **3.** $11, -44, 69, -23$ **4.** $-25, -9, 57, -12, -6$

5. Draw a box-and-whisker plot of the data. **(5.3)**

> 15, 10, 25, 9, 36, 13, 19, 45, 6, 12, 20, 27, 13, 17, 5,
> 40, 22, 8, 32, 11, 13, 49, 15, 39, 13, 6, 10, 43, 12, 9

In Exercises 6 and 7, find the percent increase or decrease. (7.7)

6. Before: $165   After: $70   **7.** Before: 38 fans   After: 109 fans

8. Using the diagram below, identify all sets of vertical angles. **(8.1)**

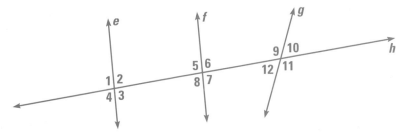

Take this test as you would take a test in class. The answers to the exercises are given in the back of the book.

1. Sketch a triangular prism and label its faces, edges, and vertices. **(9.1)**

VISUAL THINKING In Exercises 2–4, identify the solid that can be formed by folding the net. **(9.1, 9.3)**

2.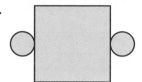

3.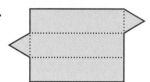

4.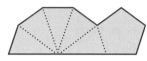

In Exercises 5–7, on graph paper, draw the net for each figure. Label the dimensions of the net. **(9.2)**

5.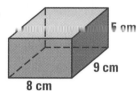
5 cm
9 cm
8 cm

6.
8 m
4 m 2 m

7.
10 ft
4 ft 6 ft

In Exercises 8–10, find the surface area of the figure. **(9.2, 9.3)**

8.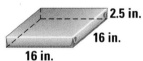
2.5 in.
16 in.
16 in.

9.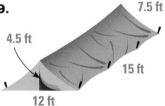
7.5 ft
4.5 ft
15 ft
12 ft

10.
2.6 in.
3.9 in.

11. Use the views to name the solid. **(9.4)**

Top

Front   Side

12. **MARKETING** You are designing a box to hold a CD-ROM. The dimensions you decide on are 12 in. by 9 in. by 2.25 in. How much area will you have to write information about the product? **(9.4)**

COOPERATIVE LEARNING

Investigating Volume

Materials Needed
- paper
- pencils or pens
- 24 cubes

Part A BUILDING PRISMS FROM CUBES

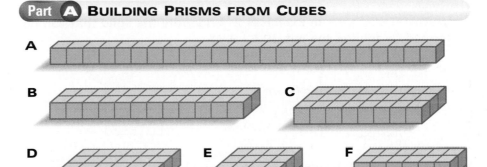

1. Because all the prisms above are built from 24 cubes, they take up the same amount of space. This means they have the same *volume*. Build each prism. Then copy and complete the following table.

   The dimensions should be given as the number of cubes that make up the length, width, and height of each prism. The dimensions for prism A are provided.

	Length	Width	Height
Prism A	24	1	1
Prism B	?	?	?
Prism C	?	?	?
Prism D	?	?	?
Prism E	?	?	?
Prism F	?	?	?

2. Each of the cubes has a volume of 1 cubic unit. Because each prism consists of 24 cubes, it must have a volume of 24 cubic units. How is the number 24 related to the lengths, widths, and heights listed in your table?

3. There are 6 different prisms shown above. Using *all 24 cubes*, can you build a prism that has dimensions different from those listed? If it is possible, build it and describe the prism. If it is not possible, explain why.

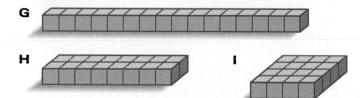

G

H   I

4. Each of the prisms above is built from 16 cubes. Build each prism and record its length, width, and height in a table. Then find a prism J with different dimensions that can be built from 16 cubes. Build it and add its dimensions to your table.

	Length	Width	Height
Prism G	16	1	1
Prism H	?	?	?
Prism I	?	?	?
Prism J	?	?	?

5. Each prism above has a volume of 16 cubic units. How is the number 16 related to the lengths, widths, and heights listed in your table?

6. Consider a prism whose dimensions are 4 by 5 by 6. What is its volume?

NOW TRY THESE

7. ACT IT OUT How many different prisms can you make with 48 cubes? Record the dimensions of each prism in a table.

8. Find the volume of each prism.
   a. 2 by 5 by 6   b. 4 by 6 by 6   c. 6 by 7 by 8

9. Consider a prism that has a volume of 54 cubic units. Name some of the possible dimensions of the prism.

10. Describe how you can find the volume of a rectangular prism whose length is l, width is w, and height is h.

9.5

Volume of a Prism

What you should learn:

Goal 1 How to find the volume of a prism

Goal 2 How to use the volume of a prism to solve real-life problems

Why you should learn it:

Knowing how to find the volume of a prism can help you compare amounts. An example is determining the amount of concrete needed for an airport runway.

Goal 1 FINDING THE VOLUME OF A PRISM

When you measure objects, you need to understand the difference between measures of length, area, and volume.

Measures of length	Measures of area	Measures of volume
Feet (ft)	Square feet $\left(\text{ft}^2\right)$	Cubic feet $\left(\text{ft}^3\right)$
Meters (m)	Square meters $\left(\text{m}^2\right)$	Cubic meters $\left(\text{m}^3\right)$

In Lab 9.5, you may have discovered this formula.

VOLUME OF A RECTANGULAR PRISM

The volume V of a rectangular prism is given by the product of its length ℓ, width w, and height h.

$$V = \ell \cdot w \cdot h$$

Example 1 **Finding the Volume of a Prism**

Find the volume of the videocassette box shown at the right.

Solution

To find the volume, multiply the three dimensions: length times width times height.

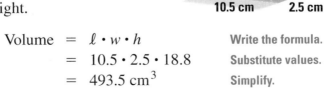

18.8 cm

10.5 cm   2.5 cm

$$
\begin{aligned}
\text{Volume} &= \ell \cdot w \cdot h & &\text{Write the formula.}\\
&= 10.5 \cdot 2.5 \cdot 18.8 & &\text{Substitute values.}\\
&= 493.5 \text{ cm}^3 & &\text{Simplify.}
\end{aligned}
$$

The volume of the videocassette box is 493.5 cm^3.

Example 2 Finding the Volume of a Runway

You are a civil engineer working for an airport.
You are replacing a section of an airport runway. The
runway is to be made of concrete. The section is $\frac{1}{2}$ mi
long, 24 ft wide, and 18 in. deep. How many cubic yards of concrete
do you need?

REAL LIFE
*Civil
Engineering*

18 in.

24 ft

$\frac{1}{2}$ mi

David P. Roberts is an
airport engineer and
architect who works for
Doohtol Infraotruoturo
Corporation. He is currently
redesigning the Hartsfield
Atlanta International
Airport.

Solution

First, rewrite each measure in the same units. Because concrete
is usually measured in cubic yards, rewrite each measure in yards.

$\frac{1}{2}$ mi = 880 yd   **Use 1760 yd = 1 mi to convert $\frac{1}{2}$ mi to 880 yd.**

24 ft = 8 yd   **Use 3 ft = 1 yd to convert 24 ft to 8 yd.**

18 in. = $\frac{1}{2}$ yd   **Use 36 in. = 1 yd to convert 18 in. to $\frac{1}{2}$ yd.**

Second, multiply the length times width times height (or depth)
to find the volume.

$$\text{Volume} = \ell \cdot w \cdot h$$
$$= 880 \cdot 8 \cdot \frac{1}{2}$$
$$= 3520 \text{ yd}^3$$

You will need about 3520 yd^3 of concrete for the runway.

The largest planes need runways that are 13,000 ft long. How many
cubic yards of concrete would be needed to pave such a runway?

ONGOING ASSESSMENT

Talk About It
· · · · · · · · · · · · · · · · ·

Suppose the runway is
$\frac{3}{4}$ mi long.

1. How many cubic yards
   of concrete do you
   need?

2. Discuss at least two
   ways to answer the
   question above.

GUIDED PRACTICE

In Exercises 1–3, match the description with the measurement.

A. 565 ft

B. 105,625 ft^2

C. 2000 ft^3

1. Area of a baseball diamond

2. Volume of a swimming pool

3. Length of a city block

4. Sketch a rectangular prism that is 4 m by 6 m by 10 m. Find the surface area and volume of the prism.

5. **ALGEBRA** The length of the side of a cube is x inches. Write an expression in terms of x that you can use to find the volume of the cube.

PRACTICE AND PROBLEM SOLVING

In Exercises 6–8, find the volume of the object.

6.

0.8 m

0.4 m

1.2 m

7.

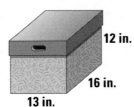

12 in.

16 in.

13 in.

8.

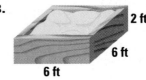

2 ft

6 ft

6 ft

9. **ICEBREAKERS** An icebreaker is a ship designed to travel through ice-covered waters and break up ice that can be as much as 8 ft thick. The ice on a section of river is $\frac{1}{2}$ mi wide, 3 mi long, and 8 ft thick. What is the volume of the ice?

In Exercises 10–12, find the dimension labeled x.

10. Volume = 390 in.^{3}

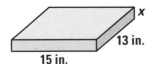

x

13 in.

15 in.

11. Volume = 1562.5 m^3

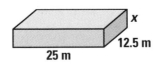

x

12.5 m

25 m

12. Volume = 1000 mm^3

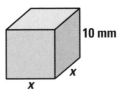

10 mm

x

x

13. Find the volume of each prism. What do you observe?

a.

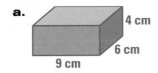

4 cm

6 cm

9 cm

b.

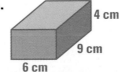

4 cm

9 cm

6 cm

c.

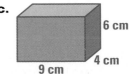

6 cm

4 cm

9 cm

In Exercises 14 and 15, sketch each rectangular prism. Then find the volume of the prism.

14. 4 yd by 8 yd by 12 yd   **15.** 2.44 m by 3.58 m by 7.04 m

16. POPCORN The largest box of popcorn in the United States measured 40 ft long, 28 ft wide, and 6.67 ft high. It was filled with popcorn at Pittsville Elementary School in Wisconsin. What was the volume of the popcorn box?

17. PHYSICAL SCIENCE Two triangular prisms make up the rectangular prism below. Find the volume of one of the triangular prisms.

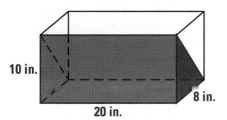

10 in.

8 in.

20 in.

STANDARDIZED TEST PRACTICE

18. Which of the following is the same as 1 ft^3?

  (A) 12 in.^3 **(B)** 144 in.^3 **(C)** 1728 in.^3 **(D)** 1 m^3

19. Which could *not* be the dimensions of a rectangular prism that has a volume of 2520 cm^3?

  (A) 6 cm by 20 cm by 21 cm   **(B)** 7 cm by 15 cm by 27 cm

  (C) 8 cm by 9 cm by 35 cm   **(D)** 10 cm by 14 cm by 18 cm

EXPLORATION AND EXTENSION

PORTFOLIO

20. BUILDING YOUR PROJECT Build a model sandbox for your playground. The dimensions for the model sandbox are 5 in. by 5 in. by 1 in. Find the volume of both the model and the actual sandbox. The scale is 1 in. : 1 ft. What would the dimensions of the real sandbox be? How much sand could it hold?

9.6

Volume of a Cylinder

What you should learn:

Goal 1 How to find the volume of a cylinder

Goal 2 How to use the volume of a cylinder to solve real-life problems

Why you should learn it:

Knowing how to find the volume of a cylinder can help you solve real-life problems. An example is finding how long it takes to fill a swimming pool.

Goal 1 FINDING THE VOLUME OF A CYLINDER

In Lesson 9.5, you learned that the volume of a rectangular prism can be found by multiplying the length times the width times the height. This product also equals the area of the base ($\ell \cdot w$) times the height. This way of thinking of the formula gives you a way to find the volume of a cylinder.

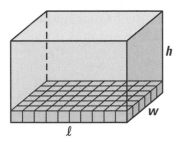

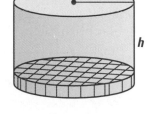

Area of base $= \ell \cdot w$ Area of base $= \pi r^2$

The area of the base equals the number of unit cubes that cover the base in 1 layer. The height tells how many layers there are. Since the base of a cylinder is a circle, the area of the base equals πr^2.

VOLUME OF A CYLINDER

To find the volume V of a cylinder, multiply the area of the base times the height h.

$$V = \pi r^2 \cdot h$$

Example 1 Finding the Volume of a Mug

The mug shown at the right has a radius of 4 cm and a height of 10 cm. Find the volume of the mug letting π equal about 3.14.

4 cm

10 cm

Solution

Volume = (Area of Base) • (Height)

$= \pi r^2 \cdot h$ Write the formula.

$\approx 3.14 \cdot 4^2 \cdot 10$ Substitute values.

$\approx 502.4 \text{ cm}^3$ Simplify.

The volume of the mug is about 502 cm^3.

Volume is commonly measured in two different ways: cubic units, such as cubic feet (ft^3) or cubic meters (m^3), and units of liquid volume, such as gallons (gal) or liters (L). A gallon is the amount of liquid that will fill a container that is 231 in.^{3} or 3785.41 cm^3. By definition, 1 mL (one milliliter) equals 1 cm^3.

Example 2 **Finding the Volume of a Pool**

You are filling a circular swimming pool with water. The water comes out of the hose at a rate of 10 gal/min. How long will it take to fill the pool? *Hint:* One cubic foot is equal to 7.48 gal.

REAL LIFE
Swimming Pools

10 ft

5 ft

Solution

Begin by finding the volume of the pool.

$$\text{Volume} = \pi r^2 \cdot h \qquad \text{Write the formula.}$$
$$\approx 3.14 \cdot 10^2 \cdot 5 \qquad \text{Substitute values.}$$
$$= 1570 \text{ ft}^3 \qquad \text{Simplify.}$$

Because 1 ft^3 is equal to 7.48 gal, the pool must contain

$$1570 \text{ ft}^3 \times \frac{7.48 \text{ gal}}{1 \text{ ft}^3} \approx 11{,}744 \text{ gal.}$$

At the rate of 10 gal/min, it would take about 1174 min, or 19.6 h, to fill the pool.

$$11{,}744 \text{ gal} \times \frac{1 \text{ min}}{10 \text{ gal}} = 1174.4 \text{ min}$$

How long would it take to fill the same size pool if water came out of the hose at a rate of 12 gal per minute?

ONGOING ASSESSMENT

Talk About It
....

Without calculating the volumes, discuss which cylinder has the greater volume. Check your result by calculating the volume of each.

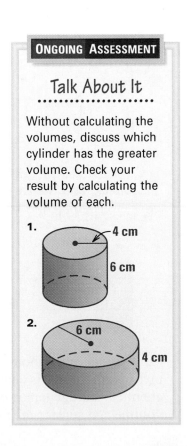

1.
4 cm
6 cm

2.
6 cm
4 cm

9.6 Exercises

Extra Practice, page 641

GUIDED PRACTICE

1. Which measures the volume of a can of orange juice? Explain.

   A. Pour the juice into cup measures.

   B. Peel the label off the can and find the area of the label.

2. **GROUP ACTIVITY** Roll two $8\frac{1}{2}$ in.-by-11 in. sheets of paper into open cylinders: one with an $8\frac{1}{2}$ in. height and the other with an 11 in. height. Discuss which you think has the greater volume. Then find the volumes.

In Exercises 3–5, use the cylinder at the right.

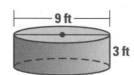

3. What is the radius of the base?

4. What is the area of the base?

5. What is the volume of the cylinder?

PRACTICE AND PROBLEM SOLVING

In Exercises 6–8, find the volume of the cylinder.

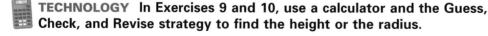

6.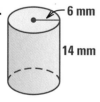

7.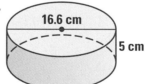

8.

 TECHNOLOGY In Exercises 9 and 10, use a calculator and the Guess, Check, and Revise strategy to find the height or the radius.

9. $V = 42.39 \text{ m}^3$

10. $V = 1017.36 \text{ m}^3$

(To find out more about the volume of cylinders, see the interactive investigation for this chapter. In the interactive investigation you will design chemical storage tanks. As part of the investigation, you will calculate the volume and surface area of cylinders and prisms.)

Tech Link

Investigation 9, Interactive Real-Life Investigations

11. **PAINTING** You are painting walls in an office building. They are 12 ft by 18 ft and the coat of paint is 0.001 in. thick. You have a cylindrical container of paint that is 8.1 in. high and has a 3.3 in. radius. How many walls can you paint?

12. **THINKING SKILLS** Find the dimensions of two cylinders so that one has the greater volume and the other has the greater surface area.

13. **LOOKING FOR A PATTERN** A cylinder has a height of 1 unit and a radius of 1 unit. What happens to its volume when the radius is doubled? Tripled? Quadrupled? Describe the pattern of the volumes.

14. **PROBLEM SOLVING** A 6 ft tall section of a northern red oak tree trunk has the cross section shown at the right. Find the volume of the bark. Explain how you solved the problem.

15. **PENCILS** You want to manufacture wooden pencils having a length of 18 cm (not including eraser) and a diameter of 0.75 cm.

    a. How much wood is needed to make one pencil?

    b. How many pencils can you make from the section of tree discussed in Exercise 14? (Assume all the wood is used and there is no waste except for the bark.)

Real Life...
Real People

Blackfeet Writing Instruments is a company that is owned and staffed by Native Americans in Montana. All their pencils have lead-free lacquer.

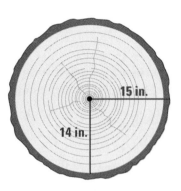

15 in.

14 in.

STANDARDIZED TEST PRACTICE

The cylinder below has a volume of 2009.6 cm^3.

16. What is the height?

    (A) 6 cm   (B) 8 cm

    (C) 10 cm   (D) 12 cm

17. What is the area of the base?

    (A) 25.12 cm^2 (B) 50.24 cm^2 (C) 100.48 cm^2 (D) 200.96 cm^2

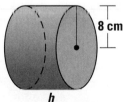

8 cm

h

18. You are pouring water from a cylindrical can that is 7 cm in diameter and 10 cm high into a pan that is 20 cm in diameter and 14 cm deep. How many full cans can you pour into the pan?

    (A) 4   (B) 7   (C) 8   (D) 11

19. BUILDING YOUR PROJECT Build a model swing set for your playground. Two posts will support the swings. The diameter of the model posts is $\frac{1}{2}$ in. They are to be 5 in. high. The model swings will hang from a bar 6 in. long and $\frac{1}{3}$ in. in diameter. Find the total volume of the model posts. How much concrete would you need to build the two actual support posts? The scale is 1 in. : 1 ft.

SPIRAL REVIEW

In Exercises 1–4, evaluate the expression. (2.2)

1. 2^5 **2.** $2 \cdot 5^2$ **3.** 4 cubed   **4.** 3 to the 4th power

In Exercises 5–12, add or subtract the integers. (4.4, 4.5)

5. $-3 + 8$ **6.** $4 + (-2)$ **7.** $7 - (-12)$ **8.** $-5 + (-7)$

9. $-16 - 13$ **10.** $-2 + (-11)$ **11.** $8 - (-8)$ **12.** $9 + (-5)$

In Exercises 13–16, solve the proportion. (6.3)

13. $\frac{4}{9} = \frac{m}{27}$ **14.** $\frac{t}{3} = \frac{22}{33}$ **15.** $\frac{2}{s} = \frac{12}{42}$ **16.** $\frac{15}{25} = \frac{k}{5}$

In Exercises 17–18, decide whether the statement is true or false. (6.6)

17. All triangles are similar.   **18.** All squares are similar.

19. SAVINGS You deposit $250 into a savings account. The annual interest rate is 5.5%. Find the simple interest you will earn in 3 months. (7.6)

In Exercises 20–22, find the area of the shaded region. Round to the nearest hundredth. (8.6)

20.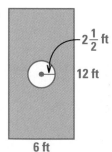

21.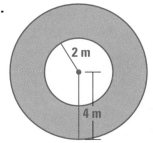

22.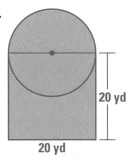

SNOW SCULPTURES

READ About It

What's a cross between an art competition and a sports competition? It's a snow sculpture contest. In Breckenridge, Colorado, each team has 4 days to shape a block of packed snow that is 10 ft by 10 ft by 12 ft. One winning entry was a hollow cube with 68 in. long sides and 10 in. wide bars. The cube's base is 10 ft by 10 ft by 3 ft.

The size of the blocks of packed snow varies between competitions. In Rockford, Illinois, the size of the block depends on the team division. State teams use blocks that are 6 ft by 6 ft by 10 ft. International teams get 12 ton cubes with 10 ft sides. High school teams work with blocks that are 4 ft by 4 ft by 6 ft. The snow used for the Rockford competition comes from airport runways.

WRITE About It

1. The snow for the Rockford, Illinois contest is molded into different-size wooden forms. Find the surface area of the wooden forms used for each of the three divisions.

2. How much does 1 ft^3 of snow weigh? How much does 1 in.^{3} of snow weigh? (*Hint:* A ton is equal to 2000 lb.) How are the two weights related?

3. Use the answer from Question 2 to find the weight of one block of snow used in the Colorado competition.

4. Estimate the dimensions of the hollow cube shown on this page. Show the dimensions on a diagram.

5. How many cubic inches of snow did the team remove to make the hollow cube? If you used the snow that was removed to make a solid cube, how long would each side of the cube be?

Investigating Similar Prisms

Part A COMPARING SIMILAR PRISMS

Materials Needed
- graph paper
- pencils or pens
- 24 cubes

1. The two prisms below are similar. Build each prism and record its length, width, height, surface area, and volume in a table. Then find the ratios of the measures of the smaller prism to the measures of the larger prism.

A   B

	Length	Width	Height	Surface Area	Volume
Prism A	?	?	?	?	?
Prism B	?	?	?	?	?
Ratios	$\dfrac{\text{Length A}}{\text{Length B}}$	$\dfrac{\text{Width A}}{\text{Width B}}$	$\dfrac{\text{Height A}}{\text{Height B}}$	$\dfrac{\text{Surface area A}}{\text{Surface area B}}$	$\dfrac{\text{Volume A}}{\text{Volume B}}$

2. The two prisms below are similar. Record each prism's length, width, height, surface area, and volume in a table. Then find the ratios of the measures of the smaller prism to the measures of the larger prism.

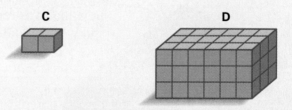

C   D

	Length	Width	Height	Surface Area	Volume
Prism C	?	?	?	?	?
Prism D	?	?	?	?	?
Ratios	$\dfrac{\text{Length C}}{\text{Length D}}$	$\dfrac{\text{Width C}}{\text{Width D}}$	$\dfrac{\text{Height C}}{\text{Height D}}$	$\dfrac{\text{Surface area C}}{\text{Surface area D}}$	$\dfrac{\text{Volume C}}{\text{Volume D}}$

3. The two prisms below are similar. Record each prism's length, width, height, surface area, and volume. Compare the ratios of the measures of the smaller prism to those of the larger prism.

E

F

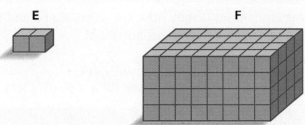

	Length	Width	Height	Surface Area	Volume
Prism E	?	?	?	?	?
Prism F	?	?	?	?	?
Ratios	$\dfrac{\text{Length E}}{\text{Length F}}$	$\dfrac{\text{Width E}}{\text{Width F}}$	$\dfrac{\text{Height E}}{\text{Height F}}$	$\dfrac{\text{Surface area E}}{\text{Surface area F}}$	$\dfrac{\text{Volume E}}{\text{Volume F}}$

4. From the examples in Exercises 1, 2, and 3, what can you say about the ratios of corresponding dimensions (lengths, widths, and heights) of similar prisms?

5. Prism G has a width of 3 in., a surface area of 22 in.^{2}, and a volume of 6 in.^{3}. Prism H is similar to Prism G and has a width of 6 inches. What is the surface area and the volume of Prism H? Explain your reasoning.

NOW TRY THESE

6. Sketch the following prisms. Which pairs of prisms are similar? Explain your reasoning.

a. 2-by-3-by-5 prism and 4-by-5-by-7 prism

b. 2-by-3-by-5 prism and 4-by-6-by-10 prism

c. 2-by-3-by-5 prism and 6-by-9-by-15 prism

d. 2-by-3-by-5 prism and 6-by-7-by-9 prism

7. Describe the ratios of lengths, widths, heights, surface areas, and volumes of similar prisms.

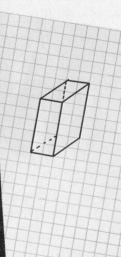

9.7

Similar Prisms

What you should learn:

Goal 1 How to identify similar prisms

Goal 2 How to describe a prism that is similar to a given prism

Why you should learn it:

Knowing how to identify similar prisms can help you build proportional models. An example is building a scale model of a box car.

Goal 1 IDENTIFYING SIMILAR PRISMS

Two prisms are similar if they have the same shape and their corresponding dimensions are proportional.

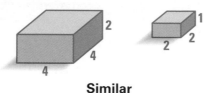

Similar

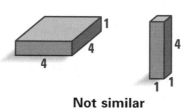

Not similar

Example 1 Identifying Similar Prisms

Show that the two rectangular prisms are similar.

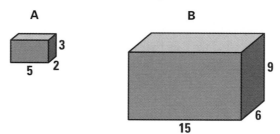

Solution

To show that the prisms are similar, find the ratios of their lengths, widths, and heights.

$$\frac{\text{Length of prism A}}{\text{Length of prism B}} = \frac{5}{15} = \frac{1}{3} \qquad \textbf{Find the ratio of lengths.}$$

$$\frac{\text{Width of prism A}}{\text{Width of prism B}} = \frac{2}{6} = \frac{1}{3} \qquad \textbf{Find the ratio of widths.}$$

$$\frac{\text{Height of prism A}}{\text{Height of prism B}} = \frac{3}{9} = \frac{1}{3} \qquad \textbf{Find the ratio of heights.}$$

Because all three ratios are equal, the corresponding dimensions of the prisms are proportional. The prisms also have the same shape. Thus, the prisms are similar.

Example 2 Describing Similar Prisms

REAL LIFE
Model Trains

You are building a scale model of the box car below. You decide to use a scale of 1 ft : 48 ft. If the length of the model is 1 ft, what will the width and height be?

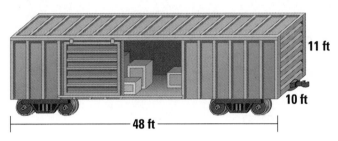

11 ft

10 ft

48 ft

Solution

Let w and h represent the width and height of your scale model.

$$\frac{\text{Length of model}}{\text{Length of box car}} = \frac{\text{Width of model}}{\text{Width of box car}}$$

$\dfrac{1}{48} = \dfrac{w}{10}$ **Substitute known dimensions.**

$10 = 48w$ **Cross multiply.**

$\dfrac{10}{48} = \dfrac{\cancel{48}w}{\cancel{48}}$ **Divide each side by 48.**

$\dfrac{5}{24} = w$ **Simplify.**

The scale model will have a width of $\dfrac{5}{24}$ foot, or $2\dfrac{1}{2}$ inches.

$$\frac{\text{Length of model}}{\text{Length of box car}} = \frac{\text{Height of model}}{\text{Height of box car}}$$

$\dfrac{1}{48} = \dfrac{h}{11}$ **Substitute known dimensions.**

$11 = 48h$ **Cross multiply.**

$\dfrac{11}{48} = \dfrac{\cancel{48}h}{\cancel{48}}$ **Divide each side by 48.**

$\dfrac{11}{48} = h$ **Simplify.**

The scale model will have a height of $\dfrac{11}{48}$ feet, or $2\dfrac{3}{4}$ inches.

ONGOING ASSESSMENT

Write About It

The scale model in Example 2 is $\dfrac{1}{48}$ the actual size of the box car. For model railroads, this is called an *O scale*. A *G scale* is $\dfrac{2}{45}$ the actual size.

1. Find the length, width, and height of a G scale model of the box car.

GUIDED PRACTICE

In Exercises 1–3, match similar prisms.

A.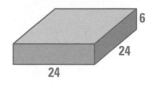
6
24
24

B.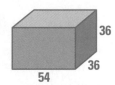
36
36
54

C.
16
16
16

1.
5
5
5

2.
8
8 2

3.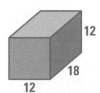
12
18
12

4. **THINKING SKILLS** Is it true that any two cubes are similar? Explain.

5. **WRITING** Explain why the two prisms at the right are *not* similar.

6. Sketch a prism that is 1 unit by 2 units by 3 units. Then sketch three similar prisms and label the dimensions.

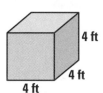
4 ft
4 ft
4 ft

6 in.
15 in.
15 in.

PRACTICE AND PROBLEM SOLVING

In Exercises 7–10, decide whether the two prisms are similar.

7.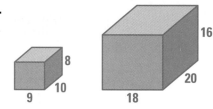
16
8
20
9 10
18

8.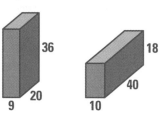
36
18
9 20
10 40

9.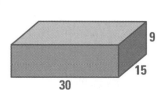
9
15
30

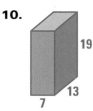
20
10 6

10.
19
10.5
7 13
28.5 19.5

11. Find the surface areas of the two prisms in Exercise 7. Is the following statement true or false? *When you double each dimension of a prism, you double the surface area of the prism.* Explain.

In Exercises 12 and 13, the two rectangular prisms are similar. Find the missing dimensions.

12. Prism A: Length $= 100$ ft   Width $= $ **?**   Height $= 37\frac{1}{2}$ ft

       Prism B: Length $= 48$ in.   Width $= 30$ in.   Height $= $ **?**

13. Prism A: Length $= 18$ cm   Width $= 75$ cm   Height $= $ **?**

       Prism B: Length $= 12$ m   Width $= $ **?**   Height $= 30$ m

In Exercises 14 and 15, the prisms are similar. Find x and y.

14.

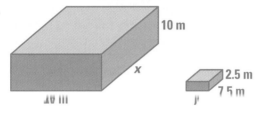

10 m x 10 m

2.5 m   7.5 m

15.

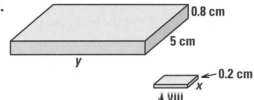

0.8 cm   5 cm y

0.2 cm x

16. CLOSETS A closet is 5 ft by 3 ft by 8 ft. Which of the following dimensions will double the closet space? Explain.

   a. 10 ft by 3 ft by 8 ft   **b.** 10 ft by 6 ft by 16 ft

   c. 5 ft by 6 ft by 8 ft   **d.** 5 ft by 3 ft by 16 ft

STANDARDIZED TEST PRACTICE

17. The dimensions of several rectangular prisms are given below. Which prism is *not* similar to the one shown at the right?

   (A) 6 in. by 9 in. by 12 in.   **(B)** 4 mm by 6 mm by 8 mm

   (C) 24 ft by 36 ft by 48 ft   **(D)** 18 cm by 21 cm by 32 cm

18. A shed is 12 ft wide, 15 ft long, and 10 ft high. A scale model of the shed is 6 in. wide and 7.5 in. long. How high is the model?

   (A) 4 in.   **(B)** 5 in.   **(C)** 6 in.   **(D)** 7 in.

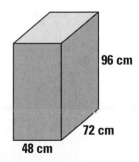

96 cm

72 cm

48 cm

EXPLORATION AND EXTENSION

19. COMMUNICATING ABOUT MATHEMATICS Using a variety of hand tools, artists can transform blocks of ice into glittering works of art.

Design your own ice sculpture. Draw a scale model of your design and label the dimensions.

WHAT *did you learn?* **WHY** *did you learn it?*

Skills

9.1	Identify polyhedrons and their parts.	Describe the shapes of skyscrapers.
9.2	Find the surface area of a prism.	Decide how much paint is needed for a set of blocks.
9.3	Find the surface area of a cylinder.	Compare the surface areas of paint cans.
9.4	Draw a top, front, and side view of a solid.	Draw a metal part from three different views.
9.5	Find the volume of a prism.	Determine the amount of concrete needed for a runway.
9.6	Find the volume of a cylinder.	Find how long it takes to fill a swimming pool.
9.7	Identify similar prisms.	Design a scale model.

Strategies

9.1–9.7	Use problem solving strategies.	Solve a wide variety of real-life problems.

Using Data

9.1–9.7	Use tables.	Organize data and solve problems.

HOW *does it fit into the bigger picture of mathematics?*

In this chapter, you studied the surface area and volume of prisms and cylinders.

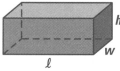

$$V = \ell \cdot w \cdot h$$

$$V = \pi r^2 \cdot h$$

If you know the formulas for the area of a triangle, a rectangle, and a circle, then you can find the surface area and volume of a prism and of a cylinder by remembering the following:

1. The surface area of a solid is the sum of the areas of its faces and lateral surfaces.
2. The area of the lateral surface of a cylinder is the product of its circumference and its height.
3. The volume of a prism or cylinder is the product of its height and the area of its base.

VOCABULARY

- polyhedron (p. 428)
- face (p. 429)
- edge (p. 429)
- vertex (p. 429)

- surface area of a polyhedron (p. 432)
- cylinder (p. 438)
- base (p. 438)

- lateral surface (p. 438)
- surface area of a cylinder (p. 438)

9.1 EXPLORING POLYHEDRONS

Example ▶ The rectangular prism at the right has 6 faces, so it is called a hexahedron. It has 12 edges and 8 vertices.

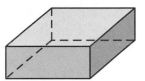

In Exercises 1–4, count the number of faces and name the polyhedron. Then find the number of edges and vertices.

1   **2.**   **3.**   **4.**

5. Sketch a rectangular prism and a triangular prism. Describe the differences between them.

9.2 SURFACE AREA OF A PRISM

Example ▶ To find the surface area of a prism, sum the areas of its faces.

Area of 2 triangular faces $= 2 \cdot \frac{1}{2} \cdot 6 \cdot 8 = 48 \text{ cm}^2$

Area of 8 cm-by-25 cm face $= 8 \cdot 25 = 200 \text{ cm}^2$

Area of 6 cm-by-25 cm face $= 6 \cdot 25 = 150 \text{ cm}^2$

Area of 10 cm-by-25 cm face $= 10 \cdot 25 = 250 \text{ cm}^2$

Surface area $= 48 + 200 + 150 + 250 = 648 \text{ cm}^2$

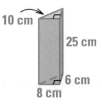

6. Sketch a rectangular prism that is 7 ft long, 3 ft wide, and 12 ft high. Find the surface area of the prism.

7. **ANT FARM** You are building an ant farm with 2 pieces of glass. Each piece of glass has the dimensions shown at the right. How many in.^{2} of glass do you need?

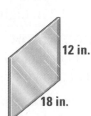

8. **STAGE SET** You are painting 3 rectangular panels for a stage set. Each panel is 10 ft by 6 ft by 1 in. Find the surface area for the 3 panels.

9.3 SURFACE AREA OF A CYLINDER

The surface area of a cylinder is the sum of the lateral surface area and the surface areas of its 2 bases.

Example Find the surface area of the cylinder.

$$\text{Surface area} = 2\pi rh + 2\pi r^2$$
$$\approx 2(3.14)(2)(5) + 2(3.14)(2^2)$$
$$\approx 87.9 \text{ cm}^2$$

2 cm

5 cm

9. A cylinder has a height of 9 cm and a radius of 3 cm. Find its surface area.

10. Find the surface area of a dart board that has a radius of 7 in. and is $\frac{3}{4}$ in. thick.

9.4 SPATIAL VISUALIZATION

Example Shown below are three views of the solid object at the left.

Top

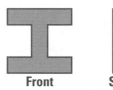

Front   Side

11. You are shown 3 views of a stack of cubes. How many cubes are in the stack?

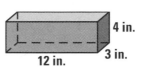

Top   Front   Side

9.5 VOLUME OF A PRISM

To find the volume of a rectangular prism, multiply the length by the width by the height.

Example Find the volume of the prism.

4 in.

12 in.   3 in.

$$\text{Volume} = \ell \cdot w \cdot h$$
$$= 12 \cdot 3 \cdot 4$$
$$= 144 \text{ in.}^3$$

12. Sketch the rectangular prism that is 15 m long, 12 m wide, and 2 m high. Then find its volume.

13. ROAD CONSTRUCTION The road base is a 2 ft thick layer of concrete. Find the volume of the base of a section of road that is 5 mi long.

14. Find the volume of asphalt needed to pave a road section that is 5 mi long.

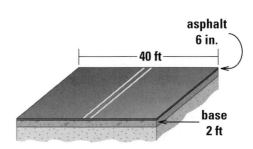

asphalt
6 in.

40 ft

base
2 ft

9.6 VOLUME OF A CYLINDER

To find the volume of a cylinder, multiply the area of the base times the height.

Example Find the volume of the cylinder at the right.

$$V = \pi r^2 \cdot h$$
$$\approx 3.14 \cdot 2.5^2 \cdot 6$$
$$\approx 117.75 \text{ m}^3$$

2.5 m
6 m

15. Sketch the cylinder that has a radius of 17 yd and is 5.8 yd high. Then find its volume.

16. JUICE CONTAINERS Which can would hold the most juice?

a.
$2\frac{11}{16}$ in.
$4\frac{13}{16}$ in.

b.
3 in.
$4\frac{7}{16}$ in.

9.7 SIMILAR PRISMS

Example To decide whether the two prisms are similar, compare the ratios of their lengths, widths, and heights to see if they are the same.

$$\frac{\text{Length of prism A}}{\text{Length of prism B}} = \frac{20}{24} = \frac{5}{6}$$

$$\frac{\text{Width of prism A}}{\text{Width of prism B}} = \frac{15}{18} = \frac{5}{6}$$

$$\frac{\text{Height of prism A}}{\text{Height of prism B}} = \frac{5}{6}$$

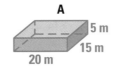

A
5 m
15 m
20 m

B
6 m
18 m
24 m

Because their corresponding dimensions have the same proportions, the prisms are similar.

17. Find *x* and *y* for the similar prisms shown at the right.

18. NESTING BOXES You are designing a set of 4 nesting boxes that are similar prisms. The smallest box is a 1 in. cube. Give the dimensions of the other 3 boxes.

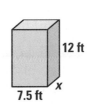

8 ft
12 ft
y   3.3 ft
7.5 ft   x

In Exercises 19 and 20, decide whether the two solids are similar.

19.

A
2
4   2

B
3
6   3

20.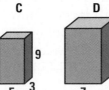

C
9
5   3

D
11
7   5

In Questions 1–3, sketch an example of the solid.

1. Prism   **2.** Pyramid   **3.** Cylinder

In Questions 4–7, find the surface area and volume of the figure.

4.
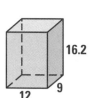
9 cm
2.5 cm
6.7 cm

5.
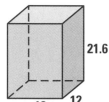
14 ft
11 ft
5 ft

6. ⊢ 21 in. ⊣
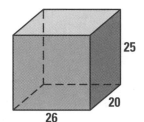
18 in.

7.
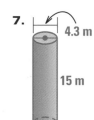
4.3 m
15 m

In Questions 8 and 9, decide whether the two prisms are similar. Explain your reasoning.

8.
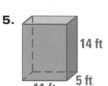
16.2
12
9
21.6
16
12

9.

10
11
8
25
20
26

CANNING In Questions 10 and 11, use the two peach cans below. The cost of Can A is $1.29 and the cost of Can B is $1.25.

10. Which can is the better buy? Explain your reasoning.

11. Find the area of each label. What is this area called?

1.3 in.
Peaches
3.5 in.
A
1.7 in.
Peaches
2.5 in.
B

12. ENGINEERING You have to design a container to hold an egg so it can be dropped from the top of a building without breaking.

You fill a cylindrical container with a sponge-like material that has a radius of 12 centimeters and a height of 20 centimeters. Find the volume of the sponge-like material.

13. FISH TANK You buy a fish tank that has a length of 18 inches, a width of 12.5 inches, and a height of 15 inches. How much glass was used to make the bottom and sides of the fish tank? How much water can the tank hold? (*Hint:* A gallon will fill 231 cubic inches.)

1. What is the name of the polyhedron?

   (A) Tetrahedron

   (B) Pentahedron

   (C) Hexahedron

   (D) Octahedron

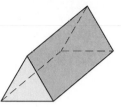

2. Which statement about the polyhedron above is *false*?

   (A) It has 5 faces.

   (B) It has 6 vertices.

   (C) It is a pyramid.

   (D) It has 9 edges.

3. Which size paper can be used to wrap the gift without cutting the paper?

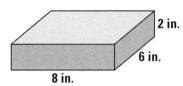

   (A) 16 in. by 20 in.

   (B) 8 in. by 19 in.

   (C) 10 in. by 15 in.

   (D) 6 in. by 30 in.

In Questions 4 and 5, you are designing an oatmeal container that has a radius of 5 cm and a height of 20 cm.

4. How much packaging is needed?

   (A) 785 cm   (B) 1570 cm^3

   (C) 785 cm^2 (D) 690.8 cm^2

5. How much can the container hold?

   (A) 628 cm^3 (B) 785 cm^2

   (C) 628 cm^2 (D) 1570 cm^3

6. Which solid best represents the different views?

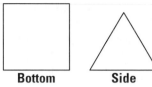

Bottom   Side   Top

   (A) Cylinder   (B) Pyramid

   (C) Prism   (D) Polyhedron

7. Which statement about the two containers is *false*?

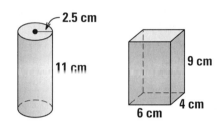

   (A) The surface area of the prism is greater than that of the cylinder.

   (B) The volume of the cylinder is greater than that of the prism.

   (C) The two containers hold about the same amount.

   (D) The prism uses more packaging than the cylinder.

8. The prisms are similar. What is the measure of the side labeled *x*?

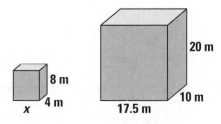

   (A) 2.3 m   (B) 7 m

   (C) 11.5 m   (D) 10 m

In Exercises 1–4, write the percent as a decimal and as a fraction in simplest form. (7.1)

1. 35%   **2.** 2.84%   **3.** 0.4%   **4.** 250%

In Exercises 5–8, write the fraction or decimal as a percent. (7.1)

5. $\frac{1}{4}$ **6.** 0.08   **7.** $\frac{5}{8}$ **8.** 0.725

LUNCH SURVEY In Exercises 9–12, use the results of a survey of 150 students. The students were asked to name their favorite school lunch. Thirty-three of the students named cheeseburgers, 42% named pizza, and 28% named submarine sandwiches. **(7.2, 7.4, 7.5)**

9. How many students liked pizza best?

10. What percent answered "cheeseburgers"?

11. What percent of students had other favorites?

12. Draw a circle graph of the data.

In Exercises 13 and 14, you are borrowing an amount P. Find the interest you will pay and the amount you must pay back. (7.6)

13. $P = \$350, r = 21\%, t = 18$ months   **14.** $P = \$1200, r = 7.5\%, t = 9$ months

In Exercises 15–18, you are having a yard sale. (7.2, 7.4, 7.7)

15. You charge 45% of the prices you originally paid. How much will you charge for a vase that cost you $15.00?

16. At noon you decide to cut the prices of all clothing in half. The price on clothing is now what percent of its original price?

17. Someone offers you $5.25 for a shirt. This is 15% of what you originally paid for it. What was the original price?

18. At the end of the day you take any reasonable offer on the yard sale items. You decide to take 95% off an electronics kit that cost $25.00. How much will you charge for it?

In Exercises 19–21, find the missing measure. (8.3, 8.6)

19. Circumference = ?   **20.** Area = ?   **21.** Circumference = 62.8 m

3 ft

5 cm

r

In Exercises 22–24, find the perimeter and area of the polygon. (8.4, 8.5)

22.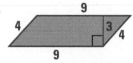

23.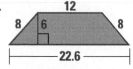

24.

In Exercises 25–27, find the missing side length. (8.8)

25.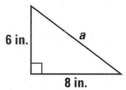

26.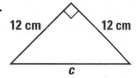

27.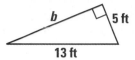

In Exercises 28–30, name the solid. Then find its surface area. (9.1–9.6)

28.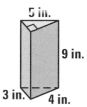

29.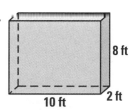

30.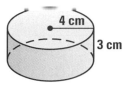

SILOS In Exercises 31 and 32, use the following information. Feed crops are stored in silos. A farmer is replacing a silo that has the shape of a rectangular prism with a silo that has the shape of a cylinder, as shown at the right. (9.2, 9.3, 9.5, 9.6)

31. Which silo holds more feed?

32. Which silo requires more material for its construction?

33. Using the results of Exercises 31 and 32, write a sentence about the advantages of using cylindrical silos.

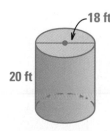

In Exercises 34 and 35, the prisms are similar. Find the values of a and b for each pair of prisms. (9.7)

34.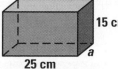

35.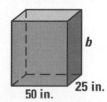

Algebra: Using Integers

TECHNOLOGY

Technology resources accompanying this chapter:
• Interactive Real-Life Investigations
• Middle School Tutorial Software

LAKE BAIKAL Located in Eastern Siberia, this lake contains 20% of the world's unfrozen fresh water. Its deepest point is 5715 ft below the surface and 4229 ft below sea level.

MAUNA KEA This Hawaiian mountain is the tallest on Earth. While its peak is only 13,796 ft above sea level, Mauna Kea rises 33,465 ft from its base on the ocean floor.

CHAPTER THEME
Earth Science

KAYANGEL ATOLL An atoll is a ring of coral that often is formed on the crater of a volcano that has sunk beneath the surface of the sea.

SURTSEY This volcano off the coast of Iceland began erupting at 426 ft below sea level in 1963. Its peak is now 567 ft above sea level.

REAL LIFE
Sea Level

Sea Level

The heights and depths of **geological formations** are measured in relation to sea level. Use the information on these two pages to answer the following questions.

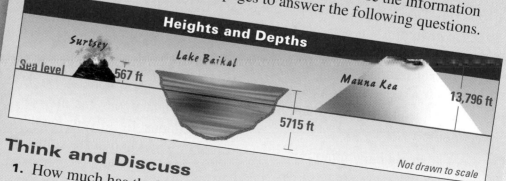

Heights and Depths

Surtsey

Sea level   567 ft

Lake Baikal

Mauna Kea

13,796 ft

5715 ft

Not drawn to scale

Think and Discuss

1. How much has the height of Surtsey increased?

2. How much above sea level is the surface of Lake Baikal? How do you know?

3. How far below sea level is the base of Mauna Kea? How did you get your answer?

PORTFOLIO

CHAPTER PROJECT

This volcano model erupted when baking soda, vinegar, and food coloring created a chemical reaction.

Researching Volcanoes

RHYOLITE *is a volcanic rock made up of fine crystals.*

PROJECT DESCRIPTION

Have you ever seen a volcano? Many people think of volcanic eruptions as explosions of hot lava. However, volcanoes can also erupt mud, rock, or gas. And not all eruptions are sudden and short-lived. Kilauea, a volcano in Hawaii, has been erupting almost continuously since 1983. Suppose you are studying volcanoes for a science project. Include information about the **TOPICS** listed on the next page.

GETTING STARTED

Talking It Over

- Discuss in your group what you know about volcanoes. What are some reasons people might study volcanoes? Make a list of things you would like to find out about volcanoes.

- Have you studied any famous eruptions? What are some of the dangers when a volcano erupts? What makes a volcano erupt? How do you think the intensity of a volcano is measured?

Planning Your Project

- **Materials Needed:** paper, pencils or pens, colored pencils or markers

- Fold several pieces of paper in half to make a booklet. Decorate your booklet with pictures of volcanoes. Go to your local library and find some volcano facts to include in your booklet. As you complete the **BUILDING YOUR PROJECT** exercises throughout the chapter, add the results to your booklet.

SNOWFLAKE OBSIDIAN
has a rougher surface than the glassy obsidian below .

Kilauea, Hawaii

Crater Lake, in Oregon, is a volcanic crater filled with water.

PUMICE *is a light, porous lava used in soaps, abrasive cleaners, and polishes.*

OBSIDIAN *is a shiny volcanic glass.*

BUILDING YOUR PROJECT

These are places throughout the chapter where you will work on your project.

TOPICS

10.1 Describe the changes in height of Mount St. Helens. *p. 483*

10.3 Investigate the length of time a volcano erupts. *p. 491*

10.4 Analyze the descent of a robot into a volcano. *p. 496*

10.5 Describe a geologist's study of a volcano's crater. *p. 503*

10.6 Find the average depth of magma reservoirs. *p. 508*

10.8 Compare the volumes of lava from different eruptions. *p. 519*

INTERNET

To find out about volcanoes, go to:
http://www.mlmath.com

LAB 10.1

COOPERATIVE LEARNING

Distances on a **Number Line**

Part A CHANGING TIME ZONES

Materials Needed
- pencils or pens
- paper

Earth is divided into 24 time zones. Each zone is labeled with the number of hours it differs from the time in Greenwich, England. For example, if it is 2:00 P.M. in Greenwich, then it is 5 hours earlier (-5), or 9:00 A.M. in Washington, D.C.

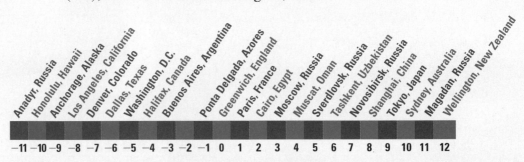

1. It is 2:00 P.M. in Greenwich, England. What time is it in each of the following cities?

   a. Honolulu, Hawaii   **b.** Buenos Aires, Argentina

   c. Ponta Delgada, Azores **d.** Muscat, Oman

   e. Tokyo, Japan   **f.** Sydney, Australia

2. Find the difference in times between the following cities.

   a. Dallas and Shanghai   **b.** Honolulu and Paris

   c. Los Angeles and Moscow **d.** Denver and Tokyo

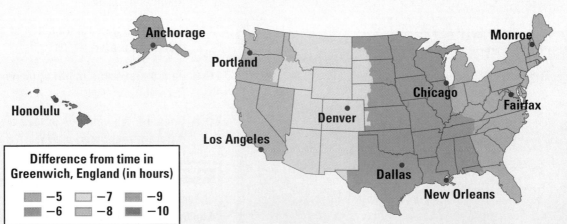

Difference from time in Greenwich, England (in hours)

-5	-7	-9
-6	-8	-10

Part B DISTANCES ON A NUMBER LINE

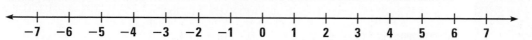

3. Use the number line to find the distance between the numbers. Descibe any patterns you see.

   a. −4 and 0   **b.** −6 and 0   **c.** 3 and 0   **d.** 5 and 0

   e. 0 and −3   **f.** 0 and 2   **g.** 0 and −5   **h.** 0 and 7

4. Explain how to find the distance between 0 and a negative number

   a. *using* a number line.   **b.** *without using* a number line.

5. Find the distance between the numbers.

   a. −4 and −1   **b.** −4 and 3

   c. −2 and −7   **d.** 3 and 5

   e. 4 and −4   **f.** 5 and   6

   g. 2 and 7   **h.** −7 and 7

NOW TRY THESE

6. You are in Paris, France. Name two cities listed on page 478 whose times differ from your time by four hours.

7. Find the difference in times between the cities.

   a. Paris and Sydney

   b. Dallas and Halifax

   c. Greenwich and Wellington

   d. Anchorage and Cairo

8. Draw a number line from −10 to 10. Which two numbers are

   a. 5 units from 0?   **b.** 3 units from 0?

   c. 2 units from 5?   **d.** 7 units from −1?

9. Explain how to find the distance between any two integers

   a. using a number line.

   b. without using a number line.

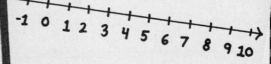

Absolute Value of a Number

What you should learn:

Goal 1 How to find the absolute value of a number

Goal 2 How to use absolute value to solve real-life problems

Why you should learn it:

Knowing how to find the absolute value of a number can help you solve real-life problems. An example is comparing the accuracy of retail clerks.

Goal 1 FINDING ABSOLUTE VALUE

Remember that opposites are numbers that are the same distance from 0 on a number line. For example, -3 and 3 are opposites. Zero is its own opposite.

LESSON INVESTIGATION

COOPERATIVE LEARNING

Investigating Absolute Value

GROUP ACTIVITY Draw a number line on patty paper or tracing paper. Label the integers from –5 to 5 on the line. Fold the number line in half with 0 at the center. Which pairs of numbers are the same distance from 0? How can you tell by looking at the folded patty paper?

The **absolute value** of a number is its distance from 0 on a number line. In the investigation above, you may have discovered that opposites have the same absolute value. The absolute value of zero is zero. An absolute value is written with two vertical rules, $|\ |$, called **absolute value signs**. For example, $|0| = 0$.

Example 1 **Finding Absolute Values**

Find the absolute value of each number.

a. -3 **b.** 5.5

Solution

You can use a number line to find the absolute value.

a. $|-3| = 3$ Absolute value of -3 is 3.

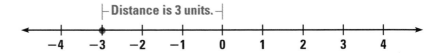

b. $|5.5| = 5.5$ Absolute value of 5.5 is 5.5.

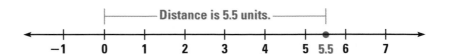

Example 2 Finding Absolute Values

REAL LIFE
Grocery Stores

Each checkout clerk at a grocery store must count the money in his or her register drawer at the end of the day. Which of the following clerks differed from the amount they were supposed to have by more than $5?

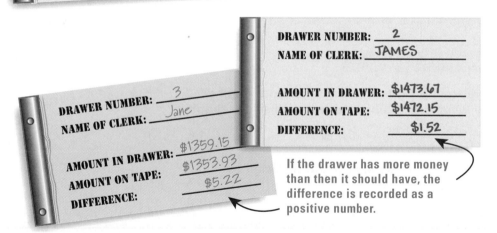

DRAWER NUMBER: ____1____
NAME OF CLERK: ___TOM___

AMOUNT IN DRAWER: $940.37
AMOUNT ON TAPE: $945.76
DIFFERENCE: −$5.39

If the drawer has less money than the register tape indicates, the difference is recorded as a negative number.

DRAWER NUMBER: ____2____
NAME OF CLERK: ___JAMES___

AMOUNT IN DRAWER: $1473.67
AMOUNT ON TAPE: $1472.15
DIFFERENCE: $1.52

DRAWER NUMBER: ____3____
NAME OF CLERK: ___Jane___

AMOUNT IN DRAWER: $1359.15
AMOUNT ON TAPE: $1353.93
DIFFERENCE: $5.22

If the drawer has more money than then it should have, the difference is recorded as a positive number.

Solution

You can find which clerk differed by more than $5 by considering the absolute value of the difference.

a. $|-5.39| = 5.39$

b. $|1.52| = 1.52$

c. $|5.22| = 5.22$

Because 5.39 > 5 and 5.22 > 5, Tom and Jane differed by more than $5.00. James differed by less than $5.00 since 1.52 < 5.

ONGOING ASSESSMENT

Write About It

Decide whether the statement is *true* or *false*. Explain your reasoning.

1. The absolute value of any number is positive.

2. Opposite numbers have the same absolute value.

3. Zero is the only number that is its own absolute value.

GUIDED PRACTICE

In Exercises 1–3, use the number line below.

```
        A       B   C           D       E       F       G
  <-----+--+--+--+--+--+--+--+--+--+--+--+--+--+--+--+--+---->
       -9  -8  -7  -6  -5  -4  -3  -2  -1   0   1   2   3   4   5
```

1. Which labeled point is the same distance from 0 as −4?

2. Which labeled point has an absolute value of 6?

3. Name two labeled points that have the same absolute value.

In Exercises 4–7, use the number line above to decide whether the statement is *true* or *false*. If it is *false*, explain why.

4. The absolute value of point *C* is −5.

5. The opposite of point *E* is 0.

6. Point *G* has a greater value than point *A*.

7. Point *G* has a greater absolute value than point *A*.

PRACTICE AND PROBLEM SOLVING

In Exercises 8–11, graph the absolute value of the integer on a number line. Then write the absolute value expression which describes the graph.

8. 3   9. −2   10. 0   11. −15

In Exercises 12–15, write the absolute value expression modeled by the number line.

12.
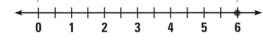

13.
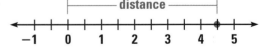

14.
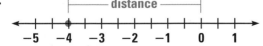

15.
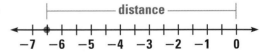

In Exercises 16–24, find the absolute value.

16. $|5|$ 17. $|-6|$ 18. $|-8|$

19. $|0|$ 20. $|-22.6|$ 21. $|-2.7|$

22. $|3.7|$ 23. $|-0.25|$ 24. $|-7.3|$

25. **PALINDROMES** Draw a number line from −5 to 5. Then use the clues to locate letters on the number line. When you are finished, you will have a *palindrome*, a word spelled the same forward and backward.

- Label as "A" all numbers whose absolute value is 1.

- Label as "D" all numbers that are their own opposites.

- Label as "R" all numbers that are 2 units from the origin.

In Exercises 26–31, complete the statement using >, <, or = .

26. 4 ? $|-4|$

27. -7 ? $|-7|$

28. $|-1|$? -2

29. $|-5|$? $|5|$

30. $|-12|$? 0

31. $|-3|$? $|-6|$

PERSONAL FINANCE In Exercises 32–35, use the circle graph showing your budget for expenses every week. Decide how much under or over budget you were for each expense.

Weekly Budget

Movies $7

Clothes $15

Food $8

32. You spent $12.95 on clothes.

33. You spent $8.25 on movies.

34. You spent $9.75 on food.

35. For which expense were you farthest off from your budget?

STANDARDIZED TEST PRACTICE

36. Which number has an absolute value less than $|-3|$?

   (A) -7 (B) -5 (C) 2 (D) 6

37. What is always true about the absolute value of a number?

   (A) It is the opposite of the number.   (B) It is positive.

   (C) It is not negative.   (D) It is greater than the number.

EXPLORATION AND EXTENSION

PORTFOLIO

38. **BUILDING YOUR PROJECT** Mount St. Helens is a volcano in Washington. It erupted in 1980 and threw ash 4 mi into the atmosphere. The mountain had been about 9400 ft tall when the eruption blew the top off. Now it stands only 8364 ft high. Find the absolute value of the difference in the heights.

10.2

Addition of Integers

What you should learn:

Goal 1 How to add integers

Goal 2 How to use addition of integers to solve real-life problems

Why you should learn it:

Knowing how to add integers can help you solve real-life problems. An example is finding an average weekly temperature.

Point Barrow is the coldest place in Alaska. The average temperature there in February is $-28°C$.

Goal 1 ADDING INTEGERS

In Lesson 4.4, you learned how to use number counters and a number line to add integers. In this lesson, you will learn *rules* that can be used to add integers.

ADDING TWO INTEGERS

1. To add two integers with the *same* sign, add their absolute values and write the common sign.
2. To add two integers with *different* signs, subtract the smaller absolute value from the greater absolute value and write the sign of the integer with the greater absolute value.
3. The sum of two opposites is 0.

Example 1 Adding Integers with the Same Sign

a. $6 + 7 = 13$ Two positive integers

b. $-3 + (-5) = -8$ Two negative integers

Example 2 Adding Integers with Different Signs

a. $-5 + 3$ **b.** $8 + (-2)$ **c.** $4 + (-4)$

Solution

a. The sum of -5 and 3 is negative because -5 has a greater absolute value than 3.

Write sign of -5.

$$-5 + 3 = -2$$

Subtract 3 from 5.

b. The sum of 8 and -2 is positive because 8 has a greater absolute value than -2.

Subtract 2 from 8.

$$8 + (-2) = 6$$

c. Since 4 and -4 are opposites, their sum is zero.

$$4 + (-4) = 0$$

Example 3 **Adding More than Two Integers**

Find the sum: $-4 + 2 + (-3) + (-2) + 5$

Solution

Method **1** Group the numbers with the same signs. Add the sum of the positive numbers and add the sum of the negative numbers. Then add the two sums.

$$-4 + 2 + (-3) + (-2) + 5 = (2 + 5) + [-4 + (-3) + (-2)]$$
$$= 7 + (-9)$$
$$= -2$$

Method **2** Add two numbers at a time, from left to right.

$$-4 + 2 + (-3) + (-2) + 5 = \underbrace{-4 + 2} + (-3) + (-2) + 5$$
$$= \underbrace{-2 + (-3)} + (-2) + 5$$
$$= \underbrace{-5 + (-2)} + 5$$
$$= \underbrace{-7 + 5}$$
$$= -2$$

Example 4 **Finding an Average**

The daily temperatures for one week in Juneau, Alaska, are 5°C, 3°C, 2°C, 0°C, −2°C, −3°C, and −4°C. What is the average temperature?

REAL LIFE
Temperatures

Solution

First, use a calculator to find the sum of the seven numbers.

5 `+` 3 `+` 2 `+` 0 `+` 2 `+/-` `+` 3 `+/-` `+` 4 `+/-` `=` ⬭ `1.`

Then divide this sum by the number of temperatures.

Average $= \dfrac{\text{Sum}}{7}$ **Divide the sum by 7.**

$\qquad\quad = \dfrac{1}{7}$ **Substitute 1 for the sum.**

$\qquad\quad \approx 0.14$ **Round to the nearest hundredth.**

The average temperature for the week was about 0.14°C.

Real Life...
Real Facts

Juneau is the capital city of Alaska. It has a larger area than any other city in the United States covering more than 3000 square miles of land.

ONGOING ASSESSMENT

Write About It
· · · · · · · · · · · · · · · · · · ·

Describe the sum of the numbers as positive, negative, zero, or "cannot be determined."

1. Two negative numbers

2. A positive number and a negative number

3. A negative number and 0

GUIDED PRACTICE

In Exercises 1–3, decide whether the sum of *a* and *b* is *positive*, *negative*, or *zero*. Explain your reasoning.

1.
a   **0**   *b*

2.
a   **0**   *b*

3.
a   **0** *b*

OPEN-ENDED PROBLEMS In Exercises 4–7, find a positive integer and a negative integer with the indicated sum.

4. The sum is less than -7.

5. The sum is greater than 16.

6. The sum is -17.

7. The sum is 0.

8. Write the addition problem represented by the phrase "The sum of negative six and negative eight." Then find the sum.

9. **TEST SCORES** You take a test that has five questions. Each question is worth 10 points. The points you missed are represented by -3, 0, -6, -1, -4. What is the sum of these five numbers? How could the sum be used to find your test score?

PRACTICE AND PROBLEM SOLVING

In Exercises 10–13, without solving the problem, decide whether the sum is *positive*, *negative*, or *zero*. Then find the sum.

10. $-9 + (-7)$ **11.** $6 + (-6)$ **12.** $-12 + 14$ **13.** $13 + (-18)$

In Exercises 14–21, find the sum.

14. $-5 + 6$ **15.** $1 + (-9)$ **16.** $0 + (-3)$ **17.** $-7 + (-7)$

18. $-10 + (-8)$ **19.** $-19 + (-20)$ **20.** $-23 + 14$ **21.** $32 + (-25)$

GUESS, CHECK, AND REVISE In Exercises 22–27, solve the equation.

22. $x - 15 = -6$ **23.** $-11 + m = -4$ **24.** $9 = t - 17$

25. $y - 13 = -22$ **26.** $-20 = -8 + n$ **27.** $k + (-27) = 23$

TECHNOLOGY In Exercises 28–30, Use a calculator to find the average of the numbers.

28. $-8, 33, -19$ **29.** $-37, 12, -6, 51$ **30.** $-24, -30, -3, 41, 26$

OPEN-ENDED PROBLEMS In Exercises 31–34, find a positive integer and a negative integer that have the indicated sum.

31. 1   **32.** 9   **33.** -2 **34.** -15

35. BANKING The bar graph at the right shows the deposits to and withdrawals from your checking account for the month of January. Did you have more money in your account at the beginning of the month or at the end of the month? How much more or less did you have? Explain your reasoning.

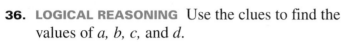

January Transactions

36. LOGICAL REASONING Use the clues to find the values of a, b, c, and d.

- $a + b = c$
- $b + c = -7$
- $b + d = -3$
- a and b are opposites.

37. GOLF The table shows the number of strokes over and under par for three golfers in a nine-hole golf game. Who won (had the lowest score)? Explain your reasoning.

Juan	3	0	2	−2	1	−1	4	−2	0
Joel	−2	1	−1	−1	2	3	0	−1	−1
Corn	1	2	2	1	0	0	1	2	−2

STANDARDIZED TEST PRACTICE

38. Which statement best completes the following sentence? The sum of two negative numbers

- **A** is always positive.
- **B** is sometimes negative.
- **C** is always zero.
- **D** is never zero.

39. Which expression has a sum less than -4?

- **A** $3 + (-6)$
- **B** $-8 + 12$
- **C** $2 + (-8)$
- **D** $-1 + 3$

EXPLORATION AND EXTENSION

PORTFOLIO

40. COMMUNICATING ABOUT MATHEMATICS (page 509) You are a marine geologist. For research purposes, you descended in a submersible lab to study the composition of the ocean floor. The ocean-floor depths (in meters) that you studied are -3850, -3895, -3625, and -3550. What is the average of the four ocean-floor depths that you studied?

10.3

Subtraction of Integers

What you should learn:

Goal 1 How to subtract integers

Goal 2 How to use subtraction of integers to solve real-life problems

Why you should learn it:

Knowing how to subtract integers can help you solve real-life problems. An example is finding the difference in times between two cities.

When it is 3:00 P.M. in Kyoto, Japan, it is 1:00 A.M. in Washington, D.C.

Goal 1 SUBTRACTING INTEGERS

You can use what you learned in Lesson 10.2 about addition to subtract integers.

LESSON INVESTIGATION

Investigating Subtraction of Integers

GROUP ACTIVITY Use a calculator to add and subtract. Describe any patterns that you see.

1. $5 - 2$
$5 + (-2)$

2. $3 - 4$
$3 + (-4)$

3. $-5 - (-6)$
$-5 + 6$

4. $-4 - (-2)$
$-4 + 2$

5. $-7 - 2$
$-7 + (-2)$

6. $8 - (-1)$
$8 + 1$

In the Lesson Investigation, you may have discovered the following rule.

SUBTRACTING TWO INTEGERS

To subtract an integer, add its opposite.

Example: $a - b = a + (-b)$

Example 1 **Subtracting Integers**

Do the following subtraction problems.

a. $-2 - 5$ **b.** $0 - (-6)$ **c.** $3 - (-7)$ **d.** $-14 - (-14)$

Solution

a. $-2 - 5 = -2 + (-5)$ Add the opposite of 5.
$= -7$ Use the rule for adding integers.

b. $0 - (-6) = 0 + 6$ Add the opposite of −6.
$= 6$ Use the rule for adding integers.

c. $3 - (-7) = 3 + 7$ Add the opposite of −7.
$= 10$ Use the rule for adding integers.

d. $14 - (-14) = -14 + 14$ Add the opposite of −14.
$= 0$ Use the rule for adding integers.

Goal 2 SOLVING REAL-LIFE PROBLEMS

Earth is divided into 24 time zones. Each zone is labeled by the number of hours its time differs from the time in Greenwich, England. The 24 time zones are shown on the number line below.

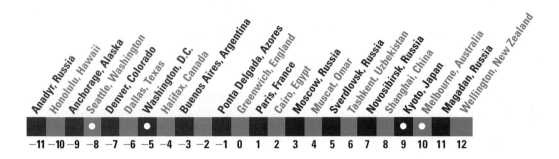

Example 2 Subtracting Integers

**REAL LIFE
Time Zones**

Find the difference in times in the following cities.

a. Kyoto, Japan and Washington, D.C.
b. Melbourne, Australia and Seattle, Washington

Solution

To find the difference in times, subtract the smaller number from the greater number.

a.
$$\begin{array}{l}\text{Kyoto's time} \\ \text{zone number}\end{array} - \begin{array}{l}\text{Washington, D.C.'s} \\ \text{time zone number}\end{array} = 9 - (-5)$$
$$= 9 + 5$$
$$= 14$$

Kyoto and Washington, D.C., have a 14-hour time difference. For example, if it is 6:00 A.M. in Washington, D.C., then it is 14 hours later, or 8:00 P.M., in Kyoto.

b.
$$\begin{array}{l}\text{Melbourne's time} \\ \text{zone number}\end{array} - \begin{array}{l}\text{Seattle's time} \\ \text{zone number}\end{array} = 10 - (-8)$$
$$= 10 + 8$$
$$= 18$$

Melbourne and Seattle have an 18-hour time difference. For example, if it is 6:00 A.M. in Seattle, then it is 18 hours later, or midnight, in Melbourne.

ONGOING ASSESSMENT

Write About It

Use the time zone information above and integer subtraction to find the time difference between the two cities.

1. Cairo and Honolulu

2. Ponta Delgada and Anchorage

3. Greenwich and Denver

GUIDED PRACTICE

In Exercises 1–3, match the subtraction problem with the equivalent addition problem. Then solve.

A. $-3 + (-5)$ **B.** $3 + 5$ **C.** $3 + (-5)$

1. $3 - 5$ **2.** $-3 - 5$ **3.** $3 - (-5)$

4. USING LOGICAL REASONING Which expression could you use to find the difference between a temperature of $-56°C$ and $-75°C$? Find the difference.

   A. $56 - 75$ **B.** $-56 - (-75)$ **C.** $-56 - 75$

HAIRCUT COSTS In Exercises 5 and 6, use the following information. The bar graph compares the cost of a man's haircut in three major cities to the cost of a man's haircut in Los Angeles. The cost of a man's haircut in Los Angeles is shown by the zero line. (Source: Runzheimer International)

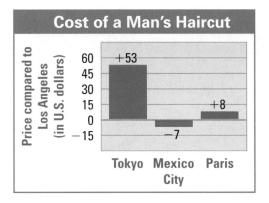

5. How much more is a man's haircut in Tokyo than it is in Paris?

6. How much more is a man's haircut in Paris than it is in Mexico City?

PRACTICE AND PROBLEM SOLVING

In Exercises 7–14, write each subtraction expression as an equivalent addition expression. Then find the sum.

7. $5 - 18$ **8.** $0 - 12$ **9.** $-3 - 19$ **10.** $-8 - 27$

11. $-12 - 25$ **12.** $0 - (-36)$ **13.** $-5 - (-27)$ **14.** $-11 - (-19)$

In Exercises 15–26, add or subtract.

15. $8 - (-3)$ **16.** $-4 + (-14)$ **17.** $-19 + 15$ **18.** $-3 - 12$

19. $-13 - 9$ **20.** $31 - (-14)$ **21.** $-25 - (-26)$ **22.** $-32 - 24$

23. $7 + (-15)$ **24.** $-7 + (-15)$ **25.** $-6 - (-24)$ **26.** $-11 - 19$

ALGEBRA In Exercises 27–34, evaluate the expression when $x = 6$ and when $x = -1$.

27. $x - 5$ **28.** $12 - x$ **29.** $-8 - x$ **30.** $x - (-3)$

31. $0 - x$ **32.** $-4 - x$ **33.** $x - (-2)$ **34.** $x - 10$

TECHNOLOGY In Exercises 35–37, match the expression with the calculator keystrokes. Then evaluate it.

A. 10 $-$ 21 $+/-$ $=$ **B.** 10 $-$ 21 $=$ **C.** 10 $+/-$ $-$ 21 $=$

35. $-10 - 21$ **36.** $10 - (-21)$ **37.** $10 - 21$

CRITICAL THINKING In Exercises 38 and 39, complete the statement using the words *positive* or *negative*. Explain your reasoning.

38. If $0 - x$ is negative, then x is __?__. **39.** If x is negative, then $0 - x$ is __?__.

BATTERY LIFE In Exercises 40–43, use the table below. The table lists the number of minutes above or below average that each of four brands of batteries lasts. The average battery lasts 19 min in a radio-controlled car. In Exercises 40–42, find the difference in the battery lives.

Brand A	Brand B	Brand C	Brand D
0 min	4 min	−2 min	−5 min

40. Brand A and Brand C **41.** Brand B and Brand D **42.** Brand B and Brand C

43. Which battery in the table would you buy? Explain.

STANDARDIZED TEST PRACTICE

44. Which number comes next in the pattern? 15, 6, -3, -12, . . .

A -22 **B** -21 **C** -20 **D** -19

EXPLORATION AND EXTENSION

PORTFOLIO

45. BUILDING YOUR PROJECT The graphics below show the first and last known eruptions of four volcanoes. Using the B.C. dates as negative numbers, determine for how long each volcano has been erupting. Which volcano has been erupting for the longest time?

1576 A.D.
1994 A.D.

6950 B.C.
1991 A.D.

1850 B.C.
1708 A.D.

6445 B.C.
1932 A.D.

Colima • Mexico Mount St. Helens • U.S.A. Mt. Fuji • Japan Mt. Pelée • Martinique

10.4

Patterns in a Coordinate Plane

What you should learn:

Goal 1 How to find patterns in a scatter plot of an equation

Goal 2 How to find patterns in a scatter plot of an absolute value equation

Why you should learn it:

Knowing how to construct a table of values can help you sketch graphs and scatter plots in a coordinate plane.

Goal 1 **TABLES OF VALUES AND GRAPHS**

In Lessons 4.2 and 5.4, you learned how to make a table of values and plot the resulting points in a coordinate plane.

Example 1 **Finding Patterns in Scatter Plots**

Use integer x-values from -3 to 3 to draw a scatter plot for the equation $y = -3 + x$. Describe any patterns that you see.

Solution

Substitute the x-values to find the corresponding y-values.

Value of x	Substitute.	Value of y
-3	$y = -3 + (-3)$	-6
-2	$y = -3 + (-2)$	-5
-1	$y = -3 + (-1)$	-4
0	$y = -3 + 0$	-3
1	$y = -3 + 1$	-2
2	$y = -3 + 2$	-1
3	$y = -3 + 3$	0

You can summarize this information in a table of values. Write the x-values and y-values in the table as a collection of ordered pairs of the form (x, y).

x	y	
-3	-6	$\longrightarrow (-3, -6)$
-2	-5	$\longrightarrow (-2, -5)$
-1	-4	$\longrightarrow (-1, -4)$
0	-3	$\longrightarrow (0, -3)$
1	-2	$\longrightarrow (1, -2)$
2	-1	$\longrightarrow (2, -1)$
3	0	$\longrightarrow (3, 0)$

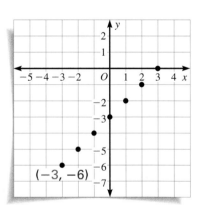

Finally, plot the points as shown. You can see from the graph that the points lie on a line. Each time the x-value increases by 1, the y-value also increases by 1.

Not all equations are lines when graphed. As you will see in Example 2, graphs can have very different shapes.

Example 2 **Finding Patterns in Scatter Plots**

Use integer x-values from -3 to 3 to draw a scatter plot for $y = |x|$. Describe any patterns that you see.

Solution

Substitute the x-values to find the corresponding y-values.

Value of x	Substitute.	Value of y
-3	$y = |-3|$	3
-2	$y = |-2|$	2
-1	$y = |-1|$	1
0	$y = |0|$	0
1	$y = |1|$	1
2	$y = |2|$	2
3	$y = |3|$	3

Make a table for the x-values and y-values. Then write these values as a collection of ordered pairs of the form (x, y) and plot the points.

x	y	
-3	3	$\longrightarrow$ $(-3, 3)$
-2	2	$\longrightarrow$ $(-2, 2)$
-1	1	$\longrightarrow$ $(-1, 1)$
0	0	$\longrightarrow$ $(0, 0)$
1	1	$\longrightarrow$ $(1, 1)$
2	2	$\longrightarrow$ $(2, 2)$
3	3	$\longrightarrow$ $(3, 3)$

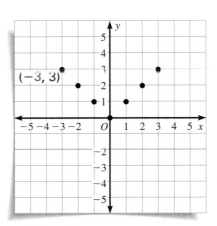

You can see from the graph that the points lie in a V-shaped pattern with the vertex at the origin. Each pair of opposite x-coordinates has the same y-coordinate.

ONGOING ASSESSMENT

Talk About It
....

Draw a scatter plot for the equation. Use integer x-values from -3 to 3. Describe the pattern.

1. $y = |x| + 1$

2. $y = -|x|$

10.4 Exercises

Extra Practice, page 642

GUIDED PRACTICE

BIOLOGY In Exercises 1–3, use the scatter plot at the right. It shows the normal maximum heart rate for people of different ages. The heart rate R is related to the person's age x by the equation $R = 220 - x$.

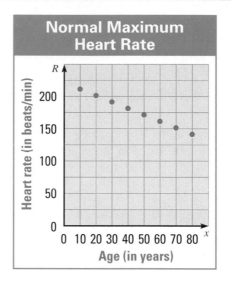

1. Use the equation to find your maximum heart rate.

2. What is the maximum heart rate for a person who is 35?

3. Is the point (65, 145) on the graph? Explain your reasoning.

In Exercises 4–6, match the scatter plot with its equation.

A. $y = x - 2$ **B.** $y = x + 2$ **C.** $y = |x| - 2$

4.

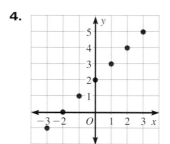

5.

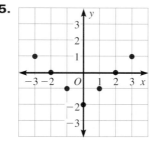

6.

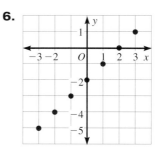

PRACTICE AND PROBLEM SOLVING

In Exercises 7–9, copy and complete the table of values.

7. $y = -8 + x$

x	−9	−6	−3	0	3
y	?	?	?	?	?

8. $y = x - 5$

x	9	6	2	−1	−5
y	?	?	?	?	?

9. $y = -10 - x$

x	−5	−2	0	3	7
y	?	?	?	?	?

In Exercises 10 and 11, write the ordered pairs shown in the table of values. Then plot the points and describe the pattern of the graph.

10.

x	−2	−1	0	1	2
y	8	7	6	5	4

11.

x	−2	−1	0	1	2
y	−7	−6	−5	−4	−3

In Exercises 12–14, make a table of values. Use *x*-values of −4, −3, −2, −1, 0, 1, 2, 3, and 4. Then plot the points and describe any patterns.

12. $y = x + 9$ **13.** $y = x - 11$ **14.** $y = -5 - x$

BUSINESS Three years ago, you became president of a company that manufactures cellular telephones. The profit or loss (in thousands of dollars) of the company for the past six years is shown in the table.

Year	1	2	3	4	5	6
Profit	−67	−42	−30	12	24	49

15. Make a scatter plot of the data.

16. Describe any patterns you see.

17. Were you a successful president? Explain.

GEOMETRY In Exercises 18 and 19, consider a rectangle that has a width of *x* centimeters and a length of 6 centimeters.

18. Copy and complete the table by finding the perimeters of the rectangles described above.

x (cm)	1	2	3	4	5	6	7	8
P (cm)	?	?	?	?	?	?	?	?

19. Make a scatter plot of the data. Describe patterns in the graph.

20. Draw a scatter plot for each equation. Use *x*-values of −3, −2, −1, 0, 1, 2, and 3. How are they alike? How are they different?

     a. $y = |x| + 2$ **b.** $y = |x| - 2$

Real Life...
Real Facts

Cellular Phones

In 1995, over 33 million people in the United States owned cellular telephones. (Source: Cellular Telecommunications Industry Association)

21. Which point is on the graph of $y = -x - 8$?

     (A) (3, 5)   **(B)** (3, −5)

     (C) (3, 11)   **(D)** (3, −11)

22. Which equation's graph is shown in the scatter plot?

     (A) $y = 6 - x$ **(B)** $y = 4 - x$

     (C) $y = x + 6$ **(D)** $y = 4 + x$

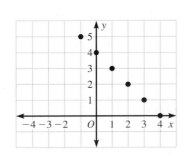

23. **BUILDING YOUR PROJECT** Researchers have used remote-controlled robots like Dante II (shown at the right) to study the conditions in dangerous volcano craters. The table below shows the possible slopes and the number of vertical feet the robot descends as it travels 100 feet down into the volcano crater. Draw a scatter plot to represent this information. Describe any patterns you see in the scatter plot.

Slope (degrees)	10	15	20	25	30	35	40	45
Descent (ft per 100 ft)	−17	−26	−34	−42	−50	−57	−64	−71

SPIRAL REVIEW

In Exercises 1 and 2, draw a box-and-whisker plot of the data. (5.3)

1. 27, 34, 32, 19, 25, 41, 38, 35, 32, 28, 26, 18

2. 96, 55, 81, 66, 86, 85, 94, 75, 86, 72, 95, 53

CARNIVAL GAME **In Exercises 3 and 4, you are playing a carnival game. You move plastic turtles by shooting water from a squirt gun. (5.7)**

3. In the game there are four turtles. Each turtle is a different color. One turtle is red, one is green, one is yellow, and one is blue. List the possible outcomes of the race. Assume there are no ties.

4. If each outcome is equally likely, what is the probability that the blue turtle will win *and* the yellow turtle will be second?

5. In a survey, 51 students, or 34% of those surveyed, said that math is their favorite subject. Use a percent equation to find the number of students that were surveyed. **(7.4)**

 TECHNOLOGY **In Exercises 6 and 7, use a calculator to find the amount of interest you owe for the loan. (7.6)**

6. $P = \$212$, $r = 19\%$, $t = 1$ year

7. $P = \$1250$, $r = 14\%$, $t = 18$ months

GEOMETRY **In Exercises 8–10, find the length of the side. (8.8)**

8.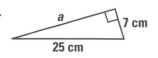

9.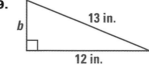

10.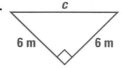

Take this test as you would take a test in class. The answers to the exercises are given in the back of the book.

In Exercises 1–3, decide whether the statement is *true* or *false*. If it is false, explain why. (10.1–10.3)

  1. The absolute value of a number is the opposite of the number.

  2. The sum of two negative integers is negative.

  3. If you subtract a negative integer from a positive integer, the result can be negative or positive.

In Exercises 4–7, find the value of the expression. (10.1)

  4. $|-1.5|$ **5.** $|4|$ **6.** $|-20|$ **7.** $|0|$

In Exercises 8–13, add or subtract. (10.2, 10.3)

  8. $12 + (-4)$ **9.** $-3 + 8$ **10.** $4 - (-15)$

  11. $-17 - 6$ **12.** $12 - 23$ **13.** $-9 + (-3)$

In Exercises 14 and 15, make a table of values for the equation. Use *x*-values of −3, −2, −1, 0, 1, 2, and 3. Then write the ordered pairs represented by the table. Plot them in a coordinate plane. (10.4)

  14. $y = 4 - x$ **15.** $y = |x| - 3$

GEOLOGY The photo at the right shows house-sized holes found in sandstone near Lake Powell in Utah. Exercises 16–18 refer to this geological feature. (10.1–10.3)

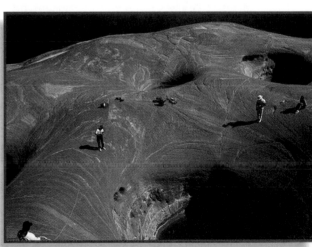

  16. Geologists are puzzled about how the holes shown in the photo were formed. They know that the holes were formed between 1,600,000 B.C. and 800,000 B.C. Which of these dates is more recent? Explain your reasoning.

  17. The first known residents of the area were the Anasazi people. They lived in the area from 10 B.C. to 1250 A.D. How many years did they live in the area?

  18. Consider the year 2000 to be 0 on a number line. What number-line values would the two dates in Exercise 17 have?

Multiplying Integers

Part A MULTIPLYING BY A POSITIVE INTEGER

Multiplying by a *positive* integer can be modeled by *putting* number counters on a mat. For example, the product 2 × 3 can be modeled by putting on 3 tan counters 2 times.

Put on 3, 2 times.   **The result is 6.**   2 × 3 = 6

Likewise, the product 3 × (−3) can be modeled by putting on 3 red counters 3 times.

Put on −3, 3 times.   **The result is −9.**   3 × (−3) = −9

1. Write the product that is being modeled.

2. Use number counters to find each product.

     a. 4 × 2   **b.** 3 × 5   **c.** 3 × (−4)   **d.** 2 × (−5)

     e. 5 × 4   **f.** 2 × (−2)   **g.** 4 × (−3)   **h.** 2 × (−4)

Multiplying by a *negative* integer can be modeled by *taking* number counters off a mat. For example, the product -2×3 can be modeled by taking off 3 tan counters 2 times. In order to have enough tan counters to take off, begin by modeling 0 with 6 zero pairs.

Make 6 zero pairs.   **Remove 3, 2 times.** $-2 \times 3 = -6$

3. Use number counters to find each product.

   a. $(-4) \times 2$ **b.** $(-3) \times 5$ **c.** $(-2) \times (-4)$ **d.** $(-3) \times (-5)$

4 Use number counters to find each product. What do you notice?

   a. $3 \times (-4)$ and $(-4) \times 3$ **b.** $(-2) \times (-5)$ and $(-5) \times (-2)$

NOW TRY THESE

5. State the multiplication fact being modeled.

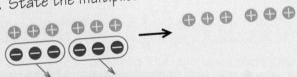

6. Use number counters to find each product.

   a. $(-4) \times 5$ **b.** $(-3) \times 6$

   c. $(-4) \times (-4)$ **d.** $(-4) \times (-5)$

7. Use the word *positive* or *negative* to complete the statement.

   a. The product of two positive integers is a **?** integer.

   b. The product of a positive integer and a negative integer is a **?** integer.

   c. The product of two negative integers is a **?** integer.

10.5

Multiplication of Integers

What you should learn:

Goal 1 How to multiply integers

Goal 2 How to use integer multiplication to solve real-life problems

Why you should learn it:

Knowing how to multiply integers can help you solve real-life problems. An example is modeling the action of a toggle switch.

Goal 1 MULTIPLYING INTEGERS

LESSON INVESTIGATION

Investigating Multiplication of Integers

COOPERATIVE LEARNING

GROUP ACTIVITY Use a calculator to find each product. Describe any patterns you see.

$4 \cdot 4 = \boxed{?}$	$4 \cdot (-4) = \boxed{?}$
$3 \cdot 4 = \boxed{?}$	$3 \cdot (-4) = \boxed{?}$
$2 \cdot 4 = \boxed{?}$	$2 \cdot (-4) = \boxed{?}$
$1 \cdot 4 = \boxed{?}$	$1 \cdot (-4) = \boxed{?}$
$0 \cdot 4 = \boxed{?}$	$0 \cdot (-4) = \boxed{?}$
$-1 \cdot 4 = \boxed{?}$	$-1 \cdot (-4) = \boxed{?}$
$-2 \cdot 4 = \boxed{?}$	$-2 \cdot (-4) = \boxed{?}$
$-3 \cdot 4 = \boxed{?}$	$-3 \cdot (-4) = \boxed{?}$
$-4 \cdot 4 = \boxed{?}$	$-4 \cdot (-4) = \boxed{?}$

To multiply two numbers, multiply their absolute values. The sign of the product is determined by the following rules.

MULTIPLYING INTEGERS

1. The product of two positive integers is positive.
2. The product of two negative integers is positive.
3. The product of a positive integer and a negative integer is negative.

CALCULATOR TIP

When multiplying negative numbers, use the +/- key. For example, to multiply $-4 \times (-4)$, use the following keystrokes.

4 +/- × 4 +/- =

Example 1 Multiplying Integers

a. $5 \cdot 6 = 30$ Product is positive.
b. $-4 \cdot (-7) = 28$ Product is positive.
c. $-3 \cdot 9 = -27$ Product is negative.
d. $12 \cdot (-4) = -48$ Product is negative.
e. $-8 \cdot 0 = 0$ Product is zero.

To multiply three or more integers, work from left to right, multiplying two numbers at a time.

Example 2 **Multiplying More Than Two Integers**

a. $2 \cdot (-3) \cdot 4 = -6 \cdot 4$ Multiply $2 \cdot (-3)$.

$= -24$ Multiply $-6 \cdot 4$.

b. $-1 \cdot (-2) \cdot (-3) \cdot (-4) = \underbrace{2 \cdot (-3)} \cdot (-4)$

$= \underbrace{-6} \cdot (-4)$

$= 24$

Example 3 **Multiplying More Than Two Integers**

Most light switches are *toggle switches*. If the light is off, flipping the switch turns the light on. If the light is on, flipping the switch turns it off. In the diagram at the right, both of the switches turn the light on or off when flipped.

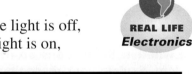

REAL LIFE
Electronics

a. The light is off. Switch 1 is flipped twice and Switch 2 is flipped once. Is the light off or on?

b. The light is on. Switch 1 is flipped three times and Switch 2 is flipped twice. Is the light off or on?

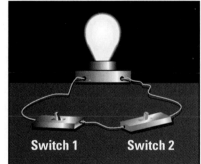

Switch 1   Switch 2

Solution

You can model the action of a toggle switch by repeated multiplication by -1. Let -1 represent "off" and 1 represent "on." Each time you flip a switch, multiply by -1.

a. -1 $\cdot$ $\underbrace{-1 \cdot -1}$ $\cdot$ $\underbrace{-1}$ $= 1$ Light is on.

Light   Flip   Flip
is off.   twice.   once.

b. 1 $\cdot$ $\underbrace{-1 \cdot -1 \cdot -1}$ $\cdot$ $\underbrace{-1 \cdot -1}$ $= -1$ Light is off.

Light   Flip three   Flip
is on.   times.   twice.

GUIDED PRACTICE

In Exercises 1–4, use the number line to decide whether the product is *positive*, *negative*, or *zero*. Explain your reasoning.

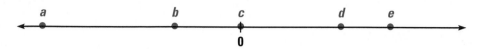

1. $a \times b$ **2.** $c \cdot d$ **3.** $a(d)$ **4.** $d \times e$

In Exercises 5–7, find the product when $m = -4$.

5. $m \cdot (-7)$ **6.** $9m$ **7.** $-1(-2)(-5)m$

8. **TIDES** The water level of an ocean bay falls 3 ft/h until low tide. Write an integer to represent the hourly change in water level. The bay reaches low tide in 6 h. How many feet did the water level fall?

PRACTICE AND PROBLEM SOLVING

In Exercises 9–14, decide whether the value is *positive*, *negative*, or *zero* without solving the problem. Explain your reasoning.

9. $-3 - (-3)$ **10.** $-4 + (-4)$ **11.** 3×12

12. $-7 \cdot 0$ **13.** $8(-2)$ **14.** $-10 \times (-5)$

In Exercises 15–20, find the product.

15. $7 \cdot 8$ **16.** $-5(0)$ **17.** $9 \times (-1)$

18. $(-2)(-13)$ **19.** $(-1)(-16)(-1)$ **20.** $(2)(-4)(-9)$

GUESS, CHECK, AND REVISE In Exercises 21–26, solve the equation.

21. $m \times 7 = 56$ **22.** $-6 \cdot y = 54$ **23.** $9 = -9t$

24. $n \cdot (-18) = 0$ **25.** $3x = -39$ **26.** $-45 = b \times (-15)$

TECHNOLOGY In Exercises 27–29, tell what sign the product will have. Then use a calculator to find the product.

27. $12.8 \cdot (-17.5)$ **28.** $\frac{4}{5}(-215)$ **29.** $(-14)(-27)(-30)$

In Exercises 30–35, evaluate the expression for $x = -6$.

30. $x \cdot (-7)$ **31.** $\frac{2}{3}x$ **32.** $x \cdot x \cdot x$

33. $x - x$ **34.** $2x + 6$ **35.** $|x| + x$

In Exercises 36 and 37, write the multiplication problem that is represented by the phrase. Then find the product.

36. The product of negative one, negative seven, and nine

37. The product of five, negative six, and zero

In Exercises 38–41, write two different multiplication problems that have the given product.

38. 0 **39.** -12 **40.** -40 **41.** 35

42. BOOKKEEPING You keep a record of your income and expenses. Copy and complete the record.

Activity	Unit Price	Units	Total
Baby-sat	$3.25 per hour	12 hours	?
Bought CDs	−$12.50 each	2	?
Played video games	−$0.25 each	14	?
Mowed lawns	$4.75 each	4	?
Bought books	−$4.50 each	3	?
Final Balance			?

STANDARDIZED TEST PRACTICE

43. If x is positive and y is negative, which expression *must* be negative?

  (A) $x + y$ **(B)** $x - y$ **(C)** $x \cdot y$ **(D)** All of these

44. Which equation is true?

  (A) $(9 - 5) \cdot (-6) = 24$ **(B)** $2 \cdot 5 - 6 \cdot (-1) = -4$

  (C) $4 \cdot (-4) \cdot (-3) = 36$ **(D)** $1 - (-3) \cdot (-2) = -5$

EXPLORATION AND EXTENSION

PORTFOLIO

45. BUILDING YOUR PROJECT Geologists measure the temperature and amounts of gases at various depths in volcanoes. A geologist is lowered 150 ft into a crater to take measurements. The geologist is then lowered 150 ft for another measurement and so on until measurements are taken at 6 locations. Use integers to represent each location. Draw a diagram to illustrate your answer.

10.6

Division of Integers

What you should learn:

Goal 1 How to divide integers

Goal 2 How to use integer division to solve real-life problems

Why you should learn it:

Knowing how to divide integers can help you solve real-life problems. An example is finding the average elevation of the bottom of a lake.

Goal 1 DIVIDING INTEGERS

In Lesson 10.5 you learned rules for determining the sign of a product of integers. The Lesson Investigation below will help you discover the rules for quotients as well.

LESSON INVESTIGATION

COOPERATIVE LEARNING

Investigating Integer Division

GROUP ACTIVITY Use a calculator to find each quotient. Discuss the results with your partner. What do you think the rules are for dividing integers?

1. $32 \div 4$ **2.** $32 \div (-4)$

3. $-32 \div 4$ **4.** $-32 \div (-4)$

To divide two numbers, divide their absolute values. The sign of the quotient is determined by the following rules.

DIVIDING INTEGERS

1. The quotient of two positive integers is positive.

2. The quotient of two negative integers is positive.

3. The quotient of a positive integer and a negative integer is negative.

The number 0 has special division rules. You cannot divide a number by 0. Expressions with 0 divisors, such as $12 \div 0$, are meaningless. When 0 is divided by a nonzero number, the result is 0.

NEED TO KNOW

Recall that the words divisor, dividend, and quotient are related as follows.

$$\text{Divisor} \rightarrow 12\overline{)168}^{\,14} \leftarrow \text{Quotient}$$

$\leftarrow$ Dividend

Example 1 Dividing Integers

a. $72 \div (-8) = -9$ The quotient is negative.

b. $-42 \div 14 = -3$ The quotient is negative.

c. $-49 \div (-7) = 7$ The quotient is positive.

d. $0 \div 3 = 0$ The quotient is zero.

✔**Check:** You can check the answer to a division problem by multiplying the quotient and the divisor. For example, you can check part (a) by writing $(-8) \cdot (-9) = 72$.

Example 2 — Finding an Average

You are exploring the bottom of a section of Lake Michigan. You take five readings of the lake bottom's elevation relative to sea level. What is the average of these elevations?

REAL LIFE
Elevations

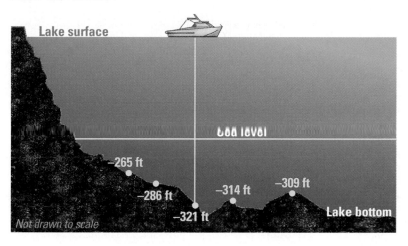

Lake surface

Sea level

−265 ft

−286 ft

−314 ft

−321 ft

−309 ft

Lake bottom

Not drawn to scale

Lake Michigan is the largest body of fresh water in the United States. Native Americans who lived near the lake called it Michi-guma. The surface is 579 ft above sea level and the deepest part is 344 ft below sea level.

Solution

To find the average, add the 5 numbers and divide by 5.

$$\text{Average} = \frac{(-321) + (-286) + (-314) + (-265) + (-309)}{5}$$

$$= \frac{-1495}{5}$$

$$= -299$$

The average elevation for this region of the bottom of Lake Michigan is −299 feet, or 299 feet below sea level.

Example 3 — Finding an Average

The average of four temperatures is −2°C. What is the sum of the four temperatures?

Solution

STRATEGY **USE LOGICAL REASONING** The average is −2°C. So the sum of the temperatures is −8 because −8 ÷ 4 = −2.

ONGOING ASSESSMENT

Talk About It

You take six other readings in the lake. Part of your record is lost, but you know that the average is −254 ft.

1. Five of the readings are −267 ft, −243 ft, −262 ft, −256 ft, and −258 ft. What was the sixth reading? Explain.

GUIDED PRACTICE

In Exercises 1 and 2, decide whether the statement is *true* or *false*. Explain your reasoning.

1. A nonzero number divided by its opposite is equal to 1.

2. A negative number divided by itself is equal to -1.

ERROR ANALYSIS In Exercises 3 and 4, explain why the division problem is incorrect.

3.

$$-12 \div 0 = -12 \; \text{✗}$$

4.

$$0 \div (-8) = -8 \; \text{✗}$$

DIVISION MAZE In Exercise 5 and 6, divide the number in a box by any other integer. If your answer is the integer in a neighboring box, you can move to that box. You cannot move diagonally.

5.

-16	11	5	-32	-20
50	29	18	-18	6
108 START	-36	36	22	3 END

6.

-85	75	30	-10	10 END
-240	240	-60	-55	15
480 START	100	135	205	40

PRACTICE AND PROBLEM SOLVING

In Exercises 7–10, decide whether the quotient is *positive* or *negative* without solving the problem.

7. $-81 \div 9$ **8.** $64 \div (-16)$ **9.** $-70 \div -10$ **10.** $45 \div 3$

In Exercises 11–22, find the quotient, if possible.

11. $42 \div (-6)$ **12.** $-33 \div 11$ **13.** $-75 \div (-25)$ **14.** $0 \div 10$

15. $52 \div (-4)$ **16.** $-125 \div 5$ **17.** $0 \div (-18)$ **18.** $-88 \div (-2)$

19. $-12 \div 0$ **20.** $-76 \div -4$ **21.** $-45 \div -9$ **22.** $19 \div 0$

AVERAGES In Exercises 23–27, find the average.

23. Temperatures: $-10°, -6°, 7°, -13°, 5°, 10°, -14°$

24. Golf scores: $-2, 1, 0, -1, -2, -1$

25. Pool depths: -15 ft, -12 ft, -6 ft, -5 ft, -4 ft, -12 ft, -10 ft, -8 ft

26. Stock price changes: $-\$2, -\$4, \$2, -\$1, -\$2, -\$3, \$2, \$0, -\$1$

27. Annual profit (in millions): $-\$21, -\$17, -\$6.5, \$4, \$10.5, \$19$

28. **GRAND CANYON** You are visiting the Grand Canyon in Arizona. You look at a tour map that tells you how many feet you will be descending into the canyon on different trails. Write the depths in miles.

Trail 1: -6336 feet   Trail 2: -1760 feet

Trail 3: -2640 feet   Trail 4: -6600 feet

ALGEBRA In Exercises 29–32, evaluate the expression when $x = 6$ and when $x = -6$.

29. $x \div 3$ **30.** $6 \div x$ **31.** $x \div -2$ **32.** $-36 \div x$

GUESS, CHECK, AND REVISE In Exercises 33 and 34, you are given the average. Find the missing number.

33. Average $= -25$; $-36, -22, -12, -20,$?

34. Average $= -4$; $-20, 15, -10, 4,$?

In Exercises 35–37, evaluate the expression.

35. $(-3 + 9) \div (-2)$ **36.** $-3 \times (20 \div (-4))$

37. $(25 \times (-2)) \div (-5 \times (-5))$

38. **WEIGHT LOSS** Changes in a person's weight, pounds, for eight weeks are shown below. What is the average change in weight per week during this time?

$-3, -2, -1, -2, 0, -1, -2, -1$

STANDARDIZED TEST PRACTICE

39. The divisor is -3. The dividend is 6. Find the quotient.

(A) -2 (B) $-\dfrac{1}{2}$ (C) $\dfrac{1}{2}$ (D) 2

40. The graph shows a company's profits (in thousands) from January to June. Find the company's average monthly profit.

(A) $-\$4500$ (B) $-\$3000$

(C) $\$3000$ (D) $\$6000$

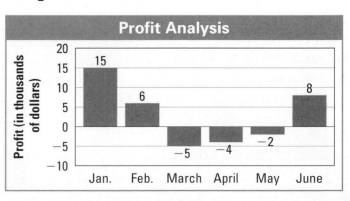

41. BUILDING YOUR PROJECT Magma that erupts from volcanoes is formed deep in Earth's interior. As pressure increases it pushes upward and collects in a magma reservoir. Geologists study this magma to try to predict eruptions. A geologist measured the depths of magma reservoirs beneath four volcanoes. The depths were −8 mi, −2 mi, −6 miles, and −10 miles. Find the average depth of the reservoirs.

Magma reservoir

SPIRAL REVIEW

1. LOOKING FOR A PATTERN The table shows the cost of becoming a member of a local swimming pool. Each price depends on the number of months, m, you sign up to be a member plus a membership fee of $18.50. Write an expression that gives the cost for m months. **(4.1)**

m	1	2	3	4
Cost ($)	43.50	68.50	93.50	118.50

In Exercises 2 and 3, find the unit rate. (6.2)

2. For taking care of your neighbor's dog for 7 days, you earn $35.

3. Your neighbor travels 495 miles in 9 hours to get to the vacation site.

GEOMETRY **In Exercises 4 and 5, describe the translation of the blue figure to the red figure. (8.2)**

4.

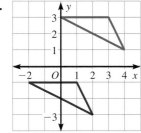

5.

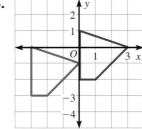

GEOMETRY **In Exercises 6 and 7, find the surface area and volume of the solid. (9.2, 9.3, 9.5, 9.6)**

6.

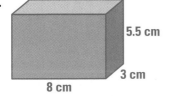

5.5 cm
3 cm
8 cm

7.

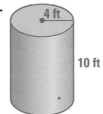

4 ft
10 ft

Mapping the Ocean Floor

READ About It

On February 29, 1956, scientists drafted a resolution asking the United States to create a national program to develop manned undersea vehicles for deep sea exploration. This resolution led to the construction of ALVIN.

ALVIN was delivered to the Woods Hole Oceanographic Institution where it made its first untethered dive on August 4, 1964, to a depth of –35 feet in relation to sea level. In 1965, ALVIN could carry three people as deep as –6000 feet for 6 to 10 hours at a time.

ALVIN has been at work inspecting deep sea sites since 1966. In 1994, ALVIN celebrated its 30th birthday. After taking six months off for an overhaul in 1996, ALVIN is back in service helping scientists investigate the deep sea world.

WRITE About It

1. What is the absolute value of the depth of ALVIN in its first untethered dive? Explain how you got your answer.

2. One of ALVIN's first manned tethered dives was to –70 feet in relation to sea level. Draw a diagram and write an expression to find the difference in depth between ALVIN's first manned tethered and untethered dives.

3. Mount Marcy in New York State stands 5344 feet above sea level. What is the distance from the top of Mount Marcy to where ALVIN sat on the ocean floor when it accidentally sunk to –5000 feet? Did you use absolute values to find the answer? Why or why not?

4. In 1973, ALVIN was fitted with a new titanium personnel sphere to double the depth the manned sub could descend in 1965. How many feet could ALVIN descend after 1973? Explain how you found the answer.

5. In 1976, ALVIN was certified to dive 1124 feet deeper than in 1973. How deep could ALVIN dive?

6. Over the course of 11 years, ALVIN made dives of –12,000 feet, –13,124 feet, –13,900 feet, and –14,764 feet in relation to sea level. What is the average of these dives? Show your work.

10.7

Integers and Exponents

What you should learn:

Goal 1 How to raise an integer to a power

Goal 2 How to recognize patterns in a coordinate plane

Why you should learn it:

Knowing how to evaluate exponential expressions can help you recognize patterns in a coordinate plane.

Goal 1 RAISING INTEGERS TO POWERS

You already know how to raise a positive number to a power. Here are two examples.

$$\text{Examples:} \quad 4^2 = 4 \cdot 4 = 16$$
$$5^3 = 5 \cdot 5 \cdot 5 = 125$$

POWERS AND ORDER OF OPERATIONS

When evaluating an expression that has a *negative* sign and a power, evaluate the power first unless parentheses indicate otherwise.

Examples: $-3^2 = -(3^2) = -9$
$(-3)^2 = (-3) \cdot (-3) = 9$

Example 1 > Using Order of Operations

a. $(-4)^2 = (-4) \cdot (-4)$ Square -4.
      $= 16$ Product of two negatives.

b. $-4^2 = -(4^2)$ Evaluate power first.
      $= -16$ Square 4.

c. $4(-2)^3 = 4 \cdot (-2) \cdot (-2) \cdot (-2)$ Cube -2.
      $= -32$ Answer is negative.

d. $4 - 2^3 = 4 - (2 \cdot 2 \cdot 2)$ Cube 2.
      $= 4 - 8$ Multiply.
      $= -4$ Subtract.

LESSON INVESTIGATION

COOPERATIVE LEARNING

Investigating Powers of Negative One

GROUP ACTIVITY Evaluate the expressions and describe the pattern in the list.

$$(-1)^1, (-1)^2, (-1)^3, (-1)^4, (-1)^5, (-1)^6$$

Use any patterns you see above to evaluate the following.

1. $(-1)^{51}$ **2.** $(-1)^{208}$ **3.** $(-1)^{533}$

Example 2 **Graphing in a Coordinate Plane**

STRATEGY **DRAW A DIAGRAM** Use integer x-values from -3 to 3 to draw a scatter plot for the equation $y = x^2$. Describe any patterns that you see.

Solution

Substitute the x-values to find the corresponding y-values.

Value of x	Substitute.	Value of y
-3	$y = (-3)^2$	9
-2	$y = (-2)^2$	4
-1	$y = (-1)^2$	1
0	$y = 0^2$	0
1	$y = 1^2$	1
2	$y = 2^2$	4
3	$y = 3^2$	9

You can summarize this information in a table of values. Write the x-values and y-values in the table as a collection of ordered pairs of the form (x, y).

x	y		
-3	9	$\rightarrow$	$(-3, 9)$
-2	4	$\rightarrow$	$(-2, 4)$
-1	1	$\rightarrow$	$(-1, 1)$
0	0	$\rightarrow$	$(0, 0)$
1	1	$\rightarrow$	$(1, 1)$
2	4	$\rightarrow$	$(2, 4)$
3	9	$\rightarrow$	$(3, 9)$

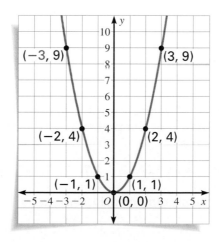

ONGOING ASSESSMENT

Talk About It
· · · · · · · · · · · · · · · · · · ·

Draw a scatter plot for the equation. Use integer x-values from -3 to 3. Describe the pattern.

1. $y = x^2 + 1$

2. $y = x^2 - 1$

Finally, plot the points as shown. If you connect the points, you will see that they lie in a U-shaped pattern, with a vertex at $(0, 0)$.

GUIDED PRACTICE

In Exercises 1 and 2, write the expression as a power. Then evaluate the expression.

1. $(-3) \cdot (-3) \cdot (-3) \cdot (-3)$

2. $(-2)(-2)(-2)(-2)(-2)$

3. **WRITING** Write a statement about the sign of a negative integer raised to an odd power and to an even power.

In Exercises 4–7, match the expression with its value.

   A. 8   B. −16   C. −10   D. 16

4. $(-4)^2$ **5.** -2^4 **6.** $-1^3 - (-3)^2$ **7.** $(-3)^2 + (-1)^3$

8. **LOOKING FOR A PATTERN** Copy and complete the table of values for $y = x^3$. Then plot the points in a coordinate plane and describe any patterns you see.

x	−3	−2	−1	0	1	2	3
y	?	?	?	?	?	?	?

9. **PARTNER ACTIVITY** Without showing your partner, write an equation of the form $y = \boxed{?}\, x^2$. Your partner should give you a value for x ($x \neq 1$), and then you give your partner the corresponding value for y. Repeat this until your partner guesses the correct equation.

PRACTICE AND PROBLEM SOLVING

In Exercises 10–18, evaluate the expression.

10. $(-9)^2$ **11.** -8^2 **12.** $-(-2^3)$

13. $4 \cdot (-2)^4$ **14.** $-(-4)^3 + 6$ **15.** $-2^5 + (-3)^3$

16. $(-7)^2 - 5^2$ **17.** $(-3)^2 - (-1^6)$ **18.** $7^2 - (-4)^2$

In Exercises 19–22, make a table of values for the equation. Use x-values of −3, −2, −1, 0, 1, 2, and 3. Then plot the points in a coordinate plane and describe any patterns you see.

19. $y = x^2 - 4$ **20.** $y = 2 \cdot x^2$ **21.** $y = -x^2$ **22.** $y = 3 - x^2$

In Exercises 23–31, complete the statement using >, <, or =.

23. $(-1)^6 \; \boxed{?} \; (-1)^8$ **24.** $(-1)^5 \; \boxed{?} \; (-1)^4$ **25.** $(-2)^6 \; \boxed{?} \; (-4)^3$

26. $-3^4 \; \boxed{?} \; -9^2$ **27.** $-6^2 \; \boxed{?} \; (-6)^2$ **28.** $-2^5 \; \boxed{?} \; -2^6$

29. $-4^3 \; \boxed{?} \; (-4)^3$ **30.** $2^3 \; \boxed{?} \; (-2)^4$ **31.** $(-3)^2 \; \boxed{?} \; 3^2$

In Exercises 32 and 33, plot the points in a coordinate plane and describe any patterns that you see.

32.

x	−3	−2	−1	0	1	2	3
y	10	5	2	1	2	5	10

33.

x	−3	−2	−1	0	1	2	3
y	7	2	−1	−2	−1	2	7

 TECHNOLOGY In Exercises 34–36, use a calculator to evaluate the expression.

34. $-2(-5)^5$ **35.** $-6^5 + (-7)^4$ **36.** $(-12)^3 - 3^7$

In Exercises 37–40, tell whether the equation is *true* or *false*. If it is false, copy the equation and insert parentheses to make it true.

37. $-4^2 + 5^2 = 9$ **38.** $-2^3 - (-3^2) = -17$

39. $-1^6 + (-2)^4 = 17$ **40.** $4^3 - (-7^2) = 113$

41. HOT AIR BALLOONS Suppose you are riding in a hot air balloon 1024 ft above the ground. You drop an object. The height of the object above the ground can be found using the equation $d = 1024 - 16t^2$ where d is the distance in feet and t is the time in seconds. Find the height of the object above the ground when the object has fallen the given amount of time.

a. 2 s   **b.** 5 s   **c.** 8 s

STANDARDIZED TEST PRACTICE

42. Identify the rule for the following pattern.

$$-2, 4, -8, 16, -32, \ldots$$

  A -2^x where $x = 1, 2, 3, 4, 5, \ldots$ **B** $-2x$ where $x = 1, 2, 3, 4, 5, \ldots$

  C $(-x)^2$ where $x = 1, 2, 3, 4, 5, \ldots$ **D** $(-2)^x$ where $x = 1, 2, 3, 4, 5, \ldots$

43. $-4^2 - (-3)^2 =$

  A 25   **B** 7   **C** −7   **D** −25

EXPLORATION AND EXTENSION

SQUARE ROOTS In Exercises 44–47, find both square roots of the number. For example, 3 and −3 are square roots of 9 because $3^2 = 9$ and $(-3)^2 = 9$.

44. 1   **45.** 49   **46.** 169   **47.** 225

In Exercises 1–3, solve the proportion. (6.3, 6.4)

1. $\dfrac{15}{x} = \dfrac{3}{4}$

2. $\dfrac{6}{9} = \dfrac{14}{b}$

3. $\dfrac{m}{12} = \dfrac{4}{16}$

TECHNOLOGY Use a calculator to find the positive square root of the number. (8.7)

4. $\sqrt{49}$

5. $\sqrt{136}$

6. $\sqrt{10.89}$

7. $\sqrt{27.04}$

BAGEL SALES Use the graphic at the right for Exercises 8–10. It shows the sales of 5 different types of bagels sold at a restaurant in a day. (7.5)

8. There are 108° in the "Onion" section of the graph. What percent of the bagels sold was onion?

9. Plain bagels accounted for 22% of the sales. How many degrees should this section of the graph contain?

10. 336 bagels, or 48%, were sesame, poppy seed, or pumpernickel. How many bagels were sold?

CAREER Interview

VOLCANOLOGIST

Christina Neal, a geologist at the Alaska Volcano Observatory, studies volcanoes to understand the role they play in shaping our planet and to assess the risk of future eruptions.

Christina Neal (L) and Ed Wolfe (R) measure the temperature of lava flow. The lava shown here at the Kilauea Volcano in Hawaii is about 2100°F.

Q What led you to this career?
I've always been interested in the outdoors and how the earth works. Volcanoes are fascinating for what they tell us about our planet and because of the important impacts they have on peoples' lives.

Q How does math help you on your job?
Arithmetic and geometry are essential for getting information about eruptions. For example, I calculate the volume of material ejected from a volcano by measuring the area over which debris has been deposited and multiplying that by the average thickness.

Q What can you tell students about the importance of math?
A lot of science is about measuring observable phenomena and trying to quantify them. You need mathematical skills to do that. More generally, there are a limitless number of wonderful things to do. You should dream big, follow your heart, and pursue a career that you really care about.

The Power of Ten

In a decimal number, you know that the place value of each digit to the left of the tens place can be written as a power of ten. By looking for a pattern, the place values of the other digits can also be written as powers of ten.

Study the chart below. What patterns do you see?

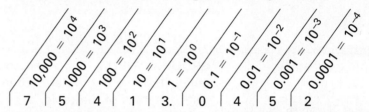

$10{,}000 = 10^4$	$1000 = 10^3$	$100 = 10^2$	$10 = 10^1$	$1 = 10^0$	$0.1 = 10^{-1}$	$0.01 = 10^{-2}$	$0.001 = 10^{-3}$	$0.0001 = 10^{-4}$
7	5	4	1	3.	0	4	5	2

Scientific calculators use powers of 10 to display numbers with more than eight or ten digits.

Example

Use a scientific calculator to multiply the numbers.

a. $2{,}500{,}000 \times 2{,}500{,}000$ **b.** 0.000052×0.00037

Solution

a. 2,500,000 ⊠ 2,500,000 ▣ [6.25 E12]

The display "6.25 E12" means 6.25×10^{12}, which is 6,250,000,000,000. This number is read as "6 trillion 250 billion."

b. 0.000052 ⊠ 0.00037 ▣ [1.924 E-8]

The display "1.924 E−8" means 1.924×10^{-8}, which is 0.00000001924.

Exercises

In Exercises 1 and 2, write the number represented by the calculator display.

1. [5.87 E7]   **2.** [2.01 E-5]

In Exercises 3–8, use a calculator. Write your answer using exponents.

3. $3{,}300{,}000 \times 550{,}000$ **4.** 0.000098×0.0025

5. 0.00033×0.0001 **6.** $1{,}255{,}000{,}000 \div 0.00005$

7. $98{,}800{,}000 \div 0.001$ **8.** $0.0000006 \div 240{,}000{,}000$

Scientific Notation

What you should learn:

Goal 1 How to evaluate powers of ten

Goal 2 How to write numbers in scientific notation

Why you should learn it:

You can use scientific notation as a convenient way to represent very large or very small numbers, such as the size of a human red blood cell.

Goal 1 USING POWERS OF TEN

In Lesson 10.7, you learned how to evaluate a power with a negative base. In the following investigation, you will see how to evaluate a power of ten with a negative *exponent*.

LESSON INVESTIGATION

COOPERATIVE LEARNING

Investigating Negative and Zero Exponents

GROUP ACTIVITY Copy and complete the first three rows of the table. Describe the pattern. Then use the pattern to complete the last four rows of the table.

$10^3 =$	1	0	0	0	.	0	0	0
$10^2 =$					.			
$10^1 =$					.			
$10^0 =$					.			
$10^{-1} =$					.			
$10^{-2} =$					.			
$10^{-3} =$					.			

In this investigation, you may have discovered the following rule for zero and negative exponents.

NEGATIVE AND ZERO EXPONENTS

Let n be a positive integer.

$$10^{-n} = \frac{1}{10^n} \text{ and } 10^0 = 1$$

Example 1 **Evaluating Powers of Ten**

a. $10^{-3} = \dfrac{1}{10^3}$ Use the rule for negative exponents.

     $= \dfrac{1}{1000}$ Evaluate the power.

     $= 0.001$ Change the fraction to a decimal.

b. $10^0 = 1$ Use the rule for zero exponent.

Goal 2 USING SCIENTIFIC NOTATION

Many numbers in real life are very large or very small. For example, a human red blood cell is about 0.000002 meters thick. A convenient way to represent this number is 2×10^{-6}.

CONNECTION
Science

$$0.000002 = \frac{2}{1,000,000} \qquad \text{Write as fraction.}$$

$$= 2 \times \frac{1}{1,000,000} \qquad \text{Write as product.}$$

$$= 2 \times 10^{-6} \qquad \text{Write fraction as a power of 10.}$$

This form is called *scientific notation*.

SCIENTIFIC NOTATION

A number is written in **scientific notation** if it has the form $c \times 10^{n}$, where c is greater than or equal to 1 and less than 10.

Notice that the exponent of 10 is the number of places the decimal point is moved. The sign of the exponent depends on whether the number is greater than or less than 1.

Decimal Form	Scientific Notation
57,000.0	5.7×10^{4}
4 places	positive exponent of **4**
0.000032	3.2×10^{-5}
5 places	negative exponent of **5**

Example 2 — Scientific Notation

Decimal Form	Product Form	Scientific Notation
a. 2500	2.5×1000	2.5×10^{3}
b. 650,000	$6.5 \times 100,000$	6.5×10^{5}
c. 0.048	$4.8 \times \dfrac{1}{100}$	4.8×10^{-2}
d. 0.000967	$9.67 \times \dfrac{1}{10,000}$	9.67×10^{-4}

ONGOING ASSESSMENT

Talk About It

Decide which of the numbers is larger. Explain your reasoning.

1. 9×10^{8} or 8×10^{9}

2. 5×10^{-6} or 5×10^{-7}

3. 4×10^{-3} or 3×10^{-4}

10.8 Exercises

GUIDED PRACTICE

In Exercises 1–3, match the power of ten with the number.

A. 1   B. $\frac{1}{10}$ C. $\frac{1}{100}$

1. 10^{-2} 2. 10^{0} 3. 10^{-1}

4. Decide whether the number is written in scientific notation. If it is not, explain why not.

     a. 21.4×3^{4} b. 0.35×10^{2} c. 1.04×10^{-3}

In Exercises 5–7, write the number in scientific notation.

5. 5280 feet in a mile

6. 3600 seconds in an hour

7. $\frac{1}{1000}$ meters in a millimeter

PRACTICE AND PROBLEM SOLVING

In Exercises 8–11, write the power of ten as a whole number or as a fraction.

8. 10^{5} 9. 10^{10} 10. 10^{-6} 11. 10^{-12}

In Exercises 12–17, write the number in scientific notation.

12. 540,000   13. 12,050,000   14. 0.062

15. 0.00035   16. 145,000,000,000   17. 0.000000667

NATURE In Exercises 18–21, write the number in scientific notation.

18. The bee hummingbird is the smallest bird. It weighs about 0.0014 kg.

19. The smallest cells are 0.0005 cm in diameter.

20. The largest known stars have a diameter of 1,600,000,000 km.

21. About 16,000,000 thunderstorms occur throughout the world each year.

Tech Link

Investigation 10, Interactive Real-Life Investigations

ERROR ANALYSIS In Exercises 22 and 23, the number is incorrectly written in scientific notation. Explain the error. Then rewrite the number correctly in scientific notation.

22. $134{,}500 = 13.45 \times 10^4$ ✗

23. $0.000056 = 5.6 \times 10^5$ ✗

In Exercises 24–29, complete the statement using $>$ or $<$.

24. 5.25×10^{-1} ? 5.25×10^1

25. 4.3×10^3 ? $430{,}000$

26. 9.8×10^1 ? 9.8

27. 3.9×10^3 ? 3.0×10^4

28. 0.00076 ? 7.6×10^{-5}

29. 1.02×10^{-2} ? 1.2×10^{-3}

USING LOGICAL REASONING In Exercises 30 and 31, choose the correct number. Explain your reasoning.

30. The number of square miles of the Atlantic Ocean is

A. 3.6×10^0.

B. 3.6×10^7.

31. The width in meters of a granule of table salt is

A. 5×10^{-4}.

B. 5×10^4.

STANDARDIZED TEST PRACTICE

32. Write the number 0.000000265 in scientific notation.

    A 2.65×10^{-7} **B** 26.5×10^{-6} **C** 2.65×10^6 **D** 2.65×10^7

33. Which number is the greatest?

    A 9×10^{-15} **B** 5.6×10^0 **C** 8.2×10^9 **D** 1×10^{10}

EXPLORATION AND EXTENSION

PORTFOLIO

34. **BUILDING YOUR PROJECT** The table at the right shows part of what is called the Volcanic Explosivity Index, or VEI. Volcanologists use this scale to determine how "big" an eruption is. The following are data about the volume of lava ejected during an eruption. Use the table to rate the eruptions with an index number.

    A. $3{,}8000{,}000$ m^3 **B.** $53{,}600{,}000{,}000$ m^3

    C. 9000 m^3 **D.** $480{,}000{,}230$ m^3

VEI	Volume of lava
0	$<1 \times 10^4$ m^3
1	$1 \times 10^4 - 1 \times 10^6$ m^3
2	$1 \times 10^6 - 1 \times 10^7$ m^3
3	$1 \times 10^7 - 1 \times 10^8$ m^3
4	$1 \times 10^8 - 1 \times 10^9$ m^3
5	$1 \times 10^9 - 1 \times 10^{10}$ m^3
6	$1 \times 10^{10} - 1 \times 10^{11}$ m^3
7	$1 \times 10^{11} - 1 \times 10^{12}$ m^3
8	$>1 \times 10^{12}$ m^3

WHAT *did you learn?*　　　　　**WHY** *did you learn it?*

Skills		WHAT did you learn?	WHY did you learn it?
Skills	10.1	Find the absolute value of a number.	Compare the accuracy of checkout clerks.
	10.2	Add integers.	Find an average temperature.
	10.3	Subtract integers.	Find the time difference between two cities.
	10.4	Find patterns in a coordinate plane.	Display biological information visually.
	10.5	Multiply integers.	Model the action of a toggle switch.
	10.6	Divide integers.	Find the average bottom elevation of Lake Michigan.
	10.7	Evaluate expressions with powers of integers.	Recognize patterns in a coordinate plane.
	10.8	Write numbers in scientific notation.	Describe very large and very small quantities more easily.
Strategies	10.1–10.8	Use problem solving strategies.	Solve a wide variety of real-life problems.
Using Data	10.1–10.8	Use tables and graphs.	Recognize patterns in equations.

HOW *does it fit in the bigger picture of mathematics?*

In this chapter, you studied three rules for finding the sign of a product and three rules for finding the sign of a quotient. It is helpful to hunt for general principles that allow you to cut down on the number of rules you need to remember. Here are two general principles that combine all six of the product and quotient rules for signs.

1. The product or quotient of two numbers that have the same sign is positive.

2. The product or quotient of two numbers that have different signs is negative.

VOCABULARY

- absolute value (p. 480)
- absolute value signs (p. 480)
- scientific notation (p. 517)

10.1 ABSOLUTE VALUE OF A NUMBER

The absolute value of a number is its distance from 0 on a number line. Opposites have the same absolute value.

Example $|-2.6| = 2.6$

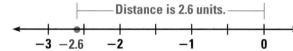
Distance is 2.6 units.

$-3 \quad -2.6 \quad -2 \quad -1 \quad 0$

In Exercises 1–3, find the absolute value.

1. $|75|$
2. $|-4.7|$
3. $|0|$

4. **BUSINESS** The table at the right shows the income and expenses for a toy company for six months. During which months did the income and expenses differ by more than \$150? Write a statement about the success of the company during the six months.

Month	Expenses	Income
January	\$500	\$375
February	\$455	\$310
March	\$480	\$640
April	\$425	\$580
May	\$670	\$750
June	\$510	\$720

10.2 ADDITION OF INTEGERS

The rules for adding integers are on page 484.

Examples
$-13 + (-9) = -22$ $2 + (-6) = -4$
$-11 + 11 = 0$ $-5 + 12 = 7$

In Exercises 5–8, find the sum.

5. $15 + (-2)$
6. $-6 + (-8)$
7. $7 + (-7)$
8. $-17 + 3$

10.3 SUBTRACTION OF INTEGERS

To subtract an integer, add its opposite.

Examples
$0 - (-9) = 0 + 9$ $-4 - 16 = -4 + (-16)$
$= 9$ $= -20$

In Exercises 9–12, find the difference.

9. $-19 - (-15)$
10. $-12 - 16$
11. $8 - (-11)$
12. $5 - 10$

10.4 PATTERNS IN A COORDINATE PLANE

To draw a scatter plot, first make a table of values. Then write the
x- and y-values in the table as a collection of ordered pairs of the
form (x, y). Plot the points. From the scatter plot, you can
determine a pattern for the points.

Example Use integer values from -3 to 3 to draw a scatter plot for $y = 4 - x$.

x	y
−3	7
−2	6
−1	5
0	4
1	3
2	2
3	1

⟶ $(-3, 7)$
⟶ $(-2, 6)$
⟶ $(-1, 5)$
⟶ $(0, 4)$
⟶ $(1, 3)$
⟶ $(2, 2)$
⟶ $(3, 1)$

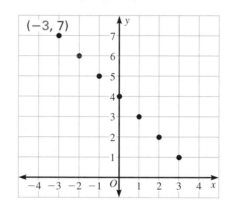

13. Copy and complete the table of values for the expression
$y = -2 + x$. Then plot the points and describe any patterns you see.

x	−3	−2	−1	0	1	2	3
y	?	?	?	?	?	?	?

**In Exercises 14–17, use integer values from -3 to 3 to draw a scatter
plot for the equation.**

14. $y = -x + 2$ **15.** $y = x - 1$ **16.** $y = |x| - 3$ **17.** $y = |x| + 4$

10.5 MULTIPLICATION OF INTEGERS

To multiply two numbers, multiply their absolute values. If the
numbers have the same sign, the product is positive. If the
numbers have different signs, the product is negative.

Examples **a.** $-4 \times (-6) = 24$ **b.** $-3 \times 5 = -15$

In Exercises 18–23, find the product.

18. $-8 \times (-9)$ **19.** -7×5 **20.** $3 \times (-1)$

21. $-9 \times (-6)$ **22.** $-14 \times (-3)$ **23.** -4×11

24. The temperature today is $-3°F$. The forecast says that the
temperature tomorrow is supposed to be four times colder. What
will the temperature be tomorrow?

10.6 DIVISION OF INTEGERS

To divide two numbers, divide their absolute values. If the numbers have the same sign, the quotient is positive. If the numbers have different signs, the quotient is negative.

Examples $\dfrac{-55}{-11} = 5$ $-14 \div 2 = -7$

In Exercises 25–28, find the quotient.

25. $-48 \div -8$ **26.** $\dfrac{-35}{7}$ **27.** $\dfrac{100}{-20}$ **28.** $-60 \div -4$

29. Find the average depth of the five Great Lakes.

Lake	Lake Superior	Lake Michigan	Lake Huron	Lake Erie	Lake Ontario
Depth (feet)	-1330	-923	-750	-210	-810

10.7 INTEGERS AND EXPONENTS

When evaluating an expression that has a negative sign and a power, evaluate the power first, unless parentheses indicate otherwise.

Examples   **a.** $-5^3 = -125$
   b. $(-3)^4 = (-3) \cdot (-3) \cdot (-3) \cdot (-3) = 81$

In Exercises 30–32, evaluate the expression.

30. $-9 - (-3)^2$ **31.** $-2^4 - 2^2$ **32.** $(-5)^3 - 10^2$

10.8 SCIENTIFIC NOTATION

Let n be a positive integer. Then $10^{-n} = \dfrac{1}{10^n}$ and $10^0 = 1$.

Example $10^{-4} = \dfrac{1}{10^4} = \dfrac{1}{10,000} = 0.0001$

A number is written in scientific notation if it has the form $c \times 10^n$ where c is greater than or equal to 1 and less than 10.

Examples $14,230,000 = 1.423 \times 10^7$ $0.000045 = 4.5 \times 10^{-5}$

In Exercises 33–38, write each number in scientific notation.

33. 34,000   **34.** 0.0061   **35.** 0.0000072

36. 570,000,000   **37.** 1000   **38.** 0.0000000008

In Questions 1 and 2, is the statement *true* or *false*? If it is false, explain why.

1. The absolute value of a negative number is negative.

2. Zero is its own opposite.

In Questions 3–11, add, subtract, multiply, or divide.

3. $4 + (-9)$

4. $-3 - 7$

5. $-17 - (-8)$

6. $-19 + 28$

7. $6 + (-6)$

8. $7 \cdot (-7)$

9. $(-3)(-12)$

10. $-72 \div (-8)$

11. $-84 \div 12$

In Questions 12–14, find the value of the expression.

12. $\left| -47 \right|$

13. $(-2)^8$

14. -3^4

In Questions 15–17, complete the statement using $>$, $<$, or $=$.

15. $\left| -2 \right|$ **?** 2

16. $-2 \cdot (-3)$ **?** $2 \cdot 3$

17. $\left| 3 - 2 \right|$ **?** $\left| 4 - 7 \right|$

In Questions 18 and 19, copy and complete the table of values. Then plot the points in a coordinate plane and describe any patterns you see.

18. $y = x + 2$

x	−3	−2	−1	0	1	2	3
y	?	?	?	?	?	?	?

19. $y = \left| x - 1 \right|$

x	−3	−2	−1	0	1	2	3
y	?	?	?	?	?	?	?

In Questions 20 and 21, write the number in scientific notation.

20. A white piano key is 0.022 m wide.

21. Volcanoes on Io, a satellite of Jupiter, are about 600,000,000 mi from Earth.

EMPLOYMENT In Questions 22–25, you are offered a job that pays $1 for the first week. Each succeeding week, your pay is doubled.

22. Make a table showing your wages for the first six weeks.

23. Plot the data in a coordinate plane.

24. If you save all of your earnings, when can you buy a $149 bicycle?

25. If you keep the job for 21 weeks, will you have earned a million dollars? Explain your reasoning.

1. Which statement is *false*?

   (A) The absolute value of 2 is 2.

   (B) The opposite of 0 is 0.

   (C) The absolute value of 7 is -7.

   (D) The opposite of -5 is 5.

2. Which expression equals -3?

   (A) $9 + (-6)$ **(B)** $-9 + 6$

   (C) $-6 + 9$ **(D)** $-6 + (-9)$

3. You are participating in a miniature golf tournament. Your score after the 17th hole is -3 (3 under par). On the 18th hole, you score 2 under par. What is your final score?

   (A) -6 **(B)** -5

   (C) -1 **(D)** 1

4. Evaluate the expression $-3 - y$ when $y = -4$.

   (A) -7 **(B)** -1

   (C) 1   **(D)** 7

5. At the beginning of the month, you deposit $100 into your checking account. You withdraw $30 during week 1, $25 during week 2, $50 during week 3, and $20 during week 4. Which statement is *false*?

   (A) You withdrew more than you deposited this month.

   (B) You withdrew $75 this month.

   (C) You withdrew more in the last two weeks than you did in the first two weeks.

   (D) In the first two weeks you withdrew $55.

6. $-5 \cdot (-8) =$

   (A) -40 **(B)** -13

   (C) -3 **(D)** 40

7. Which equation is represented by the scatter plot?

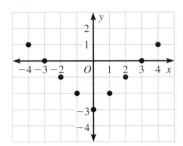

   (A) $y = |x| - 3$

   (B) $y = |x - 3|$

   (C) $y = 3 - |x|$

   (D) $y = |x| + 3$

8. What is the average of the numbers 9, -14, -10, 3, -2, and -16?

   (A) -9 **(B)** -6

   (C) -5 **(D)** 5

9. $-2^4 - (-2)^3 =$

   (A) -24 **(B)** -8

   (C) 8   **(D)** 24

10. Which expression represents the number 0.00145 written in scientific notation?

   (A) 1.45×10^{-3}

   (B) 14.5×10^{-4}

   (C) 1.45×10^{3}

   (D) 1.45×10^{4}

Probability and Discrete Mathematics

TECHNOLOGY

Technology resources accompanying this chapter:

• Interactive Real-Life Investigations

• Middle School Tutorial Software

GRAND CANYON NATIONAL PARK This park in Arizona, along the Colorado River, is an impressive example of erosion.

CHAPTER THEME
Traveling

CARLSBAD CAVERNS NATIONAL PARK
This park in New Mexico contains the nation's deepest limestone cave. It is 1597 feet deep.

BIG BEND NATIONAL PARK
This park in Texas, located on a bend of the Rio Grande, features desert, mountain, and valley terrains.

YELLOWSTONE NATIONAL PARK
The nation's first national park is where Wyoming, Idaho, and Montana meet.

A Summer Trip

REAL LIFE
Traveling

Suppose you are a travel agent, and you are planning a group tour to Grand Canyon National Park in August. You need to plan **activities** for the group members while they are there. You know that the average number of rainy days at the Grand Canyon in August is 5.

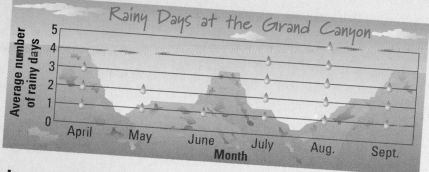

Rainy Days at the Grand Canyon

Think and Discuss

1. Do you think you would plan mostly indoor activities or outdoor activities? Explain.

2. What is the probability that it will rain on August 15?

PORTFOLIO

CHAPTER PROJECT

Planning a Tour of National Parks

PROJECT DESCRIPTION

There are more than 350 sites in the National Park System of the United States. These sites were chosen for their natural beauty, their historical significance, or for the outdoor recreation they provide. Imagine you are planning a trip for a large group to four national parks. The trip will include the activities mentioned in the **TOPICS** listed on the next page.

GETTING STARTED

Talking It Over

- Have you ever been to a national park?

- How many national parks can you name?

- For what reasons do you think these sites were chosen to be part of the National Park System?

- Why do you think it was necessary for some areas in the United States to be designated as national parks?

Planning Your Project

- **Materials Needed:** paper, pencils or pens

- Label a piece of paper with the heading "Itinerary." Make a schedule for the number of days your group will spend in each of the four parks mentioned in the **BUILDING YOUR PROJECT** list on the next page. Use your school's library or some other reference to find information about each of the parks. Add what you have learned to your itinerary.

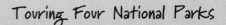

Touring Four National Parks

MT

ID

Yellowstone

WY

Grand Canyon

AZ

NM

Carlsbad Caverns

Big Bend

TX

BUILDING YOUR PROJECT

These are places throughout the chapter where you will work on your project.

TOPICS

11.1 Choose a tour at Carlsbad Caverns. *p. 533*

11.2 Plan the day at Big Bend National Park. *p. 539*

11.3 Arrange seating in a rafting trip. *p. 547*

11.4 Choose walking tours at Yellowstone National Park. *p. 552*

11.7 Choose an activity at the Grand Canyon. *p. 569*

I N T E R N E T

To find out about planning a tour of national parks, go to:

http://www.mlmath.com

11.1 Grouping Equally Likely Outcomes

What you should learn:

Goal 1 How to group equally likely outcomes

Goal 2 How to use probability to solve real-life problems

Why you should learn it:

Knowing how to group equally likely outcomes can help you make predictions. An example is finding the probability that a four o'clock flower will have a pink color.

Goal 1 GROUPING EQUALLY LIKELY OUTCOMES

In Lesson 5.7, you learned that the probability of an event is

$$\text{Probability} = \frac{\text{Number of favorable outcomes}}{\text{Total number of outcomes}}.$$

LESSON INVESTIGATION

Investigating Probability

GROUP ACTIVITY Toss 3 coins and count how many land heads up. Record each toss as 0, 1, 2, or 3 heads up. Toss the coins 30 times. Use the results to estimate the probability that exactly 2 coins will land heads up when 3 coins are tossed.

In this activity, each toss is an experiment that has 8 equally likely outcomes, as shown at the left. Probabilities found by conducting experiments are **experimental probabilities**.

Probabilities found by counting and classifying all possible outcomes are called **theoretical probabilities**.

Example 1 Grouping Equally Likely Outcomes

Find the probability of each event when 3 coins are tossed.

a. Getting at least 2 heads   **b.** Getting exactly 2 heads

Solution

Group the possible outcomes of tossing 3 coins as follows.

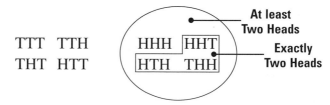

a. The event "At Least Two Heads" can occur in four ways.

$$\text{Probability} = \frac{\textbf{Ways of getting at least 2 heads}}{\textbf{Total number of outcomes}} = \frac{4}{8} = \frac{1}{2}$$

b. The event "Exactly Two Heads" can occur in three ways.

$$\text{Probability} = \frac{\textbf{Ways of getting exactly 2 heads}}{\textbf{Total number of outcomes}} = \frac{3}{8}$$

TTT

TTH

THT

HTT

HHT

HTH

THH

HHH

T = tail showing
H = head showing

Many people like to grow *hybrid* flowers. By using pollen from one plant to pollinate another plant, you can obtain offspring that have characteristics of both parents.

| Example 2 | **Probability of Inheriting Genes** |

REAL LIFE
Genetics

You grow four o'clocks as a hobby. Each plant has flowers that are red, pink, or white.

Color	Red	Pink	White
Symbol for Color Genes	RR	RW or WR	WW

Use the *Punnett square* below to find the probability that an offspring of 2 pink four o'clocks (both with RW color genes) will be pink. Each parent passes along an R or a W gene to its offspring.

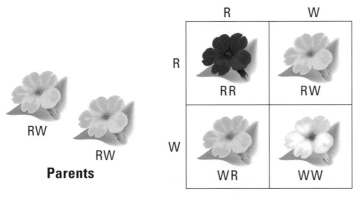

RW

RW

Parents

R   W

R
RR   RW

W
WR   WW

Offspring

Solution

From the Punnett square, you can see that there are 4 outcomes and each is equally likely. Two of the outcomes produce pink flowers. So the probability that an offspring will be pink is as follows.

$$\text{Probability} = \frac{\text{Ways of being pink}}{\text{Total number of outcomes}}$$

$$= \frac{2}{4}$$

$$= \frac{1}{2}$$

An offspring has a probability of $\frac{1}{2}$ of being pink.

Real Life...
Real Facts

Four o'clock flowers are so-named because they open up in the late afternoon (and close again by morning).

ONGOING ASSESSMENT

Write About It
. . . .

Describe the color of the four o'clock parents for the Punnett square and describe the probability of getting different colors of offspring.

1.   **R   R**

R   ??   ??

W   ??   ??

2.   **R   R**

W   ??   ??

W   ??   ??

GUIDED PRACTICE

1. Give an example of an experimental probability.

2. **BASKETBALL** You make an average of 3 out of 5 of your foul shots. What is the probability that you will *not* make a foul shot?

3. **MAKING A LIST** Find all the two-digit numbers that can be created when 2 number cubes are tossed. What is the probability that both digits are odd?

4. **GROUP ACTIVITY** Write the letters of your first name and the first name of another person in your group on separate pieces of paper and put them in a bag. Choose a piece of paper from the bag. Record whether the letter is a *vowel* or a *consonant*. Replace the letter and do this 30 times. Use the result to find the experimental probability of choosing a vowel. Then find the theoretical probability of choosing a vowel.

5. **INTERPRETING A SURVEY** The circle graph shows the results of a survey of what sounds people prefer to hear while on hold when telephoning a business. You randomly select one of the people who was polled. What is the probability that the person prefers music?

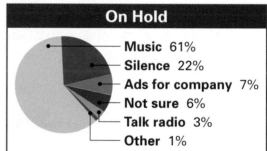

On Hold

Music 61%
Silence 22%
Ads for company 7%
Not sure 6%
Talk radio 3%
Other 1%

PRACTICE AND PROBLEM SOLVING

GENETICS A type of pea plant has genes that can produce two types of seeds: round (RR, Rr, and rR), and wrinkled (rr). In Exercises 6–9, describe the seeds of the pea plant parents and find the probability of getting offspring with each type of seed.

6.
	R	r
R	??	??
r	??	??

7.
	r	r
R	??	??
r	??	??

8.
	r	r
R	??	??
R	??	??

9.
	R	R
R	??	??
r	??	??

10. Copy the spinner and color it so that it has the indicated probabilities.

Red: $\frac{1}{6}$ Yellow: $\frac{1}{12}$ Green: $\frac{5}{12}$ Blue: $\frac{1}{3}$

11. **HORSESHOES** You are playing horseshoes. You throw 60 horseshoes and get 5 ringers. Estimate your probability of getting a ringer.

LANGUAGE CLASSES In Exercises 12–14, use the circle graph. It shows the results of a poll of 3000 Americans who enrolled in foreign language classes. You randomly select one of the people who were polled.

12. What is the probability that the person took French?

13. What is the probability that the person did *not* take Spanish?

14. For which language is the probability of choosing a person enrolled in the foreign language course $\frac{25}{1000}$?

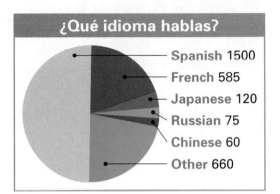

¿Qué idioma hablas?

Spanish 1500
French 585
Japanese 120
Russian 75
Chinese 60
Other 660

STANDARDIZED TEST PRACTICE

15. You and two friends join an adventure club. To determine your partner for the next adventure, you select one of the members' names from a hat. What is the probability you will select one of the two friends who joined with you?

(A) $\frac{2}{24}$ (B) $\frac{1}{24}$ (C) $\frac{2}{23}$ (D) $\frac{1}{23}$

16. You want to buy a bicycle. You can choose between a racing bike, a mountain bike, or a touring bike. Each bike can be green, blue, black, red, or yellow. How many choices are possible?

(A) 8   (B) 15   (C) 16   (D) 24

PORTFOLIO

EXPLORATION AND EXTENSION

17. **BUILDING YOUR PROJECT** There are many different tours a visitor can take at Carlsbad Caverns National Park. Of your tour group of 75 people, 50 want to take the Kings Palace Cave tour, 15 want to take the Slaughter Canyon Cave tour, and 10 want to take the Spider Cave tour.

The Slaughter Canyon Cave tour requires each person to have a flashlight. (The other two tours do not.) You hand a flashlight at random to a member of your tour group. What is the probability that this person will need the flashlight?

LAB 11.2

COOPERATIVE LEARNING

Investigating Tree Diagrams

Part A EXPERIMENTAL PROBABILITY

Materials Needed
- pencils or pens
- paper
- paper bag

Number four pieces of paper 1, 2, 3, and 4 and put them in a bag. Without looking, choose one piece of paper and write its number. Then without replacing the chosen piece of paper, choose another piece of paper and write its number.

1. In your group, discuss which of the following outcomes seems most likely: (A) both numbers are even, (B) both numbers are odd, or (C) one number is even and the other is odd.

2. Perform the experiment 10 times. Then collect the results from three other groups and write the results in a table. Based on the 40 experiments, find the experimental probability of each of the following outcomes.

   a. Both numbers are even.

   b. Both numbers are odd.

   c. One number is even and the other is odd.

Part B THEORETICAL PROBABILITY

3. To find the theoretical probability for each event, you can use a *tree diagram.* Copy the tree diagram and label each outcome as both even, both odd, or one even and one odd. For example, the first outcome "1, 2" would be labeled "one even and one odd."

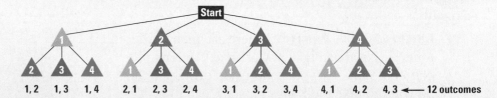

4. Use the result of Exercise 3 to find the theoretical probability of each event. Compare your results with those found in Exercise 2.

   a. Both numbers are even.

   b. Both numbers are odd.

   c. One number is even and the other is odd.

Consider this situation. To go from your home to Washington, D.C., you can travel by airplane, bus, or car. Then to go to Philadelphia, Pennsylvania, you can travel by airplane, bus, train, or car.

5. Copy the tree diagram. Complete the list of outcomes.

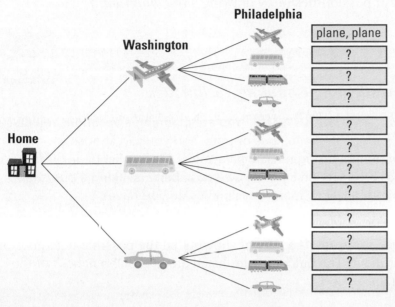

Philadelphia

Washington

Home

| plane, plane |
| ? |
| ? |
| ? |
| ? |
| ? |
| ? |
| ? |
| ? |
| ? |
| ? |
| ? |

6. How many choices do you have for this trip?

7. Suppose that each of the ways you can travel from your home to Philadelphia through Washington, D.C., is equally likely. In your group, discuss a way that you can find the probability that you will not fly on either part of the trip.

NOW TRY THESE

8. WRITING Write a real-life problem that can be modeled by the tree diagram below. Then describe a probability question that could be part of the problem.

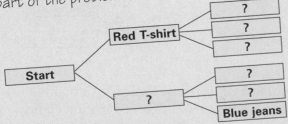

Start

Red T-shirt — ? ? ?

? — ? ? Blue jeans

11.2

Counting Techniques

What you should learn:

Goal 1 How to use a tree diagram to count the number of ways an event can happen

Goal 2 How to use the Counting Principle to count the number of ways an event can happen

Why you should learn it:

Knowing how to count the number of ways something can happen can help you figure out how many vacation choices you have.

Hikers find a water hole along a trail in Grand Canyon National Park.

Goal 1 USING TREE DIAGRAMS

You can count the number of ways something can happen by making a list of possibilities or by drawing a *tree diagram*.

LESSON INVESTIGATION

Investigating Counting Techniques

STRATEGY **MAKE A LIST** You are planning a vacation. You can travel by bus or train, and you can choose a swimming, hiking, or skiing vacation. Make a list of all the possible vacation choices. One possibility is taking a bus, then swimming. How many possibilities do you have?

A **tree diagram** is a way of showing all the possible outcomes of an experiment. The outcomes are listed along the "branches" of the diagram.

Example 1 Using a Tree Diagram

The investigation above describes vacation choices. Use a tree diagram to find the number of possible vacations you can take.

Solution

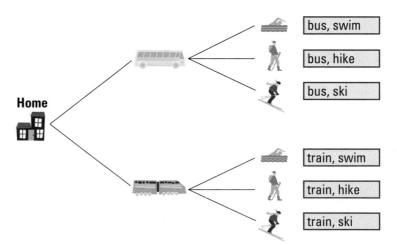

You can count the number of different choices by counting the "branches" on the tree. There are 6 different vacation choices.

Goal 2 COUNTING PRINCIPLE

In Example 1, it is easy to use a list or a tree diagram to count the possible vacation choices. In other cases, the **Counting Principle** can be helpful.

COUNTING PRINCIPLE

One item is to be selected from each of two or more sets. The total number of possible combinations is the product of the number of items in each set.

If you applied the Counting Principle to Example 1, you would obtain

$$\underset{\text{transportation}}{2 \text{ choices for}} \times \underset{\text{for activity}}{3 \text{ choices}} = \underset{\text{vacation choices.}}{6 \text{ possible}}$$

Example 2 Using the Counting Principle

REAL LIFE
Manufacturing

Your company manufactures blue jeans. You make the waist sizes, lengths, and colors shown below. How many different types of jeans does your company make?

Waist Sizes
28, 30, 32, 34, 36, 38, 40, 42

Lengths
28, 29, 30, 31, 32, 33, 34

Colors
Faded
Black
Blue

Solution

You could try making a list of all the different types, but because there are so many, it is easier to use the Counting Principle.

$$\underset{\text{sizes}}{8 \text{ waist}} \times \underset{\text{lengths}}{7} \times \underset{\text{colors}}{3} = \underset{\text{types}}{168}$$

Your company makes 168 types of jeans.

Acid washing is a process used to change the color and texture of fabrics, including denim. The fabric is washed with stones soaked in chlorine acid.

ONGOING ASSESSMENT

Write About It
....

Due to customer demand, you add two more waist sizes to your list of jeans: 33 and 35.

1. How many types of jeans does your company now make?

2. Explain how you solved the problem.

GUIDED PRACTICE

1. In your own words, state the Counting Principle.

2. How many different initials for a set of first and last names are possible? Explain how you found the number.

3. A coin and a number cube are tossed. List the possible results. Then explain how to use a tree diagram and the Counting Principle to find how many results are possible.

4. **PIZZA SHOP** A pizza shop is having a special on one-topping pizzas. You have a choice of thin, medium, or thick crust with pepperoni, sausage, onions, peppers, or mushrooms. Copy and complete the tree diagram at the right to find all the pizzas you can get.

5. **USING A DIAGRAM** In Example 1 on page 536, suppose that you can choose 5-day or 7-day vacations. Now how many vacation choices do you have? Illustrate your answer with a tree diagram.

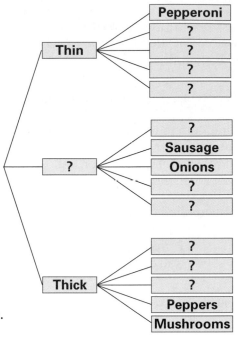

PRACTICE AND PROBLEM SOLVING

6. **WRITING** Copy and complete the tree diagram below. Then write a real-life problem that can be represented by the diagram.

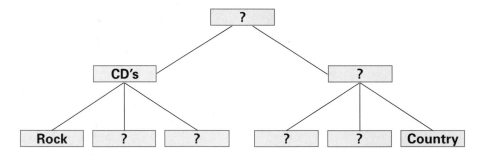

7. **LICENSE PLATES** The third letter and first number of the license plate at the right are missing. What is the probability of guessing the correct license plate? Explain your reasoning.

SNEAKERS In Exercises 8 and 9, use this information. You work for a company that makes sneakers. You make 6 types (aerobic, walking, running, volleyball, soccer, basketball), 2 colors (black, white), 9 men's sizes, and 10 women's sizes.

8. How many different pairs of sneakers does your company manufacture?

9. Due to customer requests, your company adds three more men's and two more women's sizes to its sneaker line. How many different pairs of sneakers does your company now make?

STANDARDIZED TEST PRACTICE

10. At a summer camp, you have the opportunity to canoe, hike, play tennis, or make crafts each morning. In the afternoon, you can swim, play golf, or play soccer. How many different combinations of activities can you pick?

    (A) 4   **(B)** 7   **(C)** 12   **(D)** 24

11. Using the information in Exercise 10, determine how many combinations involve at least one water sport.

    (A) 3   **(B)** 6   **(C)** 7   **(D)** 12

EXPLORATION AND EXTENSION

PORTFOLIO

12. BUILDING YOUR PROJECT During your visit to Big Bend National Park, members of your tour group will be able to select from a variety of activities in the morning, for lunch, and in the afternoon. The table below shows the possible activities scheduled for your group.

Determine how many different combinations of activities are possible for the day.

Morning	Lunch	Afternoon
go birdwatching	go on a picnic	take a nap
go hiking on the Lost Mine Trail	eat at the Chisos Mountain Lodge	browse through a visitor center
go wildlife viewing	drive to Terlingua, outside the park	go for a float trip on the Rio Grande

In Exercises 1–3, use the bar graph at the right. (5.6)

1. Explain why the bar graph is misleading.

2. Redraw the bar graph so that it is not misleading.

3. Make up a survey that the bar graph could represent.

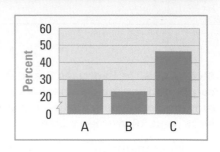

In Exercises 4 and 5, find the missing measures of the similar figures. (6.6)

4.

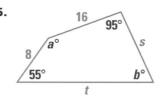
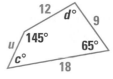

5.

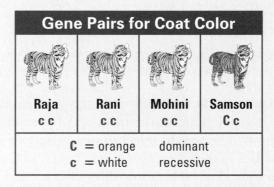

6. **SCIENCE** The total surface area of the Earth is 196,800,000 mi^2. Seventy-one percent of the total surface area is water. How many square miles of water is this? **(7.2)**

7. Write the addition problem representing the phrase "the sum of negative two and negative five." Then find the sum. **(10.2)**

Life Science Connection

GENETICS

A pair of genes determines the color of a tiger's coat. A tiger's mother and father each give one gene to the pair. The gene for an orange coat is dominant, whereas the gene for a white coat is recessive. A tiger's coat is white if both genes in a pair are recessive.

The diagram at the right shows the gene pairs for coat color of four captive tigers.

Gene Pairs for Coat Color			
Raja	Rani	Mohini	Samson
C c	C c	C c	C c

C = orange   dominant
c = white   recessive

In Exercises 1 and 2, use Punnett squares to find the probabilities.

1. Raja is mated with Rani. What is the probability that an offspring will have a white coat? Explain.

2. Mohini is mated with Samson. What is the probability that an offspring will have an orange coat? Explain.

Generating Random Numbers

The program at the left is for the TI-82 programmable calculator. It can be used to randomly choose a digit from 0 to 9 one hundred times.

Example

Using the program, the following data were obtained. Use a line plot to organize the data and describe the results.

0 0 3 4 8 6 4 6 2 4 8 8 0 6 7 0 5 1 5 4 3 0 0 6 4

2 1 8 6 7 6 5 7 2 7 7 5 3 8 7 6 1 7 5 9 0 2 8 1 2

1 9 2 5 0 3 8 3 8 6 3 5 2 4 2 3 4 3 4 8 2 0 3 9 6

4 3 3 9 9 0 8 6 9 1 6 0 6 6 4 6 3 7 4 5 4 5 3 7 4

Solution

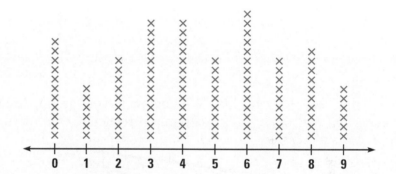

From the line plot above, you can see that each of the digits occurred between 6 and 14 times.

Exercises

1. Here are the results that we obtained when we ran the program a second time. Use a line plot to organize the results.

   4 2 6 0 5 0 1 2 2 5 9 6 4 8 8 0 7 8 2 9 2 8 6 5 2

   7 8 8 7 7 4 6 8 2 3 4 7 3 8 3 3 9 6 8 8 6 1 2 1 4

   2 2 8 6 1 0 5 2 4 7 0 4 9 4 3 5 5 4 3 6 8 0 0 6 6

   5 9 6 9 0 1 8 3 3 5 0 7 2 4 9 5 7 3 6 5 7 8 9 6 2

2. When the calculator selects 100 digits, how many 1's would you expect it to select? Explain your reasoning.

LAB 11.3

COOPERATIVE LEARNING

Investigating Order

Part A ORDERING NUMBERS

Materials Needed
- pencils or pens
- paper

1. Number four pieces of paper 1, 2, 3, and 4. Arrange them in an order and record the result. Then rearrange the pieces in a different order and record the result. For example, two possible orders are shown below. How many different orders are possible? Make a list of the possible orders.

Order: 1-2-3-4

Order: 2-3-1-4

2. With others in your group, discuss how the following tree diagram is related to the ordering problem in Exercise 1.

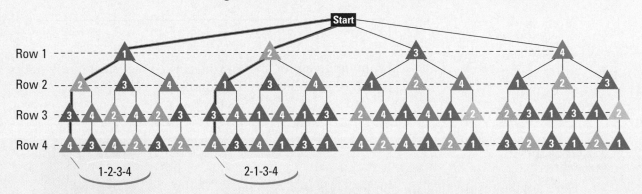

3. In the tree diagram, the number of triangles in each row is as follows. What is the pattern?

Row 1   4

Row 2 $4 \cdot 3 = 12$

Row 3 $4 \cdot 3 \cdot 2 = 24$

Row 4 $4 \cdot 3 \cdot 2 \cdot 1 = 24$

4. a. The tree diagram below shows that there are 6 ways to arrange 3 numbers in order. Use the tree diagram to list the different orders.

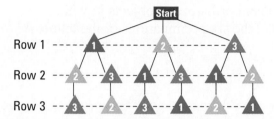

b. Describe the pattern for the number of triangles in each row in the above tree diagram.

5. a. Describe a tree diagram that shows how five numbers can be arranged in order. The first two rows of the tree diagram are shown below. How many rows are in the tree diagram? How many triangles are in each row? Explain your reasoning.

b. In how many ways can five numbers be arranged in order?

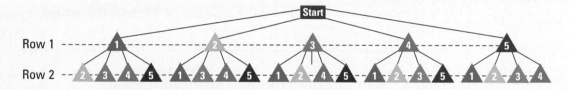

NOW TRY THESE

6. a. Sketch the first two rows of a tree diagram that could represent the number of ways six numbers can be arranged in order.

b. How many rows are in the entire tree diagram? How many triangles are in each row?

c. In how many ways can six numbers be arranged in order?

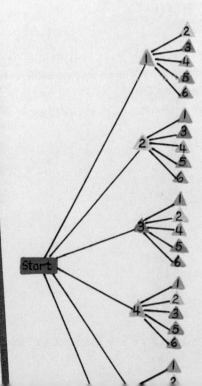

11.3

Permutations and Probability

What you should learn:

Goal 1 How to find the number of permutations of *n* objects

Goal 2 How to use permutations to solve probability problems

Why you should learn it:

Knowing how to count permutations can help you solve real-life problems. An example is analyzing the results of a chimpanzee's learning test.

Goal 1 COUNTING PERMUTATIONS

A **permutation** is an arrangement or listing of objects in which order is important. For example, the six permutations of the letters A, B, and C are shown below.

ABC	BAC	CAB
ACB	BCA	CBA

In Lab 11.3, you may have discovered that the number of permutations of *n* objects can be found by multiplying *n* times all positive integers that are less than *n*. For example, the number of permutations of 3 objects is

$$3 \cdot 2 \cdot 1 = 6.$$

PERMUTATIONS OF *n* OBJECTS

The number of permutations of *n* objects is

$$n \cdot (n - 1) \cdot (n - 2) \cdot \cdots 3 \cdot 2 \cdot 1.$$

This number is represented by the expression *n*!, which is called **n factorial**.

Example 1 Finding the Number of Permutations

Find the number of permutations of the letters A, B, C, and D.

Solution

Because there are 4 letters, the number of permutations is

$$4! = 4 \cdot 3 \cdot 2 \cdot 1 = 24.$$

✔**Check:** You can check this result by listing the permutations.

ABCD	ABDC	ACBD	ACDB
ADBC	ADCB	BACD	BADC
BCAD	BCDA	BDAC	BDCA
CABD	CADB	CBAD	CBDA
CDAB	CDBA	DABC	DACB
DBAC	DBCA	DCAB	DCBA

The 4 letters can be listed in 24 different orders.

NEED TO KNOW

The value of *n* factorial grows quickly as *n* increases. Here are the values of the first five factorials.

$1! = 1$

$2! = 2 \cdot 1 = 2$

$3! = 3 \cdot 2 \cdot 1 = 6$

$4! = 4 \cdot 3 \cdot 2 \cdot 1 = 24$

$5! = 5 \cdot 4 \cdot 3 \cdot 2 \cdot 1 = 120$

In the following investigation, you will test how often you and another person would choose three marbles in the same color order.

COOPERATIVE LEARNING

Investigating Probability

STRATEGY **ACT IT OUT** In each of two bags, place a red marble, a blue marble, and a green marble. Without looking, choose the marbles one at a time from one bag and lay them in order. Your partner should do the same with the marbles in the other bag. Record your results by writing

Same Color Order or *Different Color Order*.

If you try this experiment 24 times, how many times would you expect to choose the same color order? Discuss your reasoning. Then test your conclusion by doing the experiment 24 times.

Real Life...
Real People

Dr. Francine Patterson is a psychologist who has been working with a gorilla named Koko since 1972. Over the years, Patterson has been teaching Koko American Sign Language. Koko now uses more than 500 signs to communicate with researchers.

Example 2 **Finding a Probability**

CONNECTION
Psychology

You are training a chimpanzee to recognize colors. After working with the chimp awhile, you give it 6 colored balls and 6 colored boxes. The chimp puts all 6 balls in the correct boxes. Do you think the chimp knew what it was doing? Use probability to explain your reasoning.

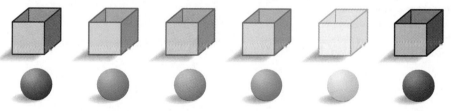

Solution

Altogether, the number of ways the chimp could have put the 6 balls in the 6 boxes is

$$6! = 6 \cdot 5 \cdot 4 \cdot 3 \cdot 2 \cdot 1 = 720.$$

This means that the probability that the chimp got the order right without knowing what it was doing is $\frac{1}{720}$. From this, it seems reasonable to conclude that the chimp *did* know what it was doing.

ONGOING ASSESSMENT

Talk About It

In Example 2, how many ways could the chimp put the balls in the boxes if there are

1. 5 balls and 5 boxes?

2. 7 balls and 7 boxes?

11.3 Exercises

Extra Practice, page 644

GUIDED PRACTICE

In Exercises 1 and 2, decide whether the list shows all permutations of the symbols shown.

1.

2. ![symbols]

BASEBALL In Exercises 3–5, match the description with the correct number of permutations.

A. 24   **B.** 6   **C.** 362,880

3. Number of possible orders in which 4 baseball teams can finish first, second, third, and fourth

4. Number of possible batting orders for 9 baseball players

5. Number of possible orders of three pitches using one fast ball, one curve ball, and one slider

6. **THINKING SKILLS** Describe a real-life situation in which you would need to know the number of permutations.

PRACTICE AND PROBLEM SOLVING

 In Exercises 7–10, use a scientific calculator to evaluate the expression.

7. 5!   **8.** 7!   **9.** 8!   **10.** 10!

In Exercises 11–13, find the number of permutations of the letters in each word. Then list the permutations to check your answer. How many of the permutations are words?

11. NO   **12.** CAT   **13.** STAR

In Exercises 14–16, find how many different numbers you can make using the given digits without repeating any digits.

14. Even digits 2 through 8   **15.** Odd digits 1 through 9   **16.** All digits 1 through 9

17. PROGRESSIVE DINNER You and 3 friends decide to have a progressive dinner. You will eat each course at a different house. The courses are appetizer, salad, main course, and dessert. In how many different ways could the dinner be organized?

18. **TECHNOLOGY** You have just written a 7-page report for social studies. On your way to school, a gust of wind scatters the pages. What is the probability that the papers will be in the correct order when you gather them back up?

CD SHUFFLE In Exercises 19–22, use this information. The shuffle feature on a CD player randomly picks a song to play. Find the probability that songs will be played in order from your most favorite to your least favorite.

19. The CD has 5 songs.

20. The CD has 6 songs.

21. The CD has 7 songs.

22. The CD has 8 songs.

Real Life... Real Facts

CD players can play the songs on a single compact disk (or on multiple compact disks) in a random order.

STANDARDIZED TEST PRACTICE

23. You are knitting an afghan that will have 6 stripes of different colors. In how many different ways can the stripes be ordered?

   A 6   **B** 36   **C** 360   **D** 720

24. The seats on an airplane are labeled by row number and one of the letters A, B, D, E, or F. You and 4 friends have tickets for Row 10. When you board the plane, all of you randomly sit in a seat in Row 10. What is the probability that you each sat in the seat that was listed on your ticket?

   A $\frac{1}{2}$ **B** $\frac{1}{120}$ **C** $\frac{4}{5}$ **D** $\frac{1}{24}$

EXPLORATION AND EXTENSION

PORTFOLIO

25. BUILDING YOUR PROJECT Mai, Pablo, and Ben have chosen to go on a float trip on the Colorado River. When they get to the river, there is one open seat in each of three rafts.

What is the probability that Mai will sit in the first raft, Pablo will sit in the second raft, and Ben will sit in the third raft?

11.4 Combinations and Probability

What you should learn:

Goal 1 How to list and count the number of combinations

Goal 2 How to use combinations to solve probability problems

Why you should learn it:

Knowing how to count combinations can help you make predictions. An example is finding the probability that you will be selected to go rafting in the same raft as your cousins.

River rafts come in different sizes and carry various numbers of passengers.

Goal 1 COUNTING COMBINATIONS

A **combination** of a set of objects is a collection of them in which order is not important. For example, the combinations of two letters taken from A, B, C, and D are

$$\{A, B\}, \{A, C\}, \{A, D\}, \{B, C\}, \{B, D\}, \{C, D\}.$$

The combination {A, B} is the same as {B, A}.

Example 1 Listing and Counting Combinations

There are 6 people in your group tour who want to go rafting. You decide to take 2 rafts, with 3 people in each raft. How many different groups of three can go in Raft 1?

Solution

Represent the people as A, B, C, D, E, and F. Organize the groups in a table. There are 20 possible rafting groups.

	A	B	C	D	E	F	Combination
1	×	×	×				{A, B, C}
2	×	×		×			{A, B, D}
3	×	×			×		{A, B, E}
4	×	×				×	{A, B, F}
5	×		×	×			{A, C, D}
6	×		×		×		{A, C, E}
7	×		×			×	{A, C, F}
8	×			×	×		{A, D, E}
9	×			×		×	{A, D, F}
10	×				×	×	{A, E, F}
11		×	×	×			{B, C, D}
12		×	×		×		{B, C, E}
13		×	×			×	{B, C, F}
14		×		×	×		{B, D, E}
15		×		×		×	{B, D, F}
16		×			×	×	{B, E, F}
17			×	×	×		{C, D, E}
18			×	×		×	{C, D, F}
19			×		×	×	{C, E, F}
20				×	×	×	{D, E, F}

Example 2 Finding a Probability

REAL LIFE
Groups

To select the rafting group, each of the 6 people chooses a letter. The letters are put in a bag and 3 letters are drawn. You (A) and your 2 cousins (B, C) want to be in Raft 1 because it will be first in the river. Find the probability of each of the following.

a. All 3 of you are selected for Raft 1.

b. You are selected for Raft 1.

c. You are selected for Raft 1 and your cousins are not.

d. Your cousins are both selected for Raft 1 and you are not.

Solution

From Example 1, you know that there are 20 different groups. Count the number of groups that satisfy the condition, and divide by 20.

	Groups	Number of groups	Probability
a.	{A, B, C}	1	$\frac{1}{20}$
b.	{A, B, C}, {A, B, D}, {A, B, E}, {A, B, F}, {A, C, D}, {A, C, E}, {A, C, F}, {A, D, E}, {A, D, F}, {A, E, F}	10	$\frac{10}{20} = \frac{1}{2}$
c.	{A, D, E}, {A, D, F}, {A, E, F}	3	$\frac{3}{20}$
d.	{B, C, D}, {B, C, E}, {B, C, F}	3	$\frac{3}{20}$

ONGOING ASSESSMENT

Write About It

Show your work and explain your steps.

1. What is the probability that you and one (but not both) of your cousins are selected?

2. What is the probability that exactly 2 of the 3 of you are selected?

GUIDED PRACTICE

1. **NAUTICAL FLAGS** Before ship crews used radios for communication purposes, they used a complicated system of flag design and codes. Six nautical flags are shown at the right. Some of the ways you can choose 2 nautical flags from the 6 are shown below. What are the other ways?

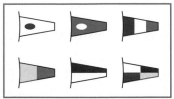

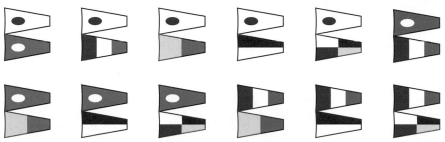

In Exercises 2 and 3, is the description a *permutation* or a *combination*? Explain.

2. How many ways can you select 5 pieces of fruit from a basket containing 7 different kinds?

3. How many ways can you arrange place cards for 11 guests of honor seated along one side of a banquet table?

PRACTICE AND PROBLEM SOLVING

In Exercises 4–6, make a table like the one in Example 1 on page 548 to count the number of combinations.

4. Choose 2 people from 4.   5. Choose 3 people from 5.   6. Choose 4 people from 6.

In Exercises 7–10, list the different combinations of digits that you can have using the digits 1 through 6.

7. 2 odd digits   8. 3 even digits

9. Any 4 digits   10. Any 5 digits

READING A MENU In Exercises 11–13, find the number of combinations.

11. 2 appetizers

12. 3 main courses

13. 2 desserts

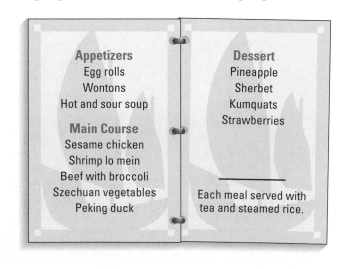

Appetizers
Egg rolls
Wontons
Hot and sour soup

Main Course
Sesame chicken
Shrimp lo mein
Beef with broccoli
Szechuan vegetables
Peking duck

Dessert
Pineapple
Sherbet
Kumquats
Strawberries

Each meal served with tea and steamed rice.

USING LOGICAL REASONING In Exercises 14–16, list the combinations.

14. Choose two letters from the set {R, S, T}.

15. Choose two letters from the set {J, K, L, M}.

16. Choose three letters from the set {J, K, L, M}.

17. LANGUAGE ARTS During the school year, you must write 4 book reports. You can choose from the books listed below. How many different combinations of book reports could you have?

The Hobbit by J.R.R. Tolkien   *Dragonsong* by Anne McCaffrey

The Clay Marble by Mingfong Ho   *Robinson Crusoe* by Daniel Defoe

Roll of Thunder, Hear My Cry by Mildred D. Taylor

In Exercises 18–21, decide whether you need to find the number of *permutations* or *combinations*. Then find the answer.

18. How many ways are there for 3 forwards to be chosen from 7 possible soccer players?

19. How many ways can 5 basketball players line up for a free-throw shooting contest?

20. You want to include a cartwheel, a forward roll, and a handstand in your gymnastics routine on the balance beam. In how many orders can you perform these 3 movements?

21. You have 6 top swimmers. How many different relay teams of 4 swimmers can be formed?

STANDARDIZED TEST PRACTICE

22. Which of the following is a combination, rather than a permutation?

  (A) How many ways can you choose a committee of 2 from 6 people?

  (B) How many ways can a club elect a president and a secretary?

  (C) How many ways can 5 bicyclists finish a race?

  (D) How many ways can you and 3 friends line up at a movie theater?

23. How many ways can your 7-member chess team choose 3 representatives to go to a competition?

  (A) 4   **(B)** 21   **(C)** 35   **(D)** 210

LAB
11.5

COOPERATIVE LEARNING

Investigating Fair Games

Materials Needed
- pencils or pens
- paper
- 2 number cubes

Consider the following number cube game for two players. Find the difference in the numbers rolled by each player.

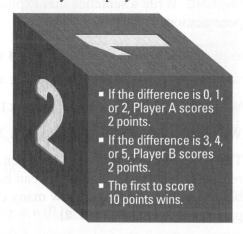

- If the difference is 0, 1, or 2, Player A scores 2 points.
- If the difference is 3, 4, or 5, Player B scores 2 points.
- The first to score 10 points wins.

1. With your partner, discuss this number cube game. If you were playing the game, would you rather be *Player A* or *Player B*? Explain your reasoning.

2. With your partner, play the game five times. Keep a record of who scores on each roll, *Player A* or *Player B*.

Part **B** TALLYING THE RESULTS

3. Collect the results of all the games that were played in your class. How many times did Player A score? How many times did Player B score?

4. Use the results of Exercise 3 to find the experimental probability that each player will score.

$$\frac{\text{Probability that}}{\text{Player A scores}} = \frac{\text{Number of times Player A scores}}{\text{Total number of rolls}}$$

$$\frac{\text{Probability that}}{\text{Player B scores}} = \frac{\text{Number of times Player B scores}}{\text{Total number of rolls}}$$

Is this game *fair*, or does it favor one of the players?

There are 36 possible differences when two number cubes are tossed.

	1	2	3	4	5	6
1	0	1	2	3	4	5
2	1	0	1	2	3	4
3	2	1	0	1	2	3
4	3	2	1	0	1	2
5	4	3	2	1	0	1
6	5	4	3	2	1	0

5. Use the table above to find the total number of ways Player A can score and the total number of ways Player B can score.

Player A

Number of ways to get a difference of 0 = ?

Number of ways to get a difference of 1 = ?

Number of ways to get a difference of 2 = ?

Player B

Number of ways to get a difference of 3 = ?

Number of ways to get a difference of 4 = ?

Number of ways to get a difference of 5 = ?

6. What is the theoretical probability that Player A will score? What is the theoretical probability that Player B will score? Compare these results with those found in Exercise 4.

NOW TRY THESE

7. In Exercises 1–6, you should have found that the number cube game is not fair. It favors Player A. Explain how you could revise the game so that it is fair.

8. Is this game fair, or does it favor one of the players? Three coins are tossed. If all the coins are the same—either all heads or all tails, then Player A scores 2 points. If the coins are different—one head and two tails or one tail and two heads, then Player B scores 1 point.

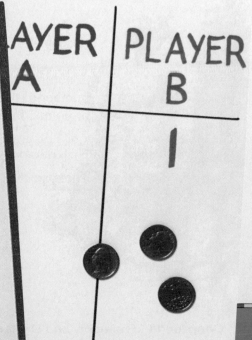

11.5

Expected Value

What you should learn:

Goal 1 How to find expected value

Goal 2 How to decide whether a game is fair

Why you should learn it:

Knowing how to find the expected value can help you analyze a player's prospects and the value of a game.

Teams often use a coin toss to decide issues such as which team has the control of the ball at the beginning of the game.

Goal 1 FINDING EXPECTED VALUE

Some games favor one player over another. The fairness of a game can be measured by computing the *expected values*. To find the **expected value** for a player, multiply the amount won by the probability of winning.

Example 1 Finding Expected Value

The spinner at the right is used in a game with two players: *Blue* and *Red*. If the spinner lands on a player's color, the player wins that number of points. Find the expected value for a turn for each player.

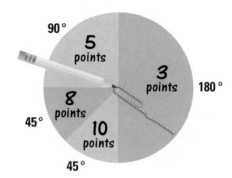

Solution

For *Blue* the expected value is

$$8 \cdot \frac{45}{360} + 3 \cdot \frac{180}{360} = 8 \cdot \frac{1}{8} + 3 \cdot \frac{1}{2} = 1 + \frac{3}{2} = \frac{5}{2}.$$

For *Red* the expected value is

$$5 \cdot \frac{90}{360} + 10 \cdot \frac{45}{360} = 5 \cdot \frac{1}{4} + 10 \cdot \frac{1}{8} = \frac{5}{4} + \frac{10}{8} = \frac{5}{2}.$$

Example 2 Finding Expected Value

A number cube is tossed. If the number is odd, Player A gets that number of points. If the number is even, Player B gets that number of points. Find the expected value for a turn for each player.

Solution

The expected value for Player A is

$$1 \cdot \frac{1}{6} + 3 \cdot \frac{1}{6} + 5 \cdot \frac{1}{6} = \frac{1}{6} + \frac{3}{6} + \frac{5}{6} = \frac{9}{6} = \frac{3}{2}.$$

The expected value for Player B is

$$2 \cdot \frac{1}{6} + 4 \cdot \frac{1}{6} + 6 \cdot \frac{1}{6} = \frac{2}{6} + \frac{4}{6} + \frac{6}{6} = \frac{12}{6} = 2.$$

A game is a **fair game** if each player has the same expected value. In a fair game, neither player has an advantage. This means that if the game is played hundreds of times, each player can expect to win about the same amount.

Example 3 ⟩ **Deciding Whether a Game Is Fair**

Decide whether the game is fair.

a. The spinner game in Example 1

b. The number cube game in Example 2

Solution

a. Each player has the same expected value, so the game is fair.

b. The players have different expected values, so the game is not fair. (The game favors Player B because Player B's expected value is greater.)

Example 4 ⟩ **A Game with More than Two Players**

In a game with three players, each player tosses a coin. Points are assigned as follows.

- Exactly 3 heads: Player X gets 12 points.
- Exactly 2 heads: Player Y gets 4 points.
- Exactly 1 or 0 heads: Player Z gets 3 points.

Is this game fair?

Solution

With three coins, there are 8 possible outcomes.

Player	Outcome	Points	Expected Value
X	HHH	12	$12 \cdot \dfrac{1}{8} = \dfrac{12}{8} = \dfrac{3}{2}$
Y	HHT, HTH, THH	4	$4 \cdot \dfrac{3}{8} = \dfrac{12}{8} = \dfrac{3}{2}$
Z	TTH, THT, HTT, TTT	3	$3 \cdot \dfrac{4}{8} = \dfrac{12}{8} = \dfrac{3}{2}$

Each player has the same expected value, so the game is fair.

ONGOING ASSESSMENT

Talk About It

A number cube game has 3 players (A, B, and C). Copy the table and assign points so that:

1. the game is fair.

2. the game is not fair.

Explain your reasoning to a partner.

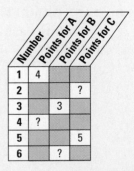

Number	Points for A	Points for B	Points for C
1	4		
2			?
3		3	
4	?		
5			5
6		?	

GUIDED PRACTICE

In Exercises 1–3, decide whether the game is fair. Explain your reasoning.

1. A number cube is tossed. If the number is even, Player A gets 2 points. If the number is odd, Player B gets 2 points.

2. Two coins are tossed. If the coins are both heads or both tails, Player A gets 4 points. If the coins are different, Player B gets 6 points.

3. Two number cubes are tossed. If the total is 6, 7, or 8, Player A gets 5 points. For any other total, Player B gets 4 points.

4. **GROUP ACTIVITY** In the game *Product*, each player rolls a number cube. If the product of the numbers is odd, Player A gets 2 points. If it is even, Player B gets 1 point. The first player to score 5 points wins. Play the game five times. Who won more games? Make a table of the possible products when two number cubes are tossed. Then find the expected value for each player. Is the game fair? If not, how could you reassign points to make the game fair?

PRACTICE AND PROBLEM SOLVING

In Exercises 5–7, is the spinner fair? If not, which color is most likely to win?

5.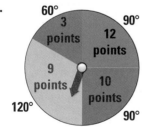

6.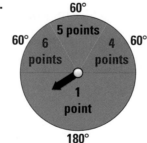

7.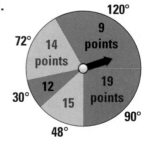

8. **DART GAME** The dart board at the right shows the points scored for hitting each region. The probability of hitting the regions is as follows.

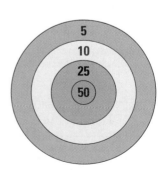

   Red $\frac{1}{10}$ Blue $\frac{1}{5}$

   Yellow $\frac{3}{10}$ Green $\frac{2}{5}$

   Assuming every dart hits the board, what is the expected value of any given throw? Explain your reasoning.

9. THINKING SKILLS Create your own game that is fair. Show that it is fair by finding the expected value for each player.

10. In a game, Player A has a three-fourths probability of winning points and Player B has a one-fourth probability of winning points. Assign points to the players so that the game is fair.

11. BASKETBALL In 1997, the probability that Shaquille O'Neal made a 2-point field goal was 0.557. The probability that he made a 1-point free throw was 0.484. Find O'Neal's expected value for each type of shot. (Source: National Basketball Association)

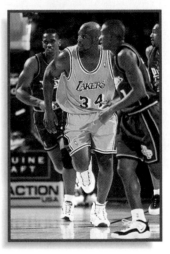

12. RAFFLE Your school's French club is selling 500 raffle tickets to raise money for a trip to Quebec, Canada. The prizes are as follows.

First Prize: $50
Second Prize: $25
Third Prize: $10

You purchase a ticket. The probability that you will win each prize is $\frac{1}{500}$. What is your expected value?

STANDARDIZED TEST PRACTICE

13. In a beanbag toss competition, there is a $\frac{1}{6}$ chance that the bag will land in the 12-point circle, a $\frac{1}{4}$ chance that it will land in the 8-point circle, and a $\frac{1}{3}$ chance that it will land in the 6-point circle. Assuming that every beanbag lands in a point circle, what is the expected value of one toss?

(A) 2 points   **(B)** 6 points   **(C)** $8\frac{2}{3}$ points   **(D)** 26 points

EXPLORATION AND EXTENSION

14. NUMBER CUBE GAME Player A rolls number cube A and Player B rolls number cube B. The player with the greater number scores 2 points. Find the expected value for each player. Is the game fair? If the game is not fair, reassign the points to make it fair.

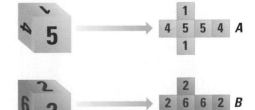

11.6

Making Predictions

What you should learn:

Goal 1 How to predict the number of times an event will occur

Goal 2 How to use probability to solve real-life problems

Why you should learn it:

Knowing how to predict the number of times an event will occur can help you plan for the future. An example is predicting the amount that an insurance company will spend on insured accidents.

Goal 1 PREDICTING EVENTS

You can predict the number of times an event will occur by multiplying its probability by the total number of trials.

Example 1 Predicting Events

Three coins are to be tossed 200 times.

a. Predict how many times all 3 coins will be heads.

b. Predict how many times 2 tails and 1 head will occur.

Solution

There are 8 possible outcomes, each with a probability of $\frac{1}{8}$.

a. To predict the number of times you will get HHH out of 200 tosses, multiply the probability by 200.

$$\frac{\text{Probability}}{\text{of 3 heads}} \cdot \frac{\text{Number}}{\text{of tosses}} = \frac{1}{8} \cdot 200 = 25$$

The coins should land with 3 heads up about 25 times.

b. Three of the 8 possible outcomes have 2 tails and 1 head, so the probability is $\frac{3}{8}$.

$$\frac{\text{Probability of}}{\text{2 tails and 1 head}} \cdot \frac{\text{Number}}{\text{of tosses}} = \frac{3}{8} \cdot 200 = 75$$

The coins should land with 2 tails and 1 head up about 75 times.

The actual number of occurrences can be more or less than your prediction. The scatter plot below shows the number of times 3 heads occurred when 3 coins were tossed. The green line shows the theoretical number of occurrences, which is one eighth of the tosses. The actual number was close to the theoretical number.

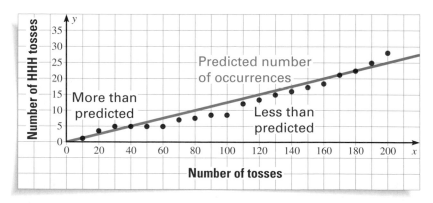

Example 2 **Predicting Events**

Your company insures 150,000 motor vehicles this year. The table shows totals for the United States from 1989 through 1994.

REAL LIFE
Insurance

a. Use the 1994 data to predict the number of accidents that your company would cover this year.

b. Use the 1994 data to predict how much your company would have to pay this year for motor vehicle accidents.

Vehicles and Accidents

	1989	1990	1991	1992	1993	1994
Vehicles (in millions)	176.0	179.3	181.5	181.5	203.6	193.4
Accidents (in millions)	34.4	33.4	31.3	31.8	32.8	33.9
Cost (in billions)	$93.9	$95.9	$93.8	$98.1	$104.1	$110.5

(Source: Statistical Abstract of the United States, 1996)

Tech Link

Investigation 11, Interactive Real-Life Investigations

Solution

a. Of 193.4 million motor vehicles in 1994, there were 33.9 million accidents. So, the probability that a vehicle will have an accident during the year is

$$\frac{33.9}{193.4} \approx 0.175.$$

Based on 150,000 vehicles insured, you can predict that your company would cover $0.175 \cdot 150{,}000$, or 26,250, accidents this year.

b. In 1994, the cost per accident was

$$\frac{110.5 \text{ billion}}{33.9 \text{ million}} = \frac{110{,}500}{33.9} \approx \$3260.$$

Because you predict 26,250 accidents, you can predict the cost to be $3260 \cdot 26{,}250$, or about 85.6, million dollars this year.

ONGOING ASSESSMENT

Talk About It

1. Discuss with a partner how your predictions would change if you used the 1993 data instead of the 1994 data.

11.6 Exercises

Extra Practice, page 645

GUIDED PRACTICE

In Exercises 1 and 2, use the spinner at the right.

1. What is the probability that the spinner will land on a prime number?

2. Predict the number of times the spinner will land on a prime number if you spin it 150 times.

3. In 1994, 7312 million pounds of bananas were consumed in the United States. That year the population was 260 million people.

   a. How many pounds of bananas were consumed per person?

   b. In 1994, California had a population of 31,220,000 people. Estimate the number of pounds of bananas eaten in California in 1994.

PRACTICE AND PROBLEM SOLVING

In Exercises 4–6, predict the number of times that the event will occur if the experiment is performed 200 times.

4. Toss 2 coins. How many times will both be tails?

5. Toss 2 number cubes. How many times will you roll double fives?

6. Choose a name from a hat in which there are the names of 15 girls and 25 boys. Replace the name. How many times will you choose a girl's name?

CONSUMERS IN CHINA In Exercises 7–9, use the table below. It shows the numbers of some items owned by households in China. It is based on a survey of 3400 households. (Source: The Gallup Organization)

Item	Bicycle	Color TV	Radio	Car
Number	2754	1360	1972	102

7. What is the probability that a household owns a color television?

8. Out of a group of 100,000 households in China, how many would you predict would own a color television?

9. Out of a group of 100,000 households in China, how many would you predict would own a bicycle?

10. ACTING IT OUT Complete the table by rolling a number cube and recording the number of times you roll a multiple of three.

Number of rolls, x	10	20	30	40	50	60
Multiples of 3, y	?	?	?	?	?	?

In Exercises 11–14, use the table you made in Exercise 10.

11. Write the data in the table as ordered pairs of the form (x, y). Then graph the ordered pairs in a coordinate plane.

12. Compute the number of times, k, you would expect to roll a multiple of 3 when you roll the number cube 60 times.

13. Draw a line that goes through the origin and through the point $(60, k)$, where k is the value found in Exercise 12.

14. How many points are over the prediction (above the line) and how many are under the prediction (below the line)?

RECYCLED PAPER In Exercises 15 and 16, use this information. In the United States, paper mills used about 34.3 million tons of recovered (recycled) paper and about 57.7 million tons of other raw materials to make new paper products in 1996. (Source: American Forest and Paper Association)

15. Find the ratio of the amount of recovered paper used to the total amount of materials used in 1996.

16. Predict the amount of recovered paper used if the total amount of materials used by paper mills in some year is 150 million tons.

STANDARDIZED TEST PRACTICE

17. A fair coin is tossed 60 times. What is the expected number of times a head will land face up?

   A 60 times   **B** 45 times

   C 30 times   **D** Not enough information

18. A school in Centerville has 300 students and 60 of those students have red hair. If Centerville has a total of 4500 students, how many students in the town would you predict have red hair?

   A 150 students   **B** 900 students

   C 90 students   **D** 15 students

19. COMMUNICATING ABOUT MATHEMATICS Parrot experts are worried that several species of parrots are becoming extinct. Of the 330 different species of parrots in the world, 71 species are endangered.

a. For a school report, you choose a species of parrot at random from an alphabetical list. What is the probability that the species you choose is endangered? Express your answer as a decimal.

b. How many students are in your class? If each of the students in your class chose a species of parrot at random for a report, predict the number of endangered species that would be chosen.

SPIRAL REVIEW

In Exercises 1 and 2, use the Venn diagram. It shows the number of students out of 100 surveyed that plant trees and recycle to help the environment. (1.7)

Recycle 52   Plant trees 45

Neither 17

1. How many students plant trees or recycle?

2. How many students just recycle?

3. The table shows the record high temperatures for Dallas-Fort Worth, Texas, for each month. Find the mean, the median, and the mode of the data. **(5.1)**

January	88	May	103	September	106
February	88	June	113	October	102
March	96	July	110	November	89
April	95	August	108	December	88

4. You have a summer job walking dogs. On Friday, you walked 4 dogs and earned $10. On Saturday, you walked 7 dogs. Write a proportion to find the amount of money you earned on Saturday. **(6.5)**

TRACK AND FIELD In Exercises 5 and 6, find the circumference and the area of the circle used for the track-and-field event. (8.3, 8.6)

5. Shot Put circle

3.5 ft

6. Discus Throw circle

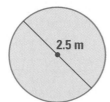

2.5 m

COMMUNICATING
About Mathematics

PARROT TALK

Just how smart can a bird be? That's what Dr. Irene Pepperberg of the University of Arizona is trying to find out. She's been teaching a parrot named Alex to understand English.

As an *easy test*, Dr. Pepperberg shows Alex a big green key and a little purple key and asks which is bigger. Alex can tell her. He even tells her how many keys she's holding.

For a *harder test*, Dr. Pepperberg shows Alex a tray with five different objects, each of a different color. She might ask him which object is red. When he's trying, Alex gets the right answer about 80% of the time. It's easy to tell when he is not trying. When Alex is tired of working, he announces, "I am going to go away," and turns his back.

1. In the easy test, what is the probability that Alex would pick the correct key if he were guessing? Explain your reasoning.

2. In the harder test, what is the probability that Alex would pick the red item on the tray? Explain your reasoning.

3. If Alex picks one item from the easy test and one item from the hard test, how many different combinations could he choose? Use a tree diagram to explain your answer.

4. What is the probability that Alex would choose the correct item in both the easy test and the hard test? Explain how this is related to your answer in Exercise 3.

5. Suppose you gave Alex the hard test twenty times, using different items and questions. Judging from his record, how many times would you expect that he would answer correctly? Express your answer as a sentence.

6. When Alex answers a question correctly, do you think that he knows what Dr. Pepperberg is asking, or do you think he is just lucky? Use the data in the article to support your answer.

11.7

Venn Diagrams and Probability

Goal 1 How to use Venn diagrams to represent sets

Goal 2 How to use Venn diagrams and compound events to solve probability problems

Why you should learn it:

Knowing how to use Venn diagrams can help you organize information. An example is finding the number of people who like pizza and different pastas.

Goal 1 USING VENN DIAGRAMS

In Lesson 1.7, you used a Venn diagram to represent a way that sets can be related to each other. For example, there are four ways that two sets, *A* and *B*, can be related.

The two sets are disjoint.

The two sets overlap.

B is a subset of *A*.

A is a subset of *B*.

Example 1 Representing Sets

STRATEGY **DRAW A DIAGRAM** Draw a Venn diagram that represents the two sets.

a. Ten people who like spaghetti and 8 people who don't

b. Five people who like spaghetti but not pizza, 3 people who like both, and 8 people who like pizza but not spaghetti

c. Twenty people who like some form of pasta and 15 people who like spaghetti

Solution

a. These sets are disjoint because one cannot like spaghetti and also not like it.

b. The sets of people who like spaghetti and of people who like pizza overlap because some people like pizza and not spaghetti, some like spaghetti and not pizza, and some like both.

c. The set of 15 people who like spaghetti is a subset of the set of 20 people who like pasta.

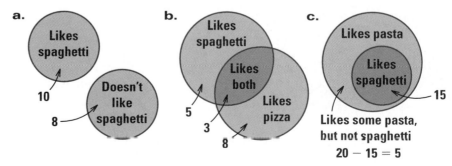

Example 2 Using a Venn Diagram

A person is chosen at random from the people described in part (c) on page 566. There are 20 people who like pasta, and 15 of these like spaghetti. The probability that the person chosen likes spaghetti is

$$\text{Probability} = \frac{15}{20}, \text{ or } \frac{3}{4}.$$

If the probability of one event occurring changes the probability of a second event occurring, then these *compound events* are **dependent**. Two events are **independent** if the occurrence of one does not affect the occurrence of the other.

Example 3 Dependent and Independent Events

You put 6 red marbles and 2 blue marbles in a bag. You draw two marbles from the bag. What is the probability of choosing a **red** marble and then a **blue** marble if

a. the first marble is replaced before the second marble is chosen?

b. the first marble is not replaced before the second one is chosen?

Solution

There are a total of 8 marbles in the bag to begin with. The probability of choosing a **red** marble on the first draw is $\frac{6}{8} = \frac{3}{4}$.

a. After replacing the first marble drawn, there are again 8 marbles in the bag. The probability of choosing a **blue** marble on the second draw is $\frac{2}{8} = \frac{1}{4}$.

Independent events

Probability of choosing red, then blue (with replacement) $= \frac{3}{4} \cdot \frac{1}{4} = \frac{3}{16}$

b. If the first marble drawn is not replaced, then there are now only 7 marbles in the bag. The probability of choosing a **blue** marble on the second draw is $\frac{2}{7}$.

Dependent events

Probability of choosing red, then blue (without replacement) $= \frac{3}{4} \cdot \frac{2}{7} = \frac{3}{14}$

ONGOING ASSESSMENT

Write About It

Find the probability that a person chosen at random from the people described in Example 1, part (b), likes

1. pizza, but not spaghetti.

2. both spaghetti and pizza.

GUIDED PRACTICE

In Exercises 1–4, match the set description with its Venn diagram.

A.

B.

C.

D.

1. Set *A* is a subset of Set *B*.

2. Sets *A* and *B* overlap.

3. Sets *A* and *B* are disjoint.

4. Set *B* is a subset of Set *A*.

In Exercises 5–7, draw a Venn diagram that represents the two sets.

5. People who like amusement park rides and people who like roller coasters

6. Animals that can fly and animals that can't

7. People who like math and people who like science

Do the statements in Exercises 8 and 9 describe *dependent events* or *independent events*?

8. You reach both hands into a barrel of apples and pull out an apple in each hand. One apple is bruised and the other one is not.

9. Today you did not need an umbrella, so tomorrow you won't need one either.

PRACTICE AND PROBLEM SOLVING

In Exercises 10–13, use the Venn diagram to find the probability.

10. *A*, but not *B* or *C*

11. *B* and *C*, but not *A*

12. *A*, *B*, and *C*

13. *A* and *C*, but not *B*

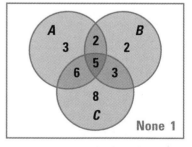

In Exercises 14–17, write a statement representing the Venn diagram.

14.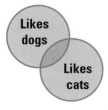

15.

16.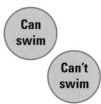

17.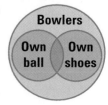

18. **MUSIC** The Venn diagram shows the results of a survey that asked students in a class if they liked country, rock, and rap music. Suppose that the students' names are written down on pieces of paper that are then put in a box. One name is chosen from the box and not returned. Then a second name is chosen. What is the probability that the name of a student who likes country music only is chosen first, then the name of a student who likes rock music only is chosen second?

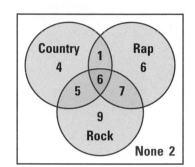

STANDARDIZED TEST PRACTICE

In Exercises 19 and 20, use the Venn diagram.

19. What does the shaded region represent?

   (A) People who own bicycles and in-line skates

   (B) All people owning bicycles and in-line skates

   (C) People who own bicycles and in-line skates, but not skateboards

   (D) People who own only skateboards

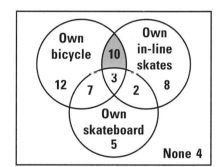

20. What is the probability that a random person owns a bicycle?

   (A) $\frac{7}{51}$ (B) $\frac{10}{51}$ (C) $\frac{32}{51}$ (D) $\frac{12}{51}$

EXPLORATION AND EXTENSION

PORTFOLIO

21. **BUILDING YOUR PROJECT** The activities available to your group at the Grand Canyon are a mule ride, a ranger-led walk, and a conservation film. All 75 of the people in your group chose at least one of these activities, 18 chose all three, 15 chose only the ride, 12 only the walk, 9 only the film, 5 both the ride and the walk, and the total number who chose the mule ride was 48.

   a. Sketch a Venn diagram to represent this information.

   b. If one person is randomly selected, what are the chances that this person chose the walk and the film but not the mule ride?

WHAT did you learn?

WHY did you learn it?

Skills

11.1 Find probabilities by grouping equally likely outcomes.

Use probability in genetics and other fields.

11.2 Count the number of ways an event can happen by using a tree diagram and by using the Counting Principle.

Study manufacturing issues such as the number of elements in a product line.

11.3 Find the number of permutations of *n* objects.

Analyze experiments involving chance.

11.4 List and count the number of combinations.

Find probabilities in problems involving group assignments.

11.5 Learn the meaning of expectation and the definition of a fair game.

Analyze a player's prospects and the value of a game.

11.6 Predict the number of times an event will occur.

Predict real-world events.

11.7 Use a Venn diagram to represent sets and subsets.

Analyze problems involving overlapping choices.

Strategies 11.1–11.7 Use problem solving strategies.

Solve a wide variety of real-world problems.

Using Data 11.1–11.7 Use tables and graphs.

Organize data and solve problems.

HOW does it fit in the bigger picture of mathematics?

Much of probability is concerned with counting the number of ways an event can occur. You have studied several counting techniques (lists, tree diagrams, and tables). Looking back on these techniques, you will see that they involve only one formula—the formula for the number of permutations of *n* objects.

Example Find the number of ways the four letters A, B, C, and D can be ordered.

Solution Order does matter (ABCD is not the same as BACD).

ABCD ABDC ACBD ACDB ADBC ADCB
BACD BADC BCAD BCDA BDAC BDCA
CABD CADB CBAD CBDA CDAB CDBA
DABC DACB DBAC DBCA DCAB DCBA

There are 24 ways to order four letters.

- **experimental probabilities** (p. 530)
- **theoretical probabilities** (p. 530)
- **tree diagram** (p. 536)
- **Counting Principle** (p. 537)

- **permutation** (p. 544)
- ***n* factorial, *n*!** (p. 544)
- **combination** (p. 548)
- **expected value** (p. 556)

- **fair game** (p. 557)
- **dependent events** (p. 567)
- **independent events** (p. 567)

11.1 GROUPING EQUALLY LIKELY OUTCOMES

To find probabilities, you can either conduct an experiment or count and classify all possible outcomes.

Example What is the probability of choosing an S from the letters in the word **MISSISSIPPI**?

Solution $\text{Probability} = \dfrac{\text{Number of \textbf{S}'s}}{\text{Total number of letters}} = \dfrac{4}{11}$

1. List the possible outcomes when two number cubes are tossed. Then find the probability of tossing a sum of 6.

2. Copy the square. Color it so that a point chosen at random from one of its parts has the following probabilities.

   White, $\dfrac{1}{2}$ Red, $\dfrac{1}{8}$ Blue, $\dfrac{3}{8}$

11.2 COUNTING TECHNIQUES

To count the number of ways an event can happen, you can use a tree diagram or the Counting Principle.

Example You are renting a pair of in-line skates. You can choose from white or tan helmets, purple or black skates, and red, white, or green knee pads. How many different skating outfits could you rent?

Solution Use the Counting Principle.

2 helmets $\times$ 2 skates $\times$ 3 knee pads = 12 different skating outfits

3. How many ways can a baby be named if the choices for a first name are Yvonne, Pearl, Tasha, and Viola, and the choices for a middle name are Renee, Lynn, and Marie? Make a tree diagram.

4. How many ways can you schedule a day at a conference if you can choose from 3 morning events, 5 afternoon events, and 4 evening events? Use the Counting Principle.

11.3   PERMUTATIONS AND PROBABILITY

Example   Find the number of permutations of the letters **E**, **A**, and **T**.
What is the probability that the permutation is a word?

Solution   There are $3! = 3 \cdot 2 \cdot 1 = 6$ permutations: **EAT, ETA, ATE, AET, TEA, TAE**

Three of the permutations are words. So the probability that

the permutation is a word is $\dfrac{3}{6} = \dfrac{1}{2}$.

In Exercises 5 and 6, use this information. Six cheerleaders are to hold letters that spell "GO TEAM," but the letters got randomly scrambled.

5. How many different ways can the cheerleaders hold up the letters?

6. What is the probability that the cheerleaders spell the correct phrase?

11.4   COMBINATIONS AND PROBABILITY

Example   You want to choose five starting players for a basketball game from a group of seven players. How many different starting teams can you have?

Solution   Represent the seven players with the letters **A, B, C, D, E, F**, and **G**. Make a list of the possible starting teams of five.

ABCDE	**ABCDF**	**ABCDG**	**ACDEF**	**ACDEG**
ADEFG	**BCDEF**	**BCDEG**	**BDEFG**	**CDEFG**

There are 10 possible starting teams.

7. You need to do three of these chores—clean your room, wash the car, cut the grass, wash the dog, and clean the garage. How many different groups of three chores can you choose?

8. In a parade, a band only has time to play four tunes from the six they have been practicing. How many groups of four tunes are there?

11.5   EXPECTED VALUE

Example   If the spinner lands on a player's color (orange or green), the player wins the points shown. Is the game fair?

Solution

$$\begin{array}{l} \text{Expected value} \\ \text{of orange} \end{array} = \begin{array}{l} \text{Probability} \\ \text{of orange} \end{array} \times \begin{array}{l} \text{Amount} \\ \text{won} \end{array} = \frac{1}{4} \times 12 = 3$$

$$\begin{array}{l} \text{Expected value} \\ \text{of green} \end{array} = \begin{array}{l} \text{Probability} \\ \text{of green} \end{array} \times \begin{array}{l} \text{Amount} \\ \text{won} \end{array} = \frac{3}{4} \times 8 = 6$$

90°   12   270°   8

The spinner is not fair because the expected value of green is greater than the expected value of orange.

9. Consider this game. *Two number cubes are tossed. If the number shown on one number cube is twice the number shown on the other, Player A gets 10 points. If it is not, Player B gets 3 points.* What is the expected value for each player? Is the game fair?

10. In a game, Player C has a two-thirds probability of winning points and Player D has a one-third probability of winning points. Assign points to the players so that the game is fair.

11.6 MAKING PREDICTIONS

Example Two coins are tossed 100 times. Predict how many times the coins will not be the same.

Solution There are 4 possible outcomes: HH, HT, TH, and TT.

$$\frac{\text{Probability of the coins}}{\text{being different}} = \frac{\text{Ways of getting different coins}}{\text{Total number of out comes}} = \frac{2}{4} = \frac{1}{2}$$

Multiply the probability by 100.

$$\frac{\text{Probability}}{\text{of event}} \times \frac{\text{Number}}{\text{of tosses}} = \frac{1}{2} \times 100 = 50$$

The coins should be different on about 50 tosses.

11. Toss 3 coins 200 times. How many times would you expect to get exactly 1 head?

12. Toss a number cube 50 times. If the cube has sides of six different colors (red, blue, green, yellow, orange, and purple), how many times would you expect the cube to land yellow side up?

11.7 VENN DIAGRAMS AND PROBABILITY

Example Use the Venn diagram at the right to find the probability of traveling on a plane and a train, but not on a boat.

Solution By adding all the numbers, you can see that there are 30 travelers. There are 3 people who have traveled on a plane and on a train, but not on a boat. The probability is $\frac{3}{30}$, or $\frac{1}{10}$.

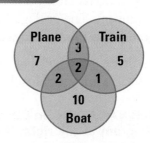

In Exercises 13 and 14, use the Venn diagram at the right.

13. Find the probability that a traveler rode in a boat and flew in a plane.

14. Find the probability of traveling only by plane.

COOKING ON THE GRILL In Questions 1 and 2, use the circle graph. It shows the results of a survey of 600 people who were asked "When do you cook on a grill?" (Source: National Cattleman's Association)

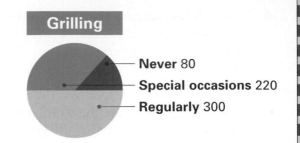

Grilling

Never 80
Special occasions 220
Regularly 300

1. What is the probability that a person surveyed never cooks on a grill?

2. What is the probability that a person surveyed cooks on a grill?

In Questions 3 and 4, use the Counting Principle to find the number of different items. Then check your answer using a tree diagram.

3. How many different types of television sets would you have to manufacture if you offered a choice of black-and-white or color, and a screen size of 13 inches, 16 inches, 19 inches, or 21 inches?

4. How many different trips are possible if you first stop in Columbus or Cincinnati, next in Pittsburgh or Philadelphia, and finally in Buffalo or Baltimore?

5. **MARCHING BAND** Your band has four sections: percussion, woodwinds, brass, and flags. In how many different orders can these four sections be lined up?

6. For this spinner, what is the probability of landing on each color? Three players (yellow, blue, and red) get the indicated number of points when they land on their own color. What is the expected value for each player? Is the game fair?

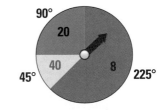

90°
20
40
45°
8
225°

7. **WORKING STUDENTS** At a college, you randomly surveyed 200 students and found that 46 of them had worked at a restaurant. The college has 3200 students. How many of them would you think have worked at a restaurant?

8. Describe an experiment that you could do to demonstrate *dependent* events, using marbles, blocks, markers, or some other item.

SUMMER VACATION In Questions 9 and 10, use the Venn diagram at the right. It shows the results of a survey of 7th graders who were asked the question "What will you do during your summer vacation?" One of the students is chosen at random. Find the probability that the student will do the following.

9. Go swimming, but not work or sleep late

10. Work and go swimming, but not sleep late

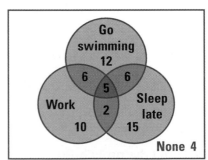

Go swimming
12
6   6
5
Work   Sleep
              late
10   2
          15
None 4

1. A survey asked 40 people to name the activity they like to do most in their spare time. What is the probability that a person randomly selected chose "listen to music?"

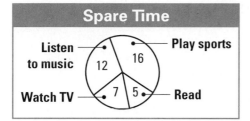

Spare Time

Listen to music — 12
Play sports — 16
Watch TV — 7
Read — 5

(A) $\frac{1}{4}$ (B) $\frac{3}{10}$

(C) $3\frac{1}{3}$ (D) 12

2. You are buying a bike. You can choose from a mountain, road, or hybrid bike in blue, green, red, or black. From how many different bikes can you choose?

(A) 7 (B) 9

(C) 12 (D) 16

3. How many ways can you select a group of 3 movies out of 5 movies to watch this weekend?

(A) 2 (B) 8

(C) 10 (D) 15

4. A spinner with seven equal regions is labeled with the numbers 20, 50, 90, 140, 200, 270, and 350. You get two points if the number spun is divisible by 4. What is your expected value?

(A) $\frac{3}{7}$ (B) $\frac{6}{7}$

(C) 2 (D) 6

5. In how many ways can 5 books be lined up on a shelf?

(A) 5 (B) 14

(C) 25 (D) 120

6. You toss a number cube 12 times. Predict the number of times the number showing will be even.

(A) 3 (B) 6

(C) 9 (D) 12

For Questions 7 and 8, use the Venn diagram.

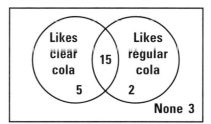

Likes clear cola
Likes regular cola
15
5
2
None 3

7. Which statement is *false*?

(A) The set of people who like clear cola is a subset of the people who like regular cola.

(B) Some people like regular cola and not clear cola.

(C) Some people do not like either kind of cola.

(D) Some people like both regular cola and clear cola.

8. What is the probability that a person chosen at random likes clear cola and not regular cola?

(A) $\frac{1}{20}$ (B) $\frac{2}{25}$

(C) $\frac{1}{5}$ (D) $\frac{3}{5}$

CHAPTER

12

Algebra: Equations and Functions

TECHNOLOGY

Technology resources accompanying this chapter:

• Interactive Real-Life Investigations

• Middle School Tutorial Software

CHINESE NEW YEAR The dragon dance symbolizes the end of this holiday's celebration and parade.

TEXAS FOLKLIFE FESTIVAL This annual event brings together more than 40 of the state's ethnic and cultural groups.

CHAPTER **THEME**
World Cultures

DANCE Many cultures use the art of dancing to celebrate special occasions or ceremonies.

FIESTA DAY People in Tampa's Ybor City celebrate their ethnic roots with this day-long street festival.

Blending Of Cultures

REAL LIFE Culture

People have been immigrating to what is now known as the United States for thousands of years. **Cultural celebrations** take place to honor the various customs and traditions brought by these travelers. The immigration process continues today as hundreds of thousands of people come to America each year. This joining of many worlds makes our society unique and allows us the great opportunity to learn about the habits of many different countries from our own neighbors.

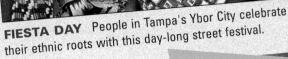

Immigrants to the United States

Period	Immigrants (thousands)
1981–1990	7338
1971–1980	4493
1961–1970	3322
1951–1960	2515
1941–1950	1035

(numbers in thousands)

Think and Discuss

1. What overall patterns or trends in immigration can you see from the data? Which time period had the greatest increase in immigration from the previous time period? How many people was it?

2. The number of people who immigrated between 1931 and 1940 was 528,000 people. What was the increase in immigration between this period and the 1941–1950 period?

CHAPTER 12

PORTFOLIO

CHAPTER **PROJECT**

International Day Bulletin Board

PROJECT DESCRIPTION

Your school is having an "International Day" to celebrate the cultural heritage of the students. Each classroom has chosen a different country to feature and makes displays to show various information about the country. To create the Bulletin Board, you will use the list of **TOPICS** on the next page.

GETTING STARTED

Talking It Over

- Discuss what types of displays you would have in your room for "International Day."

- Did any of your relatives immigrate to the United States from other countries? If so, who and when? Do you still have relatives who live in those countries? Do you plan to visit them? Does your family still practice any customs from those countries? Do you have any favorite foods from those countries?

Planning Your Project

- **Materials Needed:** poster board or construction paper, markers, scissors, glue, paper, pencils or pens

- Cut out paper letters to make a title for your bulletin board. As you answer the **BUILDING YOUR PROJECT** questions, add your results to your bulletin board for the appropriate country. Try to find facts about and pictures of your ancestor's country of origin. Be sure to include these on your bulletin board as well.

BUILDING YOUR PROJECT

These are places throughout the chapter where you will work on your project.

TOPICS

12.1 Convert between a German mark and a United States dollar. *p. 583*

12.2 Find the heights of the peaks of Mount Kilimanjaro in Africa. *p. 587*

12.3 Adjust a recipe to provide food for all visitors to the room. *p. 596*

12.4 Make scale model flags to give to students as souvenirs. *p. 601*

I N T E R N E T

To find out about other countries, go to:
http://www.mlmath.com

Chapter Project **579**

12.1

Inverse Operations

What you should learn:

Goal 1 How to model inverse operations

Goal 2 How to use inverse operations and box models to solve equations

Why you should learn it:

Knowing how to recognize inverse operations can help you solve equations.

In banking, you can think of deposit and withdrawal as inverses of each other.

Goal 1 MODELING INVERSE OPERATIONS

An **inverse operation** is an operation that "undoes" another operation. Addition and subtraction are inverses of each other. For example, the inverse of adding 2 is subtracting 2. Multiplication and division are also inverses of each other.

LESSON INVESTIGATION

COOPERATIVE LEARNING

Investigating Inverse Operations

GROUP ACTIVITY You entered 10 on a calculator, then you made a mistake. Without clearing the calculator, which keystrokes can you use to "undo" the mistake.

1. 10 **+** 8 **=**   **2.** 10 **−** 4 **=**

3. 10 **×** 3 **=**   **4.** 10 **÷** 2 **=**

Use a calculator to check your answer. When you enter your "correction", does the calculator display 10 again? What can you conclude? Discuss these results with your group.

Example 1 Modeling Inverse Operations

a. The number 9 has been subtracted from 6. You can undo this operation by adding 9.

6		6 → −3		−3 → 6
		−9		+9
Start with 6.		**Subtract 9 from 6 to get −3.**		**Add 9 to −3 to get back to 6.**

b. The number 4 has been multiplied by −2. You can undo this operation by dividing by −2.

4		4 → −8		−8 → 4
		×(−2)		÷(−2)
Start with 4.		**Multiply 4 by −2 to get −8.**		**Divide −8 by −2 to get back to 4.**

The models used in Example 1 are called **box models**. Example 2 uses box models to solve equations.

Example 2 **Solving Equations with Box Models**

Use a box model and inverse operations to solve each equation.

a. $n + 8 = -5$ **b.** $t - 3 = 6$ **c.** $4m = -28$ **d.** $y \div 3 = 8$

Solution

a.

Add 8 to n
to get -5.

Subtract 8 from
-5 to get -13.

The solution is $n = -13$.

b.

Subtract 3 from
t to get 6.

Add 3 to 6
to get 9.

The solution is $t = 9$.

c.

Multiply m by
4 to get -28.

Divide -28 by 4
to get -7.

The solution is $m = -7$.

d.

Divide y by
3 to get 8.

Multiply 8 by 3
to get 24.

The solution is $y = 24$.

ONGOING ASSESSMENT

Write About It
. . . .

Use a box model to
solve each equation.
Show your work.

1. $m + 3 = 2$

2. $x - 5 = -2$

3. $5n = 30$

4. $p \div 8 = 4$

12.1 Exercises

Extra Practice, page 646

GUIDED PRACTICE

In Exercises 1–4, describe the operation represented by the box model. Then describe the inverse operation.

1.

2.

3.

4.

In Exercises 5–8, write the equation that is being modeled. Copy and complete the box model to solve the equation.

5.

6.

7.

8.

9. Use a box model to solve the equation $-3x = -18$.

10. PLAYING A CD You want to play a CD using your stereo system. To play a CD, you must select the CD you want to listen to, turn on the stereo system, remove the CD from the jewel case, insert it into the CD player, and press the play button. Describe what you could do to reverse the process and return the CD to its storage place.

PRACTICE AND PROBLEM SOLVING

In Exercises 11–14, name the inverse operation.

11. Add 12. **12.** Subtract -3. **13.** Multiply by -4. **14.** Divide by 10.

In Exercises 15–22, copy and complete the box model.

15.

16.

17.

18.

19.

20.

21.

22.

In Exercises 23–30, write a box model for the equation. Then use an inverse operation to solve the equation.

23. $m - 7 = -13$ **24.** $y + 15 = 8$ **25.** $x + 4.7 = 9.2$ **26.** $k - (-4) = 10$

27. $-3b = 42$ **28.** $\dfrac{t}{3} = 2$ **29.** $n \div 1 = -2$ **30.** $a \cdot (-6) = -54$

In Exercises 31–36, explain whether the real-life activity can be reversed.

31. Freeze water. **32.** Stand up. **33.** Burn a log.

34. Open a door. **35.** Read a book. **36.** Break a glass.

In Exercises 37–40, write an equation that represents the box model. Then solve the equation.

37.
+10
| b | → | 6 |

38.
− (−2)
| m | → | −12 |

39.
÷ $\frac{1}{4}$
| y | → | 8 |

40.
×(−3)
| c | → | −24 |

41. MAZE Find the path the mouse would travel to get to the cheese. Describe the steps the mouse would take to get back out of the maze.

42. You are riding your bike from your home to your friend's home. To get there you must ride north 5 blocks, turn west and ride 3 blocks, turn south and ride 1 block, then turn west and ride $\frac{1}{2}$ block.

Describe how to reverse the process.

STANDARDIZED TEST PRACTICE

43. What is the inverse operation of adding 8 to a number?

A Subtracting −8 from the number.

B Subtracting the number from 8.

C Subtracting 8 from the number.

D Adding the number to 8.

44. Solve the equation: $16m = 64$.

A $\frac{1}{4}$ **B** 4   **C** 28   **D** 1024

PORTFOLIO

EXPLORATION AND EXTENSION

45. BUILDING YOUR PROJECT The classroom that featured Germany made a sign describing the exchange rate between the German marks and U.S. dollars. Make a box model to show the exchange rates between the two currencies. Use the box model to determine how many German marks you would get in exchange for 27 U.S. dollars.

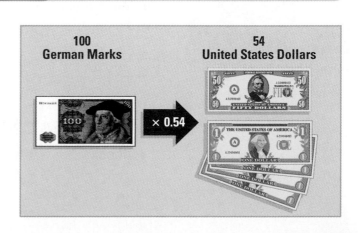

100 German Marks → × 0.54 → 54 United States Dollars

What you should learn:

Goal 1 How to use an inverse operation to solve an addition equation

Goal 2 How to use an inverse operation to solve a subtraction equation

Why you should learn it:

Knowing how to solve addition and subtraction equations can help you solve problems. An example is finding out how long baseball gloves have been used.

Baseball legend Ty Cobb, 1921.

Goal 1 SOLVING ADDITION EQUATIONS

In Lesson 4.6, you learned to solve an addition equation by using inverse operations. To do this, you subtracted the same number from both sides of the equation. This gives you the variable by itself on one side of the equation and the numerical solution to the equation on the other side. This process is called **isolating the variable**. It works because subtraction is the inverse operation of addition.

Example 1 › Solving an Addition Equation

Solve each equation.

a. $x + (-4) = 8$ **b.** $9 = 3 + n$

Solution

a.

$x + (-4) = 8$	Write original equation.
$x + (-4) - (-4) = 8 - (-4)$	Subtract -4 from each side.
$x + (-4) + 4 = 8 + 4$	Subtract by adding the opposite.
$x = 12$	Solution: x is by itself.

The solution is $x = 12$. Check this as follows.

✔**Check:**		
	$x + (-4) = 8$	Write original equation.
	$12 + (-4) \stackrel{?}{=} 8$	Substitute 12 for x.
	$8 = 8$	Both sides are the same. ✔

The equation in part (a) of this example could have also been solved in another way. Because you are adding a negative number to the variable, the equation could have been rewritten as the subtraction equation $x - 4 = 8$ before being solved. In the third step of our solution, 4 was added to both sides of the equation. This is the same way the equation $x - 4 = 8$ would be solved.

b.

$9 = 3 + n$	Write original equation.
$9 - 3 = 3 - 3 + n$	Subtract 3 from each side.
$6 = n$	Solution: n is by itself.

The solution is $n = 6$. Check this as follows.

✔**Check:**	$9 = 3 + n$	Write original equation.
	$9 \stackrel{?}{=} 3 + 6$	Substitute 6 for n.
	$9 = 9$	Both sides are the same. ✔

In Lesson 4.7, you learned to solve a subtraction equation by adding the same number to both sides. As with addition equations, your goal is to isolate the variable.

Example 2 Solving a Subtraction Equation

Solve each equation.

a. $b - 5 = -6$ **b.** $12 = m - (-5)$

Solution

a.
$$b - 5 = -6$$ Write original equation.
$$b - 5 + 5 = -6 + 5$$ Add 5 to each side.
$$b = -1$$ Solution: b is by itself.

The solution is $b = -1$. Check this as follows.

✔Check: $b - 5 = -6$ Write original equation.
$$-1 - 5 \stackrel{?}{=} -6$$ Substitute -1 for b.
$$-6 = -6$$ Both sides are the same. ✔

b.
$$12 = m - (-5)$$ Write original equation.
$$12 = m + 5$$ Rewrite as addition equation.
$$12 - 5 = m + 5 - 5$$ Subtract 5 from each side.
$$7 = m$$ Solution: m is by itself.

The solution is $m = 7$. Check this as follows.

✔Check: $12 = m - (-5)$ Write original equation.
$$12 = m + 5$$ Rewrite as an addition equation.
$$12 \stackrel{?}{=} 7 + 5$$ Substitute 7 for m.
$$12 = 12$$ Both sides are the same. ✔

Notice that the subtraction equation in part (b) was rewritten as an addition equation because it made it a simpler equation to solve.

$$12 = m - (-5) \longrightarrow 12 = m + 5$$

This can be done because addition and subtraction are inverse operations of one another.

ONGOING ASSESSMENT

Write About It
· · · · · · · · · · · · · · · · · · · ·

Decide whether it is easier to solve each equation as an addition equation or as a subtraction equation. Explain your reasoning. Then solve it that way. Show your work. Explain each step.

1. $m + (-6) = -10$

2. $-4 = c - (-5)$

GUIDED PRACTICE

In Exercises 1 and 2, complete the solution.

1. $w + (-8) = -9$

$w + (-8) - \boxed{?} = -9 - \boxed{?}$

$w = \boxed{?}$

2. $24 = z - (-7)$

$24 + \boxed{?} = z - (-7) + \boxed{?}$

$\boxed{?} = z$

In Exercises 3–6, match the equation with its solution.

A. $n - 4 = -1$
B. $-3 + n = -\dfrac{10}{3}$
C. $n - 4 = -7$
D. $n - 3 = -\dfrac{8}{3}$

3. $n = -3$
4. $n = 3$
5. $n = \dfrac{1}{3}$
6. $n = -\dfrac{1}{3}$

7. ERROR ANALYSIS You are a math teacher. Write the correct solution to the students incorrect work at the left.

$x - (-21) = 17$

$x - (-21) + 21 = 17 + 21$ ✗

$x = 38$

Tech Link

Investigation 12, Interactive Real-Life Investigations

8. Solve the equation $t - 6 = 13$. Show your steps.

PRACTICE AND PROBLEM SOLVING

In Exercises 9–11, decide whether $p = -6$ is a solution.

9. $-6 + p = -12$
10. $p - 6 = 0$
11. $p - (-12) = 6$

In Exercises 12–14, rewrite the equation in a simpler form. Then solve the equation.

12. $d - (-3) = 10$
13. $-18 = x + (-5)$
14. $-13 = b - (-1)$

GEOMETRY **In Exercises 15–17, write and solve an addition equation to find the side length or angle measure labeled x.**

15. Perimeter $= 14$

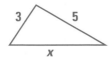

16.

17.

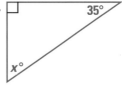

In Exercises 18–23, solve the equation and check your solution.

18. $m + (-1) = 9$
19. $s - 12.2 = -9.8$
20. $16 = y - (-2)$

21. $11 = 3 + t$
22. $\dfrac{1}{2} + x = \dfrac{7}{2}$
23. $\dfrac{2}{3} = b - \dfrac{5}{6}$

24. BASEBALL Use the illustration at the right to find out how many years ago baseball gloves were first used. Use the verbal model below to write an equation. Then solve.

$$\begin{array}{c}\text{Year baseball}\\\text{gloves first used}\end{array} + \begin{array}{c}\text{Number of}\\\text{years ago}\end{array} = \begin{array}{c}\text{Current}\\\text{Year}\end{array}$$

First used
1877   **1901**   **1951**   **Modern**

PRESIDENTIAL ELECTIONS The bar graph shows the electoral vote results for the 1860 Presidential election. Match the equation with the question. Then solve the equation and answer the question.

A. $x + 12 = 180$ **B.** $x + 12 = 303$ **C.** $x + 180 = 303$

25. How many electoral votes did candidates other than Abraham Lincoln receive?

26. How many more electoral votes did Lincoln receive than Stephen Douglas?

27. How many electoral votes did candidates other than Douglas receive?

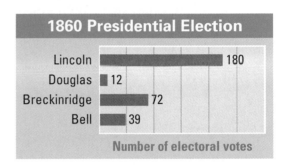

1860 Presidential Election

Lincoln — 180
Douglas — 12
Breckinridge — 72
Bell — 39

Number of electoral votes

STANDARDIZED TEST PRACTICE

28. 14 is a solution to which equation?

Ⓐ $20 - (-m) = 6$ **Ⓑ** $20 + (-m) = 34$

Ⓒ $m - (-16) = -2$ **Ⓓ** $m + (-10) = 4$

29. Solve the equation: $s - (-24) = 4$.

Ⓐ -20 **Ⓑ** 6   **Ⓒ** 20   **Ⓓ** 28

EXPLORATION AND EXTENSION

PORTFOLIO

30. BUILDING YOUR PROJECT The class that featured the country of Kenya in Africa made a display about Mount Kilimanjaro. Kilimanjaro lies on the border between Kenya and Tanzania and has 2 summits. One of these, Kibo, is the highest peak in Africa. The lesser, Mawensi, is 16,890 ft high and 2,450 ft lower than Kibo. Write and solve an equation to find the height of Kibo.

1. Here are the average temperatures (in °F) from January through December in the Greater Ohio Valley.

   36, 32, 39, 55, 64, 72, 75, 80, 71, 62, 50, 39

   a. Find the mean, median, and mode of the data. **(5.1)**

   b. Draw a box-and-whisker plot of the data. **(5.3)**

2. What is 15% of 280? **(7.4)**

3. 25 is what percent of 1000? **(7.4)**

In Exercises 4–6, use the figure at the right. (8.2)

4. Write the coordinates of the vertices of the figure.

5. Slide the figure 3 units to the left and 2 units up. What are the new coordinates of each point?

6. Describe the slide that would move the leftmost point of the figure to the origin.

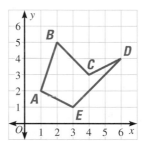

HISTORY Connection

CALENDARS

The ancient Chinese calendar is a lunar calendar, based on the cycles of the moon. Each year generally has 12 months and each month begins on a day when there is a new moon. Since the cycle of the moon goes from new to full and back to new every 29.5 days, the Chinese calendar contains both "big months" of 30 days and "small months" of 29 days. The Chinese calendar is also broken up into cycles of twelve years, each defined an animal. The year 2000 is the year of the dragon.

New Moon

First Quarter

Full Moon

Last Quarter

New Moon

1. Suppose M = days in a "big month." Which equation shows when a full moon takes place. How many days into the month is it? Explain.

   A. $M + 2$ **B.** $M - 2$ **C.** $2M$ **D.** $\dfrac{M}{2}$

In Exercises 2–5, use the time line below. Match the animal's year with the equation that relates it to the year 2000. Then solve the equation to determine the year of each event.

2. $x + 12 = 2000$ A. Next year of the dog

3. $x - 6 = 2000$ B. Next year of the sheep

4. $x + 7 = 2000$ C. Last year of the rooster

5. $x - 3 = 2000$ D. Last year of the dragon

Inverse Operation Game

Here is a calculator game to find inverse operations.

Example

With a partner, use the following steps to play this *One-Step Inverse Game*.

1. Player A enters any integer on the calculator.

2. Player B enters three keystrokes.

Choice 1	Choice 2	Choice 3
− , + , × , ÷	1, 2, 3, 4, 5, 6, 7, 8, 9	=

3. Player A enters three keystrokes from the same choices. Player A's goal is to obtain the original integer.

Solution

Here is one example of how the game could be played.

	Step 1	Step 2	Step 3
Player A	18 [+/−]		[+] 4 [=]
Player B		[−] 4 [=]	

−18.	−22.	−18.

Exercises

1. Play the *One-Step Inverse Game* several times with a partner. Take turns being Player A. Then describe a winning strategy for Player A.

2. Is there a strategy that Player B can use to stop Player A from reaching his or her goal? Explain your reasoning.

3. The *Two-Step Inverse Game* is the same as above, but uses the keystrokes

− , + , × , ÷	1, 2, 3, 4, 5, 6, 7, 8, 9	=	− , + , × , ÷	1, 2, 3, 4, 5, 6, 7, 8, 9	=

Write 4 examples of games in which Player A reaches his or her goal.

4. Describe a winning strategy for Player A in the *Two-Step Inverse Game*. Is there a strategy that Player B can use to stop Player A from reaching his or her goal? Explain your reasoning.

LAB 12.3

COOPERATIVE LEARNING

Investigating Multiplication Equations

Part A MODELING EXPRESSIONS

Materials Needed
- algebra tiles
- pencils or pens
- paper

Algebra tiles can be used to model expressions. Here are some examples.

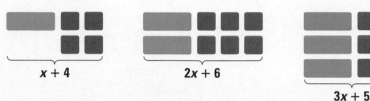

$x + 4$ $2x + 6$

$3x + 5$

1. Use algebra tiles to model each expression.

   a. $5x + 6$ **b.** $4x + 8$ **c.** $2x + 9$ **d.** $3x + 1$

Part B MODELING EQUATIONS

In Lab 4.6, you learned how to use algebra tiles to model addition equations. The tiles can also be used to model multiplication equations. Here is an example.

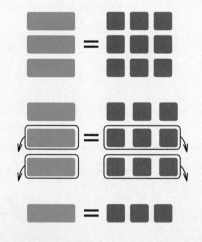

Original equation: $3x = 9$

To isolate x, divide each side into three groups and remove two of the groups.

The solution is $x = 3$.

2. Use algebra tiles to model and solve each equation.

   a. $4x = 8$ **b.** $2x = 6$ **c.** $3x = 12$ **d.** $4x = 12$

3. Discuss how you could solve the multiplication equations in Exercise 2 without using algebra tiles.

In Lesson 12.1, you learned how box models and inverse operations can be used to solve equations. For instance, you can solve the equation $3x = 42$ with a box model as follows.

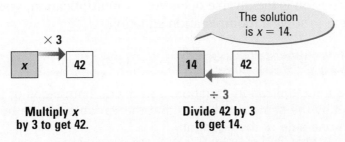

The solution is $x = 14$.

Multiply x by 3 to get 42.

Divide 42 by 3 to get 14.

4. Use a box model to solve each equation.

    a. $6x = 12$ **b.** $-2x = 12$ **c.** $6x = -18$ **d.** $24x = -12$

NOW TRY THESE

5. Write the equation that is modeled with algebra tiles. State the solution and check it by substituting in the original equation.

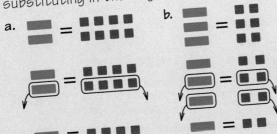

a.   **b.**

6. Solve each equation with algebra tiles or with a box model. Draw a sketch of your work.

    a. $5x = 10$ **b.** $5x = -10$ **c.** $-3x = 9$

In Exercises 7–9, match the equation with its solution. Then simplify the solution and check it.

7. $2x = 8$ **A.** $x = 8 \div (-2)$

8. $-2x = 8$ **B.** $x = (-8) \div (-2)$

9. $-2x = -8$ **C.** $x = 8 \div 2$

6.a.

12.3

Multiplication Equations

What you should learn:

Goal 1 How to use an inverse operation to solve a multiplication equation

Goal 2 How to use multiplication equations to solve real-life problems

Why you should learn it:

Knowing how to solve multiplication equations can help you solve real-life problems. An example is finding a person's share of a profit or loss.

Goal 1 SOLVING MULTIPLICATION EQUATIONS

Because division is the inverse operation of multiplication, you can use division to solve a multiplication equation.

SOLVING A MULTIPLICATION EQUATION

To solve a multiplication equation, you divide both sides of the equation by the same number so that the variable will be by itself on one side of the equation.

Example 1 Solving a Multiplication Equation

Solve each equation.

a. $5y = -42$ **b.** $2.4n = 144$

Solution

a. $5y = -42$ Write original equation.

$\dfrac{5y}{5} = \dfrac{-42}{5}$ Divide each side by 5.

$y = -8.4$ Solution: y is by itself.

The solution is $y = -8.4$. Check this as follows.

✔Check: $5y = -42$ Write original equation.

$5(-8.4) \stackrel{?}{=} -42$ Substitute -8.4 for y.

$-42 = -42$ Both sides are the same. ✔

b. $2.4n = 144$ Write original equation.

$\dfrac{2.4n}{2.4} = \dfrac{144}{2.4}$ Divide each side by 2.4.

$n = 60$ Solution: n is by itself.

The solution is $n = 60$. Check this as follows.

✔Check: $2.4n = 144$ Write original equation

$2.4(60) \stackrel{?}{=} 144$ Substitute 60 for n.

$144 = 144$ Both sides are the same. ✔

STUDY TIP

When you solve a multiplication equation, check that your solution has the correct sign. Here is the pattern.

$(+) \cdot (+) = (+)$

$(+) \cdot (-) = (-)$

$(-) \cdot (+) = (-)$

$(-) \cdot (-) = (+)$

Example 2 Modeling a Real-Life Problem

In social studies class, you are a member of an 8-person team that is studying the stock market. Each person on your team "buys" $2000 worth of stocks and sells them at the end of a month. As part of your assignment, you are asked to combine all 8 profits and losses and find each person's share. The profits and losses are as follows.

REAL LIFE
Business

Stock Brokers are agents who buy or sell stocks or other securities.

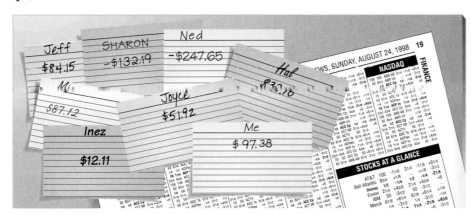

What is each person's share?

Solution

Begin by adding all of the profits and losses to obtain a total of −$14.40. Then use a verbal model to find each person's share.

Verbal Model	**Number of people** · **Share per person** = **Total profit or loss**

Labels   Number of people = **8**
Share per person = x
Total profit or loss = **−14.40**

Equation $8x = -14.40$ Write original equation.

$$\frac{8x}{8} = \frac{-14.40}{8}$$ Divide each side by 8.

$x = -1.8$ Solution: x is by itself.

Each person's share is −$1.80. This means that, overall, your group averaged a *loss of* $1.80 per person.

12.3 Exercises
Extra Practice, page 646

GUIDED PRACTICE

In Exercises 1–3, write the equation represented by the box model. Then solve the equation and check the solution.

1. × (−4)

m → 32

2. × 6

b → −78

3. × (−3)

y → −51

In Exercises 4–7, match the equation with its solution.

A. $x = -0.8$ **B.** $x = -2$ **C.** $x = 1.25$ **D.** $x = 2$

4. $4x = 5$ **5.** $4x = -8$ **6.** $-4x = -8$ **7.** $-5x = 4$

8. The following list represents the number of points a student missed on five 100-point tests.

$$-9, -3, -27, -6, -15$$

Use the verbal model below to find the mean of these five numbers. What does the mean represent?

Number of tests · Mean = Total points incorrect

PRACTICE AND PROBLEM SOLVING

In Exercises 9–12, without solving the equation, decide whether the solution is *positive* or *negative*. Then solve the equation.

9. $5n = -17$ **10.** $26 = 2x$ **11.** $-3t = -54$ **12.** $-4m = 38$

MAKING AN ESTIMATE In Exercises 13–21, use mental math to estimate the solution of the equation. Then solve the equation.

13. $2k = 101$ **14.** $31 = -10b$ **15.** $-60 = 8a$

16. $-15b = -9$ **17.** $-9m = 94.5$ **18.** $3.2t = -48$

19. $-5x = -36.2$ **20.** $4x = 0.5$ **21.** $\frac{1}{3} = 2x$

In Exercises 22–30, solve the equation. Then check the solution.

22. $8y = 32$ **23.** $-72 = 6m$ **24.** $2x = 4$

25. $5k = 0$ **26.** $3n = -7.2$ **27.** $12p = 9$

28. $-15a = -18$ **29.** $19t = -57$ **30.** $132 = -11z$

31. **FOOTBALL** Your team gains 90 yards on 12 plays. Use the verbal model below to determine your team's average gain per play.

Number of plays · Average yards per play = Total yards

In Exercises 32–35, write the equation represented by the verbal sentence. Then solve the equation.

32. A number multiplied by -5 is 0.

33. -22 is -8 times a number.

34. -6 is the product of 9 and a number.

35. The product of -7 and a number is 91.

GEOMETRY In Exercises 36–38, write an equation using the given information. Then solve the equation to find *x*.

36. Area = 135 in.^{2}

9 in.

x

37. Area = 120 ft^2

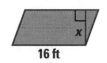
x

16 ft

38. Area = $2\frac{2}{5}$ m^2

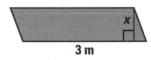
x

3 m

FINDING A PATTERN In Exercises 39 and 40, solve each equation. Then describe the pattern.

39. $-2d = 16, -4d = 16, -8d = 16$

40. $1.5x = -3, 1.5x = -6, 1.5x = -9$

WATERFALLS OF THE WORLD In exercises 41–44, write a multiplication equation using the variables given to represent the statement. Then use the values in the pictograph at the right to check that the equation is correct.

41. The height of Angel, *A*, is 20 times greater that the height of Niagara Falls, *N*.

42. The height of Takkakaw, *T*, is twice that of Skykje, *S*.

43. The height of Skykje, *S*, is 2.5 times greater than the height of Comet, *C*.

44. The height of Feather, *F*, is $\frac{1}{5}$ of the height of Angel, *A*.

Waterfalls of the World

Height (in meters)

Angel 1000
Takkakaw 500
Feather 200
Comet 100
Skykje 250
Niagara Falls 50

STANDARDIZED TEST PRACTICE

45. If $y = -3$, which equation is false?

(A) $4y = -12$ (B) $-0.6y = 1.8$ (C) $y \cdot (-1) = -3$ (D) $y \cdot 5 = -15$

46. Solve the equation: $24t = 4$.

(A) $\frac{1}{6}$ (B) $\frac{1}{3}$ (C) 6   (D) 20

47. BUILDING YOUR PROJECT One of the students in the room that featured China brought in a recipe for Honey-Glazed Chicken Wings.

The class made arrangements with the home economics teacher to cook the wings. The class needed to make enough wings so that each of the 64 students coming to their room could each have 3 wings. How many wings needed to be made? Write and solve multiplication equations to determine how much of each ingredient the students needed. Make a revised recipe card for the bulletin board and include a description of how the original recipe was changed.

Honey-Glazed Chicken Wings

8 chicken wings
1/4 cup soy sauce
1/4 cup water
1 tablespoon honey
2 cloves garlic, crushed
1 tablespoon chopped fresh ginger

1. Mix the soy sauce, water, honey, garlic, and ginger in a large baking dish. Add the chicken wings and turn to coat. Let the wings marinate for at least 15 minutes.

2. Broil the wings for 10 minutes. Turn them over and broil for another 10 minutes, then serve.

SPIRAL REVIEW

GEOMETRY In Exercises 1–3, find the perimeter (or circumference) and area of the figure. **(8.3–8.6)**

1.
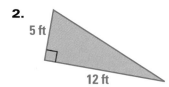
22 cm
20 cm   16 cm   20 cm
46 cm

2.
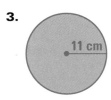
5 ft
12 ft

3.
11 cm

GEOMETRY In Exercises 4–6, find the surface area of the solid. **(9.2–9.5)**

4.
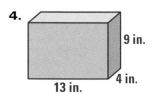
9 in.
13 in.   4 in.

5.
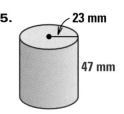
23 mm
47 mm

6.
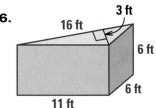
3 ft
16 ft
6 ft
11 ft   6 ft

7. BUSINESS The table below shows the profit and loss for each of the first four months of a small business. How much profit or loss did the business have after the first four months? **(10.2, 10.3)**

May	June	July	August
−$450	−$275	−$90	$385

Take this test as you would take a test in class. The answers to the exercises are given in the back of the book.

In Exercises 1–4, match the box model with the equation. Then use the box model to solve the equation. (12.1)

a.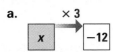

b.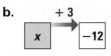

c.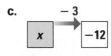

d.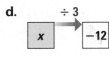

1. $x - 3 = -12$ **2.** $3x = -12$ **3.** $x \div 3 = -12$ **4.** $x + 3 = -12$

5. SCIENCE For ice to turn into water, the temperature must increase to 32°F. For water to turn into steam, the temperature must increase to 212°F. Describe the steps that must happen for steam to turn into water and then into ice. **(12.1)**

In Exercises 6–8, write the equation in a simpler form. Then solve the equation. (12.2)

6. $n + (-3) - -4$ **7.** $-5 - x - (-4)$ **8.** $m - (-3) - 6$

ERROR ANALYSIS **In Exercises 9–11, find and correct any errors. (12.2, 12.3)**

9.
$$n - (-4) = -6$$
$$n - (-4) + 4 = -6 + 4$$
$$n = -2 \quad \text{✗}$$

10.
$$6 = x - 5$$
$$6 - 6 = x - 5 - 6$$
$$0 = x \quad \text{✗}$$

11.
$$3p = -15$$
$$\frac{3p}{3} = \frac{-15}{3}$$
$$p = 5 \quad \text{✗}$$

In Exercises 12–14, solve the equation. Then check your solution. (12.3)

12. $5x = -15$ **13.** $-2x = 6$ **14.** $-4x = -18$

15. ACCOUNTING You are an accountant and are checking the records of a business. The records show that the business lost a total of $4780 over 6 months. Use the following verbal model and labels to write an equation that can be used to find the average monthly loss. Then solve the equation to find this average. **(12.3)**

| Number of months | • | Loss per month | = | Loss for 6 months |

Number of months = 6

Loss per month = x

Loss for 6 months = -4780

12.4

Division Equations

What you should learn:

Goal 1 How to use an inverse operation to solve a division equation

Goal 2 How to use division equations to solve real-life problems

Why you should learn it:

Knowing how to solve division equations can help you solve real-life problems. An example is estimating the amount of food needed to feed a gorilla.

Goal 1 SOLVING DIVISION EQUATIONS

Inverse operations can be used to solve division equations. You can use multiplication to solve a division equation.

SOLVING A DIVISION EQUATION

To solve a division equation, multiply both sides of the equation by the same number so that the variable will be by itself on one side of the equation.

Example 1 Solving a Division Equation

Solve each equation.

a. $\dfrac{x}{3} = 7.5$ **b.** $\dfrac{n}{3.1} = -20$ **c.** $y \div \dfrac{1}{6} = -5$

Solution

a.
$$\dfrac{x}{3} = 7.5 \qquad \text{Write original equation.}$$
$$3 \cdot \dfrac{x}{3} = 3 \cdot 7.5 \qquad \text{Multiply each side by 3.}$$
$$x = 22.5 \qquad \text{Solution: } x \text{ is by itself.}$$

The solution is $x = 22.5$. Check this in the original equation.

b.
$$\dfrac{n}{3.1} = -20 \qquad \text{Write original equation.}$$
$$3.1 \cdot \dfrac{n}{3.1} = 3.1 \cdot (-20) \qquad \text{Multiply each side by 3.1.}$$
$$n = -62 \qquad \text{Solution: } n \text{ is by itself.}$$

The solution is $n = -62$. Check this in the original equation.

c.
$$y \div \dfrac{1}{6} = -5 \qquad \text{Write original equation.}$$
$$y \div \dfrac{1}{6} \cdot \dfrac{1}{6} = -5 \cdot \dfrac{1}{6} \qquad \text{Multiply each side by } \dfrac{1}{6}.$$
$$y = -\dfrac{5}{6} \qquad \text{Solution: } y \text{ is by itself.}$$

The solution is $y = -\dfrac{5}{6}$. Check this in the original equation.

Example 2 Solving a Proportion

You work in a zoo and help feed a 340-pound gorilla that eats about 22 pounds of food each day. The zoo is getting another gorilla that weighs 260 pounds. About how much food will it eat each day?

REAL LIFE
Zoos

Solution

To solve this problem, assume that the amount of food a gorilla eats is proportional to its weight.

Verbal Model

$$\frac{\text{Food for small gorilla}}{\text{Food for large gorilla}} = \frac{\text{Weight of small gorilla}}{\text{Weight of large gorilla}}$$

Labels

Food for small gorilla = x lbs

Food for large gorilla = **22** lbs

Weight of small gorilla = **260** lbs

Weight of large gorilla = **340** lbs

Algebraic Model

$\dfrac{x}{22} = \dfrac{260}{340}$ Write original equation.

$22 \cdot \dfrac{x}{22} = 22 \cdot \dfrac{260}{340}$ Multiply each side by 22.

$x \approx 17$ Solution: x is by itself.

You can also solve this problem by cross multiplying.

$\dfrac{x}{22} = \dfrac{260}{340}$ Write original equation.

$340 \cdot x = 22 \cdot 260$ Cross multiply.

$\dfrac{340 \cdot x}{340} = \dfrac{22 \cdot 260}{340}$ Divide each side by 340.

$x \approx 17$ Solution: x is by itself.

The small gorilla will eat about 17 pounds of food each day.

Real Life...
Real People

George Schaller, one of the greatest naturalists of the 20th century, spent nearly two years in a hut in Zaire studying the nature, behavior and habitat of mountain gorillas.

ONGOING ASSESSMENT

Talk About It

The zoo is getting a third gorilla. It has been eating 20 pounds of food each day.

1. Estimate the third gorillas weight.

2. Discuss how you got your answer.

GUIDED PRACTICE

In Exercises 1 and 2, complete the statement using the words *multiply* or *divide*.

1. To solve $\frac{n}{12} = -60$, _?_ both sides of the equation by 12.

2. To solve $12n = -60$, _?_ both sides of the equation by 12.

HOLLYWOOD In Exercises 3–5, use the following information. It took 700 hours and 170 gallons of white paint to repaint the "Hollywood" sign on Mt. Lee in California. Match the question with the equation you would use. Then use the equation and a calculator to solve the problem. (Source: Dutch Boy Paints)

A. $x = 9 \cdot 700$ **B.** $700x = 170$ **C.** $170 = 9x$

3. What is the average number of gallons of paint it took to paint each letter?

4. Suppose painters earned $9 per hour to paint the sign. What was the total cost for painters?

5. How many gallons of paint were used per hour?

6. Why can't you solve the equation $\frac{x}{0} = 6$?

PRACTICE AND PROBLEM SOLVING

In Exercises 7–14, solve the equation. Then check your solution.

7. $\frac{d}{10} = 12$ **8.** $\frac{t}{28} = 9$ **9.** $n \div \frac{1}{4} = 5$ **10.** $\frac{x}{-8} = -15$

11. $\frac{p}{2.3} = 4.9$ **12.** $a \div \frac{5}{8} = \frac{3}{4}$ **13.** $\frac{y}{5.5} = -10.2$ **14.** $\frac{b}{-3.7} = 8.2$

15. JOGGING You are recording the number of calories you use while jogging. The number of calories used is proportional to the distance you jog. Yesterday you jogged 1.2 miles and used 117 calories. Today you jogged 2.7 miles. Use the verbal model below to estimate the number of calories you used.

$$\frac{\text{Total calories used today}}{\text{Total calories used yesterday}} = \frac{\text{Distance jogged today}}{\text{Distance jogged yesterday}}$$

GEOMETRY In Exercises 16–18, write a division equation to find the area x of the figure. Solve the equation to find the area.

16. Area $= x$

12 cm

15 cm

17. Area $= x$

13 yd

13 yd

18. Area $= x$

2.5 m

2.6 m

In Exercises 19–22, decide whether the solution is positive or negative *without* solving the equation.

19. $\dfrac{m}{5} = -15$

20. $s \div -42 = -6$

21. $\dfrac{z}{-11} = 4$

22. $c \div 15 = 3$

LOOKING FOR A PATTERN In Exercises 23–25, solve the equations. Describe any patterns that you see.

23. $s \div 5 = 2$

$s \div 5 = 4$

$s \div 5 = 6$

24. $r \div 0.2 = -20$

$r \div 0.2 = -25$

$r \div 0.2 = -30$

25. $p \div 11 = 0.54$

$p \div 11 = 0.63$

$p \div 11 = 0.72$

STANDARDIZED TEST PRACTICE

26. Which equation has a solution of $m = 5$?

(A) $m \div 20 = 0.2$

(B) $m \div 2 = 2.5$

(C) $-m \div 10 = 0.5$

(D) $-m \div 3 = -1.3$

27. Solve the proportion: $\dfrac{t}{1.2} = \dfrac{7.5}{18}$.

(A) 0.5

(B) 2.88

(C) 9

(D) 112.5

EXPLORATION AND EXTENSION

PORTFOLIO

28. BUILDING YOUR PROJECT The classroom that featured Colombia handed out miniature paper versions of the country's flag as souvenirs. Each souvenir flag was 6 in. long. Use the flag at the right as a model. Write and solve proportions to determine the height of the souvenir flags and the width of each stripe on the flags.

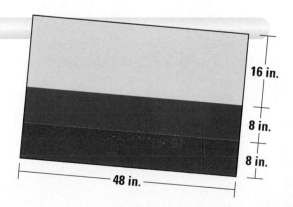

16 in.

8 in.

8 in.

48 in.

LAB 12.5

COOPERATIVE LEARNING

Investigating Two-Step Equations

Part A MODELING EQUATIONS

Materials Needed
• algebra tiles
• pencils or pens
• paper

Some equations contain a single operation. Here are some examples.

$$x + 3 = 7, \qquad x - 4 = -2, \qquad 2x = 21, \qquad \frac{x}{3} = 7$$

These equations are called *one-step equations* because they can be solved with just one step. (For example, you can solve the first equation by subtracting 3 from each side of the equation.)

Other equations, such as $3x + 4 = 10$, contain two operations. This type of equation is called a *two-step equation*. One way to solve a two-step equation is to use algebra tiles.

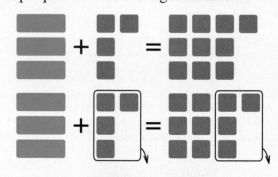

Original Equation:
$3x + 4 = 10$

As a first step, subtract four red tiles from each side of the equation.

Simplify the equation.

As a second step, divide each side into 3 groups and remove two of the groups.

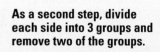

The solution is $x = 2$.

1. Use algebra tiles to solve each equation.

   a. $2x + 3 = 7$ **b.** $3x + 5 = 14$ **c.** $4x + 1 = 13$

2. In the equation modeled above, explain how inverse operations are used to isolate the variable.

Two-step equations can also be modeled with box models. For example, the equation $4x - 3 = 13$ is modeled below.

The solution is
$x = 4$.

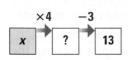

×4   **−3**

| x | ? | 13 |

Multiply x by 4. Then subtract 3 to get 13.

| x | 16 | 13 |

+3

Add 3 to 13 to undo subtracting 3.

| 4 | 16 | 13 |

÷4

Divide 16 by 4 to undo multiplying by 4.

3. Use a box model to model and solve each equation. Draw a sketch of your models.

   a. $5x + 2 = -8$ **b.** $2x - 7 = 5$

   c. $\dfrac{x}{3} + 4 = -2$ **d.** $\dfrac{x}{4} - 5 = 1$

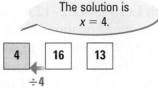

NOW TRY THESE

4. Use algebra tiles to model and solve each equation. Draw a sketch of your steps.

   a. $2x + 3 = 9$ **b.** $4x + 7 = 11$ **c.** $5x + 4 = 24$

5. Write the equation that is being modeled by the box model. Then use the box model to solve the equation. Check your solution.

   a.   **×2**   **−2**

   | b | ? | 11 |

   b.   **÷4**   **+5**

   | y | ? | −21 |

6. Use a box model to model and solve each equation. Draw a sketch of your steps.

   a. $5x - 4 = -19$ **b.** $2x + 3 = -11$

   c. $\dfrac{x}{2} - 3 = 2$ **d.** $\dfrac{x}{6} + 4 = -2$

7. **WRITING** Write a paragraph that summarizes how to solve a two-step equation. Use an example to explain your reasoning.

GUIDED PRACTICE

In Exercises 1 and 2, describe each step of the solution.

1.
$$\frac{n}{2} + 6 = 3$$
$$\frac{n}{2} + 6 - 6 = 3 - 6$$
$$\frac{n}{2} = -3$$
$$2 \cdot \frac{n}{2} = 2 \cdot (-3)$$
$$n = -6$$

2.
$$9y - 13 = -4$$
$$9y - 13 + 13 = -4 + 13$$
$$9y = 9$$
$$\frac{9y}{9} = \frac{9}{9}$$
$$y = 1$$

3. Write the equation represented by the verbal sentence. Then solve the equation. *The sum of* -2 *times a number and 5 is* -7.

4. BOWLING At a bowling alley, shoes cost $0.75 to rent and each game is $2.25. Use the verbal model below to find the number of games you can bowl with $12.

$$\begin{array}{c}\text{Cost for}\\ \text{shoes}\end{array} + \begin{array}{c}\text{Cost per}\\ \text{game}\end{array} \cdot \begin{array}{c}\text{Number}\\ \text{of games}\end{array} = \begin{array}{c}\text{Total cost}\\ \text{of bowling}\end{array}$$

PRACTICE AND PROBLEM SOLVING

In Exercises 5–7, describe the first step you would take towards solving the equation.

5. $3x + 10 = 4$

6. $-16 + 4m = 12$

7. $-2 = \frac{z}{4} - 5$

In Exercises 8–10, write the equation represented by the box model. Then solve the equation and check the solution by filling in the empty square of the box model.

8. × 2   − 8

| t | → | ? | → | 14 |

9. × (−5)   + 3

| b | → | ? | → | 28 |

10. ÷ 3   + 1

| m | → | ? | → | −9 |

In Exercises 11–19, solve the equation. Then check the solution.

11. $15 + 4m = -1$

12. $-6x - 12 = 6$

13. $(a \div 3) - 2 = 5$

14. $\frac{n}{8} - 3 = -3$

15. $7 = \frac{b}{5} + 9$

16. $\frac{k}{12} + \frac{1}{3} = \frac{1}{2}$

17. $2t - 8 = -10$

18. $9.3 + 3z = -5.7$

19. $-11 + 2y = 0$

GEOMETRY In Exercises 20–22, solve the equation. Then use the solution to find the angle measures.

20. $8x + 2 = 90$

$(5x + 2)°$

$3x°$

21. $6x + 12 = 180$

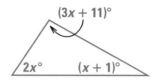

$(3x + 11)°$

$2x°$ $(x + 1)°$

22. $10x + 10 = 180$

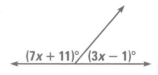

$(7x + 11)°$ $(3x - 1)°$

23. USING LOGICAL REASONING Use the clues to find the values of a, b, c, and d.

$$\frac{d}{8} - b = c \qquad \frac{a}{3} + b = 0 \qquad 4c - b = a \qquad b = 2$$

24. CLUB MEMBERSHIP You want to join a swimming club for the summer. *Swim USA* has a membership fee of $25 plus $18 a month. *Swimmers Club* has a membership fee of $40 plus $12 a month. You have saved $91 for your membership. Use the verbal model below for each club and solve the resulting equation. Which membership would you choose? Explain your reasoning.

$$\text{Cost per month} \cdot \text{Number of months} + \text{Membership fee} = \text{Amount saved}$$

25. FUNDRAISING Your class is having a fundraiser with a goal of raising $600. You get $175 from the magazine company plus $1.25 per subscriber. Write a verbal model, labels, and an equation to find the number of magazine subscribers you need to reach your goal.

STANDARDIZED TEST PRACTICE

26. Your aunt's age is 3 less than 4 times your cousin's age. Your aunt is 29 years old. Which equation can you use to determine your cousin's age?

  A $29 = 3x + 4$ **B** $29 = 4x + 3$

  C $29 = 3x - 4$ **D** $29 = 4x - 3$

27. The total cost for a school field trip is $212. The total cost consists of transportation costs and student costs. The transportation costs are $86. If 35 students go on the field trip, what is the cost per student?

  A $2.48   **B** $3.60   **C** $6.06   **D** $8.51

28. COMMUNICATING ABOUT MATHEMATICS You can determine which women's and men's shoe sizes will fit a certain foot length using the following equations.

$\frac{1}{3}$(Women's shoe size $-$ 1) = Foot length in inches $-8\frac{5}{12}$

$\frac{1}{3}\left(\text{Men's shoe size} - 5\frac{1}{2}\right)$ = Foot length in inches $-$ 10.08

a. Solve to find out what foot length a women's size 7 shoe will fit. What length will a men's size 7 shoe fit?

b. Analyze the equations. What do you think are the smallest women's and men's shoe sizes? What length foot do they fit?

c. Write a verbal model that would apply to both of these shoe size equations.

In Exercises 1–4, write the equation that represents the statement. Then solve the equation. (4.6, 4.7, 12.3, 12.4)

1. The sum of nine and a number is negative fourteen.

2. Negative seven is the difference of a number and fifteen.

3. Forty-two is three and a half times a number.

4. Negative twenty is one fourth of a number.

5. MINIATURE GOLF The table below shows your score (above and below par) for the first nine holes of miniature golf. Draw a scatter plot of the data using the *hole* numbers as *x*-coordinates and the *score* numbers as *y*-coordinates. In what two quadrants are all the points located? **(5.4)**

Hole	1	2	3	4	5	6	7	8	9
Score	1	-1	2	0	-1	-2	3	1	-2

In Exercises 6–9, use cross products to solve the proportion. Then check the solution. (6.4)

6. $\frac{x}{8} = \frac{27}{72}$ **7.** $\frac{40}{m} = \frac{5}{6}$ **8.** $\frac{5.6}{7} = \frac{4}{b}$ **9.** $\frac{8}{12} = \frac{t}{21}$

10. You work for a company that manufactures T-shirts. You make 2 styles (v-neck and round neck) in 7 colors (red, yellow, white, black, gray, green, blue), and in 5 sizes (small, medium, large, extra large, extra extra large). How many different T-shirts does your company manufacture? **(11.2)**

The Size that FITS

READ About It

They come in different colors. Some have lights that flash with each step. Designers even have plans to build in video games and heaters or coolers. But whatever gadgets your sneakers have, the most important thing is that they fit.

Between the ages of four and eleven, your feet grow about $\frac{1}{3}''$ longer each year. It is important to have your feet measured each time you buy new shoes. The length of the foot is the most important factor in determining shoe size. Infant shoes start at size 0 for feet that are $3\frac{11}{12}$ inches long.

The smallest girl's size is 7. These are for a foot length of $5\frac{11}{12}''$. Girls go to a women's size 1 when their feet measure $8\frac{5}{12}''$. The smallest boy's size is 8. These are for a foot length of $6\frac{5}{12}''$. Boys go to men's size $5\frac{1}{2}$ when their feet measure 10.08 inches.

In all of the kinds of sizes (girl's, boy's, women's, and men's) each whole size is $\frac{1}{3}$ inch longer than the previous whole size.

WRITE About It

1. Describe in words how to figure out how many inches your feet might grow between the ages of 4 and 11. Write an equation and solve it to find out how many inches they grow.

2. Using the format $\frac{1}{3} \cdot (Shoe\ size - Minimum\ size) = Foot\ length$ (in.) $- Foot\ length\ of\ minimum\ size$ (in.), write equations relating foot size and shoe size for infants', girls', boys', mens', and womens' feet.

3. In what way are the equations you wrote in Question 2 the same? In what way are they different?

4. Does a girl's size 9 shoe fit the same length foot as a boy's size 9 shoe? Use the equations in Question 2 to help find the answer.

5. NBA player Bob Lanier wears a size 22 sneaker. Use the equation you wrote in Question 2 to determine the length of his feet. Express your answer as a sentence.

Investigating Functions

Materials Needed
- pencils or pens
- paper

Part **A** A FUNCTION MODEL

A *function* is a rule that accepts an input and produces an output. Here is an example.

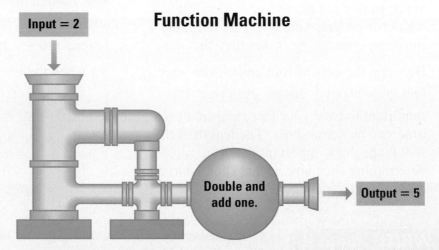

Function Machine

Input = 2

Double and add one.

Output = 5

1. Use the function machine above to copy and complete the table.

Input, x	1	2	3	4	5	6	7
Output, y	?	?	?	?	?	?	?

2. The function described above is "double and add one." Which of the following equations represents this function? Explain your reasoning.

   a. $y = 2x + 1$ **b.** $y = 2(x + 1)$

   c. $y = 2 + x$ **d.** $y = 2x + 2$

Part **B** A FUNCTION MODEL

3. Copy and complete the input-output table for each function.

Input, x	0	1	2	3	4	5	6	7
Output, y	?	?	?	?	?	?	?	?

   a. $y = 3x - 5$ **b.** $y = 4 - x$ **c.** $y = \dfrac{x}{2} + \dfrac{1}{2}$ **d.** $y = 6 + 4x$

Part C Writing Equations for Functions

4. Write an equation for each function.

a.

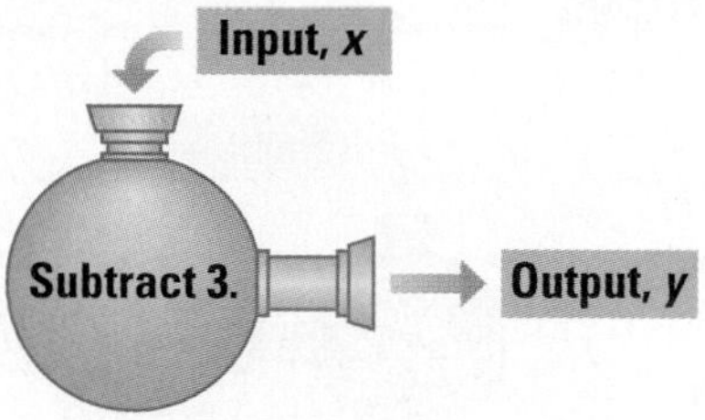

Input, x
Subtract 3.
Output, y

b.

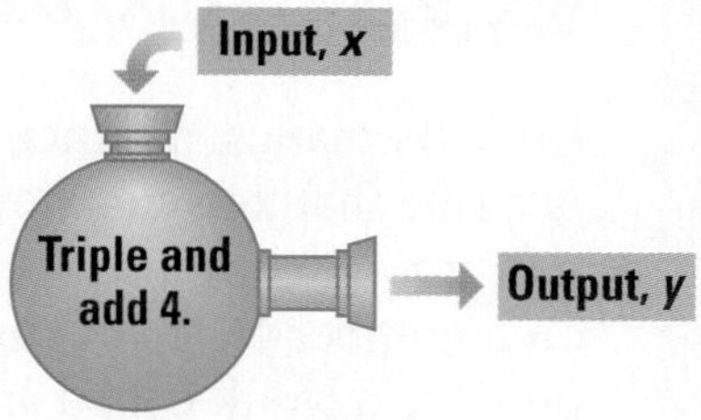

Input, x
Triple and add 4.
Output, y

c.

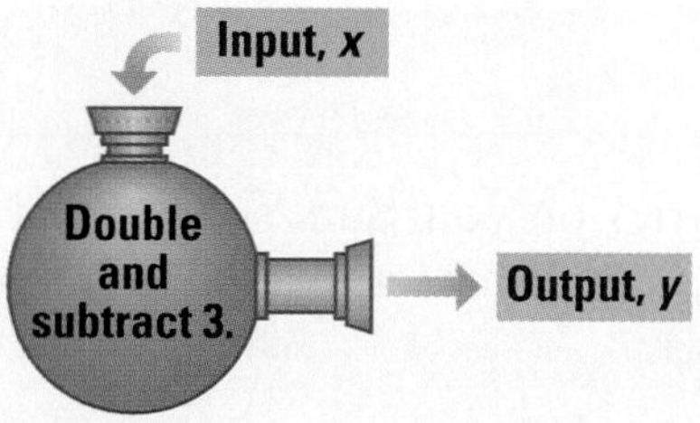

Input, x
Double and subtract 3.
Output, y

d.

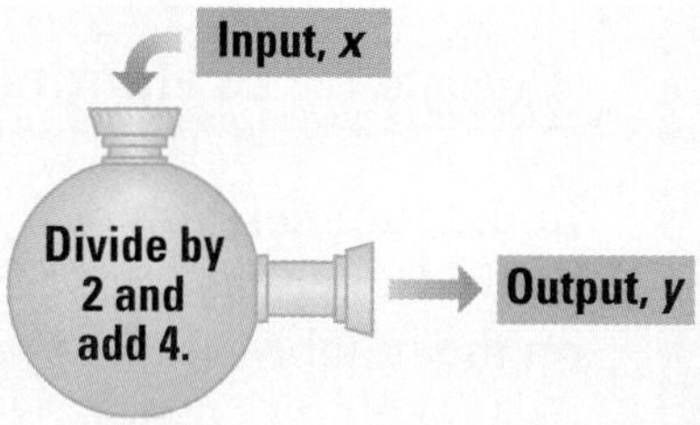

Input, x
Divide by 2 and add 4.
Output, y

5. Use the input-output table to write an equation for the function.

a.

Input, x	0	1	2	3	4	5
Output, y	1	4	7	10	13	16

b.

Input, x	0	1	2	3	4	5
Output, y	12	10	8	6	4	2

NOW TRY THESE

6. Write a sentence that describes each function.

   a. $y = 3x - 7$ b. $y = 4 - 5x$ c. $y = \frac{x}{3} + 8$

7. One of the following descriptions fits the equation $y = 4(x + 3)$ and the other fits the equation $y = 4x + 3$. Which is which? Are the two functions the same? Explain.

   a. Multiply the input by 4 and then add 3.

   b. Add 3 to the input and multiply by 4.

8. Use the input-output table to write an equation for the function.

Input, x	0	1	2	3	4	5
Output, y	0	4	8	12	16	20

12.6 Functions

What you should learn:

Goal 1 How to evaluate a function

Goal 2 How to write a rule for a function

Why you should learn it:

Knowing how to evaluate functions can help you find patterns in real life. An example is finding a pattern for the amount you can earn picking strawberries.

Goal 1 EVALUATING FUNCTIONS

In mathematics, a **function** is a rule that tells you how to perform one or more operations on a number called an **input** to produce a result called an **output**.

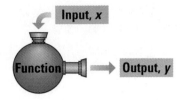

Input, *x*

Function → Output, *y*

Example 1 Evaluating a Function

In the summer, you pick strawberries on your aunt's farm. You are paid $10 per day, plus $0.25 per quart. Your total daily pay P depends on the number of quarts n you pick.

$$P = 0.25n + 10$$

Use this function to find your total pay for picking 8, 16, 24, 32, 40, and 48 quarts.

Solution

You can make a list to organize your work.

Input	Function	Output
$n = 8$	$P = 0.25(8) + 10$	$P = 12$
$n = 16$	$P = 0.25(16) + 10$	$P = 14$
$n = 24$	$P = 0.25(24) + 10$	$P = 16$
$n = 32$	$P = 0.25(32) + 10$	$P = 18$
$n = 40$	$P = 0.25(40) + 10$	$P = 20$
$n = 48$	$P = 0.25(48) + 10$	$P = 22$

Once you have evaluated your pay P for each value of n, you can use a table of values to summarize your results.

Input, n	8	16	24	32	40	48
Output, P	$12	$14	$16	$18	$20	$22

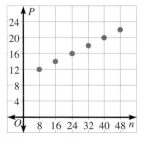

Drawing a scatter plot of the data from the table makes it easier to see the relationship between the input and the output of the function. In this case, you can see that for every 8 quarts of strawberries picked your total pay went up $2.00.

Example 2 ❯ **Writing a Function Rule**

STRATEGY **LOOK FOR A PATTERN** Find the number of tiles in each figure. Organize the results in a table. Look for a pattern between the number of tiles in the top row of each figure and the total number of tiles in each figure. Then describe the pattern and write a rule for the function.

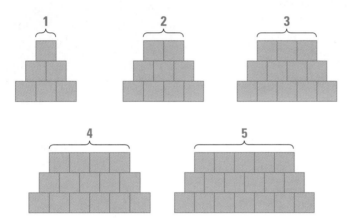

Solution

You can organize the number of tiles in a table of values.

Tiles in Top Row, Input, x	1	2	3	4	5
Total Number of Tiles, Output, y	6	9	12	15	18

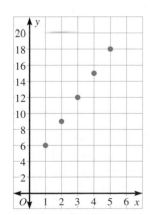

When x is 1, the total number of tiles is 6. Each time x increases by 1, the total number of tiles increases by 3. A rule for this function is

$$y = 3 \cdot x + 3.$$

A scatter plot can help you visualize this relationship. Begin by writing the data as ordered pairs of the form (x, y).

(1, 6), (2, 9), (3, 12) (4, 15), (5, 18)

Then, plot the points onto a coordinate plane. The coordinate plane will look like the one at the left.

ONGOING ASSESSMENT

Write About It
. . . .

The perimeters of the figures in example 2 also have a pattern. Assume each tile is a 1-by-1 square.

1. Find the perimeter of each figure and describe the pattern for the perimeters, P.

2. Write a function rule that gives P in terms of the number of tiles, x.

GUIDED PRACTICE

In Exercises 1–3, match the function description with its equation.

A. $y = 4(x + 1)$ **B.** $y = 4x + 1$ **C.** $y = \frac{x}{4} + 1$

1. Multiply by 4 and add 1.   **2.** Divide by 4 and add 1.   **3.** Add 1 and multiply by 4.

In Exercises 4–6, you are planning a camping trip for you and some friends.

4. The cost for renting a cabin at Sleepy Hollow is $55.00 for the cabin, plus $8.00 for each person. The cost in dollars is $C = 55 + 8n$, where n is the number of people. Copy and complete the table.

Input, n	1	2	3	4	5	6
Output, C ($)	?	?	?	?	?	?

5. The cost for renting a cabin at Maple Creek is $75.00 for the cabin, plus $4.00 for each person. Write a function that you can use to find the cost for x people. Then make an input-output table like that above.

6. Six people will be taking the trip. Which campground would you choose? Explain.

PRACTICE AND PROBLEM SOLVING

In Exercises 7–12, make an input-output table for the function. Use x-values of 1, 2, 3, 4, 5, and 6.

7. $y = 5x + 2$ **8.** $y = \frac{x}{3} + 2$ **9.** $y = -3x - 1$

10. $y = 5(x - 1)$ **11.** $y = \frac{x}{6} + 1$ **12.** $y = 2.5x - 5$

In Exercises 13–16, use the input-output table to write an equation for the function.

13.

Input, x	1	2	3	4	5	6
Output, y	14	12	10	8	6	4

14.

Input, x	1	2	3	4	5	6
Output, y	6	9	12	15	18	21

15.

Input, x	1	2	3	4	5	6
Output, y	8	11	14	17	20	23

16.

Input, x	1	2	3	4	5
Output, y	2.5	4.5	6.5	8.5	10.5

SCIENCE In Exercises 17 and 18, use the graph at the right. It shows the distance d that sound travels in air in the time t.

17. Make a table of the input t and output d.

18. Write an equation that represents how many miles sound travels in air in t seconds.

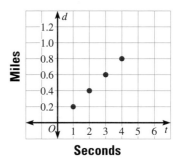

VOLUME In Exercises 19 and 20, you are given the function to find the volume of the solid for a given length x. Make a table using x-values of 1, 2, 3, 4, and 5. Then draw a scatter plot.

19. $V = 1.5 \cdot 2 \cdot x$

20. $V = 3.14 \cdot 0.5^2 \cdot x$

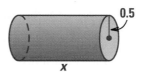

21. SURFACE AREA Decide which of the following functions you can use to find the surface area of a cube of side length x. Then make a table for the surface area of a cube with sides $x = 1, 2, 3, 4,$ and 5 inches.

A. $S = x^2 + 6$ **B.** $S = 4x^2$ **C.** $S = 6x^2$

STANDARDIZED TEST PRACTICE

22. Your sister pays $65.00 to have a phone line installed. Each call made costs her $0.10 per minute. Which function represents the amount she will pay, P, if she talks for m minutes during the first month?

(**A**) $0.1P + 65 = m$ (**B**) $65 - 0.1m = P$

(**C**) $65 + 0.1m = P$ (**D**) $0.1m + P = 65$

23. In the function $Z = 48 - 1.5d$, what is the value of Z when $d = 18$?

(**A**) 5   (**B**) 21   (**C**) 24   (**D**) 837

EXPLORATION AND EXTENSION

24. EYES The average diameter (in millimeters) of a person's pupil in daylight can be represented by the equation *Size of pupil (in mm) = 5.5 + 0.04 · age*. What is the diameter of a 25-year old's pupil? What is the diameter when the person reaches 65?

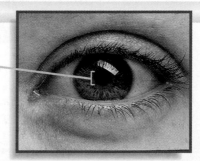

Pupil

WHAT *did you learn?*   **WHY** *did you learn it?*

		WHAT did you learn?	WHY did you learn it?
Skills	12.1	Write the inverse of an operation.	Solve various algebraic equations.
	12.2	Solve addition and subtraction equations.	Use equations to solve real-life problems.
	12.3	Solve multiplication equations.	Find each person's share of a profit or a loss.
	12.4	Solve division equations.	Estimate the amount of food needed to feed a gorilla.
	12.5	Solve two-step equations.	Find the number of booklets that can be printed.
	12.6	Evaluate a function. Write a rule for a function.	Find how much money you can earn picking strawberries.
Strategies	12.1–12.6	Use problem solving strategies.	Solve a wide variety of real-world problems.
Using Data	12.1–12.6	Use tables, graphs, and time lines.	Organize data and solve problems.

HOW *does it fit in the bigger picture of mathematics?*

One of the things you learned this year is that mathematics has many different parts. We hope this book has opened windows for you to see several of these parts: number operations, algebra, geometry, statistics, and probability. In addition, we hope that you have learned that there are many connections among the different parts of mathematics. For example, in this chapter you learned that a table of function values can be graphed as a scatter plot. This is a connection between algebra and geometry.

$y = 2x + 3$ →

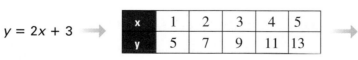

x	1	2	3	4	5
y	5	7	9	11	13

→

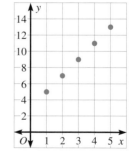

Continue to look for many connections among the different parts of mathematics. Finding connections between differing sections of mathematics helps open windows so that you can see more of the bigger picture of mathematics.

VOCABULARY

- inverse operation (p. 580)
- box models (p. 581)
- isolating the variable (p.584)
- function (p. 612)
- input (p. 612)
- output (p. 612)

12.1   INVERSE OPERATIONS

Inverse operations "undo" the action of another operation.

Example   Solve $n \div 3 = -2$ using box models.

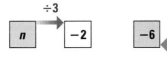

The solution is $n = -6$.

In Exercises 1–4, write a box model for each equation and then solve.

1. $x + 18 = 10$ **2.** $f - 9 = -4$ **3.** $84 = 6t$ **4.** $\dfrac{m}{4} = 6.5$

12.2   ADDITION AND SUBTRACTION EQUATIONS

To solve addition or subtraction equations, use an inverse operation and isolate the variable. Then check your solution.

Example   Solve the equation $b - 4 = 5$. Then check the solution.

Solution $b - 4 = 5 \longrightarrow b - 4 + 4 = 5 + 4 \longrightarrow b = 9$

✔**Check:** $b - 4 = 5 \longrightarrow 9 - 4 \stackrel{?}{=} 5 \longrightarrow 5 = 5$

In Exercises 5–8, solve the equation and then check your solution.

5. $m + (-3) = 5$ **6.** $-8 = x - 5$ **7.** $-7 - k = 0$ **8.** $-12 = d + 17$

12.3   MULTIPLICATION EQUATIONS

To solve a multiplication equation, divide both sides of the equation by the same number to isolate the variable.

Example   Solve the equation $6c = 45$. Then check the solution.

Solution $6c = 45 \longrightarrow \dfrac{6c}{6} = \dfrac{45}{6} \longrightarrow c = 7.5$

✔**Check:** $6c = 45 \longrightarrow 6(7.5) \stackrel{?}{=} 45 \longrightarrow 45 = 45$

In Exercises 9–12, solve the multiplication equation and check your solution.

9. $-2.3x = 11.5$ **10.** $124 = 8c$ **11.** $0.44z = 22$ **12.** $37.5 = 5w$

12.4 DIVISION EQUATIONS

To solve a division equation, multiply both sides of the equation by the same number to isolate the variable. Then check your solution.

Example Solve the equation $m \div 4 = 7$. Then check the solution.

Solution $m \div 4 = 7 \longrightarrow m \div 4 \cdot 4 = 7 \cdot 4 \longrightarrow m = 28$

✔**Check:** $m \div 4 = 7 \longrightarrow 28 \div 4 \overset{?}{=} 7 \longrightarrow 7 = 7$

In Exercises 13–16, solve the division equation and check your solution.

13. $\frac{m}{5} = 12.5$ **14.** $a \div \frac{2}{3} = 6$ **15.** $-13 = \frac{w}{3.5}$ **16.** $p \div \frac{7}{3} = 9$

12.5 TWO-STEP EQUATIONS

To solve two-step equations simply use two different inverse operations to isolate the variable. Then check your solution.

Example Solve the equation $4x - 6 = 10$. Then check the solution.

$$4x - 6 = 10 \longrightarrow 4x - 6 + 6 = 10 + 6 \longrightarrow 4x = 16 \longrightarrow \frac{4x}{4} = \frac{16}{4} \longrightarrow x = 4$$

✔**Check:** $4x - 6 = 10 \longrightarrow 4(4) - 6 \overset{?}{=} 10 \longrightarrow 10 = 10$

In Exercises 17–20, solve the two-step equation and check your solution.

17. $8 - \frac{c}{4} = 5$ **18.** $-3 + 5d = 1$ **19.** $3.5s + 13 = 23.5$ **20.** $\frac{m}{6} - 3 = 2$

12.6 FUNCTIONS

To evaluate a function, substitute a number, called the input, for the variable and simplify. The result is the output.

Example Evaluate the function $P = 5n + 3$ for $n = 0, 1, 2, 3$.

Solution

Input	Function	Output
$n = 0$	$P = 5(0) + 3$	$P = 3$
$n = 1$	$P = 5(1) + 3$	$P = 8$
$n = 2$	$P = 5(2) + 3$	$P = 13$
$n = 3$	$P = 5(3) + 3$	$P = 18$

21. Make an input-output table for $y = 2x - 3$ for $x = 0, 1, 2, 3, 4, 5, 6$. Then plot the points on a scatter plot.

22. Describe the pattern of the numbers in the table. Then write an equation for the function given by the table and plot the points on a scatter plot.

x	1	2	3	4	5	6
y	-6	-5	-4	-3	-2	-1

In Questions 1–3, write the equation that is being modeled. Copy and complete the box model to solve the equation.

1.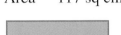

2.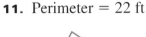

3.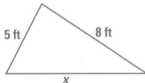

In Questions 4–6, solve the equation. Then check the solution.

4. $x - (-5.8) = -19.2$ **5.** $7m - 1 = -36$ **6.** $3 = \dfrac{n}{10} + 6$

In Questions 7–9, without solving the equation, decide whether the solution is positive or negative. Explain your reasoning.

7. $-4y = -68$ **8.** $-9p = 0.75$ **9.** $\dfrac{a}{6.5} = -4$

GEOMETRY In Exercises 10 and 11, write an equation to find the side length labeled x. Then solve the equation to find the length.

10. Area = 117 sq cm

9 cm

x

11. Perimeter = 22 ft

5 ft   8 ft

x

In Questions 12 and 13, write an equation for the function represented by the input-output table.

12.

Input, x	0	1	2	3	4	5
Output, y	16	13	10	7	4	1

13.

Input, x	0	1	2	3	4	5
Output, y	1	5	9	13	17	21

14. ANGEL FISH One angel fish needs 2 gallons of water. Use a proportion to find the number of angel fish that you could put in a 20-gallon aquarium.

15. HIKING You are buying a pair of hiking boots. The sporting goods store is having a sale on hiking boots. The regular price for the boots is $65.90. You pay $46.13 (excluding tax). Use the verbal model below to find the percent discount of the sale.

$$\begin{array}{c}\text{Regular}\\\text{Price}\end{array} = \begin{array}{c}\text{Regular}\\\text{Price}\end{array} \cdot \begin{array}{c}\text{Percent}\\\text{Discount}\end{array} + \begin{array}{c}\text{Sale}\\\text{Price}\end{array}$$

1. What value of x will complete the box model?

(A) -15 **(B)** -3

(C) 3 **(D)** 15

2. Which equation can be used to find the angle measure in the rectangle?

(A) $x + 38 = 90$

(B) $x - 38 = 90$

(C) $x - 38 = 180$

(D) $x + 38 = 180$

3. You can wash 3 cars in 20 minutes. Which equation can be used to find the number of cars you can wash in 3 hours?

(A) $\dfrac{3}{20} = \dfrac{c}{3}$ **(B)** $\dfrac{c}{3} = \dfrac{20}{180}$

(C) $\dfrac{c}{20} = \dfrac{3}{180}$ **(D)** $\dfrac{3}{20} = \dfrac{c}{180}$

In Questions 4 and 5, use the multiplication equation $4x = 7$.

4. Which statement can be used to represent the equation?

(A) You buy 7 pencils for $4.

(B) You earn $4 each day for 7 days.

(C) The temperature fell 7° in 4 h.

(D) It costs $7 to bowl 4 games.

5. What is the solution of the equation?

(A) $\dfrac{4}{7}$ **(B)** 1.75

(C) 11 **(D)** 28

6. What solution is next in the pattern?

$m \div 5 = 2, m \div 10 = 2,$
$m \div 15 = 2, \ldots$

(A) $\dfrac{1}{10}$ **(B)** 10

(C) 30 **(D)** 40

7. Which equation represents the verbal statement: The difference of a number and -4 is 4?

(A) $y + (-4) = 4$ **(B)** $n - 4 = 4$

(C) $b - (-4) = 4$ **(D)** $z - 4 = -4$

In Questions 8 and 9, use the following information. You make a long-distance telephone call to your pen pal. The call costs $1 for the first minute and $0.18 for each additional minute.

8. The call came to $10. How many minutes did you talk?

(A) 8.5 **(B)** 50

(C) 51 **(D)** 61.1

9. The long-distance telephone company is offering a promotion that decreases the cost for each additional minute. How much is each additional minute for the promotion if the call is 26 minutes and costs $4?

(A) $0.11   **(B)** $0.12

(C) $0.15   **(D)** $0.16

10. Which equation represents the function?

Input, x	1	2	3	4	5	6
Output, y	5	4	3	2	1	0

(A) $y = x + 4$ **(B)** $y = -x + 6$

(C) $y = x - 6$ **(D)** $y = -2x + 7$

11. What number comes next in the pattern: 0, 1, 3, 6, 10, 15, . . .?

(A) 19   (B) 20

(C) 21   (D) 22

12. What is the greatest common factor of 45, 75, and 105?

(A) 3   (B) 5

(C) 9   (D) 15

13. Which equation demonstrates the Distributive Property?

(A) $(a + b) + c = a + (b + c)$

(B) $a(b + c) = ab + bc$

(C) $ab = ba$

(D) $(a \cdot b) \cdot c = a \cdot (b \cdot c)$

14. Which point has the coordinates $(-3, 2)$?

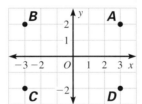

(A) A

(B) B

(C) C

(D) D

15. Find the surface area of the prism.

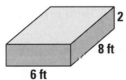

(A) 96

(B) 120

(C) 128

(D) 152

16. Evaluate the expression $(-8)^2 - (-4^2)$.

(A) -80 (B) -48

(C) 48   (D) 80

17. Solve the proportion $\dfrac{6}{n} = \dfrac{9}{15}$

(A) 8   (B) 9

(C) 10   (D) 12

18. 63 is 75% of what number?

(A) 47.25   (B) 84

(C) 110.24   (D) 4725

19. Find the circumference and area of the circle.

(A) $C = 31.4$ cm; $A = 78.5$ cm^2

(B) $C = 31.4$ cm^2; $A = 78.5$ cm^2

(C) $C = 78.5$ cm^2; $A = 31.4$ cm

(D) $C = 62.8$ cm; $A = 314$ cm^2

20. Find the mean, median, and mode of the following data.

10, 12, 15, 12, 12, 15, 10, 18, 12, 14

(A) mean = 12, median = 12, mode = 12

(B) mean = 13, median = 13.5, mode = 12

(C) mean = 13.5, median = 12, mode = 10

(D) mean = 13, median = 12, mode = 12

21. You take a car to the garage for repairs. The total cost (parts and labor) of the repair bill is $456. The cost of the new parts is $240. If a mechanic worked on the car for 6 hours, how much does the garage charge per hour for labor?

(A) $36   (B) $40

(C) $76   (D) $112

In Exercises 1–4, complete the statement. (7.2, 7.7)

1. 75 is 48% of ? .

2. ? is 75% of 140.

3. 126 is ? % of 315.

4. 175% of 48 is ? .

 In Exercises 5–7, find the length of the side of the triangle that is labeled *x*. Round your result to hundredths if possible. (8.8)

5.
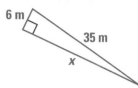
6 m

35 m

x

6.
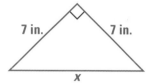
7 in.   7 in.

x

7.
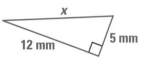
x

12 mm   5 mm

In Exercises 8–10, find the volume and surface area of the solid. (9.3–9.5)

8.
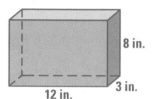
8 in.

12 in.   3 in.

9.
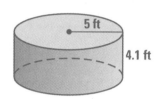
5 ft

4.1 ft

10.
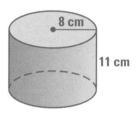
8 cm

11 cm

In Exercises 11–18, add, subtract, multiply, or divide. (10.2–10.6)

11. $14 - 27$

12. $3 + (-6)$

13. $-7 + 12$

14. $-18 - 10$

15. $2 - (-7)$

16. $17 + (-3)$

17. $4 \cdot (-8)$

18. $-3 \cdot (-7)$

In Exercises 19–22, consider an experiment in which two number cubes are tossed. Find the probability of the indicated total. (11.1)

19. A total that is an even number

20. A total of 7 or 11

21. A total greater than 4

22. A total greater than 1

In Exercises 23–31, name the inverse of the operation. (12.1)

23. $+ 3$

24. $- 6$

25. $\times 12$

26. $\div 8$

27. $- (-7)$

28. $+ (-10)$

29. $\div (-2)$

30. $\times (-9)$

31. $\div (-\frac{4}{3})$

In Exercises 32–40, solve the equation. (12.2–12.5)

32. $b + 7 = 5$

33. $15 + c = -4$

34. $-7 + t = -1$

35. $3g = 27$

36. $-2 \cdot f = 30$

37. $r \div 16 = -4$

38. $2m + 3 = 31$

39. $6 + 3j = 27$

40. $4 + 7k = -24$

Student Resources

Table of Contents

Use after Lesson 1.1, page 4

1. Make a list of the two-color combinations you can make from blue, white, red, green, and grey.

2. You are buying pencils. A pack of 10 costs $.95. A pack of 12 costs $1.00. Which is the better bargain? Explain your reasoning.

Use after Lesson 1.2, page 8

1. Describe any patterns that you see. Then use the pattern or patterns to find the next 3 sums.

$$1 = 1$$
$$1 + 3 + 1 = 5$$
$$1 + 3 + 5 + 3 + 1 = 13$$
$$1 + 3 + 5 + 7 + 5 + 3 + 1 = 25$$

2. Thirty-two players are competing in a chess tournament. After each game, the loser drops out. How many games will be played? Describe your problem solving strategy.

Use after Lesson 1.3, page 16

In Exercises 1–3, use the rectangle at the right.

1. Find the perimeter and area of the rectangle.

2. Use four of these rectangles to form a similar rectangle. What are its dimensions?

3. Find the perimeter and area of the similar rectangle. Compare the two perimeters and the two areas.

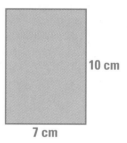

10 cm

7 cm

Use after Lesson 1.4, page 20

1. You randomly draw marbles from a bag. In your first 5 draws, you get 2 red, 2 green, and 1 blue marble. How many of each color would you expect to get in 20 draws?

2. Design a simulation to estimate how many questions you will answer correctly on a 30-point true-false test, if you guess at every answer.

Use after Lesson 1.5, page 26

In Exercises 1 and 2, use the Guess, Check, and Revise strategy to find the side length of a square with the given area.

1. Area = 484 square meters

2. Area = 51.84 square miles

3. When you subtract me from 75, you get 4 times my value. What number am I?

Use after Lesson 1.6, page 30

In Exercises 1–6, check the given value of the variable in the equation. Is it a solution? If not, find the solution.

1. $d - 17 = 4, d = 22$ **2.** $i \div 8 = 24, i = 3$ **3.** $n \times 4 = 36, n = 9$

4. $31 - t = 11, t = 52$ **5.** $7 \times j = 56, j = 8$ **6.** $12 + r = 17, r = 8$

7. Each week you save $15 from your paycheck. You have saved a total of $345. Use the verbal model below. Assign labels and write an equation for this problem. Then solve the equation to find the number of weeks.

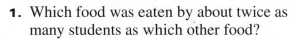

Amount saved each week × Number of weeks = Total amount saved

Use after Lesson 1.7, page 36

1. Matt, Juan, and Ted have unusual pets: a mouse, an iguana, and a grass snake. Juan's pet is a mammal. Matt doesn't own the iguana. Which boy owns which pet?

In Exercises 2–4, use the Venn diagram at the right. The diagram represents students' answers when asked if they have a skateboard, in-line skates, or roller skates.

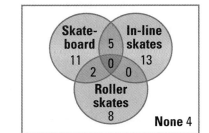

2. How many students answered the question?

3. How many students own a skateboard?

4. How many students own either in-line skates or roller skates?

Use after Lesson 1.8, page 40

1. How many different combinations of 3 even numbers have a sum of 20? (Consider $2 + 2 + 16$ to be the same as $16 + 2 + 2$.)

2. Each question on a 3 question quiz has 3 answers to choose from. How many different combinations of answers can you choose?

3. You have 1 quarter, 2 dimes, and 1 nickel. Not including a total of zero, how many different total amounts can you make?

Use after Lesson 1.9, page 44

In Exercises 1–3, use the graph at the right. The graph shows what students ate for breakfast on a given day.

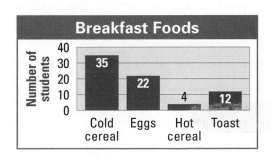

1. Which food was eaten by about twice as many students as which other food?

2. Which food is less popular than toast?

3. How many fewer students ate hot cereal than eggs?

Use after Lesson 2.1, page 58

In Exercises 1–6, evaluate the expression.

1. $4 - 6 \div 3 + 8$ **2.** $10 \div 5 + 5 \cdot 2$ **3.** $(4 + 12) \div 4 - 1$

4. $3 \times 8 \div (4 + 4)$ **5.** $27 + 6 \div 3 - 1$ **6.** $16 \div 8 - 4 \div 2$

In Exercises 7–9, evaluate $7(n - 1)$ for the given values of n.

7. $n = 1$ **8.** $n = 2$ **9.** $n = 3$

In Exercises 10–12, evaluate the expression when $m = 3$.

10. $(m + 7) \div 5$ **11.** $16 - 2 \cdot m$ **12.** $12 \div m \times 3$

Use after Lesson 2.2, page 64

In Exercises 1–9, evaluate the expression.

1. 4^2 **2.** 3^3 **3.** 5^2

4. 2^6 **5.** 4^4 **6.** 6^3

7. 1 to the sixth power **8.** 10 cubed **9.** 5^4

In Exercises 10–12, write each number in the pattern as a power.

10. $36, 25, 16, 9, 4, 1$ **11.** $2, 4, 8, 16, 32, 64$ **12.** $3, 9, 27, 81, 243, 729$

Use after Lesson 2.3, page 70

In Exercises 1–9, use divisibility tests to decide whether the number is divisible by 2, 3, 4, 5, 6, 9, and 10.

1. 519 **2.** 722 **3.** 1875

4. 8620 **5.** 11,925 **6.** 47,851

7. 159,234 **8.** 254,526 **9.** 873,558

10. A band teacher is trying to decide whether to have 90 members or 100 members in the marching band. Which will allow more possibilities for rectangular formations?

Use after Lesson 2.4, page 76

In Exercises 1–3, decide whether the number is prime or composite.

1. 77 **2.** 151 **3.** 279

In Exercises 4–6, write the prime factorization of each number.

4. 88 **5.** 133 **6.** 294

In Exercises 7–12, find the number with the given prime factorization.

7. $2 \cdot 3 \cdot 11$ **8.** $2^3 \cdot 5 \cdot 7$ **9.** $3 \cdot 5 \cdot 13$

10. $3^2 \cdot 5^2$ **11.** $2^2 \cdot 5$ **12.** $3^2 \cdot 17$

Use after Lesson 2.5, page 82

In Exercises 1–6, find the greatest common factor of the numbers.

1. 24, 60

2. 42, 66

3. 51, 34

4. 9, 11, 17

5. 44, 28, 52

6. 18, 33, 51

7. Three math classes have 16, 28, and 20 students. The teachers want to divide the students of each class into equal-sized teams for a semester project. How many students should be on each team? How many teams will there be altogether?

Use after Lesson 2.6, page 86

In Exercises 1–4, find a denominator for the fraction so that the greatest common factor of the numerator and denominator is 4.

1. $\dfrac{16}{?}$

2. $\dfrac{32}{?}$

3. $\dfrac{20}{?}$

4. $\dfrac{44}{?}$

In Exercises 5–8, write the fraction in simplest form.

5. $\dfrac{24}{40}$

6. $\dfrac{60}{84}$

7. $\dfrac{66}{78}$

8. $\dfrac{64}{192}$

In Exercises 9–12, write three other fractions that are equivalent to the given fraction. Include the simplest form.

9. $\dfrac{21}{49}$

10. $\dfrac{51}{85}$

11. $\dfrac{16}{72}$

12. $\dfrac{48}{64}$

Use after Lesson 2.7, page 94

In Exercises 1–4, write the fraction that is equivalent to the given expression. Then write the equivalent decimal.

1. $3 \div 4$

2. $1 \div 5$

3. $15 \div 25$

4. $13 \div 20$

TECHNOLOGY **In Exercises 5–12, write the fraction as a decimal. Round your answer to the nearest hundredth.**

5. $\dfrac{17}{20}$

6. $\dfrac{4}{7}$

7. $\dfrac{5}{13}$

8. $\dfrac{3}{16}$

9. $\dfrac{1}{3}$

10. $\dfrac{6}{25}$

11. $\dfrac{10}{11}$

12. $\dfrac{1}{6}$

Use after Lesson 2.8, page 98

In Exercises 1–4, plot the numbers on a number line. Then order them from least to greatest.

1. 3.5, 3.85, 2.83, 3.08, 2.58, 3.8

2. $\dfrac{1}{4}, \dfrac{5}{8}, \dfrac{1}{3}, \dfrac{3}{4}, \dfrac{2}{3}, \dfrac{3}{8}$

3. $\dfrac{2}{5}$, 0.52, 0.528, 0.45, $\dfrac{3}{7}$

4. 0.92, 0.095, $\dfrac{9}{10}$, 0.902, $\dfrac{1}{11}$

Use after Lesson 3.1, page 114

In Exercises 1–4, find the least common multiple of the numbers.

1. 5, 20   **2.** 7, 3   **3.** 12, 18   **4.** 6, 15, 21

5. There are 10 hot dogs in a package and 8 buns in a package. You want to buy one bun for each hot dog. What is the fewest number of packages you could buy? How many hot dogs and buns will you have?

Use after Lesson 3.2, page 118

In Exercises 1–8, rewrite the improper fraction as a mixed number.

1. $\dfrac{23}{6}$ **2.** $\dfrac{17}{3}$ **3.** $\dfrac{29}{7}$ **4.** $\dfrac{39}{4}$

5. $\dfrac{27}{5}$ **6.** $\dfrac{20}{9}$ **7.** $\dfrac{37}{10}$ **8.** $\dfrac{51}{8}$

In Exercises 9–16, rewrite the mixed number as an improper fraction.

9. $2\dfrac{7}{8}$ **10.** $3\dfrac{1}{4}$ **11.** $6\dfrac{1}{9}$ **12.** $4\dfrac{3}{10}$

13. $7\dfrac{1}{2}$ **14.** $2\dfrac{5}{6}$ **15.** $1\dfrac{14}{15}$ **16.** $3\dfrac{2}{11}$

In Exercises 17–20, rewrite the number as a decimal.

17. $\dfrac{21}{4}$ **18.** $\dfrac{10}{3}$ **19.** $5\dfrac{3}{4}$ **20.** $2\dfrac{7}{8}$

Use after Lesson 3.3, page 126

In Exercises 1–8, add or subtract. Simplify if possible.

1. $\dfrac{2}{9}+\dfrac{5}{9}$ **2.** $\dfrac{3}{4}+\dfrac{5}{12}$ **3.** $\dfrac{7}{8}-\dfrac{3}{8}$ **4.** $\dfrac{13}{15}-\dfrac{2}{3}$

5. $\dfrac{1}{2}+\dfrac{3}{7}$ **6.** $\dfrac{5}{6}+\dfrac{5}{8}$ **7.** $\dfrac{7}{9}-\dfrac{1}{3}$ **8.** $\dfrac{7}{12}-\dfrac{2}{15}$

Use after Lesson 3.4, page 130

In Exercises 1–8, simplify the mixed number.

1. $3\dfrac{11}{7}$ **2.** $8\dfrac{13}{12}$ **3.** $5\dfrac{17}{10}$ **4.** $7\dfrac{14}{9}$

5. $9\dfrac{10}{5}$ **6.** $12\dfrac{7}{3}$ **7.** $1\dfrac{6}{4}$ **8.** $4\dfrac{14}{8}$

In Exercises 9–16, add or subtract. Simplify if possible.

9. $2\dfrac{2}{5}+3\dfrac{1}{5}$ **10.** $4\dfrac{1}{4}+2\dfrac{3}{8}$ **11.** $3\dfrac{2}{3}-1\dfrac{1}{3}$ **12.** $1\dfrac{1}{7}+5\dfrac{6}{7}$

13. $7\dfrac{3}{4}+2\dfrac{1}{3}$ **14.** $8\dfrac{7}{9}+4\dfrac{5}{6}$ **15.** $7\dfrac{1}{2}-3\dfrac{1}{3}$ **16.** $3\dfrac{5}{12}+3\dfrac{8}{9}$

Use after Lesson 3.5, page 138

In Exercises 1–8, multiply. Simplify if possible.

1. $\frac{4}{5} \times \frac{1}{4}$

2. $4 \cdot \frac{3}{8}$

3. $\frac{7}{10} \cdot 12$

4. $11 \times 2\frac{1}{2}$

5. $2\frac{3}{4} \cdot 3\frac{1}{6}$

6. $\frac{2}{7} \cdot 8\frac{7}{8}$

7. $2\frac{1}{8} \cdot 5\frac{1}{4}$

8. $5\frac{1}{7} \times \frac{7}{9}$

In Exercises 9–11, find the area of the region.

9. 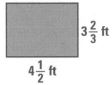 $3\frac{2}{3}$ ft

$4\frac{1}{2}$ ft

10. $\frac{3}{4}$ yd

$\frac{3}{4}$ yd

11. 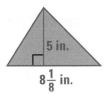 5 in.

$8\frac{1}{8}$ in.

Use after Lesson 3.6, page 142

In Exercises 1–9, rewrite the expression using the Distributive Property. Then evaluate.

1. $24\left(\frac{1}{8} + 2\right)$

2. $20(10 + 7)$

3. $8\left(\frac{1}{16} + \frac{1}{2}\right)$

4. $19 \times 6 + 21 \times 6$

5. $\frac{3}{7} \times 25 + \frac{11}{7} \times 25$

6. $5 \times 5 + 5 \times 7$

7. $\left(\frac{1}{12} + \frac{1}{6}\right)36$

8. $(2 + 30)8$

9. $\left(1 + \frac{2}{7}\right)14$

In Exercises 10–15, use the Distributive Property to rewrite the expression.

10. $12(n + 9)$

11. $7y + 10y$

12. $(k + 8)30$

13. $4b + 6b$

14. $5(a + b)$

15. $7(x + y)$

Use after Lesson 3.7, page 150

In Exercises 1–8, write the reciprocal of the number.

1. $\frac{1}{4}$

2. $\frac{3}{8}$

3. 7

4. 1

5. $3\frac{1}{5}$

6. $4\frac{2}{7}$

7. $1\frac{2}{3}$

8. $8\frac{1}{2}$

In Exercises 9–17, divide. Simplify if possible.

9. $3\frac{1}{2} \div 2$

10. $4 \div \frac{1}{6}$

11. $\frac{5}{9} \div 3$

12. $5\frac{1}{3} \div \frac{1}{3}$

13. $2\frac{2}{5} \div 1\frac{1}{6}$

14. $10 \div 2\frac{1}{2}$

15. $\frac{5}{8} \div \frac{5}{6}$

16. $\frac{22}{25} \div 10\frac{1}{2}$

17. $4\frac{1}{6} \div 2\frac{2}{9}$

Use after Lesson 4.1, page 168

In Exercises 1–4, make a table of values. Use $x = 1, 2, 3, 4, 5$, and 6.

1. $2x + 5$ **2.** $14 - 2x$ **3.** $x \div 5$ **4.** $6x + 7$

In Exercises 5 and 6, write an expression that describes the pattern.

5.

x	1	2	3	4	5	6
y	4	7	10	13	16	19

6.

x	1	2	3	4	5	6
y	9	8	7	6	5	4

Use after Lesson 4.2, page 172

In Exercises 1–4, plot the points on a coordinate plane.

1. $A(3, 8)$ **2.** $B(0, 4)$ **3.** $C(8, 3)$ **4.** $D(5, 0)$

In Exercises 5–8, draw a scatter plot that represents the equation. Use x-values of 1, 2, 3, 4, 5, and 6.

5. $y = \frac{1}{2}x$ **6.** $y = x - 1$ **7.** $y = 9 - x$ **8.** $y = 2x + 3$

Use after Lesson 4.3, page 178

In Exercises 1–3, graph the numbers on a number line. Describe the pattern and find the missing integers.

1. $-6, -4, -2, 0, \boxed{?}, \boxed{?}$ **2.** $13, 10, 7, 4, \boxed{?}, \boxed{?}$ **3.** $-5, -4, -2, 1, \boxed{?}, \boxed{?}$

In Exercises 4–6, order the numbers from least to greatest.

4. $2, -5, 5, 0, -2$ **5.** $-7, 10, -12, 4, -3$ **6.** $4.4, \frac{2}{3}, -6.1, 0, -5\frac{1}{4}$

In Exercises 7–10, write the integer represented by the real-life situation.

7. 12 feet below sea level   **8.** Mountain elevation of 10,322 feet

9. Deposit $300 in the bank   **10.** Withdraw $20 from an account

Use after Lesson 4.4, page 184

In Exercises 1 and 2, write the addition problem that is illustrated by the number line. Then solve the problem.

1.
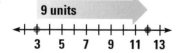

2.
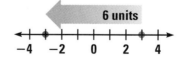

In Exercises 3–10, use a number line to find the sum.

3. $7 + (-8)$ **4.** $12 + (-3)$ **5.** $-4 + 17$ **6.** $-20 + 8$

7. $0 + (-13)$ **8.** $-5 + (-1)$ **9.** $-7 + (-7)$ **10.** $10 + (-14)$

11. The low temperatures for a week were 5°F, −1°F, 3°F, −7°F, −10°F, −8°F, and 4°F. Find the average low temperature for the week.

Use after Lesson 4.5, page 192

In Exercises 1 and 2, write the subtraction problem that is illustrated by the number line. Then solve the problem.

1.

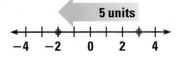

2.

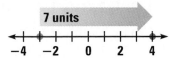

In Exercises 3–6, use a number line to find the difference.

3. $5 - 8$ **4.** $3 - (-2)$ **5.** $-7 - 6$ **6.** $-4 - 8$

7. At noon the temperature was $-3°F$. By midnight the temperature had dropped to $-16°F$. How much did the temperature drop?

Use after Lesson 4.6, page 198

In Exercises 1–8, solve the equation. Then check your solution.

1. $d + 11 = 20$ **2.** $m + 15 = 0$ **3.** $7 + r = -10$ **4.** $9 + p = 7$

5. $-20 = v + 31$ **6.** $a + \dfrac{1}{8} = \dfrac{1}{2}$ **7.** $-1 - \dfrac{3}{4} + m$ **8.** $-3.5 = k + 0.2$

In Exercises 9–11, write the equation that represents the statement. Then solve the equation.

9. The sum of eighteen and a number is thirty-two.

10. A number added to twelve is zero.

11. Negative four is the sum of nine and a number.

12. Suzanna collects baseball cards. After buying 5 cards, she counted a total of 87 cards in her collection. Write and solve an addition equation to find the number she had before buying the 5 cards.

Use after Lesson 4.7, page 204

In Exercises 1–8, solve the equation. Then check your solution.

1. $t - 7 = 3$ **2.** $g - 4 = 12$ **3.** $b - 9 = -5$ **4.** $q - (-2) = -5$

5. $x - 4 = -11$ **6.** $k - \dfrac{1}{2} = \dfrac{3}{4}$ **7.** $9.3 = z + 4.1$ **8.** $a - 1.7 = 0$

In Exercises 9–11, write the equation that represents the statement. Then solve it the equation.

9. Eight is the difference between a number and fourteen.

10. The difference between a number and negative three is seventeen.

11. The difference between a number and 15 is negative three.

12. Paul opened a package of cookies and ate 7 of them. He counted the cookies he had left, and there were 29. Write and solve a subtraction equation to find the number of cookies in the unopened package.

Use after Lesson 5.1, page 220

In Exercises 1 and 2, find the mean, median, and mode of the data.

1. Number of siblings of 21 students in a class:
   0, 1, 0, 2, 2, 1, 1, 2, 1, 2, 3, 0, 1, 1, 2, 0, 1, 4, 3, 1, 2

2. Wind speed (mi/h) by month at Block Island, Rhode Island:
   20, 20, 19, 17, 15, 14, 13, 12, 14, 17, 19, 20

Use after Lesson 5.2, page 226

In Exercises 1–3, use the data below. It gives the number of U.S. farms (in thousands) by state in 1995. (Source: U.S. Dept. of Agriculture)

AL 47	CO 25	HI 5	KS 66	MA 6	MT 22	NM 14	OK 71	SD 33	VA 47
AK 1	CT 4	ID 22	KY 89	MI 54	NE 56	NY 36	OR 39	TN 81	WA 36
AZ 7	DE 3	IL 77	LA 27	MN 87	NV 3	NC 58	PA 50	TX 202	WV 20
AR 43	FL 39	IN 62	ME 8	MS 42	NH 2	ND 32	RI 1	UT 13	WI 80
CA 80	GA 45	IA 100	MD 14	MO 105	NJ 9	OH 74	SC 22	VT 6	WY 9

1. Make a frequency table of the data. Use intervals of 20: 1−20, 21−40, ...

2. Make a histogram of the data.

3. Write a statement about the distribution of U.S. farms in 1995.

Use after Lesson 5.3, page 234

In Exercises 1 and 2, use the data below. It gives the average monthly temperatures in degrees Fahrenheit for November through October for some regions in the U.S. (Source: Old Farmer's Almanac)

New England: 49, 35, 28, 32, 39, 46, 57, 65, 75, 74, 66, 59

Florida: 72, 66, 67, 59, 63, 74, 78, 81, 81, 82, 81, 75

Southwest Desert: 55, 55, 49, 57, 62, 69, 79, 75, 92, 89, 86, 57

Pacific Northwest: 43, 37, 32, 37, 48, 52, 59, 63, 66, 67, 64, 50

1. For each region, draw a box-and-whisker plot of the data.

2. For each region, use your box-and-whisker plot to write a statement about the climate. Then compare the climates of the regions.

Use after Lesson 5.4, page 238

In Exercises 1 and 2, plot the points in a coordinate plane.

1. $(-3, 6), (-1, 5), (2, 3), (4, 0), (5, -2)$ 2. $(-5, -3), (4, 2), (0, 6), (3, -4), (2, -4)$

3. The table shows a car's total braking distance at different speeds. Draw a scatter plot of the data. Describe any patterns you see.

Speed (mi/h)	10	20	30	40	50	60	70
Distance (ft)	20	45	78	125	188	272	381

Use after Lesson 5.5, page 244

In Exercises 1 and 2, use a line graph or a bar graph to represent the data. Use your graph to write a statement about the data.

1. Recommended daily servings or amounts for a diet of 2200 calories

Food group	Bread	Vegetable	Fruit	Milk	Meat (oz.)
Servings or amounts	9	4	3	2–3	6

2. Percent of U.S. population that is foreign born

Year	1920	1930	1940	1950	1960	1970	1980	1990	1995
Percent	13.2	11.6	8.8	6.9	5.4	4.8	6.2	7.9	8.8

Use after Lesson 5.6, page 248

In Exercises 1–4, use the bar graph. It shows the net weight of 6 different sizes of eggs.

1. Look at the bars of the graph, not the scale, and write a statement comparing the weight of Jumbo eggs to the weight of Pee Wee eggs.

2. Use the scale to write a statement comparing the weight of Jumbo eggs to the weight of Pee Wee eggs.

3. Explain why the graph is misleading.

4. Make a bar graph that is *not* misleading.

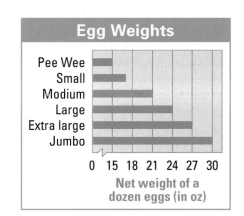

Egg Weights

Net weight of a dozen eggs (in oz)

Use after Lesson 5.7, page 256

In Exercises 1–5, match the event with its probability.

A. 1   B. 0.75   C. 0.5   D. 0.33   E. 0

1. The spinner at the right will land on a blue region when spun once.

2. The sun will come up tomorrow.

3. You get "heads" when flipping a coin.

4. March will have 35 days next year.

5. In a bag are 1 blue marble and 3 white ones. You do not pick the blue marble.

6. The table gives the probability of each hair color in a randomly selected population. Of 100 randomly selected people, how many would you expect to have each hair color?

Hair Color	Brown	Black	Red	Blonde
Probability	$\frac{7}{10}$	$\frac{1}{10}$	$\frac{1}{16}$	$\frac{1}{7}$

Use after Lesson 6.1, page 272

In Exercises 1 and 2, which ratio is not equal to the others?

1. $\dfrac{5\text{ cm}}{8\text{ cm}}, \dfrac{25\text{ cm}}{40\text{ cm}}, \dfrac{8\text{ cm}}{5\text{ cm}}$

2. $\dfrac{2\text{ yards}}{3\text{ yards}}, \dfrac{9\text{ feet}}{12\text{ feet}}, \dfrac{3\text{ yards}}{4\text{ yards}}$

In Exercises 3–5, use the table at the right. It gives the enrollment at Sacajawea Middle School.

3. Find the ratio of males to females in Grade 7.

4. Find the ratio of Grade 8 females to Grade 7 females.

5. Find the ratio of Grade 7 students to Grade 6 students.

	Female	Male
Grade 6	82	76
Grade 7	80	84
Grade 8	75	75

Use after Lesson 6.2, page 276

In Exercises 1–4, simplify the quotient. Is it a rate or a ratio?

1. $\dfrac{105\text{ mi}}{3\text{ h}}$

2. $\dfrac{5\text{ m}}{20\text{ m}}$

3. $\dfrac{32\text{ people}}{8\text{ cars}}$

4. $\dfrac{45\text{ questions}}{60\text{ minutes}}$

In Exercises 5 and 6, find the unit rate.

5. Earn $46 in 8 hours.

6. Type 285 words in 5 minutes.

7. An 8 oz box of crackers costs $1.49, and a 12 oz box costs $1.99. Which is the better buy?

Use after Lesson 6.3, page 284

In Exercises 1–4, decide whether the statement is true.

1. $\dfrac{9}{15} \overset{?}{=} \dfrac{3}{5}$

2. $\dfrac{5}{8} \overset{?}{=} \dfrac{10}{24}$

3. $\dfrac{25}{30} \overset{?}{=} \dfrac{4}{6}$

4. $\dfrac{3}{11} \overset{?}{=} \dfrac{9}{44}$

In Exercises 5–7, write the description as a proportion. Then solve the proportion.

5. 3 is to p as 15 is to 20.

6. 9 is to 6 as c is to 10.

7. 4 is to 5 as 28 is to n.

In Exercises 8–11, solve the proportion.

8. $\dfrac{d}{12} = \dfrac{1}{3}$

9. $\dfrac{20}{30} = \dfrac{4}{n}$

10. $\dfrac{12}{x} = \dfrac{3}{16}$

11. $\dfrac{4}{5} = \dfrac{m}{40}$

Use after Lesson 6.4, page 288

Use cross products to decide whether the proportion is true.

1. $\dfrac{6}{16} \overset{?}{=} \dfrac{9}{24}$

2. $\dfrac{21}{9} \overset{?}{=} \dfrac{7}{3}$

3. $\dfrac{15}{10} \overset{?}{=} \dfrac{9}{8}$

4. $\dfrac{20}{13} \overset{?}{=} \dfrac{6}{3.9}$

Use cross products to solve the proportion. Then check the solution.

5. $\dfrac{12}{k} = \dfrac{8}{10}$

6. $\dfrac{v}{14} = \dfrac{6}{21}$

7. $\dfrac{9}{15} = \dfrac{3}{x}$

8. $\dfrac{4}{3} = \dfrac{z}{7.8}$

Use after Lesson 6.5, page 294

In Exercises 1 and 2, decide which of the equations you could not use to solve the problem. Then solve the problem.

1. A sink is dripping so that it fills a 3-gallon bucket in 5 hours. How long would it take the drip to fill a 24-gallon bucket?

   a. $\dfrac{3 \text{ gal}}{24 \text{ gal}} = \dfrac{5 \text{ h}}{z \text{ h}}$ **b.** $\dfrac{5 \text{ h}}{24 \text{ gal}} = \dfrac{z \text{ h}}{3 \text{ gal}}$ **c.** $\dfrac{3 \text{ gal}}{5 \text{ h}} = \dfrac{24 \text{ gal}}{z \text{ h}}$

2. A punch recipe that serves 12 people calls for 8 cups of grape juice. How many cups of juice would you need to use if you wanted to serve 27 people?

   a. $\dfrac{8 \text{ c}}{x \text{ c}} = \dfrac{27 \text{ people}}{12 \text{ people}}$ **b.** $\dfrac{27 \text{ people}}{x \text{ c}} = \dfrac{12 \text{ people}}{8 \text{ c}}$ **c.** $\dfrac{27 \text{ people}}{12 \text{ people}} = \dfrac{x \text{ c}}{8 \text{ c}}$

In Exercises 3 and 4, write a proportion to solve the problem.

3. A 3 cm-by-2 cm negative is to be enlarged into a photograph whose longer side is 21 cm. How long will the shorter side be?

4. Charles rode his bike 42 miles in 3 hours. At this rate, how far will he ride in 7 hours?

Use after Lesson 6.6, page 300

1. Show that the two polygons are similar. Then draw a polygon of a different size that is similar to them.

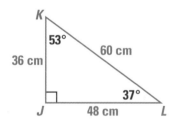
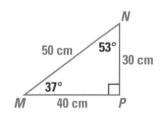

2. A tall building casts a 25 ft shadow. At the same time, a 10 ft sign casts a 6 ft shadow. Draw similar triangles to represent this situation. Let h be the height of the building.

3. Lindsay is 45 inches tall, and her shadow is 20 inches long. At the same time, her mother's shadow is 28 inches long. Estimate the height of Lindsay's mother.

Use after Lesson 6.7, page 306

1. The Wright brothers' first airplane had a wingspan of about 40 feet. You are building a model of the plane with a scale factor of 1 to 60. What is the wingspan of the model in inches?

In Exercises 2–5, you are given a distance on a map. The scale factor on the map is 2 cm to 55 miles. Find the actual distance.

2. 3 cm   **3.** 14 cm   **4.** 8.5 cm   **5.** 22 cm

Use after Lesson 7.1, page 322

In Exercises 1–4, write the percent as a decimal and a fraction in simplest form.

1. 60%   **2.** 95%   **3.** 75%   **4.** 30%

In Exercises 5–8, write the fraction as a decimal and as a percent.

5. $\dfrac{1}{5}$ **6.** $\dfrac{3}{8}$ **7.** $\dfrac{18}{25}$ **8.** $\dfrac{9}{20}$

9. A family has 6 children, 5 boys and 1 girl. The fraction of boys in the family is $\dfrac{5}{6}$. Find the percent of boys and the percent of girls.

Use after Lesson 7.2, page 328

In Exercises 1–4, find the value.

1. 80% of 90   **2.** 62% of 75   **3.** 8% of 225   **4.** 55% of 120

5. Pam scored 85% on a test with 20 questions, each worth one point. How many questions did Pam answer correctly on the test?

6. A sweatshirt priced at $40 is on sale "30% off." How much is saved by buying the sweatshirt on sale?

Use after Lesson 7.3, page 336

In Exercises 1–4, write the percent as a decimal and a fraction in simplest form.

1. 350%   **2.** 0.01%   **3.** $\dfrac{3}{10}$%   **4.** 290%

In Exercises 5–8, write the fraction or decimal as a percent.

5. 4.95   **6.** $\dfrac{1}{250}$ **7.** 0.0072   **8.** $\dfrac{5}{2}$

In Exercises 9–11, use mental math.

9. 300% of 40   **10.** 0.6% of 2000   **11.** 125% of 480

Use after Lesson 7.4, page 342

In Exercises 1–6, use a percent equation to solve the problem.

1. 36 is 40% of what number?   **2.** What number is 80% of 75?

3. What number is 224% of 200?   **4.** What percent of 120 is 210?

5. What number is 35% of 80?   **6.** 14% of what number is 70?

7. Of 625 students who answered a survey, 68% were girls. How many girls answered the survey?

8. About 30% of the students in a middle school are in seventh grade. There are 165 seventh graders. About how many students are there?

Use after Lesson 7.5, page 348

In Exercises 1–3, find the angle measures for a circle graph with the given parts.

1. 55%, 39%, 6%   **2.** 32%, 40%, 11%, 17%   **3.** 70%, 2%, 28%

4. Three parts of a circle graph with four parts use the percents 22%, 15%, and 31%. Find the percent for the fourth part.

5. Three parts of a circle graph with four parts use the measures 60°, 45°, and 150°. Find the angle measure for the fourth part.

6. Students were asked how many pets they have. The results are shown in the table. Draw a circle graph of this data.

7. Of the first 1000 customers at a frozen yogurt stand, 386 chose vanilla, 154 chose peach, and 460 chose twist. Draw a circle graph of this data.

Number of pets	Percent
0	25%
1	40%
2	18%
3	7%
More than 3	10%

Use after Lesson 7.6, page 354

In Exercises 1–4, find the amount of simple interest paid on $400 borrowed for 9 months at the given annual interest rate.

1. 9%   **2.** 13%   **3.** 18%   **4.** 21%

In Exercises 5–8, find the simple interest you earn for the given amount of time on a deposit of $2000 in a savings account that pays 5% annual interest.

5. 3 months   **6.** 4 months   **7.** 6 months   **8.** 9 months

In Exercises 9–11, Find the interest you will pay for borrowing the given principal. Then find the total you must pay back.

9. $P = \$900, r = 15\%,$
   $t = 6$ months

10. $P = \$5000, r = 9\%,$
   $t = 24$ months

11. $P = \$1500, r = 12\%,$
   $t = 1$ year

Use after Lesson 7.7, page 358

In Exercises 1–6, find the percent increase or percent decrease.

1. Before: 80   **After:** 100   **2. Before:** 150   **After:** 175

3. Before: 30   **After:** 70   **4. Before:** 240   **After:** 200

5. Before: 350 **After:** 70   **6. Before:** 27   **After:** 36

In Exercises 7–12, is the percent decrease about 10%, 25%, 50%, or 75%?

7. Original: $50.00   **Sale:** $38.00   **8. Original:** $90.00   **Sale:** $80.00

9. Original: $15.00   **Sale:** $4.25   **10. Original:** $39.99   **Sale:** $19.99

11. Original: $85.00   **Sale:** $65.00   **12. Original:** $59.89   **Sale:** $14.89

13. The enrollment of a club doubled. Find the percent increase.

14. Aaron spent half his money. Find the percent decrease.

Use after Lesson 8.1, page 374

In Exercises 1–5, use the diagram. Line *n* and line *p* are parallel.

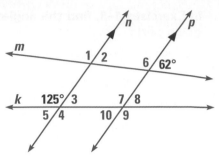

1. Find the measure of ∠2.

2. Find the measure of ∠4.

3. Name three angles congruent to ∠3.

4. ∠7 and ∠9 are called __?__ angles.

5. ∠6 and ∠7 are called __?__ angles.

Use after Lesson 8.2, page 380

In Exercises 1 and 2, describe the translation of triangle *ABC* to triangle *DEF*.

1. *A*(0, 0), *B*(3, 3), *C*(6, 0)
   D(−2, −4), *E*(1, −1), *F*(4, −4)

2. *A*(4, 3), *B*(7, 5), *C*(6, −2)
   D(−2, 3), *E*(1, 5), *F*(0, −2)

A quadrilateral has vertices at (−2, 0), (−2, 2), (1, 4), and (3, −1). Give the coordinates of the vertices of the quadrilateral after each translation.

3. 8 units right

4. 2 units down

5. 1 unit left and 6 units up

Use after Lesson 8.3, page 386

In Exercises 1–3, find the circumference of the circle. Use π ≈ 3.14.

1.

6 in.

2.

9 ft

3.

5.5 cm

4. If you order a 12-inch circular pizza, is the 12-inch measure the *radius*, the *diameter*, or the *circumference* of the pizza?

Use after Lesson 8.4, page 390

In Exercises 1–3, find the area of the parallelogram.

1.
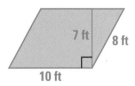
7 ft, 8 ft, 10 ft

2.
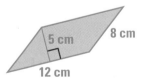
5 cm, 8 cm, 12 cm

3.
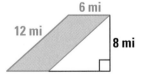
6 mi, 12 mi, 8 mi

In Exercises 4–6, find the dimension labeled *x*.

4. *A* = 600 sq mm
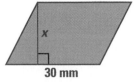
x, 30 mm

5. *A* = 91 sq ft
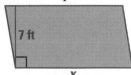
7 ft, *x*

6. *A* = 72 sq m
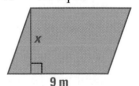
x, 9 m

Use after Lesson 8.5, page 396

In Exercises 1–3, find the area of the trapezoid.

1.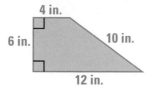
4 in.
6 in.
10 in.
12 in.

2.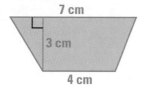
7 cm
3 cm
4 cm

3.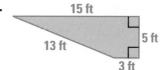
15 ft
13 ft
5 ft
3 ft

In Exercises 4–6, find the dimension labeled _x_.

4. $A = 22.5$ sq cm

x
5 cm
7 cm

5. $A = 96$ sq in.

5 in.
x
11 in.

6. $A = 108$ sq mm

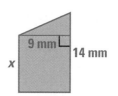
9 mm
14 mm
x

Use after Lesson 8.6, page 400

In Exercises 1–3, find the area of the circle. Use $\pi \approx 3.14$.

1. Radius = 5 in.

2. Diameter = 16 ft

3. Diameter = 9 m

In Exercises 4–6, find the area of the shaded region.

4.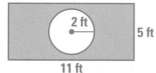
2 ft
5 ft
11 ft

5.
2 m
1 m

6.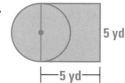
5 yd
5 yd

Use after Lesson 8.7, page 406

 In Exercises 1–4, use a calculator to find the square root of the number.

1. $\sqrt{441}$

2. $\sqrt{196}$

3. $\sqrt{49}$

4. $\sqrt{53.29}$

 In Exercises 5–8, use mental math to estimate the square root. Then use a calculator to check your estimate.

5. $\sqrt{20}$

6. $\sqrt{104}$

7. $\sqrt{35}$

8. $\sqrt{123}$

Use after Lesson 8.8, page 412

In Exercises 1–3, find the length of the missing side.

1.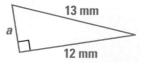
13 mm
a
12 mm

2.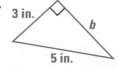
3 in.
b
5 in.

3.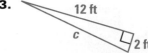
12 ft
c
2 ft

Use after Lesson 9.1, page 428

Name the polyhedron and state the number of faces, edges, and vertices.

1.

2.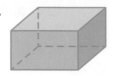

3.

4.

5. For each of Exercises 1–4, match the polyhedron with its description.

A. triangular prism   **B.** triangular pyramid
C. rectangular prism   **D.** rectangular pyramid

Use after Lesson 9.2, page 432

In Exercises 1–4, find the surface area of the prism.

1.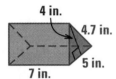
4 in., 4.7 in., 5 in., 7 in.

2.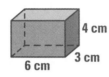
4 cm, 3 cm, 6 cm

3.
2 ft, 2 ft, 2 ft

4.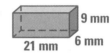
9 mm, 6 mm, 21 mm

5. A cube has a surface area of 384 centimeters. What is the length of one edge? Sketch the cube and label its edges.

Use after Lesson 9.3, page 438

Decide whether the net can be folded to form a cylinder.

1.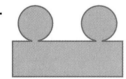

2.

3.

Use can A and can B shown at the right. Each can has a paper label that covers the entire curved surface.

4. Which can has the label with the greater area?

5. Will a rectangular label that measures 9 in. by 12 in. completely cover can B?

6. The two cans hold the same amount of liquid. Which can has the greater surface area?

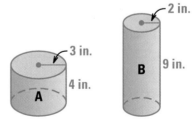
2 in., 3 in., 4 in., 9 in., A, B

Use after Lesson 9.4, page 442

In Exercises 1–3, draw a top view, a front view, and a side view.

1.

2.

3.

Use after Lesson 9.5, page 450

In Exercises 1–3, find the volume of the box.

1.
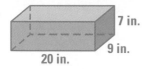
7 in.
9 in.
20 in.

2.
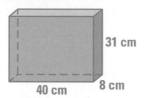
31 cm
40 cm   8 cm

3.
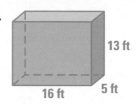
13 ft
16 ft   5 ft

4. Bonnie wants to spread 3 inches of peat moss over her rectangular flower bed that measures 2 feet by 14 feet. One package of peat moss contains 3.8 cubic feet. How many packages does she need?

5. The dimensions of two rectangular suitcases are given. Which suitcase will hold more?

    A. 20 cm by 32 cm by 44 cm   **B.** 15 cm by 30 cm by 50 cm

Use after Lesson 9.6, page 454

In Exercises 1–3, find the volume of the cylinder.

1.
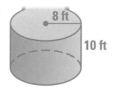
8 ft
10 ft

2.
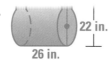
22 in.
26 in.

3.
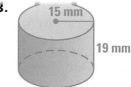
15 mm
19 mm

In Exercises 4–6, find the missing measurement.

4.
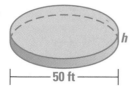
h
50 ft
$V = 8635 \text{ ft}^3$

5.

r
20 in.
$V = 4019.2 \text{ in.}^3$

6.
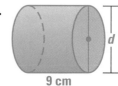
d
9 cm
$V = 706.5 \text{ cm}^3$

Use after Lesson 9.7, page 462

In Exercises 1 and 2, decide whether the two prisms are similar.

1.
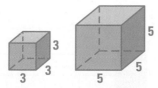
5
3
3   3   5   5

2.
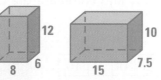
12   10
8   6   15   7.5

3. The heights of two similar rectanglar prisms are 15 cm and 20 m, respectively. What is the ratio of the heights?

4. Sketch a rectangular prism with dimensions 2 units by 5 units by 8 units. Then sketch a similar prism that is smaller and a similar prism that is larger. Label the dimensions.

Use after Lesson 10.1, page 480

In Exercises 1–8, find the absolute value.

1. $|-6|$ **2.** $|5|$ **3.** $|7|$ **4.** $|-4|$

5. $|10|$ **6.** $|-17|$ **7.** $|-4.7|$ **8.** $|12\frac{1}{3}|$

In Exercises 9–12, complete the statement using $<$, $>$, or $=$.

9. -3 ? $|3|$ **10.** 0 ? $|-2|$ **11.** $|-6|$? $|6|$ **12.** 8 ? $|-8|$

Use after Lesson 10.2, page 484

In Exercises 1–8, find the sum.

1. $17 + (-6)$ **2.** $4 + (-12)$ **3.** $-15 + 20$ **4.** $-11 + (-4)$

5. $9 + (-9)$ **6.** $-12 + 14$ **7.** $-13 + (-8)$ **8.** $7 + (-18)$

In Exercises 9–14, find the average of the numbers.

9. $12, -4, 13, -9$ **10.** $-5, -1, -3, 11$ **11.** $45, -23, 15, -37$

12. $98, -30, -3, -11, -4$ **13.** $21, -9, 27, -17, -12$ **14.** $7, 9, 9, 6, -30$

Use after Lesson 10.3, page 488

In Exercises 1–8, write each subtraction expression as an equivalent addition expression. Then find the sum.

1. $8 - 15$ **2.** $-9 - 12$ **3.** $3 - (-6)$ **4.** $-6 - (-8)$

5. $-20 - 3$ **6.** $30 - 42$ **7.** $21 - (-17)$ **8.** $-30 - (-47)$

In Exercises 9–16, add or subtract.

9. $12 + (-4)$ **10.** $-3 - (-17)$ **11.** $-11 + 19$ **12.** $7 - (-9)$

13. $25 - 38$ **14.** $19 + (-29)$ **15.** $-18 - (-16)$ **16.** $-11 + (-21)$

In Exercises 17–20, evaluate the expression when $x = 2$ and when $x = -8$.

17. $17 - x$ **18.** $8 - x$ **19.** $x - (-20)$ **20.** $0 - x$

Use after Lesson 10.4, page 492

In Exercises 1–3, copy and complete the table of values.

1. $y = -12 + x$ **2.** $y = x - 4$ **3.** $y = -x + 6$

x	−10	−5	0	5	10
y	?	?	?	?	?

x	−4	−2	0	2	4
y	?	?	?	?	?

x	−3	−1	0	1	3
y	?	?	?	?	?

In Exercises 4–7, use integer values from −3 to 3 to draw a scatter plot for the equation.

4. $y = x - 5$ **5.** $y = x + 8$ **6.** $y = |x| + 2$ **7.** $y = -1 - x$

Use after Lesson 10.5, page 500

In Exercises 1–8, find the product.

1. $3 \times (-5)$ **2.** $(-7) \cdot (-9)$ **3.** $(-4)(2)$ **4.** $(3)(-2)(3)$

5. $-6 \cdot 6$ **6.** $15 \cdot (-3)$ **7.** $(8)(-7)$ **8.** $-6 \cdot 2 \cdot 3$

In Exercises 9–12, evaluate the expression when $x = -4$ and when $x = 5$.

9. $-8x$ **10.** $|x| \cdot x$ **11.** $3x + 9$ **12.** $11 \cdot x$

Use after Lesson 10.6, page 504

In Exercises 1–8, find the quotient.

1. $-49 \div (-7)$ **2.** $52 \div (-4)$ **3.** $-144 \div 12$ **4.** $-99 \div (-11)$

5. $-21 \div 3$ **6.** $-48 \div 6$ **7.** $-120 \div (-12)$ **8.** $35 \div (-7)$

In Exercises 9 and 10, find the average of the numbers.

9. $-15, 3, -22, 12, 10, -8, 2, 6$ **10.** $-14, -16, -6, 18, -8, -10, -8, -9, 17$

In Exercises 11–14, evaluate the expression when $x = 2$ and when $x = -3$.

11. $-18 \div x$ **12.** $x \div 6$ **13.** $12 \div x$ **14.** $x \div (-8)$

Use after Lesson 10.7, page 510

In Exercises 1–8, evaluate the expression.

1. $(-6)^2$ **2.** -5^2 **3.** $2(-4)^2$ **4.** $(-3)(-2)^3$

5. $(4 \cdot 2)^2$ **6.** $-(-3)^3 \times (-3)$ **7.** $(-5)^3 - 50$ **8.** $4 \times 3 - 2^4$

In Exercises 9–12, make a table of values for the equation. Use x-values of $-3, -2, -1, 0, 1, 2,$ and 3. Then plot the points in a coordinate plane and describe any patterns you see.

9. $y = 5 - x^2$ **10.** $y = x^2 - 3$ **11.** $y = \frac{1}{3} \cdot x^3$ **12.** $y = 9 - x^2$

Use after Lesson 10.8, page 516

In Exercises 1–4, write the power of ten as a whole number or as a fraction.

1. 10^4 **2.** 10^1 **3.** 10^{-8} **4.** 10^0

In Exercises 5–10, write the number in scientific notation.

5. 0.0000009 **6.** $200,000,000$ **7.** 0.0000715

8. 0.0026 **9.** $389,000,000,000$ **10.** $42,100,000$

In Exercises 11–16, complete the statement using $>$, $<$, or $=$.

11. 7.03×10^4 ? 7030 **12.** 8.3 ? 8.3×10^{-1} **13.** 6.2×10^6 ? 8.5×10^5

14. 9.2×10^{-4} ? 0.00092 **15.** 6219 ? 6.2×10^3 **16.** 4×10^{-3} ? 4×10^{-2}

Use after Lesson 11.1, page 530

In Exercises 1–4, use the spinner at the right. Find the
probability of spinning the letter.

1. L

2. P

3. U or P

4. G

A couple plans to have four children. Assume "boy" and "girl" are
equally likely. In Exercises 5–7, list all the possible outcomes for the
given genders of the children. Then find the probability.

5. two boys and two girls

6. three boys and one girl

7. all the same gender

Use after Lesson 11.2, page 536

In Exercises 1–3, find the number of possible outcomes in the situation.
Use a tree diagram or the Counting Principle.

1. You want to buy a radio, a remote control vehicle, and a science kit.
The store stocks 3 models of radios; 2 remote control cars, a dune
buggy and a truck; and science kits for both chemistry and physics.

2. There are 4 bus routes that stop by your house. On any of the 4 routes
you can get off at 6 places.

3. On each of the 4 bus routes in Exercise 2, the transit authority adds
2 more stops.

Use after Lesson 11.3, page 544

In Exercises 1–4, use a scientific calculator to evaluate the expression.

1. 4!

2. 6!

3. 3!

4. 9!

In Exercises 5–7, find the number of permutations of the letters in each
word. List the permutations. How many are words?

5. CUP

6. PINE

7. TEA

8. In how many different ways can 4 people be elected President,
Vice President, Secretary, and Treasurer of a club?

Use after Lesson 11.4, page 548

In Exercises 1–3, decide whether you need to find the number of
permutations or *combinations*. Then find the answer.

1. How many ways are there to choose 3 out of 4 players?

2. In how many ways can 8 players be put in a batting line up?

3. In how many ways can you and 3 friends wait in a line at the movies?

In Exercises 4 and 5, list the combinations.

4. Choose 2 even digits from the digits 1 through 8.

5. Choose 3 digits from the digits 1 through 5.

Use after Lesson 11.5, page 556

In Exercises 1 and 2, decide whether the game is fair. Explain.

1. Two number cubes are tossed. Player A gets 8 points if both numbers are even. Player B gets 2 points if they are both odd or if one is even and one is odd.

2. A spinner is labeled with each of the 12 months. Player A gets 12 points if the month spun ends in "ber"; otherwise, player B gets 6 points.

In Exercises 3–5, if the spinner lands on a player's letter, the player wins that number of points. Decide if the spinner is *fair*. If not, which player is most likely to win?

3.
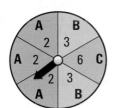

4.

5.
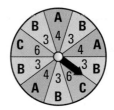

Use after Lesson 11.6, page 560

In Exercises 1 and 2, predict the number of times the event will occur if the experiment is performed 500 times.

1. Toss 2 number cubes. The sum is 10 or greater.

2. A spinner marked with the twelve months of the year lands on a month that begins with the letter J.

3. Nearly 60% of American households includes a cat or a dog. You plan to open a pet store in a town with about 1000 households. There is no other pet store in town. About how many households might you expect to shop at your store?

4. The probability of at least one inch of snow on December 25 in Burlington, Vermont, is 77%. If you spend four years in Burlington, how many times would you expect snow on December 25?

Use after Lesson 11.7, page 566

In Exercises 1–3, draw a Venn diagram that represents the two sets.

1. Boats and canoes   2. Dog owners and cat owners   3. Fish and birds

In Exercises 4 and 5, use the following information. Of 30 people surveyed, 21 ate soup for lunch, 18 ate salad, and 11 ate both.

4. How many people ate salad but not soup? How many ate soup but not salad? Sketch a Venn diagram to support your answers.

5. What is the probability that one of these people chosen at random ate neither soup nor salad for lunch?

Use after Lesson 12.1, page 580

In Exercises 1–3, write the equation that is being modeled. Copy and complete the box model to solve the equation.

1.
$$+3$$
| a | → | 7 |

2.
$$-6$$
| z | → | 5 |

3.
$$\times(-8)$$
| n | → | 16 |

In Exercises 4–11, write a box model for the equation. Then use an inverse operation to solve the equation.

4. $y + 5 = 12$ **5.** $g - 4 = 11$ **6.** $n \cdot 5 = 35$ **7.** $w + (-3) = -1$

8. $p \div 4 = -3$ **9.** $c - 7 = -2$ **10.** $\dfrac{x}{-6} = -36$ **11.** $-9d = 45$

Use after Lesson 12.2, page 584

In Exercises 1–3, decide whether $x = 5$ is a solution.

1. $-7 + x = -12$ **2.** $-x + 4 = -1$ **3.** $-3 - x = 2$

In Exercises 4–6, rewrite the equation in a simpler form. Then solve.

4. $f - (-8) = 8$ **5.** $m + (-2) = 9$ **6.** $h - (-5) = 13$

In Exercises 7–14, solve the equation. Then check your solution.

7. $14 + g = 5$ **8.** $\dfrac{1}{3} + n = 2\dfrac{2}{3}$ **9.** $s - 8 = -6$ **10.** $z - \dfrac{7}{8} = \dfrac{3}{8}$

11. $k + 9.6 = 1.2$ **12.** $0.5 + y = 0.75$ **13.** $a - (-6) = 8$ **14.** $u + (-11) = 7$

Use after Lesson 12.3, page 592

In Exercises 1–3, without solving the equation, decide whether the solution is *positive* or *negative*. Then solve the equation.

1. $3g = 27$ **2.** $-40 = 8m$ **3.** $-6x = -16$

In Exercises 4–11, solve the equation. Then check your solution.

4. $24 = -4n$ **5.** $-0.4h = -63$ **6.** $7d = -77$ **7.** $-\dfrac{1}{3}y = 28$

8. $0 = 8a$ **9.** $-14r = -42$ **10.** $-1.5p = 7.5$ **11.** $-k = 22$

In Exercises 12 and 13, write the equation represented by the verbal sentence. Then solve the equation.

12. 14 is the product of -2 and a number.   **13.** The product of a number and -3 is -24.

14. You can make $.015 per word writing magazine articles. You sent one article and got a check for $93.75. Use the verbal model below to assign labels and write an equation. Then find how many words were in the article you sent.

$$\dfrac{\text{Number}}{\text{of words}} \cdot \dfrac{\text{Rate per}}{\text{word}} = \text{Earnings}$$

Use after Lesson 12.4, page 598

In Exercises 1–3, decide whether the solution is positive or negative *without* solving the equation. Then solve the equation.

1. $\dfrac{t}{-7} = -39$ **2.** $f \div 9 = -21$ **3.** $\dfrac{p}{-14} = 6$

In Exercises 4–12, solve the equation. Then check your solution.

4. $\dfrac{m}{5} = 11$ **5.** $a \div 13 = -3$ **6.** $\dfrac{v}{-4} = -7$

7. $c \div (-12) = -8$ **8.** $\dfrac{s}{-8} = 64$ **9.** $n \div \dfrac{3}{4} = \dfrac{1}{6}$

10. $\dfrac{t}{3.6} = -72$ **11.** $w \div \left(-\dfrac{3}{2}\right) = \dfrac{4}{9}$ **12.** $\dfrac{h}{-3.4} = -7.5$

Use after Lesson 12.5, page 604

In Exercises 1–9, solve the equation. Then check your solution.

1. $12 + 5m = -43$ **2.** $6w - 9 = 39$ **3.** $3t - 11 = -23$

4. $\dfrac{u}{-9} + 7 = 13$ **5.** $\dfrac{d}{6} - 1 = 12$ **6.** $\dfrac{k}{-5} + 11 = 6$

7. $-3x + 5 = 11$ **8.** $2.5z - 7 = 4.5$ **9.** $14 - 2y = 0$

10. Your brother is setting up a lemonade stand. His goal is to make $10. He spent $4.99 on supplies and has enough lemonade for about 50 cups. Use the verbal model to figure what to charge per cup.

$$\dfrac{\text{Number}}{\text{of cups}} \cdot \dfrac{\text{Charge}}{\text{per cup}} - \dfrac{\text{Start-up}}{\text{costs}} = \text{Profit}$$

11. Admission to an amusement park is $6.50. Each ride ticket costs $1.25. You have $20 to spend. How many ride tickets can you buy?

Use after Lesson 12.6, page 612

In Exercises 1–3, make an input-output table for the function. Use *x*-values of 1, 2, 3, 4, 5, and 6.

1. $4x + 7 = y$ **2.** $y = \dfrac{x}{4} + 5$ **3.** $y = -6x - 2$

In Exercises 4 and 5, use the input-output table to write an equation for the function.

4.

Input, x	1	2	3	4	5	6
Output, y	−3	0	3	6	9	12

5.

Input, x	1	2	3	4	5	6
Output, y	6	5	4	3	2	1

6. Draw scatter plots of the ordered pairs in Exercises 4 and 5.

TOOLBOX

Using a Pattern

Example 1 Describe the pattern. Then write the next three terms.

3, 9, 27, 81, 243, ?, ?, ?, ...

Solution Each number is 3 times the previous one. Multiply by 3 to find the next numbers.

$243 \cdot 3 = 729$ $729 \cdot 3 = 2187$ $2187 \cdot 3 = 6561$

The next three numbers are 729, 2187, and 6561.

Example 2 Describe a pattern in the products. Then predict the value of the product 100000001 · 100000001.

$101 \cdot 101 = 10201$ $1001 \cdot 1001 = 1002001$ $10001 \cdot 10001 = 100020001$

Solution In each product, a power of ten plus 1 is multiplied by itself. The result has a 1 at each end and a 2 in the middle. Zeros separate these digits. Notice that the number of zeros matches the number of zeros in the original factors.

Using this pattern, you can predict that

100000001 · 100000001 = 10000000200000001.

7 zeros   7 zeros   7 zeros   7 zeros

PRACTICE AND PROBLEM SOLVING

In Exercises 1–10, describe the pattern. Then write the next three terms.

1. 16, 20, 24, 28, ?, ?, ?, ...

2. 2, 10, 50, 250, ?, ?, ?, ...

3. 10, 7, 4, 1, ?, ?, ?, ...

4. 12, 121, 1212, 12121, ?, ?, ?, ...

5. 80, 40, 20, 10, ?, ?, ?, ...

6. $\frac{1}{2}, \frac{2}{3}, \frac{3}{4}, \frac{4}{5}$, ?, ?, ?, ...

7. Z, A, Y, B, ?, ?, ?, ...

8. A, C, E, G, ?, ?, ?, ...

9. Z, W, T, Q, ?, ?, ?, ...

10. B, C, D, F, G, H, J, ?, ?, ?, ...

In Exercises 11 and 12, describe a pattern in the products. Then predict the next three products.

11. $2 \cdot 99 = \mathbf{198}$

$3 \cdot 99 = \mathbf{297}$

$4 \cdot 99 = \mathbf{396}$

$5 \cdot 99 = \mathbf{495}$

$6 \cdot 99 = \mathbf{594}$

12. $12 \cdot 99 = \mathbf{1188}$

$13 \cdot 99 = \mathbf{1287}$

$14 \cdot 99 = \mathbf{1386}$

$15 \cdot 99 = \mathbf{1485}$

$16 \cdot 99 = \mathbf{1584}$

Using a Table or List

Example 1 Use a table or list to find how many different ways you can combine quarters, dimes, and nickels to make $.40.

Solution Make an organized list.

Quarters	Dimes	Nickels
1	1	1
1	0	3
0	4	0
0	3	2
0	2	4
0	1	6
0	0	8

These combinations use a quarter.

These combinations do not use a quarter.

They are listed according to the number of dimes.

There are seven ways of getting $.40 using only quarters, dimes, and nickels.

PRACTICE AND PROBLEM SOLVING

In Exercises 1–8, use a table or list to find the answer.

1. How many ways can you make $1.00 using quarters and dimes?

2. How many ways can you make $.75 using quarters and nickels?

3. How many ways can you make $.50 using quarters, dimes, and nickels?

4. List the multiples of 5 between 0 and 100 that are also multiples of 3.

5. You have a red sweatshirt, a white sweatshirt, and a gray sweatshirt. You have black pants and blue pants. List all possible combinations of sweatshirt and pants.

6. You can have one or two toppings on your pizza. The toppings that are available are pepperoni, mushroom, onion, and extra cheese. List all the possible types of pizza you can have.

7. How many different ways can you arrange your Math, English, History, and Science books in a row on a shelf?

8. Organize this information into a table:

   • The ingredients for pancakes are 2 c. baking mix, 1 c. milk, and 2 eggs.

   • The ingredients for waffles are 2 c. baking mix, $1\frac{1}{3}$ c. milk, 1 egg, and 2 T. oil.

   • The ingredients for biscuits are $2\frac{1}{4}$ c. baking mix, and $\frac{2}{3}$ c. milk.

Using a Graph or a Diagram

Example 1 Use the bar graph to estimate the percent of people in Los Angeles who use each kind of transportation to get to work.

Solution The scale at the left tells you that each grid mark represents 10% of the working population.

About 65% drive alone, and about 15% carpool to work.

About 10% use public transit, and about 10% use some other kind of transportation.

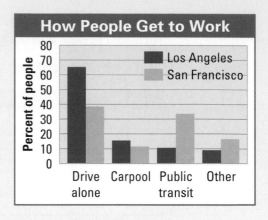

How People Get to Work

Example 2 The length and width of a rectangle are integers. The area is 24 square units. What such rectangle has the smallest perimeter?

Solution Draw a diagram of the possibilities. The rectangle with the smallest perimeter is 4 units by 6 units.

P = 50   24   1

P = 28   12   2   P = 22   8   3   P = 20   6   4

PRACTICE AND PROBLEM SOLVING

In Exercises 1 and 2, use the bar graph in Example 1.

1. Estimate the percent of people in San Francisco who use each kind of transportation to get to work.

2. Which methods of getting to work are more popular in San Francisco than in Los Angeles?

In Exercises 3–6, draw a diagram to find the answer.

3. The length and width of a rectangle are integers. The area is 36 cm^2. Which such rectangle has the smallest perimeter?

4. The length and width of a rectangle are integers. The perimeter is 20 m. Which such rectangle has the largest area?

5. Four students are playing tennis. They want to make sure that everyone gets to play everyone else. How many games do they need to play?

6. In a city with square city blocks, you walk 2 blocks east, 3 blocks north, 4 blocks west, then 5 blocks south. How should you walk to get back to where you started?

Working Backward

Example 1   Your aunt gives you and your two sisters some money. You divide it equally. You spend half and save half. After 3 yr, your savings have earned $35 interest and the total in your savings account is $385. How large was your aunt's gift amount?

Solution   Draw a diagram.

$$\boxed{?} \rightarrow \div 3 \rightarrow \boxed{?} \rightarrow \div 2 \rightarrow \boxed{?} \rightarrow + 35 \rightarrow \boxed{385}$$

gift   **your share**   **savings**   **balance**

Work backward on the diagram to find the original gift amount.

$$\boxed{2100} \leftarrow \times 3 \leftarrow \boxed{700} \leftarrow \times 2 \leftarrow \boxed{350} \leftarrow - 35 \leftarrow \boxed{385}$$

gift   **your share**   **savings**   **balance**

Your Aunt's original gift was $2100.

PRACTICE AND PROBLEM SOLVING

In Exercises 1–4, copy and complete the diagram.

1. $\boxed{?} \rightarrow \times 5 \rightarrow \boxed{?} \rightarrow + 3 \rightarrow \boxed{8}$

2. $\boxed{?} \rightarrow \div 6 \rightarrow \boxed{?} \rightarrow + 4 \rightarrow \boxed{?} \rightarrow \times 3 \rightarrow \boxed{15}$

3. $\boxed{?} \rightarrow + 12 \rightarrow \boxed{?} \rightarrow \times 3 \rightarrow \boxed{?} \rightarrow - 8 \rightarrow \boxed{10}$

4. $\boxed{?} \rightarrow \div 10 \rightarrow \boxed{?} \rightarrow - 3 \rightarrow \boxed{?} \rightarrow \times 2 \rightarrow \boxed{4}$

In Exercises 5–8, write an equation that models the question. Then solve the equation.

5. What number can be added to 92 to get 103?

6. From what number can you subtract 6 to get 17?

7. What number can be multiplied by 6 to get 90?

8. What number can be divided by 4 to get 52?

In Exercises 9–11, solve by making a diagram and working backwards.

9. Your violin lesson begins at 4:00 P.M. You want to be there 15 min early to warm up. To get to your lesson, you have a 20 min bus ride. It takes you 5 min to walk to the bus stop. What time should you leave?

10. You bake some cookies. You take half of them to the school bake sale and leave half at home. While you are at school, your parents eat 9 cookies and your brothers and sisters eat 12 cookies. When you get home, there are 19 cookies left. How many cookies did you bake?

11. One side of a rectangle is 15 in. long. The perimeter is 38 in. How long is the shorter side of the rectangle?

Place Value

Our number system is a place-value system. The value of each digit depends on its place. For example, in the number 592, the digit 5 has a value of 500 because it is in the hundreds' place.

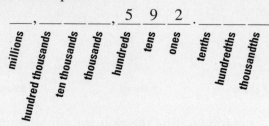

Example 1 Write the number 432.7 in expanded form.

Solution
$$432.7 = 400 + 30 + 2 + 0.7$$
$$= 4 \cdot 100 + 3 \cdot 10 + 2 \cdot 1 + 7 \cdot \frac{1}{10}$$

Example 2 Write the number in decimal form.

a. Three million four hundred thousand fifty   **b.** Seven and 19 hundredths

Solution **a.** Put 3 in the millions' place, 4 in the hundred thousands' place, and 5 in the tens' place. Use zeros as placeholders. The answer is 3,400,050.

b. Put 7 in the ones' place, 1 in the tenths' place, and 9 in the hundredths' place. The answer is 7.19.

PRACTICE AND PROBLEM SOLVING

In Exercises 1–4, write the number in expanded form.

1. 1254   **2.** 6,000,750   **3.** 380.2   **4.** 12.045

In Exercises 5–11, write the number in decimal form.

5. $6 \cdot 10{,}000 + 4 \cdot 1000 + 8 \cdot 10 + 7 \cdot 1$

6. $5 \cdot 100 + 4 \cdot 1 + 3 \cdot \frac{1}{10} + 7 \cdot \frac{1}{100}$

7. One million six hundred eighty thousand nineteen

8. Fifty-three thousand eight hundred

9. Four hundred seven and sixteen hundredths

10. Sixty-four and seven tenths

11. Nine and fifty-three thousandths

In Exercises 12–15, write the number in words.

12. 1208   **13.** 3,078,205

14. 12.003   **15.** 1.15

TOOLBOX

Add, Subtract, Multiply, and Divide Whole Numbers

Example 1   **Add or subtract.**

       a. $145 + 297$ **b.** $330 - 96$

Solution   **a.**
$$
\begin{array}{r}
\overset{1\ 1}{145} \\
+\ 297 \\
\hline
442
\end{array}
$$
442 — $5 + 7 = 12$
        $1 + 4 + 9 = 14$
        $1 + 1 + 2 = 4$

   b.
$$
\begin{array}{r}
\overset{2\ 1}{3\cancel{3}0} \\
-\ 96 \\
\hline
234
\end{array}
$$
234 — $10 - 6 = 4$
        $32 - 9 = 23$

Example 2   **Multiply or divide.**

       a. 83×9 **b.** $85 \div 6$

Solution   **a.**
$$
\begin{array}{r}
\overset{2}{83} \\
\times\ 9 \\
\hline
747
\end{array}
$$
747 — $3 \times 9 = 27$
        $9 \times 8 + 2 = 74$

   b. $14\frac{1}{6}$

$6\overline{)85}$

$\underline{6}$ — $10 \times 6 = 60$

25 — $85 - 60 = 25$

$\underline{24}$ — $4 \times 6 = 24$

1 **1** is the remainder.

PRACTICE AND PROBLEM SOLVING

In Exercises 1–12, add or subtract.

1. $125 + 67$ **2.** $35 + 225$ **3.** $48 - 27$ **4.** $370 - 124$

5. $500 - 9$ **6.** $924 - 862$ **7.** $153 + 296$ **8.** $126 + 391 + 402$

9. $2000 + 200 + 2$ **10.** $326 + 127 - 81$ **11.** $429 - 98 + 11$ **12.** $600 - 60 - 6$

In Exercises 13–24, multiply or divide.

13. 15×8 **14.** 37×6 **15.** $900 \div 5$ **16.** $360 \div 9$

17. $824 \div 6$ **18.** $255 \div 11$ **19.** 200×16 **20.** 26×12

21. 80×70 **22.** $200 \div 45$ **23.** 293×50 **24.** $690 \div 15$

25. To pay for a sweatshirt that costs $18 and a belt that costs $15, you hand the sales clerk two $20 bills. How much change should the clerk give you?

26. A camp counselor asks a group of 163 campers to form teams of 6 campers each. How many teams are formed, and how many campers are "left over"?

27. To start a game of *Monopoly*®, the person playing the banker gives each player two $500 bills, two $100 bills, two $50 bills, six $20 bills, five $10 bills, five $5 bills, and five $1 bills. How much money does each player get?

Add and Subtract Decimals

Example 1 **Add or subtract.**

a. $2.4 + 0.86 + 6$ **b.** $15.10 - 3.94$

Solution Write each problem in vertical form. Line up the decimal points. Use zeros as place holders.

a.
$$
\begin{array}{r}
2.40 \\
0.86 \\
+\ 6.00 \\
\hline
9.26
\end{array}
$$

b.
$$
\begin{array}{r}
^{4\ 10\ 1} \\
1\cancel{5}.1\cancel{0} \\
-\ 3.94 \\
\hline
11.16
\end{array}
$$

PRACTICE AND PROBLEM SOLVING

In Exercises 1–8, add.

1. $2.8 + 3.1$ **2.** $12 + 5.5$ **3.** $1.01 + 4.3$ **4.** $0.66 + 0.04$

5. $3.28 + 6.12$ **6.** $35.012 + 6.32$ **7.** $9.999 + 0.001$ **8.** $0.105 + 1.02$

In Exercises 9–16, subtract.

9. $5.6 - 1.4$ **10.** $9.25 - 3.72$ **11.** $10.4 - 0.57$ **12.** $16 - 1.2$

13. $8.8 - 2.02$ **14.** $10 - 1.8$ **15.** $102.5 - 30.6$ **16.** $36.85 - 32.006$

In Exercises 17–22, simplify.

17. $15.3 + 0.65 - 10.4$ **18.** $96 + 10.2 - 75.4$

19. $0.65 + 3.20 - 1.09$ **20.** $42.06 - 32.1 + 0.68$

21. $32.14 - 6.23 + 4.07$ **22.** $89.123 - 64.07 - 15.7$

In Exercises 23–27, add or subtract to solve the problem.

23. To pay for milk that costs $3.62, you hand the clerk a $5 bill. How much change should you receive?

24. You buy a pair of soccer shorts for $5.95 and a team shirt for $8.50. How much do you spend?

25. Normal body temperature is about 98.6°F. A nurse finds that a patient's temperature is 101°F. By how many degrees is the patient's temperature above normal?

26. The student music club has a three-day bake sale to raise money for a tour. Their sales on the three days are $63.85, $47.25, and $22.05. What are the total sales?

27. You bring $10 to the beach, buy an iced drink for $1.95 and a snack for $2.25, and on your way home you find $.35 in the parking lot. How much money do you have at the end of the day?

Multiply and Divide Decimals

Example 1 **Multiply.**

    a. 4.25×1.4 **b.** 1.24×0.06

Solution   Write each problem vertically. You do not need to line up the decimal points. The total number of decimal points in the factors is the number of decimal places in the answer.

a.	4.25	two decimal places
	$\times$ 1.4	one decimal place
	1700	
	425	
	5.950	three decimal places

b.	1.24	two decimal places
	$\times$ 0.06	two decimal places
	0.0744	four decimal places

Example 2 **Divide: $0.086 \div 0.2$.**

Solution   Write the problem in long division form.

$$0.2\overline{)0.086}$$

Move the decimal points in the divisor and dividend the same number of places until the divisor is a whole number. Then divide.

$$0.2.\overline{)0.0.86} \qquad\qquad 2\overline{)0.86}^{\,0.43}$$

Move one place to the right.

PRACTICE AND PROBLEM SOLVING

In Exercises 1–8, multiply.

1. 8.5×2.5 **2.** 2.5×0.04 **3.** 0.00002×16 **4.** $500{,}000 \times 0.0003$

5. 6.2×4.5 **6.** 3.05×2.7 **7.** 9.33×0.1 **8.** 0.04×260

In Exercises 9–16, divide.

9. $600 \div 0.3$ **10.** $36.36 \div 1.2$ **11.** $6.024 \div 0.04$ **12.** $85.02 \div 0.006$

13. $2.75 \div 0.005$ **14.** $59.18 \div 0.011$ **15.** $31.28 \div 9.2$ **16.** $6.71 \div 2.2$

In Exercises 17–19, multiply or divide to solve the problem.

17. To convert kilograms to pounds, multiply the number of kilograms by 2.2. What is the weight in pounds of a dog that weighs 15 kg?

18. To convert pounds to kilograms, divide the number of pounds by 2.2. What is the weight of a baby that weighs 6.75 lb?

19. How much do you pay for 6 gal of gasoline if the price is $1.2999 per gallon?

Add and Subtract Fractions

Example 1   **Add or subtract.**

     a. $\dfrac{4}{15} + \dfrac{1}{15}$ **b.** $\dfrac{2}{3} - \dfrac{1}{2}$

Solution   **a.** The two fractions have the same denominator, 15, so you add the numerators.

$$\frac{4}{15} + \frac{1}{15} = \frac{4+1}{15} = \frac{5}{15}$$

Because the numerator and denominator have a common factor of 5, the answer can be simplified.

$$\frac{5}{15} = \frac{5 \cdot 1}{5 \cdot 3} = \frac{1}{3}$$

b. The two fractions do not have the same denominator. You need to rewrite them with the same denominator.

$$\frac{2}{3} - \frac{1}{2} = \frac{2 \cdot 2}{2 \cdot 3} - \frac{3 \cdot 1}{3 \cdot 2} \qquad \text{Rewrite each fraction.}$$

$$= \frac{4}{6} - \frac{3}{6} \qquad \text{The common denominator is 6.}$$

$$= \frac{1}{6}$$

PRACTICE AND PROBLEM SOLVING

In Exercises 1–8, add or subtract. Simplify your answer if possible.

1. $\dfrac{2}{3} + \dfrac{1}{3}$ **2.** $\dfrac{3}{4} - \dfrac{1}{4}$ **3.** $\dfrac{5}{16} + \dfrac{3}{8}$ **4.** $\dfrac{2}{5} - \dfrac{1}{10}$

5. $\dfrac{7}{8} + \dfrac{1}{4}$ **6.** $\dfrac{2}{3} - \dfrac{1}{9}$ **7.** $\dfrac{1}{10} + \dfrac{5}{6}$ **8.** $\dfrac{5}{9} - \dfrac{1}{2}$

In Exercises 9–12, add or subtract to solve the problem.

9. A soup recipe calls for $\dfrac{3}{4}$ c. of grated cheese. Of this, $\dfrac{1}{2}$ c. will be stirred into the soup. How much will be left to sprinkle on top?

10. To make a baby quilt, you buy $\dfrac{3}{4}$ yd of blue print fabric and $\dfrac{1}{3}$ yd of pink print. How much fabric do you buy?

11. Over three days, a city had these amounts of rainfall: $1\dfrac{1}{8}$ in., $\dfrac{3}{4}$ in., and $\dfrac{1}{2}$ in. How much rain fell in these three days?

12. In a survey of seventh graders, half said that they preferred early lunch and a third said that they preferred late lunch. What fraction of the seventh graders had no opinion?

TOOLBOX

Multiply and Divide Fractions

Example 1   **Multiply or divide.**

     a. $\dfrac{3}{7} \cdot \dfrac{2}{9}$ **b.** $3\dfrac{1}{5} \div \dfrac{4}{5}$

Solution   **a.** To multiply fractions, multiply the numerators and denominators.

$$\dfrac{3}{7} \cdot \dfrac{2}{9} = \dfrac{3 \cdot 2}{7 \cdot 9} \qquad \text{Rewrite the product.}$$

$$= \dfrac{6}{63} \qquad \text{Multiply.}$$

$$= \dfrac{2}{21} \qquad \text{Simplify.}$$

     b. To divide fractions, multiply by the reciprocal of the divisor.

$$3\dfrac{1}{5} \div \dfrac{4}{5} = \dfrac{16}{5} \div \dfrac{4}{5} \qquad \text{Express } 3\tfrac{1}{5} \text{ as } \tfrac{16}{5}.$$

$$= \dfrac{16}{5} \cdot \dfrac{5}{4} \qquad \text{To divide by } \tfrac{4}{5}, \text{ multiply by } \tfrac{5}{4}.$$

$$= \dfrac{16}{4} \qquad \text{Multiply.}$$

$$= 4 \qquad \text{Simplify.}$$

PRACTICE AND PROBLEM SOLVING

In Exercises 1–12, multiply or divide.

1. $\dfrac{3}{4} \cdot \dfrac{1}{5}$ **2.** $\dfrac{3}{5} \cdot \dfrac{10}{11}$ **3.** $\dfrac{2}{3} \div \dfrac{1}{3}$ **4.** $\dfrac{16}{9} \div \dfrac{2}{3}$

5. $\dfrac{2}{15} \cdot \dfrac{5}{8}$ **6.** $\dfrac{2}{3} \cdot \dfrac{2}{3}$ **7.** $\dfrac{5}{4} \div 10$ **8.** $\dfrac{6}{5} \div \dfrac{1}{10}$

9. $\dfrac{9}{4} \cdot 8$ **10.** $\dfrac{1}{3} \cdot 4\dfrac{1}{5}$ **11.** $\dfrac{7}{3} \div 7$ **12.** $\dfrac{5}{8} \div 2\dfrac{1}{4}$

In Exercises 13–16, multiply or divide to solve.

13. $\dfrac{2}{3}$ of a pie is left over after a party. You and three friends share it equally. What fraction of a pie does each of you get?

14. On a map, $\dfrac{3}{4}$ in. represents 150 mi. How many miles does $2\dfrac{1}{4}$ in. represent? Explain.

15. A store advertises televisions on sale for $\dfrac{1}{3}$ off the original price. How much would you save on a television that was originally priced at $210?

16. You run $3\dfrac{1}{2}$ times around a quarter-mile track. How far did you run?

In the metric system, the basic unit of length is the *meter* (m), which is a little longer than a yard. The basic unit of weight is the *gram* (g), which is about the weight of a dollar bill.

The metric system uses prefixes to express larger and smaller measurements.

Prefix	Meaning	Length	Weight
kilo-	one thousand	kilometer (km) = 1000 m	kilogram (kg) = 1000 g
centi-	one hundredth	centimeter (cm) = 0.01 m	centigram (cg) = 0.01 g
milli-	one thousandth	millimeter (mm) = 0.001 m	milligram (mg) = 0.001 g

Example 1 **Complete the statement.**

a. 6300 g = $\boxed{?}$ kg

b. 0.03 m = $\boxed{?}$ cm

Solution

a. $6300 \text{ g} = \dfrac{6300 \text{ g}}{1} \cdot \dfrac{1 \text{ kg}}{1000 \text{ g}}$ Multiply by a fraction equal to 1.

$\phantom{6300 \text{ g}} = \dfrac{6300 \text{ g}\!\!\!\diagup}{1} \cdot \dfrac{1 \text{ kg}}{1000 \text{ g}\!\!\!\diagup}$ Cancel units in numerator and denominator.

$\phantom{6300 \text{ g}} = 6.3 \text{ kg}$ Simplify.

So, 6300 g = 6.3 kg.

b. $0.03 \text{ m} = \dfrac{0.03 \text{ m}}{1} \cdot \dfrac{100 \text{ cm}}{1 \text{ m}}$ Multiply by 1.

$\phantom{0.03 \text{ m}} = \dfrac{0.03 \text{ m}\!\!\!\diagup}{1} \cdot \dfrac{100 \text{ cm}}{1 \text{ m}\!\!\!\diagup}$ Cancel units.

$\phantom{0.03 \text{ m}} = 3 \text{ cm}$ Simplify.

So, 0.03 m = 3 cm.

PRACTICE AND PROBLEM SOLVING

In Exercises 1–16, complete the statement.

1. 1 m = $\boxed{?}$ mm

2. 1 m = $\boxed{?}$ km

3. 1 cm = $\boxed{?}$ mm

4. 1 g = $\boxed{?}$ mg

5. 1 mg = $\boxed{?}$ cg

6. 1 kg = $\boxed{?}$ mg

7. 8.2 kg = $\boxed{?}$ g

8. 250 cm = $\boxed{?}$ m

9. 0.07 g = $\boxed{?}$ cg

10. 8200 m = $\boxed{?}$ km

11. 34 cg = 34 $\boxed{?}$

12. 0.4 g = 40 $\boxed{?}$

13. The length of a pen is about $\boxed{?}$ cm.

14. The weight of a nickel is about 5 $\boxed{?}$.

15. The diameter of a skateboard wheel is about 55 $\boxed{?}$.

16. A liter of water weighs about $\boxed{?}$ kg.

TOOLBOX

Line Plots

Example 1 Use a line plot to organize the numbers of goals scored in the championship games of World Cup soccer tournaments.

World Cup Soccer Goals					
Year	Goals	Year	Goals	Year	Goals
1930	6	1958	7	1978	4
1934	3	1962	4	1982	4
1938	6	1966	6	1986	5
1950	3	1970	5	1990	1
1954	5	1974	3	1994	0

Solution Make a number line that includes the integers from 0 to 7. Place an X above the number line for each soccer tournament.

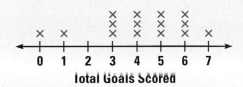

Total Goals Scored

PRACTICE AND PROBLEM SOLVING

In Exercises 1–3, match the line plot with the description.

A. includes 10 numbers   **B.** has a range of 5   **C.** has a mode of 3

1.

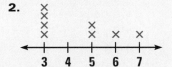

2.

3.

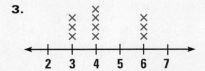

In Exercises 4–6, use the information about number cube rolls.

You roll a pair of number cubes 40 times. Here are the totals: 10, 6, 12, 6, 6, 5, 11, 7, 5, 4, 8, 8, 6, 5, 11, 10, 5, 8, 9, 8, 8, 7, 6, 8, 4, 4, 5, 5, 6, 4, 6, 7, 6, 6, 11, 10, 5, 7, 2, and 7.

4. Use a line plot to organize the totals.

5. What is the range for the number cube roll data?

6. Which total appeared most frequently?

In Exercises 7 and 8, use the information about television sets.

In a consumer survey, 25 people were asked how many television sets their family owned. Their responses were: 3, 1, 2, 3, 0, 1, 5, 2, 2, 2, 3, 1, 0, 1, 1, 1, 1, 2, 1, 3, 1, 0, 2, 2, and 1.

7. Use a line plot to organize the results.   **8.** What was the most frequent response?

Stem-and-Leaf Plots

Example 1 **The table shows the number of games won by teams in the Eastern Conference of the National Basketball Association in a recent year.**

a. Make a stem-and-leaf plot to organize the data.

b. What is the median number of games won?

Atlantic Division		Central Division	
Team	**Games won**	**Team**	**Games won**
Orlando	60	Chicago	72
New York	47	Indiana	52
Miami	42	Cleveland	47
Washington	39	Atlanta	46
Boston	33	Detroit	46
New Jersey	30	Charlotte	41
Philadelphia	18	Milwaukee	25
		Toronto	21

Solution **a.** The data ranges from 18 to 72, so use stems of 1 through 7 for the tens digits. The units digit of each number is a leaf.

unordered plot

```
7 | 2
6 | 0
5 | 2
4 | 7 2 7 6 6 1
3 | 9 3 0
2 | 5 1
1 | 8
```
Key
3 | 9 = 39 games won

ordered plot

```
7 | 2
6 | 0
5 | 2
4 | 1 2 6 6 7 7        median
3 | 0 3 9
2 | 1 5
1 | 8
```
Key
3 | 9 = 39 games won

b. If you order the leaves then you can find the middle number. Since there are 15 numbers in the data, the eighth number is the median. The median number of games won is 42.

PRACTICE AND PROBLEM SOLVING

In Exercises 1–4, use the data and plot below.

Data: 9, 27, 7, 17, 39, 6, 8, 27, 1, 14, 2, 34, 26, 11, 16, 31, 8, 1, 22

1. Copy the stem-and-leaf plot and add any missing numbers.

2. Give a key for the plot.

3. Make an ordered stem-and-leaf plot.

4. What is the median for the data?

```
2 | 7 7 6 2
1 | 7 4 1 6
0 | 9 7 6 8 1 2 8 1
```

Bar Graphs

Example 1 The table shows the number of endangered animal species in the United States. Make a bar graph to display this information.

Animal group	Number of species
Mammals	55
Birds	74
Reptiles	14
Fishes	65
Crustaceans	14
Insects	20

Solution

The graph has a title.

The scale is chosen to fit all the data.

Grid lines are evenly spaced and start a 0.

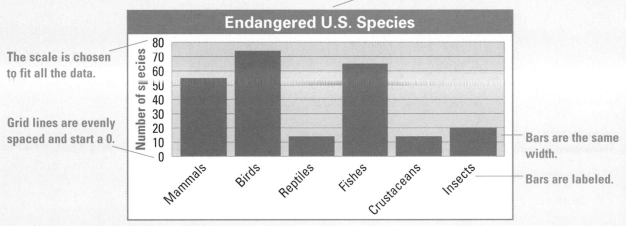

Bars are the same width.

Bars are labeled.

PRACTICE AND PROBLEM SOLVING

In Exercises 1 and 2, make a bar graph to display the information.

1.

Animal	Speed (mi/h)
Black Mamba Snake	20
Cheetah	70
Elephant	25
Giraffe	30
Greyhound	39

2.

National park	Visitors (millions)
Great Smoky Mountains	9.3
Grand Canyon	4.6
Yosemite	3.8
Rocky Mountain	2.9
Yellowstone	2.8

3. Explain how you chose scales for the bar graphs you made in Exercises 1 and 2.

4. **OPEN-ENDED PROBLEM** Find some data in a newspaper or book and make a bar graph to display it.

5. Explain why it is important to start the scale of a bar graph at zero.

Line Graphs

TOOLBOX

Example 1 ▸ The table shows the number of passenger cars manufactured in the United States from 1970 to 1995. Make a line graph of the data.

Year	1970	1975	1980	1985	1990	1995
Millions of cars	6.6	6.7	6.4	8.2	6.1	6.4

Solution

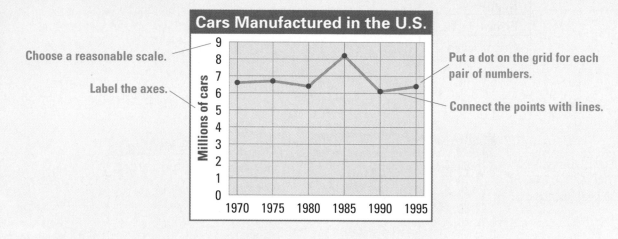

Choose a reasonable scale.

Label the axes.

Cars Manufactured in the U.S.

Put a dot on the grid for each pair of numbers.

Connect the points with lines.

PRACTICE AND PROBLEM SOLVING

In Exercises 1 and 2, refer to the line graph in Example 1.

1. Between 1970 and 1995, when was the biggest increase in the manufacture of passenger cars? the biggest decrease?

2. Describe the trend in the manufacture of cars during this time.

In Exercises 3 and 4, refer to the table showing the value of a car.

Age (years)	0	1	2	3	4	5
Value	$25,000	$17,500	$12,000	$8500	$6000	$4000

3. Make a line graph of the data.

4. Predict the value of the car after 6 yr.

In Exercises 5–7, use the line graph showing business profits at the right.

5. When did this business begin to make a profit?

6. Did profits increase every year? How can you tell from the line graph?

7. Estimate the 1999 profit.

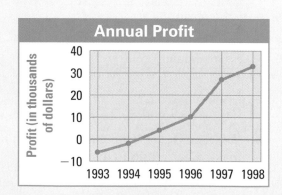

Annual Profit

Ratio and Proportion

A *ratio* is a comparison of two numbers by division. A *proportion* is an equation stating that two ratios are the same.

Example 1 In the rectangle shown, what is the ratio of the *length* to the *width*?

[rectangle: 18 in. by 8 in.]

Solution $\dfrac{length}{width} = \dfrac{18 \text{ in.}}{8 \text{ in.}}$ Write the ratio.

$= \dfrac{18}{8}$ The units cancel in a ratio.

$= \dfrac{9}{4}$ Simplify.

Example 2 Solve the proportion.

$$\frac{3}{5} = \frac{x}{20}$$

Solution Multiplying the numerator *and* the denominator of $\frac{3}{5}$ by 4 will give an equivalent fraction with a denominator of 20.

$$\frac{3}{5} \cdot \frac{4}{4} = \frac{12}{20}$$

So, $x = 12$.

PRACTICE AND PROBLEM SOLVING

In Exercises 1–6, write each expression as a ratio and simplify.

1. 55 cents to 15 cents

2. 30 min to 6 h

3. 4 yd to 8 ft

4. $1.75 to $.75

5. 5 days to 10 h

6. 3 in. to 2 ft

In Exercises 7–12, solve each proportion.

7. $\dfrac{2}{5} = \dfrac{18}{p}$

8. $\dfrac{q}{7} = \dfrac{10}{35}$

9. $\dfrac{3}{4} = \dfrac{r}{16}$

10. $\dfrac{5}{3} = \dfrac{s}{9}$

11. $\dfrac{4}{t} = \dfrac{80}{60}$

12. $\dfrac{4}{10} = \dfrac{v}{25}$

In Exercises 13 and 14, the two rectangles have the same ratio of length to width. Write and solve a proportion to find the missing length.

13.

[rectangle: 8 cm by 2 cm]

[rectangle: x by 4 cm]

14.

15. A recipe for lemonade calls for 3 c. lemon juice, 2 c. sugar, and 21 c. water. You have only 1 c. lemon juice. How much sugar and water should you use?

Angles and Their Measures

An angle is formed by two rays joined at their endpoints.

- Angles with measures **between 0° and 90°** are *acute*.
- Angles with measures of **90°** are *right*.
- Angles with measures between **90° and 180°** are *obtuse*.

Example 1   **Use the protractor to find the measure of each angle. Tell whether the angle is *acute*, *right*, or *obtuse*.**

    a. $\angle AOB$

    b. $\angle AOC$

    c. $\angle AOD$

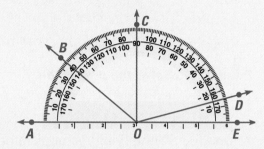

Solution   **a.** $\angle AOB$ has a measure of 40°. It is acute.

       b. $\angle AOC$ has a measure of 90°. It is right.

       c. $\angle AOD$ has a measure of 165°. It is obtuse.

PRACTICE AND PROBLEM SOLVING

In Exercises 1–4, refer to the diagram in Example 1. Find the measure of each angle.

1. $\angle BOC$ **2.** $\angle COD$ **3.** $\angle BOE$ **4.** $\angle DOE$

5. Use a protractor to find the measure of each angle in the shape at the right.

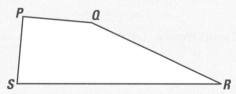

In Exercises 6–11, use a protractor to find the measure of each angle. Tell whether the angle is *acute*, *right*, or *obtuse*.

6. $\angle AGB$ **7.** $\angle DGF$

8. $\angle CGE$ **9.** $\angle BGE$

10. $\angle CGF$ **11.** $\angle CGD$

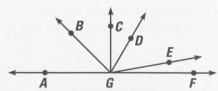

In Exercises 12–14, draw a shape that matches the description.

12. a triangle with one obtuse angle

13. a quadrilateral with exactly two right angles

14. a pentagon with three right angles

Area and Perimeter

Example 1 **Find the perimeter of the parallelogram.**

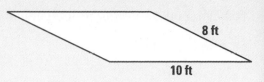

Solution   Because the figure is a parallelogram,
opposite sides have the same length.
The perimeter is the distance around the figure.

8 ft + 10 ft + 8 ft + 10 ft = 36 ft

The perimeter is 36 ft.

Example 2 **Find the area of the figure.**

a.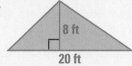

b.

Solution   **a.** Area of a triangle $= \frac{1}{2} \cdot$ base $\cdot$ **height**

$$= \frac{1}{2} \cdot 20 \cdot 8$$

$$= 80$$

The area of the triangle is 80 ft^2.

b. Area of figure = Area of rectangle + Area of triangle

$$= 12 \cdot 9 + \frac{1}{2} \cdot 4 \cdot 9$$

$$= 108 + 18$$

$$= 126$$

The area of the figure is 126 cm^2.

PRACTICE AND PROBLEM SOLVING

In Exercises 1–3, find the perimeter and area of the figure.

1.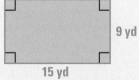

2.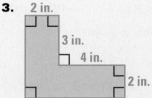

3.

4. Explain what happens to the perimeter and area of a square if you double the length of its sides. Show several examples.

5. Explain what happens to the perimeter and area of a rectangle if you triple the lengths of its sides. Show several examples.

TOOLBOX

Add and Subtract Integers

You can model addition of integers on a number line.

Example 1 Add.

a. $2 + (-6)$ b. $-5 + 3$

Solution a.

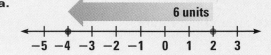

Start at 2.

Move 6 units to the left.

$2 + (-6) = -4$

b.

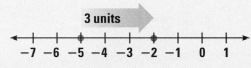

Start at -5.

Move 3 units to the right.

$-5 + 3 = -2$

Example 2 Subtract.

a. $6 - (-4)$ b. $-5 - 2$

Solution Subtracting is the same as adding the opposite.

a. $6 - (-4) = 6 + 4$ The opposite of -4 is 4.

$\qquad = 10$

b. $-5 - 2 = -5 + (-2)$ The opposite of 2 is -2.

$\qquad = -7$

PRACTICE AND PROBLEM SOLVING

In Exercises 1–6, model each problem on a number line to find the sum.

1. $10 + (-6)$ 2. $-12 + (4)$ 3. $-1 + (-2)$

4. $5 + (-5)$ 5. $-3 + (-1)$ 6. $-7 + 0$

In Exercises 7–12, add or subtract.

7. $-15 + (-6)$ 8. $14 - 19$ 9. $5 + (-6)$

10. $6 - (-9)$ 11. $7 + (-7)$ 12. $-16 - (-14)$

In Exercises 13 and 14, add or subtract to solve.

13. In the morning, the temperature was $-9°F$. By noon, the temperature was $15°F$. By how many degrees did the temperature rise?

14. A football team loses 14 yd, then gains 8 yd, then gains 3 yd. How many yards did the team gain or lose overall?

Solve Addition and Subtraction Equations

Example 1 Solve.

  a. $x + 2.3 = 5.1$ **b.** $-1.4 = y - 2.8$

Solution **a.**

$x + 2.3 = 5.1$	This is an addition equation.
$x + 2.3 - \mathbf{2.3} = 5.1 - \mathbf{2.3}$	Subtract 2.3 from both sides.
$x = 2.8$	Solution: x is by itself.

b.

$-1.4 = y - 2.8$	This is a subtraction equation.
$-1.4 + \mathbf{2.8} = y - 2.8 + \mathbf{2.8}$	Add 2.8 to both sides.
$1.4 = y$	Solution: y is by itself.

Example 2 **Use an equation to model the problem. Then solve the equation.**

Zoe bought a compact disk for $12.50. She then had $10.25 left. How much money did she start out with?

Solution Let m stand for the original amount of money Zoe started out with.

Original amount − Cost of CD = Amount left

$m - 12.50 = 10.25$	This is a subtraction equation.
$m - 12.50 + \mathbf{12.50} = 10.25 + \mathbf{12.50}$	Add 12.50 to both sides.
$m = 22.75$	Solution: m is by itself.

Zoe started out with $22.75.

PRACTICE AND PROBLEM SOLVING

In Exercises 1–4, tell whether the given number is a solution to the equation.

1. $w - 12 = -7; w = 5$

2. $y + 1.4 = -2.6; y = -2.2$

3. $0 = z - 8; z = 0$

4. $15 = x + 9; x = 6$

In Exercises 5–8, solve.

5. $y + 3.4 = 5.5$

6. $z - 0.6 = 0.07$

7. $a + \dfrac{3}{10} = \dfrac{2}{5}$

8. $b - \dfrac{1}{6} = \dfrac{4}{9}$

In Exercises 9 and 10, use an equation to model the problem, then solve.

9. After adding a $12.50 tip, a restaurant bill was $75. What was the cost of the meal?

10. You cut $\dfrac{5}{8}$ yd from a length of fabric. The remaining length is $\dfrac{7}{8}$ yd. How long was the original piece of fabric?

TOOLBOX

U.S. CUSTOMARY MEASURES

■ LENGTH

12 inches (in.) = 1 foot (ft)
3 feet = 1 yard (yd)
36 inches = 1 yard
5280 feet = 1 mile (mi)
1760 yards = 1 mile

■ CAPACITY

1 cup (c) = 8 fluid ounces (fl oz)
2 cups = 1 pint (pt)
2 pints = 1 quart (qt)
2 quarts = 1 half-gallon
4 quarts = 1 gallon (gal)

■ WEIGHT

16 ounces (oz) = 1 pound (lb)
2000 pounds = 1 ton

■ AREA

144 square inches (in.^2) = 1 square foot (ft^2)
9 ft^2 = 1 square yard (yd^2)
640 acres = 1 mi^2

■ VOLUME

1728 cubic inches (in.^3) = 1 cubic foot (ft^3)
27 ft^3 = 1 cubic yard (yd^3)

■ TIME

60 seconds (s) = 1 minute (min)
3600 seconds = 1 hour (h)
60 minutes = 1 hour
24 hours = 1 day
7 days = 1 week

360 days = 1 business year
365 days = 1 year
366 days = 1 leap year
10 years = 1 decade
10 decades = 1 century = 100 years

■ CONVERTING MEASUREMENT WITHIN THE U.S. CUSTOMARY SYSTEM

When you rewrite a measurement in another unit, you can use the relationships between the units to write a fraction that equals 1.

STUDY TIP

To change 45 miles per hour to feet per second:

$$\frac{45\ \text{miles}}{\text{hour}} \times \frac{5280\ \text{feet}}{1\ \text{mile}} \times \frac{1\ \text{hour}}{3600\ \text{seconds}}$$

$$= \left(\frac{45 \times 5280}{3600}\ \frac{\text{feet}}{\text{second}}\right) = 66\ \text{ft/s}$$

STUDY TIP

To change 120 ounces per square inch to pounds per square foot:

$$\frac{120\ \text{oz}}{\text{in}^2} \times \frac{144\ \text{in}^2}{1\ \text{ft}^2} \times \frac{1\ \text{lb}}{16\ \text{oz}} =$$

$$\left(\frac{120 \times 144}{16}\right)\frac{\text{lb}}{\text{ft}^2} = \frac{1080\ \text{lb}}{\text{ft}^2}$$

REFERENCES & TABLES

METRIC MEASURES

In the metric system, the units are related by powers of 10.

Table of Units				
PREFIX	POWER of 10	LENGTH	CAPACITY	MASS
kilo (k)	1000 units	kilometer	kiloliter*	kilogram
hecto (h)	100 units	hectometer*	hectoliter*	hectogram*
deka (da)	10 units	dekameter*	dekaliter*	dekagram*
	1 unit	meter	liter	gram
deci (d)	0.1 unit	decimeter*	deciliter*	decigram*
centi (c)	0.01 unit	centimeter	centiliter*	centigram*
milli (m)	0.001 unit	millimeter	milliliter	milligram

*These units are seldom used.

■ LENGTH

10 millimeters (mm) = 1 centimeter (cm)
10 cm = 1 decimeter (dm)
100 cm = 1 meter (m)
1000 m = 1 kilometer (km)
100,000 cm = 1 km

■ AREA

100 square millimeters (mm^2) =
  1 square centimeter (cm^2)
100 cm^2 = 1 square meter (m^2)
100,000 m^2 = 1 square kilometers (km^2)

■ CAPACITY

1000 milliliter (mL) = 1 liter (L)
10 deciliter (dL) = 1 L

■ MASS

1000 milligrams (mg) = 1 gram (g)
1000 g = 1 kilogram (kg)

■ VOLUME

1,000,000 cubic centimeters (cm^3) =
  1 cubic meter (cm^3)
1 cm^3 = 1 mL
1000 cm^3 = 1 L

■ CONVERTING MEASURES WITHIN THE METRIC SYSTEM

Use the relationships between units, which are shown in the table at the top of this page, to convert measures within the Metric System.

STUDY TIP

When you rewrite a measurement using a smaller unit, you multiply.

0.24 m = [?] cm

In the Table of Units, there are 2 steps from meters to centimeters, so multiply by 10^2, or 100.

0.24 m × 100 = 24 cm

STUDY TIP

When you rewrite a measurement using a larger unit, you divide.

3500 mg = [?] kg

In the Table of Units, there are 6 steps from milligrams to kilograms, so divide by 10^6, or 1,000,000.

3500 mg ÷ 1,000,000 = 0.0035 kg

Example 1

Find 54^2.

Solution

Find 54 in the column labeled n. Read across that line to the column labeled n^2. So, $54^2 = 2916$.

n	n^2	$\sqrt{n}$
51	2601	7.141
52	2704	7.211
53	2809	7.280
54	2916	7.348
55	3025	7.416
56	3136	7.483

Example 2

Find a decimal approximation of $\sqrt{54}$.

Solution

Find 54 in the column labeled n. Read across that line to the column labeled $\sqrt{n}$. This number is a three-decimal place approximation of $\sqrt{54}$, so $\sqrt{54} \approx 7.348$.

n	n^2	$\sqrt{n}$
51	2601	7.141
52	2704	7.211
53	2809	7.280
54	2916	7.348
55	3025	7.416
56	3136	7.483

Example 3

Estimate $\sqrt{3000}$.

Solution

Find the two numbers in the n^2 column that 3000 is between. Read across these two lines to the column labeled n; $\sqrt{3000}$ is between 54 and 55, but closer to 55. So, $\sqrt{3000} \approx 55$. A more accurate approximation can be found using a calculator: 54.772256.

n	n^2	$\sqrt{n}$
51	2601	7.141
52	2704	7.211
53	2809	7.280
54	2916	7.348
55	3025	7.416
56	3136	7.483

REFERENCES & TABLES

SQUARES AND SQUARE ROOTS

n	n^2	$\sqrt{n}$	n	n^2	$\sqrt{n}$	n	n^2	$\sqrt{n}$
1	1	1.000	33	1089	5.745	69	4761	8.307
2	4	1.414	34	1156	5.831	70	4900	8.367
3	9	1.732	35	1225	5.916	71	5041	8.426
4	16	2.000	36	1296	6.000	72	5184	8.485
5	25	2.236	37	1369	6.083	73	5329	8.544
6	36	2.449	38	1444	6.164	74	5476	8.602
7	49	2.646	39	1521	6.245	75	5625	8.660
8	64	2.828	40	1600	6.325	76	5776	8.718
9	81	3.000	41	1681	6.403	77	5929	8.775
10	100	3.162	42	1764	6.481	78	6084	8.832
11	121	3.317	43	1849	6.557	79	6241	8.888
12	144	3.464	44	1936	6.633	80	6400	8.944
13	169	3.606	45	2025	6.708	81	6561	9.000
14	196	3.742	46	2116	6.782	82	6724	9.055
15	225	3.873	47	2209	6.856	83	6889	9.110
16	256	4.000	48	2304	6.928	84	7056	9.165
17	289	4.123	49	2401	7.000	85	7225	9.220
18	324	4.243	50	2500	7.071	86	7396	9.274
19	361	4.359	51	2601	7.141	87	7569	9.327
20	400	4.472	52	2704	7.211	88	7744	9.381
21	441	4.583	53	2809	7.280	89	7921	9.434
22	484	4.690	54	2916	7.348	90	8100	9.487
23	529	4.796	55	3025	7.416	91	8281	9.539
24	576	4.899	56	3136	7.483	92	8464	9.592
25	625	5.000	57	3249	7.550	93	8649	9.644
26	676	5.099	58	3364	7.616	94	8836	9.695
27	729	5.196	59	3481	7.681	95	9025	9.747
28	784	5.292	60	3600	7.746	96	9216	9.798
29	841	5.385	61	3721	7.810	97	9409	9.849
30	900	5.477	62	3844	7.874	98	9604	9.899
31	961	5.568	63	3969	7.937	99	9801	9.950
32	1024	5.657	64	4096	8.000	100	10000	10.000
			65	4225	8.062			
			66	4356	8.124			
			67	4489	8.185			
			68	4624	8.246			

SYMBOLS

■ **ARITHMETIC AND ALGEBRA**

$=$	Is equal to
$\neq$	Is not equal to
$>$	Is greater than
$<$	Is less than
$\approx$	Is approximately equal to

$$\left.\begin{array}{l} ab \\ a(b) \\ a \cdot b \end{array}\right\} \quad a \text{ times } b$$

a^n	A number a raised to the nth power
10^{-n}	$\dfrac{1}{10^n}$
10^0	1
$(\ )$	Grouping symbols
5, or $+5$	Positive 5
-5	Negative 5
$|a|$	Absolute value of a number a
$\sqrt{a}$	Square root of a number a
$a:b$, or $\dfrac{a}{b}$	Ratio of a to b
$n!$	n factorial

■ **GEOMETRY**

(a, b)	Ordered Pair a, b
$\sim$	Is similar to
$\cong$	Is congruent to
$\overline{AB}$	Segment AB
AB	Measure of segment AB
$\angle A$	Angle A
π	Pi

FORMULAS AND NUMBER PROPERTIES

Formulas

Perimeter and Circumference

$P = 4 \cdot s$	Square (*p. 17*)
$P = 2 \cdot \ell + 2 \cdot w$	Rectangle (*p. 17*)
$C = \pi \cdot d$	Circle (*p. 386*)

Area

$A = s^2$	Square
$A = \ell \cdot w$	Rectangle (*p. 17*)
$A = b \cdot h$	Parallelogram (*p. 390*)
$A = \frac{1}{2}b \cdot h$	Triangle (*p. 17*)
$A = \frac{1}{2} \cdot (b_1 + b_2) \cdot h$	Trapezoid (*p. 396*)
$A = \pi \cdot r^2$	Circle (*p. 400*)

Surface area

Surface area of polyhedron = Sum of the areas of the faces (*p. 432*)

Surface area of a cylinder = Lateral surface area + Area of 2 bases (*p. 438*)

Lateral surface area = $2 \pi r \cdot h$

Area of 2 bases = $2 \cdot \pi r^2$

Volume

$V = s^3$	Cube (*p. 65*)
$V = \ell \cdot w \cdot h$	Rectangular prism (*p. 488*)
$V = \pi r^2 \cdot h$	Cylinder (*p. 454*)

Miscellaneous

$I = P \cdot r \cdot t$	Simple interest (*p. 354*)
$a^2 + b^2 = c^2$	Pythagorean Theorem (*p. 413*)

Number properties

Let a, b, and c, represent any numbers.

Addition	**Multiplication**	
$a + b = b + a$	$a \cdot b = b \cdot a$	Communicative Properties (*p. 63*)
$a + (b + c) = (a + b) + c$	$a \cdot (b \cdot c) = (a \cdot b) \cdot c$	Associative Properties (*p. 63*)
	$a \cdot (b + c) = a \cdot b + a \cdot c$	Distributive Properties (*p. 142*)

absolute value of a number (p. 480) The distance the number is from 0 on a number line.

absolute value signs (p. 480) The symbol "| |" that denotes absolute value. For example, $|0| = |0|$.

acute angle (p. 412) An angle whose measure is between 0° and 90°.

acute triangle (p. 412) A triangle with three acute angles.

adjacent angles (p. 375) Two angles that share a side and a vertex but do not overlap.

angle (p. 372) A figure formed by two rays that begin at the same point.

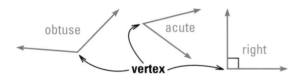

annual interest rate (p. 354) The percent of the principal earned (or paid) as interest based on one year.

area (p. 17) A measure of how much surface is covered by a figure. Area is measured in square units.

Associative Property of Addition (p. 63) If a, b, and c are any numbers, then
$(a + b) + c = a + (b + c)$.

Associative Property of Multiplication (p. 63) If a, b, and c are any numbers, then
$(a \times b) \times c = a \times (b \times c)$.

average (p. 220) The sum of a set of numbers divided by how many numbers are in the set. It is also called the *mean*.

balance (p. 355) The amount available for your use in a savings account or checking account, or the amount owed on a debt.

base of a cylinder (p. 438) A circular face of the cylinder. *See also* **cylinder.**

base of a parallelogram (p. 390) Any side of a parallelogram.

base of a percent (p. 342) The number from which a portion is to be found. In the percent equation $\frac{a}{b} = \frac{p}{100}$, the base is b.

base of a power (p. 64) In the power 2^3, 2 is the base.

bases of a trapezoid (p. 396) The two parallel sides. *See also* **trapezoid.**

base of a triangle (p. 17) Any side of the triangle.

box-and-whisker plot (p. 234) A diagram that shows the first, second, and third quartiles; the least number; and the greatest number of a set of data.

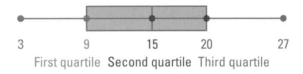

box model (p. 581) A model used in operations with positive and negative numbers.

center of a circle (p. 386) The point inside a circle that is the same distance from all the points on the circle.

circle (p. 386) A closed curve in a plane for which every point on the curve is the same distance from a given point called the *center.*

circle graph (p. 348) A graph that represents data as parts of a circle. The whole circle represents the entire collection.

circumference of a circle (p. 386) The perimeter of a circle.

combination (p. 548) A collection of a set of objects in which order is not important.

common denominator (p. 126) The same denominator used in two or more fractions. For example, $\frac{7}{8}$ and $\frac{3}{8}$ have a common denominator of 8.

common factor (p. 82) A number that divides two or more given numbers evenly.

common multiple (p. 114) A number that is a multiple of two or more given numbers. For example, 12 is a common multiple of 2 and 3.

Commutative Property of Addition (p. 63) If *a* and *b* are any numbers, then changing the order in which they are added will not change the sum; that is, $a + b = b + a$.

Commutative Property of Multiplication (p. 63) If *a* and *b* are any numbers, then changing the order in which they are multiplied will not change the product; that is, $a \times b = b \times a$.

complements (p. 375) Two angles are complements if their measures add up to 90°.

composite number (p. 76) A number that has more than two factors.

cone (p. 444) A solid that has a circular base, a vertex, and a lateral surface.

congruent angles (p. 374) Angles that have the same measure.

congruent figures (p. 385) Figures that have exactly the same shape and size.

coordinate plane (p. 172) A plane formed by a horizontal number line called the *x*-axis, and a vertical number line called the *y*-axis.

coordinates of a point (p. 172) The two numbers of an ordered pair that locate a point in a coordinate plane.

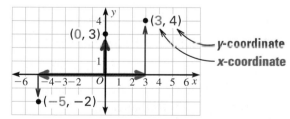

corresponding angles (p. 300) Matched angles of two polygons. For example, angle B and angle E are corresponding angles.

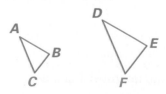

corresponding sides (p. 300) Matched sides of two polygons. For example, $\overline{AB}$ and $\overline{DE}$ are corresponding sides.

Counting Principle (p. 537) When one item is selected from each of two or more sets, the total number of possible combinations is the product of the number of items in each set.

cross multiply (p. 288) To find the cross products of a proportion.

cross products (p. 288) In the proportion $\frac{a}{b} = \frac{c}{d}$, $a \cdot d$ and $b \cdot c$ are the cross products. They are equal.

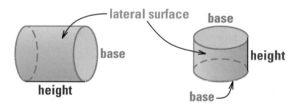

cube (p. 65) A rectangular prism whose faces are squares.

cube of a number (p. 65) The third power of the number.

cylinder (p. 438) A solid figure that has two circular bases and a curved lateral surface.

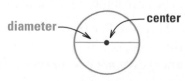

data (p. 4) A collection of numbers or facts.

denominator (p. 86) The number below the line in a fraction. It tells into how many pieces the whole has been divided. For example, the denominator of $\frac{2}{3}$ is 3.

dependent events (p. 567) If the probability of one event occurring changes the probability of a second event occurring, then these are dependent events.

diameter of a circle (p. 386) The distance across the circle through its center.

disjoint sets (p. 566) Two or more sets that have no common members.

Distributive Property (p. 142) If *a*, *b*, and *c* are any numbers, then
$a \times (b + c) = a \times b + a \times c.$

divide (p. 504) To find the quotient and remainder of two numbers.

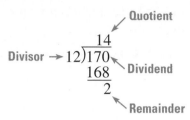

dividend (p. 504) *See* **divide.**

divisibility test (p. 70) A test used to decide when one number is evenly divisible by another.

divisor (p. 504) *See* **divide.**

double bar graph (p. 44) A graph that uses two colors of bars to show how quantities compare to each other.

edge of a polyhedron (p. 429) A line segment where two faces meet. *See also* **polyhedron.**

equally likely outcomes (p. 530) Outcomes that have the same probability of occurring.

equation (p. 30) A mathematical statement with an equal sign "=" in it.

equivalent fractions (p. 86) Two fractions that represent the same quantity. For example, $\frac{2}{3}$ and $\frac{4}{6}$ are equivalent fractions.

evaluating an expression (p. 58) Finding the value of an expression after all variables are replaced by numbers.

even number (p. 37) A multiple of 2.

expected value (p. 556) A way of measuring the fairness of a game. The expected value for a player is the product of the amount that can be won by the probability of winning.

experimental probability (p. 530) A probability based on the frequency of outcomes that have occurred after performing an experiment many times.

exponent (p. 64, p. 516) The number of times a base is used as a factor. For example, in the power 2^4, 4 is the exponent. $2^4 = 2 \times 2 \times 2 \times 2$, or 16.

expression (p. 58) A collection of numbers, variables, and symbols such as $+$, $-$, $\times$, and $\div$.

face of a polyhedron (p. 429) A polygon that is a side of the polyhedron. *See also* **polyhedron.**

factor (p. 64) A number that is multiplied in an expression. For example, in the equation $2 \cdot 4 = 8$, 2 and 4 are factors.

fair game (p. 557) A game in which each player has the same expected value.

first quartile (p. 234) *See* **quartiles**.

frequency (p. 226) The number of times an item occurs within an interval.

frequency table (p. 226) A table that groups large amounts of data into intervals.

function (p. 612) A rule that tells you how to perform one or more operations on a number called the *input* to produce a result called the *output*.

greatest common factor (p. 82) The largest common factor of two numbers.

height *See* **cylinder, parallelogram, prism,** and **trapezoid.**

hexagon (p. 15) A 6-sided polygon.

hexahedron (p. 428) A polyhedron with six faces.

histogram (p. 227) A bar graph that represents data in a frequency table. There is a bar (or space for a bar) for each interval of the frequency table.

hypotenuse (p. 412) The side of a right triangle that is opposite the right angle. *See also* **right triangle.**

improper fraction (p. 118) A fraction that is greater than or equal to 1. For example, $\frac{3}{2}$ and $\frac{2}{2}$ are improper fractions.

independent events (p. 567) If the occurrence of one event does not effect the occurrence of a second event, then these are independent events.

input (p. 612) The number that replaces a variable in an equation.

integers (p. 178) The set of whole numbers and their opposites.

interest (p. 354) The cost of borrowing money or the income from money saved in a bank.

intersecting lines (p. 374) Two lines in a plane that meet at a common point.

inverse operation (p. 580) An operation that "undoes" another operation. For example, addition is the inverse operation of subtraction.

isolating the variable (p. 584) Getting a variable by itself on one side of an equation.

lateral surface (p. 438) The curved surface that connects the two bases of a cylinder. *See also* **cylinder.**

least common denominator of two fractions (p. 126) The least common multiple of their denominators.

least common multiple (p. 114) The smallest common multiple of two or more numbers. For example, the least common multiple of 2 and 3 is 6.

legs of a right triangle (p. 412) The two perpendicular sides. *See also* **right triangle.**

line graph (p. 245) A graph on which the plotted points are connected with line segments.

mean (p. 220) The sum of a set of numbers divided by how many numbers are in the set. It is also called the *average.*

measure of central tendency (p. 220) A single number that is used to represent a set of data. The mean, median, and mode are measures of central tendency.

median (p. 220) The middle number (or the mean of the two middle numbers) of a set of numbers written in numerical order.

mixed number (p. 118) A number such as $2\frac{3}{5}$ that is the sum of a whole number and a fraction.

mode (p. 220) The number that occurs most often in a set of data.

modeling a real-life problem (p. 31) Writing an equation that represents a real-life problem.

multiple of a number (p. 114) The product of the number and any whole number greater than zero. For example, the multiples of 2 are 2, 4, 6, 8, ...

n factorial (p. 544) The expression $n!$ that represents the number of permutations of n objects. It is the product of the numbers from 1 to n.

negative integer (p. 178) An integer that is less than 0.

negative sign (p. 178) The symbol " − " that represents a negative number.

net (p. 426) A flat pattern that can be folded to form a solid.

nonahedron (p. 431) A polyhedron with 9 faces.

number line (p. 98) A line to which numbers have been assigned.

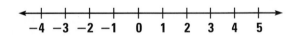

numerator (p. 86) The number above the line in a fraction. It shows the number of equal portions out of the whole.

numerical expression (p. 58) An expression that has only numbers and symbols.

obtuse angle (p. 412) An angle whose measure is greater than 90° and less than 180°.

obtuse triangle (p. 412) A triangle that has one obtuse angle.

octahedron (p. 428) A polyhedron with eight faces.

odd number A whole number that is not even.

opposites (p. 184) Two numbers that are the same distance from 0 on a number line. For example, −4 and 4 are opposites.

Order of Operations (p. 59, p. 64) A procedure for evaluating an expression that has more than one operation.

1. First do operations within grouping symbols.

2. Then evaluate powers.

3. Then multiply and divide from left to right.

4. Finally add and subtract from left to right.

ordered pair (p. 172) A pair of numbers such as (3, 2) that locates a point in a coordinate plane.

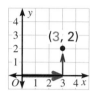

ordering (p. 98) Arranging numbers from least to greatest or greatest to least.

origin (p. 172) The point (0, 0) on the coordinate plane. It is the intersection of the *x*-axis and the *y*-axis.

outcome (p. 256) The result of an experiment. For example, heads is an outcome of tossing a coin.

output (p. 612) The result produced by evaluating a function using a specific input.

parallel lines (p. 374) Two lines in a plane that are the same distance apart at all points.

parallelogram (p. 390) A quadrilateral whose opposite sides are parallel.

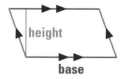

pentagon (p. 15) A polygon with five sides.

pentahedron (p. 428) A polyhedron with five faces.

percent (p. 322) Per hundred. A ratio whose denominator is 100.

percent decrease (p. 358) The ratio of the amount of decrease to the original amount, expressed as a percent.

percent equation (p. 342) The statement "*a* is *p* percent of *b*" can be written as the percent equation $\frac{a}{b} = \frac{p}{100}$.

percent increase (p. 358) The ratio of the amount of increase to the original amount, expressed as a percent.

perfect square (p. 406) A number whose square root is a whole number. For example, 0, 1, 4, and 9 are perfect squares.

perimeter (p. 17) The distance around a figure.

permutation (p. 544) An arrangement or listing of objects in which order is important.

pi (π) (p. 386) The number that is the ratio of the circumference of a circle to its diameter. It is approximately 3.14.

pictograph (p. 244) A graph that uses pictures or symbols to represent data.

plane (p. 374) A flat surface that extends in all directions.

polygon (p. 10) A plane figure such as a triangle or a quadrilateral whose sides are line segments.

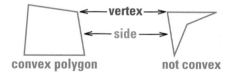

polyhedron (p. 428) A solid figure that has polygons as sides.

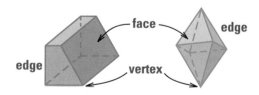

positive integer (p. 178) An integer that is greater than 0.

power (p. 64) An expression such as 5^4 that has a base (5) and an exponent (4).

powers of 10 (p. 515) The numbers 10^1, 10^2, 10^3, 10^4, ... They can also be written as 10, 100, 1000, 10,000, ...

prime factorization (p. 76) A number written as the product of prime numbers.

prime number (p. 76) A number that has exactly two factors, itself and 1.

principal (p. 354) The amount of money borrowed, loaned, or in savings.

prism (p. 428) A polyhedron with two congruent and parallel faces.

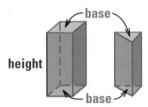

probability of an event (p. 256) A measure of the likelihood that the event will occur.

proper fraction (p. 118) A fraction that is less than 1.

proportion (p. 284) An equation that equates two ratios.

proportional sides (p. 300) The sides of polygons are proportional if the ratios of their lengths are equal.

protractor (p. 372) A device that is used to measure angles.

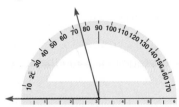

pyramid (p. 428) A polyhedron whose base is a polygon and whose other faces are triangles that share a common vertex.

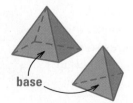

base

Pythagorean Theorem (p. 413) For any right triangle, the sum of the squares of the lengths of the legs equals the square of the length of the hypotenuse.

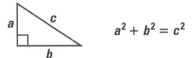

$$a^2 + b^2 = c^2$$

quadrant (p. 238) One of the four regions in a coordinate plane formed by the coordinate axes.

quadrilateral (p. 15) A 4-sided polygon.

quartiles (p. 234) Three numbers that separate a collection of ordered numbers into four groups that contain about the same number of pieces of data.

quotient (p. 504) *See* **divide.**

radical sign (p. 406) The symbol "$\sqrt{}$" that denotes square root. For example, $\sqrt{16}$ means the square root of 16.

radius of a circle (p. 396) The distance from the edge of a circle to its center.

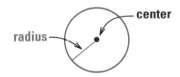

range (p. 226) The difference between the greatest and least numbers in a set of numbers.

rate (p. 276) A fraction in which the numerator and denominator have different units of measure.

ratio (p. 272) A quotient of two numbers that have the same unit of measure.

reciprocals (p. 150) Two numbers whose product is 1. For instance, $\frac{5}{6}$ and $\frac{6}{5}$ are reciprocals because $\frac{5}{6} \times \frac{6}{5} = 1$.

rectangle (p. 6) A parallelogram that has four right angles.

regrouping (p. 131) Rewriting a mixed number to take a value of one from the whole number and add it to the fraction. For example, $3\frac{1}{5}$ can be regrouped as $2\frac{6}{5}$.

right angle (p. 412) An angle whose measure is 90°.

right triangle (p. 412) A triangle that has a right angle.

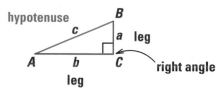

round a number (p. 13) To replace a number with another one of approximately the same value that is easier to use.

scale drawing (p. 306) A drawing in which the measurements are proportional to the actual dimensions of an object.

scale factor (p. 306) The ratio of measurements in a scale drawing to the actual measurements.

scatter plot (p. 173) A collection of points in a coordinate plane that represents a relationship between two quantities.

scientific notation (p. 517) A number in the form $c \times 10^n$ where c is greater than or equal to 1 and less than 10.

second quartile (p. 234) The median of an ordered set of numbers.

sequence (p. 166) A list of numbers in a specific order.

similar geometric figures (p. 16) *See* **similar polygons**.

similar polygons (p. 300) Polygons whose corresponding angles have the same measure and whose corresponding sides are proportional.

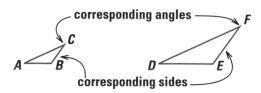

similar prisms (p. 462) Prisms that have the same shape and proportional corresponding dimensions.

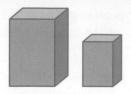

simple interest (p. 354) The product of the principal, the annual interest rate, and the time in years.

simplest form of a fraction (p. 86) A fraction is in simplest form if its numerator and denominator have a greatest common factor of 1.

solution of an equation (p. 30) The value of the variable that makes the equation true.

solve an equation (p. 30) Find the value of the variable that makes the equation true.

spreadsheet (p. 231) A software program used for organizing and analyzing data.

square (p. 6) A rectangle with four sides of the same length.

square of a number (p. 64) The second power of the number.

square root of a number (p. 406) A number that when multiplied by itself equals the given number.

subset (p. 566) Set B is a subset of set A if every member of B is also in A.

supplements (p. 375) Two angles are supplements if their measures add up to 180°.

surface area of a cylinder (p. 438) The sum of the areas of the bases and the area of the lateral surface.

surface area of a polyhedron (p. 432) The sum of the areas of the faces of a polyhedron.

table of values (p. 168) A table that is used to organize several values of an expression.

tessellation (p. 385) A covering of a plane with congruent figures so that the figures do not overlap or leave gaps.

tetrahedron (p. 428) A polyhedron with four faces.

theoretical probability (p. 530) A probability that is found by counting and classifying all possible outcomes.

third quartile (p. 234) *See* **quartiles**.

translation (p. 380) Movement of a figure so that every point on the figure slides the same direction and the same distance.

trapezoid (p. 396) A quadrilateral that has two opposite sides that are parallel and two opposite sides that are not parallel.

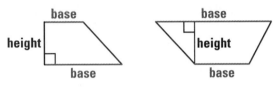

tree diagram (p. 76, p. 536) A diagram that shows the factorization of a number. Also, a diagram that shows all the possible outcomes of an experiment. Outcomes are listed along the "branches" of the diagram.

triangle (p. 15) A polygon with 3 sides.

unit rate (p. 276) A rate with a denominator of 1 unit.

variable (p. 30) A letter in an equation that can be replaced by a number.

variable expression (p. 58) An expression that has at least one variable.

Venn diagram (p. 37) A drawing that uses geometric shapes to show relationships among sets of objects.

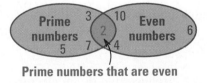

verbal model (p. 199) An equation written using words and symbols.

vertex of an angle (p. 372) The initial point of both rays of an angle. *See also* **angle.**

vertex of a polygon (p. 10) A point at which two sides meet. *See also* **polygon.**

vertex of a polyhedron (p. 429) A point where two edges meet. *See also* **polyhedron.**

vertical angles (p. 374) Intersecting lines form two pairs of vertical angles. Angle 1 and angle 3 are vertical angles. Angle 2 and angle 4 are vertical angles.

volume (p. 65) A measure of how much space is occupied by a solid figure. Volume is measured in cubic units.

x-axis (p. 172) The horizontal axis in a coordinate plane.

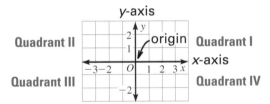

x-coordinate (p. 172) The first coordinate of a point in the coordinate plane.

y-axis (p. 172) The vertical axis in a coordinate plane.

y-coordinate (p. 172) The second coordinate of a point in the coordinate plane.

absolute value of a number/valor absoluto de un número (p. 480) Distancia entre un número y el 0 en una línea numérica.

absolute value signs/signos de valor absoluto (p. 480) El símbolo "$|\ \ |$" que denota un valor absoluto. Por ejemplo, $|0| = |0|$.

acute angle/ángulo agudo (p. 412) Angulo que mide entre 0° y 90°.

acute triangle/triángulo agudo (p. 412) Triángulo con tres ángulos agudos.

adjacent angles/ángulos adyacentes (p. 375) Dos ángulos que comparten un lado y un vértice pero no se superponen.

angle/ángulo (p. 372) Figura formada por dos rayos que comienzan en el mismo punto.

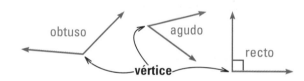

annual interest rate/tasa de interés anual (p. 354) Porcentaje del capital que se gana (o paga) como interés sobre la base de un año.

area/área (p. 17) Medida de la superficie cubierta por una figura. El área se mide en unidades cuadradas.

Associative Property of Addition/propiedad asociativa de la adición (p. 63) Para cualesquier números a, b, y c $(a + b) + c = a + (b + c)$.

Associative Property of Multiplication/ propiedad asociativa de la multiplicación (p. 63) Para cualesquier números a, b, y c $(a \times b) \times c = a \times (b \times c)$.

average/promedio (p. 220) Suma de los números de un conjunto dividida entre la cantidad de números del conjunto. También se le llama *media*.

balance/saldo (p. 355) Importe disponible para el uso en una cuenta corriente o en una cuenta de ahorros o importe adeudado sobre una deuda.

base of a cylinder/base de un cilindro (p. 438) Cara circular del cilindro. *Ver también* **cylinder/cilindro.**

base of a parallelogram/base de un paralelogramo (p. 390) Cualquier lado de un paralelogramo.

base of a percent/base de un porcentaje (p. 342) Número del que se debe hallar una porción. En la ecuación porcentual $\dfrac{a}{b} = \dfrac{p}{100}$, la base es b.

base of a power/base de una potencia (p. 64) En la potencia 2^3, 2 es la base.

base of a trapezoid/base de un trapezoide (p. 396) Los dos lados paralelos. *Ver también* **trapezoid/trapezoide.**

base of a triangle/base de un triángulo (p. 17) Cualquier lado del triángulo.

box-and-whisker plot/gráfico de caja y costados (p. 234) Diagrama que muestra el primero, el segundo y el tercer cuartil, el número menor y el número mayor de un conjunto de datos.

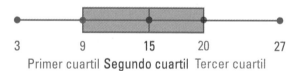

box model/modelo de caja (p. 581) Modelo usado en operaciones con números positivos y negativos.

center of a circle/centro de un círculo (p. 386) Punto interior a un círculo que está a la misma distancia de todos los puntos del círculo.

circle/círculo (p. 386) Curva cerrada en un plano cuyos puntos están todos a la misma distancia de un punto dado llamado *centro*.

circle graph/gráfico circular (p. 348) Gráfico que representa datos como partes de un círculo. La totalidad del círculo representa la totalidad del conjunto.

circumference of a circle/circunferencia de un círculo (p. 386) Perímetro de un círculo.

combination/combinación (p. 548) Colección de un conjunto de objetos en el que el orden no tiene importancia.

common denominator/común denominador (p. 126) Igual denominador usado en dos o más fracciones.

Por ejemplo, $\frac{7}{8}$ y $\frac{3}{8}$ tienen un común denominador que es 8.

common factor/factor común (p. 82) Número que divide exactamente a dos o más números dados

common multiple/común múltiplo (p. 114) Número que es múltiplo de dos o más números dados. Por ejemplo, 12 es común múltiplo de 2 y de 3.

Commutative Property of Addition/propiedad conmutativa de la adición (p. 63) Para dos números cualesquiera a y b, cambiar el orden en que se los suma no cambiará la suma; esto es, $a + b = b + a$.

Commutative Property of Multiplication/ propiedad conmutativa de la multiplicación (p. 63) Para dos números cualesquiera a y b, cambiar el orden en que se los multiplica no cambiará el producto; esto es, $a \times b = b \times a$.

complements/complementarios (p. 375) Dos ángulos son complementarios si sus medidas suman 90°.

composite number/número compuesto (p. 76) Número que tiene más de dos factores.

cone/cono (p. 444) Un sólido que tiene una base circular, un vértice y un curva lateral.

congruent angles/ángulos congruentes (p. 374) Angulos que tienen la misma medida.

congruent figures/figuras congruentes (p. 385) Figuras que tienen exactamente el mismo tamaño y la misma forma.

coordinate plane/plano de coordenadas (p. 172) Plano formado por una línea numérica horizontal llamada eje de las x y una línea numérica vertical llamada eje de las y.

coordinates of a point/coordenadas de un punto (p. 172) Dos números de un par ordenado que ubican un punto en un plano de coordenadas.

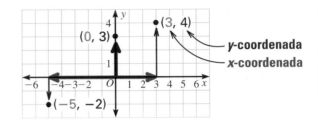

corresponding angles/ángulos correspondientes (p. 300) Angulos coincidentes de dos polígonos. Por ejemplo, los ángulos B y E son ángulos correspondientes.

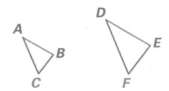

corresponding sides/lados correspondientes (p. 300) Lados coincidentes de un polígono. Por ejemplo, los lados $\overline{AB}$ y $\overline{DE}$ son lados correspondientes.

Counting Principle/principio de conteo (p. 537) Cuando se selecciona un elemento de cada uno de dos o más conjuntos, el número total de posibles combinaciones es el producto del número de elementos de cada conjunto.

cross-multiply/multiplicación cruzada (p. 288) Hallar los productos cruzados de una proporción.

cross products/productos cruzados (p. 288)
En la proporción $\frac{a}{b} = \frac{c}{d}$, $a \cdot d$ y $b \cdot c$ son productos cruzados. Son iguales.

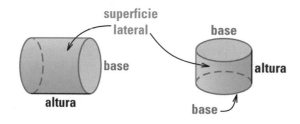

cube/cubo (p. 65) Prisma rectangular cuyas caras son cuadrados.

cube of a number/cubo de un número (p. 65) Tercera potencia del número.

cylinder/cilindro (p. 438) Figura que tiene dos bases circulares y una superficie lateral curva.

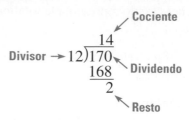

data/datos (p. 4) Conjunto de números o hechos.

denominator/denominador (p. 86) Número situado debajo de la línea de una fracción y que indica en cuántas partes se ha dividido el entero.

Por ejemplo, el denominador de $\frac{2}{3}$ es 3.

dependent events/sucesos dependientes (p. 567) Si la probabilidad de que ocurra un suceso cambia la probabilidad de que ocurra un segundo suceso, entonces se trata de sucesos dependientes.

diameter of a circle/diámetro de un círculo (p. 386) Distancia a través de un círculo que pasa por su centro.

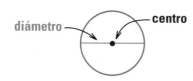

disjoint sets/conjuntos inconexos (p. 566) Conjuntos que no tienen miembros comunes.

Distributive Property/propiedad distributiva (p. 142) Para cualesquiera números $a \times (b + c) = a \times b + a \times c$.

divide/dividir (p. 504) Hallar el cociente de dos números.

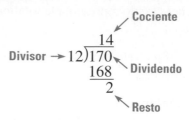

dividend/dividendo (p. 504) *Ver* **divide/dividir.**

divisibility test/prueba de divisibilidad (p. 70) Prueba usada para decidir si un número se puede dividir exactamente entre otro.

divisor/divisor (p. 504) *Ver* **divide/dividir.**

double bar graph/gráfico de doble barra (p. 44) Gráfico que usa dos colores de barras para mostrar una comparación entre cantidades.

edge of a polyhedron/arista de un poliedro (p. 429) Segmento de línea donde se unen dos caras. *Ver también* **polyhedron/poliedro.**

equally-likely outcomes/resultados igualmente posibles (p. 530) Resultados que tienen la misma probabilidad de ocurrir.

equation/ecuación (p. 30) Aseveración matemática que incluye un signo de igual "=".

equivalent fractions/fracciones equivalentes (p. 86) Dos fracciones que representan la misma cantidad. Por ejemplo, $\frac{2}{3}$ y $\frac{4}{6}$ son fracciones equivalentes.

evaluating an expression/evaluar una expresión (p. 58) Hallar el valor de una expresión después de que todas las variables se sustituyen por números.

even number/número par (p. 37) Número que es múltiplo de 2.

expected value/valor esperado (p. 556) Forma de medir la imparcialidad de un juego. El valor esperado para un jugador es el resultado de multiplicar la cantidad que puede ganar por la probabilidad de ganar.

experimental probability/probabilidad experimental (p. 530) Probabilidad basada en la frecuencia de los resultados que han ocurrido después de realizar un experimento muchas veces.

exponent/exponente (p.p. 64, 516) Número de veces que una base se usa como factor. Por ejemplo, en la expresión 2^4, 4 es el exponente. $2^4 = 2 \times 2 \times 2 \times 2$, ó 16.

expression/expresión (p. 58) Conjunto de números, variables y símbolos tales como $+$, $-$, $\times$, y $\div$.

face of a polyhedron/cara de un poliedro (p. 429) Polígono que es lado del poliedro. *Ver también* **polyhedron/poliedro.**

factor/factor (p. 64) Número que se multiplica en una expresión. Por ejemplo, en la expresión $2 \cdot 4 = 8$, son factores.

fair game/juego imparcial (p. 557) Juego en el que cada jugador tiene el mismo valor esperado.

first quartile/primer cuartil (p. 234) *Ver* **quartiles/cuartiles.**

frequency/frecuencia (p. 226) Número de veces que ocurre un elemento dentro de un intervalo.

frequency table/tabla de frecuencias (p. 226) Tabla que agrupa en intervalos grandes cantidades de datos.

function/función (p. 612) Regla que indica cómo realizar una o más operaciones en un número llamado *entrada* para lograr un *resultado.*

greatest common factor/mayor factor común (p. 82) Mayor factor común de dos números.

height/altura *Ver* **cylinder/cilindro, parallelogram/paralelogramo, prism/ prisma** y **trapezoid/trapezoide.**

hexagon/hexágono (p. 15) Polígono de seis lados.

hexahedron/hexaedro (p. 428) Poliedro con seis caras.

histogram/histograma (p. 227) Gráfica de barras que representa datos en una tabla de frecuencias. Hay una barra (o un espacio de barra) por cada intervalo de la tabla de frecuencia.

hypotenuse/hipotenusa (p. 412) Lado de un triángulo recto que está opuesto al ángulo recto. *Ver también* **right triangle/triángulo recto.**

improper fraction/fracción impropia (p. 118) Fracción que es mayor o igual que 1. Por ejemplo, $\frac{3}{2}$ y $\frac{2}{2}$ son fracciones impropias.

independent events/sucesos independientes (p. 567) Si la ocurrencia de un suceso no afecta la ocurrencia de un segundo suceso los sucesos son independientes.

input/entrada (p. 612) Número que sustituye a una variable en una ecuación.

integers/enteros (p. 178) Conjunto de números no fraccionarios y sus opuestos.

interest/interés (p. 354) Costo de tomar dinero en préstamo o renta del dinero depositado en un banco.

intersecting lines/líneas intersectadas (p. 374) Dos líneas en un plano que se encuentran en un punto común.

inverse operation/operación inversa (p. 580) Operación que deshace otra operación. Por ejemplo, la adición es la operación inversa de la sustracción.

isolating the variable/aislar la variable (p. 584) Colocar una variable sola en un lado de una ecuación.

isosceles triangle/triángulo isósceles (p. 438) Triángulo que tiene al menos dos lados congruentes.

lateral surface/superficie lateral (p. 438) Superficie curva que conecta las dos bases de un cilindro. *Ver también* **cylinder/cilindro.**

least common denominator of two fractions/mínimo común denominador de dos fracciones (p. 126) Mínimo común múltiplo de sus denominadores.

least common multiple/mínimo común múltiplo (p. 114) Múltiplo común mínimo de dos o más números. Por ejemplo, el mínimo común múltiplo de 2 y 3 es 6.

legs of a right triangle/cateto de un triángulo recto (p. 412) Los dos lados perpendiculares. *Ver también* **right triangle/triángulo recto.**

line graph/gráfica de líneas (p. 245) Gráfica en la que los puntos marcados se conectan con segmentos de línea.

mean/media (p. 220) Suma de un conjunto de números dividida entre la cantidad de números que hay en el conjunto. También se le llama *promedio.*

measure of central tendency/medida de la tendencia central (p. 220) Número único que se usa para representar un conjunto de datos. La media, la mediana y el modo son medidas de la tendencia central.

median/mediana (p. 220) Número medio (o promedio de los dos números medios) de un conjunto de números que han sido escritos en orden numérico.

mixed number/número mixto (p. 118) Número tal como $2\frac{3}{5}$, que es la suma de un número entero y una fracción.

mode/modo (p. 220) En un conjunto de datos, el número que aparece con mayor frecuencia.

modeling of a real life problem/modelaje de un problema de la vida real (p. 31) Escribir una ecuación que representa un problema de la vida real.

multiple of a number/múltiplo de un número (p. 114) Producto de dicho número y cualquier número entero mayor que cero. Por ejemplo, 2, 4, 6, 8, . . . son múltiplos de 2.

n-factorial/factorial n (p. 544) Expresión n que representa el número de permutaciones de n objetos. Es el producto de los números de 1 hasta n.

negative integer/entero negativo (p. 178) Entero inferior a 0.

negative sign/signo negativo (p. 178) Símbolo " − " usado para representar números negativos.

net/red (p. 426) Molde plano que puede plegarse para formar un sólido.

nonahedron/nonaedro (p.431) Poliedro con nueve caras.

number-line/línea numérica (p. 98) Línea a la que se han asignado números.

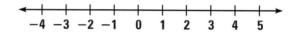

numerator/numerador (p. 86) Número situado encima de la línea de una fracción que muestra el número de partes iguales del entero.

numerical expression/expresión numérica (p. 58) Expresión que solamente incluye números y símbolos.

obtuse angle/ángulo obtuso (p. 412) Angulo que mide más de 90° y menos de 180°.

obtuse triangle/triángulo obtuso (p. 412) Triángulo que tiene un ángulo obtuso.

octahedron/octaedro (p. 428) Poliedro con ocho caras.

odd number/número impar Número entero que no es divisible entre dos.

opposites/opuestos (p. 184) Dos números que están a la misma distancia del 0 en una línea numérica. Por ejemplo, 4 y −4 son opuestos.

Order of Operations/orden de las operaciones (pp. 59, 64) Procedimiento para evaluar las expresiones que tienen más de una operación.

1. Realizar las operaciones dentro de los símbolos de agrupamiento;

2. Hallar el valor de las potencias;

3. Multiplicar y dividir de izquierda a derecha;

4. Finalmente, sumar y restar de izquierda a derecha.

ordered pair/par ordenado (p. 172) Par de números, tal como (3, 2), que ubica un punto en un plano de coordenadas.

ordering/ordenar (p. 98) Disponer números de menor a mayor o de mayor a menor.

origin/origen (p. 172) En un plano de coordenadas, el punto (0, 0). Es la intersección entre el eje de las *x* y el eje de las *y*.

outcome/resultado (p. 256) Resultado de un experimento. Por ejemplo, "cara" es un resultado de tirar al aire una moneda para ver de qué lado cae.

output/salida (p. 612) Resultado producido al evaluar una función usando una entrada específica.

parallel lines/líneas paralelas (p. 374) Dos líneas en un plano que están a la misma distancia en todos sus puntos.

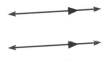

parallelogram/paralelogramo (p. 390) Cuadrilátero cuyos lados opuestos son paralelos.

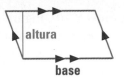

pentagon/pentágono (p. 15) Polígono de cinco lados.

pentahedron/pentaedro (p. 428) Poliedro con cinco caras.

percent/porcentaje (p. 322) Por ciento. Razón cuyo denominador es 100.

percent decrease/reducción porcentual (p. 358) Razón de la magnitud de la reducción con respecto a la cantidad original, expresada como porcentaje.

percent equation/ecuación porcentual (p. 342) El enunciado "*a* es un porcentaje *p* de *b*" puede escribirse con la ecuación porcentual $\frac{a}{b} = \frac{p}{100}$.

percent increase/aumento porcentual (p. 358) Razón de la magnitud del aumento con respecto a la cantidad original, expresada como porcentaje.

perfect square/cuadrado perfecto (p. 406) Número cuya raíz cuadrada es un número entero. Por ejemplo, 0, 1, 4 y 9 son cuadrados perfectos.

perimeter/perímetro (p. 17) Distancia en torno a una figura.

permutation/permutación (p. 544) Disposición o enumeración de objetos en la que el orden es importante.

pi/pi (π) (p. 386) Número aproximadamente igual a 3,14 que representa la relación entre la circunferencia de un círculo y su diámetro.

pictograph/pictografía (p. 244) Gráfica que usa imágenes o símbolos para representar datos.

plane/plano (p. 374) Superficie plana que se extiende en todas las direcciones.

polygon/polígono (p. 10) Figura plana cerrada tal como un triángulo o un cuadrilátero cuyos lados son segmentos de recta.

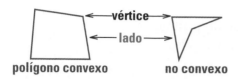

polígono convexo   no convexo

polyhedron/poliedro (p. 428) Figura sólida que tiene lados que son polígonos.

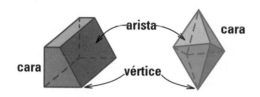

positive integer/entero positivo (p. 178) Todo entero mayor que cero.

power/potencia (p. 64) Expresión tal como 5^4, que tiene una base (5) y un exponente (4).

powers of 10/potencias de 10 (p. 515) Los números 10^1, 10^2, 10^3, 10^4, . . . , que también pueden escribirse como 10, 100, 1.000, 10.000, ...

prime factorization/descomposición en números primos (p. 76) Número escrito como el producto de números primos.

prime number/número primo (p. 76) Número que tiene exactamente dos factores, el mismo número y 1.

principal/capital (p. 354) Cantidad de dinero que se toma en préstamo, se presta o se ahorra.

prism/prisma (p. 428) Poliedro con dos caras congruentes y paralelas.

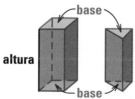

probability of an event/probabilidad de un suceso (p. 256) Medición de la probabilidad de que el suceso ocurra.

proper fraction/fracción propia (p. 118) Fracción que es menor que 1.

proportion/proporción (p. 284) Ecuación que iguala dos relaciones.

proportional sides/lados proporcionales (p. 300) Los lados de los polígonos son proporcionales si los coeficientes de sus longitudes son iguales.

protractor/transportador (p. 372) Instrumento usado para medir ángulos.

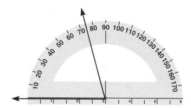

pyramid/pirámide (p. 428) Poliedro cuya base es un polígono y cuyas demás caras son triángulos que comparten un vértice común.

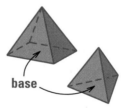

base

Pythagorean Theorem/teorema de Pitágoras (p. 413) En cualquier triángulo recto, la suma de los cuadrados de las longitudes de los catetos es igual al cuadrado de la longitud de la hipotenusa.

$$a^2 + b^2 = c^2$$

quadrant/cuadrante (p. 238) Cada una de las cuatro regiones de un plano de coordenadas formadas por los ejes de coordenadas.

quadrilateral/cuadrilátero (p. 15) Polígono de cuatro lados.

quartiles/cuartiles (p. 234) Tres números que separan un conjunto de números ordenados en cuatro grupos que contienen aproximadamente el mismo número de elementos de datos.

quotient/cociente (p. 504) *Ver* **divide/dividir.**

radical sign/signo de radical (p. 406) Símbolo "$\sqrt{}$" que denota una raíz cuadrada. Por ejemplo, $\sqrt{16}$ significa la raíz cuadrada de 16.

radius of a circle/radio de un círculo (p. 396) Distancia entre el centro de un círculo y su borde.

range/rango (p. 226) Diferencia entre los números máximo y mínimo de un conjunto de números.

rate/razón (p. 276) Fracción en la que el numerador y el denominador tienen unidades de medida diferentes.

ratio/coeficiente (p. 272) Cociente de dos números que tienen la misma unidad de medida.

reciprocals/números recíprocos (p. 150) Dos números cuyo producto es 1. Por ejemplo, $\frac{5}{6}$ es el número recíproco de $\frac{6}{5}$ porque $\frac{5}{6} \times \frac{6}{5} = 1$.

rectangle/rectángulo (p. 6) Paralelogramo que tiene cuatro ángulos rectos.

regrouping/reagrupar (p. 131) Reescribir el formato de un número mixto de manera que tome el valor de un número entero sumándolo a la fracción. Por ejemplo, $3\frac{1}{5}$ puede reagruparse como $2\frac{6}{5}$.

right angle/ángulo recto (p. 412) Angulo que mide 90°.

right triangle/triángulo recto (p. 412) Triángulo con un ángulo recto.

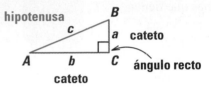

round a number/redondear un número (p. 13) Sustituir un número por otro de aproximadamente el mismo valor y que sea más fácil de usar.

scale drawing/dibujo a escala (p. 306) Dibujo en el cual las medidas son proporcionales a las dimensiones reales de un objeto.

scale factor/factor de escala (p. 306) Razón entre las medidas de un dibujo a escala y las medidas reales.

scatter plot/diagrama de dispersión (p. 173) Conjunto de puntos en un plano de coordenadas que representa una relación entre dos cantidades.

scientific notation/notación científica (p. 517) Número expresado como $c \times 10^n$ donde c es mayor o igual que 1 y menor que 10.

second quartile/segundo cuartil (p. 234) Mediana de un conjunto ordenado de números.

sequence/secuencia (p. 166) Listado de números en orden específico.

similar geometric figures/figuras geométricas semejantes (p. 16) *Ver* **similar polygons/polígonos semejantes.**

similar polygons/polígonos semejantes (p. 300) Polígonos cuyos ángulos correspondientes tienen la misma medida y cuyos lados correspondientes son proporcionales.

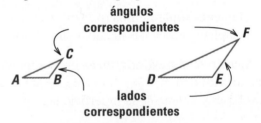

similar prisms/prismas semejantes (p. 462) Prismas que tienen la misma forma y dimensiones correspondientes proporcionales.

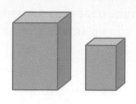

simple interest/interés simple (p. 354) Producto del capital por la tasa de interés anual y por el tiempo en años: Interés (I) = capital (C) $\times$ tasa (%) $\times$ tiempo (t).

simplest form of a fraction/forma más simple de una fracción (p. 86) Una fracción está en su forma más simple si el mayor factor común del numerador y el denominador es 1.

solution of an equation/solución de una ecuación (p. 30) Valor de la variable que hace que una ecuación se cumpla.

solve an equation/resolver una ecuación (p. 30) Hallar el valor de la variable que hace que la ecuación se cumpla.

spreadsheet/hoja electrónica de cálculo (p. 231) Programa de computación usado para organizar y analizar datos.

square/cuadrado (p. 6) Rectángulo con cuatro lados de la misma longitud.

square of a number/cuadrado de un número (p. 64) Segunda potencia del número.

square root of a number/raíz cuadrada de un número (p. 406) Número que al multiplicarse por sí mismo es igual al número dado.

subset/subconjunto (p. 566) El conjunto *B* es un subconjunto del conjunto *A* si todos los elementos de *B* están también en *A*.

supplements/suplementos (p. 375) Dos ángulos son suplementos si sus medidas suman 180°.

surface area of a cylinder/área de la superficie de un cilindro (p. 438) Suma de las áreas de las bases y el área de la superficie lateral.

surface area of a polyhedron/área de la superficie de un poliedro (p. 432) Suma de las áreas de las caras de un poliedro.

table of values/tabla de valores (p. 168) Tabla que se usa para organizar varios valores de una expresión.

tessellation/mosaico (p. 385) Cobertura de un plano con figuras congruentes de manera tal que las figuras no se traslapen ni dejen vacíos.

tetrahedron/tetraedro (p. 428) Poliedro con cuatro caras.

theoretical probability/probabilidad teórica (p. 530) Probabilidad que se determina contando y clasificando todos los resultados posibles.

third quartile/tercer cuartil (p. 234) *Ver* **quartile/cuartil.**

translation/traslación (p. 380) Movimiento de una figura de tal forma que todos los puntos de la misma se deslicen en la misma dirección y a la misma distancia.

trapezoid/trapezoide (p. 396) Cuadrilátero que tiene dos lados opuestos que son paralelos y dos lados opuestos que no son paralelos.

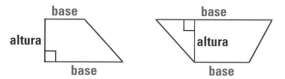

tree diagram/diagrama de árbol (pp. 76, 536) Diagrama que muestra la factorización de un número. Asimismo, un diagrama que muestra todos los resultados posibles de un experimento. Los resultados se enumeran a lo largo de las "ramas" del diagrama.

triangle/triángulo (p. 15) Polígono de tres lados.

unit rate/razón unitaria (p. 276) Razón con un denominador de 1.

variable/variable (p. 30) Letra de una ecuación que puede sustituirse por un número.

variable expression/expresión variable (p. 58) Expresión que tiene por lo menos una variable.

Venn diagram/diagrama de Venn (p. 37) Diagrama que usa formas geométricas para mostrar relaciones entre conjuntos de objetos.

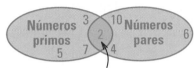

Números primos que son pares

verbal model/modelo verbal (p. 199) Ecuación escrita usando palabras y símbolos.

vertex of an angle/vértice de un ángulo (p. 372) Punto inicial de ambos rayos de un ángulo. *Ver también* **angle/ángulo.**

vertex of a polygon/vértice de un polígono (p. 10) Punto en el que se unen dos lados. *Ver también* **polygon/polígono.**

vertex of a polyhedron/vértice de un poliedro (p. 429) Punto donde se unen dos aristas. *Ver también* **polyhedron/poliedro.**

vertical angles/ ángulos verticales (p. 374) Las líneas intersectadas forman dos pares de ángulos verticales. En la figura, los ángulos 1 y 3 son ángulos verticales y los ángulos 2 y 4 son ángulos verticales.

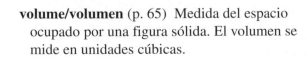

volume/volumen (p. 65) Medida del espacio ocupado por una figura sólida. El volumen se mide en unidades cúbicas.

x*-axis/eje de las *x (p. 172) Eje horizontal de un plano de coordenadas.

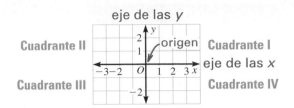

x*-coordinate/coordenada de las *x (p. 172) Primera coordenada de un punto en el plano de coordenadas.

y*-axis/eje de las *y (p. 172) Eje vertical de un plano de coordenadas.

y*-coordinate/coordenada de las *y (p. 172) Segunda coordenada de un punto en el plano de coordenadas.

B

Credits

Cover Image

Photography by Ralph Mercer; Origami airplane designed and folded by Michael G. LaFosse

Stock Photography

vi Peter Rauter/Tony Stone Images (t); Rob Crandall/Stock Boston (b); **vii** David A. Harvey/National Geographic Society (t); Wesley Bocxe/Photo Researchers, Inc. (b); **viii** Tony Freeman/PhotoEdit (t); K. Preuss/The The Image Works (b); **ix** Michael Newman/PhotoEdit (t); Mark E. Gibson (b); **x** Daniel Olson/Unicorn Stock Photos (t); Jeff Isaac Greenberg/Photo Researchers, Inc. (b); **xi** Worldsat International, Inc./Photo Researchers, Inc. (t); Tony Freeman/PhotoEdit (b); **xii** Schafer & Hill/Tony Stone Images (t), Nancy Sheehan/PhotoEdit (b); **xiii** Tim Bieber/The Image Bank (t); Maslowski/Photo Researchers, Inc. (b); **xiv** Kaz Mori/The Image Bank (t); Julie Houck/Stock Boston (b); **xv** Krafft/Photo Researchers, Inc. (t); Ray Atkeson/The Stock Market (b); **xvi** Lowell Georgia/Photo Researchers, Inc. (t); Tim Eagan/Woodfin Camp & Associates (b); **xvii** Bob Daemmrich/Stock Boston (t); Alastair Laidlaw/Tony Stone Images (b); **xix** Tom McHugh/Photo Researchers, Inc. (tl); Uniphoto, Inc. (tr); Telegraph Colour Library/FPG International (r); Andy Sacks/Tony Stone Images (bl); Nancy Sheehan (b); **xx** Courtesy of Christina Neal (t); Scott Warren (tl); Superstock (cl, br); Momatiuk/Eastcott/Woodfin Camp and Associates (bl); **xxi** Tony Freeman/PhotoEdit (t); RMIP/Richard Haynes (c); Ralph Mercer (b); **xxii** Frank Niemeier/The Atlanta Constitution (t); Sygma (c); D. Young-Wolff/PhotoEdit (b); **xxiii** Arthur Tilley/FPG International; Photri, Inc (b); **xxiv** RMIP/Richard Haynes; **xxv** David Epperson/Tony Stone Images; **xxvi** D. Young-Wolff/PhotoEdit (t); Robert Beck (c); Krafft/Photo Researchers, Inc.; **xxvii** Julie Houck/Stock Boston (t); Emory Kristof/National Geographic Image Collection (br); C/B Productions/The Stock Market (bl); **0** Peter Rauter/Tony Stone Images; (t); Comstock (b); **1** Mark Harvey/DDB Stock Photo (tr); Kent Wood/Peter Arnold, Inc. (tl); **2** Rob Crandall/Stock Boston; **3** Superstock (tl); NOAA/Science Source (b); **4** Jeff Zaruba/Tony Stone Images; **7** Phil Schofield; **11** Werner H. Muller/Peter Arnold, Inc. (t); Peter Gridley/FPG International (b); **12** Courtesy of Barbara McNaught Watson; **15** School Division, Houghton Mifflin Company (b); **16** Superstock; **21** Michael Covington/Phototake; **22** School Division, Houghton Mifflin Company; **23** School Division, Houghton Mifflin Company; **24** Keith Kent/Science Photo Library/Photo Researchers, Inc.; **26** Jeffrey Sylvester/FPG International; **29** Ken O'Donoghue (t); Peter Miller/Photo Researchers, Inc. (b); **31** David Young-Wolff/PhotoEdit (l); School Division, Houghton Mifflin Company (r); **32** David Young-Wolff/PhotoEdit; **33** Ralf-Finn Hesthoft/SABA; **34** Keren Su/Tony Stone Images; **35** Keren Su/Tony Stone Images; **36** Jeffrey Dunn Studios; **38** Bob Daemmrich/The The Image Works; **40** Jeff Greenberg/Unicorn Stock Photo; **43** Howard Bluestein/Photo Researchers, Inc.; **45** J. Gordon Miller/Superstock (l); Donovan Reese/Tony Stone Images (r); **47** Robert Herko/Tony Stone Images (l); Jim Corwin/Photo Researchers, Inc. (r); **52** Robert Beck, **54** Superstock (b); Mark C. Burnett/Photo Researchers, Inc.(t); School Division, Houghton Mifflin Company (br); **55** David A. Harvey/National Geographic Image Collection; **56** Jonathan Blair/National Geographic Image Collection (t); School Division, Houghton Mifflin Company (b); **57** Momatiuk/Eastcott/Woodfin Camp and Associates (bl); Wesley Bocxe/Photo Researchers, Inc. (tr); School Division, Houghton Mifflin Company (tl, cl); **58** David Young-Wolff/PhotoEdit; **61** Superstock; **63** School Division, Houghton Mifflin Company (b); **64** Alfred Pasieka/Science Photo Library/Photo Researchers, Inc.; **67** Hans Deryk/AP Worldwide Photos, Inc.; **68** H. Talman; **69** Pedrick/The The Image Works; **71** Wendy Chan/The Image Bank; **75** School Division, Houghton Mifflin Company (l); **77** Denise Applewhite/Sygma; **79** School Division, Houghton Mifflin Company; **80** North Wind Picture Archives; **81** Cathlyn Melloan/Tony Stone Images; **85** Werner Forman/Art Resource, NY; **90** Gordon Gahan/National Geographic Image Collection; **91** PhotoDisc,Inc. (t); Superstock (l); Al Kooistra/Sportschrome (b); **94** Jonathan Nourok/PhotoEdit; **96** Ken O'Donoghue; **97** Raffi Van Chromes; **99** Bohdan Hrynewych/Stock Boston; **100** Anne B. Keiser/National Geographic Image Collection; **101** Francis & Donna Caldwell/Visuals Unlimited; **106** Brooks Walker/National Geographic Image Collection; **108** William Taufic/The Stock Market (t); PhotoDisc, Inc. (b); **109** Will & Deni McIntyre/Photo Researchers, Inc. (l); Henryk T. Kaiser/Envision (r); **110** Michael Newman/PhotoEdit; **111** Gayna Hoffman

Smithsonian Institution; **333** Arthur Tilley/FPG International.; **335** Gerard Fritz/FPG International; **336** C/B Productions/The Stock Market; **339** Tony Stone Images; **340** PhotoDisc, Inc. (l, br); **343** Courtesy of Levi Strauss & Co. Archives, San Francisco, CA; **344** Don Smetzer/Tony Stone Images; **346** Ken Levine/Allsport; **347** Sisse Brimberg/National Geographic Image Collection; **348** Richard Hutchings/PhotoEdit; **351** B. Bachman/The Image Works; **352** Will & Deni McIntyre/Tony Stone Images; **353** Flip Nicklin/Minden Pictures; **355** David Young-Wolff/PhotoEdit; **356** Michael A. Dwyer/Stock Boston; **357** William Taufic/The Stock Market; **361** Dallas & John Heaton/Stock Boston (l); Peter Pearson/Tony Stone Images (c); Allan A. Philiba (r); Flip Nicklin/Minden Pictures (b); **366** Thayer Syme/FPG International; **368** Bieber/The Image Bank (c); PhotoDisc, Inc. (t, b); **369** Dennis MacDonald/Unicorn Stock Photo (l); Alice M. Prescott/Unicorn Stock Photo (r); **370** Maslowski/ Photo Researchers, Inc.; **371** Tommy Dodson/Unicorn Stock Photo; **373** School Division, Houghton Mifflin Company; **374** Bullaty Lomeo/The Image Bank; **378** School Division, Houghton Mifflin Company; **381** Courtesy of Lynn Smith; **384** Susan Doheny; **386** Gale Zucker/Stock Boston; **388** Jeff Greenberg/Peter Arnold, Inc.; **389** Brian Drake/Sportschrome (l); B. Drake/Sportschrome (r); David Parker/Science Photo Library/Photo Researchers, Inc. (b); **393** Frank Pennington/Unicorn Stock Photo; **394** PhotoDisc, Inc. (l); **395** David Young-Wolff/ PhotoEdit; **396** Dannielle B. Hayes/Omni Photo Communications; **399** James Martin/Tony Stone Images (t); **402** PhotoDisc, Inc.; **403** Stacy Pick/Stock Boston; **405** David Parker/Science Photo Library/Photo Researchers, Inc.; **412** D. MacDonald/PhotoEdit; **422** Ron Haisfield (t); Tony Freeman/PhotoEdit (b); **423** Kaz Mori/The Image Bank (l); Bill Pogue/Tony Stone Images (r); **424** Cindy McIntyre/The Picture Cube; **425** Ken Karp/Omni Photo Communications (tr); Julie Houck/Stock Boston (tl); Bob Daemmrich/The Image Works (b); **427** School Division, Houghton Mifflin Company (b); **428** Telegraph Colour Library/FPG International; **431** M. Antman/The Image Works; **436** Ted Rose/Unicorn Stock Photo; **438** Uniphoto; 441 Bob Daemmrich/The Image Works; **442** Jeff Greenberg/MR/Unicorn Stock Photo; **445** Dennis MacDonald/PhotoEdit (l); Malcolm S.Kirk/Tony Stone Images (c); Andre Jenny/Unicorn Stock Photo (r); **446** Bob Donnan Photography; **447** School Division,

Houghton Mifflin Company; **450** Will McIntyre/Photo Researchers, Inc.; **451** Superstock (l); Bill Lisenby (r); **453** Uniphoto, Inc. (t); Roy Gumpel/Liaison International (b); **454** School Division, Houghton Mifflin Company; **457** Robert Clarkson; **459** Scott Warren; **461** School Division, Houghton Mifflin Company (b); **465** Comstock; **470** John M. Roberts/The Stock Market; **472** Bob Daemmrich/Stock Boston; **474** Novosti Press Agency/Science Photo Library (t); Franco Salmoiraghi/ Photo Resource Hawaii (b); **475** Douglas Faulkner/Photo Researchers, Inc. (tl); Ragnar Larusson/Photo Researchers, Inc. (br); **476** Andrew J. Martine/Photo Researchers, Inc. (b); **477** Brad Lewis/Photo Resource Hawaii (r); Ray Atkeson/The Stock Market (l); Bucky Reeves/Photo Researchers, Inc. (t); Prentice K. Stout/Photo Researchers, Inc. (cl); A. J. Copley/Visuals Unlimited (bl); **479** School Division, Houghton Mifflin Company (b); **480** Bob Daemmrich/ The Image Works; **483** Gary Braasch/Woodfin Camp and Associates; **484** Edith G. Haun/Stock Boston; **485** Jeff Greenberg/ Omni Photo Communications; **487** Emory Kristof/ National Geographic Image Collection; **488** Jean Higgins/Unicorn Stock Photo; **495** Michael Mancuso/ Omni Photo Communications; **496** Sygma; **497** Dennis Netoff; **503** Barron Claiborne (t); Krafft/Photo Researchers, Inc. (b); **505** James Blank/Stock Boston; **507** Mark Newman/Photo Researchers, Inc.; **509** Emory Kristof/National Geographic Image Collection; **514** Courtesy of Christina Neal (b); PhotoDisc, Inc. (t); **516** Ken Eward/Photo Researchers, Inc.; **517** NASA/ Science Source/Photo Researchers, Inc.; **518** Ron Chapple/FPG International; **524** NASA/Omni Photo Communications; **526** Bill Terry/Viesti Associates, Inc.; **527** Jeff Foot (bl); Bob Daemmrich Photo, Inc. (r); David L. Brown/The Picture Cube (tl); **528** C. C. Lockwood/ Animals Animals; **529** Gary A. Conner/Index Stock International (t); Marshall Prescott/Unicorn Stock Photo (c); PhotoDisc, Inc. (bl, br); **531** Rod Planck/Photo Researchers, Inc.; **533** Mark E. Gibson/Visuals Unlimited; **535** PhotoDisc, Inc.; **536** Mark E. Gibson/ Visuals Unlimited; **537** Bob Daemmrich/Stock Boston; **539** Michael Shedlock/New England Stock Photo; **540** C. G. Randall/FPG International; **541** School Division, Houghton Mifflin Company; **545** UPI/Bettmann; **546** Frank Niemeier/The Atlanta Constitution; **547** David Young-Wolff/PhotoEdit (t); Tom Bean/The Stock Market (b); **548** Gary A. Conner/PhotoEdit; **551** Tony Duffy/NBC/Allsport;

SELECTED ANSWERS

Chapter 1

1.1 Exercises, pp. 6–7

1. *Sample answer:* b   **3.** *Sample answer:* 15 to 18 stars in a square and from 120 to 144 total stars in the rectangle. Results will vary slightly, depending on where the template is placed. **5.** white: 18 ft; whitetip: 10 ft; tiger: 15 ft   **7.** 16 **9.** 25 to 30 acres; *sample answer:* Since one household uses 5 to 6 acres, five households will need five times the number of acres.   **11.** C

1.2 Exercises, pp. 10–11

1. 4; 9; 16; *sample answer:* The sum of each set of numbers is the middle number multiplied by itself.   **3.** *Sample answer:* Look for a pattern between the number of rows and the number of flowers. The total number of flowers is one half the product of the number of rows and one more than the number of rows. So, for 20 rows, multiply 20 by 21 and then divide by 2.   **5.** 25; add 4 the first time, then add 5, then add 6, and so on. **7.** 62; add 4, then add 8, then add 16, then add 32, and so on, doubling the previous amount added each time.   **9.** Start with 1, then add 2, then add 3, then add 4, and so on; 210; *sample answer:* Solving a Simpler Problem, Drawing a Diagram, or Looking for a Pattern.   **11.** 304 ft; *sample answer:* The person falls 32 ft farther each second than in the previous second. Add 32 ft another seven times to get to the tenth second.   **13.** 42; *sample answer:* Because there are 43 players, there will be 42 players who must lose a game, and there must be 42 games.   **15.** D

Spiral Review, p. 12

1. 3.1   **3.** 0.27   **5.** $\frac{12}{16}, \frac{3}{4}$ **7.** 48   **9.** 18

Using a Calculator, p. 13

1. 22.00, 11.00, 7.33, 5.50, 4.40, 3.67, 3.14

1.3 Exercises, pp. 18–19

1. *Sample answer:* Similar geometric figures have the same shape, though they may have different sizes.   **3.** 44 cm, 105 cm^2 **5.** 40 cm, 60 cm^2 **11.** 32 m, 64 m^2 **13.** 30 ft, 30 ft^2 **15.** 80 cm, 384 cm^2 **17.** 56 in., 180 in.^{2} **19.** no; *sample answer:* The right triangles on page 18 do not have the same shape.   **21.** Yes; they are the same.   **23.** No; they have different shapes. **25.** Yes; they have the same shape but are different sizes.

27. *Sample answer:*

29. No; the perimeter doubles, while the area increases by four times.   **31.** C

1.4 Exercises, pp. 22–23

1.

+	1	2	3	4	5	6
1	2	3	4	5	6	7
2	3	4	5	6	7	8
3	4	5	6	7	8	9
4	5	6	7	8	9	10
5	6	7	8	9	10	11
6	7	8	9	10	11	12

7; there are more ways to get a sum of 7 than any other sum.   **3.** about 8   **7.** about 5 (On average, the coins are worth about $.10.)   **9.** *Sample answer:* Pick several small areas of the region at random, count the populations in those areas, and then use the average population for these areas to estimate the population for the whole region, assuming that the population density remains about the same over the whole region.   **11.** A

Spiral Review, p. 24

1. five thousand, fifteen   **3.** four hundred twelve thousand, three   **5.** 14.5   **7.** 0.3   **9.** 36 ft^2 **11.** 54 mi^2 **13.** A   **15.** B   **17.** cheetah

Mid-Chapter Assessment, p. 25

1. 24; 4 (MAT, HAT, TAM, HAM)   **2.** 4 square units; it quadruples; it increases nine-fold; it increases sixteen-fold. When the lengths of the sides of a square are multiplied by a number, the area of the square is multiplied by that number squared. It increases twenty-five-fold.

3. A and C; they have the same shape but are different sizes.   **4.** 42 in.^{2}

5. *Sample answer:*

6. 6 in.   **7.** 8 cm   **8.** 5 m   **9.** 40; *sample answer:* Four of the five spinner choices are below full price, so out of 50 spins, you would expect 40 videos to be sold below full price.
10. 30; *sample answer:* One-sixth of the possible combinations of the two cubes are doubles, and one-sixth of 180 is 30.   **11.** *Sample answer:* Count the number of grains in a teaspoon or a tablespoon. Then look up how many spoonfuls are in a cup and multiply the number of grains of rice by the number of spoonfuls in a cup.

1.5 Exercises, pp. 28–29

1. *Sample answer:* You need a number that when multiplied by itself gives 144. The guess 36 is too large.   **3.** TWO = 764, FIVE = 1528   **5.** 18 m, 1 m   **7.** 5 km, 2 km   **9.** 11 yd, 3 yd

11.   **13.**

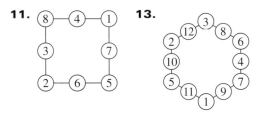

15. 26   **17.** 33 ft by 11 ft   **19.** 5   **21.** 25
23. B

1.6 Exercises, pp. 32–33

1. *Sample answer:* The letter in an equation stands for a number that you want to find. To solve an equation, find a number that can be substituted for the variable so the equation is true.   **3.** solution
5. D   **7.** C   **9.** Number of CDs = 7; Cost of a CD = c; Total cost = $83.93; $7 \times c = \$83.93$; the solution is $11.99, so each CD costs $11.99.
11. no; 8   **13.** yes   **15.** no; 6   **17.** 25; 14 + 25 = 39   **19.** 35; 35 − 17 = 18   **21.** 14; 2 × 14 = 28   **23.** 63; 63 ÷ 9 = 7   **25.** $n - 16 = 7$; 23   **27.** $n \div 18 = 2$; 36   **29.** 19.03   **31.** 13.2
33. 13.65   **35.** the original number   **37.** Number of people = 4; Cost per person = c; Cost of a pack = $1.80; $4 \times c = \$1.80$; the solution is $.45, so each person's share is $.45.   **39.** C

SA2   *Selected Answers*

Spiral Review, p. 34

1. A   **3.** D   **5.** 12   **7.** 40 cm^2 **9.** 12 m^2

1.7 Exercises, pp. 38–39

1.

	Center	Forward	Guard
Cindy	0	X	X
Shawna	X	X	0
Sheila	X	0	X

Cindy: center; Shawna: guard; Sheila: forward

3.

	Ski	Drama	Pep
Juan	X	0	X
Linda	X	X	0
Ed	0	X	X

Juan: drama club; Linda: pep club; Ed: ski club

5.

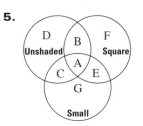

7. Ben; Jen   **9.** 6   **11.** A

1.8 Exercises, pp. 42–43

1. 70   **3.** 2 supers and 4 large   **5.** 3 different sizes, with a total of 28 triangles   **7.** *Sample answer:* Go all the way across the top first, then go all the way down the diagonal to the left.

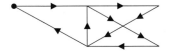

9. 24
11. yes

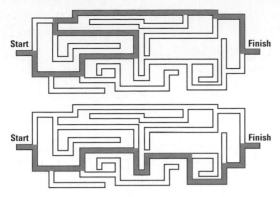

13. B

1.9 Exercises, pp. 46–47

1. giraffe: 18 ft; elephant: 13 ft; *sample answer:* Guess, Check, and Revise   **3.** true; *sample answer:* The difference is 7, the largest difference of any season.   **5.** 24   **7.** $35; *sample answer:* Work Backward   **9.** *Sample answer:* The temperature increased quickly from 9:00 A.M. to noon, and then increased slowly from noon to 4:00 P.M.   **11.** 12:00–1:00, 2:00–3:00, and 3:00–4:00   **13.** $5.50; *sample answer:* Guess, Check, and Revise or Write an Equation   **15.** C

Chapter 1 Review, pp. 49–51

1. Delicious apples; *sample answer:* The price per pound of Macintosh apples is already given. Find the price per pound of Delicious apples and then compare the two prices.   **3.** 99; the number of squares in each figure is given by successive odd numbers.   **5.** perimeter: 24 cm and 20 cm; area: 36 cm^2 and 25 cm^2 **7.** 33   **9.** 15   **11.** A, C, G, F, D, B   **13.** 29   **15.** *Sample answer:* Multiply 68° by 5 to get 340°. From this, subtract the other four temperatures. The result is the missing temperature.

Chapter 2

2.1 Exercises, pp. 60–61

1. A numerical expression contains only numbers and symbols; $4 \times 3 + 7$. A variable expression contains at least one variable; $(12 + n) \times 8$.
3. a. the cost of making n pins   **b.** the selling price of n pins   **c.** the profit in selling n pins   **d.** the profit margin for one pin   **e.** the profit in selling n pins   **5.** Addition was done before division; $12 + 6 \div 2 = 12 + 3 = 15$ **7.** 16   **9.** 19   **11.** 6   **13.** 12   **15.** 36   **17.** 15   **19.** true   **21.** false; $(9 + 4) - (3 + 7) = 3$ **23.** false; $15 \div (5 - 2) + 14 = 19$ **25.** true   **27.** false; $(7 + 2) \div (7 - 4) = 3$ **29.** $14 + 6 \times 3 = 32$ **31.** $25.2 - 2.8 \times 3 = 16.8$ **33.** 40; 28; 18; 10; answers decrease by twice the value of the number added to the variable in the previous expression.   **35.** B

2.2 Exercises, pp. 66–67

1. 8^2 **3.** B   **5.** D   **7.** *Sample answer:* 2×3 involves the multiplication of 2 times 3. 2^3 involves multiplying 2 times 2 times 2.   **9.** c^3 **11.** m^5 **13.** 81   **15.** 125   **17.** 64   **19.** 1   **21.** 32   **23.** 4, 16, 64, 256, 1024, 4096; all are sequential powers of 4.   **25. a.** Incorrect; 4^2 does not equal 8.   **b.** Incorrect; once exponents are evaluated, division must take place before addition.   **27.** 0, 26   **29.** 4, 16   **31.** 8, 56   **33.** $<$ **35.** $<$ **37.** $<$ **39.** *Sample answer:* The numbers in each row increase by an increment that is one greater than the previous row.   **41.** D

Spiral Review, p. 68

1. 96; double the preceding value.   **3.** 27; divide the preceding value by 3.   **5.** 3 nickels, 2 dimes, 2 quarters   **7.** no; 37   **9.** 16   **11.** 51

Using a Calculator, p. 69

1. 2187   **3.** 1024   **5.** 4096   **7.** 512   **9.** 11   **11.** about 5 years

2.3 Exercises, pp. 72–73

1. 360; *sample answer:* Test likely numbers recursively using divisibility tests.   **3.** yes; *sample answer:* If a number ends in 0, it must be divisible by 5.   **5.** always; *sample answer:* 36   **7.** sometimes; *sample answer:* 18   **9.** none   **11.** 2, 3, 4, 6   **13.** 2   **15.** 2, 4, 5, 10   **17.** 0, 6   **19.** 0, 3, 6, 9   **21.** *Sample answer:* 1035   **23.** yes; *sample answer:* A lower power of a given base is always a factor of a higher factor of that base.   **25.** A number is divisible by 8 if the last three digits of the number are divisible by 8.   **27.** no   **29.** D

2.4 Exercises, pp. 78–79

1.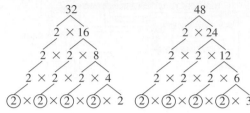
$2^2 \times 3 \times 7$

84
2 × 42
2 × 6 × 7
2 × 2 × 3 × 7

3. 2 **5.** composite **7.** 1-neither, 2-prime, 3-prime, 4-composite, 5-prime, 6-composite, 7-prime, 8-composite, 9-composite, 10-composite, 11-prime, 12-composite, 13-prime, 14-composite, 15-composite, 16-composite, 17-prime, 18-composite, 19-prime, 20-composite, 21-composite, 22-composite, 23-prime, 24-composite, 25-composite **9.** $2^3 \times 7$
11. $2^4 \times 3^2$ **13.** $2^4 \times 3^2 \times 5$
15. $2 \times 3 \times 5 \times 7 \times 11$ **17.** 105 **19.** 54
21. 90 **23.** 26; composite
25. *Sample answer:* The sum of its digits is 18, a multiple of 3. **27.** 13 rows of 15 beads; 3 rows of 65 beads; 1 block of 195 beads; *sample answer:* Using 5 rows of 39 allows for some variety in color selection, without excessive packaging costs. **29.** 36 **31.** 1×2, 1×3, 1×4, 1×6, 1×12, 2×2, 2×3, 2×4, 2×6, 2×12, 4×2, 4×3, 4×4, 4×6, 4×12, 8×2, 8×3, 8×4, 8×6, 8×12 **33.** D

Spiral Review, p. 80

1. 9×5, 15×3, 45×1 **3.** 9×8, 12×6, 18×4, 24×3, 36×2, 72×1 **5.** 27 **7.** 57
9. E **11.** C **13.** F **15.** 39, 78 **17.** 101, 104

Mid-Chapter Assessment, p. 81

1. $5 \times (9 + 2) = 55$ **2.** $45 - 6 \times (2 + 3) = 15$ **3.** $36 \div (3 + 6) \div 2 = 2$ **4.** $(27 - 18) \div (6 - 3) = 3$ **5.** 125 **6.** 64 **7.** 243 **8.** 64
9. C **10.** A **11.** D **12.** B **13.** 84×1, 42×2, 28×3, 21×4, 14×6, 12×7
14. 130 **15.** 132 **16.** 225 **17.** 252
18. False; 2^3 is the same as $2 \times 2 \times 2$, or 8.
19. true **20.** False; the expression $(6 \times 8) - (6 \div 2)$ is equal to 45. **21.** true **22.** Yes; three divides evenly into both the length and the width.

2.5 Exercises, pp. 84–85

1. 1; the number itself **3. a.** 32: 1, 2, 4, 8, 16, 32; 48: 1, 2, 3, 4, 6, 8, 12, 16, 24, 48; GCF: 16

b.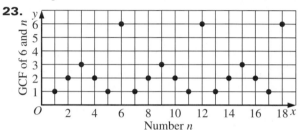

32
2 × 16
2 × 2 × 8
2 × 2 × 2 × 4
② × ② × ② × ② × 2

48
2 × 24
2 × 2 × 12
2 × 2 × 2 × 6
② × ② × ② × ② × 3

GCF: $2 \times 2 \times 2 \times 2 = 16$

c. *Sample answer:* I prefer listing factors, because fewer steps are involved. **5.** B **7.** C **9.** 14: 1, 2, 7, 14; 21: 1, 3, 7, 21; GCF: 7 **11.** 72: 1, 2, 3, 4, 6, 8, 9, 12, 18, 24, 36, 72; 84: 1, 2, 3, 4, 6, 7, 12, 14, 21, 28, 42, 84; GCF: 12 **13.** 44; $2 \times 2 \times 11$ **15.** 9; 3×3 **17.** *Sample answer:* 9 and 15
19. *Sample answer:* 36 and 48 **21.** sometimes

23.

(A graph with horizontal axis "Number *n*" from O to 18 and vertical axis "GCF of 6 and *n*" from 1 to 6.)

Sample answer: The distribution of greatest common factors repeats at regular intervals.
25. C

2.6 Exercises, pp. 88–89

1. B **3.** A **5.** B, D, and E **7.** *Sample answer:* 15 **9.** *Sample answer:* 45 **11.** $\frac{2}{3}$ **13.** $\frac{3}{7}$
15. $\frac{7}{11}$ **17.** $\frac{1}{6}$ **19.** $\frac{3}{5}$ **21.** $\frac{72}{81}, \frac{8}{9}, \frac{24}{27}$
23. $\frac{15}{25}, \frac{75}{125}, \frac{3}{5}$ **25.** *Sample answer:* $\frac{6}{7}, \frac{12}{14}, \frac{24}{28}$
27. $\frac{3}{8}$ **29.** $\frac{1}{6}$ **31.** $\frac{19}{72}$ **33.** B **35.** A

Spiral Review, p. 90

1. 16 **3.** 1 head and 1 tail; *sample answer:* There are two possible combinations that yield one head and one tail but only one combination that yields two heads or two tails, respectively.
5. $(22 - 10) \times (16 \div 8) = 24$ **7.** 125 **9.** 49
11. $3^3 \times 5^2$ **13.** 7×13^2

2.7 Exercises, pp. 96–97

1. always **3.** sometimes

5. *Sample answer:*

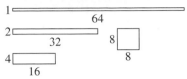

7. A   **9.** $\frac{4}{5}$; 0.8   **11.** $\frac{6}{8}$; 0.75   **13.** 0.67

15. 0.78   **17.** $\frac{2}{27}$, 0.07; $\frac{2}{27}$, 0.07; $\frac{2}{27}$, 0.07;

$\frac{2}{9}$, 0.22; $\frac{5}{27}$, 0.19; $\frac{5}{27}$, 0.19; $\frac{5}{27}$, 0.19   **19.** 0.19

21. 0.35   **23.** $0.\overline{1}, 0.\overline{2}, 0.\overline{3}, 0.\overline{8}$; *sample answer:*
All are repetitions of the given numerator.

25. $\frac{1}{10}$ **27.** $\frac{1}{25}$ **29.** C

2.8 Exercises, pp. 100–101

1. *Sample answer:* ordering finish times in a race;
ordering wrenches in a tool set

3. false

5.

$\frac{5}{4}, \frac{8}{3}$, 2.85, 2.9, 3.3, $\frac{7}{2}$

7. 0.25, 1.8; $0.25 < 1.8$

9. *Sample answer:*

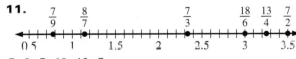

11.

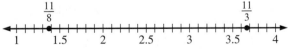

$\frac{7}{9}, \frac{8}{7}, \frac{7}{3}, \frac{18}{6}, \frac{13}{4}, \frac{7}{2}$

13. true

15.

The numbers increase by 0.3; 1.7, 2.0.

17. B

Chapter 2 Review, 103–105

1. 6   **3.** $24 \div (8 - 2) + 6 \cdot 3 = 22$ **5.** 12
7. $1 \times 64, 2 \times 32, 4 \times 16, 8 \times 8$

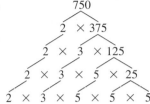

9.

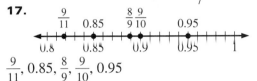

$750 = 2 \times 3 \times 5^3$

11. The greatest common factor of 80 and 36 is 4,
but tiles must be 2×2 in order to fit the dimensions of each room evenly.   **13.** $\frac{6}{7}$ **15.** 0.12

17.

$\frac{9}{11}$, 0.85, $\frac{8}{9}, \frac{9}{10}$, 0.95

Chapter 3

3.1 Exercises, pp. 116–117

1. False; the least common multiple of 12 and 15
is 60.   **3.** true   **5.** *Sample answer:* 24 and 126
7. 2, 4, 6, 8, 10, 12, 14, 16; 7, 14, 21, 28, 35, 42,
49, 56; 14   **9.** 4, 8, 12, 16, 20, 24, 28, 32; 20, 40,
60, 80, 100, 120, 140, 160; 20   **11.** 4, 8, 12, 16,
20, 24, 28, 32; 6, 12, 18, 24, 30, 36, 42, 48; 8, 16,
24, 32, 40, 48, 56, 64; 24   **13.** 230   **15.** 576
17. $23,088; $23,244; $23,400; $23,556; $23,712,
$23,868   **19.** 6, 9; 18   **21.** $2 \cdot 3 \cdot n$ **23.** yes, at
18 ft and 36 ft from the beginning   **25.** C

3.2 Exercises, pp. 120–121

1. proper if less than 1, such as $\frac{5}{6}$; improper if
greater than or equal to 1, such as $\frac{9}{7}$
3. $8\frac{2}{3} = 8 + \frac{2}{3} = \frac{24}{3} + \frac{2}{3} = \frac{26}{3}$ **5.** 2.75 lb
7. improper; equal to 1   **9.** proper; less than 1
11. D   **13.** C   **15.** $1\frac{5}{6}$ **17.** $3\frac{1}{9}$ **19.** $\frac{16}{11}$
21. $\frac{25}{3}$ **23.** 4.25   **25.** 9.5   **27. a.** $\frac{7}{4}, \frac{5}{4}$
b. 7, 5; they are the numerators of the improper
fractions.   **29.** D

Spiral Review, p. 122

1. 10 mi   **3.** false; $20 \div (2 \times 5) + 7 = 9$ **5.** 1
7. 3   **9.** $\frac{2}{9}$ **11.** $\frac{5}{7}$

Using a Calculator, p. 123

1. 1.08   **3.** 0.60   **5.** 0.67   **7.** 0.23

3.3 Exercises, pp. 128–129

1. 24; find the least common multiple of 12 and 8.
3. your friend; $\frac{1}{10}$ mi   **5.** $\frac{9}{7}$ **7.** $\frac{23}{35}$ **9.** $\frac{1}{10}$
11. $1\frac{1}{8}$ **13.** yes; for example, $\frac{3}{4} + \frac{3}{4} = 1\frac{1}{2}$
15. $\frac{7}{10}, \frac{9}{10}, \frac{11}{10}; \frac{4}{5} + \frac{1}{2} = \frac{13}{10}, \frac{5}{5} + \frac{1}{2} = \frac{15}{10}$
17. $\frac{1}{4}$ **19.** $\frac{1}{3}$ **21.** $\frac{1}{6}$ **23.** $\frac{14}{25}$ **25.** $\frac{31}{100}$ **27.** D

3.4 Exercises, pp. 132–133

1. C, A, D, B   **3.** 11   **5.** 13   **7.** $5\frac{4}{5}$ **9.** $2\frac{2}{11}$
11. 3   **13.** 9   **15.** $8\frac{1}{9}$ **17.** $1\frac{4}{5}$ **19.** 7   **21.** $1\frac{3}{8}$
23. $3\frac{2}{3}$ **25.** $4\frac{5}{12}$ **27.** $9\frac{1}{5}$ **29.** $2\frac{1}{4}$ **31.** $6\frac{1}{3}$ ft;
$60 - 53\frac{2}{3} = 6\frac{1}{3}$ **33.** $5\frac{7}{12}$ ft; $40 - 34\frac{5}{12} = 5\frac{7}{12}$
35. 19 h   **37.** $3\frac{3}{4}$ in.   **39.** C

Spiral Review, p. 134

1. 4 square units   **3.** 3 m by 6 m   **5.** 72 in.^{2}
7. 256   **9.** $2 \times 2 \times 2 \times 2 \times 2 \times 2$
11. $3 \times 5 \times 7$ **13.** $2 \times 2 \times 2 \times 2 \times 5$

Mid-Chapter Assessment, p. 135

1. 42   **2.** 68   **3.** 110   **4.** 60   **5.** every
12 weeks   **6.** B   **7.** D   **8.** C   **9.** A   **10.** $\frac{4}{25}$
11. $\frac{39}{100}$ **12.** $\frac{9}{100}$ **13.** 1   **14.** $1\frac{7}{9}$ **15.** $6\frac{3}{5}$
16. $4\frac{4}{9}$ **17.** $9\frac{11}{24}$ **18.** $3\frac{1}{10}$ **19.** $2\frac{1}{4}$ **20.** $5\frac{17}{24}$
21. $\frac{2}{5}$, 0.4   **22.** $\frac{2}{3}$, 0.67   **23.** $\frac{1}{2}$, 0.5   **24.** $\frac{1}{2}$, 0.5

3.5 Exercises, pp. 140–141

1. $\frac{5}{6} \times 2\frac{1}{3} = 1\frac{17}{18}$ **3.** First rewrite as improper
fractions. Then multiply numerators and
denominators.   **5.** Both are correct.   **7.** always
9. never   **11.** $\frac{10}{27}$ **13.** $2\frac{1}{2}$ **15.** $12\frac{3}{8}$ **17.** $1\frac{1}{18}$
19. 13   **21.** $8\frac{2}{5}$ **23.** $7\frac{1}{3}$ ft^2 **25.** $4\frac{3}{8}$ m^2 **27.** D

3.6 Exercises, pp. 144–145

1. $\times, \times, \times$ **3.** The two 3's were added instead of
being used as a factor in applying the Distributive
Property; $3(10) + 3(15) = 3(10 + 15) = 3(25) =$
75   **5.** $5(t), 5 \times t, 5 \cdot t, 5t$ **7.** $5(4 + 3)$,
$5 \cdot 4 + 5 \cdot 3$ **9.** 55   **11.** 71   **13.** $3\frac{1}{5}$
15. $3t + 12$ **17.** $4c + 6c$ or $10c$ **19.** $x + 24$
21. 48, 48; they are the same.   **23.** 33.6
25. 125   **27.** 97.2   **29.** $20(2 + \frac{1}{2} + 5) =$
150 min, or $2\frac{1}{2}$ h   **31.** \$200.50   **33.** B

Spiral Review, p. 146

1. 15   **3.** 9   **5.** 9 people   **7.** 2, 3, 6   **9.** 17
11. 1   **13.** 35   **15.** $\frac{1}{2}$ **17.** $\frac{3}{4}$ **19.** $\frac{2}{5}$ **21.** $\frac{2}{5}$
23. $\frac{4}{5}$ **25.** $\frac{4}{5}$, 1.04, $\frac{7}{5}$, 1.45, $1\frac{1}{2}$, 1.7, $\frac{7}{4}$

3.7 Exercises, pp. 151–153

1. $2\frac{1}{2} \div \frac{5}{6} = 3$ **3.** Rewrite as improper fractions.
Multiply by reciprocal. Simplify fraction.
5. yes; 10   **7.** D   **9.** A   **11.** $1\frac{24}{25}$ **13.** $\frac{4}{11}$
15. $1\frac{17}{39}$ **17.** $\frac{3}{4}$ **19.** $\frac{1}{5}$ **21.** $1\frac{1}{2}$
23. $\frac{8}{3}$ **25.** $2\frac{1}{24}$ ft; $1\frac{1}{2}$ times   **27.** C

Chapter 3 Review, pp. 155–157

1. 18   **3.** 176   **5.** $6\frac{4}{5}$ **7.** 4.375   **9.** $2\frac{5}{12}$ ft
11. $7\frac{1}{24}$ **13.** $5\frac{3}{4}$ **15.** $6\frac{9}{10}$ million   **17.** $\frac{7}{12}$
19. 22.4   **21.** $\frac{5}{6}$

Chapters 1–3 Cumulative Review, pp. 160–161

3. similar   **5.** 8 m by 10 m   **7.** $102 - n = 54$; 48
9. $x \div 8 = 9$; 72   **11.** 17   **13.** 2   **15.** 1
17. False; *sample answer:* change 3 to 12.
19. true   **21.** False; *sample answer:* change 5
to 25.   **23.** $\frac{1}{10}$ **25.** $\frac{5}{7}$ **27.** $\frac{1}{6}$ **29.** 0.38
31. 0.17   **33.** 0.20   **35.** $\frac{2}{9}, \frac{1}{4}, \frac{3}{11}, \frac{2}{5}$
37. $\frac{4}{9}$, 0.49, 1.04, $\frac{7}{5}$ **39.** 77   **41.** 120   **43.** 80
45. $\frac{11}{25}$ **47.** $\frac{13}{20}$

Chapter 4

4.1 Exercises, pp. 170–171

1. 1, 6, 11, 16, 21   **3.** A   **5.** B

7.

x	1	2	3	4	5	6
$3x - 1$	2	5	8	11	14	17

9.

x	1	2	3	4	5	6
$4 + 5x$	9	14	19	24	29	34

11.

x	1	2	3	4	5	6
$7 - 4x$	3	–1	–5	–9	–13	–17

13. $2 + 3m$

m	1	2	3	4	5	6
$2 + 3m$	5	8	11	14	17	20

15. $10(m - 1)$

m	1	2	3	4	5	6
$10(m - 1)$	0	10	20	30	40	50

17. *Sample answer:* The value of the expression begins at 50. Each time n increases by 1, the value of the expression increases by 6.   **19.** *Sample answer:* For fewer than 7 letters, the first company offers the better deal. For 7 letters, both companies' prices agree. For more than 7 letters, the second company offers the best deal.   **21.** D

4.2 Exercises, pp. 174–175

1. C   **3.** D   **5.** A   **7.** (0, 0)   **9.** (0, 3)
11. (0, 0)   **13.** (3, 3)   **15.** (1, 2), (2, 4), (3, 6), (4, 8), (5, 10), (6, 12)

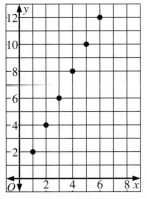

17.

x	1	2	3	4	5
y	4	8	12	16	20

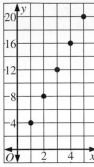

Sample answer: The points increase at regular intervals from left to right and appear to form a straight line.

19.

x	1	2	3	4	5
y	28.5	27	25.5	24	22.5

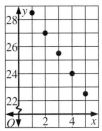

Sample answer: The points decrease at regular intervals from left to right and appear to form a straight line.

21.

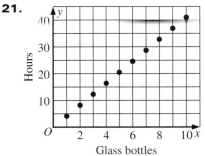

Sample answer: The points increase at regular intervals from left to right and appear to form a straight line.   **23.** B

Spiral Review, p. 176

1. *Sample answer:* With each fold, the number of regions doubles.   **3.** 28   **5.** 14   **7.** 4   **9.** >
11. >   **13.** $17\frac{4}{5}$ ft, $18\frac{7}{10}$ ft²

Using a Calculator, p. 177

1. 9.2; yes; *sample answer:* The area is the sum of the two widths.   **3.** 24.2; yes; *sample answer:* The area is the sum of the two widths.   **5.** *Sample answer:* Yes; for frames whose outer width is more than one greater than its inner width, the product of the difference of the widths and the sum of the widths of the two squares is the area of the frame.

4.3 Exercises, pp. 180–181

1. $3.5, -6\frac{1}{2}, -2.75$;

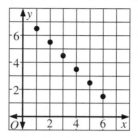

3. 0 **5.** *Sample answer:* $-5 < -2$ **7.** $-4, -6$; *sample answer:* The numbers are decreasing by two. **9.** 7, 13; *sample answer:* The numbers are increasing by increments that are also increasing by one. **11.** $>$ **13.** $<$ **15.** false;

17. -12 **19.** -45

21. $-9, -8, -3, 0, 3$ **23.** $-7, -5, -4.25, -\frac{7}{2}, -1\frac{3}{4}$
25. sole **27.** B **29.** D

4.4 Exercises, pp. 186–187

1. B **3.** A **5.** sometimes **7.** *Sample answer:* The subtraction keystroke should be a $\boxed{+/-}$ keystroke. **9.** $-6 + 5 = -1$ **11.** 13 **13.** 7
15. -15 **17.** 23 **19.** C; -1 **21.** A; 1
23. $-9, -5$ **25.** 5 **27.** 0 **29.** zero **31.** -4
33. 0 **35.** -367 ft **37.** A

Spiral Review, p. 188

1. three 3 lb bags and one 5 lb bag **3.** 36
5. 2, 5, 8 **7.** 2, 5, 8 **9.** $\frac{1}{3}$ **11.** 5
13. $\frac{1}{4}(8) + \frac{1}{4}(6); 3\frac{1}{2}$ **15.** $2(3.2 + 4.8); 16$

Mid-Chapter Assessment, p. 189

1.

x	1	2	3	4	5	6
$3x + 8$	11	14	17	20	23	26

2.

x	1	2	3	4	5	6
$100 - 5x$	95	90	85	80	75	70

3.

x	1	2	3	4	5	6
$120 \div x$	120	60	40	30	24	20

4. *Sample answer:* Cost increases $5 for every one unit of change in x. **5.** *Sample answer:* Cost decreases $7 for every one unit of change in x.
6. (2, 6), (3, 5), (4, 4), (5, 3), (6, 2), (7, 1)
7. $\left(1, 2\frac{1}{2}\right)$, (2, 3), $\left(3, 3\frac{1}{2}\right)$, (4, 4), $\left(5, 5\frac{1}{2}\right)$, (6, 6)
8.

x	1	2	3	4	5	6
y	1.5	2.5	3.5	4.5	5.5	6.5

(1, 1.5), (2, 2.5), (3, 3.5), (4, 4.5), (5, 5.5), (6, 6.5);

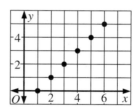

Sample answer: The points increase at regular intervals from left to right.

9.

x	1	2	3	4	5	6
y	$6\frac{1}{2}$	$5\frac{1}{2}$	$4\frac{1}{2}$	$3\frac{1}{2}$	$2\frac{1}{2}$	$1\frac{1}{2}$

$\left(1, 6\frac{1}{2}\right), \left(2, 5\frac{1}{2}\right), \left(3, 4\frac{1}{2}\right), \left(4, 3\frac{1}{2}\right), \left(5, 2\frac{1}{2}\right), \left(6, 1\frac{1}{2}\right)$;

Sample answer: The points decrease at regular intervals from left to right.

10.

x	1	2	3	4	5	6
y	0	1	2	3	4	5

(1, 0), (2, 1), (3, 2), (4, 3), (5, 4), (6, 5);

Sample answer: The points increase at regular intervals from left to right.

11. $-10, -5, -1, 4$ **12.** $-15, -13, -12, -11$
13. -11 **14.** 4 **15.** 4, -3, 0, -2; *sample answer:* His time for this race was 1 second faster than his previous best time.

4.5 Exercises, pp. 194–195

1. negative **3.** positive **5.** -10%
7. The model shows the addition of 3 units instead of the subtraction of 3 units;

$; -4 - 3 = -7$

9. B **11.** A **13.** -19 **15.** 17 **17.** -11
19. -48 **21.** -101 **23.** 111 **25.** 35 **27.** -34
29. 382 **31.** $2\frac{3}{4}$ in. **33.** $2\frac{1}{2}$ in. **35.** B

4.6 Exercises, pp. 200–201

1. *Sample answer:* -12 was added to both sides of the equation. **3.** B **5.** C **7.** yes; *sample answer:* Only the order of the equations has been changed. **9.** -14 **11.** -23 **13.** -50 **15.** 0.9 **17.** $\frac{1}{2}$ **19.** 1991; 1994; *sample answer:*
1990–1991: $x + 983 = 1017$, $x - 34$;
1991–1992: $x + 1017 = 1119$, $x = 102$;
1992–1993: $x + 1119 = 1458$, $x = 339$;
1993–1994: $x + 1458 = 2254$, $x = 796$;
1994–1995: $x + 2254 = 2517$, $x = 263$
21. $x + 10 = 10$; 0 **23.** $-20 = 14 + x$; -34
25. $x + 32 = 212$; $180°$ **27.** Amount to be spent on CDs + Cost of blank cassettes = Total amount; Amount to be spent on CDs = x; Cost of blank cassettes = \$8.75; Total amount = \$28.00; $x + 8.75 = 28$; $x = \$19.25$; *sample answer:* You could buy two CD singles for \$8.50 each or one album CD for \$15.85. You could not buy a double CD set for \$24.50. **29.** C

Spiral Review, p. 202

1. 34 mm, 48 mm^2 **3.** 3^4 **5.** $2^4 \times 7$ **7.** $\frac{3}{5}$
9. $\frac{8}{9}$ **11.** D **13.** B **15.** -3 **17.** 10

4.7 Exercises, pp. 206–207

1. Subtract 11 from both sides of the equation.
3. Add 15 to both sides of the equation. **5.** A
7. B **9.** 65 **11.** negative; -8 **13.** positive; 23
15. *Sample answer:* $-9 = b + 7$, $-20 = b - 4$
17. 0 **19.** 34 **21.** -23 **23.** 3.33 **25.** $3\frac{1}{2}$
27. $26 = n + 40$; -14 **29.** yes; *sample answer:*
By the Commutative Property of Addition $-3 + x$ is the same expression as $x + (-3)$, which also can be written as $x - 3$. So, $-3 + x = 5$ and $x - 3 = 5$ represent the same equation and must have the same solution. **31.** 3 **33.** Original price $-$ Amount off original price = Sale price; Original price = p, Amount off original price = \$9, Sale price = \$27; $p - 9 = 27$; $p = \$36$ **35.** C

Chapter 4 Review, pp. 209–211

1.

n	1	2	3	4	5	6
$n + 4$	5	6	7	8	9	10

3.

n	1	2	3	4	5	6
$3n - 13$	-10	-7	-4	-1	2	5

5. *Sample answer:* The value of the expression begins at 23. Each time t increases by 1, the value of the expression decreases by 1; $23 - t$.
7. $(4, 3)$ **9.** $(1, 5), (2, 4), (3, 2), (4, 3), (5, 1)$

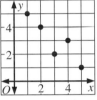

11. $-70, -54, -48, -46, -45, -35, -34, -32$
13. -17 **15.** 0 **17.** $-5 + 6 + (-2) + 1 = 0$; yes **19.** 16 **21.** -5 **23.** 26 **25.** $3.25 + x = 8.00$; \$4.75 **27.** 0

Chapter 5

5.1 Exercises, pp. 222–223

1. The median is 15.5, not 15. **3.** The median is 14, not 16. **5.** 120 **7.** \$2.45, \$2.45, \$3.00, \$3.15, \$3.25, \$3.25, \$3.25, \$4.00, \$4.00, \$5.00; \$3.38, \$3.25, \$3.25 **9.** 1, 1, 3, 3, 3, 3, 3, 3, 3, 4, 4, 4, 4, 4, 5, 5, 6, 6, 7, 8; 4, 4, 3 **11.** 8.24, 8, 8; 8; the measures of central tendency are all about 8. **13.** *Sample answer:* 25, 25, 25, 25, 30 **15.** The mean would be about \$41,457, but the median and mode would not change. **17.** D

5.2 Exercises, pp. 228–229

1.

Interval	Tally	Frequency
1–1.9	IIII	4
2–2.9	₩ III	8
3–3.9	₩	5
4–4.9	III	3
5–5.9	₩ II	7
6 plus	III	3

Sample answer: The table in Ex. 1 best represents the data because the intervals in the table in Ex. 2 are so large that the data are too condensed.
3. 0–14; 75–99

5.

Interval	Tally	Frequency
1–9	### IIII	9
10–19	### ### I	11
20–29	### ### I	11
30–39	### I	6
40–49	IIII	4
50–59	II	2
60–69	II	2
70–79	I	1
80–89	III	3
90–99	I	1

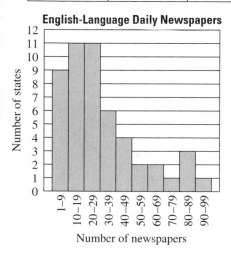

7. B

Spiral Review, p. 230

1. A, 0; B, 9; C, 1; D, 8; E, 2; F, 7; G, 3; H, 6; I, 4; J, 5   **3.** *Sample answer:* 28   **5.** *Sample answer:* 80   **7, 9.** *Sample answer:* Points appear to form a straight line.

7.

x	y
1	$\frac{1}{5}$
2	$\frac{2}{5}$
3	$\frac{3}{5}$
4	$\frac{4}{5}$
5	1
6	$\frac{6}{5}$

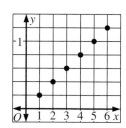

9.

x	y
1	10
2	8
3	6
4	4
5	2
6	0

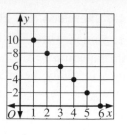

Using a Spreadsheet, p. 231

1.

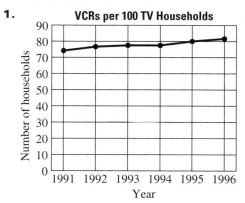

about 84 VCRs per 100 TV households

5.3 Exercises, pp. 236–237

1. first   **3.** upper

5.

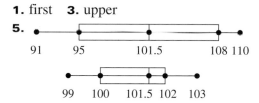

7. B   **9.** D

11.

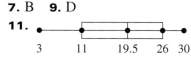

13. *Sample answer:* The women's winning times are greater than the men's; the women's winning times have a wider range than the men's.   **15.** C

5.4 Exercises, pp. 240–241

1. (–5, 1)   **3.** (0, 0)   **5.** (6, 0)   **7.** II   **9.** I
11. At least one is zero.

13.

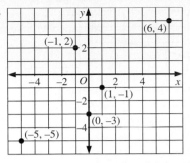

15.

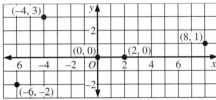

17.

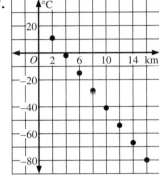

Sample answer: As height increases, temperature decreases.

19.

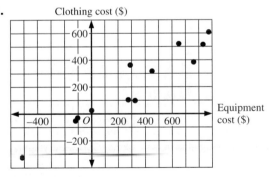

21. about $140   **23.** C

Spiral Review, p. 242

1. 7   **3.** 10   **5.** 50   **7.** 1 ft-by-1 ft: 768;
2 ft-by-2 ft: 192; 4 ft-by-4 ft: 48; 8 ft-by-8 ft: 12
9. *E*   **11.** –9   **13.** 0   **15.** 14.4

17. *Sample answer:*

Interval	Tally	Frequency
42–45	II	2
46–49	### I	6
50–53	### III	8
54–57	### ### ###	15
58–61	###	5
62–65	IIII	4
66–69	II	2

Mid-Chapter Assessment, page 243

1. 3.6, 4, 4   **2.** $49, $45, $45   **3.** 17, 19, 21
4. *Sample answer:*

Interval	Tally	Frequency
1–5	### ###	10
6–10	### III	8
11–15	### IIII	9
16–20	IIII	4
21–25		0
26–30	IIII	4
31–35	###	5
36–40	I	1
41–45	II	2
46–50	II	2
51 +	II	2

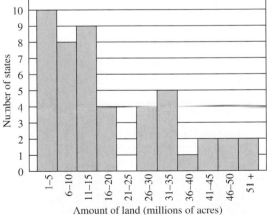

5.

41   62 70.5 81   100

6. *Sample answer:* Half the soaps give you between 62 and 81 hand washes.

7.

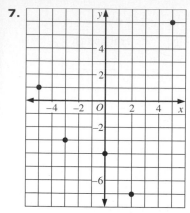

8.

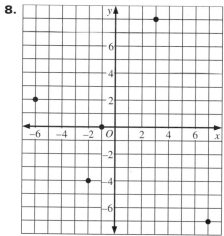

9. Score

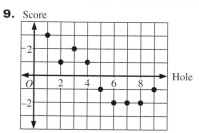

10. *Sample answer:* The first four scores are positive and the last five scores are negative.

5.5 Exercises, pp. 246–247

1.

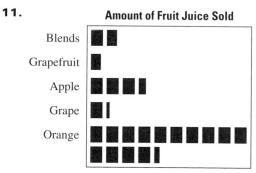

3. 5 ft/s, 10 ft/s, 9 ft/s, 6 ft/s, 2 ft/s **5.** 5 ft/s

7.

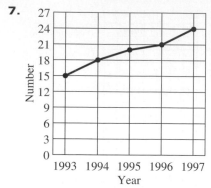

Sample answer: As the year increases, the number increases.

9.

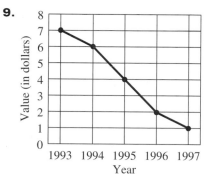

Sample answer: As the year increases, the dollar value decreases.

11.

Amount of Fruit Juice Sold

Blends, Grapefruit, Apple, Grape, Orange

Key: = 50 gallons

13.

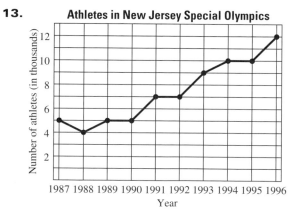

Athletes in New Jersey Special Olympics

15.

Favorite Pickles

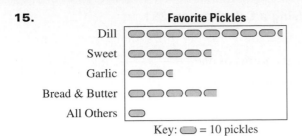

Key: ⬭ = 10 pickles

17. B

5.6 Exercises, pp. 250–251

1. *Sample answer:* A broken scale distorts the data. **3.** The number of hours for 1996 is about $1\frac{1}{2}$ times the number for 1991. The graph is misleading because the broken scale distorts the data. **5.** A little more than twice as many people play basketball as volleyball; the graph is misleading because the broken scale distorts the data.

7. It appears that about $2\frac{1}{2}$ times as many people in the West prefer Winter Olympics, that people in the Central and Northeast United States greatly prefer the Winter Olympics, and that people in the South prefer the Summer Olympics; the broken scale distorts the data, so the preferences seems larger. **9.** The amount spent increased from 1990 to 1996. **11.** about $3\frac{1}{3}$ billion dollars **15.** D

Spiral Review, p. 252

1. dining room, family/living room, kitchen, bedroom **3.** D **5.** A
7. $d = -3 + 2c$;

c	0	1	2	3	4	5
d	−3	−1	1	3	5	7

9. 0, 1, 2, 2, 3, 3, 4, 4, 4, 4, 4, 4, 5, 5, 5, 7; about 3.6, 4, 4

5.7 Exercises, pp. 258–259

1. A or B **3.** F **5.** C **7.** B **9.** A **11.** $\frac{12}{77}$, or about 0.16 **13.** $\frac{2}{13}$, or about 0.15 **15.** 0.47
17. 0.95 **19.** D

Chapter 5 Review, pp. 261–263

1. $350 **3.** $400
5. (Histogram for Ex. 4)

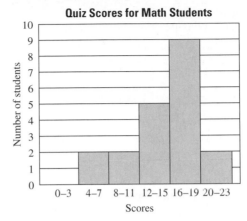

Quiz Scores for Math Students

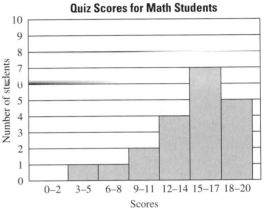

Quiz Scores for Math Students

Sample answer: The data in the second histogram are less condensed than the data in the first histogram.

7. 26
9.

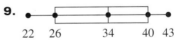

11.

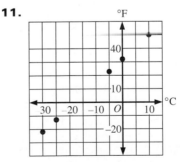

As degrees Celsius increase, degrees Fahrenheit increase, and the points lie on a line.
13. The broken scale distorts the data. **15.** The vertical scale is not distorted. **17.** 1; the sun rises every day.

Chapter 6

6.1 Exercises, pp. 274–275

1. $\frac{1}{3}$ **3.** $\frac{5 \text{ balloons}}{3 \text{ balloons}}$ **5.** $\frac{9 \text{ ft}}{15 \text{ ft}}$; $\frac{3 \text{ yd}}{5 \text{ yd}}$; yes   **7.** No; in a ratio, units of measure must be the same.

9. Yes; in a ratio, units of measure must be the same.   **11.** $\frac{0.75 \text{ yd}}{2 \text{ yd}} = \frac{3}{8}$; $\frac{27 \text{ in.}}{72 \text{ in.}} = \frac{3}{8}$; yes

13. $\frac{5280 \text{ ft}}{2640 \text{ ft}} = \frac{2}{1}$; $\frac{1 \text{ mi}}{0.5 \text{ mi}} = \frac{2}{1}$; yes   **15.** $\frac{2}{3}$ **17.** $\frac{6}{7}$

19. $\frac{5}{176}$ **21.** $\frac{21}{13}$ **23.** A

6.2 Exercises, pp. 278–279

1. *Sample answer:* A ratio is a fraction in which the numerator and denominator have the same unit of measure, while a rate is a fraction in which the numerator and denominator have different units of measure. For example, $\frac{1 \text{ cup}}{4 \text{ cups}} = \frac{1}{4}$ is a ratio, while $\frac{8 \text{ cups}}{1 \text{ gal}}$ is a rate.   **3.** 50 mi/h

5. $\frac{28 \text{ mi}}{1 \text{ gal}}$; rate   **7.** $\frac{33}{25}$; ratio   **9.** $\frac{\$.0273}{1 \text{ sheet}}$, or $\frac{2.73\cancel{c}}{1 \text{ sheet}}$

11. $\frac{\$15}{1 \text{ day}}$ **13. a.** $\frac{\$1.08}{2 \text{ lb}} = \frac{\$.54}{1 \text{ lb}}$ **b.** $\frac{\$2.10}{5 \text{ lb}} = \frac{\$.42}{1 \text{ lb}}$

c. $\frac{\$3.95}{10 \text{ lb}} = \frac{\$.40}{1 \text{ lb}}$; *sample answer:* The potatoes in (c) are the best buy, since they cost least per pound of potatoes.   **15.** typical adult: 2500 cal/day; Olympic athlete: 10,000 cal/day

17. 48.6 h/year; about 32 movies/year

19. Chung: $\frac{126 \text{ words}}{3 \text{ min}} = \frac{42 \text{ words}}{1 \text{ min}}$;

Shana: $\frac{240 \text{ words}}{5 \text{ min}} = \frac{48 \text{ words}}{1 \text{ min}}$;

Randy: $\frac{180 \text{ words}}{4 \text{ min}} = \frac{45 \text{ words}}{1 \text{ min}}$; Shana typed the fastest, since her rate per minute is the highest.

21. C

Spiral Review, p. 280

1. 81   **3.** 256   **5.** 0.56   **7.** 0.27   **9.** $\frac{9}{10}$

11. 25   **13.** −10

15.

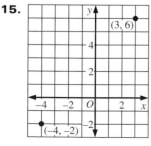

Using a Calculator, p. 281

1. 68.2 mi/h   **3.** 117.3 ft/s; multiplying 80 mi/h by the forms of one $\frac{1 \text{ h}}{60 \text{ min}}$, $\frac{1 \text{ min}}{60 \text{ s}}$, and $\frac{5280 \text{ ft}}{1 \text{ mi}}$ gives an equivalent rate in ft/s.

6.3 Exercises, pp. 286–287

1. B   **3.** A   **5.** C; 1   **7.** not true   **9.** true

11. $\frac{p}{21} = \frac{11}{33}$; 7   **13.** $\frac{9}{6} = \frac{m}{18}$; 27   **15.** $\frac{28}{w} = \frac{36}{9}$; 7

17. $\frac{13}{52}$ **19.** 1   **21.** 1   **23.** 12   **27.** 55.1 lb

29. $x = 5.5$, so the image will be 5.5 in. wide.

31. D

6.4 Exercises, pp. 290–291

1. a. $\frac{4}{13} = \frac{n}{52}$

$\frac{4 \cdot 4}{4 \cdot 13} = \frac{n}{52}$

$\frac{16}{52} = \frac{n}{52}$

Because the denominators are equal, it follows that $n = 16$.

b. $\frac{4}{13} = \frac{n}{52}$

$4 \cdot 52 = 13 \cdot n$

$\frac{208}{13} = \frac{13 \cdot n}{13}$

$16 = n$

3. D   **5.** C   **7.** true   **9.** not true   **11.** true

13. not true   **15.** 12   **17.** 87   **19.** 4   **21.** 4.5

23. $\frac{54 \text{ in.}}{90 \text{ in.}} = \frac{3}{5}$, $\frac{57 \text{ in.}}{95 \text{ in.}} = \frac{3}{5}$ **25.** 24.14   **27.** 63.64

29. true; *sample answer:* If $\frac{3}{4} = \frac{9}{12}$, then $\frac{12}{4} = \frac{9}{3}$ is true because each side equals 3.   **31.** 9.6 h, or 9 h 36 min   **33.** C   **35.** C

Spiral Review, p. 292

1. $\frac{17}{24}$ **3.** $\frac{17}{30}$ **5.** $5\frac{1}{3}$ **7.** −15   **9.** 5   **11.** $\frac{1}{2}$

13. $\frac{5}{16}$

Mid-Chapter Assessment, p. 293

1. $\frac{49}{300}$ **2.** $\frac{32}{25}$ **3.** $\frac{11}{15}$ **4.** $\frac{74 \text{ cal}}{1 \text{ oz}}$, or 74 calories per ounce   **5.** $\frac{500 \text{ pieces}}{1 \text{ in.}}$, or 500 pieces per inch   **6.** $\frac{k}{12} = \frac{5}{60}$; 1   **7.** $\frac{x}{6} = \frac{6}{2}$; 18   **8.** $\frac{4}{7} = \frac{m}{35}$; 20

9. $\frac{72}{9} = \frac{s}{4}$; 32   **10.** true   **11.** not true   **12.** true

13. Sam Houston: about $.19/mi, Delaware: about $.11/mi, Daniel Boone: about $.03/mi, Chicago: about $.26/mi; the Chicago Skyway is most expensive because it costs about 26¢ per mile.
14. Equation (b); $x = 152.9$, so Geoff took about 153 steps per minute.   **15.** $x = 857{,}143$, so you must mine about 857,000 pounds of rock to produce 1 ounce of diamonds.

6.5 Exercises, pp. 296–297

1. 330 min, or 5 h 30 min   **3.** 2 in. wide, 3 in. long; $\frac{2 \text{ in.}}{3 \text{ in.}} = \frac{x}{154}$; 103 in.   **5.** You cannot use C; 9 in.; *sample answer:* Cross multiply and then divide both sides of the equation by 2.
7. *Sample answer:* The $250 in a savings account grows with interest to $275. If you had put $1200 in this account instead, how much would it be worth? Let $x =$ the amount $1200 would be worth. Then $\frac{\$275}{\$250} = \frac{\$x}{\$1200}$, so $x = \$1320$.
9. *Sample answer:* $\frac{\$1300}{\$2500} = \frac{325 \text{ ft}^2}{x \text{ ft}^2}$; 625 ft^2
11. *Sample answer:* $\frac{4 \text{ people/mi}^2}{3 \text{ people/mi}^2} = \frac{97 \text{ people/mi}^2}{p \text{ people/mi}^2}$; 73 people/mi^2 **13.** C

6.6 Exercises, pp. 302–303

3. no   **5.** 60°   **7.** $\frac{24}{41.6} = \frac{15}{26}$, since the cross-products are equal.
9. *Sample answer:* Angles K and S measure 270°, and all other angles measure 90°; $\frac{GH}{PQ} = \frac{3}{4}, \frac{HJ}{RQ} = \frac{3}{4}, \frac{JK}{RS} = \frac{3}{4}, \frac{KL}{ST} = \frac{3}{4}, \frac{LM}{UT} = \frac{3}{4}, \frac{MG}{UP} = \frac{3}{4}$; because corresponding angles are equal and the corresponding sides are proportional, the polygons are similar.   **11.** Yes; all angles measure 90°, and the ratio of any two sides is $\frac{1}{1}$.   **13.** 27
15. angle $F = 45°$, angle $G = 45°$, $FG = 21$, $XZ = 25$
17. $\frac{\text{Height of building}}{\text{Height of Ferris wheel}} = \frac{\text{Length of building's shadow}}{\text{Length of Ferris wheel's shadow}}$; 344.5 ft
19. A

Spiral Review, p. 304

Spiral Review, p. 304

1. three 2 gal containers and two 0.5 gal containers   **3.** $=$ **5.** B   **7.** A   **9.** $\frac{5}{9}$ **11.** $\frac{1}{7}$
13. $-9 = n - 16$; 7   **15.** $\frac{7}{3}$ **17.** $\frac{1}{12}$

6.7 Exercises, pp. 308–309

1. C   **3.** B   **5.** 40 in.   **9.** $2\frac{2}{3}$ mi   **11.** 21.6 mi
13. 384 ft   **15.** 299 mi   **17.** 143 mi   **19.** 1.5 in.
21. 100 ft   **23.** D

Chapter 6 Review, pp. 311–313

1. $\frac{10}{3}$ **3.** $\frac{64}{3}$ **5.** $\frac{1}{4}$ **7.** $\frac{26 \text{ mi}}{1 \text{ gal}}$ **9.** 3   **11.** $\frac{7}{9}$
13. 65   **15.** 51
17. $\frac{\text{Amount of water flow each second}}{\text{Total amount of flow}} = \frac{1 \text{ second}}{\text{Total seconds}}$; Total time $= x$; $\frac{750{,}000 \text{ gal}}{3{,}000{,}000 \text{ gal}} = \frac{1 \text{ s}}{x \text{ s}}$; 4 s
19. 4 in. long, 3 in. wide

Chapters 1–6 Cumulative Review, pp. 316–317

1. shape with 4 sides   **3.** shape with 3 sides
5. Kay, May, Ray, Fay   **7.** 16   **9.** $2^3 \cdot 3^2$
11. $2^4 \cdot 7$ **13.** 2; 42   **15.** 5; 150   **17.** B
19. A   **21.** 1.05, 1.1, $\frac{9}{8}, \frac{6}{5}$, 1.25, $\frac{3}{2}$ **23.** $\frac{3}{20}$
25. $10\frac{1}{24}$ **27.** $8\frac{1}{2}$ **29.** $\frac{25}{24}$

31.

x	1	2	3	4	5	6
y	4	2	0	−2	−4	−6

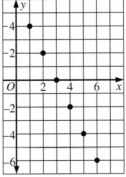

33. −25 ft   **35.** 136, 133, 131

37.

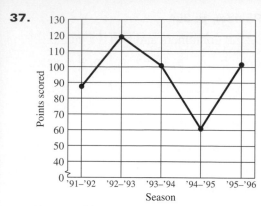

Points scored vs. Season graph

39. 5   **41.** 12

Chapter 7

7.1 Exercises, pp. 324–325

1. *Sample answer:* Words with "cent" have to do with one hundred (cents in a dollar, centimeter, Centigrade, centipede). So, percent means per hundred, and a percent is a fraction with a denominator of 100—the numerator tells how many of something there are per 100.   **3.** *Sample answer:* The decimal 0.625 is another way to write the fraction $\frac{625}{1000}$. Then you can divide the numerator and denominator by 10 to rewrite $\frac{625}{1000}$ as $\frac{62.5}{100}$. Because this is now a ratio with a denominator of 100, you can rewrite it as a percent, 62.5%.

7. 0.08; $\frac{2}{25}$ **9.** 0.45; $\frac{9}{20}$ **11.** $\frac{78}{100}$; 78%

13. $\frac{9.5}{100}$; 9.5%   **15.** 56%   **17.** 87.5%   **19.** 44%

21. 27%   **23.** $\frac{14}{25}$; this is equivalent to $\frac{56}{100}$, while all of the other numbers are equivalent to $\frac{68}{100}$.

29. Science and Nature: 37.5%; Geography: 15.625%; Sports and Leisure: 15.625%; Art and Literature: 6.25%; Entertainment: 6.25%; History: 18.75%; the total of the percents is 100%; this means that all 160 people in the survey are accounted for.   **31.** B

7.2 Exercises, pp. 330–331

1. 2.5 miles; 75 miles   **3.** 0.45 orange; 27 oranges

5. a. 66 baseball cards

200 baseball cards

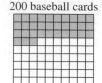

Each square represents 2 cards.

b. *Sample answer:* Find the value of 1% of the cards, which is 2 cards. Then multiply this value by the given percent (33). Or, multiply 200 by 0.33.   **7.** 54%, 27 hours   **9.** 92%, 460 cups

11. 40 questions   **13.** 0.5; 20   **15.** 8; 320

17. 156   **19.** 120   **21.** 45   **23.** 54

25. *Sample answer:* 34   **27.** 219   **29.** D

Spiral Review, p. 332

1. $\frac{9}{36}$, $\frac{1}{4}$ **3.** $\frac{16}{28}$, $\frac{4}{7}$ **5.** 1 ft 2 in., or 14 in., or $1\frac{1}{6}$ ft

7. 35   **9.** 27

Using a Calculator, p. 333

1. 31,000   **3.** 700,000

7.3 Exercises, pp. 338–339

1. 164%   **3.** B   **5.** A   **7.** 390   **9.** 72 in.

11. 1.7, $1\frac{7}{10}$ or $\frac{17}{10}$ **13.** 0.00375, $\frac{3}{800}$ **15.** 4.5,

$4\frac{1}{2}$ or $\frac{9}{2}$ **17.** 650%   **19.** 0.875%   **21.** 55 points

23. 0.5 day   **25.** >   **27.** =   **29.** 165, 240, 325, 420; *sample answer:* Add 75, then 85, then 95, and so on; 525, 640.   **31.** about 13,200

33. D

7.4 Exercises, pp. 344–345

1. $\frac{17}{20} = \frac{p}{100}$; 85%   **3.** $\frac{25}{b} = \frac{20}{100}$; 125   **5.** The

equation should be $\frac{36}{150} = \frac{p}{100}$; 24%   **7.** 750

9. 200   **11.** 18   **13.** 25%   **15.** 9   **17.** 8; 8; 8; the percents double, the bases are halved, and the numbers are all 8.   **19.** 15; 30; 45; the percents increase by 25, the bases stay the same, and the numbers are multiples of 15.   **21.** 72   **23.** A

Spiral Review, p. 346

1. $\frac{2}{3}$ **3.** $1\frac{2}{3}$ **5.** $\frac{25}{36}$ ft^2, or 100 in.^{2} **7.** $3\frac{3}{8}$ yd^2

9. −7   **11.** −2   **13.** 61   **15.** about 84 bowlers per day

Mid-Chapter Assessment, p. 347

1. 12.4% **2.** 35% **3.** 6.7% **4.** 75% **5.** 289%
6. $\frac{5}{9}$% **7.** 3.7% **8.** 406.25% **9.** 75%, 180 ft
10. 65%, 16.25 muffins **11.** 22%, 35.2 lb
12. $<$ **13.** $>$ **14.** $=$ **15.** 132 **16.** 600
17. 117 **18.** 8 **19.** $100 **20.** $24.75
21. a. 25,000 **b.** 1900

7.5 Exercises, pp. 350–351

1. *Sample answer:* Find out what percent of the total data fit into each category. Then you can multiply this percent by the 360° in a circle to find out how large to make the angle for the section of the circle a given category occupies. To check, make sure that the percents add to 100% and that the degrees add to 360°. **3.** fractions clockwise from top: $\frac{3}{20}$, $\frac{1}{5}$; angles clockwise from top: 72°, 36°, 198° **5.** *Sample answer:* You can make a circle graph because the six categories total 200, which is the number of people in the survey.

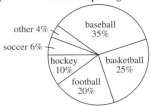
Favorite Sporting Event

baseball 35%
other 4%
soccer 6%
hockey 10%
basketball 25%
football 20%

7. 95 **9.** 4
11. *Sample answer:*

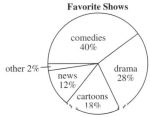
Favorite Shows

comedies 40%
other 2%
news 12%
drama 28%
cartoons 18%

13. *Sample answer:* Show that the percents total 100%: 40% + 28% + 18% + 12% + 2% = 100%.
15. *Sample answer:*

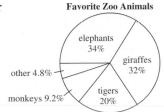
Favorite Zoo Animals

elephants 34%
giraffes 32%
other 4.8%
tigers 20%
monkeys 9.2%

17. C **19.** C

Spiral Review, p. 352

1. 48; each number is 3 less than the preceding number. **3.** 100 **5.** 320

7.

x	1	2	3	4	5
y	2	1	0	−1	−2

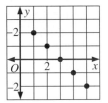
The points all lie on a line that slopes down to the right. When the x-value increases by 1, the y-value decreases by 1.

9. 4.25, 4.3, 4.4 **11.** 10 ft **13.** 625%; *sample answer:* All of the other numbers are ways to write $\frac{5}{8}$, but 625% is the same as $6\frac{1}{4}$.

7.6 Exercises, pp. 356–357

1. C **3.** D **5.** *Sample answer:* No; even if your friend kept the money for a whole year, the interest would only be $5. **7.** $\frac{1}{4}$ **9.** $\frac{2}{3}$ **11.** $20
13. $200 **15.** $320 **17.** $560
19. about $35.3 billion **21.** $18.75; $1268.75
23. $1350; $13,350 **25.** $135; $1035
27. $12.89 **29.** $13.08 **31.** A

7.7 Exercises, pp. 360–361

1. C **3.** A **5.** true; 100% is the same as one times the number, which is the number itself.
7. *Sample answer:* If you do not have a very low score, you might prefer to have the scores increased by 5%. Then, for example, if your original score was 160, your score would increase to 168, instead of just to 165 as under the other option. **9.** 50% increase **11.** 60% decrease
13. 25% increase **15.** about 9.06%
17. about 50% **19.** about 75%
21. about 10.0% **23.** about 12.2% **25.** D

Chapter 7 Review, pp. 363–365

1. 32% **3.** 0.4, $\frac{2}{5}$ **5.** 0.72, $\frac{18}{25}$ **7. a.** 28%
b. 126 ft **9.** 5.88 **11.** 0.025 **13.** 300
15. 60% **17.** 180 **19.** $2.25 **21.** 11.1%
23. about 18.5%

Chapter 8

8.1 Exercises, pp. 376–377

1. ∠1 and ∠3, ∠2 and ∠4, ∠5 and ∠7, ∠6 and ∠8 **3. a.** false **b.** false **c.** true **d.** true
5. 60° **7.** 90° **9.** never **11.** sometimes
13. never **15.** ∠1: 45°, ∠2: 90° **17.** 50° **19.**
Sample answer: vertical angles: ∠1 and ∠3, ∠2 and ∠4; adjacent angles: ∠1 and ∠2, ∠2 and ∠3, ∠3 and ∠4, ∠1 and ∠4; supplementary angles: ∠1 and ∠2, ∠2 and ∠3, ∠3 and ∠4, ∠1 and ∠4

21. Main Street and Oak Street **23.** B

8.2 Exercises, pp. 382–383

1. 5 units to the right and 6 units up **3.** *Sample answer:* 1 and 3, 2 and 4, 5 and 7, 6 and 8
5. 4 units to the left and 3 units down
7. $G(2, 2)$, $H(8, 2)$, $J(8, -4)$ **11.** A and F; 36 units to the right and 1 unit down **13.** B

Spiral Review, p. 384

1. 1 quarter, 2 dimes, and 4 nickels **3.** 6 **5.** 42
7. 60 **9.** $\frac{1}{21}$ **11.** 2 **13.** $1\frac{25}{27}$

8.3 Exercises, pp. 388–389

1. *Sample answer:* The circumference is the distance around a circle. The diameter is the width of the circle at its widest point. The radius is the distance from the circle's edge to its center.
3. 12.56 ft **5.** 14.915 in. **7.** 31.4 in.
9. 62.8 ft **11.** It doubles. For example, a circle of diameter 5 has circumference 5π, while a circle of diameter 10 has circumference 10π. It doubles. For example, a circle of radius 3 has diameter 6 and therefore circumference 6π, while a circle of radius 6 has diameter 12 and therefore circumference 12π. **13.** C **15.** about 1.80 cm
17. about 0.16 in. **19.** 37.68 ft **21.** C

8.4 Exercises, pp. 392–393

1. 6 units, 3 units **3.** 18 units² **5.** 12 cm
7. 49 ft²
9. *Sample answer:*

11. *Sample answer:*

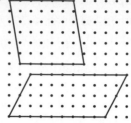

13. 17 in. **15.** $4\frac{1}{8}$ ft **17.** All; by definition, a parallelogram is a quadrilateral whose opposite sides are parallel. **19.** Some; a parallelogram doesn't have to be a rectangle, since it doesn't have to have right angles. **21.** $3\frac{1}{2}$ in.² **23.** D

Spiral Review, p. 394

1. false; $3 + 7 \times (9 - 5) = 38$ **3.** true
5. false; $(13 - 5) \div 4 + 2 = 4$ **7.** 10.9, 9.5, 9
9. 15.33, 17, 12 **11.** 15 **13.** 6 **15.** left figure: 25 cm, right figure: side 6 cm and top 8 cm

Mid-Chapter Assessment, p. 395

1. false **2.** true **3.** true **4.** true **5.** *Sample answer:* ∠3 is congruent because ∠1 and ∠3 are vertical angles. ∠5 is congruent because ∠2 is supplementary to both ∠1 and ∠5, so ∠1 and ∠5 must be congruent. **6.** ∠1 and ∠4, ∠3 and ∠4, ∠2 and ∠3, ∠1 and ∠2, ∠5 and ∠8, ∠7 and ∠8, ∠6 and ∠7, ∠5 and ∠6 **7.** 125°; ∠4 and ∠2 are congruent because they are vertical angles, so ∠2 measures 55°. Because ∠2 and ∠5 are supplementary, ∠5 has measure $180° - 55° = 125°$.
8. $L(-5, 2)$, $M(-6, -2)$, $N(0, 1)$ **9.** $G(-1, 6)$, $H(-3, 3)$, $J(2, 2)$, $K(4, 5)$ **10.** about 3 m
11. about 25 mm **12.** 4.5 cm **13.** 224 in.²
14. 80 in.²

8.5 Exercises, pp. 398–399

3. C **5.** The height is perpendicular to the bases, so the height is 40, not 42. The area is $26 \cdot 40 = 1040$ cm². **7.** 9000 mm² **9.** 11.96 ft²
11. 14.24 m² **13.** $18\frac{1}{16}$ mi²
15. *Sample answer:*

17. 2 mi **19.** 60 units² **21.** C

8.6 Exercises, pp. 402–403

1. A **3.** D **5.** about 92.86 ft²

7. about 730.2 cm² **9.** about 200.96 in.²
11. about 314 cm², about 62.8 cm
13. about 615.44 mi², about 87.92 mi
15. about 110.79 ft² **17.** a
19. about 17,662.5 mi² **21.** about 651.1 in.²
23. about 1157.5 in.² **25.** C

Spiral Review, p. 404

1. 1, 3, 5, 7, 9 **3.** D **5.** A **7.** zero; 0
9. negative; –6 **11.** positive; 28 **13.** $LM = 9$
15. 25 **17.** 24

8.7 Exercises, pp. 408–409

1. The number 9 times itself is 81. The square root of 81 is 9. **3.** *Sample answer:* 121, 144, 169
5. C; $\sqrt{108}$ is between 10 and 11. **7.** 5 **9.** 1
11. 9.1 **13.** about 7.75 **15.** 9.7 yd; the area of a square is s^2, so $s = \sqrt{94.09}$. **17.** about 7.75 yd; the area of the triangle is 30 yd², so the area of a square with sides of length s is 60. The area of a square is s^2, so $s = \sqrt{60}$. **19.** about 3.16
21. about 13.53 **23.** about 4.90
25. about 20.02 **27.** $a = 256$, $b = 16$, $c = 4$, $d = 2$ **29.** 32 units²; $4\sqrt{2}$ units **31.** C

8.8 Exercises, pp. 414–415

1. right, legs, hypotenuse **3.** 900, 2500, 1600, 40
5. $\overline{DF}$ **7.** obtuse **9.** acute **11.** right; about 5.66 cm **13.** about 39.05 **15.** about 114.13
17. 36 in. **19.** about 10.11 ft **21.** C

Chapter 8 Review, pp. 417–419

1. $\angle 3 = 35°$, $\angle 7 = 90°$, $\angle 8 = 35°$, $\angle 9 = 55°$
3. (3, 0), (6, 3), (8, 4), (7, –2) **5.** 34.54 ft **7.** 8 m
9. 8 units² **11.** 7.5 units² **13.** 54 units²
15. about 113.04 in.² **17.** 5.8 **19.** about 9.49
21. right; 26

Chapter 9

9.1 Exercises, pp. 430–431

1. No; faces are not polyhedrons. **3.** yes; triangular prism **5.** face, vertex, edge
9. **11.** **13.** yes; 5

15. yes; 6 **17.** C; the nets in A and B would fold into boxes with a missing face. **19.** B

9.2 Exercises, pp. 434–435

1. 12 in.², 12 in.², 100 in.², 100 in.², 160 in.²
3. A **5.** A; 52 units² **7.** $13\frac{1}{8}$ in.²
9. 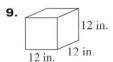 **11.** 204.8 cm²

12 in.
12 in. 12 in.

13. A; the dimensions of a sugar cube are about $\frac{1}{2}$ in. $\times$ $\frac{1}{2}$ in. $\times$ $\frac{1}{2}$ in. Its surface area is about $6\left(\frac{1}{4}\text{ in.}^2\right) = 1.5$ in.². **15.** 402 in.² **17.** D

Spiral Review, p. 436

1. $\frac{1}{12}$ **3.** 12 **5.** $\frac{33}{8}$, or $4\frac{1}{8}$ **7.** $\frac{19}{9}$, or $2\frac{1}{9}$
9. *Sample answer:*

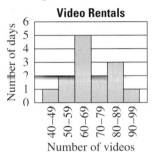

line graph or bar graph
11. 24 **13.** 125% **15.** 95

Using a Spreadsheet, p. 437

1. yes

9.3 Exercises, pp. 440–441

1. base, circumference, height, radius, lateral surface **3.** D **5.** A **7.** *Sample answer:* Paint cans, soup cans, and oil cans all hold liquids.
9. No; the rectangle would roll to be the lateral surface, but both circles would fold on the same end. **11.** Yes; the rectangles would roll to form the lateral surface and the circles would be folded to be the top and bottom bases. **13.** 1155.52 ft²
15. A; 4873.28 mm² **17.** B; 62.8 in.²
19. *Sample answer:*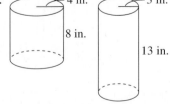

21. no; surface area of sack = 2059.84 in.², surface area of bag = 5172 in.² **23.** A

9.4 Exercises, pp. 444–445

1.

Top   Front and Side

3.

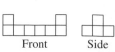

Top   Front   Side

5.

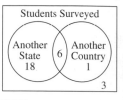

7. A   **9.** triangular prism

11. rectangular prism   **13.** A   **15.** B

Spiral Review, p. 446

1. 6 students;

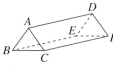

Students Surveyed

Another State 18   6   Another Country 1

3

3. 3.25

5.

5 10 14   27   49

7. about 186.8%

Mid-Chapter Review, p. 447

1.

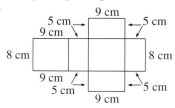

faces: *ABC, ADFC, BCFE, ADEB, DEF*; edges: $\overline{AB}, \overline{BC}, \overline{AC}, \overline{CF}, \overline{AD}, \overline{DE}, \overline{EF} \overline{DF}, \overline{BE}$; vertices: *A, B, C, D, E, F*   **2.** cylinder

3. triangular prism   **4.** pentagonal prism

5. *Sample answer:*

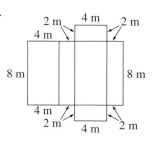

9 cm
5 cm   5 cm
9 cm
8 cm   8 cm
9 cm
5 cm   5 cm
9 cm

6. *Sample answer:*

2 m   4 m   2 m
4 m
8 m   8 m
4 m
2 m   4 m   2 m

7. *Sample answer:*

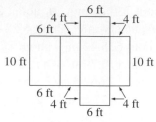

6 ft
4 ft   4 ft
6 ft   6 ft
10 ft   10 ft
6 ft
4 ft   4 ft
6 ft

8. 672 in.^{2} **9.** 459 ft^2 **10.** 42.45 in.^{2}
11. triangular prism   **12.** 310.5 in.^{2}

9.5 Exercises, pp. 452–453

1. B   **3.** A   **5.** x^3 **7.** 2496 in.^{3}
9. 334,540,800 ft^3 **11.** 5 m   **13.** The prisms have the same volume.   **a.** 216 cm^3 **b.** 216 cm^3
c. 216 cm^3 **15.** 61.5 m^3 **17.** 800 in.^{3} **19.** B

9.6 Exercises, pp. 456–457

1. A; A gives you the volume, B gives you the lateral surface area.   **3.** 4.5 ft   **5.** ≈190.755 ft^3
7. ≈1081.573 cm^3 **9.** ≈6 m   **11.** ≈8.9 walls, or 8 entire walls   **13.** The volume is multiplied by 4; the volume is multiplied by 9; the volume is multiplied by 16; if you multiply the radius by *n*, the volume is multiplied by n^2.
15. a. ≈7.9 cm^3 **b.** 91,915 pencils   **17.** D

Spiral Review, p. 458

1. 32   **3.** 64   **5.** 5   **7.** 19   **9.** –29   **11.** 16
13. 12   **15.** 7   **17.** false   **19.** $3.44
21. 37.68 m^2

9.7 Exercises pp. 464–465

1. C   **3.** B   **5.** The ratio of the lengths and the ratio of the heights are not equal; $\frac{4}{15} \neq \frac{4}{6}$.   **7.** yes
9. yes   **11.** 484 units^2; 1936 units^2; false; the surface area is multiplied by 4.   **13.** width: 50 m; height: 45 cm   **15.** $x = 1.25$ cm, $y = 8$ cm
17. D

Chapter Review, pp. 467–469

1. 7, pentagonal prism; 15, 10   **3.** 5, triangular prism; 9, 6

5.

A rectangular prism has 2 rectangular bases and 4 lateral rectangular faces. A triangular prism has 2 triangular bases and 3 rectangular lateral faces.

7. 432 in.² **9.** 226.08 cm² **11.** 9
13. 2,112,000 ft³
15.

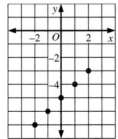 ; about 5263.268 yd³

17. $x = 4.95$ ft, $y = 5$ ft **19.** yes

Chapters 7–9 Cumulative Review, pp. 472–473

1. 0.35, $\frac{7}{20}$ **3.** 0.004, $\frac{1}{250}$ **5.** 25% **7.** 62.5%
9. 63 **11.** 8% **13.** $110.25, $460.25
15. $6.75 **17.** $35 **19.** ≈18.84 ft **21.** ≈10 m
23. 50.6 units, 103.8 units² **25.** 10 in.
27. 12 ft **29.** rectangular prism; 232 ft²
31. the cylinder **33.** Cylindrical silos hold more
than rectangular silos with about the same surface
area. **35.** $a = 20$ in., $b = 60$ in.

Chapter 10

10.1 Exercises, pp. 482–483

1. G **3.** D, F **5.** true **7.** false; $|-8| > 4$
9. $|-2| = 2$ **11.** $|-15| = 15$ **13.** $|4.5|$
15. $|-6.5|$ **17.** 6 **19.** 0 **21.** 2.7 **23.** 0.25
25. RADAR **27.** < **29.** = **31.** <
33. $1.25 over **35.** clothes **37.** C

10.2 Exercises, pp. 486–487

1. zero; a and b are opposites. **3.** negative;
$a > b$ **5.** *Sample answer: $-3 + 21$* **7.** *Sample
answer: $-6 + 6$* **9.** -14; $50 - 14 = 36$, $\frac{36}{50} =$
72% **11.** zero; 0 **13.** negative; -5 **15.** -8
17. -14 **19.** -39 **21.** 7 **23.** 7 **25.** -9
27. 50 **29.** 5 **31.** *Sample answer: $5 + (-4)$*
33. *Sample answer: $1 + (-3)$* **35.** more at the
end of the month by $15; $95 - 80 = 15$
37. Joel; Juan: 5, Joel: 0, Sara: 2 **39.** C

10.3 Exercises, pp. 490–491

1. C; -2 **3.** B; 8 **5.** $45 **7.** $5 + (-18)$; -13
9. $-3 + (-19)$; -22 **11.** $-12 + (-25)$; -37
13. $-5 + 27$; 22 **15.** 11 **17.** -4 **19.** -22
21. 1 **23.** -8 **25.** 18 **27.** 1, -6
29. $-14, -7$ **31.** $-6, 1$ **33.** 8, 1 **35.** C; -31
37. B; -11 **39.** Positive; subtracting a negative
value results in addition of a positive value.

41. 9 min **43.** Brand B; it lasts 4 min longer
than average.

10.4 Exercises, pp. 494–495

3. no; $220 - 65 = 155$ **5.** C **7.** $-17, -14, -11,$
$-8, -5$ **9.** $-5, -8, -10, -13, -17$
11. $(-2, -7), (-1, -6), (0, -5), (1, -4), (2, -3)$;

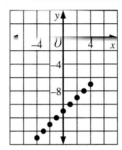

Points lie in a line, where for
each increase of 1 in the
x-value, the y-value increases
by 1.

13.

x	-4	-3	-2	-1	0	1	2	3	4
y	-15	-14	-13	-12	-11	-10	-9	-8	-7

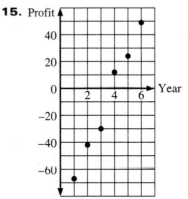

Points lie in a line, where
when x increases by 1,
y increases by 1.

15.

Points graph showing Profit vs Year with values 40, 20, 0, −20, −40, −60 and Year axis 2, 4, 6

17. Yes; the company has generated yearly profits, with the amount of profit increasing each year.

19.

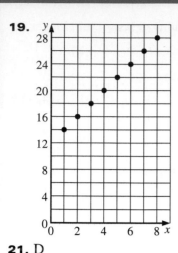

For each increase of 1 in the x-value, the y-value increases by 2.

21. D

Spiral Review, p. 496

1.

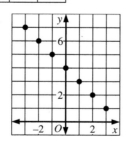

18   25.5 30 34.5   41

3. RGYB, RGBY, RBYG, RBGY, RYBG, RYGB, GRYB, GRBY, GBYR, GBRY, GYBR, GYRB, BRYG, BRGY, BGYR, BGRY, BYRG, BYGR, YRBG, YRGB, YGBR, YGRB, YBGR, YBRG
5. 150   **7.** \$262.50   **9.** 5 in.

Mid-Chapter Assessment, p. 497

1. False; absolute value of a positive number equals itself.   **2.** true   **3.** False; subtracting a negative number results in adding a positive number, and the sum of two positive numbers is positive.   **4.** 1.5   **5.** 4   **6.** 20   **7.** 0   **8.** 8
9. 5   **10.** 19   **11.** –23   **12.** –11   **13.** –12

14.

x	–3	–2	–1	0	1	2	3
y	7	6	5	4	3	2	1

$(-3, 7), (-2, 6), (-1, 5), (0, 4),$
$(1, 3), (2, 2), (3, 1)$

15.

x	–3	–2	–1	0	1	2	3
y	0	–1	–2	–3	–2	–1	0

$(-3, 0), (-2, -1), (-1, -2),$
$(0, -3), (1, -2), (2, -1), (3, 0)$

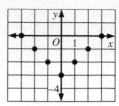

16. 800,000 B.C.; 800,000 B.C. is closer to 0, and thus, closer to the current year.   **17.** 1260 years
18. –2010, –750

10.5 Exercises, pp. 502–503

1. Positive; the product of two negative numbers is positive.   **3.** Negative; the product of a negative number and a positive number is negative.   **5.** 28   **7.** 40   **9.** Zero; subtracting a negative number results in addition, and addition of opposites is zero.   **11.** Positive; the product of 2 positive numbers is positive.   **13.** Negative; the product of a positive number and a negative number is negative.   **15.** 56   **17.** –9   **19.** –16
21. 8   **23.** –1   **25.** –13   **27.** negative; –224
29. negative; –11,340   **31.** –4   **33.** 0   **35.** 0
37. $5 \cdot (-6) \cdot 0; 0$ **39.** *Sample answer:* $-2 \cdot 6$; $4 \cdot (-3)$ **41.** *Sample answer:* $5 \cdot 7; -5 \cdot (-7)$
43. C

10.6 Exercises, pp. 506–507

1. False; it equals –1.   **3.** You cannot divide by zero.   **5.** $\frac{108}{-3} = -36, \frac{-36}{-1} = 36, \frac{36}{2} = 18,$
$\frac{18}{-1} = -18, \frac{-18}{-3} = 6, \frac{6}{2} = 3$ **7.** negative
9. positive   **11.** –7   **13.** 3   **15.** –13   **17.** 0
19. not possible   **21.** 5   **23.** –3°   **25.** –9 ft
27. –\$1.83   **29.** 2, –2   **31.** –3, 3   **33.** –35
35. –3   **37.** –2   **39.** A

Spiral Review, p. 508

1. $C = 18.50 + 25m$ **3.** 55 mi/h   **5.** 3 units to the right and 1 unit up   **7.** 351.8 ft^2; 502.4 ft^3

10.7 Exercises, pp. 512–513

1. $(-3)^4$; 81   **3.** Raised to an odd power, the product is negative. Raised to an even power, the product is positive.   **5.** B   **7.** A   **11.** –64
13. 64   **15.** –59   **17.** 10

19.

x	–3	–2	–1	0	1	2	3
y	5	0	–3	–4	–3	0	5

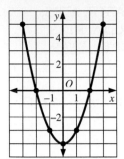 The points form a U-shaped pattern.

21.

x	-3	-2	-1	0	1	2	3
y	-9	-4	-1	0	-1	-4	-9

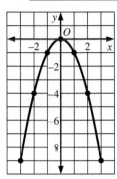 The points form an upside-down U-shaped pattern.

23. $=$ **25.** $>$ **27.** $<$ **29.** $=$ **31.** $=$

33. 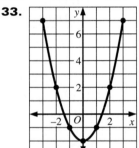 The points form a U-shaped pattern.

35. -5375 **37.** true
39. false; $-1^6 + (-2)^4 = 17$ **41. a.** 960 ft
b. 624 ft **c.** 0 ft **43.** D

Spiral Review, p. 514

1. 20 **3.** 3 **5.** 11.66 **7.** 5.2 **9.** 79.2°

10.8 Exercises, pp. 518–519

1. C **3.** B **5.** 5.280×10^3 **7.** 1×10^{-3}
9. 10,000,000,000 **11.** $\dfrac{1}{1,000,000,000,000}$
13. 1.205×10^7 **15.** 3.5×10^{-4}
17. 6.67×10^{-7} **19.** 5×10^{-4} **21.** 1.6×10^7
23. When the decimal point moves to the right, the exponent is negative; 5.6×10^{-5}. **25.** $<$
27. $<$ **29.** $>$ **31.** A; a granule is small, and $10^{-4} < 10^4$. **33.** D

Chapter 10 Review, pp. 521–523

1. 75 **3.** 0 **5.** 13 **7.** 0 **9.** -4 **11.** 19
13. $-5, -4, -3, -2, -1, 0, 1$

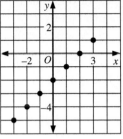 For each increase of 1 in the x-value, the y-value increases by 1.

15. 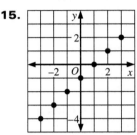 **17.**

19. -35 **21.** 54 **23.** -44 **25.** 6 **27.** -5
29. -804.6 ft **31.** -20 **33.** 3.4×10^4
35. 7.2×10^{-6} **37.** 1×10^3

Chapter 11

11.1 Exercises, pp. 532–533

1. *Sample answer:* counting the number of heads in 10 tosses of a coin

3.
11	21	31	41	51	61
12	22	32	42	52	62
13	23	33	43	53	63
14	24	34	44	54	64
15	25	35	45	55	65
16	26	36	46	56	66

The probability that both digits are odd is $\dfrac{1}{4}$.

5. $\dfrac{61}{100}$ **7.** One parent is round, one is wrinkled; offspring: probability of round $= \dfrac{1}{2}$, probability of wrinkled $= \dfrac{1}{2}$. **9.** Both parents are round; offspring: probability of round $= 1$, probability of wrinkled $= 0$. **11.** $\dfrac{1}{12}$ **13.** $\dfrac{1}{2}$ **15.** C

11.2 Exercises, pp. 538–539

1. *Sample answer:* If you have choices for each of several decisions, you multiply those numbers of choices to find out how many choices are possible.

3. H1, H2, H3, H4, H5, H6, T1, T2, T3, T4, T5, T6; *sample answer:* For the tree diagram, each of the 2 branches for the coin has 6 branches for the number cube, so the diagram has 12 outcomes. For the Counting Principle, the product of 2 choices for the coin and 6 choices for the number cube is 12.   **5.** 12 choices

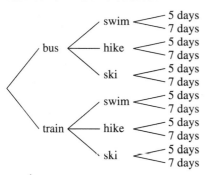

7. $\frac{1}{260}$; *sample answer:* There are 26 choices for the third letter and 10 choices for the first number, or 260 choices. There is 1 correct answer, so the probability of guessing that correct answer is $\frac{1}{260}$.
9. 288   **11.** B

Spiral Review, p. 540

1. *Sample answer:* The vertical scale is broken. The graph makes it seem that C is twice as much as A and three times as much as B.   **3.** *Sample answer:* In a survey of 3 classrooms, students were asked whether or not they had pets. In classroom A, 30% had pets; in classroom B, 22% had pets; and in classroom C, 46% had pets.
5. $a = 145, b = 65, c = 55, d = 95, s = 12$, $u = 6, t = 24$ **7.** $-2 + (-5) = -7$

Using a Calculator, p. 541

1.

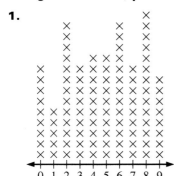

11.3 Exercises, pp. 546–547

1. yes   **3.** A   **5.** B   **7.** 120   **9.** 40,320
11. 2; <u>NO</u>, <u>ON</u>; 2

13. 24; ARST, <u>ARTS</u>, ASRT, ASTR, ATRS, ATSR, RAST, <u>RATS</u>, RSAT, RSTA, RTAS, RTSA, SART, SATR, SRAT, SRTA, <u>STAR</u>, STRA, <u>TARS</u>, TASR, TRAS, TRSA, <u>TSAR</u>, TSRA; 5
15. 120   **17.** 24   **19.** $\frac{1}{120}$ **21.** $\frac{1}{5040}$ **23.** D

11.4 Exercises, pp. 550–551

1.

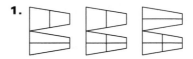

3. Permutation; order is important.
5. 10;

	A	B	C	D	E	Combination
1	X	X	X			{A, B, C}
2	X	X		X		{A, B, D}
3	X	X			X	{A, B, E}
4	X		X	X		{A, C, D}
5	X		X		X	{A, C, E}
6	X			X	X	{A, D, E}
7		X	X	X		{B, C, D}
8		X	X		X	{B, C, E}
9		X		X	X	{B, D, E}
10			X	X	X	{C, D, E}

7. {1, 3}, {1, 5}, {3, 5}   **9.** {1, 2, 3, 4}, {1, 2, 3, 5}, {1, 2, 3, 6}, {1, 2, 4, 5}, {1, 2, 4, 6}, {1, 2, 5, 6}, {1, 3, 4, 5}, {1, 3, 4, 6}, {1, 3, 5, 6}, {1, 4, 5, 6}, {2, 3, 4, 5}, {2, 3, 4, 6}, {2, 3, 5, 6}, {2, 4, 5, 6}, {3, 4, 5, 6}   **11.** 3   **13.** 6
15. {J, K}, {J, L}, {J, M}, {K, L}, {K, M}, {L, M}   **17.** 5   **19.** permutations; 120
21. combinations; 15   **23.** C

Spiral Review, p. 552

1. 6 fringetail and 2 popeye   **3.** $3 \cdot 5 \cdot 13$
5. $2 \cdot 11 \cdot 11$ **7.** 384 in.^{2} **9.** 12   **11.** 9   **13.** 4

Mid-Chapter Assessment, p. 553

1. 24   **2.** 720   **3.** 5040   **4.** 362,880
5. *Sample answer:* The 9 starters on a baseball team and 1 coach line up for a picture. How many different ways can they stand in a line? (answer: 3,628,800)   **6.** *Sample answer:* A permutation is a list of outcomes in which order is important.
7. $\frac{1}{16}$ **8.** $\frac{1}{16}$ **9.** $\frac{1}{4}$ **10.** 16   **11.** 64,000

12.

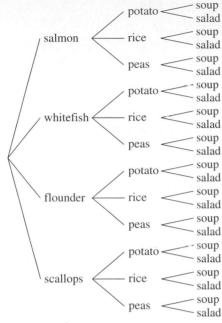

13. 24   **14.** $\frac{1}{24}$ **15.** 18   **16.** 8

11.5 Exercises, pp. 558–559

1. fair; *sample answer:* Odd and even are equally likely, and the players get the same number of points for a win.   **3.** fair; *sample answer:* Player A's probability of winning is $\frac{16}{36}$, so the expected value of each toss is $\left(\frac{16}{36}\right)(5) = \frac{20}{9}$, while Player B's probability of winning is $\frac{20}{36}$ and the expected value of each toss is $\left(\frac{20}{36}\right)(4) = \frac{20}{9}$.

5. yes   **7.** no; orange   **11.** 1.114; 0.484   **13.** B

11.6 Exercises, pp. 562–563

1. $\frac{2}{5}$ **3. a.** about 28.1   **b.** about 878 million
5. about 5 or 6   **7.** $\frac{2}{5}$, or 0.4   **9.** about 81,000
15. about 0.37   **17.** C

Spiral Review, p. 564

1. 83   **3.** 98.8, 99, 88   **5.** about 22.0 ft, about 38.5 ft^2

11.7 Exercises, pp. 568–569

1. D   **3.** C

5.

likes roller coasters   likes amusement park rides

7.

likes math   likes science

9. independent events   **11.** $\frac{1}{10}$ **13.** $\frac{1}{5}$

15. *Sample answer:* All of the people who play musical instruments like music.   **17.** *Sample answer:* Some people own bowling shoes, some people own bowling balls, and some own both; and all those people are bowlers. Also, there are bowlers who do not own bowling balls or bowling shoes.   **19.** C

Chapter 11 Review, pp. 571–573

1.

+	1	2	3	4	5	6
1	2	3	4	5	6	7
2	3	4	5	6	7	8
3	4	5	6	7	8	9
4	5	6	7	8	9	10
5	6	7	8	9	10	11
6	7	8	9	10	11	12

$; \frac{5}{36}$

3. 12 ways;

Yvonne — Renee, Lynn, Marie
Pearl — Renee, Lynn, Marie
Tasha — Renee, Lynn, Marie
Viola — Renee, Lynn, Marie

5. 720   **7.** 10   **9.** Player A: $\frac{60}{36} = \frac{5}{3}$; Player B: $\frac{90}{36} = \frac{5}{2}$; not fair   **11.** 75   **13.** $\frac{1}{15}$

Chapter 12

12.1 Exercises, pp. 582–583

1. Add 9 to –3 to get 6. Subtract 9 from 6 to get –3.   **3.** Divide –8 by –4 to get 2. Multiply 2 by –4 to get –8.

5. $y + 7 = 0$

$+7$
y → 0
Add 7 to y to get 0.

-7
-7 ← 0
Subtract 7 from 0 to get –7.

The solution is $y = -7$.

7. $n - 8 = -10$

The solution is $n = -2$.

Subtract 8 from n to get –10.   Add 8 to –10 to get –2.

9.

The solution is $x = 6$.

Multiply x by –3 to get –18.   Divide –18 by –3 to get 6.

11. Subtract 12.   **13.** Divide by –4.

15.

The solution is $s = 9$.

Subtract 14 from s to get –5.   Add 14 to –5 to get 9.

17.

The solution is $y = -11$.

Add 7 to y to get –4.   Subtract 7 from –4 to get –11.

19.

The solution is $t = \dfrac{2}{3}$.

Divide t by 2 to get $\frac{1}{3}$.   Multiply $\frac{1}{3}$ by 2 to get $\frac{2}{3}$.

21.

The solution is $n = -9$.

Multiply n by –3 to get 27.   Divide 27 by –3 to get –9.

23. ; –6   **25.** ; 4.5

27. ; –14   **29.** ; –2

31. Yes; you can let ice melt back into water.
33. No; you cannot recreate the log from the smoke and ash.   **35.** No; once you have read a book, you cannot "unread" a book.

37. $b + 10 = 6$; –4   **39.** $y \div \dfrac{1}{4} = 8$; 2

41. To get to the cheese: the mouse should enter the maze, then go left at the first intersection, then continue past a second intersection, then continue past a third intersection to the cheese. To get back out of the maze: the mouse should go past the first intersection, then continue past the second intersection, then turn right at the third intersection, then continue out of the maze.   **43.** C

12.2 Exercises, pp. 586–587

1. –8, –8, –1   **3.** C   **5.** D   **7.** $x = -4$ **9.** yes
11. yes   **13.** $-18 = x - 5$; –13   **15.** $x + 8 = 14$; 6   **17.** $x + 125 = 180$; 55   **19.** 2.4   **21.** 8
23. $1\dfrac{1}{2}$ **25.** C; 123   **27.** B; 291   **29.** A

Spiral Review, p. 588

1. a. 56.25, 58.5, 39
b.

3. 2.5%   **5.** $A(-2, 4)$, $B(-1, 7)$, $C(1, 5)$, $D(3, 6)$, $E(0, 3)$

Using a Calculator, p. 589

1. *Sample answer:* Player A should perform the inverse operation with the same number that Player B performed the operation with. For example, if B adds 5, then A subtracts 5; if B divides by 3, then A multiplies by 3, and so on.   **3.** *Sample answer:* If the original number is 33 and Player B enters "– 8 = × 7 =" to obtain 175, then Player A should enter "÷ 7 = + 8 =" to return to 33.

12.3 Exercises, pp. 594–595

1. $-4m = 32$; –8   **3.** $-3y = -51$; 17   **5.** B
7. A   **9.** negative; –3.4   **11.** positive; 18
13–21. Estimates will vary.   **13.** 50.5   **15.** –7.5
17. –10.5   **19.** 7.24   **21.** $\dfrac{1}{6}$ **23.** –12   **25.** 0
27. 0.75, or $\dfrac{3}{4}$ **29.** –3   **31.** 7.5 yards per play
33. $-22 = -8x$; 2.75, or $2\dfrac{3}{4}$ **35.** $-7x = 91$; –13
37. $16x = 120$; $7\dfrac{1}{2}$ ft   **39.** –8, –4, –2; the coefficient of d doubles each time, and d is multiplied by $\dfrac{1}{2}$.   **41.** $A = 20N$; $1000 = 20(50)$
43. $S = 2.5C$; $250 = 2.5(100)$ **45.** C

Spiral Review, p. 596

1. 108 cm, 544 cm^2 **3.** 22π cm (about 69.08 cm), 121π cm^2 (about 379.94 cm^2)
5. about 3220π mm^2 (about 10,110.8 mm^2)
7. a loss of $430

Mid-Chapter Assessment, p. 597

1. c; –9   **2.** a; –4   **3.** d; –36   **4.** b; –15
5. For steam to turn into water, the temperature must decrease to 212°F. Then for the water to turn into ice, the temperature must fall to 32°F.
6. $n - 3 = -4$; –1   **7.** $-5 = x + 4$; –9
8. $m + 3 = 6$; 3   **9.** The second step should be $n - (-4) + (-4) = -6 + (-4)$, which gives $n = -10$.   **10.** The second step should be $6 + 5 = x - 5 + 5$, which gives $x = 11$.

11. The third step should be $p = -5$.   **12.** -3

13. -3 **14.** $4\frac{1}{2}$ **15.** $6x = -4780$; \$796.67

12.4 Exercises, pp. 600–601

1. multiply   **3.** C; $18\frac{8}{9}$ gal, or about 18.9 gal

5. B; $\frac{17}{70}$ gal, or about 0.24 gal   **7.** 120   **9.** $\frac{5}{4}$, or $1\frac{1}{4}$ **11.** 11.27   **13.** -56.1

15. about 263 calories   **17.** $\frac{x}{13} = 13$; 169 yd^2

19. negative   **21.** negative   **23.** 10; 20; 30; the quotient increases by 2 each time, while the dividend increases by 10.   **25.** 5.94; 6.93; 7.92; the quotient increases by 0.09 each time, while the dividend increases by 0.99.   **27.** A

12.5 Exercises, pp. 606–607

1. Subtract 6 from each side; simplify; multiply each side by 2; solution: n is by itself.

3. $-2x + 5 = -7$; 6   **5.** Subtract 10 from each side.   **7.** Add 5 to each side.   **9.** $-5b + 3 = 28$; $-5, 23$ **11.** -4 **13.** 21   **15.** -10 **17.** -1

19. $5\frac{1}{2}$ **21.** 28; 29°, 56°, and 95°   **23.** $a = -6$, $b = 2$, $c = -1$, $d = 8$ **25.** Income per subscriber · Number of subscribers + Fixed income = Total income; Income per subscriber = \$1.25, Number of subscribers = n, Fixed income = \$175, Total income = \$600; $1.25n + 175 = 600$; the solution is 340, so you need 340 subscribers to reach your goal.   **27.** B

Spiral Review, p. 608

1. $9 + x = -14$; -23 **3.** $42 = 3\frac{1}{2}x$; 12

5. 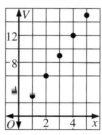 ; Quadrants I and IV

7. 48   **9.** 14

12.6 Exercises, pp. 614–615

1. B   **3.** A

5. $C = 75 + 4x$

Input, x	1	2	3	4	5	6
Output, C (\$)	79	83	87	91	95	99

7.

Input, x	1	2	3	4	5	6
Output, y	7	12	17	22	27	32

9.

Input, x	1	2	3	4	5	6
Output, y	-4	-7	-10	-13	-16	-19

11.

Input, x	1	2	3	4	5	6
Output, y	$1\frac{1}{6}$	$1\frac{1}{3}$	$1\frac{1}{2}$	$1\frac{2}{3}$	$1\frac{5}{6}$	2

13. $y = -2x + 16$ **15.** $y = 3x + 5$

17.

Input, t	1	2	3	4	5	6
Output, d (mi)	0.2	0.4	0.6	0.8	1	1.2

19.

Input, x	1	2	3	4	5
Output, V	3	6	9	12	15

21. C

Input, x	1	2	3	4	5
Output, S (in.^{2})	6	24	54	96	150

23. B

Chapter 12 Review, pp. 617–618

1. $x + 18 = 10$

The solution is $x = -8$.

Add 18 to x to get 10.   Subtract 18 from 10 to get -8.

3. $84 = 6t$

The solution is $t = 14$.

Multiply t by 6 to get 84.   Divide 84 by 6 to get 14.

5. 8   **7.** -7 **9.** -5 **11.** 50   **13.** 62.5

15. -45.5 **17.** 12   **19.** 3

21.

Input, x	0	1	2	3	4	5	6
Output, y	-3	-1	1	3	5	7	9

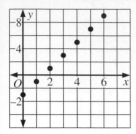

Chapters 7–12 Cumulative Review, p. 622

1. 156.25   **3.** 40   **5.** 34.48 m   **7.** 13 mm

9. about 321.85 ft^3; about 285.74 ft^2 **11.** –13

13. 5   **15.** 9   **17.** –32   **19.** $\frac{1}{2}$ **21.** $\frac{5}{6}$

23. subtracting 3   **25.** dividing by 12

27. adding –7   **29.** multiplying by –2

31. multiplying by $-\frac{4}{3}$ **33.** –19   **35.** 9

37. –64   **39.** 7